The Widening Gate

The New Historicism: Studies in Cultural Poetics
Stephen Greenblatt, General Editor

A CENTENNIAL BOOK

One hundred books
published between 1990 and 1995
bear this special imprint of
the University of California Press.
We have chosen each Centennial Book
as an example of the Press's finest
publishing and bookmaking traditions
as we celebrate the beginning of
our second century.

UNIVERSITY OF CALIFORNIA PRESS

Founded in 1893

The Widening Gate

*Bristol and the Atlantic Economy,
1450–1700*

David Harris Sacks

UNIVERSITY OF CALIFORNIA PRESS
Berkeley • Los Angeles • London

Cover illustration: Early modern Bristol's coat of arms.
(Detail from James Millerd's View of Bristol, 1673.)

University of California Press
Berkeley and Los Angeles, California

University of California Press, Ltd.
London, England

© 1991 by
The Regents of the University of California

First Paperback Printing 1993

Library of Congress Cataloging-in-Publication Data

Sacks, David Harris, 1942–
    The widening gate : Bristol and the Atlantic economy, 1450–1700 /
David Harris Sacks.
        p.   cm.—(The New historicism ; 15)
    "A Centennial book."
    Includes bibliographical references and index.
    ISBN 0-520-08449-7
    1. Bristol (England)—Economic conditions. 2. Capitalism—
England—Bristol—History. 3. Bristol (England)—Commerce—
History. I. Title. II. Series.
HC258.B76S23   1991
330.9423'93—dc20   90-19878
                                                        CIP

Printed in the United States of America

9 8 7 6 5 4 3 2 1

For Eleanor

Contents

Illustrations

Tables

Preface

Bristol is the city that John Cabot sailed from and Thomas Chatterton dreamed, that Hugh Latimer preached to and Oliver Cromwell seized, that entertained Parliaments in the Middle Ages and rioted for Reform in the nineteenth century. Since the Norman Conquest, it has always had an important place in English history, experiencing events and contributing to developments that stirred the nation. What follows is an account of its connection with one small piece of that history, the rise of the Atlantic economy in the early modern period and the accompanying transformation of English economic ideas and practices. But this book is not about economics alone. It is grounded on the belief that we can no more abstract the economy from politics, culture, and society than we can separate intentional human action from thought and judgment. It also rejects the notion that the life of a city like Bristol could ever be treated as a self-contained whole. Instead it views such cities as social organisms living in close relationship with their surroundings. What gives them their structure is the set of internal codes they carry. And what enables them to survive is their ability to adapt to or transform their environment, which itself is always changing.

It was beyond my capacity to write this kind of history encyclopedically. Even if the evidence necessary to define every relevant interrelationship had survived—it has not—I could not have distilled it all into words. Hence in place of a comprehensive treatment analyzing every aspect of Bristol's history in depth, I offer an extended essay, one that attempts to turn what I have been able to learn about early modern Bristol into a coherent story. Given the city's importance in this period, a number of such stories were possible, each with different terminal dates and a different emphasis. But the one that interested me most was Bristol's transition from medieval trading center to Atlantic entrepôt. This development has important implications for our understanding of the growth of capitalism in England, for it allows us to see how "merchant capital"—that weak limb of capitalism, according to many scholars[1]—fit into the social and political order of the sixteenth and seventeenth centuries and helped to transform it. This book, then, is an essay in the local history of capitalism, viewing this historical development from the perspective of a provincial town in the west of England whose traders long had looked to the Atlantic for their livelihoods. As such, it centers the story of this great transformation far from the financial, commercial, and manufacturing capitals of Europe where other important processes of economic, social, intellectual, and political change were under way.

Ever since Marx, the history of capitalism has been a central subject for all students of early modern European history. But its study has oscillated among only a limited number of established positions. On the one hand, there has been a lengthy debate—primarily among Marxists—about whether the transition to capitalism arises principally from internal contradictions within the feudal order or from the dissolution of feudal relationships produced by the so-called commercial revolution. On the other, there has been an equally lengthy debate—this time primarily between Marxists and non-Marxists such as Max Weber and his followers—about whether we should look for the origins of capitalism principally in material changes in the economy or in spiritual changes in mentalité and moral outlook. Fruitful as these controversies have been in unearthing new knowledge, they seem forever to repeat themselves, despite employing hitherto unknown facts and more and more refined terminologies. Such repetition generally signals a problem less of inadequate evidence than of conceptualization. A hidden assumption or a false dichotomization makes resolution of the debate impossible.

The history of Bristol between 1450 and 1700 offers a way out of this dilemma, since developments there defy conventionally accepted distinctions between internal and external forces. In their place, the evidence reveals a strong pattern of reciprocal relationships between the city and the wider world that shaped contemporary outlooks and in turn were affected by them. Bristol's story, then, provided a good opportunity to rethink some of the heretofore unresolved issues posed by the development of modern capitalism. This book is the result. It does not purport to give a final answer to any question, but if it has succeeded in casting some fresh light on its subject I shall be pleased.

Because this history seeks to explain an economic transformation, its starting place is the central economic fact of Bristol's fifteenth-century history: England's loss of Bordeaux in 1453. Thereafter the narrative unfolds by examining the complex interplay of economic, social, cultural, and political changes that followed this event. Part 1 traces the rivalry between Bristol's merchants and shopkeepers that emerged as the city adapted to a new pattern of trade in the sixteenth century. Part 2 looks to the prevailing patterns of culture in the city in the later Middle Ages, focusing especially on ideas of community and authority. It considers how these concepts and the practices associated with them changed during the sixteenth and early seventeenth centuries. In Part 3, the story moves into the second half of the seventeenth century, concentrating on the 1660s and 1670s, to explore how the peculiar structural features of the city's life that had emerged in the Elizabethan and early Stuart era came undone as the growth of the Atlantic economy went hand in hand with the establishment of a new kind of politics and prompted the development of new ways of economic thought and action. The book concludes by considering the state of social and economic understanding in Bristol at the end of the seventeenth century.

The approach I have followed has meant giving primacy to the long-term economic history of Bristol while omitting to mention the Exclusion Crisis and the Glorious Revolution and relegating the Reformation and the Civil War to a secondary position. The danger is that these important occurrences will therefore be thought of as no more than effects of the economic history recounted here. Nothing could be further from my intention. The story told by this book is one of human choices, not of determinism. But to develop its theme, many important subjects have had to be presented only as subordinate, not independent, topics. Other books written for different purposes surely will give those subjects the central position and full treatment they deserve, and in such works my own subject no doubt will be mentioned only in passing.

A word should perhaps be said about the relation of this volume to "cultural poetics." This term has been used primarily in studies of literary culture. What has it to do with a book about urban history in which reliance on the techniques and scholarly equipment of the social scientist is so evident? Or, to put this point the other way around, why should a work concerned with a form of cultural interpretation depend

so much on statistical tables? How can they aid, to use Stephen Greenblatt's words, in studying "the collective making of distinct cultural
practices" and inquiring "into the relations among these practices"?[2]
These questions are especially grounded in the recent development of
economic history as a field. In the 1930s, as F. J. Fisher has pointed out,

> the main requirement of an economic historian was that he should be able
> to read, since most of his sources were literary. The archetype of the learned
> monograph consisted of a thin rivulet of text meandering through wide and
> lush meadows of footnotes. . . . Today, the first requirement of an economic
> historian is that he should be able to count, for his materials are largely sta-
> tistical. The archetype of our modern fashion is one in which a stream, often
> a less than limpid stream, of text tumbles from table to table and swirls
> around graph after graph.[3]

As the scope of economic history has widened, and as its reliance on
economic theory has grown, this assessment has become almost a truism. Economic history is now more properly denominated "quantitative history" or, as Robert Fogel has called it, "new economic history"—history, as it were, by equation.[4] This highly sophisticated
approach has generated many new and important insights into the
study of economic laws and practices. But for all its technical brilliance,
it has not solved the historian's main problem, which remains interpretive, not statistical. The figures having been collected, what do they
mean? Given the time, the place, and the enterprise, should we have expected the results we found, or do they require further explanation? As
always, the most important questions call upon our understanding and
not just our analytical skills, so arriving at a satisfactory account of our
subject demands comprehension of the milieu and the motives of the
participants, and not just measurement of structures and conjunctures.[5]
To grasp the meaning and significance of economic history requires a
careful attention to the changing norms of the market and their relation
to broad developments in religion, society, and politics that the term
"cultural poetics" captures very effectively. Put another way, economic
history demands attention to literary documents and cultural artifacts
as well as statistical sources, and an ability to read and observe as well
as to count.

What, then, of the connection of this book to the so-called New Historicism itself? As used among literary critics, this term usually refers to
an interest in historically grounded studies of ideology and power in
cultural production. For many historians, however, the concept of historicism stands for two seemingly contradictory—and equally nox-

ious—notions. On the one hand, it refers to a form of determinism which argues that history reveals discoverable rhythms and patterns to human life or is governed by discernible laws of social development. On the other, it refers to a form of relativism. The truths it unearths are time-bound; they depend on differences in culture and on the particular historical situation in which events occur or institutions are found. When put together, these two notions lead to a highly artificial view in which each period is reified into a self-standing historical object with its own spirit or principle of organization that fits into a deterministic evolutionary scheme. The end result is a necessary progress of ideas, an iron logic of modes, a forced march of social development in discrete stages.

Nevertheless, it would be impossible to study history without accepting some elements of the historicist's view. The foundation of historical scholarship, as Marc Bloch argues in *The Historian's Craft,* is that it is about human beings living in time. But this simple truth, which every working historian would probably accept, is no mere truism, since "historical time" understood in Bloch's sense is not an abstraction—not a simple unit of measurement—but, as Bloch says, "a concrete and living reality with an irreversible onward rush. It is the very plasma in which events are immersed, and the field in which they become intelligible." Accordingly, it demonstrates continuity, in that one event may lead to others, and it reveals difference, in that periods or cultures are shown to have self-standing characters arising and disappearing in "the uninterrupted sequence of the ages." But even though "a historical phenomenon can never be understood apart from its moment in time," a given moment can either unite a particular phenomenon with or separate it from what had come before and what would follow. For historians, then, the "very *raison d'être*" of scholarship is to be able to decide, as Bloch says, "to what extent . . . the connection which the flow of time sets between" two consecutive periods predominates or fails to predominate "over the differences born out of the same flow[.] Should the knowledge of earlier periods be considered indispensable or superfluous for the understanding of the later?" This view of historical time transforms historicism into a methodology, a source of research questions rather than of metaphysical certainties.[6]

Employed in this heuristic fashion, historicism of Bloch's kind simultaneously recognizes the importance of historical causality in shaping events and the possibility that their consequences might have been otherwise. This book proceeds from a similar perspective. It aims to account for historical change without assuming its inevitability or explaining away its significance. It rests on the conviction that a culture is not simply a collection of norms and values but a complex and continuously altering arrangement of beliefs and practices governing the whole of social life. This kind of culture is neither monolithic nor uncontested. As Stephen Greenblatt has stressed, every aspect of it involves negotiation: "a subtle, elusive set of exchanges, a network of trades and trade-offs, a jostling of competing representations" that takes place in time and that is repeated and developed across time.[7] To grasp the nature of this process requires attention to nuances of meaning, to caesurae in meter and to ambiguities of manner in what is said and done. Although many New Historicists will find this book concerned with issues far different from their usual fare and employing methods not normally encountered in cultural studies, and others no doubt will disagree with its emphasis on contingent events and human choices and intentions, all should recognize a reliance on common assumptions about the importance of historical understanding in interpreting cultural processes.

This kind of historical understanding proceeds from what might be called a position of methodological realism, a sense of the past as independent of ourselves, a sense that it is capable of teaching us something about the possibilities of human life that we can discover in no other way. Those of us who study history in this fashion write as though we are describing and analyzing places we might actually have visited. Our professed goal is to illuminate what happened to the people who lived there, to see how the events that affected them unfolded, and to account for why they took the course they did. Hence, our scholarly disputes normally are more about whether we have gotten the story right than about the theories we have employed in reaching our conclusions. We worry about anachronism, about distinguishing between our ways of living and those followed by the societies we study. Some practitioners of this approach even try "to vanish before their subjects," as Steven Ozment has said.[8]

Nevertheless, it is a mistake to treat the past as a metaphysical entity, cut off from the present, existing timelessly in independence of our minds and methods—something we can actually recover whole whenever sufficient evidence has survived. What we know of any past culture or society is available to us because of the remnants it has left behind: its texts, its documents, its artifacts. The significance of these items becomes apparent only by virtue of the questions we ask and the techniques we use to answer them. It depends on interpretation, an always daunting task that we would not escape even if by some miraculous means we could be transported in time to view history as it happened. We would still find ourselves, as do historians of contemporary events, translating back and forth from our own social and cultural frameworks to what we can understand of the meanings and purposes of our subjects. Our questions and techniques arise because of our particular interests in the past, which depend on our motives—often ideological as well as academic—for studying it. These in turn vary according to history and therefore according to our relation to the past itself. In consequence, we can never actually see the world through the eyes of our subjects, although we sometimes insist that we should try. We can only imagine how it might have appeared to them, depending as best we can on our critical self-awareness to correct the distortions created by our biases and prejudices. But we can never erase ourselves entirely from what we study. Nor should we want to.[9]

It is never easy to say where a project such as the present one found its origin. In one sense, it began in the late Professor W. K. Jordan's graduate seminar at Harvard, in which I wrote a paper on Bristol in the Civil War. This research so intrigued me that upon its completion I made it the proposed subject of my dissertation. But my first foray into English archives taught me a salutary lesson. Nearly everything I had concluded about Bristol from printed sources quickly came undone when I saw my first manuscripts, and the social and political divisions I had established in my seminar paper turned out to be illusory. What had seemed a plausible way to cover the facts I had gleaned from the books in Widener Library could in no way account for the evidence I had now discovered. Gradually, however, a new understanding emerged, one beginning with the perception that early modern English cities were, not self-contained social organisms, but places open to the wider world of national and even international affairs. My Ph.D. thesis, completed under Professor Wallace MacCaffrey's direction and subsequently published in a dissertation series, explored the implications of this view of urban society for the lives and outlooks of the Bristolians, never reaching the Civil War period about which I had first intended to write.[10] But using 1640 as a terminal date created something of a false sense of finality to the story, since events in the late 1630s seemed to settle all the outstanding political and economic issues of Bristol's history in the later sixteenth and the early seventeenth century. Of course this was only an artifact of the chronological limits of the study; the Civil War and its aftermath almost immediately undid nearly all that happened. Upon completing my dissertation, then, I was left with the dilemma of how to deal with this awkward fact.

The solution came somewhat serendipitously in response to an inquiry from Bernard Bailyn, who had read my dissertation soon after its completion. He was interested in Bristol's role in American immigration during the later seventeenth century and wanted to know something about its system for registering indentured servants bound for the American plantations. During my research I had made some notes about the origins of this system in 1654 but had given little thought to them at the time. When looked at closely, however, this registration scheme posed a genuine puzzle, since, as is argued in Chapter 8, the remedy it instituted simply did not fit the crime it claimed to punish. What, then, was this ordinance about and what had provoked it? Discovery of the case that had brought the Bristol Common Council to action began to reveal what was at stake, since the main targets of the registration scheme turned out to be interlopers in overseas trade and sectaries as well. In 1654 the activities of these individuals were highlighted at the calling of the first Protectorate Parliament, the elections for which in Bristol had produced victory for conservative merchants and outraged protest from the city's radicals and sectaries. Many of these radicals turned out to be important colonial traders who frequently supplied indentured labor to the American market. In this light the ordinance and the register seemed designed less to protect servants than to control the traders; it was not so much a mechanism of economic regulation as a weapon of political attack.

Once I had reached this conclusion, much else began to become clear about the role of American trade in Bristol's life. The nature of the American market, I realized, made it impossible to regulate trade with it under the rules on which Bristol's major overseas merchants had previously relied. As a result, their victories in the late 1630s were incapable of coping with the new economic order taking shape among the colonial traders. I knew then that I had a solution to the dilemma posed by my dissertation, and I began pursuing the implications of my findings where they would lead. This book is the outcome.

A NOTE ON DATES AND QUOTATIONS

Unless otherwise indicated, all dates are given Old Style, except that the year is taken to begin on 1 January. Spelling and punctuation in the quotations follow the original, but I have expanded the abbreviations.

Acknowledgments

Although this book is about the beginnings of impersonal exchange in the modern market economy, the history of its research and writing testifies to the persistence in our own age of more venerable traditions of generosity, friendship, and support. I am especially grateful for the financial aid that has made this book possible. Early in my training I received assistance from a Woodrow Wilson National Fellowship and from Harvard University. Later a Frank Knox Memorial Fellowship from Harvard funded my first research trip to British archives. Additional research was furthered in part by other generous grants from Harvard, from the American Philosophical Society, and from the Folger Shakespeare Library. In recent years, Reed College has also helped with summer grants which have made possible the purchase of important research materials.

I also want to thank the staffs of the many libraries and collections that I visited in the course of writing this book. Throughout the project, my labors were immeasurably lightened by the kindness, skill, and knowledge of the archivists of the City of Bristol, especially Elizabeth Ralph and her successor Mary E. Williams. They have made the Bristol Record Office one of the best depositories in Britain in which to pursue local history. I am also indebted to the Treasurer of the Society of Merchant Venturers of the City of Bristol and to the Vicar of St. Mary, Redcliffe, Bristol, for permission to consult and quote from papers in their care and for courtesies extended to me during my visits. Grateful thanks are due as well to the staffs of the Bristol Central Library, the Bristol

City Museum, the University of Bristol Library, the Bodleian Library, the Cambridge University Library, the Friends' House Library, the Library of the Institute of Historical Research, the British Library, and the Public Record Office in Britain; the Harry Elkins Widener Memorial Library, the Houghton Library, the Harvard-Andover Library, the Law School Library, and the Kress Library of Business and Economics at Harvard University; the Folger Shakespeare Library and the Library of Congress in Washington, D.C.; the Huntington Library in San Marino, California; the Newberry Library in Chicago; the New York Public Library; the University of Wisconsin libraries in Milwaukee and Madison; the library of the University of Massachusetts–Boston; and the Reed College Library.

I am also pleased to acknowledge the permissions I have received to use portions of my earlier work in the present volume. Chapter 4 employs material from "The Demise of the Martyrs: The Feasts of St. Clement and St. Katherine in Bristol, 1400–1600," which was published originally in *Social History* 11, 2 (May 1986): 141–69. Chapter 5 depends in part on my essay "Celebrating Authority in Bristol, 1475–1640," which appeared in *Urban Life in the Renaissance,* pp. 187–223, edited by Susan Zimmerman and Ronald F. E. Weissmann and published in 1989 by the University of Delaware Press for the University of Maryland's Center for Renaissance and Baroque Studies. Portions of the Introduction, Chapters 6 and 7, and the Conclusion draw on and reproduce material from my article "The Corporate Town and the English State: Bristol's 'Little Businesses,' 1625–1641," which first appeared in *Past and Present: A Journal of Historical Studies,* no. 110 (February 1986): 69–105 (World Copyright: The Past and Present Society, Oxford). Several illustrations also are included in this book with the generous consent of those who hold the originals. Figure 1 is from Sloane MS 2596, f. 77 and appears by permission of the British Library. Figures 4 and 5 come from Robert Ricart's *The Maire of Bristowe Is Kalendar,* Bristol Record Office, MS 04270 (1), ff. 5^v and 152^v respectively, and appear by permission of the City of Bristol Record Office.

My deepest thanks are owed to the many teachers, colleagues, friends, and family who have stood by and guided me as I worked and reworked the ideas and arguments put forward in this book. As an undergraduate I had the benefit of studying with an extraordinary group of teachers at Brooklyn College, who together taught me what it meant to analyze, argue, think, and learn. I especially want to mention the late Raymond de Roover, who gave me my first training in late medieval and early modern economic history, and Madeline Robinton, who introduced me to the study of British history. I am forever grateful to them. In many respects this book is the product of their teaching. At Harvard I was equally blessed. This book first took form under the tutelage of W. K. Jordan, from whose wide learning, sympathetic encouragement, and kindly supervision I benefited during the early stages of my career. After Professor Jordan's retirement and death, my work was directed by Wallace MacCaffrey, who saw my dissertation through all of its stages. His probing questions, careful attention to detail, and generous criticism not only saved me from many errors but led my researches in a number of new directions which have occupied me since I completed my doctoral degree. I am very pleased that we have remained in close touch over the years, and I want to thank him here for his continued wise advice, warm friendship, and generous support. Only those of us who have worked closely as students with Wallace can truly know the breadth of his learning and the depth of his judgment. He has always seemed to me the perfect exemplar of a gentleman and scholar. A third figure among my teachers at Harvard also played an important role in shaping my understanding: the late Elliott Perkins, with whom I did not study in a formal sense, nonetheless taught me immensely important lessons about the close relationship of teaching to scholarship and about the larger ethical purposes of an academic career. I shall always cherish the friendship and moral support he gave me while I was a graduate student and for many years afterwards. I am not alone in remembering the warmth, hospitality, and human decency he and his wife Mary always managed to show when they were most needed.

I benefited over the years from the interest Bernard Bailyn has taken in my work and from the late John Clive's friendly regard for my progress. I am also grateful for the thoughtful questions, warm encouragement, and wise advice of John Brewer and Simon Schama. I must thank Carole Shammas and Jonathan Barry as well. At crucial stages in my work, each of them stepped in to help me obtain otherwise inaccessible source materials. My former colleagues and students in History and Literature at Harvard and my present ones in History at Reed College also deserve acknowledgment. They provided the first sounding board for many of my ideas, and their encouraging responses gave me the impetus to go forward. In addition, I want to thank the scholars who attended my presentations of portions of my work at conferences and other occasions, including meetings of the Social Science History

Association, the North American Conference on British Studies, the Cambridge Seminar on Early Modern History, and the Harvard History and Literature Staff Seminar. Their comments and questions helped sharpen the focus and extend the perspective of the present work.

Numerous friends and colleagues have read my work in whole or in part, and their advice, judgment, and criticism have been of great assistance to me. Along with those already mentioned, I especially want to thank Harold J. Cook, Natalie Zemon Davis, Sigmund Diamond, Stephen Diamond, Stephen Greenblatt, Harold J. Hanham, Clive Holmes, the late Roger Howell, Richard Marius, J. G. A. Pocock, Lawrence Stone, and Stephen White. In this connection, the readers for the University of California Press deserve special mention. Paul Seaver's and A. J. Slavin's reader's reports were models of insightful criticism, as was the written commentary I received from Buchanan Sharp, who read the manuscript as a member of the Press's editorial committee. Their remarks and suggestions for revision have without a doubt helped make this a better book. I also want to thank the editors at the University of California Press itself for the care they have taken with my manuscript and for easing my burdens as I have seen the book through its last stages. Stephen Greenblatt and Doris Kretschmer had faith in this project from the time they first encountered it, and I am certain it would not have appeared in its present form without their patience and confidence. Once the final version was submitted, Jane-Ellen Long stepped in as copy editor. I especially thank her for the numerous improvements she has made in the manuscript. Rose Vekony gave the book the benefit of her expert skills in seeing it through the press.

Finally I must say a few words about my greatest debts of all. My dissertation, out of which this present volume has grown, was dedicated to my mother and the memory of my father. That dedication inadequately acknowledges the care and love my parents always gave to me and that I still receive. I hope that this book answers in some small measure their aspirations for me. The present dedication is to my wife, Eleanor, and it too cannot fully acknowledge all she has contributed. Nor can it fully express my gratitude to her. Suffice it to say that without her love and faith, *The Widening Gate* would never have been completed. I must also note that she has commented on every one of its many drafts and that much of the statistical work presented here would have been impossible without her assistance. Throughout this book's long gestation she has been its most faithful friend and helpful critic. Her sharp eye for detail

has saved me from innumerable errors of omission and commission, and
her excellent ear for the English language has helped remove many in-
felicities and inconsistencies in my prose. This book is not just for
Eleanor; it is Eleanor's as well as mine.

David Harris Sacks
January 1991

Introduction: The Closed Arena and the Open Gate

The sixteenth century was a great age of mapmaking, and among the many surviving examples, city maps are especially common. An aerial view shows us a city, usually fortified, with high church steeples rising majestically above the rooftops and numerous houses crowded tightly together along narrow streets. Around it are hills and forests and fields, in which few buildings or other marks of human settlement can be seen. The city appears as a bounded world, an artifact of man rising up out of the order of nature, rather like the megaliths of the ancient Britons that rise up as from nowhere on the Salisbury plain. These maps seem to show us, in the words of Oscar Handlin, "self-contained entities walled off from their surroundings, each one a separate universe . . . whole and entire of itself."[1]

Among the city maps drawn in the sixteenth century is one of Bristol dating from 1568 (Figure 1).[2] It depicts just such a compact place. Although some churches and dwellings are to be observed in the suburbs, its medieval walls and its powerful castle, protected by a moat, still dominate it and define its form. Its stone churches and red-roofed houses show us an environment created by human hands, standing apart from the green fields and woodlands of the nearby countryside. It appears very much its own world.

But we also see two other characteristic, if sometimes neglected, features of this geography: its highways and its waterways. Moving out from the city are roads to Wales and the city of Gloucester to the north, to the cities of Wells and Bath to the south, and to the great metropolis

Fig. 1. William Smith's View of Bristol, 1568. (British Library, Sloane MS 2596, f. 77. By permission of the British Library.)

of London to the east, linking Bristol with the rest of the kingdom. Even more prominent are the rivers Avon and Frome, on which the city is situated. Together they form the city's harbor, as we can see from the tall-masted ships docked along the Back and Key. These rivers were as much a part of Bristol's human geography as were its walls, buildings, and roads. The Frome, as we find it here, was itself the handiwork of man, its channel having been remade by the citizens of the thirteenth century in order to expand the number of docking places near the city center.[3] The Avon with its enormous tides, which emptied the channel twice a day, was the principal avenue of communication for the city, leading through Hungroad and Kingroad, at which ships docked as they waited for wind and tide, to the Severn and the Bristol Channel, and thence to the wider world of commerce beyond the seas.

The draftsman of this first authentic map of Bristol was William Smith, a scholar primarily devoted to heraldry, an art of symbols, not to mapmaking.[4] In the upper right-hand corner of his carefully "measured & laid in Platforme" view of Bristol, he gives us an example of

Fig. 2. Early Modern Bristol's Coat of Arms. (Detail from James Millerd's View of Bristol, 1673.)

this other talent. There, in what would be the northeast quadrant of the map, we find tricked out the arms of the city of Bristol. These arms, which also appeared on Bristol's common seal, were very much the mark of the city's status as a corporation, a union of head and body for common action in pursuit of common interests and goals made possible by the express grant of liberties and franchises from the Crown.[5] They signaled at one and the same time the city's life as an independent community and its subordination to the authority of the king and the law. In their modern form, these arms show us a fortress upon a hill near a riverbank or seashore with a ship in full sail passing by. However, the version in use in medieval and early modern times depicts the ship sailing through the gates of a great castle (Figure 2). Both images have resonance for us; they symbolize a community that lived by trade and was thus connected to the wider world. But the latter with its gate is the better emblem. It stresses that a late medieval and early modern English city was not only a stronghold, marked by a jurisdictional as well as a physical boundary that distinguished its inhabitants from their fellow Englishmen, but a passage point for people and commodities. Depicting a castle gate with a ship sailing through juxtaposed strength of community with successful enterprise as if to say, as the poet Thomas Churchyard in fact did say for Bristol,

> Our traed doth stand on Siuill lief
> And thear our glory lies.[6]

Any inquiry into the history of an early modern English city must come to terms with this reciprocal relationship between its political and its economic life. Urban society is characterized primarily by the concentration of diverse socioeconomic functions in a densely built-up center of population, which is dependent on markets located outside the authority of its own government. Urban social order, then, is always vulnerable to regional, national, and even international economic developments beyond the political control of its inhabitants. But an English city of the fifteenth, the sixteenth, or the seventeenth century was primarily a legal and political unit, defined by precise jurisdictional boundaries that offered no real barrier to economic and social change. What held it together were its corporate existence and its sense of community, which separated its freemen and their dependents from their surroundings and gave them a unity and a capacity for collective action they would not otherwise have possessed. This combination of openness to the world of commerce and industry and closeness behind protective walls was the energizing force in city life. It meant that civic society was never at rest, but was always acting on its environment and adapting itself to any changes in it. The town was not a closed arena which drew in upon itself and made of the connections and rivalries of its inhabitants the sole source of local life, but an open gate in which the larger world penetrated into the community and helped shape it.

In modern historiography, the prevailing view of English urban life from the fifteenth to the eighteenth century has been closer to Handlin's than to the one implicit in Bristol's coat of arms. Until recently most writers have considered the typical English town of the period not as part of an integrated realm but as a "self-conscious and coherent community with a distinct life of its own," separate from that of the kingdom at large.[7] Or in the words of Mrs. J. R. Green, it was "a free self-governing community, a state within the state . . . a little principality" carrying on an "isolated self-dependent life."[8] At the heart of this understanding is a vision, familiar enough to anyone who has read Thomas Hobbes, that juxtaposes the state to society and its constituent communities. Hobbes saw all corporate bodies, the towns included, "as many lesser Commonwealths in the bowels of a greater, like wormes in the entrayles of a naturall man," and thought the state could not tolerate them. "For what is it to divide the Power of a Common-wealth, but to Dissolve it," he says, "for powers divided mutually destroy each other."[9] Hence for him, and for those historians who follow his model, the existence of independent, self-standing communities that command the primary loyalties of their members implies the absence of a strong state, just as the rise of the state entails their disappearance.

At its inception this idea focused on politics. According to Green, a town's autonomy consisted in its freedom to arm its own soldiers and defend its own territory; elect its own rulers and officials; draw up its own constitutions and ordinances; assess, levy, and raise its own taxes; settle its own trading relations; and administer the law through its own courts. But more recent scholarship has added an emphasis upon sociology, as revealed by the use of the term "community." In everyday language the word can mean no more than a collectivity of people having common interests and sharing common activities. It need not imply competition with the larger social organisms of which it may be a part. In this sense the village or neighborhood, the county or town, the district or region, and the kingdom or nation can each be called a community in its own right. Localists following Green's lead, however, consider the community more narrowly, as a bounded social system of a particular type, or, in Alan Everitt's words, "a little self-centered kingdom on its own."[10] The type is what sociologists sometimes call a *Gemeinschaft,* a small community characterized by multifaceted, face-to-face, and permanent social relationships in contrast to the partial, impersonal, and transitory relationships found in the larger society. According to theory, such communities are homogeneous, self-sufficient, and slow-changing, marked by a continuous corporate existence and a high degree of interaction and common endeavor among their members. Typically they are dominated by the institution of the extended family, which through patriarchal authority and close ties of affinity provides the community with a strong bond of social solidarity.[11]

Most of the sociologists of the small community have found a particular place for it in a broad view of social history. According to their model, the earliest societies were simple, undifferentiated, tiny social organisms of men and women living in isolation, close to nature and bound by tradition. More intricately organized forms of social existence, marked by a highly articulated division of labor and governed by rational principles, developed only in the modern world. As this evolutionary process unfolds, the world changes from a place in which social cohesion is the dominant motif to one where competition and the rational pursuit of self-interest hold supreme sway. In the course of the history, small communities gradually disappear as meaningful entities because their members become integrated into larger and larger social organizations.

Similar ideas, amounting to a theory of modernization, are deeply embedded in the approach of localist historians of English rural and urban life. H. P. R. Finberg, for example, tells us that the self-conscious local communities in which he is interested are "not much in evidence today." Rather, they—or most of them, at any rate—have undergone a strict course of development from birth, often in the distant past, to death "the day before yesterday." The archetypical local history, then, tells the story of "the Origin, Growth, Decline and Fall of a Local Community," emphasizing that present-day towns and rural districts lack "the old degree of social cohesion" that characterized communities of the past.[12] Finberg also suggests some reasons for this change. "A railwayman or a mill-owner today," he says,

> pretty certainly feels himself more closely linked in sympathies and interests and aspirations with his fellow-railwaymen or fellow manufacturers up and down the country than with the majority of his fellow townsmen. Moreover Leviathan, as we all know, looks with no friendly eye upon allegiances that are not centered on its omnicompetent self. It may be that just as the family, once so powerful a unit, has withered into social impotence, so the local community is destined to wither in its turn. But while it flourished it yielded only to the nation, and not always even to the nation, in its hold over men's loyalties.[13]

Thus the local community is a form of social life peculiar to a particular phase of history. With the growth of the modern economy and the rise of the state, its existence becomes increasingly problematic and it gradually disappears from view.

This theory of localism has had its uses. By reminding us that state and society have not always existed in their present forms, it has helped us to break new ground in urban history and to reveal much that we did not know about the fabric of social and cultural life in early modern England. Where history once was little more than the study of grand politics, political institutions, and constitutional ideas, it has become all-encompassing, covering everything from architecture to xenophobia, each understood in the context of lives lived by ordinary men and women at home. Nothing human—or inhuman, for that matter—is alien to us anymore. Nevertheless, there is something anachronistic in the approach of the localists, since it relies upon an understanding of political and social reality that emerged only at the end of the early modern period and did not become widely held until very much later. The views of those living through this era usually depended upon different premises, ones that accepted a dimension of communal autonomy without also implying a rivalry with the nation or the central authorities.

According to the Elizabethan civil lawyer Thomas Wilson, early modern English cities were highly independent places. "They are not taxed," he says, "but by their owne officers of the[ir] owne brotherhoodes," and "no other officer of the Queen nor other" possessed "authority to entermeddle amongst them." The queen, indeed, placed no "governor in any Towne through out the whole Realme"; rather, a city's mayor, chosen locally without reference to royal nomination, served in the capacity of "Queens Lieftenant." It was his duty "to governe the Citty in good order," and, with the consent of the Common Council, "to make lawe and constitutions for the benifitt of the Citty." In addition, Wilson points out, "every citty hath a peculiar jurisdiction among themselves . . . by which jurisdiction . . . they have the authority to Judge all matters Criminell and Cyvill." For these reasons, Wilson thought of cities as privileged enclaves within the structure of government and society. "Every citty," he said, has "as it were, a Comon Wealth among themselves."[14]

But despite this use of the term "commonwealth," Wilson recognized—as Green did not—that at no time were English cities entirely free from the fabric of royal rule. Their privileges did not completely liberate them from the system of royal justice or from the obligation to pay taxes. Nor did city governments exercise jurisdiction over wide territories as did some of their continental counterparts. In no sense, therefore, were they classical city-states, radically separated from the hierarchy of rights and obligations that shaped neighboring communities. Wilson stresses that a city's "peculier jurisdiction" was the consequence of individual and explicit grants "by the King in divers times . . . confirmed by letters patent under the great seale," and operated under the important "restraynt that still all Civill causes may be removed from theirs to the highest Courts at Westminster." Cities, then, were effectively subordinated to both the will and the jurisdiction of the Crown. Although they enjoyed a great deal of self-government, they were not completely self-contained worlds, whole unto themselves.[15]

This conclusion is carried even further by early modern London's great antiquary, John Stowe. He refrains from using the word "commonwealth" in discussing his city, but instead conceives of a more encompassing commonwealth of which London was but a part. At the conclusion of his *Survey of London* Stowe prints a long "Apologie" for his city, written probably by the lawyer James Dalton. It argues that

> [i]t is besides the purpose to dispute, whether the estate of the gouernement here bee a *Democratie,* or *Aristocracie,* for whatsoeuer it bee, being considered in it selfe, certayne it is, that in respect of the whole Realme, London is but a Citizen, and no Citie, a subiect and no free estate, an obendienciarie, and no place indowed with any distinct or absolute power.

Not only are its citizens governed by the same law as "the rest of the Realme . . . a few customes onely excepted," but in Parliament

> they are but a member of the Comminaltie . . . and are as straightly bound by such lawes as any part of the Realme is, for if a contribution in subsidie of money to the Prince bee decreed, the Londoners haue none exemption, no not so much as to assesse themselues: for the prince doth appoint the Commissioners. If Souldiers must be mustered, Londoners haue no law to keepe themselues at home, if prouision for the Princes housholde bee to bee made, their goods are not priuileged. In summe, therefore, the gouernment of London differeth not in substance, but in ceremonie from the rest of the realm.[16]

London was without doubt the most highly privileged and independent city in England. If Stowe could agree to this view of its participation in the life of the kingdom, he surely would have said at least as much about the provincial towns.

This model, however, offers a dual vision of urban life. For within its boundaries a city may be said to have a community of its own, existing for the fellowship and mutual aid and affection that citizens give to one another. "[W]hereas commonwealthes and kingdomes cannot haue, next after God, any surer foundation than the loue and goodwill of one man towardes another," Stowe's apologist says, the same is "also closely bred and maintayned in Citties, where men by mutual societie and companying together, doe grow to alliances, comminalties and corporations."[17] Such a community could be a democracy or an aristocracy, since as a corporate body it must consist of a head to lead and members to obey, whether the head be selected by a free vote, co-optation, or inheritance.

Neither this approach nor Wilson's leads us inevitably to a localist interpretation of city life, since neither begins with a vision of the state or society as the necessary enemy of community or the individual. Each focuses our attention on different issues: Wilson's on the relation of civic to national institutions; Stowe's on the relation of the civic to the national community. The former stresses civic autonomy but recognizes the city's dependency on the nation for its freedoms. The latter offers a more complex view. On the one hand, the city is seen as part of a larger polity—a subsidiary body of the commonwealth of England. On the other, it is said to have its own communal integrity and common purposes. From this second viewpoint, the essence of urban society is the fellowship that citizens have with one another. Put in other words, from the perspective of the national polity a city is an organization with important functions to perform; from the perspective of the inhabitants it is a moral community in which head and body work together for common ends. Or, as F. W. Maitland says, it is "both organ and organism."[18]

These more complex approaches to early modern urban history have important consequences for research strategy and interpretation. One of the advantages of the localist's stress on communal solidarity is that the supposed compactness and distinctiveness of each community make it possible to study any particular county or town as a complete social organism having its own interlocking system of social relations. As Alan Everitt puts it, local history is the study of "some particular local community *as a whole*, as a complete society or organism, with a more or less distinct and continuous life of its own."[19] Hence it is a field concerned primarily with "structure," and above all with "social structure," understood as a systematic arrangement of interconnected parts.[20] In other words, this approach owes a heavy debt to the structural-functionalism of British social anthropology, in the sense that all the elements of the social order are seen to fit together to form a single, integrated system.[21] Such studies begin by assuming the existence of an autonomous collectivity of men and women, the boundaries of which mark the limits of a self-standing society and so help us to restrict the range of our inquiries to sources concerned primarily with relations within those boundaries.

But both Thomas Wilson and John Stowe force us to cast our nets more widely, to consider the community in its context and hence to devote as much attention to events and developments outside its boundaries as to those within them. The members of every society ordinarily are aware of qualitative differences in their degree of personal involvement with others, their formal rights and obligations, and their more informal moral responsibilities and social duties. They commonly recognize a division between Them and Us. But when a community is contained within a larger polity, as were the English towns, the lines of demarcation are often unclear. For there are overlapping levels of authority and overlapping markets, and the community's boundary is rather more like an open border than a guarded frontier. Men and materials, ideas and influences can pass through in either direction without passport or visa. This means, in turn, that groups within the town were free to form differing relationships to this wider context of action. Hence along with examining the ways the various components of urban society held together among themselves, we shall also have to explore how the city held together with the larger social order of which it was a part, and to look for breakdowns in internal and external relations and for conflicts within the community and between it and the wider world.

This emphasis on the way cities like Bristol were open to the world also has important consequences for the story we shall tell. The structural-functional model employed by localist historians is essentially static. It treats the ways social institutions fit together to make working mechanisms and how social actions promote social cohesion. In this view, conflict is seen as reinforcing the structure of society, because the parties engaged in it compete in the same arena and for the same ends. The theory leaves little room for self-generating change. Studies written according to this model do not completely exclude consideration of change, of course. But change, when it does occur, is understood to come from outside forces. The consequent imbalances in the local social order are then treated as working toward a new equilibrium.[22] But if the inhabitants of a city live in a setting of open relationships, in which different groups could form different connections with their surroundings, change is not the exclusive product either of external forces affecting the stable structures of tradition or of internal contradictions.

Instead it must be the consequence of a counterpoint between internal and external developments, in which the processes of change are neither accidental nor inevitable, but the outcome of human intelligences addressing the world as they find it. As Marx says, "men make their own history, but they do not make it just as they please; they do not make it under circumstances chosen by themselves, but under circumstances directly encountered." For Marx this confrontation could be a nightmare, but we must also recognize that it could be the wellspring of creativity, as human beings shape and reshape the world "given and transmitted" to them "from the past."[23]

Finally, our focus on the city's openness requires us to study social meanings. For structural-functionalists, and for many Marxists as well, only social uses are important. Functionalism begins with the concept of social structure as its foundation; it assumes the existence of a single fabric of social relations to which all action and thought are directed. Ideas have a place in the story only as they reflect society and reinforce it. But if the members of a community live within open borders and participate, through their choices, in the processes of historical change, we can expect to find among them more than one understanding of how society works and more than one set of goals for it. Society can no longer be thought of as a single system which we can observe in its entirety from on high. It becomes instead the product of different and competing viewpoints, which we must understand both jointly and severally if we are ever to put together a coherent story. This can be accomplished only if we take meanings seriously by placing people's words and gestures in the context of their thought and values as well as of their needs and interests.

In Bristol's coat of arms the controlling feature is the gate; it makes the connection between the city and the world. But "gate" in early English usage meant not only an opening or passing place in a wall, but sometimes also a way. It could be a road or path—a way to distant places; or it could be a manner or method—a way of doing or living. The word "trade" has a similarly complex meaning. At its root it refers to a course trodden by a person, but by extension it becomes a way or manner of life, a course of action, a mode of procedure or method, the practice or habit of doing something. Hence it is synonymous on the one hand with "craft" or "occupation," and on the other with "commerce" or "the buying and selling of commodities for a profit." To trade is both to follow a course and to traffic in goods. Bristol's life in the late medieval and early modern period was founded on trade understood in both these senses. Its citizens looked for their sustenance to the pathways that led beyond its boundaries, and in doing so they developed a distinctive outlook and pattern of action in the pursuit of their ends.

At the outset of our period, the trade of Bristolians depended upon the annual exchange of English woolens for French wines at Bordeaux. This traffic set the pace of life for the entire city, determining its social structure and its relations with its own hinterland and with the institutions of the English state. Two and a half centuries later, Bristol's trade touched nearly every important international market, and Bristol itself was an entrepôt of the Atlantic economy. From the fifteenth century, then, Bristol was more and more an open city with wider gateways bringing the world economy into closer relation with the local community. There was also a widening gate as its economy and its social and political structure were transformed. More and more of its inhabitants became engaged in the city's expanding Atlantic commerce, the networks of trade and credit deepened and broadened, and politics and religion converged with this new economic order. Out of this conjunction emerged new habits and action in society that were the beginnings of a modern form of capitalism, focused on credit and commerce.

For many scholars it may seem inappropriate to study the rise of modern capitalism in this fashion. If, as Eric Wolf says, "the world of humankind constitutes . . . a totality of interconnected processes" and capitalism touches "the four corners of the globe," no single case could ever be thought complete enough to serve as an illustrative example, and the only way to study the subject would be encyclopedically, "as a whole, a totality, a system."[24] But this conclusion depends on how the genre of local history is understood. Among English historians in recent years two main approaches have prevailed. The first involves the search for representative examples of general types. Here the historian, anxious to avoid the pitfalls of antiquarianism, focuses on themes typical of all similar places, not on local peculiarities, and his work aims to illuminate our understanding of broad developments in the same fashion as experimental results in the sciences are supposed to exemplify the truth of general laws. The second form of local study emphasizes the particular, even the unique, rather than the typical or universal. In these works the historian is interested in revealing the diversity of life in a society as it was lived away from the centers of action. Such a history tells us stories that "enlighten us about the common run of chaps" as they lived "at their home address[es]."[25] But neither type suits the study of a large-scale historical process like the growth of capitalism, for the former focuses on the part, not the whole, whereas the latter treats only the variegated periphery, not the unifying core.

There is a third kind of local history, one that searches for the paradigmatic rather than the typical or the unique. Paradigms have achieved a certain currency in recent historical studies. Usually the word means a conceptual model or frame of reference, but as employed in the history of science, it can also refer to a transforming experiment, a procedure and result that change the way problems are viewed and become a pattern for further experimentation. It is a term that implies a relationship between an experiment and its context and that treats the two as integral parts of a process of change.[26] Local history can be like this as well: it can concentrate on the ways a particular place and its inhabitants participated in and contributed to the transformation of an established pattern of thought and action.

In the great revolution in historical learning that accompanied the English Renaissance, local history of this kind was among the first subjects to be extensively studied. Edmund Gibson's 1695 edition of Camden's *Britannia,* for example, lists in its bibliography 162 separate items of local scholarship for England alone, and more still for Wales, Scotland, Ireland, and the Channel Islands.[27] Most of these were works in which the author sought to establish the standing of his town or county in the grand history of the kingdom; they were local in their outlook only in that they told the story of a particular place, not in the themes they treated. The purpose of this kind of history was to show the beauties and antiquities of a place and the greatness and virtue of those who peopled it, so that both place and people could become exemplars of the good life and of right action. But this period also witnessed two other momentous developments in the study of society, namely, the rise of "political arithmetic" and of "Whig" history. Both have made genuine contributions to our understanding, the former by showing us that we can measure the dimensions of human life and the latter by showing us that we can see the present emerge from the past. But both accomplished their work by enormous feats of abstraction. To do political arithmetic requires concentration on a limited range of questions and sources and a disregard of those many aspects of society that cannot be quantified.[28] Similarly, to do Whig history demands a neglect of past events, ideas, and social structures that have no demonstrable link to the present.[29] These features have perhaps nowhere been more evident than

in the study of early modern capitalism, where various forms of clio-
metrics, rooted in neoclassical economic theories, often compete with
various kinds of teleology in shaping interpretation.

The paradigmatic approach employed in the following chapters pur-
sues a different line in attempting to put both economy and society
back into the life of a particular place at a particular time. These chapters treat Bristol as simultaneously typical, in that it helped set a pattern
for all who related to it, and unique, in that its history depends on its
particular relationship to the world, which changes as its story unfolds.
In periods of rapid change, the existence of such places marks the transition from one form of life to another. At those times, when the old
rules no longer apply and new ones have not yet come to dominate, the
world is made up of a rich array of community types, each combining
in its own fashion new ideas and social arrangements with fragments of
the old order. Each type, then, can reveal something important about
the underlying patterns of change in thought and social interaction.[30]

In many studies of the growth of modern capitalism, however, it has
become commonplace to think of the newly emerging world economy
as a single structure, in which each region or place has its particular
niche either at the core or at the margins.[31] For those who use this
model, the perspective is that of an omniscient observer looking down
upon the globe from distant space. At that altitude everything appears
in an ordered hierarchy, with economic surpluses flowing to the dominating center and new ideas and values flowing to the outlying depen-
dencies. But from such an elevated viewpoint neither the fine details that
distinguish place from place nor the everyday comings and goings of individuals will be discernible. The risk is that the structures we see will
be rather like the canals of Mars, creations of our eye and brain. These
problems disappear if we cease to think of capitalism as a universal
structure—a single system or organization—and view it instead as a
way of thinking and acting, a form of life. A form of life can exist along-
side other forms. It can take shape slowly, emerging in one place and
then another until it widens its range sufficiently to link these places together. It can broaden its reach, setting rules for more and more kinds
of behavior, and it can deepen in the ways it commits the people living
under it to following those rules. Moreover, just as the emergence of a
new species of animal will force all other creatures in the environment
to adjust their relations to it, the development of a form of life can effect
changes in the habits of thought and action of those living according to

a different set of rules. The result, however, will be a new pattern of diversity, not a modernized unity produced by the extinction of all but one form.

Capitalism conceived in this way is the joint product of a distinctive point of view and a particular context. It is, then, rather like a language—a set of gestures, signs, and meanings linked together by grammar, syntax, and logic. To comprehend what is said and how its significance has changed over time, however, we need to attend not only to the general rules of usage being followed but, as Hilary Putnam argues, to what the speaker "wants or intends," which is relative to "the nature of the environment" in which he finds himself.[32] This will be the subject of our history of early modern Bristol, whose Atlantic perspective gives us an excellent vantage point from which to see an urban form of modern capitalism emerge as the fragments of an older social and cultural order combined and recombined with new ideas and social arrangements.

PART I

Opening the Way, 1450–1650

CHAPTER I

Feats of Merchandise

At the end of the seventeenth century Bristol was, after London, the pre-eminent Atlantic port in England. Two centuries before, it had been the first seafaring town from which Englishmen had sailed in search of the Northwest Passage. These facts make it tempting to think of Bristol as destined by geography and history "for the role of Empire builder."[1] But such a view obscures more than it explains. It assumes that Bristol's Atlantic commerce grew steadily and along a predetermined natural course, like a great tree from a seed, when in fact its growth was the result of no single developmental process. As Bristol became increasingly involved in trans-Atlantic enterprise, the world around it also changed. In consequence, the events that account for the city's rise as a center of exploration at the close of the Middle Ages bear little relation to those that explain its dominant position as a colonial entrepôt at the time of the Glorious Revolution. During these centuries Bristol's history was, nevertheless, inextricably intertwined with that of the Atlantic world. Most of the tale, however, is of a mundane character, involving the workaday activities of conventional traders engaging in the steady pursuit of profit along well-traveled avenues of commerce on the Atlantic shores of Europe—what early sixteenth-century Bristolians themselves called "feats of marchaundises."[2] Innovations, when they came, were more often the consequence of makeshift efforts to cope with immediate social and economic problems than the result of heroic actions by seafaring adventurers or bold commercial experiments by rationalizing entrepreneurs. The story begins with the close of the Hundred Years' War, thirty years before the first voyages in quest of newfound lands, and its opening chapter takes us from the so-called economic depression of the fifteenth century to the tobacco boom of the early seventeenth century.

In the early fifteenth century there was no question of Bristol's place among English commercial cities.[3] Although it could not hope to match the wealth and distinction of London, it was at the very height of its vigor, as was manifest in the grandeur and elegance of the church of St. Mary, Redcliffe, beautified by William Canynges's benefactions.[4] Indeed, Canynges, probably the richest Bristolian of this period, easily rivaled any merchant in the realm.[5] Many of his Bristol contemporaries, such as Thomas Strange, Robert Sturmy, or John Jay, though hardly as wealthy, were themselves great merchants capable of risking vast fortunes in ventures into untried waters.[6] But this picture is somewhat false, since from the middle of the century the foundations of this medieval prosperity had been shattered by events the Bristolians could not control.

Throughout the later Middle Ages Gascony was Bristol's principal market. From the very start the demand for wine was at the heart of this traffic. It was imported through the city at least as early as King John's reign, when it began to supplant the vintages of Picardy on the English table. During the fourteenth century, the relationship between Gascony and Bristol deepened as Bordeaux and other Gascon ports became major outlets for English cloth, with Bristol responsible for the largest part of this traffic.[7] Indeed, in Gascony cloth and wine stood in symbiotic relation with one another, with the former serving as the principal medium of exchange used in acquiring the latter. In consequence, the trade levels in the two commodities displayed the same rhythm of upward and downward movement.[8] To a large degree this pattern in Bristol's trade persisted throughout the first half of the fifteenth century.[9] To be sure, Bristolians were rapidly developing new commercial interests in the Iberian peninsula, especially in Portugal,[10] but this expansion rested firmly upon the solid ground provided by the city's Gascon trade.

The key to this long-term commercial relationship was its security. So long as Bordeaux and its environs remained the possession of the English Crown, English and Gascon merchants were specially protected in each other's home districts. In peacetime the trade was as certain as the changing of the seasons. Each fall, large convoys of English vessels, sometimes amounting to fifty ships or more, could be expected to arrive for the new vintage. Small communities of Gascon merchants resided in Bristol and nearly every other English port that dealt with the wine districts, while, for their part, the English enjoyed advantageous trading rights in Gascony. At various periods, including most of the first half of the fifteenth century, the English were even able to trade their own wares duty-free in Gascony. In addition, the English king was anxious to sustain close and friendly relations with his prized French dependency. In times of dearth he invariably licensed shipments of English grain, even when supplies were scarce at home. With this guarantee of necessary food supplies, and with the certainty of a large English market in which to sell wine, the Gascons were free to devote nearly every available plot of land to the cultivation of the vine. In turn, the English supplied cloth as well as grain to Bordeaux and its environs.[11] This trade provided the principal market for Bristol's cloth merchants. Cargoes sent to Gascony consisted almost entirely of woolen fabric, with only small quantities of hides, fish, and coal making up the exports used to purchase wine. At Bordeaux this link between cloth and wine was so intimate that the one was often bartered directly for the other by Bristolians.[12]

In the mid-fifteenth century, these ties were rent asunder by the English defeat in the Hundred Years' War. The final stages took more than fifteen years to complete. Until 1438, the Bordelais itself had been relatively free of the devastation of war. But the destructive invasion of marauding bands of soldiers in that year ended this period of immunity, and an era of marked instability in trade ensued. In 1449 the battles were renewed almost at the very moment of the vintage. Bordeaux fell to the French in June 1451, only to be recovered in the autumn of the following year. Finally, in July 1453 the French again seized the city, this time for good. Although trade persisted at reduced levels throughout the period of fighting and immediately thereafter, in the fall of 1455 it was almost completely brought to a halt by French cutbacks in the issuance of safe-conducts to the English. The impact of this new policy was devastating. Between 1453 and 1455 Bristol had imported an average of over seventeen hundred tons of wine per year (Table 1). For the six subsequent years, however, imports were only half this figure. The cloth trade suffered the same setback, with an annual average shipment in the 1460s almost 40 percent below what had been common in the first half of the century (Table 2).[13]

These events had profound effects on Bristol's commerce, making the third quarter of the fifteenth century the low point in Bristol's late medieval economic history. A stable traffic was replaced by a trade subject

TABLE I NONSWEET WINE TRADE, 1400–1500
(FIVE-YEAR AVERAGES TO THE NEAREST TON)

Mich.–Mich.	Bristol	London	Southampton	Devon Ports
1400–1405[a]	1,452	3,853	698	337[b]
1405–1410	1,255	3,788	1,262	682[c]
1410–1415	1,144	5,646	1,420	621
1415–1420	1,357	5,584	1,692[d]	611
1420–1425[e]	1,940	4,325	831	421
1425–1430[f]	1,129	4,013	665	326
1430–1435	1,258	3,493[g]	532	659
1435–1440[h]	1,255	2,626	332	397[i]
1440–1445	2,411	4,135	997[j]	575
1445–1450	1,915	2,855[k]	723	595
Annual avg.	1,499	4,098	947	563
1450–1455	1,810	2,520	438	270
1455–1460	814	1,409	340	132
1460–1465	834	2,013	502	240
1465–1470	1,075[l]	1,900	489	300
1470–1475	—[m]	1,828	688[n]	193
1475–1480	1,549[o]	2,592	746[n]	336[p]
1480–1485	1,323[q]	3,511[r]	517	458[s]
1485–1490	1,627	3,359	407	426
1490–1495	2,201	3,567	350	595
1495–1500	2,197	3,621	330[t]	838
Annual avg.	1,504	2,614	487	377

SOURCE: M. K. James; *Studies in the Medieval Wine Trade*, ed. E. M. Veale, with introduction by E. M. Carus-Wilson (Oxford: Clarendon Press, 1971), pp. 112–15.

[a]No figures are available for 1400–1403.

[b]Figures for 1404–1405 are incomplete and not used.

[c]Figures for 1405–1407 are incomplete and not used.

[d]Figures for 1415–1416 are incomplete and not used.

[e]Denizen subsidy ceased 31 August 1422 to 31 July 1425, hence the figures for 1421–1425 are not used.

[f]Denizen subsidy ceased 11 November 1427 to 5 December 1429, hence the figures for 1427–1429 are not used.

[g]Figures for 1433–1434 are incomplete and not used.

[h]Denizen subsidy ceased 11 November 1436 to 1 April 1437, hence the figures for 1436–1437 are not used.

[i]Figures for 1437–1438 are incomplete and not used.

[j]Figures for 1442–1443 are incomplete and not used.

[k]Figures for 1448–1449 are incomplete and not used.

[l]Figures for 1466–1467 are missing.

[m]Figures are available only for 1470–1471 (765 tuns).

[n]Figures for 1474–1475 and 1475–1476 have been estimated by dividing the single figure of 1926 tuns given for the two years together.

[o]Figures for 1475–1477 are missing.

[p]Figures for 1475–1476 are missing; figures for 1476–1477 are incomplete and not used.

[q]Figures for 1484–1485 are missing.

[r]Figures for 1482–1483 are incomplete and not included.

[s]Figures for 1483–1485 are missing.

[t]Figures for 1498–1500 are missing.

TABLE 2 CLOTH EXPORTS, 1400–1500
(DECENNIAL AVERAGES TO THE NEAREST WHOLE CLOTH OF ASSIZE)

Mich.–Mich.	Bristol		London		Southampton		Exeter	
	No. cloths	(% denizen)	No. cloths	(% denizen)	No. cloths	(% denizen)	No. cloths	(% denizen)
1400–1410	3,079	(98.7)	13,845[a]	(41.9)	5,639[b]	(12.8)	307	(85.1)[c]
1410–1420	2,281	(99.1)	13,595	(30.0)	2,284	(34.7)	471	(88.0)
1420–1430	4,427	(99.3)	17,155	(32.2)	6,154	(27.9)	386	(88.6)
1430–1440	4,087	(99.8)	17,597	(49.8)	8,414	(15.9)	1,122	(93.3)
1440–1450	5,106	(98.6)	19,082	(43.0)	9,957	(19.0)	1,875	(96.8)[d]
Annual avg.	3,796	(99.1)	16,304	(39.8)	6,507	(20.0)	824	(93.1)
1450–1460	3,355	(98.5)	16,444	(50.1)[e]	7,058	(21.3)	1,256	(98.9)[f]
1460–1470	2,413	(97.3)[g]	18,308	(61.9)[e]	5,233	(18.9)	946	(93.8)
1470–1480	5,052	(98.7)[b]	28,886	(57.2)	3,972	(23.4)	1,241	(87.6)[i]
1480–1490	5,245	(92.4)[j]	35,909	(42.5)	1,345	(38.7)	3,021	(76.1)
1490–1500	6,515	(95.5)	39,495	(43.0)[k]	3,346	(28.1)[l]	3,893	(87.0)
Annual avg.	4,522	(95.8)	27,322	(49.5)	4,226	(23.2)	2,124	(85.7)

SOURCE: Compiled from E. M. Carus-Wilson and Olive Coleman, *England's Export Trade, 1275–1547* (Oxford: Clarendon Press, 1963), pp. 97–111.

[a]Figures for 1400–1401 are missing.

[b]Figures for 1401–1402 are missing.

[c]Figures for 1404–1405 are incomplete and not used; 1407–1408 includes Plymouth until 11 August 1408.

[d]Figures for 1449–1450 are incomplete and not used.

[e]The London accounts for 1459–1460 and 1460–1461 run from 29 September 1459 to 31 July 1460 and from 31 July 1460 to 29 September 1461, respectively. For purposes of these decennial averages I have taken the mean of these two years in order to provide an annual figure for each of the years involved.

[f]Figures for 1450–1451 are incomplete and not used.

[g]Figures for 1466–1468 are incomplete and not used.

[h]There is a large gap in the figures from 1471–1477. In the first year of this decade a total of only 2,074 cloths were shipped from Bristol; at the end of the decade the average was 6,044 cloths.

[i]Figures for 1475–1477 are missing.

[j]Figures for 1484–1485 are missing. In addition, denizen figures for 1485–1487 contain an unspecified number of cloths shippped by Spaniards.

[k]Figures for 1494–1496 are missing.

[l]Figures for 1498–1500 are missing.

to unpredictable interruptions and sharp fluctuations of volume. With
the end of the war and the period of reduced commercial exchanges that
followed, the change in the framework of Anglo-Gascon relations solidi-
fied. Although trade with Gascony did not cease entirely, Bristolians
now dealt with it as foreigners in the territories of a former enemy, not
as privileged parties in the dominions of their own king. At the same
time, the Iberian trades grew in importance. At the end of the century,
they easily rivaled commerce with France, taking the bulk of the city's
cloth and other exports and supplying a list of valuable imports, including wax, sugar, spices, fruit, iron, and dyestuffs, as well as wines. On
this foundation, the fourth quarter of the fifteenth century witnessed
the last flowering of Bristol's medieval prosperity. After reaching a low
ebb in the 1460s, the city's trade figures bounced back to new heights
by the 1490s. In that decade woolen exports achieved an average of
sixty-five hundred cloths per annum and wine shipments were significantly higher than they had been in any period except the 1440s (see Tables 1 and 2). Other valuable commodities such as olive oil, woad,
sugar, and spices also poured into the port. When judged by customs
revenue for this period, Bristol was easily the third most important
commercial center in southern England, outranked only by London and
Southampton.[14] Following the loss of Gascony, the focus of Bristol's
trade had shifted southward. Although Bordeaux and its environs still
remained important to the city's merchants, the diverse commodities of
Spain and Portugal now had a greater attraction than before.

If the closing years of the fifteenth century provided Bristol with a rich
harvest, the beginning of the sixteenth century brought the city into a
bleak new season in its economic history. Every aspect of commerce suffered in some measure. According to the merchants, the city's shipping,
in which the wealth of its merchant magnates had been heavily invested
in the fifteenth century, severely decayed during Henry VIII's reign. By
the 1540s bitter complaints were heard that "where as ther grett shippes
haue customably made towe or thre viages in the yere, now by reason
of small vtteraunce of their warres & merchantdise the[y] make but
one viage in the yere."[15] Bristol's drapers also protested a depression in
their trade, asserting that in the time span in which two hundred cloths
used to be sold, now but twenty could be vented.[16] We should discount
the exaggeration of these remarks made by men begging special favors.
But the trend they manifest cannot be denied. Bristol's economy had

suffered a sharp blow. It fell further and further behind London in economic position and was rapidly overtaken by Exeter, its chief rival in the western districts, whose access to divers new kinds of woolen fabrics gave it advantages in the French trade, when it revived, that Bristol lacked.[17]

The most severe effects of this early sixteenth-century commercial difficulty were felt by the cloth trade. In the closing years of Henry VII's reign, its boom in Bristol simply ended. In the first five years of the century, annual average exports were about 30 percent below the figures achieved in the 1490s. The tailspin continued during the next five quinquennial periods, until the averages were barely one-third of those for the last decade of the fifteenth century. Indeed, only in the 1530s and again in the years between 1550 and 1555 were there slight upturns in the trend, but even these were almost immediately halted in the following period. Over the whole first sixty years of the sixteenth century, moreover, the city exported an average of only slightly over twenty-seven hundred cloths per year, a figure rivaling the worst decennial averages of the fifteenth century (Table 3). Bristol's exports of English woolens had simply stagnated. By the beginning of Elizabeth's reign they were not only at their lowest ebb but were being traded by higher percentages of alien merchants than ever before.

In conjunction with this direct blow to Bristol's chief export came a more general decline in the city's commercial well-being. The wine trade, for example, suffered a considerable diminution. As with cloth, the first years of the sixteenth century witnessed a sharp initial contraction, in this case of about 50 percent from the high figures of the 1490s, and even though there was some improvement after 1515, the levels neither returned to the peaks of the last decade of the fifteenth century nor remained consistently strong (Table 4). Only the goods subject to ad valorem duties appear to have escaped this gloomy fate, although here, too, there was a decline from the very high figures reached in the late fifteenth century and an increase in the number of non-denizens engaging in the trade (Table 5). During the last five years of Henry VIII's reign, the average value of these goods for customs purposes was about 25 percent higher than the average figures at the beginning of his reign. This suggests a double shift away from cloth as an export to other items such as metals, hides, and foodstuffs, which were assessed ad valorem, and a corresponding shift to more expensive imports, also assessed ad valorem, though with many items now brought to Bristol by merchant strangers.[18]

TABLE 3 CLOTH EXPORTS, 1500–1561
(FIVE-YEAR AVERAGES TO THE NEAREST WHOLE CLOTH OF ASSIZE)

Mich.–Mich.	Bristol		London		Southampton		Exeter	
	No. cloths	(% denizen)	No. cloths	(% denizen)	No. cloths	(% denizen)	No. cloths	(% denizen)
1500–1505	4,612	(96.8)	46,610	(45.5)	6,851	(20.8)[a]	9,329	(95.1)
1505–1510	3,219	(99.1)	52,390	(52.2)	13,504	(13.1)	7,207	(97.9)
1510–1515	3,140	(97.7)	62,257	(53.8)	10,732	(34.2)	4,840	(93.2)
1515–1520	3,025	(98.8)	63,084	(57.8)	13,428	(17.3)	4,087	(95.1)
1520–1525	2,440	(94.1)	61,854	(57.5)	8,481	(26.2)	3,782	(90.9)
1525–1530	2,176	(96.9)	73,513	(58.7)[b]	6,995	(23.5)	4,533	(93.7)
1530–1535	2,344	(95.8)	75,503	(54.3)	7,482	(37.4)	4,429	(91.4)
1535–1540	2,816	(93.8)	91,731	(50.9)	3,816	(50.9)	5,624	(88.1)
1540–1545	2,191	(82.4)	99,535	(49.9)[c]	3,840	(39.5)	5,064	(79.1)
1545–1550	2,663	(84.5)	123,797	(57.2)[d]	2,285	(58.7)[e]	2,433	(89.8)
1550–1555	3,362	(94.9)[f]	111,091	(69.8)[g]	1,990	(90.7)[h]	3,205	(94.1)[i]
1555–1561	1,176	(71.2)[j]	101,743	(77.9)[k]	1,139	(79.6)[l]	3,005	(97.8)[m]
Annual avg.	2,743	(93.7)	76,331	(57.0)	7,042	(28.2)	4,850	(92.3)

SOURCE: E. M. Carus-Wilson and Olive Coleman, England's Export Trade, 1275–1547 (Oxford: Clarendon Press, 1963), pp. 112–19; J. D. Gould, The Great Debasement: Currency and the Economy in Mid-Tudor England (Oxford: Clarendon Press, 1970), pp. 173–81.

[a] Account for 1500–1501 is incomplete and consequently not used.
[b] Account for 1528–1529 is incomplete and consequently not used.
[c] No account exists for 1544–1545.
[d] There are incomplete accounts for 1546–1547 and 1548–1549.
[e] No accounts exist for 1546–1547 and 1548–1549.
[f] No accounts exist for 1551–1553.
[g] No accounts exist for 1552–1553 and 1554–1555.
[h] No accounts exist for 1552–1554.
[i] No accounts exist for 1551–1553. Accounts for 1553–1554 do not distinguish shipments by denizens; hence figures for this year have been omitted in calculating the percentage.
[j] No accounts exist for 1556–1557.
[k] No accounts exist for 1555–1556 and 1557–1559.
[l] No account exists for 1559–1560.
[m] No account exists for 1556–1557.

TABLE 4   NONSWEET WINE IMPORTS TO BRISTOL, 1480–1547
(FIVE-YEAR AVERAGES TO THE NEAREST TON)

Mich.–Mich.	Tonnage
1480–1485[a]	1,323
1485–1490	1,627
1490–1495	2,201
1495–1500	2,197
Annual avg.	1,864
1509–1514	1,079
1514–1519	1,965
1519–1524	1,624
1524–1529	1,195
1529–1534	1,638
1534–1539	1,629
1539–1544	1,512
(1544–1547)	1,294
Annual avg.	1,503

SOURCE: 1480–1500: M. K. James, *Studies in the Medieval Wine Trade*, ed. E. M. Veale, introduction by E. M. Carus-Wilson (Oxford: Clarendon Press, 1971), pp. 114–16. 1509–1547: Georg von Schanz, *Englische Handelspolitik gegen Ende des Mittelalters mit besonderer Berücksichtigung des Zeitalters der beiden ersten Tudors, Heinrich VII. und Heinrich VIII.*, 2 vols. (Leipzig: Duncker und Humblot, 1881), vol. 2, pp. 132–33. The format and the gaps are a consequence of the fact that the two sources do not form a completely sequential series.
[a]Data for the year 1484–1485 are missing.

Nevertheless, not all of Bristol's markets were equally affected by the general collapse of its trade. Ireland and France were the worst hit. There was perhaps a 50 percent fall in cloth exports to the Irish market, and, although commerce in other commodities still remained brisk, there was also a falling away from the high levels achieved in the last years of the fifteenth century.[19] As regards France, not only did shipping between Bristol and the major Atlantic ports decline and then stagnate, but the volume of French wine coming to Bristol was also severely reduced.[20] In these markets, therefore, conditions were especially dark. But Bristol appears to have held its own more successfully in the Iberian peninsula. In Portugal, old commercial ties and a continued demand for English cloth insured a reasonable traffic for the city.[21] In Spain the picture was brighter still. Although there had been a dramatic decline in the number of cloths shipped there from Bristol during the first decade of the sixteenth century, by 1517–18 the figures had risen again almost to equal those from 1485–86. Despite the strained relations between England and Spain after 1527 or so, a steady trade continued throughout the remainder of Henry VIII's reign and persisted right to the end of the century, though at a somewhat lower volume than in the teens

TABLE 5   VALUE OF GOODS SUBJECT TO AD VALOREM DUTIES
ENTERED AT BRISTOL IN THE REIGN OF HENRY VIII
(THREE-YEAR AVERAGES TO THE NEAREST £)

Mich.–Mich.	Value	% Denizen
1509–1512	11,455	97.1
1512–1515	12,249	91.7
1515–1518	12,584	95.5
1518–1521	13,441	94.3
1521–1524	9,895	93.0
1524–1527	11,163	93.9
1527–1530	9,852	91.9
1530–1533	13,935	87.5
1533–1536	12,728	92.2
1536–1539	14,068	92.5
1539–1542	14,477	94.1
1542–1545	13,427	85.6
(1545–1547)	17,977	79.0
Annual avg.	12,731	91.4

SOURCE: Georg von Schanz, *Englische Handelspolitik gegen Ende des Mittelalters, mit besonderer Berücksichtigung des Zeitalters der beiden ersten Tudors, Heinrich VII. und Heinrich VIII.*, 2 vols. (Leipzig: Duncker und Humblot, 1881), vol. 2, p. 64.

and twenties. Bristol's import trade from Spain and Portugal also was remarkably healthy. Wine shipments stayed high, and the value of other imports rose to levels substantially in excess of those for the pre-1490 period. Despite diminished totals in Bristol's cloth exports, the cloth trade still remained important in the Iberian peninsula, where Bristolians exchanged cloth for a wide variety of valuable goods. But cloth was no longer the backbone of Bristol's commercial activity. Over the first half of the sixteenth century, the fall in its export substantially outstripped the declines experienced in other sectors of the city's commerce. As a result, Bristol's ancient connection with the production and distribution of cloth was weakened, and those inhabitants who depended on the cloth trade faced depressed circumstances and disrupted businesses.[22]

To a considerable degree, the movement of the woolen trade away from Bristol was part of a larger process of English economic history, just beginning in this period, which saw a general reordering of the nation's urban hierarchy as commerce came to be centered upon London. Viewed from the perspective of Bristol's traditional economy, this story appears as one of straightforward decline, especially for those whose livelihood depended primarily upon the cloth industry. But seen in terms of the emerging national urban system, the tale is rather more complicated, for it involved a recasting of urban functions and not simply a linear descent into long-term depression. Developments of this type almost invariably bring a mood of crisis with them, because they catch particular individuals and groups unable to adapt, economically or intellectually, to the new circumstances. But they sometimes bring new opportunities as well. In examining this era of urban crisis in Bristol, we must keep our eyes open for shifts in function within the larger urban network and the varied effects these changes had on the city's internal structure and on different groups within it.[23] Nevertheless, taken by themselves, as many of the most hard-hit Bristolians necessarily would have perceived them, the economic conditions revealed by the raw trade statistics for the early sixteenth century show Bristol's situation vis-à-vis London to have been rather grim.

In the mid-fifteenth century London commanded only something less than 50 percent of cloth exports; a hundred years later the figure was 90 percent. At the same time the traffic in imports concentrated there. Much of this change was due to the growth of the Antwerp mart, through which London's merchants could readily exchange the vast quantities of cloth at their disposal for the riches of Europe and Asia. But these developments were accomplished primarily at the expense of the outports, whose own growth could not keep pace. Judging from customs revenues collected between 1485 and 1547, London's share of England's commerce rose from approximately half to nearly two-thirds of the total, and the proportion of trade in the hands of provincial merchants declined nearly everywhere. When set in the context of national trends these Bristol figures are all the more revealing, since the city's decline as a center for the cloth trade corresponded to a period of expansion in the export of the same traditional woolen fabrics in which Bristol had previously specialized. Although the rise in these exports may not have been quite so "meteoric" as F. J. Fisher claimed on the basis of London's figures alone, it is clear that during much of this period shipments of broadcloth from Southampton and Exeter and its member ports remained stronger than from Bristol.[24]

From early in the sixteenth century, outcries against the decay of Bristol's clothing industry and the intrusion of Londoners into its economic affairs were common among Bristolians. In 1518, for example, Sheriff William Dale complained that

> thenhabitauntes of [Bristol] beyng as Cloythers wevers dyers tookers and other sundry Crafty men dayly lak work and runne in Idylnes. And the

towne by Reason of the same [is] broughte vnto great desolacion and about
viii c howseholdes in the same towne desolate vacante and decayed to the vt-
ter decay and distruccion of the said towne.[25]

Twenty years later the lamentations were even louder. The mayor himself complained that "[m]any tenements are fallen into decay for want
of timber and stones, and the quay and town walls are in like ruin."[26]
Much of the blame for this dismal state was placed on London. In the
1540s it was said that Londoners not only had captured the business of
Gloucestershire, Somerset, and other counties neighboring Bristol but
had invaded the city's own industrial districts. Redcliffe parish, in
which once "spinsters, carders and dyverse substancyall & riche men
[made] ther dwelling & levyed well by ther occupacions and occupyeng
of clothmakyng," now would no longer supply the Bristolians with
workmen for their cloths. The Londoners, with their large capital resources, were able to give better credit terms than their rivals from the
western port.[27]

Although Bristol was well located to tap the cloth production of
western England and to travel to and from the Iberian peninsula, its decay in the early sixteenth century made it difficult to acquire the necessary cloth supplies for this commerce. As a result, the city's wealthiest
and most successful entrepreneurs had pulled up stakes and reestablished themselves in London, the hub of the cloth trade. These entrepreneurs include such well-known men of affairs as Paul Withypoll, the
younger Robert Thorne, and George Monox, each of whom was a
leader first of Bristol's, then London's, merchant community. Monox
and Thorne both served as mayor of Bristol before leaving for London,
while Withypoll came on his mother's side from a family with a long
record of similar service.[28] All three primarily traded with Spain and
Portugal. From this base, they appear to have been attracted by the
riches of the Levant and of the Indies, even to the point of trading directly with those distant places rather than relying on shipments via Iberian ports. Withypoll was among the earliest traders to the Isle of Candy
(Crete), and Thorne was not only a depositor in the famous bank of St.
George in Genoa and a dealer in Italian and Levantine goods but was
also one of the first group of Englishmen to deal regularly with the West
Indies.[29] After leaving Bristol, Monox became a leading London Draper
and for a time the master of Blackwell Hall; Withypoll and Thorne were
Merchant Taylors. As well as holding major posts in London's government, both Monox and Withypoll acted as master of their livery companies; indeed, Monox served seven times.[30]

That these men made their choice of London over Bristol not without regret is revealed in Robert Thorne's will, for among his many substantial benefactions he made several for charitable purposes in his home town, including monies to help found a free school and for the care of the city's poor. He even set aside £200 for the redemption of the fee farm and the prisage of wines collected at the port.[31] Although he may have replanted his roots in London, his ties to his home remained strong.

The way cloth and its availability affected the cloth merchant is made clearer by the career of Thomas Howell. Howell, who traded with Spain and Portugal, was a regular business associate of the various members of the Thorne family. Not only did he have frequent dealings in Seville with Robert Thorne and his brother Nicholas, but at the beginning of his career he was servant or apprentice to Hugh Eliot, the business partner of Robert Thorne the elder, and later as his factor in Seville he used Thomas Maillard, who was a regular business partner of the younger Robert Thorne. Like Withypoll, Monox, and Thorne, Howell was an expatriate Bristolian who settled in London in the midst of his career. Like them, too, he was a cloth trader, undertaking his activities in London as a member of the livery of the Drapers Company. Judging from his commercial records, he was among the foremost of Iberian merchants in the first half of the sixteenth century, trading in Andalusia and in Portugal, and also with the Spanish ports on the Bay of Biscay. Howell must be listed, along with Thorne and Maillard, as among the earliest Englishmen who traded directly with the Spanish possessions in the Caribbean. In 1527, for example, he shipped £50 worth of "Sartane stofe" (i.e., cloth of some type), to John de Morsynes, his factor in Santo Domingo.[32]

Howell's ledger offers insight into his motive for abandoning residence in Bristol to set up business in London. The book, which gives a full account of Howell's commercial affairs from 1517 to 1527, reveals his domestic business to have been almost entirely devoted to cloth. Even his imports were largely complementary to these cloth shipments. Apart from the iron that he brought from northern Spain in substantial quantities, his foreign purchases were primarily supplies for the production of cloth, such as oil, alum, woad, and other commodities used in the dyeing and finishing of textiles. The fabrics he shipped, moreover, were of every variety, dyed and undyed, many of them types originating in the manufacturing districts only a short distance from Bristol. The clothiers with whom Howell dealt, however, were residents of East

Anglia and the home counties. They came from Norfolk, Suffolk, Essex, Berkshire, Middlesex, and Kent; one was even a Merchant Tailor in London itself. This fact is especially revealing because Howell, like Thorne and Monox as well as other Bristolians become Londoners, did a good deal of his importing through Bristol as well as London.[33] Hence it seems it was less London's geographical position than its role in the marketing of cloth that attracted Howell and his fellows to the capital. With tens of thousands of cloths coming into London every year, not only were supplies for export readily available, but the skilled craftsmen necessary to support the industry, especially dyers and shearmen, were concentrated there as well. As Howell's ledger shows, he frequently bought unfinished cloths and put them out himself to be barbed, folded, pressed, sheared, and dyed by London specialists, sometimes even paying them in woad, alum, soap, or other raw materials that he imported from the continent. The volume of his trade permitted him to combine his disparate dealings into a single orbit of commerce in which each element complemented the others.[34] As Bristol's merchants eventually came to recognize, this capacity for integration in London's cloth industry neutralized their own city's geographical advantages in trade with the Iberian peninsula and left them unable to compete effectively with their rivals in the capital. In the face of this hard fact, ambitious Bristolians sought a foothold in London.

This transfer of many of Bristol's leading merchants to London was not only a symptom of their city's economic crisis but a cause in its own right. Their departures represented more than a choice based on London's comparative economic advantage. Unlike young apprentices who came to the capital without wives and children and usually with little more than a small stake or the hope of an inheritance, these established Bristolians had substantial personal fortunes as well as deeply rooted personal connections in their home city. Withdrawal of their wealth was itself a significant blow to the city's prosperity, further reducing its attractiveness as a theater for the ambitions of others.[35] Even though by the second half of the sixteenth century London's own cloth-finishing industry was in decline, the changes wrought in the overall character of English economic life by London's domination of these crafts in the first half of the century proved irreversible.[36]

The earliest signs of change in the direction of Bristol's commerce are to be found in Robert Sturmy's ventures into the Mediterranean in the mid-fifteenth century, even though they proved unsuccessful. Trade with this region had long held a special fascination for the merchants of Bristol. Its products—sweets and spices, rich and delicate textiles, and other finery of the luxury trade—were highly valued and highly profitable. But in the fifteenth century this traffic was a monopoly of the Italians, who frequented London and Southampton but rarely ventured to Bristol. Still, Bristolians traded regularly in Eastern luxuries, shipping cloth and other wares by road to Southampton to be exchanged with the Venetians and Genoese for silks and spices.[37] But it was not until the trouble in Gascony that the Bristolians were willing to risk the ire of the Italians by passing through the Straits of Gibraltar on their own.

Two separate voyages were attempted. The first took place in 1446–47 when Sturmy sent the Coq Anne to Pisa and thence to Jaffa, carrying one hundred and sixty pilgrims probably laden with cloth, tin, and wool. Although the occasion for this voyage was the ouster of the Venetians from Egypt, which opened the Levant to English enterprise, the altered conditions in Gascony also provided a stimulus in this search for quick profits and a new market. Unfortunately, on its return the Coq Anne, sailing off the island of Modon, was struck by a fierce storm that destroyed the ship with its crew of thirty-seven Bristolians. The second of Sturmy's adventures into the Levant dates from ten years later, when Gascony was already lost and the Bristolians undoubtedly were left with great quantities of cloth on their hands. In late winter 1457, Sturmy was licensed to ship in three vessels large quantities of tin, lead, wool, cloth, and grain "beyond the mountains by the Straits of Marrock." But once again hopes of high profits were foiled. After a successful journey purchasing pepper and other spices in the Levant, Sturmy's small fleet was met off Malta by several Genoese ships that spoiled two vessels. In all, some £6,000 damage was done to Sturmy and his associates, and it appears that Sturmy himself died in the engagement.[38]

Remarking upon these events, Fernand Braudel insists that they do not "necessarily signify the beginning of an enterprise that was spread over a period of centuries."[39] But these voyages nevertheless represent a new mode of commercial thinking in Bristol. What Sturmy and his fellow merchants were after was both an outlet for their surplus cloth and an opportunity to tap the riches of the East for their own gain. If cloth could no longer be sold in its former quantities in Gascony, it was necessary either to find another market for it, or to increase the return from each transaction, or to find new products in which to deal. Trade to the Levant, if established on a regular basis, satisfied all these criteria. It not only provided a good outlet for cloth, but the import of pepper, spices, rich fabrics, and other luxuries made an especially attractive substitute for wine. The large returns on the sale of these goods in England meant that dealings in cloth might proceed at reduced levels without adversely affecting the income of the merchants. If the market for exports had decayed, greater stress must be laid upon imports; if risks increased, so must the prospects of gain.

Similar considerations stimulated the Bristolians' search for markets and trade routes in other parts of the world. The history of Bristol's dealings in the southern Atlantic, for example, also began in the period following the loss of Gascony. From the mid-fifteenth century Madeira sugar regularly found its way into the city via Lisbon.[40] By May 1480 there was a direct trade, with Bristolians shipping cloth and no doubt seeking the valuable sugars of the island at their source. The earliest recorded inward voyage dates from September 1486, when Portuguese merchants carried sugar and bowstaves to Bristol. There appears to have been some dealing with the Azores as well.[41] And North Africa was visited by Bristolians in the latter half of the fifteenth century.[42]

More dramatic than these ventures in the southern Atlantic and North Africa was Bristol's search in the 1480s for the mythical Isle of Brasil in the western Atlantic, which was reputed to lie somewhere in the temperate zone to the north of Madeira or west of the Azores.[43] Two Bristol voyages in search of Brasil are definitely known, one in 1480 and another in the following year. Both appear to have been the result of licenses granted to Thomas Croft, King's Customer in Bristol, and William Spencer, Robert Straunge, and William de la Fount, merchants of the city, to trade to any parts for three years with any goods save staple goods, in two or three ships of sixty tons or less. The first voyage sailed in a single vessel on the fifteenth of July 1480, from King-road toward "the Island of Brasylle on the west part of Ireland," but was turned back by storms and forced to put into harbor along the Irish coast, probably sometime in September of the same year. The following July, two other ships, an eighth part of each being owned by Thomas Croft, set forth "not by cause of merchaundise but thentent to serce and fynd a certain Ile callid the Isle of Brasile." The vessels were each supplied with forty bushels of salt "for the repacion and sustenacions of the said shippys."[44]

What did these venturesome Bristolians hope to find? One possibility is that they were searching for new fishing grounds. During most of the

fifteenth century they had regularly fished for cod on the banks near
Iceland, but contact with this northern island was already in decline by
1480. The lading of large quantities of salt on each of the vessels suggests a cod-fishing venture employing the stockfish technique. In itself
this offers a significant clue to the economic goals of the Bristolians. Salt
fish were in high demand in the Iberian peninsula, especially in Portugal
and Andalusia. Discovery of a new source of supply would have provided a good means to secure the highly valued imports Bristolians
sought in these markets.[45] But the Isle of Brasil may have held out other
prospects as well. If it was situated in the vicinity of Madeira and the
Azores, the newfound island might be expected to yield riches similar
to those of its near neighbors. More than simply finding new fishing
grounds, then, the Bristolians might have been hoping to discover their
own Madeira, on which sugar and other valuable subtropical crops
could be planted.

The exact purpose of Bristol's earliest Atlantic explorations remains
uncertain, but the same cannot be said of the projects of John Cabot.
Arriving in Bristol sometime in 1495 or 1496, he persuaded a group of
Bristolians, several of whom had previously been interested in the quest
for the Isle of Brasil, to help finance yet another voyage across the Atlantic. Like Columbus, Cabot believed in a western route to the riches of
Asia, and he was determined to find it in northern waters. In March
1496 he acquired a royal patent on behalf of himself and his three sons
that permitted him to sail westward with up to five ships "to find, discover and investigate whatsoever islands, countries, regions or provinces of heathens and infidels, in whatsoever part of the world places,
which before this time were unknown to all Christians." The role of
Bristol in this was to be paramount, for all ships in the venture were
"bound and holden only to arrive" there.[46] If this project had been fully
successful, Bristol would have become the major entrepôt of the spice
trade, bypassing the Levant and thereby supplanting Southampton,
London, and even Antwerp and rivaling and probably surpassing Lisbon as well. All that Robert Sturmy had hoped for and more would
have been gained.[47]

John Cabot, of course, never found the Northwest Passage. His first
voyage, in 1496, was abortive. But the second, in 1497, met with success; after thirty-three days at sea his little ship, the *Matthew*, made
landfall at Belle Isle off Newfoundland.[48] Cabot was convinced that he
had struck northeastern Asia and that by following the coast he would

inevitably reach "an island which he calls Cipango, situated on the equi-
noctal region, where he believes that all the spices of the world have
their origin, as well as the jewels."[49] According to a contemporary observer, those who had participated in the voyage also reported the new
lands to be "excellent and temperate" and believed "that Brizil wood
and silk are native there." In addition, "they asserted that the sea there
is swarming with fish, which can be taken not only with the net, but in
baskets let down with a stone, so that it sinks in the water." "These
same English," he went on, "say that they could bring so many fish that
[England] would have no further need of Iceland, from which place
there comes a very great quantity of the fish called stockfish."[50] On the
basis of this exciting news a third expedition was mounted by Cabot in
1498, this time consisting of five vessels laden with coarse cloth, caps,
laces, and other small wares, one fitted out by the king himself and four
by merchants of Bristol and London. Although fishing may also have
been intended, trade was clearly the principal aim.[51] This venture ended
in disaster, but it reveals the interest of Cabot and his investors in a new
world of trade beyond the established continental centers. As far as the
Bristolians were concerned, it suggests that the quest for imports, which
would characterize their trade for the next two centuries or more,
had begun.

By the middle of Elizabeth's reign this new import-driven pattern of
commerce was firmly established. At a time when English overseas traffic was focused primarily on the Netherlands, Bristol specialized as a
center for the Spanish and Portuguese trades, assembling diverse cargoes of exports in order to supply England with this market's lucrative
wares. In later years this same interest in highly profitable commodities
became the foundation for extending trade beyond the Iberian peninsula into the Mediterranean and to the New World. Before proceeding
to a description and analysis of this expansion, let us look at the overall
structure of Bristol's trade as it had formed by the second half of the sixteenth century, examining the commerce of a single trading year to get
a snapshot view. This technique is somewhat problematic, since the evidence of a single year hardly guarantees a general trend, any more,
as Aristotle said, than a single swallow makes a summer. Each trading
year has its peculiarities caused as much by chance events—of wind,
weather, war, and international politics—as by underlying features of
the trade cycle. But we need a clear picture of the interrelationships existing among the various elements of Bristol's commerce and, given the

spottiness of the surviving customs records, the only way we can draw
it is by looking at a single complete year, focusing primarily on the
structure of trade and checking our findings against related records
for different years. The year chosen runs from Michaelmas 1575 to
Michaelmas 1576, the first year for which Bristol was treated separately
from Gloucester in the customs.[52]

When we compare Bristol's trade for this year with annual shipments
in the fifteenth century, it seems extremely meager. In all, only a little
over six hundred tons of wine and seven hundred and forty-nine cloths
were shipped—hundreds, even thousands, less than were traded in the
best periods of the previous century.[53] Nor had much happened to take
up the slack. Lead and coal were being exported, but not in large
amounts. In addition, a trade developed in cheap-quality "cottons" and
friezes, both of which were coarse woolen fabrics, and in lightweight
half-worsteds. But these were not exported in large enough quantities
to counterbalance the diminished shipments of traditional woolens. For
imports the picture is much the same. Salt, a relatively cheap commodity, was shipped in substantial amounts, and olive oil, train oil, woad,
and spices also were brought to Bristol. It is doubtful, however, that
they made up for the decay in the wine trade.[54]

Nevertheless, Bristol's character as a port specializing in trade with
southern Europe gave it a commercial strength that belies these dismal
figures. If we concentrate on the grand totals for shipping for 1575–76,
Bristol's trade seems remarkably in balance, with ninety vessels of just
over four thousand tons burden departing the port and eighty-two vessels, also totaling just over four thousand tons, entering during these
twelve months. But analysis of the various geographical components of
Bristol's trade shows this image of commercial equilibrium to be illusory. Comparing voyages to and from the continent or the Atlantic islands belonging to Portugal and Spain reveals inbound traffic to have
been one-tenth greater in tonnage than the outbound and one-sixth
greater in the number of vessels involved. Even more startling is the distribution of shipping. In the northern trades, nearly equal numbers of
vessels were used in the inbound and outbound traffic, but almost 40
percent more tonnage left the city than entered. In the south, however
there were about 40 percent more inbound ships, totaling about 50 percent more tonnage. In other words, import trade from the south dominated the picture. Almost equal tonnage departed Bristol for northern
and for southern ports, but about twice as much arrived from the latter
as the former. The tonnage of all southern voyages, moreover, exceeded

the figure for northern voyages by over 40 percent, even though the number of ships used in the north was almost 70 percent greater than in the south.[55]

But tonnages alone do not tell very much, since often the largest vessels did not carry the most valuable goods.[56] To understand the relative importance of the various aspects of Bristol's commerce, we must study the goods in which the city traded. The northern trades were dominated by imports of salt and iron, and exports of lead, coal, and cheap textiles. Only relatively meager shipments of wine and citrus fruit break the monotony of this workaday traffic. By using the customs rates to determine the value of the city's dealings in the north, we can see that the trade was heavily concentrated around La Rochelle and the Bay of Biscay, largely bypassing Bordeaux. Assuming that the customs rates for goods taxed ad valorem varied roughly in proportion to their market value—admittedly, a somewhat risky assumption—the figures also suggest, very tentatively, a trade imbalance in favor of imports of at least 60 and perhaps as much as 100 percent, since on a conservative estimate the woolen fabric shipped to this region was worth perhaps £8 per whole cloth, whereas the wine imported was worth between £10 and £15 per ton.[57]

As we move south, however, we enter a different world, one in which subtropical and tropical wares were preeminent. Seventeen ships totaling about sixteen hundred and fifty tons left Bristol for markets in this region during 1575–76, and twenty-four vessels totaling some twenty-five hundred tons returned thence. But trade in this market was richer and more vibrant, focused primarily on high-priced wares, some of them necessary raw materials such as olive oil and dyestuffs and most of the remainder luxury items such as fruits, spices, sugars, and fine wines. The only bulky cheap commodity in the traffic was salt. The city's exports to the south consisted largely of textiles, although lead also played an important role. The picture is of a commerce in which Bristol sought to tap the riches of the southern trades with outgoing cargoes assembled for their barter value from its own hinterland in south Wales, the Severn valley, and the west Midlands, within which it in turn distributed the fruits of its foreign enterprises. The key was the value of the imports, not the worth of the exports. As measured by value, the import trade exceeded exports by an even larger percentage than was true in the north. Using the same tentative wholesale prices for cloth and wine we just employed in estimating the value of the northern trades, imports from Bristol's southern markets were worth anywhere from 120 to 150 percent more than its exports to that region (Table 6).[58]

TABLE 6   VALUE OF BRISTOL'S EUROPEAN TRADE, 1575–76

| | Outward | | Inward | | |
	Goods[a]	Cloth (cloths of assize)	Goods[a]	Wine (tons)	Total
Northern	£1,151	87	£ 1,171	190	£ 6,042
Southern	£1,527	662	£10,861	415	£25,233
Total	£2,678	749	£12,032	605	£31,275

SOURCE: Public Record Office, E 190/1129/11, 1129/12. Value estimated using £10 per whole cloth and £15 per ton of wine, to the nearest £.
[a]Goods subject to customs paid ad valorem to the nearest £.

Comparing the estimated values of the northern and the southern trades leads to two firm conclusions. First, for the European trade as a whole, Bristol's imports were worth between two and two and a half times the value of its exports. Second, the southern trades, concentrated primarily in the Iberian peninsula, overwhelmed the northern. Bristol's European trade was largely focused on its highly valued riches, particularly of the southern trades, which the city purchased primarily with less expensive English goods. Although the prices of Bristol's imports and exports were no doubt lower at their sources, where they were in relatively good supply, than in their final markets, where they were scarce, this trade pattern implies regular deficits which had to be made up in coin or by bills of exchange. In addition, since the textile and mining industries, which provided the bulk of Bristol's exports, were highly labor-intensive, Bristol was acquiring the high-priced commodities of Europe not only with the resources of its hinterland in the Severn valley, the Midlands, and the West Country, but indirectly with the plentiful labor of the region as well.

The Irish trade was the other major component of Bristol's commercial economy. It accounted for almost 40 percent of the ships entering and leaving Bristol in 1575–76 and for about 13 percent of the tonnage. Virtually all of this traffic was in the hands of the Irish themselves.[59] In terms of goods shipped, this trade had the classic form of colonial commerce. Ireland sent its English customers basic foods, industrial raw materials—particularly agricultural products such as wool—and cheap manufactures, in return for which it received better-quality manufactures, reexports of luxury wares from Europe, and some essential agricultural commodities, such as hops, that it did not produce itself.[60] The most striking feature of this trade is the large quantities of small wares that made their way to Ireland through Bristol. These were acquired at the two Bristol fairs, one in January and one in July, to which great throngs of Irish merchants and tradesmen came each year in their small vessels.[61] But the Irish trade only complemented Bristol's traffic with its European markets. In terms of value, Ireland accounted for probably less than 10 percent of the total trade of the city.

It might be protested that too much attention is paid in studies of sixteenth-century trade to high-price, high-profit goods, since these commodities were usually sold only in small quantities. In 1575–76, for example, Bristol imported only eighty hundredweight of sugar, while salt, which was much more useful, was carried in far greater quantity. But the customs value of sugar was thirty-three times higher than salt, while retail prices for sugar were on the order of three thousand times higher than for salt. For the same volume of trade, then, the profits were much higher for sugar than for salt.[62] From the point of view of the merchant, as Fernand Braudel has observed, what mattered most was not the tonnage shipped but "the rate and facility of gain, the accumulation of capital."[63] Because the Bristolians followed this precept, by the middle of Elizabeth's reign their trade had become settled primarily on the southern routes, with the Iberian coast from Lisbon to Puerta Santa Maria absorbing the bulk of the trade. The shift away from the city's old market in Gascony had now firmly established Bristol as an Iberian port. At the same time, the emphasis on imports begun in Henry VII's reign was continued. Bristol, once a great exporter of cloth and outlet for commerce with Bordeaux, had become primarily a trader of foreign wares drawn from the subtropical regions of the known world.

A similar pattern is discernible in the customs accounts for the rest of Elizabeth's reign and for the early Stuart period.[64] The southern trades remained the most important part of the city's traffic, providing the richest returns and commanding the greatest attention from the Bristol merchants. But there were significant changes within this structure of commerce. Activity increased and new markets were opened up with the addition of trades to the Netherlands, the Baltic, and the western Atlantic, while interest in the Atlantic islands and the Mediterranean was strengthened. Bristol's old haunts on the Iberian peninsula came to play a smaller role as a more complex trading system emerged. This expansion, moreover, helped to stimulate a number of developments in the domestic economy, including the growth of the mining, shipping, cloth, and other industries. But throughout the period the underlying theme was the quest for imports, which yielded the highest profits and therefore encouraged the undertaking of risky new ventures. We can see the persistence of this pattern if we look closely at trade in

1624–25, fifty years after the annual trade cycle we have just studied. Again, this procedure has obvious shortcomings, but employed with appropriate caution it allows us to see in some measure how the overall structure of Bristol's trade evolved during this period.[65]

Again, a conservative estimate, using tentative wholesale prices for cloth and wine as well as the totals for goods paying customs ad valorem, suggests that import value was at least double that of exports (Table 7).[66] In addition, whereas the outward trade for the year is almost equally divided between the northern and the southern region, with the south having a slight edge, for the inbound trade the southern region shows a marked advantage. But the great strength of the southern trades now lay away from the Iberian peninsula. On the inward leg, Marseilles, together with Toulon, accounted for 40 percent of the goods paying ad valorem duties, while Marseilles alone accounted for the bulk of exports to the southern region in this year. In part this was a consequence of the impending war with Spain, which caused Bristolians to bring back their investments from the Iberian peninsula as quickly as they could and prompted them to invest their profits in southern France and Italy. But, as we shall see, the main reason behind this pattern is that the Mediterranean and other southern markets were playing a greater role in Bristol's trade in the early seventeenth century than they had in the previous period. The wine trade also showed dramatic improvement in 1624–25. The total shipments for this year are almost three times greater than they were in 1575–76, with the traffic in French wine more than five times what it had been fifty years before. This, too, is part of a general pattern of trade in the early seventeenth century. French wines led the recovery, with Bordeaux's position as the queen of the trade restored, if not to glory, at least to respectability. In addition, wines from the Iberian peninsula, the Atlantic islands, and the Mediterranean were gaining in significance, with direct shipments from Málaga and the Canaries now playing a major role. The picture for the Irish trade is virtually the same as in 1575–76. The general impression is that by the mid-1620s the value of Bristol's trade had grown considerably from its level in the middle of Elizabeth's reign.[67]

Even though Bristol's trade in the early seventeenth century showed the same interest in southern wares as in Elizabeth's reign, there were several important new developments. Markets in the Netherlands and Norway, in North Africa, and in the eastern Mediterranean grew, while in the Iberian peninsula itself there was a shift in Bristol's trade away

TABLE 7   BRISTOL'S CUSTOMS PAYMENTS, 1624–25

Ports	Outward		Inward	
	Subsidy (£-s-d)	No. cloths[a]	Subsidy (£-s-d)	Wine
A. Northern European:				
Norway	9-11-03		9-13-03	
Amsterdam	18-14-00		39-00-08	
Le Havre				
St. Malo, St. Briac-sur-mer	35-10-07	4¼	56-04-04	9 tons 1 butt[b]
Le Croisic	1-02-04		5-01-00	9 tons
Le Pouliguen			15-00-00	
Nantes	13-12-00		5-00-00	
Lucon	0-10-00			
Bourgneuf Bay	7-05-08		1-10-08	
St. Martin	1-05-00		1-15-00	
La Rochelle	30-12-01		30-08-04	9 tons 1 pipe
Bordeaux	141-08-02	103⁵/₁₂	34-14-05	986 tons 1 terce
Bayonne	4-03-00			
St. Jean de Luz	42-12-00	2⅙	10-01-00	
San Sebastian			8-19-06	
Bilbao	24-11-06		10-01-00	
Customs A	330-17-07	109⅚	227-09-02	1,014 tons 1 terce
Value A	6,617-11-08		4,549-03-04	

B. Southern European:

Oporto			83-06-08	18 tons 1 butt
Lisbon			77-05-10	444 tons
San Lucar			10-18-00	
Cádiz	8-10-00		38-06-10	138 tons 1 pipe 1 hhd
Málaga	40-12-00	11	123-11-10	2 tons
Madeira	3-01-00	16⅔	49-08-04	78 tons 1 pipe
Canaries	30-18-07	20	36-13-08	
São Miguel	15-00-06	23¾	25-12-06	
Marseilles	251-12-04	50⅔	222-03-10	
Toulon			76-19-06	
Leghorn	1-13-10	2⅔		
Candia (Crete)				100 tons muscadels
Customs B	351-08-03	124¾	744-07-10	781 tons 1 butt 1 hhd
Value B	7,028-05-00		14,887-00-00	
Customs A–B	682-05-10	237 7/12	971-17-00	1,795 tons 1 butt 1 hhd 1 terce
Value A–B	13,645-16-08		19,436-03-04	

C. Atlantic:

Newfoundland	2-00-00		45-01-01	
New England	1-16-00		0-18-00	
Somers Islands			57-10-00	
Customs C	3-16-00		103-09-01	
Value C	76-00-00		2,069-01-08	

D. British Isles:

Scotland			2-04-08	
Ireland	384-01-04	14⅔	617-06-06	
Customs D	384-01-04	14⅔	619-11-02	
Value D	7,681-06-08		12,391-03-04	
Customs A–D	1,070-02-02	249¼	1,694-17-03	1,795 tons 1 butt 1 hhd 1 terce
Value A–D	21,403-03-04		33,896-08-04	

SOURCE: Public Record Office, E 190/1135/6.
[a]In whole cloths of assize.
[b]Spanish wine.

from the Bay of Biscay, Lisbon, and the Guadalquivir valley to new centers of trade on Spain's Mediterranean coast. There were also important
developments in exports as Bristol's merchants sought to find new commodities to sell to their foreign customers. Calfskins, butter, lead, iron,
and coal all played an increasingly significant role in the city's trade,
and textile shipments became much more varied as cheap "cottons" and
friezes and expensive worsteds joined the older varieties of broadcloth
in the holds of Bristol ships. The cheaper fabrics found a good market
in the north, and the lighter-weight and finer-quality goods were in high
demand on the southern routes.[68] At the same time, a whole new world
of trade opened across the Atlantic. In general, then, the early Stuart period witnessed the emergence of a more widespread and complex system of commerce, knitting together a greater diversity of commodities
and overseas ports than in the sixteenth century.

Amsterdam provides the key to understanding the changes in the
northern trades. In the course of the later sixteenth century it had become the principal emporium of Baltic and Scandinavian wares. With
the wealth accumulated by the city's traders and the low freight charges
on their shipping, the merchants of Amsterdam were able to enter the
Mediterranean markets themselves, acting as carriers for its commerce
and bringing wealth to their home city. Bristol's trade with Amsterdam
reflects the historic rise of the Dutch city in the early seventeenth century. The Bristolians shipped such goods as coal, lead, some iron, Welsh
butter, Welsh cottons, and molasses, produced from imported Madeira
sugar.[69] The return shipments were divided in origin. The bulk came
from Scandinavia and the Baltic, but some Mediterranean goods were
also purchased in Amsterdam. Grain from the Baltic was an especially
important commodity in times of dearth.[70] Other northern wares
shipped in this year included tar, pitch, Norway deal boards, cable yarn,
rough hemp, battery, old iron, rod iron, steel, frying pans, hops, and
shellfish. Occasional additions were made in the form of such southern
items as madder and cinnamon.[71]

But the more interesting changes in the overall pattern of Bristol's
trade occurred in the southern markets. In 1575–76, southern commercial routes had focused on Lisbon and the Guadalquivir valley ports of
San Lucar de Barrameda, Cádiz, and Puerta Santa Maria. During the
late sixteenth century these together accounted for over 80 percent of
the tonnage in the southern trades. The seventeenth century, however,
saw a significant shift; trade with Lisbon remained strong, but Oporto
was added as a stopping place for the Bristolians. Bristol's contacts with

southern Spain also moved eastward. San Lucar and Cádiz continued to claim a significant share of the trade, but Málaga became a major center of Bristol's dealings in the Iberian peninsula, and Almería and Alicante, east of the Straits of Gibraltar, were also frequented upon occasion. Trade in Spain beyond Gibraltar was not entirely new to the seventeenth century,[72] of course, but it had been only intermittent in the mid-sixteenth century and, despite the English reentry into the Mediterranean after 1573, seems to have remained so down to 1600.[73] Hence the growth of commercial dealings inside the Pillars of Hercules in the early seventeenth century represents something of a new development in Bristol's trade.

What attracted the Bristolians to this market? The customs evidence suggests that it was a fine outlet for exports, particularly lightweight worsteds, traditional broadcloths, and calfskins. But the heart of this commerce, as with all the southern trades, was the imports, which included sugar, white soap, olive oil, dried fruit, and wine, all highly profitable, high-priced wares. These were commodities that in the sixteenth century Bristolians had acquired almost exclusively in San Lucar and Cádiz, even though in many instances they were produced elsewhere in Spain. In this period, then, the Bristolians were content to deal in these wares through intermediary markets and middlemen. But after 1600 they were more anxious to buy "at the first hand," as the saying went, where the goods were produced.[74]

One possible reason for the move to Málaga and Alicante was that these ports, serving a region new to market agriculture, offered better prices or better-quality commodities than were available in Guadalquivir ports.[75] But a more fundamental development was at work as well. Throughout the sixteenth century, commercial exchange with Spain had operated under the stimulus of the American trade. Although Bristolians participated to a degree in this colonial commerce through Seville, it was not so much the presence of American products such as tobacco that excited their interest as the buoyancy of the market created by Spanish involvement in the New World. The resulting inflation and generally high demand for consumer products encouraged trade in English wares. At the same time, Spanish wage levels ran well ahead of English in the sixteenth century, growing between 1520 and 1620 by more than 200 percent, whereas English wages rose only 44 percent; real wages fell in England during this period, but they remained high in Spain. This meant not only that English manufactures were relatively cheap in Spanish terms, but that there was a large Iberian market with cash to pay for these English wares.[76] The Spanish importation of New World gold and silver also encouraged trade, by helping to ease credit in the Iberian peninsula.[77] Since Seville, by virtue of its privileged position in the colonial trade, was the financial center through which Bristolians raised capital, made exchanges, and settled accounts, it kept Bristol's trade focused on the Guadalquivir valley throughout the sixteenth century.[78]

But the boom in Spain's American commerce ended early in the seventeenth century. Silver imports peaked in the decade between 1600 and 1610. At about the same time, real wages in Spain rose sharply, reflecting the movement of capital from overseas ventures to domestic production. Wages stayed high throughout most of the first forty years of the seventeenth century.[79] In the early 1620s, after a thirty-year period of stagnation, Spain's economic relations with the New World entered a long period described by Pierre Chaunu as "la grande dépression." This extended depression began in 1620–1622 with a sharp decline in traffic, particularly outbound traffic, from which Spain's American trade never recovered. These troubles had a direct impact on the main Spanish centers of the colonial traffic. By 1624–1626, Andalusian prices were depressed, and investment in New World activities slowed in Seville and other Guadalquivir ports. The buoyancy of the Guadalquivir market was lost, and the Bristolians and their English compatriots were encouraged to seek further afield for trading partners.[80] The change in the southern trades, however, was not confined to the growth of new commercial relationships with Málaga and Alicante. There was also significant growth in Bristol's dealings with Madeira and other Atlantic islands and with ports in southern France, Italy, and the eastern Mediterranean. By the mid-1630s, this non-Iberian portion of the southern commerce accounted for half the inbound and more than half the outbound traffic. Bristol, while continuing to maintain its firm foothold in Spain and Portugal, more and more was reaching beyond the Iberian peninsula in search of the high-valued commodities that they had long purchased only there.[81]

These developments conditioned Bristol's activities in nearly every other part of its southern market. Commerce with North Africa illustrates the pattern. This trade, as we know, has a history dating to at least the 1480s,[82] but a regular English traffic along the Barbary Coast of Morocco probably did not begin until 1551.[83] Even then contacts remained intermittent and of very low volume until the 1590s, when the

Spanish war helped deflect a portion of the Iberian commerce onto the North African coast. By the early seventeenth century Bristol's dealings in Barbary both became more regular and increased in volume.[84] The Barbary trade proved to be exceptionally lucrative. Sugar, molasses, dates, oranges and lemons, figs, raisins, marmalade, candied fruit, almonds, capers, aniseed, cumin, indigo, saltpeter, gum arabic, raw silk, ostrich feathers, and even gold could be obtained there. In return, it was a brilliant market for fine English cloth, for lead and tin, for manufactured items, for European reexports, and for timber.[85]

Along with trading to Barbary, Bristolians also frequented other ports in the Mediterranean, although a large and steady traffic began only in the early seventeenth century. Between 1573 and 1593, for example, among the vessels recorded as arriving at Leghorn only three are specified as originating at Bristol. Still, Bristol's interest was an early one; for example, the *Swallow of Bristol* sailed for the Mediterranean in 1576.[86] Leghorn and Marseilles were the keys to the traffic, but by the 1630s Toulon also played an important part. Leghorn was a well-established entrepôt for commerce with the entire eastern Mediterranean, a place where credit or coin might be found and from which it was possible to mount trading expeditions throughout the Mediterranean basin. It dominated Bristol's interest in the Mediterranean during the later sixteenth century. Marseilles entered the picture only after 1600. As the chief port of Provence, through which the trade of much of southern France passed, it was a close cousin of Leghorn, linked to the Iberian peninsula by regular trade routes and serving as a center for commerce in North African and Levantine wares. In the 1630s Lewes Robertes called it "[t]he principall seate of *Trade* in *Provence* . . . famous for the great concourse of *Merchants,* and for the commerce that it maintaineth with *Turkie, Barbarie, Spain, France, Italy, Flanders* and *England.*" Its own commodities, as Robertes tells us, were only "*Oyles, Wines, Wools, Almonds,* and *Verdigrace.*" It was much the same with Toulon, which lay ten leagues from Marseilles. Toulon, according to Robertes, "aboundeth onely in *Oyles,* which hence is laden in great aboundance." But, unlike Toulon, Marseilles was also an entrepôt for wares "from other Countries, such as *Alexandria, Aleppo, Acria, Constantinople, Naples, Leghorne,* or the coasts of *Spaine* doth yield." Equally important, it was a financial capital where coin, particularly Spanish reals, could be acquired and licensed for exportation, which, as Robertes says, "is the onely meanes whereby the *trade* of *Turkie* is preserved."[87] Marseilles, then, was a place, like Leghorn, for mounting ventures further to the east where currency was absolutely essential.

When we examine Bristol's trade with the Provençal ports, however, we observe little of these more exotic trades. In both exports and imports, Bristol's commerce there resembled that with the Iberian peninsula. Lead and lead ore were the most important exports. Calfskins and tanned Irish hides came second. Other goods traded included "cottons," short jersey stockings, linsey-woolsey, and some woolen cloths. Little distinguishes this list from that of the cargoes sent to the Iberian peninsula in the same year. In return for these wares, the goods the Bristolians brought back directly from Marseilles and Toulon consisted primarily of olive oil, though, in addition, there was white soap, similar to the well-known product of Castile, as well as capers from Marseilles and rice from Toulon. Nevertheless, trade in Levantine wares through these southern French ports was fairly common in the first forty years of the seventeenth century, primarily because the monopoly of the Levant Company made it necessary. In these years Bristolians regularly returned from the Mediterranean with substantial shipments of currants and muscadel wine, as well as Egyptian cottons, mohair, dyestuffs such as galles, and aniseed and wormseed, both Levantine drugs. Some of these goods undoubtedly were purchased in Marseilles or in Leghorn from local middlemen, but some probably came directly from the Levant Company's privileged markets, within which Bristolians had a special license to buy currants.[88]

Closely tied to the expansion of Bristol's European trades was the evolution of commercial interests in the New World. Three main lines of development may be distinguished. The North Atlantic had the great fisheries off Newfoundland and New England. Further south there was traffic in the commodities of Virginia and the West Indies. Finally, the search for a Northwest Passage remained a recurring theme in Bristol's history. Each in its way was related to the older southern trades; the fishery provided a highly marketable commodity to sell in the Iberian peninsula and the Mediterranean, while the other ventures sought "at the first hand" the same type of profitable imports that Bristolians commonly acquired on the southern routes.

Bristol's knowledge of the Newfoundland fishery was already well established by the beginning of Elizabeth's reign. Following Cabot's discovery, during the early sixteenth century the Bristolians maintained a steady interest in Newfoundland cod.[89] The midcentury ushered in a period of reduced English presence on the Grand Banks: by 1570 the entire English fishing fleet amounted, according to the Bristolian Anthony Parkhurst, to no more than "iiii sayle of small barkes."[90] The English returned in force to Newfoundland, however, in the mid-1570s, with a doubling or even quadrupling in the number of English on the Grand Banks. But Bristol became involved in a large way only in the 1590s. There were three returning ships in 1591–92, ten in 1594–95, twelve in 1598–99, and sixteen between 1600 and 1602. In the 1610s and 1620s eight to sixteen vessels made the journey each year, and in the 1630s, when Bristol's American interests had become more widely diversified, about half that number made a direct return to the city from Newfoundland and New England.[91] The stimulus for this turnabout was undoubtedly Elizabeth I's war with Spain, which disrupted the settled patterns of Bristol's trade in the sixteenth century. The war left much shipping idle; if not employed in privateering, these ships were available for the time-consuming enterprise of fishing or trading for fish across the Atlantic. In the same years, rich new fishing grounds were discovered in American waters off Ramea.[92] And, finally, the Spanish conflict stimulated aggressive new enterprises in the Mediterranean, where salt fish were in high demand.[93]

In the late sixteenth and early seventeenth centuries, Bristol's interest in the New World was largely one of trade. For most of the period little thought was given to colonial settlement, although in Elizabeth's reign Anthony Parkhurst of Bristol lobbied for it. But even he was concerned with founding a permanent establishment primarily in order to sustain the fishery. Better facilities, he argued, would improve the catch by permitting salt to be produced on the spot, thus lowering costs, and by enabling the residents to fish beyond the early fall, when the prospect of winter storms forced the fleets to sail homeward.[94] The joint London-Bristol Newfoundland Company, founded in 1610, which managed to plant a colony at Conception Bay, conformed closely to this scheme. The Newfoundland colony established in James I's reign was very much a Bristol venture. Eleven residents of the city, ten of them leading merchants, were charter members. Trade in fish was the principal aim. Although no outright monopoly was claimed, the settlement was intended primarily to give its backers special advantages in the fishery, particularly by permitting a longer fishing season and by offering the settlers opportunity to monopolize the best fishing grounds. The proximity of the settlement to the fishing grounds, moreover, placed the Company's agents in an exceptionally good position to buy the catches

of non-Company fishermen and transport them to the continent. The
Company also hoped to sell fishermen pine boards and timber for barrel
hoops and staves.[95]

Since, throughout the early seventeenth century, it was the fishery
and the prospects of trade rather than the idea of a colony in its own
right that attracted the Bristolians, when this interest was outweighed
by other pressures they avoided participation. Above all, they sought independence for their own enterprises. By 1614, John Guy, their leader
in Newfoundland, had fallen out with the Londoners of the Company
over administrative policy and had withdrawn from membership, probably taking the other Bristolians with him. Still, the advantages of a settlement near the fishing grounds remained, and in 1617 a group of city
merchants, possibly including some of the original members, formed
their own settlement at Bristol's Hope on Conception Bay. Richard
Hayman, an Exeter man but brother-in-law to the Bristolian John
Barker, styled it "Bristol's Hope of Wealth."[96]

This same desire for independence and commercial gain conditioned
Bristolians' responses to other colonial ventures. When in 1621 Sir Ferdinando Gorges attempted to bring them into a joint stock venture for
planting New England they vigorously resisted the idea, although by
this time they were interested in fishing off the New England coast, "in
regard that the Newfoundland fishing hath fayled of late years." They
were willing, however, to seek a license from Gorges to maintain their
fishery there.[97] During the later 1620s and the 1630s, however, the reluctance of at least some Bristolians to hold land in New England was
eased, but, as in Newfoundland in 1610 and 1617–18, fish remained the
foundation of these settlements. In 1626 Robert Aldworth, who had
previously invested in Martin Pring's 1602–03 and 1606 explorations
of the New England coast and in the Newfoundland Company of 1610,
bought Monhegan Island from Abraham Jennings of Plymouth, another Newfoundland Company investor. In 1630–31, moreover, Aldworth and his son-in-law Giles Elbridge acquired twelve thousand acres
on the Pemaquid peninsula. Both Monhegan and Pemaquid were used
regularly by the English in the early seventeenth century as bases for
fishing ventures. Thus, for Aldworth, perhaps the greatest Iberian and
Mediterranean trader of his day, the hope for gain was much the same
as it had been in Newfoundland. Whatever other benefits might follow
from his enterprise, they began with the acquisition of fish to sell in European markets.[98]

Just as Bristol's activities in Newfoundland and New England helped
the city's merchants acquire the high-value commodities upon which

their commerce depended, traffic to and from the West Indies and Virginia was also tied to Bristol's southern trade routes. The commodities they sought there substituted for the profitable wares they purchased in their commerce with the Iberian peninsula, the Atlantic islands, and the Mediterranean. And they were used in the Mediterranean trade in just the way fish were. We have already seen that Bristol's ties to the West Indies extend back into the early sixteenth century, when such men as Robert Thorne and Thomas Tison of Bristol maintained a direct trade through Seville with the Spanish possessions in the region.[99] As Anglo-Spanish relations soured in the mid-sixteenth century, however, this open and legitimate traffic came to an end and was replaced by a long period of commercial warfare in which Bristol played its share. In 1576, for example, John and Andrew Barker, in reprisal for the loss of their goods in the Canaries to the Inquisition the previous year, mounted an expedition of two ships, the *Ragged Staff* and the *Beare,* "to the coast of Terra Firma and the Bay of Honduras in the West Indies," which, unfortunately for the Barkers, ended in disaster. Despite this outcome, at least one Bristol ship was privateering in the West Indies in the 1590s. Caribbean and South American waters exerted a powerful attraction for the Bristolians. Even the Barkers maintained an interest. In 1612–13, John Barker, nephew of Andrew and son of Andrew's partner John, mounted an expedition to the Marowijne River in Guyana. The voyage was aboard the *Sea Bright of Bristol,* with Martin Pring as master.[100]

If fishing and the tobacco trade were both aspects of Bristol's quest for the highly profitable wares of the southern trades, the epitome of this mode of commerce was the city's recurring search for a short route to the riches of the Orient, the search for the Northwest Passage. As we have seen, Bristol had conceived of such a westerly route with John Cabot's voyages in the 1490s. From then on, it was a continuing theme of commercial life in the city, lying dormant for a time only to be excited by some new prospect of discovery. About the year 1508, for example, Bristolians aided Sebastian Cabot in an exploration of the American coast in search of a southwestern passage to the Orient. In 1521, they were involved with Cabot's proposals for a venture to find the Northwest Passage. In Elizabeth's reign they aided Frobisher, at least indirectly, on his second voyage, in which the suspected discovery of gold and the prospect of the city as the site of a smelting works tantalized them as much as the Northwest Passage itself. They were even more intimately involved in Humphrey Gilbert's 1583 voyage, when Richard Hakluyt the Younger, who was prebend of Bristol Cathedral, approached the merchant community there about a venture, and Walsingham wrote them directly endorsing Gilbert's plan. The sum they eventually invested came to £1,000. Finally, in 1631, their appetite was whetted again: a large group of Bristol merchants financed the voyage of Thomas James of Bristol in search of the Northwest Passage. James himself says he was encouraged by the merchants who furnished him his ship, which seems to have been mounted to insure that a London-based voyage by Luke Foxe did not capture all the wealth and glory.[101]

There is no mystery about the aims of these voyages. They were intended to find an easy way to the Orient and thereby convert Bristol, already interested in the spice trade, into a major entrepôt in its own right. This heady dream manifested itself in a variety of other ways during this period. Edward Pryn of Bristol, for example, was a member of the Muscovy Company, hoping, with the rest of its members, to find a Northeast Passage and settling, as the others did, for a route to the wealth of Persia that bypassed the Levant. About the year 1611, Thomas Aldworth, brother of Robert, joined the service of the East India Company as an agent. Perhaps through his agency, Martin Pring entered the same service about 1614. Other Bristolians also found the power of the East irresistible in this period. James Oliver, for example, sailed to Mokha in 1625 and established a factory there. These Bristolians wanted a direct trade to the East that would permit them to bypass Lisbon and the Levant and bring home pepper, cinnamon, nutmeg, ginger, and the rest without having to deal through middlemen. To have accomplished this would have converted the port from a significant provincial center to a boomtown such as Leghorn had been earlier in the sixteenth century. Whether they pointed their vessels west or east, these venturesome Bristolians sought to become the intermediaries in the spice traffic and in dealing in other Eastern riches. It was a vain hope, as Thomas James, locked in ice and in fear for his life, discovered, but to the heroes of commerce engaged in these feats of merchandise the prospect of success made it worth the risk and the investment.[102]

⁂

In the aftermath of the Hundred Years' War Bristol's place in the English commercial economy had been transformed as its dependence on the manufacture and export of traditional kinds of woolen cloth and the import of French wines diminished and it became a major redistribution point for foreign wares to the Severn valley, South Wales, and the west Midlands, on whose products—raw materials and agricultural commodities as well as manufactures—it relied for its exports. Hence, as London grew in population and economic power, coming to dominate and give order to England's urban hierarchy, Bristol gradually settled into its niche as "the metropolis of the west," a role it would play with increasing definition in the later seventeenth and the eighteenth century.[103] What drove Bristol's trade in the sixteenth and early seventeenth centuries was the pursuit of high margins of profit and quick gain, rather than economic concentration and expanding control over capital resources. The entrepreneur's object was to multiply small investments into large returns by understanding and playing the market, not by efficiently converting raw materials into salable manufactured wares. Small reliance was put upon fixed capital assets. The emphasis was on distribution, not production, and on imports that could be marketed after little or no investment in labor. But there was an elusiveness to the Bristolians' quest. The more successful the pursuit of scarce and much-prized wares, the greater the supply; the greater the supply, the lower the unit price and profits. The problem of the southern trades, then, was the problem of a traffic in luxuries and other scarce commodities gradually becoming a trade in staples. In the long run this outcome was inescapable. In the short run, however, it was possible to resolve the dilemma by pushing beyond the established trading centers to markets with more plentiful supplies or less competition and by trading whenever possible at the first, not the second, hand. The expansion of Bristol's commerce in the early seventeenth century was guided by these considerations, which help to account for the movement of the city's trade into the Mediterranean and the Atlantic and for the continuing search for the Northwest Passage.

CHAPTER 2

Mere Merchants

As Bristol moved from being a cloth exporter of the first rank to become a principal center for imports, a new and more complex system of commerce emerged. Export commodities were diversified to include significant quantities of metals and metal wares, fish, leather, butter, coal, and more varieties of textiles, while at the same time the city's leading markets shifted away from Gascony to the Iberian peninsula, the Mediterranean, and the Atlantic. In making this transformation Bristol was not alone. Similar changes took place in nearly the whole of English commerce of the Tudor and Stuart period. Bristol, however, was at the forefront of the development, under the pressure of a dismal level of cloth exports in Henry VIII's reign, whereas for London and much of the rest of England similar changes came only in the later sixteenth and early seventeenth centuries, with the trade depressions of the 1550s and 1620s providing the stimulus.[1] In this chapter we shall explore the consequences of these new directions in commercial history for the structure of Bristol's trading community, as the city became a home for the type of overseas traders whom sixteenth-century commentators called "mere merchants"—traders who lived exclusively by their large-scale dealings in foreign commerce.

New markets and new commodities inevitably called forth new strategies from traders for winning profit and new relationships within the trading community. In the fifteenth century, commercial practices had been quite simple. In the Iberian peninsula a form of "tramping" was followed, in which a vessel laden with export wares sailed from port to port with an itinerant merchant aboard looking for the best prices.[2] Even in Gascony, the most sophisticated sector of the city's commerce, trade was a type of barter. Cloth, manufactured in or near Bristol, was carried annually in large fleets to Bordeaux to be exchanged for wine, with the French dealers usually paid directly in textiles for the vintage.[3] No elaborate system of credit or arrangement for the clearing of balances was necessary, although the use of loans and reliance on attorneys or factors were hardly unknown. Many merchants combined overseas operations with the maintenance of a workshop or retail establishment, making the merchant community both large and diverse. For example, between September 1479 and July 1480 over two hundred and fifty Bristolians engaged in overseas trade, a very considerable number in a town of only about ten thousand inhabitants. As a result, quite humble men found it possible to enter in significant numbers into the city's merchant leadership.[4] In the sixteenth century much of this would change. Not surprisingly, the starting place is the connection between clothmaking and overseas trade.

Just as Bristol's prosperity in the fourteenth and early fifteenth centuries depended on the cloth trade, the structure of the medieval trading community was founded on cloth manufacture. In the oldest legislation governing this industry, dating from the fourteenth century, we can catch a glimpse of its early organization as its members idealized it. Manufacture was to take place in small, domestic units located within the boundaries of the city, and each producer was to operate independently, not as the agent of an entrepreneur who put out work to him. Weavers not only were expected to keep the instruments of their craft "in halls and rooms next the road," where only two or three looms could have been worked at one time, but also were forbidden to receive yarn "from anyone except . . . their husbands and wives." Similarly, fullers were expected to work only their own cloths, presumably buying them from the weavers, then in turn selling their work to the drapers. Finally, cloth was to be sold primarily in the weekly cloth market held in Tucker Street, which all the city's merchant drapers were obliged to attend. Only if cloth failed to find a buyer there could it be offered privately.[5]

The wistful tone of these old ordinances makes clear, however, that even at this early date these arrangements survived solely as ideals from a distant past. We can identify two major lines of development in the cloth industry. First, by the 1340s Bristol's boundaries no longer successfully contained its burgesses' involvement in woolen manufacture. The combing of wool, spinning of yarn, and weaving, fulling, finishing, buying, and selling of cloth by Bristolians or their employees now took place in the countryside as well as the city.[6] Second, a distinct group of entrepreneurs operating on a large scale had emerged to dominate the industry. To be sure, the industry still sustained a relatively large number of independent producers in Bristol. In 1346, for example, eighty-eight fullers resided in the city, most presumably still using the old walking technique to treat their cloth. But even among these men significant signs of change abounded. Although various ordinances stipulate wages to be paid workers at the stocks and the perch, instruments associated with the older techniques for shrinking and thickening woolens, much of the actual fulling appears to have occurred at mills located in the Mendip and Cotswold hills, with only the "rekkyng, pleyting and amending" of the cloth taking place in Bristol itself. Some of the fullers, then, seem to have become clothiers responsible for organizing the finishing stages of production.[7] At the same time, weaving seems to have fallen under the control of a small group of entrepreneurs, who put out woolen yarn to weavers in both country and town. From other sources we know of the existence of individuals such as Thomas Blanket who maintained large workshops in their own houses, containing "divers instruments for weaving" operated by a number of "weavers and other workmen." Many of these men participated actively as merchant drapers and as cloth exporters to the overseas markets. Some traded in a wide variety of goods, including dyestuffs, wine, and oil among imports; leather and wool as well as cloth among exports. Thus in place of the antique ideal upheld by the city's ordinances, we have an industry organized along distinctly proto-capitalist lines.[8]

Unfortunately, it is impossible to reconstruct in detail the pattern of occupations in Bristol during this period. Our best guess is that 20 percent of the city's population, and probably more, were employed at least part of the time in the various stages of textile production.[9] But we can do somewhat better in establishing an economic profile for the city's elite, the members of its Common Council. Almost all the fifty-six known councillors from the late fourteenth and the early fifteenth century engaged in overseas trade to some degree, but there was as yet no differentiation of retail shopkeeping from wholesale trading or from the financing of cloth production. Many held properties, usually in the form of tenements and workshops, in the clothmaking districts. They seem very much a group of general entrepreneurs dependent on commerce in cloth, but not yet committed exclusively to overseas trade.[10] Where specialization occurred in this period, it was less in commerce than in real estate and shipping. According to E. M. Carus-Wilson, William Canynges the Younger, one of Bristol's, and indeed England's, richest men in the fifteenth century, held "fourteen shops, at least seventeen tenements, a close and two gardens in Bristol, and lands in Wells, the hundred of Wells and Westbury on Trym." He also owned at least ten ships, which William Worcester tells us directly employed about eight hundred men. Nevertheless, Canynges, once a merchant in his own right, had ceased to trade. Trade in this period, focused as it was narrowly on cloth and wine, exchanged among only a small network of traders in a handful of ports, did not readily lend itself to great concentrations of wealth. For the Bristol entrepreneurs, the only avenues for long-term investment were property and ships, and many of the leading men in the fifteenth century put their hard-earned profits into these ventures as they drew back from the risks of everyday dealings. But for most of the others, trade remained centered on cloth, until the great changes of the second half of the fifteenth century altered this pattern forever.[11]

By the early sixteenth century the social effects of the decline in Bristol's cloth trade were already quite clear. Judging from apprenticeship records, which give us a rough idea of the demand for labor in particular industries, the proportion of those directly engaged in making cloth during the 1530s and 1540s had fallen to something less than 15 percent (Table 8).[12] About a third of these men were weavers, but they produced mainly cheap cloths, such as friezes, that were a far cry from the fine-quality "Broadmeads" that had made the city's looms so famous in the fourteenth century. Most of the remainder of the textile manufacturers were engaged in the dyeing and finishing trades. Since the work of several weavers normally was required to employ a single dyer, fuller, and shearman, this imbalance implies that Bristol was receiving the fabrics not only of its own weavers but of country producers as well. Bristol, in other words, had become something of a center for cloth finishers. Many of these individuals used their position at the end of the production process to command the market and to finance and manage manufacture through its various stages. The fullers or, as they were called in sixteenth-century Bristol, tuckers, were especially active entrepreneurs, successfully outmaneuvering the shearmen during a nearly century-long battle for control of the industry. The catastrophic fall in Bristol's cloth exports and the heavy emphasis upon the manufacture of

TABLE 8   DISTRIBUTION OF OCCUPATIONS AMONG
BRISTOL APPRENTICES, 1532–1542 AND 1626–1636

	1532–1542		1626–1636	
	No.	%[a]	No.	%[a]
Men				
Leading entrepreneurs				
Merchants	119	8.51	142	5.22
Major retailers	145	10.37	317	11.65
Soapmakers and chandlers	18	1.29	89	3.27
Total	282	20.17	548	20.13
Textile production	196	14.02	369	13.56
Leather production	150	10.73	103	3.78
Clothing production and other				
secondary users of cloth				
and leather	287	20.53	393	14.44
Metal crafts	121	8.66	317	11.65
Building trades	35	2.50	197	7.24
Shipping and related trading				
and port activities	155	11.09	521	19.14
Food production and related				
industries	91	6.51	171	6.28
Woodworking	18	1.29	20	0.73
Professional and service				
industries	42	3.00	68	2.50
Miscellaneous	21	1.50	15	0.55
Total known	1,398		2,722	
Total unknown	7		12	
Total	1,405	96.43[b]	2,734	95.86[b]
Women[c]	52	3.57[b]	118	4.14[b]
Total Men and Women	1,457		2,852	

SOURCE: 1532–1542: D. Hollis, ed., *Calendar of the Bristol Apprentice Book, 1532–1565.* Part 1: *1532–1542* (Bristol Record Society 14, 1949). 1626–1636: Bristol Record Office, *Apprentice Book, 1626–1640,* ff. 1ʳ–333ʳ.
[a]Percentage of known men.
[b]Percentage of total.
[c]The occupations of female apprentices in Bristol were almost completely gender-specific in 1532–1542 and 1626–1636. Women were apprenticed primarily in domestic service or in knitting and needlework, crafts to which men were not apprenticed in these two periods. In 1532–1542, however, four women were apprenticed to crafts that otherwise employed men, one to a pinmaker and three to mercers, but the latter may have been trained only in the art of needlework: see David Harris Sacks, *Trade, Society and Politics in Bristol, 1500–1640,* 2 vols. (New York: Garland Publishing, 1985), vol. 2, p. 763.

coarse and cheap fabrics, however, made this victory somewhat pyrrhic. By the beginning of the seventeenth century, the place of textile manufacture in the city had fallen even a bit further, despite efforts to build up the industry through production of new, lighter-weight fabrics such as worsteds, fustians, and serges.[13]

There is more here than merely a dismal tale of dwindling trade. Beneath the statistics also lie signs of renewal. In the early sixteenth century the city was already characterized by a new and distinctive distribution of occupations. Just as Coventry, Worcester, and Norwich possessed occupational structures typical of textile towns, and Northampton of a leather-producing one, Bristol now had an occupational structure typical of commercial towns, with a heavy emphasis on trade-related crafts. In the 1530s over a third of all apprentices in the city specialized in overseas trade and retailing or in serving the port; the figure would be even higher if we included among the retailing shopkeepers such small craftsmen as shoemakers, tailors, and other clothing manufacturers, many of whom ordinarily sold at retail what they produced. By the 1620s, this pattern had developed further, with almost half of the apprentices employed in commerce, merchandising, and shipping. In this same period, a similar proportion of the city's freemen came from this sector of Bristol's economy. Again, these already large percentages would be still more striking if we also counted the small craftsmen engaged in clothing manufacture. Where once Bristol had itself been primarily a center of cloth production and its trade, it had now become a center of more general overseas commerce and regional distribution.[14]

The driving force in these processes of social and economic change was the growth of the Iberian trade, which, with its emphasis on valuable, exotic, and highly profitable import goods such as spices, dyestuffs, silks, sugar, and tobacco, ended the domination of the cloth traders and turned Bristol into a city of "merchantmen, grocers, mercers, haberdashers," dealing largely in the wares of southern Europe.[15] This same transformation of Bristol's commerce brought into being a more complicated trading network that became evident by the early seventeenth century. In order to acquire the riches of the Iberian peninsula and the Mediterranean, for example, fish were transported from the Grand Banks, which in turn demanded purchases of ships' timber in Amsterdam, sailcloth in France, and salt in Spain and Portugal. To accomplish this, a variety of export wares were necessary, most of them far different from the English goods demanded in Marseilles, Leghorn, or Madeira. At the same time, a more integrated system emerged that demanded sophisticated financial and managerial techniques. Few traders operating entirely on their own were able successfully to marshal the capital or the managerial skill to conduct enterprises linking Welsh butter and calfskins; Mendip lead; Kingswood coal; Dean's Wood iron; western, northern, and Welsh cloth; Newfoundland fish; French, Spanish, and Portuguese salt; and American, Mediterranean, Iberian, and French specialties into one system of commerce.

One of the first consequences of this new demand for coordination was a contraction in the size of the trading community, even though Bristol's population remained remarkably constant, at ninety-five hundred to ten thousand inhabitants, until about 1575.[16] Around 1550, for example, a leading Bristolian, probably himself a merchant, thought that only about one hundred and twenty-five of his fellow citizens then had the wherewithal or credit to be merchants in the city, compared to the two hundred and fifty who had traded fifty or seventy-five years earlier.[17] By the mid-1570s the number of active overseas merchants had fallen to fewer than one hundred; from Michaelmas 1575 to Michaelmas 1576, for example, only ninety-five Bristolians shipped goods to or from foreign markets, and this figure seems to have remained fairly constant into the early seventeenth century, when Bristol's population had grown by at least 25 percent.[18]

These quantitative changes not only show a contraction in the number of traders engaged in foreign commerce but suggest a concentration of their activities. They signal the emergence of a new commercial order in Bristol. Entrepreneurs whose businesses encompassed a full range of undertakings from the Grand Banks to the Levant required the assistance of their fellows both at home and abroad to achieve their goals even more than did those who had less far-flung or ambitious businesses. Sitting in their countinghouses with their ledgers and journals, they necessarily conducted their affairs through agents and colleagues. The new forms of commercial organization that emerged in Bristol during the sixteenth century depended first upon the existence of these close personal ties and the mutual trust they engendered among overseas merchants.

No matter how cautious or wealthy the entrepreneur, a great variety of events, often of the most prosaic kind, stood ready to disrupt his affairs and threaten his businesses. John Browne, merchant of Bristol and the author of *The Marchants Avizo,* saw this as a basic fact of a trader's life. "Let not thy expenses be equall with they gaines," he warned, "for either sicknes, naughtie debtors, let of trade and misfortune at sea or land, may soone ouerthrow thee."[19] Merchants were men who might

encounter danger at every turn of their professional existence, by placing their goods and sometimes their lives in jeopardy in hopes of returning a profit.[20] According to Alderman John Whitson, this made for an
exceptionally "burthensome kind of Life." "Abundance of Riches . . .
rob a Man of his Quiet," he said,

> and take away his Time either in the account of 'em or in the Disposing of
> 'em. For what Care is there to be had of Rents? What Caution and Wariness
> to be had of bad Debtors? What Fear of Losses and Casualties? What Dis-
> trust and Suspicion of our best Friends? What Vigilance and Diligence, that
> we be not over-charged in our Bargains? What Grief, if we be overthrown
> in our Suits, and vex'd with Fines and Amercements? To be brief, what Toil
> and Weriness throughout our whole lives? Eithere we are troubled with get-
> ting or cumber'd with keeping, or afflicted and heart-broken with losing, and
> never at Rest, paying and receiving.[21]

Whitson knew whereof he spoke. The inventory of his estate at his
death showed him to be owed £3,000 in "desparate debts" in addition
to the more than £5,400 in moneys, bonds, leases, merchandise, household stuff, and other movables for which his executors acknowledged
responsibility. His "goods debts" and his "hopeful debts" came only to
about £1,400.[22] To other Bristolians the truth of Whitson's remarks
was confirmed by numerous examples of fellow citizens brought low by
accident or circumstance—of multiple mishaps destroying men "heretofore of some wealth and nobility," or poor judgment and bad practice
bringing calamity down upon men's heads.[23]

Whitson's lament envisions the mercantile profession as composed of
isolated individuals, each single-handedly confronting the pitfalls of the
marketplace, but nothing could have been further from the truth.
Rather than plying their trades alone, Bristol's merchants habitually
aided one another by dealing in partnership, by serving as factors and
agents, by acting as intermediaries in the delivery or receipt of coin or
goods, and by jointly transporting merchandise. Precisely because trade
was such a precarious form of endeavor, it was essential for everyone
to be certain of his fellows' trustworthiness. Only those who were
known to be competent and honest in their trade could be relied on to
pay their just debts or to handle another's wares and monies safely. A
close community of merchants was a necessary precondition to the conduct of business. Signs of its existence appear nearly everywhere, making it—somewhat paradoxically—difficult to study. Nevertheless, a
convenient method can be employed to study its operating principles in
the mid-sixteenth century.

We have already mentioned a document dating from about 1550 naming those men who were deemed worthy of membership in the merchant community. It lists one hundred and twenty-seven individuals.[24] Not all were exclusively overseas traders; several, such as "Smythe the boke bynder," must have maintained retail shops. Unfortunately, the author's hand is unknown, but since the list is found inserted in the ledger of John Smythe, one of Bristol's most important merchants in this period, we can assume it came from one of his circle and that the names in it represent the vast majority of those in Bristol for whom long-distance wholesale trade was the foundation of business. It was just such men who became known as "mere merchants."[25] Smythe, in his capacity as an exporter of cloth, lead, and leather, an importer of wine, iron, oil, woad, fruit, and the like, and a shipowner, had economic ties with fifty-seven of the men named in the list. He depended on them to aid in his business dealings from time to time, to freight his ship the *Trinity Smythe*, and to serve him either as suppliers of export goods or as a subsidiary market for imports. A survey of his dealings with them can help us see something of the socioeconomic bonds that held together the Bristol merchants of his day.

Smythe's overseas trade was centered in the Iberian peninsula. There he often relied on his fellow Bristolians for help in conducting business. Cash loans were sometimes necessary to complete transactions. Edward Pryn, for example, acting as the "taker" on a bill of exchange, lent Smythe £25 to be received in Andalusia through Hugh Tipton, Pryn's agent there. On other occasions Smythe himself lent money in Spain to facilitate the trade of fellow citizens, for which he was repaid at home, sometimes in goods. Merchant colleagues were also frequently entrusted with valuables for Smythe, as when 100 ducats were left for safekeeping with Thomas Harris in Seville, or when Francis Codrington carried a large sum of money overland to Smythe's resident servant in San Sebastian. But in most instances these duties were left in the hands of Smythe's own servants who traveled overseas with his goods.[26]

More important were the partnerships and other joint ventures in which Smythe engaged with his Bristol colleagues. In 1539, for example, Smythe joined with John Cutt and Giles White, who was Smythe's servant at the time, for the sale of Málaga raisins. But unlike some of his colleagues, Smythe participated in few such short-term partnerships as this. Joint export licenses were more important to his business. He combined with Edward Pryn and Robert Poole of Gloucester in a license for the export of leather in 1539, and he sold shares in his licenses for grain exports to a number of fellow Bristolians. Several of these ventures were conducted as true partnerships, with the participants buying, shipping, and selling the goods together under the terms of the license. Such an agreement seems to have been in force with Francis Codrington and William Carr, with whom Smythe participated in several licenses between 1538 and 1540. Edward Pryn, too, was a frequent partner in the shipment of restricted commodities. But more often the licensees were merely shareholders, lading their goods independently.[27]

Usually partnership agreements among merchants were for a single voyage. They came into being to combine capital or spread risk in only one enterprise and ended with the clearing of accounts several months later, after the venture had been completed. However, longer-term associations occasionally existed in which a number of individuals combined for mutual benefit, either to trade generally for a period of time or, less commonly, to trade jointly in one commodity over several years. Smythe belonged to one "firm" of the latter type in the early 1540s. Its purpose was to "Adventure in company" to the Azores for woad for six years. Eleven merchants participated in it, including seven of those mentioned in our list of merchants. The total capital was 5,200 Portuguese ducats, worth £1,300, divided into eight shares. Nicholas Thorne, William Spratt, and Smythe himself each held one full share. Single shares were also held by three partnerships, with one possessed by Edward Pryn and Robert Butler, another by Francis Codrington and William Carr, and a third by William Ballard and Francis Fowlar. The final two shares were jointly in the hands of the partnership of Francis Blanckley and Pedro Goncalez. To manage the firm's interests a simple administrative structure was established, with Edward Pryn "admytted for mynester here in Ynglande & the seid Frances Blanckelley & Pedro Goncalez for mynesters beyond the see." Thus, the Azorean woad enterprise reveals the existence not only of the main partnership but of several smaller merchant firms of sufficient permanence to hold shares in it.[28]

Shipping is another way that Smythe was bound with the membership of the Bristol merchant community in mutual endeavor. Of the fifty-seven merchants on the 1550 list with whom Smythe dealt, twenty-six used his ship at one time or another to conduct their trade. The vessel was occasionally chartered for long voyages, as by Francis Codrington and William Carr in 1538. More usually, however, merchants merely laded their goods aboard Smythe's vessel either in Bristol or abroad when it was in his own charge. As an overseas merchant, however, Smythe's own shipping needs could not be satisfied by his *Trinity.* Given the risks involved in all seaborne traffic, he would in any case have often sought to ship a portion of his exports and imports on vessels belonging to others. Frequently he laded his goods aboard vessels owned by fellow Bristolians. At one time or another, charter parties for ships owned by Thomas Tison, John Gorney, and Thomas Harris were recorded in Smythe's accounts. Occasionally Smythe chartered vessels jointly with merchant colleagues, as when he and Edward Pryn together hired the *Primrose of Bristol* to carry beans and wheat for them to Spain. Sometimes these ties were renewed several times over a relatively short period, reflecting the common business interests of the parties. For example, the *Harry of Bristol,* owned by Thomas Hickes, Francis Codrington, and William Carr, frequently carried Smythe's cargoes from 1538 through 1540, when all four men were engaged in other enterprises together.[29]

Foreign trade was not the only realm in which Smythe's ties to the Bristol merchant community proved significant. His activities in the domestic market also depended heavily upon his economic relations with his fellow merchants. Perhaps most important, these merchants provided a major outlet for his imported goods. Although they traded overseas in their own right, Smythe supplied many of them with commodities to supplement their businesses. Thirty-two of the fifty-seven merchants on the 1550 list with whom he dealt were his customers at one time or another. Spanish iron was the most frequently purchased item, perhaps reflecting Smythe's special command of this market, but he also sold wine, olive oil, woad, and raisins to other Bristol merchants. In return, Smythe sometimes received goods for his own stock from his fellow merchants. John Gorney and Thomas Harris both sold him wine, and Harris also sold him prunes; Thomas Tison, raisins and alum; William Appowell, cork and spices; John Cutt, cordovan, the red or purple dye known as orchil, and oakum; John Capes, salmon; James Bailey, orchil; William Cary, Walter Roberts, and Robert Saxy, various fabrics. In many of these instances the goods were exchanged to clear debts owed Smythe. Tison and Cutt, for example, paid their freight charges on the *Trinity* in the goods mentioned; Roberts paid for iron and wine, and Appowell for iron, wine, and woad. John Capes provided the salmon in return for an advance payment for the fish and the sale of wine and vinegar to him for his enterprises.[30]

Along with buying and selling with each other, Smythe and his colleagues also indirectly facilitated trade by acting as intermediaries for one another in domestic transactions. Often merchants well known to Smythe stood surety for lesser tradesmen who bought on credit from him. Usually the bonds were issued to strangers with no long-term ties to Smythe. Richard Pryor, for example, stood surety for William Bemer of Langford on a bond for the payment of £24 for a butt of sack; similarly, William Ballard provided the security on a bond for Richard Apris of Hereford for £10 worth of wine. Sometimes Bristolians whose credit was unknown or suspect also found it necessary to have surety for their bonds, as Richard Browne of Bristol, grocer, did for £6 worth of iron bought in 1540. A more common action was for merchants to pay the debts of their own business associates. This was particularly convenient when the debtor was a stranger, resident at a distance from Bristol. For example, the money owed by William Nowle of Bromwich for iron was paid for him by William Spratt, who in turn probably owed Nowle money. Smythe himself had such an arrangement with William North of Bruton, vintner, who often purchased wine from Smythe. In January 1543, Smythe paid a debt of £8 owed by North to John Gorney, in return for which North paid John Yerberry of Bruton, clothier, for cloths that Smythe had bought. The Bristol merchants also cleared their debts with each other in this fashion, as when Francis Codrington paid Smythe for freight charges owed by Thomas Hickes and Hickes paid Codrington for debts owed by Smythe.[31]

Behind the multifaceted ties connecting Smythe and his fellow merchants stands the credit relationship. Nearly all the fifty-seven merchants whose associations with Smythe have been traced were indebted to him at least once in the years 1538 to 1550. In some cases the form of the debt was a direct loan of cash, as when John Gorney received 20s from him in London in 1546 or when Thomas Harris received £10 in 1547–48. More often, however, it represented shop credit carried on the sale of goods or for the payment of freight charges. The terms were usually "3 monthes and 3 monthes" or "half in hand" and half at a stated date in the future, usually three months or six months hence. Rarely was the full amount paid on the spot for anything. No mention is made of interest charges, but higher prices on credit sales probably concealed them. Just what was done when payments were late, as often occurred, is not revealed. Just as credit helped sustain ties between a merchant and his suppliers or clientele, a network of close personal relationships grew as indebtedness was spread throughout the merchant community. At any given moment Smythe, or any of his contemporaries, not only owed large sums to his fellows for freight or goods or

both, but also carried substantial "accounts receivable" on his books.
Only those without sufficient credit or reputation were required to find
formal security for their obligations. In most cases the evidence of the
account book alone was sufficient to prove the debt. Indebtedness created recurring, even nearly permanent, links among close business associates. Often merchants became newly obligated to their creditors as
their old accounts were cleared, reinforcing and perpetuating their
relationship.[32]

Smythe's ledger is, unfortunately, a unique document in Bristol's economic history. No record as detailed or comprehensive survives for the
period following its terminal date in 1550. But *The Marchants Avizo*,
issued as a guide to apprentices and young merchants in the Iberian
trades, offers a starting point for comparison and analysis. Published in
1589 by John Browne, it contains the accounts and commercial papers
of a single large venture to Portugal and Spain conducted on behalf of
Thomas Aldworth of Bristol by Robert and John Aldworth of the same
city, Thomas's nephews and apprentices.[33]
    The venture that provided Browne with his documentation was a
complex one, conducted in the fall and winter of one of the years between 1577 and 1584, during which Robert Aldworth was in his uncle's
service. Probably it took place after February 1582, since the dates on
documents sent from the Iberian peninsula appear to depend on the
new-style, Gregorian calendar in use there from that time.[34] Five vessels, the *Joseph*, the *Gabriel*, the *Minion*, the *Unicorne*, and the *Pleasure*, were involved, all sailing together or associating with each other
in the voyage. Robert Aldworth was aboard the *Joseph*, which was
laden with both broadcloth and stammel, as well as wax and lead. The
other vessels carried similar cargoes, including additional varieties of
cloth such as "bayes" and "reading kersies." At least three of these
ships, the *Joseph*, the *Minion*, and the *Gabriel*, set sail from Bristol on
29 September, bound first for Portugal. After a brief setback caused by
a storm that drove them into Milford Haven six days later, they arrived
in Lisbon on 24 October, according to the letter Robert sent to his uncle
on his arrival there. (The voyage actually took only nine days, not nineteen: there is a ten-day difference between the new-style calendar and
the old.)
    Thereafter, business proceeded relatively briskly. By 7 November,
New Style, the first sales of Thomas Aldworth's goods had been accomplished and six kintals, two roves of pepper and one kintal of cloves had

been purchased and laden aboard the *Gabriel;* indeed, plans were already afoot "to go for Andalozia" to carry out further business. But this journey into Spain did not occur until the beginning of December, when the *Joseph,* unaccompanied by the *Gabriel,* made its way to San Lucar.[35] With ongoing activities in two ports, Robert Aldworth's task became somewhat more complicated. During December and early January, cloth and wax continued to be sold in Lisbon, while lead and bayes were sold in San Lucar. At the same time, such wares as pepper, cloves, mace, and cinnamon were purchased in Lisbon and olive oil and sack were purchased in the Guadalquivir valley. All in all, Robert Aldworth handled the following goods in the course of this single voyage: broadcloth, stammels, bayes, kerseys, wax, and lead as exports, and pepper, cloves, mace, cinnamon, cochineal, olive oil, and sack as imports. And in doing so, he dealt with at least five different merchants in Lisbon and four in San Lucar.[36]

During this fall and winter, Robert Aldworth not only purchased goods for his master but carried out a variety of other items of business as well. To begin with, he undertook to buy and sell as agent or factor for a number of Bristol merchants other than his uncle Thomas. According to a bill of lading dated 20 January, for example, he bought three roves of cochineal and five butts of sack for John Barker and another eight butts of sack for Thomas James, all of which were placed aboard the *Pleasure* along with the pepper, olive oil, and sack that he had acquired for his master. He also relied on various other merchants to act as his factors in markets that he could not reach. While resident in Seville, for instance, he wrote a friend in Lisbon to receive 100 ducats from one P. R., draper of that city, "to imploie it all in good pepper," and to lade the same aboard the *Pleasure* for shipment to Thomas Aldworth in Bristol. He wrote to another friend in San Lucar asking him to meet the *Gabriel* there and receive from it six tons of lead containing one hundred and five pieces "& to doe so much as make present sale of it, the best you can as time serueth." With the money earned from this transaction, moreover, this same factor was ordered "to ride vnto Sheres and buy for me 8. Buts of very good Secke the best that possible can be gotten, though they cost a Ducket or two the more in a But."[37]

Of equal importance was the financial business undertaken both in England and in the Iberian peninsula. In September, for example, Thomas Aldworth caused his ship the *Gabriel* to be insured in London by two resident merchants of that city and by one of his Bristol compatriots. Much additional activity concerned the settling of debts and accounts and the exchanging of monies. Inevitably, these procedures also involved dependence on associates and friends among overseas traders in the area. Before he set sail, Robert Aldworth authorized one T. M. "to recouer & receaue of G. H. marchant of the aforesaid City of Bristow the summe of 25. pounds, due vnto me as appeareth by this bill." During the busy month of January, young Robert also served in this capacity for one of his Bristol principals, while later in the month he authorized yet another fellow townsman to collect a debt owed him in Lisbon. Bills of exchange also were issued. By their very nature these financial instruments required the services of friendly intermediaries who either lent the original sum, delivered the bill, or made the exchange.[38]

Just as in Smythe's day, the factor remained key to the success of commercial enterprise. It was the factor's activity that permitted the Bristol merchant to conduct his affairs from his countinghouse rather than the deck of a ship, and therefore to spread his interests over a wider and wider area. Often cargoes laded in Bristol were placed under the charge of a servant, such as Robert Aldworth, or a young merchant acting for a group of merchants. Commonly the ship carried a supercargo who was responsible for the welfare of the vessel and its freight and who usually also served as factor for the sale of the goods that were otherwise unaccompanied. But more and more, Bristol's merchants were relying on resident factors in foreign ports who were independent professionals rather than servants to a particular merchant or group. Many of these "commission agents" were themselves Bristolians. In the 1520s, for example, Leonard Osborn agreed to act as factor in Bordeaux for Gerom Grene; and in the 1540s Robert Tyndall was resident in San Sebastian. Early in the next century, John Hopkins resided in Venice, where John Whitson used him; in the 1630s, William Colston, Junior, served the interests of his fellow Bristolians from his home in Lisbon. These factors were servants to their native merchant community as much as they were agents for individual traders. Bristolians turned to them, not only for their familiarity with local market conditions, but because they were known and trusted.[39]

The institution of partnership reflects the same reliance on the community of merchants as does the use of factors. Most partnerships existed for short periods and for strictly limited purposes; they were more like trading fellowships than business firms. Frequently, they were no more than convenient arrangements that grew out of extremely short-term market conditions and were typically designed to fill only the most immediate trading needs of the members. In John Whitson's letter book, for example, we note that one of the alderman's factors in France, complaining of the high current price of salt, offered to "goe in partabell" terms with his principal if he "canne fynde anny that will goe upon reasonable termes." Even the long-term trading relations of kinsmen, such as the "cumpany" that was formed between the brothers William and Robert Tyndale in the mid-1540s, had something of this informal and intermittent character, as the surviving records of their accounts reveal.[40] Customs records reinforce this view of fluid relations among merchants and of their small reliance upon permanent companies or firms. In 1636–37, only about 2 percent of the cockets issued by the Bristol customs officers for exports were in the name of a partnership. Trading in company was somewhat more common in inward traffic. For example, about 14 percent of the import cockets in 1637–38 were in the name of more than one merchant or of an association, with wine shipments almost always being made in this fashion. In nearly all of these cases, however, the parties traded independently as well as with co-partners. Indeed, there was nothing to prevent them from combining with more than one group of partners at the same time.[41]

The primary economic function of a partnership was the pooling of liquid resources, not the concentrated exploitation of the market through rational organization and the division of labor.[42] According to the classic seventeenth-century definition, a partnership exists

> where one man doth aduenture a thousand pounds, another fiue hundred pounds, another three hundred pounds, and another four hundred pounds, more or lesse as they agree amongst themselves to make a stock, euery man to haue his profit, or to beare losses and aduenture according to their seuerall stocks in one or many voyages, for one or more years . . . to be diuided into so many parts as they agree.[43]

Yet few commercial enterprises had the permanence of the woad partnership in which John Smythe participated, and almost none had a comparable organization. At the end of the fifteenth and the beginning of the sixteenth century, for example, Hugh Eliot and Robert Thorne traded jointly at home and abroad for two decades, but they reckoned their books and settled accounts after each voyage rather than maintaining their profits and losses in a joint account from year to year. Half a century later, William Gittens and John Carr managed their joint ownership in the same way, each paying his share of expenses at the end of a venture. Those long-lived partnerships that did exist usually were family affairs. For almost twenty years in the 1620s and 1630s, for instance, Robert Aldworth and Giles Elbridge, his nephew, former apprentice, and adoptive heir, regularly traded together and engaged in other joint activities such as the plantation on the Pemaquid peninsula in New England. But they also maintained independent commercial establishments, taking apprentices and conducting business on their own. The pattern was the same for the brothers Erasmus and Thomas Wright in the 1630s. Although such arrangements necessarily required joint records and orderly procedures in settling accounts, there was little to differentiate them from partnerships for a single voyage. As with the partnership of the Tyndales in the early sixteenth century, their purpose was preservation of family interests by concentrating capital resources into a single stock, not the creation of specialized firms with highly structured internal organizations. Moreover, long-term partnerships that lacked a strong family character seem to have been especially vulnerable to dispute and litigation when accounts could not be balanced, as happened in turn to Eliot and Thorne and to Gittens and Carr, among others.[44] Only extraordinary investments requiring lengthy and systematic joint endeavor to turn a profit, such as Smythe's woad partnership or the early seventeenth-century colony at Bristol's Hope, Newfoundland, seem to have required more highly structured business organizations.

Even among shipowners, economic associations lacked the character of the modern business firm. Although sailing vessels were typically the property of small and apparently close-knit groups of merchants, individual members were continually divesting themselves of their interests, and, just as in commerce, partnerships were in a constant state of flux. Comparison of two lists of Bristol ships and shipowners, compiled in November 1626 and March 1629, respectively, shows an extraordinarily high turnover in both equipment and personnel. In 1626, Bristolians owned forty-two vessels; two and a half years later, they owned forty-eight vessels. However, only nineteen ships are common to both lists. In 1626, 50 percent of the vessels were individually owned: four by Robert Aldworth, four by John Brooke, three by Thomas Wright, two by Edward Ballash, and one each by Nathaniel Butcher, George Gibson, William Haskins, Richard Woodward, Thomas Rogers, John Came, William Owfield, and Edward Peters. With war increasing the risks of shipowning, only 25 percent of the vessels were in the possession of a single merchant in March 1629: three owned by Thomas Wright, two each by Giles Elbridge and Edward Peters, and one each by Robert Aldworth, William Owfield, Thomas Heathcott, Charles Driver, and John Brooke. Most merchants, however, preferred to own shares, often in several vessels. In 1626, for example, Humphrey Browne, John Gonning, and Nathaniel Butcher each held an interest in four ships, while John Barker, Richard Long, and William Wyatt were concerned in three and Francis Creswick, Richard Holworthy, and Humphrey Hooke in two. Between fall 1626 and spring 1629, moreover, the ownership of thirteen of the nineteen ships which appear on both lists was significantly altered. Either new shareholders had been added, or shares had changed hands. Twenty of the fifty individuals named as owners on the first list do not appear on the second, and seventeen of the forty-seven names on the second list do not appear on the first. A portion of this turnover is no doubt due to the maritime warfare that plagued these years, but not all the vessels were used for such purposes. Wartime conditions merely exaggerated what was already commonplace in more settled times.[45]

In the commercial economy of Elizabethan and early Stuart Bristol, the role played by rationalized firms, joint enterprises, and highly organized, permanent partnership was small. The social foundations of trade were provided, rather, by the existence of networks of regular mercantile contacts among Bristolians. Capital was extremely mobile, not only permitting the diversification of a merchant's interests into many markets and many commodities but also encouraging the formation of a variety of commercial ties with numerous overseas traders. To a remarkable degree, the conduct of most individual merchant businesses showed little difference in principle from the pattern revealed by partnerships. Judging from John Smythe's ledger, merchants usually considered each investment as a separate enterprise, accounting profits and losses in compartments. Smythe practiced a form of "venture accounting" in which individual enterprises and dealings with particular persons were kept in separate entries. This method permitted him to distinguish his many interests from one another and to keep a close watch on the balances in each one. He grouped his exports under the markets to which they were sent, and a profit-and-loss account was kept by voyages to a particular region for a stated period, usually a year. Import items were each given a separate profit-and-loss account. Hence for most undertakings individual and joint ventures were treated the same in the accounts.[46]

The highly fluid character of partnerships and of shipowning arrangements was a manifestation of the social principle on which trade was based. The commodities market also reveals that principle at work. When large stocks of merchandise were brought into Bristol, their first market frequently was not a retailer but a fellow merchant, whose business contacts could help distribute the goods. Early in James I's reign, for example, Thomas Aldworth and Francis Doughty imported substantial quantities of sugar, Canary wine, sumac, and perhaps also currants aboard the *White Stag of Bristol* from Madeira. Aldworth sold a portion of his goods to Walter Williams, merchant, and Doughty conveyed his share to Humphrey Fitzherbert, Peter Miller, and William Barker, merchants. This helped spread the risk among a number of individuals, who for their part were happy to have the supplies. In place of a world of established business firms anxious to exploit a specialized market for the utmost profit to the exclusion of all competition, there existed a community of merchants, men personally known to one another by reputation and credit, who cooperated as well as competed in the marketplace.[47]

As in John Smythe's day, credit was the binding force in this community in the early seventeenth century. Usually a merchant was both creditor and debtor, waiting on the payments of one tradesman in order to clear his accounts with another. To Alderman John Guy this was an inevitable consequence of the calling. "Neither the borrower nor the lender have any money," he said, "and only he that neither borrows nor lends; for the borrower commonly as he receives with one hand he pays with the other, and for the lender it is ever out of his hands, he will borrow a small sum to make up a greater to put it out."[48] Merchant inventories reveal something of this ubiquity of indebtedness. At Richard Pley's death in 1639, for instance, over 55 percent of his total assets were in thirty-eight separate debts owed him by forty-one different individuals. Thirteen of these debtors were fellow Bristol merchants. Among them was Walter Stephens, who owed a total of over £2,100, of which £675 was exclusively in his own name and the remainder in conjunction with four others. John Gonning, Junior, was responsible for another £130 or thereabouts, and Richard Aldworth was personally indebted for almost £150 and joined with Stephens and three others in a further sum of nearly £900. With these men Pley conducted business "on Accompte," suggesting either commodity sales or partnerships. But there were also a number of bonds, including one for £104 in the names of Thomas and Erasmus Wright, who perhaps purchased property or capital equipment from Pley.[49] The inventory does not record Pley's own debts, since those were not assets for which the executors of his estate were liable. But Pley's account book, had it survived, probably would reveal sums owed others from whom he bought goods or with whom he jointly traded. As Sir Arthur Ingram said in 1624, "if the trade of the kingdom were divided into 4 parts, 3 of them at least are carried on credit."[50]

The Marchants Avizo indicates that this hard-won credit was to be directed primarily toward obtaining the scarce luxuries carrying high profit margins that came from the import trade. According to John Browne, a young merchant was to have an expert knowledge of such wares as pepper, cloves, mace, cinnamon, nutmeg, ginger, sugar, calicos, cochineal, olive oil, white soap, and wine.[51] To this list we should add alum, woad, madder, indigo, tobacco, dried and fresh fruit, sweet wines, and such items of mercery and haberdashery as silks, velvets, laces, ribbons, linens, hats, handkerchiefs, fancy gloves, and other finery. The motives for purchasing such wares is suggested in the "caueat" Thomas Aldworth gave to his young nephew John:

> [N]euer think the same ware which is best cheape and is most bought vp, that it will be best to bestowe your money theron, for ordinarily it falleth out, that the best cheape wares that is brought home, hath smaller vtterance and lesse profite, than such deare wares as there commeth but verie little quantitie of.[52]

The scarce, the exotic, and the small and easy to transport were the ideal wares. They might carry the highest prices abroad, but they yielded the greatest profits at home.

In consequence, overseas trade was essentially a well-orchestrated effort on the part of the city's merchants to maximize imports. Monies received abroad were immediately paid out again to purchase spices, wine, oil, or some other scarce commodity. Restrictions on carrying coin or bullion out of Spain and other markets made this procedure essential for returning home with the proceeds of one's sales. "And if after you haue bought al these wares," Thomas Aldworth wrote to his factor, "there may be any surplus money remaining: do you bestow it in good cochenele, so far as it will rise." The attraction of the import market was so strong that Bristolians were also willing to borrow or to use ready cash in order to participate in it. John Smythe in the 1540s not only transferred funds to the Iberian peninsula by bill of exchange but also shipped coin to Bordeaux and northern Spain to acquire commodities there. Thirty years later Robert Aldworth, acting for his uncle Thomas, borrowed money in England on bills of exchange to make his purchases in Spain. For the Levant trade, paying in cash was essential.

TABLE 9   JOHN SMYTHE'S TRADING PROFITS,
19 JANUARY 1540 TO 27 SEPTEMBER 1543

Exports	£-s-d	Imports	£-s-d	Total £-s-d
Gains				
Bordeaux	7-06-08	Oils	117-16-03	
Biscay	301-15-01	Iron	481-12-07½	
Lisbon and		Woad	43-17-09	
Andalusia	282-18-03	Raisins	3-05-09	
Leather license	1-04-08	Salmon	15-00-00	
		Wine[a]	289-12-01	
Total	588-04-08		951-04-05½	1,539-09-01½
Losses				
Bordeaux	1-14-04	Salt	6-18-03	
Lisbon and		Sack	22-13-04	
Andalusia	20-07-02	Bad debts	60-00-00	
Total	22-01-06		89-11-07	111-13-01
Grand Total	566-03-02		861-12-10½	1,427-16-00½

SOURCE: Jean Vanes, ed., *The Ledger of John Smythe, 1538–1550* (Bristol Record Society 28, 1974), pp. 132–33.
[a] Consists of Gascon, £55-01-05; sack, £112-03-02; bastard, £38-04-10; teynt, £3-17-09; ossey, £7-08-01; and "of Andalusia," £72-16-10.

Currants, it was said, "haue such an attractive power that noe discouragement can withhould the marchants of England from sending readie money and shippes to buy and lade the same" and "noe Commodities of this Kingdome (worthy the mentioning)" could be vented to purchase them "according to the vsual course of commerce."[53]

A good picture of commerce conducted on these principles is offered by Smythe's ledger. Despite his preference for venture accounting, periodically Smythe cast up his total profits from his export-import tallies. A look at his summary for the period January 1540 to November 1543 shows a gross profit of about £1,540, of which sales of exports accounted for about 38 percent and sales of imports for about 62 percent. Against these gains was almost £112 in losses, making a net profit of nearly £1,428, of which about 40 percent came from exports and about 60 percent from imports (Table 9). When Smythe's exports are closely examined, his difficulties in turning a profit on them become clear. The English commodities upon which his outward trade relied in 1540–1543 were cloth, leather and skins, and beans and wheat. Later in the 1540s he also traded in lead, either newly smelted from the Mendips or old lead from the roofs and furnishings of the local monasteries. Cloth was his major trading item, but his profits on its sale were very meager. In August 1540, he laded thirty-eight of John Yerberry's better fabrics

TABLE 10   JOHN SMYTHE'S PROFITS
AND LOSSES ON SALES,
24 MARCH 1540 TO 27 SEPTEMBER 1543

Exports	Gains (%)	Imports	Gains (%)
Bordeaux	3.10	Oils	16.51
Biscay	11.06	Iron	14.88
Lisbon and		Woad	15.62
Andalusia	16.31	Raisins	7.26
Leather license	3.84	Salmon	31.25
		Wine[a]	21.11
		Salt	−10.63
Average	12.55		16.40

SOURCE: Jean Vanes, ed., *The Ledger of John Smythe, 1538–1550* (Bristol Record Society 28, 1974), pp. 132–33. The table does not include bad debts or losses at sea that do not reveal profit margin.

[a] Consists of Gascon, 13.31; sack, 19.48; bastard, 38.62; teynt, 32.77; ossey, 31.05; and "of Andalusia," 29.43.

aboard two vessels bound for Lisbon and Andalusia. Their value "clere abord" was £4 per cloth, or £152. When sold in Lisbon they earned net just about 8 percent profit. In several instances cloth was sold at no profit. For example, fabrics worth £150 were taken to Biscay aboard the *Trinity* in December 1539. When their sales were complete in June 1540, they had earned Smythe only about £145, a loss of over 3 percent. Two voyages to Lisbon and Andalusia in 1539–40 and one to Bordeaux in 1541 showed net losses as a result of similarly poor sales of cloth. In one case, sixteen trunkers were left unsold in Spain and were finally disposed of six months later for £6 less than they had cost. Profits were earned, however, on wheat and leather.[54]

Smythe's ledger suggests that mid-sixteenth-century Bristol merchants were assembling their outbound cargoes largely as a means to transfer capital to foreign markets. Exports produced only uncertain profits, with cloth sometimes showing losses, leather and wheat requiring licenses for legal shipment, and the demand for grains depending upon fluctuating harvests both in England and abroad. Imports, however, consistently produced handsome returns, with salmon and wine leading (Table 10). Through the inward-bound commodities traffic not only were Smythe's foreign earnings brought home, but gains were regularly made on domestic sales.

The experiences of John Smythe and his fellow merchants in the 1540s were conditioned by English currency devaluations, ending in 1551, which drove up domestic prices while stimulating cloth exports.

Smythe also relied more heavily upon the Biscayan trade than merchants did in the second half of the sixteenth century. Nevertheless, Bristol's merchants of Elizabeth's reign conducted their business affairs on much the same basis as Smythe had. As is revealed by the Aldworth papers in *The Marchants Avizo,* imports remained the foundation of commerce. The particular remembrance which Thomas Aldworth supplied his apprentice gives the prices at which fine broadcloths, stammel, and wax had been purchased; Robert Aldworth's accounts show the prices at which these goods were sold in Lisbon. The broadcloths, for example, cost "clear on board" £12 per piece and were bargained for 53 ducats 4 reals each in Portugal, or approximately £13 7s; the stammel cost £17 and was sold for 75 ducats, or about £18 15s. Together these transactions provided a gross profit of almost 9 percent. But deducted from the final sale prices were charges for "barking," "landing," "Marco customs," "measuring," "wyndage," "brokerage," and "auerage," plus a 2.5 percent factor's fee. This reduced the net profit to a bit less than 5 percent. The sale of wax was even less lucrative. It had cost Thomas Aldworth £5 12s per hundredweight and was sold for 23 ducats 5 reals per hundredweight in Lisbon, or just under £6 the hundredweight. The gross profit here was about 5 percent, and the additional charges and fees reduced this already meager sum to only a bit over 1 percent.

For Aldworth's imports there are no equivalent figures; only the prices paid in the Iberian peninsula have survived. But we can estimate the profit margins. According to merchant custom, sale of pepper by the dozen pounds was considered a wholesale transaction. Aldworth paid 52 ducats per kintal of one hundred twelve pounds in Lisbon, or just over 27s per dozen pounds. Between 1575 and 1584 the average price of a dozen pounds of pepper in England was around 36s, which suggests a profit margin of about 23 percent, less freight charges and customs in England. For other commodities it is necessary to rely on English retail prices as a guide. Sack was bought by Aldworth for about £5 per butt, or 9.5d per gallon. In the years 1575–1584, a gallon of sack usually sold for 2s 8d, for an estimated gain of just over 70 percent between original purchase and final sale, less freight, customs, and other charges in England, which were steep. Still, this suggests a merchant's profit in the same range as that achieved by Smythe in the 1540s. The picture we get is of an import-driven trade, in which a merchant could expect to make a substantial profit on the goods he brought from abroad, but little, if any, gain from his exports.

The forms of overseas commercial enterprise prevalent in sixteenth- and early seventeenth-century Bristol would have been quite familiar to the city's late medieval merchants. The factor, the partnership, the existence of shares in ships, and the dependence on credit that characterized the businesses of Smythe, Aldworth, and Whitson were already well-known in the fifteenth century. What was new was the degree to which the forms had become elaborated over a wide network of trade in a variety of different markets. Because of their relatively unstructured character, these older institutions had proven admirably adaptable to new commercial conditions. For Bristol's overseas trade, the early modern era had been born without revolutionary changes in accepted practices. But the same cannot be said for the organization of the domestic economy. Here shifts in business arrangements redefined the relationship of trade to the economy and recast the social structure of the city.

We can see the clearest signs of these changes in the ways that the merchants' relations with the domestic market altered in the sixteenth century. The city's ancient rules for dealing with strangers required them to bring their goods to a central place to be weighed, to have toll paid, and to be sold only to burgesses, by wholesale, not retail. After 1459, the place settled upon was Spicer's Hall, named after Richard Spicer, who had given it to the city; later it was called the Backhall. There all persons not burgesses were to bring their woad, woolen cloth, wine, and grocery wares. Sales of livestock and goods were also subject to toll and were to be conducted only in the established open markets and at fixed hours. Private dealings between strangers and burgesses were forbidden; instead, every citizen was to have an equal opportunity to view and purchase the goods. But by the mid-sixteenth century these rules were no more than an ideal continually appealed to but regularly violated. In the 1530s and 1540s, for example, John Smythe maintained close ties with a number of country cloth manufacturers who sold exclusively to him in return for the oil, alum, woad, madder, and other dyestuffs he provided them. His chief supplier, John Yerberry of Bruton, clothier, was even paid directly in woad for his fabrics. Smythe also undertook to finish cloth himself, taking unfinished fabrics from country clothiers and employing Bristol shearmen, tuckers, and dyers to ready it for market. As a result of practices like these, the Backhall was moribund in the sixteenth century, used more for weighing and warehousing goods than for regulating their sale.[55]

The history of the Bristol fairs reveals the same story. The fairs of medieval Bristol, of which there were as many as eight at one time or another, were great open marketplaces. Tolls and customs were suspended to encourage strangers and foreigners to bring their "goodes cattell and merchandiszes" to them. Merchants set up stalls in the Marsh, St. James churchyard, Spicer's Hall, or the city streets to display wares. Negotiations took place on the spot, without guarantee that every item brought to market would be sold. Goods were examined, prices debated, and agreements reached in full publicity. Private dealings with foreigners may also have taken place, but the essence of the fair was sale in "market overt," primarily between Bristolians and strangers, made in the presence of other marketgoers and subject to regulations imposed by the city and enforced in the market court. By the mid-sixteenth century, however, this had changed. Although there were certainly still booths and stalls around which buyers gathered to bargain in the manner of an Oriental bazaar, and the market court still survived, a fair was no longer primarily such an open marketplace. It had become, rather, an occasion at which "seller & . . . byer do appoynt to mete . . . & there do bargayne." The great annual St. James Fair took place at Whitsuntide, seven weeks after Easter. After 1529 a winter fair was added, first at Candlemas, in early February, and then, from 1548 on, at the Feast of the Conversion of St. Paul at the end of January. Together these fairs gave a distinct seasonal rhythm to inland trade. They provided two established periods, some six months apart, during which merchants from all over southern and western England congregated to place orders, pay debts, and settle accounts. In consequence, the fairs became financial as well as mercantile institutions, used as convenient clearinghouses not only by Bristolians but by merchants of the Midlands, the West Country, South Wales, Ireland, and London, who maintained continuous ties with each other year in and year out.[56]

The Backhall and the fairs, two institutions designed to insure open trading between burgess and "foreigner," were either circumvented or transformed to serve a new economic order in which private contractual arrangements between townsmen and outsiders were the common pattern. As if to mark this change, the collection of tolls at the city gates was abandoned in 1546; the income from newly purchased monastic properties made up for the lost revenue. Medieval restrictions against strangers trading freely with the city remained in force, but Bristol's leading men no longer relied on them to protect their interests. They did not usually buy and sell in the city markets, either the Backhall or the fairs, but maintained steady working relationships with individual dealers and customers, with whom they were linked by credit.[57]

Credit again dictated the structure of social relations, this time in a distinctly asymmetrical pattern. Dealings in cloth were almost invariably conducted on account by the city's merchants. John Smythe, for example, usually deferred payments to his country suppliers for three or, more often, six months. Only for such relatively low-priced goods as "lether corne buttar chese tallow calveskyns" and the like did he and his brethren pay in ready cash. In effect, the merchant received his cloths out of the "clothier's stok" usually for "halff year and halff year," which permitted the overseas trader not only to sell his fabrics abroad but to pay his debts with the proceeds of the import trade. The trade depended on a clear division of labor from which each side normally benefited. The clothier was relieved of managing his affairs, with all the attendant risks, in foreign as well as domestic markets. The merchant was saved the difficult task of coordinating the various stages of cloth production at home, leaving him free to worry about the state of sales in distant places. Since the merchant controlled access to the final market abroad, he had the advantage over the clothier, even though he was in the clothier's debt. However, if accounts were to be cleared and new ventures undertaken, rapid, secure, and profitable marketing of imports was absolutely essential to the merchant.[58] For this reason merchants felt an intense interest in their outlet for foreign wares, the domestic retail trade.

The relationship between merchant and retailer ideally was also a symbiotic one. As the merchants themselves said,

> A merchant cannot be a retailer for want of skill and acquaintance of customers, which requires an apprenticeship to bring him to it; neither can he have a fit place to dwell in, for all the houses that stand in place of retail are already in the hands of retailers.[59]

A legal dispute between Daniel Bishop, vintner, Edward Coxe, merchant, et al. reveals these close ties.[60] In October 1618, Bishop, together with one James Glover of Bristol, had leased a tavern called the King's Head and Merchant's Arms, in which wine was to be sold. Over a period of three years these two men, acting as partners, had become indebted to divers persons for upwards of £300, which they were unable to pay on time. On a thorough examination of their joint estates, Glover decided it was wise to leave the partnership and was willing to grant to Bishop all his rights in the tavern as well as all the personal property of the partnership, if Bishop in turn would dispose of all their outstanding debts. At first Bishop was unwilling to agree to this, but two of his creditors, Edward Coxe, merchant of Bristol, and John Gibbens, baker, encouraged him and promised to stand surety for the debts of the partnership and to use their credit to provide Bishop with the wine he needed to continue his trade. This is a most revealing act on their part. In their efforts to save their debtor from bankruptcy they were not only hoping to recover the money owed them but were also preserving the access to the market that Bishop provided. Moreover, as Bishop was paying his old debts he was becoming further obligated to these benefactors for additional extensions of credit. Had this arrangement been successful the result would have been a tavern tied to the wholesalers who supplied it.

As the relationship between debtor and creditors developed, Coxe and Gibbens required Bishop to sign over to them his rights to the tavern as well as all of the debts owed him—a sum of £200 or so—with the understanding that the conveyance of the tavern would be null and void if Bishop should pay off all his creditors within fifteen months. Bishop paid the first installment on this plan, but found it impossible to meet the second one. Still, the tavern held out a powerful attraction to merchant capital. Even in the depths of Bishop's financial difficulties, Edward Peters, merchant, was willing to replace Gibbens as co-guarantor of Bishop's debts. Unfortunately for Bishop, this intervention came too late. By March 1623, Coxe and Gibbens had already sued process in the Bristol Tolzey, where the Sheriffs' Court was located, and, as a result, a *capias* had been issued and Bishop's property had been attached. Fearful of the outcome of his case in the Tolzey, Bishop fled the city—over the rooftops, according to one story—taking with him all the plate and other valuables he could manage to transport. He thereby made himself not only a bankrupt but a thief and outlaw to boot. Undaunted, Coxe and Gibbens pursued him with legal process into Gloucestershire and from there across the country to London, where he was found and arrested a year later. Soon thereafter they joined with Robert Aldworth and John Gonning, merchants, and sued a commission of bankruptcy out of the Chancery, which put a final end to Bishop's career.

Despite the sad end of this ill-starred association of merchant and tavernkeeper, merchant interest in such domestic enterprises was not an unusual phenomenon in the sixteenth and early seventeenth centuries. During this long period, a number of overseas traders maintained their own inns or taverns or informally linked themselves to others. William Pepwell, for example, owned The Starr in the 1560s; and in the 1580s his son-in-law, Philip Langley, was proprietor of the George in High Street. During the early seventeenth century, such important figures as Thomas Wright and Richard Vickris leased other Bristol taverns, while several leading merchants, including Thomas James, John Barker, and Richard Aldworth, had rights to country inns near Bristol.[61] A review of Bristol wills and other surviving family papers reveals at least twelve hostelries in the hands of overseas merchants in the years from 1550 to 1640. Most of these investors were either specialists in grocery wares, such as Pepwell, Langley, and Vickris, or large-scale dealers in wines, such as Barker, James, and Wright. Like Edward Coxe and Edward Peters, they no doubt looked upon their inns and taverns primarily as ready markets for their imports.

This evidence of merchant investment in taverns and inns reveals Bristol's overseas traders to have been dependent, if only in small degree, upon their customers among the city's retailers. This dependency was mutual. So long as it was possible to turn a profit of as much as 25 to 35 percent on retail sales, as some shopkeepers were said to do,[62] it was to the advantage of the grocer, mercer, and vintner to maintain good relations with their sources of supply. Merchants, moreover, usually sold their wares to shopkeepers on credit, thereby supplying them with the necessary capital to renew their retail trading stocks.[63] This meant that the merchant ordinarily enjoyed a double hold on his customers among the retailers. Not only were they in his debt, but without him they would have lacked the necessary stocks to run their businesses.

What Bristol's merchants wanted from the import trade was a quick turnover of their investments. Keeping full storehouses was not a typical pattern; it only idled capital and blocked credit. When stocks built up, merchants sometimes retailed their wares, either openly or illicitly, especially if perishable goods were involved.[64] At times the Privy Council was even enlisted to stimulate sales, as when the Bristol merchants petitioned "to haue the vyntners of this Citty to take from the Marchant yeerly a competent quantity of wines . . . for that they haue great quantities of wines vpon their Hands which are not taken of as formerly haue ben don."[65] But because many of the imports were expensive, scarce commodities, their markets were highly elastic and volatile; a small oversupply could dramatically drop prices and cut profits. It was thus necessary for merchants also to control import prices through a form of "ingrossing," which, according to theory, kept

commodities in reputation to maintain a trade thereby: as when men of meanes do ingrosse and by vp a commoditie, and for a reasonable gaine they

sell the same again to shop keepers and retailers. This is much vsed amongst
Merchants of all nations, otherwise when aboundance of a commodity doth
so much abate the price of it, that Merchants do become losers and discour-
aged, then the traffique and trade is thereby ouerthrowne, to the generall
hurt of the Commonwealth: in which respect it is better to pay somewhat
more for Commodities, than to haue them altogether ouercheape.[66]

Such a procedure introduced a degree of predictability into the import
trade without which commerce in all but staple items would have been
too risky to undertake.

These conditions meant that the relationship between merchants and
retailers was always in delicate balance. There was an inherent rivalry
between the wholesale trader and the shopkeeper. When the latter invested in overseas commerce on his own account, not only did he keep
the merchant's share of the profits, but he could afford to buy at a somewhat higher price and to sell at a somewhat lower price than his competition. It was not even necessary for the shopkeeper to travel overseas
to undertake this business. The services of a factor could be used to
carry out his orders. These men, usually young merchants traveling
abroad on their own business or resident in some foreign city, regularly
acted as commission agents for merchants living at home. Their charges
were moderate, typically only 2.5 percent for each transaction, far
cheaper than the rates received by merchant middlemen, so that the
shopkeeper's final price was lower even though he now had to pay the
freight charges and customs. The incentive for retailers to become their
own suppliers thus was large.[67]

Wholesale merchants were especially concerned about this form of
competition, for it threatened their control of the market. "The rich retailers," the merchants warned, "as the grocer, mercer, haberdasher,
soapmaker, vintner, &c., adventuring themselves, must needs undo all
the poorer sort who do not adventure, and eat out the meer merchants,
who have but those to whom they make their vent."[68] The fear was
rooted in economic reality. Provided the shopkeeper conducted his overseas ventures on a cash-and-carry basis and not on credit, he was free
to buy when prices were at their lowest, at the peak of supply, and to
hold his purchases from the market until consumer demand was at its
highest.[69] For many of the items in which he traded, these periods were
readily predictable; they came at fair times and festivals in the winter,
spring, and summer. If grocers, vintners, and other retailers maintained
their own stocks of foreign commodities, however, the market became
difficult for the wholesale merchant to judge, since there was no telling

when a hitherto unknown supply of a particular commodity would appear for sale. But unless the true state of local supplies could be estimated, the decision to purchase additional imports as prices rose was extremely risky. Buying the remains of the previous fall's vintage, for example, might be a worthwhile investment if local supplies were nearly exhausted, but it could prove disastrous if the vintners were maintaining an independent stock. The entrance of retailers into foreign trade significantly increased the uncertainties of commercial dealing for the wholesaler.

On the whole, however, the relations between individual overseas traders and retailers were not troubled by competition. Only the very richest shopkeeping grocers, drapers, mercers, or vintners were likely to engage frequently in foreign commerce. For most of the rest, as Smythe's ledger suggests, ties with merchant suppliers typically were extremely stable, with the shopkeeper dependent on the wholesaler for the continued conduct of his business. Yet relations between wholesale merchants and retail shopkeepers deeply affected the underlying social order of sixteenth- and early seventeenth-century Bristol. As those Bristolians who engaged in overseas trade became an increasingly tight-knit community exclusively engaged in wholesale enterprise, separate from other crafts and trades of the city, a reorganization of society occurred that touched nearly every aspect of social life in the city, as we shall see in the following chapters.

✦

Judged on the basis of the foregoing evidence, Bristol's trading society in the sixteenth and early seventeenth centuries was composed of two contrasting types of social order, the one a fluid fellowship, the other focused more sharply on precisely defined relationships between particular individuals. The difference is largely a consequence of the credit system. Where merchants were often both creditors and debtors in their dealings with fellow overseas traders, dealings with domestic dealers usually were restricted to one mode or the other. Clothiers, for example, tended to be creditors, while vintners and grocers tended to be debtors. To assure payment of these debts, heavy reliance was placed upon continually trading with known, trusted, and credit-worthy individuals. Under these conditions, transactions in the open market became more and more rare as each domestic dealer became dependent upon particular merchants for his business.

Those credit arrangements gave life to the city's social order and formed its characteristic shape. At the pinnacle stood a cohesive group of overseas merchants, whose relationships with one another defined the framework within which commerce was conducted. Among the membership of this elite the institution of the firm, relying upon highly specialized skills or equipment and exploiting a single market, was present only in primitive form. Stability and order were provided, rather, by the network of economic ties that bound the commercial community together. The links between these overseas merchants and their principal domestic suppliers and customers, however, were dramatically different. Instead of a regime in which co-equals freely associated with one another according to circumstances, fixed business arrangements, even contracts, tied individual merchants to particular suppliers and retailers.

CHAPTER 3

Organizing the Society

During the late fifteenth and the early sixteenth century, as Bristol's economy ceased to be based on trade in wine and woolens with western France and came to depend on much riskier dealings in high-priced and exotic imports from southern Europe, a close community of whole-sale merchants, specializing in this southern trade, differentiated itself from the larger body of tradesmen and craftsmen in the city. So far, however, we have treated this development as though it were the natural product of an evolution in which environmental changes produce new forms of social organization to meet altered requirements for survival. But that kind of determinism neglects the way human agency drives such historical processes. In this chapter we shall begin correcting this shortcoming.

In the conventions of sociology and anthropology, social organization has commonly been considered the equivalent of social structure— simply another way of speaking about the "arrangement in which the elements of social life are linked together."[1] According to the stand-ard definition, " 'social organization' refers . . . to the observed regular-ities in the behavior of people that are due to . . . social conditions . . . rather than to their physiological or psychological characteristics as individuals."[2] But, as Raymond Firth has stressed, "the more one thinks of a society in abstract terms, as of group relations or of ideal patterns, the more necessary it is to think separately of social organiza-tion in terms of concrete activity." Social organization understood in this way is "a social process, the arrangement of action in sequence in conformity with selected social ends." It may "imply a putting together of diverse elements into common relation" according either to "existing structural principles" or to newly adopted procedures; but it also leaves room for the possibility of conscious change in society as choices, backed by the power to impose them, are made about the primacy of some elements over others and the best arrangement of the parts. If social structure expresses "the element of continuity in social life," setting limitations on the making of decisions, social organization exploits the resulting potential for variations and alterations in social behavior. Hence social organization, understood as "the systematic ordering of social relations by acts of choice and decision," necessarily enters the realm of politics. It depends on formal or informal mechanisms "to take decisions on behalf of the totality." It also enables the challenging of those decisions according to conflicting principles and varied interests. In this way it raises issues regarding the exercise of authority and the distribution of power.[3]

One of the principal means of converting social structure into social organization involves the self-conscious creation of what sociologists and political scientists sometimes call "formal organizations." These differ from the patterned social arrangements of which we have just been speaking: they are distinct institutions deliberately established for expressing the interests and goals of specific groups within the social order.[4] Nevertheless, by providing ways of shaping the social world in which their members find themselves, they can play a major role in social organization more broadly construed. The very establishment of a formal organization tends to fix the boundaries of social relations, putting up barriers where previously there were only signposts, and thereby hardening the lines of social and political conflict. Under these conditions formal organizations cease to be responses to existing social arrangements—ways of coping within an existing order—and become features of social organization itself—ways of remaking that order on a new model.

The evolution of a distinct fellowship of merchants in Bristol during the years following 1453 represents just such a reorganization of society. Rather than being a mere reflexive adaptation to a profound change, the emergence of this separate commercial group was very much the product of the conscious exercise of authority and the willful extension of power that together recast the economic and social environment in which Bristolians found themselves in the sixteenth and early seventeenth centuries. Changes in structure promote changes in organization; changes in organization encourage changes in structure. The turning point came in 1552, when the successful establishment of a separate Society of Merchant Venturers transformed what had previously been no more than a convenient set of commercial connections among the leading members of Bristol's commercial elite into a formal organization for the protection of their interests and advancement of their power. The troubling economic conditions of the later fifteenth and the early sixteenth century did not by themselves dictate this solution. They merely presented a dilemma. Domination of the trading community by a narrow, self-designated group of privileged traders was not the only method available for coping with that dilemma. Since customary commercial practices and the ethos of medieval urban life also emphasized the mutual support owed fellow townsmen in times of economic distress,[5] Bristol's traditions could have led to the sharing of its ancient commercial franchises by the commonalty of freemen rather than the emergence of the leading merchants in a separate gild. We need to understand how and why the second choice came to prevail.

The Master, Wardens, and Commonalty of Merchant Venturers of the City of Bristol—which is the official corporate name of the Society— was the focus of much of the city's political, social, and economic life during the later sixteenth and early seventeenth centuries. As a commercial gild, it stood at the heart of the city's mercantile community, regulating trade and defending the interests of Bristol's merchants at home and abroad. Of equal importance was its social role, for in helping to organize the activities of the city's leading overseas traders it gave coherence to this group as a local elite. In consequence, the Merchant Venturers formed a distinct element within the city's social order, one whose influence was discernible in almost every facet of urban life. This is especially true of politics. Whether in conflict with other groups or divided among themselves, the Society's membership is usually found in the thick of controversy over the uses of power and the direction of policy within the city. Most of these disputes and conflicts were initiated by the Merchant Venturers in advancing their own vision of the urban social order.

But the Society did not spring full-grown into Bristol's history in 1552. During the century preceding the Society's first royal charter, Bristol's merchants participated in a series of experiments in commercial organization designed to help them cope with the new conditions under which they traded after the loss of Bordeaux. The earliest attempt to establish an organization of overseas merchants dates from the period immediately following England's ouster from Gascony. This organization had very limited purposes. In 1467, when commerce with France was still deep in the doldrums, a city ordinance created a society of merchants to assure that the city's diminished trade would benefit its freemen, not outsiders. The legislation covered iron, olive oil, wax, and "meteoyle," probably tallow, the first three of which were major Iberian imports. To control the sale of these wares, the ordinance instructed the Common Council to elect from its own membership each year a master, two wardens, and two beadles to serve a newly created merchant fellowship. This group was granted the use of a chapel and a room in Spicer's Hall, to which all the merchants of the city periodically were to be summoned to set the prices at which the four commodities might be sold to strangers. Although there was no specific provision for this "fellowship" to make regulations for its own governance, in drawing a distinction between its members and the rest of the city's "merchants" the ordinance appears to have created a separate society of "adventurers," defined as those who traded in bulk beyond the seas. The larger body of merchants in this period would have been primarily retail shopkeepers, not large-scale or wholesale traders.[6]

No evidence has survived of the activities of the body brought into being by this ordinance. It may well have dissolved within a decade of its foundation, when economic conditions improved sufficiently to relieve pressure on the sale of the four commodities.[7] But following Bristol's receipt of a new royal charter in 1499, a second attempt was made by the city Corporation to organize a company of merchants. Very probably this effort was the work of the newly created bench of aldermen, which was made up of the wealthiest citizens. In 1499 it was granted extraordinary powers to shape governmental policy and to lead the Common Council. The new company, like the society of 1467, was also organized to attend to the Iberian trades.[8] Its stated purpose was to solve an ancient urban problem, the "colourable and crafty dealyng" by certain burgesses who habitually "colored" the goods of strangers; that is to say, bought and sold them as their own, contrary to the burgess oath, to the profit of the outsiders.[9] To cope with this old problem, the Corporation established a merchant fellowship, separate and distinct from every other organized group of tradesmen and craftsmen in the city. Only "merchant adventurers," as the ordinance called them, were permitted to join. The main aim seems to have been the exclusion of all clothiers—men trained in the crafts—from participation in overseas trade. Members of the newly founded company were forbidden to act as agents for nonmembers, whether stranger or citizen, either in shipping goods from Bristol or in receiving them abroad for return to Bristol. If any nonmember freighted a vessel for a voyage to or from the port, no member was to join with him or lade his goods aboard the same vessel.[10]

By implication, these and similar regulations defined the membership of the new company. They insured that members would give over trading as agents for nonmembers—neighbors or foreigners—and that those unable to sustain their businesses without this source of income would cease trading abroad altogether. A rough line was drawn, therefore, between overseas merchants and other tradesmen. Artisans were forbidden membership outright, but there was no prohibition of retailing on the part of the membership, and many merchants undoubtedly continued to sell small quantities of their stock for immediate consumption. Nevertheless, the distinction between the major "merchant adventurers," who depended primarily on foreign commerce, and lesser figures, who only occasionally ventured abroad for foreign wares, had emerged more clearly than in 1467.[11]

Limiting the competition facing the merchant adventurers was only one intended effect of the new fellowship. Equally important was the way it sought to enhance their social cohesion. For example, all members were expected to trade to and from foreign parts together, under company rule, rather than individually. No merchant of Bristol was to lade any ship, either at home or abroad, with any goods without the advice, assent, and license of the master and wardens or the approval of the majority of the membership. Company members were to share the same vessels for all their overseas traffic.[12] Moreover, the fellowship itself was to settle all controversies among its members. Twice every week, if necessary, the master and wardens were to call together the entire membership to discuss not only their "feats of marchaundises," but also

> to here complayntes and sett direccions accordyng to reason and good conscience bitweene partees of the same company beyng atte variaunce or debate, or to send the said parties with their causes as they have founde theym certifyed unto the maire of Bristowe . . . further to be ordred or directed as the case rightfully shall requyre.[13]

To further prevent members from going to law against each other, every merchant adventurer was forbidden to "vex trouble or sue" any of his brethren in any court before first bringing "the matier hangyng in variaunce" to the master and wardens. By relying on the common interests of each disputant in maintaining his reputation and goodwill with his fellow merchants, and by using the services of friends and partners to resolve disagreements quickly, the ordinance sought to preserve the internal harmony among the membership that it presupposed.[14]

Had this company of merchants accomplished all it set out to do, it would have given Bristol's overseas traders a cohesive communal structure and a privileged organization on which to build their personal and business relationships. Unfortunately, no records of its activities have survived and nothing is known about how it met the economic crises that struck Bristol soon after its creation. It may well have continued to operate in some form throughout the first half of the sixteenth century. The mariners' chapel, dedicated to St. Clement of Alexandria and built in 1493, with which the fellowship of 1500 was associated, survived intact until the dissolution of the chantries in 1549. The chapel's property eventually became the site of the Merchant Venturers' almshouse, established to perform the charitable functions associated with the original foundation. The ordinances of 1500 also passed into the hands of the Merchant Venturers as its earliest surviving documentary record. But by 1508 the city government's powers to make ordinances regarding "the colouring of strangers goods" were already under challenge, and it may be that the merchant fellowship ceased to enforce its wideranging regulations on this subject soon thereafter. There is certainly no reference to it in the Common Council acts of 1520 and 1527 regarding "strangers goods."[15] Perhaps the maintenance of the chapel provided sufficient institutional basis to keep the fellowship together.

In addition to experimenting with local companies during the century preceding 1552, Bristol's merchants participated in the commercial organizations established during Henry VIII's reign by English traders in Spain: the Brotherhood of St. George, founded at San Lucar de Barrameda in 1517 by letters patent from the duke of Medina Sidonia, and the Andalusia Company, founded by Henry VIII's letters patent in 1530.[16] However, neither body possessed a constitution well suited to the needs and interests of the Bristol merchants. The privileges of the Brotherhood of St. George, for example, amounted to little more than the right to build a church at San Lucar and to elect a consul with authority to hear and decide civil and criminal cases, especially those arising from debts between Englishman and Englishman or Englishman and Spaniard.[17] Even the much more elaborately organized Andalusia Company was not ideally suited to the Bristolians, since its jurisdiction remained confined to traders in southern Spain, with no permanent organization in England itself, and its leadership was dominated by Londoners, whose interests were not always the same as those of provincial merchants. Perhaps not surprisingly, the Company ceased effective existence by the end of Henry VIII's reign. All that was left of a once quite important organization was the consul of the English nation, who could hardly be effective without a united community behind him.[18]

Bristol's experiments with various forms of company organization during the century preceding 1552 demonstrate the desire of many of its overseas merchants for some kind of common institution within which to conduct their individual commercial activities. What they sought was not a joint-stock company that would carry on business as a single firm, but a corporate status through which commerce might be regulated, competition limited, and exclusive trading rights enjoyed. The benefits from such an organization would have been large under any economic conditions, but they were a particular boon in times of economic distress, since membership in a company would assist merchants in securing credit and pooling resources under tight financial conditions, in establishing common policies to address mutual problems, and in seeking royal privileges and governmental protection to cope with crises. Finally, by limiting participation in foreign commerce, a company could insure its members a larger share of the reduced profits. Hence the incentives for creating a formal organization of merchants multiplied when trade was in decline, as was the case in the years immediately preceding Edward VI's grant of letters patent in 1552.

We already know that the first half of the sixteenth century was one of the worst periods in Bristol's commercial history, with trade receding on nearly every front. In the early 1550s, this general malaise combined with two more immediate crises that deepened the city's economic troubles. The first and more significant of these crises concerned the state of the Spanish market, already crucial to Bristol's prosperity. Just at the beginning of the 1550s Spain entered a period of serious economic difficulty, as commerce to and from her American colonies fell victim in 1549 or 1550 to what Pierre Chaunu has called a "*grande récession intercyclique*" that began with a rapid decline and lasted for the remainder of the decade. As Chaunu describes it, this recession resulted from

the extraordinary conditions under which trans-Atlantic commerce
proceeded in the sixteenth century, conditions affected by the vast distances that had to be covered and the consequent high costs of transportation.[19]

In the early period of Spanish colonial enterprise, times of expansion
such as occurred in the years preceding 1550 generally encouraged the
export of such high-priced wares as English cloth, since these made the
most efficient and profitable use of the available shipping. As a result,
during expansions stocks of relatively cheap and bulky goods built up
in Spain, while shipping accumulated in American waters waiting for
lucrative cargoes to bring home. Eventually, however, serious scarcities
of shipping developed in the Iberian ports, and Spanish merchants, already anxious to recover at least some of their investment from abroad,
brought home their vessels, often with inadequate cargoes, to cope with
the growing inventories of less profitable wares in their storehouses.
This flood of returning ships then caused the prices of American commodities to collapse, with a consequent loss of profits, setting off a recession, first among Spain's own merchants and later among foreigners
like the Bristolians, whose prosperity depended on the buoyancy of the
Iberian markets. The recession in Spain during the 1550s was exactly
of this type. With increased shipping available in Spain in 1549, freight
charges dropped, and it became profitable to reduce the heavy inventories of cheaper and bulkier goods that had been growing in Andalusia
during the expansion of the 1540s. Demand declined for the wares that
the English and other non-Spaniards usually sold in Spain. In addition,
foreign shipping, which had been attracted to Spain by inflated freight
charges, was no longer required in the same quantities as before. Hence
foreigners engaged in colonial commerce—such as the Bristolians based
in Seville, San Lucar, and Cádiz, who operated in the American market
by license—felt the effects of the recession before most other merchants
and tradesmen.[20]

Within a short time the recession touched nearly everyone trading in
Spain, whether or not they were directly dependent on colonial commerce. By the mid-sixteenth century, the American trade had become
systematically integrated into the Spanish, and particularly the Andalusian, economy, causing Spanish prices to fluctuate with changes in this
traffic. As the flood of ships returning in the early 1550s created an incentive to export, old stocks were cleared out. By 1552 the prices of domestic Spanish commodities began a steep rise. In Spain at large, prices

increased by nearly 3 percent between 1551 and 1552, while in the Guadalquivir valley, where the Bristolians did the majority of their business, the rise was more on the order of 12 percent.[21] The prices Bristolians paid increased especially for certain key trading items that they regularly bought in Spain. Between 1551 and 1552, olive oil rose by 8.5 percent, sugar by 10.5 percent, and pepper by more than 22 percent, while wine, which had been relatively cheap throughout the 1540s, jumped by almost 43 percent, to a new plateau at which it would remain throughout the 1550s.[22] These facts meant that in 1552 Bristolians and other foreigners frequenting Spanish ports were faced with inflated prices both on the goods they imported from Spain and on the victuals and other goods they needed to fit out their ships in Spanish harbors. Although it is possible that their own goods also rose in price during this year, we have already learned that they earned very small profits, if any, from sales of these exports. Moreover, the general condition of the Spanish economy suggests that any increase in the price of English wares in Spain would have compensated only partially for their extra outlays.[23]

All in all, the merchants of Bristol were confronted by extremely worrisome circumstances in Spain. By 1552 the more experienced among them would have known that they were in the midst of an extremely unstable and dangerous season. They were bound to have felt anxiety about their long-term prospects and the correct commercial strategy to follow. These fears would only have been compounded by the troubles into which the English economy itself descended in the early 1550s as a result of the chaotic state of monetary policy. From 1542 to 1551, English coinage had undergone a series of debasements that doubled or more than doubled the amount of currency in circulation. This policy undoubtedly contributed in some degree to the inflation and falling exchange rates that England experienced in the 1540s and early 1550s, though recent scholarship has shown that the correlations among the value of English coin, domestic prices, and foreign exchange rates are very rough. This same debasement of the currency also seems to have promoted the expansion of English cloth exports in this period, but in a significant way only during 1549–1551. The sharp rise in cloth exports from Bristol in this two-year period supports this conclusion. In April 1551, however, Edward VI's council began a policy of "calling down" or deflating the currency. This course was followed very haphazardly for almost a year until, in March 1552, the metal content of the coinage was once again restored to its pre-debasement level. The effect of this new policy was to reduce by half the existing circulating medium, thereby severely tightening credit.[24]

The initial effect of the announced calling-down of the currency in April 1551 was just the reverse of what was intended, which was to cool the overheated economy and consequently lower domestic prices. But prices rose rather than fell. The currency exchanges appeared in disarray and were at most only intermittently in operation. The main cause was that the government proceeded with the revaluation using a series of half-measures, which themselves were undermined by confusions and missteps. For example, it announced in April 1551 that in four months English currency would be worth 25 percent less than at present, but in the interval it issued the most debased currency of the period. The English appropriately began to hoard goods, to settle their outstanding debts in the newly debased coin, and to buy whatever was available on the open market. At the same time, foreigners ceased or nearly ceased all exchange transactions until the dust settled. Matters were only made worse when announcement of a further 25 percent revaluation was made in August and new coins were issued twice before the following March. Since no one could be certain what course events would take, the adverse effects of this initial calling-down of the currency in the spring and summer of 1551 lingered well into 1552.[25]

As might be expected, English cloth exports dropped dramatically in 1552. But the depression was probably felt more severely in London, where trade was already tied more closely to the exchange markets, than in the outports, where local merchants might have been able to profit from London's difficulties.[26] In Bristol, however, disarray in the Spanish economy almost certainly wiped away any such short-term advantage.[27] Whatever the immediate effect of the recoinage on Bristol's trade, its merchants must have become extremely wary of conditions, unwilling perhaps to forego the profits that might be won during this unsettled period, yet fearful of committing their wealth to new business while prices, currency values, and exchange rates fluctuated so wildly. Their instincts would have warned them to be cautious and draw in their investments, but they must also have found it necessary to continue to trade at or near their usual levels just to stay even with inflation. In such times, the hope of security often supplants the desire for profits as the primary economic goal.

The crisis of the Hispano-American trade and the great debasement and recoinage set the background for the Bristol merchants' petition to the Crown for a chartered company. Events in another quarter gave added urgency to the situation and made such an effort all the more essential. The dissolution of the chantries had destroyed St. Clement's Chapel, the last vestige of their common efforts. In December 1550, moreover, the building and its lands had been ceded to Sir Ralph Sadler and Laurence Winnington, who quickly made a bargain with the city government for its use, thereby eliminating the direct control over the property previously exercised by the merchants.[28] Whatever remnants of commercial organization had survived in Bristol into the mid-sixteenth century were no more. For those merchants who looked to an institutionalized fellowship among themselves to limit competition and provide mutual aid and protection, a new company was now required.

The belief in the need to keep the craft of merchants separate from all others emerged, or reemerged, as a theme of Bristol's life in the mid-1540s. Roger Edgeworth, the conservative city preacher, speaking at the end of Henry VIII's reign, expanded on the principle that each man should remain within the vocation to which he had been called, exhorting his congregation

> to medle not to muche with other mens occupations that you cannot skyll on, leaste whyle ye be so curious in other mens matters not perteininge to your lerning you decaye as well in your owne occupation, as in the other, so fallinge to penurye, extreme pouertye, and very beggery. For when a tayler forsakyng his owne occupation wyll be a marchant venterer, or a shomaker to become a groser, God sende him well to proue.[29]

The moral principle was hardly new—Plato had articulated it in his *Republic*—but the definition of what constituted a proper occupation is of some significance. Edgeworth is concerned with protecting crafts or arts with trading functions—merchants and grocers—from encroachment by those engaged in manufacturing. As we already know, "marchant venterer" was no ancient craft in the 1540s.[30]

But it was only in 1552 that this spirit was transformed into a plan to acquire a royal charter for the creation of a new company of merchants in Bristol. The principal movers were Edward Pryn, Thomas Hickes, and Robert Butler, all prominent Iberian merchants who called themselves "marchant Venterers" and who described their businesses "as putting themselves their factors servants goods and marchandice in perill uppon the Sea."[31] To justify their request for letters patent, these men submitted a "lamentable petition" which, as is common with such

documents, complained bitterly of a severe decay of trade. Bristol's
principal problem, according to the petitioners, was

> that divers Artificers and men of manuell arte inhabitinge the saide Citty
> haveinge alsoe occupacions to get theire liveinge (whoe were never appren-
> tice or brought upp to or in the recourse or trade of the arte of marchants . . .
> nor haveinge anie good knowledge in the same Arte) Doe commonly exercise
> use and occupie the saide recourse or trade of marchandize to and from the
> partes beyond the seas.[32]

As in 1500, the merchants desired to remove artificers from overseas
trade and thereby convert the art of merchandise into a separate craft,
although this time the complaints focused on the tradesmen's lack of
training and the consequent harm to the commonweal it caused, instead
of their illicit dealings on behalf of strangers. Ignorant and untrained
handicraftsmen who engaged in overseas trade, it was asserted, ordinarily relied for their business on foreign shipping, on board which English goods were secretly conveyed away to the defrauding of the royal
Customs and the detriment "of the Navye and marriners and the porte
of the saide Citty . . . and chiefly of the said marchants."[33]

Most of Edward VI's charter is devoted to incorporating the Society
of Merchant Venturers as a legal entity. Unlike the merchant fellowship
of 1500, this company was not merely authorized to elect its own officers and make its own ordinances, as any officially sanctioned city gild
might do, but to have a common seal and to be "capeable and fitt in ye
lawe" to act as a corporation in administering property and conducting
its collective business in "perpetual succession."[34] Nevertheless, it was
not entirely independent of the city government, since each year its master and wardens were required to take a corporal oath before the mayor
and aldermen, just as the officers of other, lesser gilds did. In addition,
the jurisdiction of its ordinances was limited only to its own membership and to the "Misterie or Arte" of the merchant adventurers. As we
shall see, this limitation created a loophole through which passed much
of the city's politics for the next century or more.[35]

Since the newly formed Society's power to regulate trade was restricted, what gave it its life were the rights and rules governing
membership. "[N]oe Artificer of the Citty," the charter said,

> shall exercise the recourse of marchandize into the kingdome or dominions
> of the parties beyond the seas unlesse he shalbee admitted into the said So-
> cietie and State [of Merchant Venturer] by the . . . Maister and wardens, Nei-
> ther that any other but onelie those who have bine, or hereafter shalbee ap-

prentice to ye saide Misterie or Arte of Marchaunts . . . or have used the
same Misterie by the space of seauen yeeres.[36]

On its face, this amounted to a grant of monopoly in overseas trade to
the Society's membership, although it was not clear whether they could
enforce it with their own ordinances. Moreover, it is not entirely certain
who exactly were to be the beneficiaries of the grant, since the patent
provides no list of members and does not define what was meant by
merchant venturer. The exclusion of artificers barred those trained as
craftsmen unless they had been expressly admitted to the Society. Were
the members also to be "mere merchants," as contemporary usage had
it, who would devote their businesses entirely to wholesale dealings, es-
chewing even occasional retail transactions? We do not know. In the absence of company ordinances, all we can say for certain is that merchant
venturers devoted themselves primarily to "adventuring" or risk-taking
in overseas trade.[37]

Nevertheless, the question of membership stirred great controversy
from the moment the Society was born. If only those who had been admitted to its fellowship indeed could legally trade beyond the seas, it
was perhaps inevitable that those excluded would cry out against the
loss. Fortunately, one document suggests some of the contested points.
Among the papers kept with John Smythe's ledger for 1538–1550 is a
list of "such as be marchauntes and hath the sporonge of marchauntes,"
which we have already examined for other purposes.[38] "Sporonge" here
means "purse" or "credit." These individuals, the author urges, were
"not to be denied to be of the mystery." This document apparently was
written either just before or just after the founding of the Society, probably in opposition to the denial of admission to some of those mentioned. It is perhaps related to the "matter at variaunce" in February
1552 between Smythe and Thomas Chester, mayor of Bristol when the
Society was founded, who was one of the most ardent harrowers of retailers later in his life.[39] As we know, the list gives the names of one hundred and twenty-seven individuals, considerably more than appear in
most later lists of Merchant Venturers. Twenty of them were grocers,
drapers, mercers, vintners, and haberdashers (Table 11). These occupations typically were retail trades dealing in relatively high-priced goods.
Over time, of course, the more successful of these men may have given
over their retailing to specialize in wholesale trade. In effect, they would
have become "mere merchants," who rarely if ever had to indulge in retail sales to reduce unwanted inventory or turn a quick profit. Hence
their presence in the list, as summarized in Table 11, need not be a sign

TABLE 11   JOHN SMYTHE'S LIST OF "SUCH AS BE
MARCHAUNTES AND HATH THE SPORONGE
OF MARCHAUNTES I THINCK NOT TO BE DENYED
TO BE OF THE MYSTERY," CIRCA 1550

Occupation	No.	% of Known Men
Merchants	52	59.09
Other large-scale dealers[a]		
Grocer	7	7.96
Draper	7	7.96
Mercer	3	3.41
Haberdasher	1	1.14
Vintner	2	2.27
Total	20	22.73[b]
Miscellaneous		
Scrivener	1	1.14
Bookbinder	1	1.14
Baker	3	3.41
Brewer	1	1.14
Ropemaker	1	1.14
Tailor	2	2.27
Tucker (clothier)	1	1.14
Pewterer	2	2.27
Skinner	2	2.27
Saddler	1	1.14
Soapmaker	1	1.14
Total	16	18.18[b]
Total known	88	100.00
Total unknown	39	—
Total	127	—

SOURCE: Jean Vanes, ed., *The Ledger of John Smythe, 1538–1550* (Bristol Record Society 28, 1974), pp. 315–17.
[a] I have assigned two questionable cases so as to minimize, rather than exaggerate, the number of retailers.
[b] Discrepancies due to rounding errors.

that the Society remained open to Bristolians who still operated primarily as shopkeepers. But the same cannot be said of the bakers, skinners, tailors, pewterers, and others who appear in Table 11 in the miscellaneous category. Nearly all of these sixteen men were known to have been practicing their craft during the middle years of Henry VIII's reign and none appears to have become sufficiently wealthy in his subsequent career to have entirely abandoned this craft work.[40] These men, along with a few of the retailers, probably were marginal overseas traders who only occasionally ventured their capital or their goods in foreign markets.

We can get some measure of the significance of this matter by taking the tailors as an example. As an occupational group, they were primarily craftsmen, who worked to order and who were usually supplied the necessary fabric by their customers. But many were also retail shopkeepers who kept their own supplies of cloth and reserved to themselves the right to sell it by wholesale when they were overstocked.[41] The more adventuresome probably also kept supplies of linen, silk, velvet, lace, and ribbons, which were usually foreign wares. There was a temptation, then, for tailors to seek their own sources for these accessories to their craft, and it seems likely that the two tailors who appear in the list did so on a sufficiently regular basis to warrant their inclusion. Similar stories can be told for almost all the other handicrafts represented in the list. Hence even if all the merchants, grocers, drapers, mercers, haberdashers, and vintners in Table 11 dealt exclusively by wholesale—an unlikely prospect—the author of the list apparently contemplated the inclusion of some craftsmen in the membership of the new Society. This viewpoint apparently won the day in 1552. According to Bristol's tuckers, Edward VI's charter did not exclude all shopkeepers and artisans from participation. It failed, they said, "to make the marchants and [sic] Crafte."[42]

Although the subsequent history of the Bristol Merchant Venturers was by no means smooth, the royal letters patent of 1552 created a local organization that has survived as a corporate body to the present day. As it appeared in the early seventeenth century, it had a relatively large establishment of officers, including a master, two wardens, a treasurer, a clerk, and a beadle, as well as a board of twelve assistants. In addition, there was the Hall, made up of all the members, which met periodically through the year to elect the principal officials of the Society, approve or amend the Society's bylaws, and carry out a number of other important duties.[43] Separately and together these elements performed a multiplicity of functions that were vital both to the commercial life of the city and to the welfare of the members themselves.

One major area of corporate activity was the maintenance of shipping. By the early seventeenth century, for example, many of the responsibilities for maintenance of Bristol's port facilities previously borne by the city government had fallen to the Society, whose officers collected keyage, craneage, plankage, and wharfage to pay for them. As a result, the Hall regularly took account of the competency of pilots and port officials, the care of harbor facilities, and related matters.[44] In addition, the protection of ships on the high seas was an important issue, especially in wartime or when pirates were marauding in the Bristol Channel or in nearby English waters. Consequently, the Hall gave considerable attention to this subject, often in response to the Crown's demands for money to mount naval expeditions.[45] The Society's charitable activities—which by the early seventeenth century included not only the maintenance of an almshouse for aged seamen but also a schoolmaster for poor mariners' children—were also a significant area of collective concern.[46]

Although these areas, with their demands for collective decisions and permanent commitments, helped to build a spirit of community among the Merchant Venturers, they were not the center of the Society's corporate life. Bristol's great overseas merchants depended to a considerable degree on national economic policy for their privileges and wealth. They were of necessity engaged in the affairs of the kingdom at large, and one of the main functions of their Society was to serve as their political agent with the state. As Patrick McGrath has put it, the Society was in some measure an economic "pressure group" for its members.[47] Sometimes the favors requested were very limited in scope, as when an official license had to be secured from the Lord Treasurer to land goods in the port from a stranger's ship.[48] Sometimes they were large, as when new powers were begged from the Crown in the form of letters patent.[49] But often there was an air of crisis in dealings with royal officials, as when there was trouble with the royal purveyors, or when new impositions were set upon imported goods, or when disagreements arose with the Customs officers. Urgent meetings were called and streams of letters sent to the king pleading for redress of the wrong, sometimes carried by delegations of merchants ready to appeal personally to their connections in Westminster. To the Merchant Venturers the state was a source of bounty, a reservoir of favors and privileges to be tapped if they could. But in its demands for money and control, it was also a threat to commercial enterprise, something to be kept at a distance if at all possible. On the whole, the Society's lobbying of the Crown was successful. If it did not always achieve its members' more ambitious goals, it usually managed to alleviate the difficulties they had with royal officials.[50]

This capacity to intercede with the Crown in the interests of its membership also brought benefits to the economic lives of the Merchant Venturers. Strictly speaking, the Society was a regulated company under whose ordinances individual traders conducted their business on a private basis. Although the principle of individual enterprise generally prevailed, if a royal license was required to export a particular commodity only the action of the Society as a whole made it possible. There was joint stock, for example, to ship eighteen hundred barrels of butter a year under a license held by George Henley of London. For this purpose the entire membership of the Society acted as Henley's partner.[51] A similar arrangement for exporting calfskins was made in 1615 between the Crown and Francis Knight, John Whitson, Mathew Haviland, Robert Aldworth, and Abell Kitchen, merchants acting in effect as feoffees for their fellow Merchant Venturers, with William Lewis, Collector of Customs at Bristol, serving as the Crown's agent for the grant. When Knight died two years later, a new agreement was reached between Lewis and twenty-eight Merchant Venturers acting on behalf of themselves and their fellows.[52] In both cases, the licenses were acquired by a joint-stock venture managed by the Society, then divided among the participants, who shipped the licensed commodity abroad for their own account.

By far the most important public business transacted by the Society concerned the protection of trade against official or semi-official intrusion. The case of the New England fishery, which by the early seventeenth century had come to play an important part in Bristol's trading economy, provides a useful illustration of how problems arose and how the Society fended them off. In 1621, Sir Ferdinando Gorges, acting in his role as President of the Council for New England, approached all the western ports with a scheme for the plantation of New England and for government of fishing ventures on its shores. The plan involved the creation of six "staple" towns, each with its own treasurer and group of commissioners, through which all Englishmen desiring to participate in New England enterprise must "putt in his aduenture into the Common stock of one of these Citties . . . Corporate togeather with the rest to bee managed by the Treasourer & Commissioners for the publique good of the Adventurers." This proposed arrangement was heartily supported by the Privy Council, which not only threatened summary punishment of all those who might violate Gorges's letters patent but also severely chastised the city governments of Bristol, Exeter, and Plymouth when they refused to submit to the newly formed Council for New England.[53]

The Bristol Merchant Venturers, however, were extremely reluctant to enter into such a complex and risky undertaking and used every available tactic of delay to avoid doing so, including sending responses to Gorges's letters to a place they knew he would not be. They found his articles of plantation "so difficult," they said, "that . . . they cannot

Conclude" to join in his enterprise without a conference with him, followed by further deliberations among themselves. In the interim, they hoped that "if . . . any particular men of their Company shall set forth any shipping on a fishing voyadg for that Country," Gorges would accept "an indifferent rate" from them for the privilege. At the conference, held in October, Gorges informed the merchants that even though his patent did not give him the power to restrain fishing, it did permit him to forbid the use of the shore to salt and dry fish, which is what he proposed to do. Since commercial fishing would then have become fruitless, the Merchant Venturers asked Gorges what he would require from those who wished to send ships just for the purpose of fishing. Gorges's initial demand was for 10 percent of each venture, valued in shipping as well as the profits of the catch itself, but after much debate he agreed to allow them fishing rights provided they each carried over one man and £10 of provisions for every thirty tons of shipping they used, with the merchants bearing the costs of the provisions.[54]

Some of the Merchant Venturers found this an acceptable arrangement, but many hoped to avoid agreeing to it. Since Parliament was in session, they wrote to the city's members, both Merchant Venturers themselves, requesting that these men acquire a copy of Gorges's patent to see if he did indeed have the power to restrain Bristol's fishing and also to seek protection in Parliament or elsewhere for "the quiet engaging of fishing."[55] Here Bristol was especially fortunate, since it possessed at least one good friend on the Council for New England, the earl of Arundel, who earlier that year—soon after he had joined the Council—had been allowed to name the city's new town clerk.[56] Through Arundel's efforts and the concerted attack on Gorges's patent mounted by the West Country fishermen in the Commons, a further concession was wrenched from the Council. Gorges finally wrote that "it is not . . . intended to debar any Regular or honest [traders] from a free recourse" to New England, so long as they conformed themselves to the reasonable conditions and just and lawful orders made by his Council for the advantage of the plantation. He agreed, therefore, to permit the treasurer at Exeter to grant Bristolians licenses if they wished to frequent New England, even for purposes other than fishing.[57]

What troubled the Merchant Venturers was the loss of independence that Gorges's plan entailed. As reported by the two Bristol members of Parliament in London, the city's merchants and shipowners liked neither the idea of forming a joint stock with the merchants of other western ports nor the prospect of being governed by the President and

Council for New England. This same concern surfaced whenever the Bristolians were threatened with a loss of local autonomy in their trade, as they were at various times during the early seventeenth century in regard to the Spanish Company, the French Company, and the Levant Company.[58] To prevent this from happening they were able to use a variety of political resources at their disposal—their prominence in the city government, their service in Parliament, and their connections in London—all made the more effective by their ability to present a united front to the authorities. Had Gorges been able to win over even a minority of the Merchant Venturers to his demands, he no doubt would have been able, with the Privy Council's assistance, to exact his due from the rest. But the concerted resistance of the Society, acting for the Merchant Venturers as a whole, made it impossible to adopt such a strategy of divide and conquer.

The initial impulse behind the foundation of the Merchant Venturers was to give the city's new community of overseas merchants the capacity to defend its common interests in an era of severe economic constraint. What from the perspective of economic history was little more than an effect of large and impersonal social processes soon became a social force on its own. The merchants who brought the Merchant Venturers into being transformed their relations with one another from a mere feature of the economic environment into an active shaper of their world. Like the beaver whose dam-building creates a habitat to suit its form of life, they remade their social landscape. We can perhaps best see the effects of these changes by looking closely at what happened to the patterns of social mobility in Bristol in the years following the Society's foundation.

The phrase "social mobility" can refer to two very different social processes. In communities that highly value an individual's or a family's command over goods and services, change in real wealth is the primary criterion. Here a person—before recent times usually it would be a man—might improve his position in society simply by increasing his income or the number or worth of his possessions while remaining in his particular social niche or occupation all his life. As he goes from being a poor or middling farmer, shoemaker, or lawyer to a rich one, he ascends the social ladder. In other kinds of community, however, social recognition and deference are granted principally according to social rank, defined as the place held in a fixed hierarchy of social stations assigned by birth or career. To move upward in this form of society it is

necessary to marry well, thereby improving family bloodlines and connections, or to rise in rank by changing career or acquiring honored office. But even the most status-conscious societies maintain a close link
between wealth and social position, since an individual's social standing
helps determine his access to wealth, and fulfillment of his social obligations requires material resources. If wealth is wisely used, moreover, it
offers increased opportunity for improved status, if not for the individual, then for his posterity.

Sixteenth- and early seventeenth-century Bristol was a hierarchical
society in which legal and quasi-legal distinctions such as those between
freemen and non-freemen, ruler and ruled, were of crucial significance.
But, because it was a commercial city, its inhabitants were also deeply
concerned with the acquisition of wealth. Indeed, the achievement of social rank was founded as much on the accumulation of money and possessions as on birth: as successful individuals or families increased their
wealth, they were often able to move upward in rank. Unfortunately, direct study of patterns of social mobility based solely on accumulated
capital or liquid assets is impossible. We can, however, use an individual's occupation as a useful guide to his place in the social order. Not
only did a man's occupation define his economic role, it helped shape
his social connections and his chances to achieve both riches and recognition. Hence, occupational mobility can serve as a general, if limited,
indicator of social mobility more broadly construed. Admittedly, we
shall be using a rather crude instrument to accomplish this goal. Occupation alone can tell us very little of any particular individual's life history. Knowing whether an early modern Bristolian identified himself as
a grocer or weaver, merchant or wiredrawer, cannot help us to predict
his actual achievements accurately. But such information in the aggregate gives some insight into the relative chances the members of particular groups had to acquire wealth, status, and power and how these
chances may have changed over time. Provided we want no more than
a general estimate of the overall pattern of mobility and a general sense
of the direction of change, this technique seems worth pursuing, even
though the aggregation of our data, with its tendency to lump dissimilar
cases into common categories, necessarily exaggerates some features
of the story while flattening others. Allowing for these shortcomings
in our method, what can we determine about the relative openness of
Bristol's social structure before and after the foundation of the Merchant Venturers?

The study of occupational mobility in the sixteenth and early seven-teenth centuries necessarily begins with the institution of apprentice-ship. In conjunction with training a young man in the skills of his cho-sen trade or craft, it established him within the network of business relations in the trading community. For merchants, this process took place in the actual course of trade, as the young apprentice, after receiv-ing the rudiments of training in his master's household, was allowed considerable opportunity to make his own judgments and decisions in the marketplace. In nearly every other trade, however, apprenticeship also involved both a social and an economic aspect. Under the protec-tion and discipline of a master, young men were not merely trained in the techniques of a craft but were sent on errands to buy raw materials, to settle debts, and to bring finished goods to customers, or, alterna-tively, were left to look after the shop for short periods while their mas-ters saw to these tasks. If they were to fulfill their purpose as servants, it could not be otherwise. Just how a particular individual was used de-pended on his years of service, his trustworthiness, and the nature of his craft. Among retailers, the apprentice's contacts were more likely to be with customers frequenting the shop than with merchant suppliers; among craftsmen, they were more likely to be with the middlemen and other manufacturers in the chain of production with whom his master ordinarily dealt. In these ways service as an apprentice helped to estab-lish the economic opportunities the young man might later have as a master in his own right and also set him in a social network that af-fected both his future livelihood and his way of life.[59]

The institution of apprenticeship was also tied to occupational mo-bility in a much more direct way. In many urban families, children stayed at home only until they were old enough to find places in the ser-vice of others. This was more than a consequence of the peculiar fact, often remarked upon by foreigners, that the English sent their children at an early age to be raised as apprentices or servants outside the family.[60] It was also the result of hard economic realities. Many fathers and mothers died young, leaving their children orphans who had to be placed with strangers if they were to survive and find livelihoods of their own. Even when one or both parents remained alive, it was often impos-sible for the family to employ all its children within the household or provide them with formal educations in the professions or set them up on the land. Since many other households simultaneously found them-selves needing extra labor to manage their affairs, a regular system developed to exchange children between families in both urban and rural communities. Although, as we shall see for Bristol, many sons simply followed in their father's footsteps when pursuing their livelihood, many others did not, either because they were unable to or because they had been placed elsewhere to better themselves. In effect, there was a market for their services, conditioned by the individual family's ability to employ its own children, the supply of and demand for servant labor in particular industries, and the economic and social connections of the people involved. Where premiums were charged for taking on the care and training of young men, as they often were in lucrative trades such as that of overseas merchant, the ability of the family to pay the going rate was a factor. Seen in the aggregate, the resulting distribution of occupations reflects in a concrete fashion the state of the labor market at any particular time and the differences between periods encapsulates the changes in that market. In so saying, however, we note only the fact of movement. We need not assume that a young man's father or guardian necessarily sought the best possible service for him, although surely many—probably most—did so, since it was in their interests and those of their kin that each member of the family be placed where he could do the others the most good.

Apprenticeship was the most formal type of "fostering" arrangement for children, if it may be so called. In most urban places apprenticeship already had a long history in local custom before the passage of the Statute of Artificers in 1563 incorporated it into national law. What makes it an especially useful institution for our present purposes is that its administration depended on the use of written instruments, called indentures, which in Bristol were carefully enrolled in the central city records kept at the Tolzey. The earliest of these records survive from 1532. These indentures typically name the father of the apprentice, giving his occupation, and the young apprentice's new master, giving his occupation as well. Using these indentures in their enrolled form, we can glimpse the overall patterns of occupational mobility in Bristol from one generation to another by comparing the occupations into which the sons of Bristolians were apprenticed with those of their fathers. In studying this material we need to look, as it were, at both the outward and the inward traffic in apprentices. To which trades were fathers in particular industries most likely to apprentice their sons? From which trades were those in particular industries most likely to have attracted their apprentices? For our purposes the more important information is the former, since it tells us in some measure about the ways the life chances of members of particular groups were affected over time. Records for two ten-year periods have been chosen for this purpose: 1532–1542 and 1626–1636.[61]

Let us take the history of the leather trades as an example, counting those engaged in leather production together with those who used the finished product to make such items as saddles, aprons, and gloves. In the period from 1532 to 1542, some two hundred and seventy-six men were apprenticed in Bristol in these industries, of whom sixty, just under a quarter, were Bristolians. From 1626 to 1636, two hundred and ninety-three men were apprenticed in the same industry, of whom ninety-five, nearly a third, were Bristolians. Given the fact that Bristol's population had grown by at least 25 percent between the two periods, however, the difference in the total number of apprentices in these industries represents a net decline in demand for apprentices of 20 percent or more. This fall was sharpest in the crafts engaged in leather production itself; between 1532 and 1542, one hundred and fifty men were apprenticed there; in the period from 1626 to 1636, the number had fallen to one hundred and three men, which, in light of the population growth, means a real fall in the demand for apprentices in this sector of the economy of something in excess of 50 percent. The slack was taken up largely by an increase of more than 100 percent in the number of shoemakers apprenticed in the city, as we might expect in response to its own population growth and its growing role as a center of regional trade in the west.[62]

Turning now to the Bristol-born apprentices in the leather trades, we find that in the 1530s and 1540s the fathers of almost 50 percent of all these apprentices were themselves involved in the manufacture of leather or of leather products, and just over 63 percent of those Bristolians in the leather crafts who apprenticed sons in this period put them out in the leather trades. In the 1620s and 1630s the rates were somewhat lower, with both figures at about 46 percent, which almost certainly reflects the diminished demand for labor in these industries rather than increased social mobility. In addition, an impressive percentage in each period were apprenticed not merely in the industry but in their father's specific occupation—shoemakers' sons to shoemakers and whitawers' sons to whitawers. These same data also yield a second significant result. In both periods the sons of leather craftsmen apprenticed outside their father's own industry were placed largely in the minor crafts or in the noncommercial sectors of the economy, not among the large-scale entrepreneurs. Between the two periods, however, the

TABLE 12 BRISTOLIANS IN THE LEATHER INDUSTRIES
(PRODUCTION AND SECONDARY USE), 1532–1542 AND 1626–1636

| | 1532–1542 | | | | 1626–1636 | | | |
| | Sons[a] | | Fathers[b] | | Sons[a] | | Fathers[b] | |
	No.	%	No.	%	No.	%	No.	%
Leading entrepreneurs								
Merchants	3	5.00	2	2.60			3	3.13
Major retailers	5	8.33	5	6.49			12	12.50
Soapmakers, chandlers					3	3.15	3	3.13
Total	8	13.33	7	9.09	3	3.15	18	18.75
Textile industries	7	11.67	8	10.40	13	13.68	5	5.21
Leather industries	38	63.33	38	49.35	44	46.32	44	45.83
Metal industries	3	5.00	1	1.30	14	14.74	5	5.21
Building trades			3	3.90	6	6.32	4	4.17
Shipping and related trading and port activities	2	3.33	12	15.58	10	10.53	8	8.33
Woodworking					3	3.15		
Food production	1	1.67	7	9.09	1	1.05	7	7.29
Professional and service trades								
Gentlemen, esquires							1	1.05
Miscellaneous	1	1.67	1	1.30	1	1.05	4	4.17
Total known	60		77		95		96	
Total unknown			12				4	
Total	60		89		95		100	

SOURCE: 1532–1542: D. Hollis, ed., *Calendar of the Bristol Apprentice Book, 1532–1565. Part 1: 1532–1542* (Bristol Record Society 14, 1949), 1626–1636: Bristol Record Office, *Apprentice Book, 1626–1640*, ff. 1ʳ–333ᵛ.

[a] I.e., the occupations of apprentices whose fathers were in the leather industries.

[b] I.e., the occupations of fathers whose sons were apprenticed in the leather industries.

proportion of leather craftsmen's sons indentured in the most lucrative trades had become smaller. In the period 1532–1542 it was just over a third; in the 1626–1636 period it was only about 5 percent. This fall is perhaps indicative of the declining position of the leather industry in Bristol, which left its members less able to support the capital requirements of overseas trade and large-scale commercial dealing, demands which themselves may have been growing in this period. It suggests an increasing gulf between the leather trades and the merchants and leading retailers of the city (Table 12).

This interpretation of the data presented in Table 12 is complicated by the comparatively large increase in the number and proportion of apprentices entering the industry who were the sons of major entrepreneurs. From 1626–1636, eighteen of the new apprentices in the leather industry came from this kind of social background. But only seven were placed with shoemakers at the lower end of the scale in the industry, and none of these came from the ranks of the merchants, grocers, mercers, drapers, or great soapmakers, but from the haberdashers and innholders, who rarely achieved the wealth or power of the other occupations in this classification. Of the remaining eleven, nine were bound to whitawers, the one leather craft in Bristol that served more than the immediate local market and that maintained a high demand for labor in the seventeenth century. The sons of the city's leading entrepreneurs thus seem to have competed heavily with the children of leather craftsmen only for the most lucrative positions in the industry, largely leaving the remaining leather trades to others.[63]

Similar patterns of occupational mobility reveal themselves in the textile trades, where the demand for labor had more or less stabilized during these years (Table 13). Between 1532 and 1542, three hundred and fifty-two men were apprenticed in Bristol in crafts engaged in the production of cloth and woolen clothing, of whom seventy-two, or a fifth, were Bristolians. Between 1626 and 1636, five hundred and sixty-two men were apprenticed in this same group of industries, of whom one hundred and seventy-three, or just under a third, were Bristolians. Taking population growth into account, the increase in the total number of new apprentices between the two periods amounts to about 20 percent, but demand for labor ran significantly ahead of the general population expansion only among cappers or feltmakers and tailors; weavers also show some increase, but this occurred primarily among those making cheaper-quality woolens.[64] From 1532 to 1542, nearly 53 percent of all Bristol-based clothiers, weavers, dyers, clothworkers,

TABLE 13   BRISTOLIANS IN THE TEXTILE INDUSTRIES
(PRODUCTION AND SECONDARY USE), 1532–1542 AND 1626–1636

	1532–1542				1626–1636			
	Sons[a]		Fathers[b]		Sons[a]		Fathers[b]	
	No.	%	No.	%	No.	%	No.	%
Leading entrepreneurs								
Merchants	4	5.56	5	5.75	3	1.75	3	1.61
Major retailers	4	5.56	3	3.45	7	4.09	10	5.38
Soapmakers, chandlers	2	2.78	2	2.30	1	0.58	4	2.15
Total	10	13.89	10	11.49	11	6.43	17	9.14
Textile industries	38	52.78	38	43.68	94	54.97	94	50.54
Leather industries	8	11.11	6	6.90	6	3.51	13	6.99
Metal industries	4	5.56	8	9.20	19	11.11	7	3.76
Building trades			6	6.90	8	4.68	9	4.84
Shipping and related trading and port activities	4	5.56	7	8.05	18	10.53	13	6.99
Woodworking					1	0.58	1	0.54
Food production	3	4.17	6	6.90	10	5.85	10	5.34
Professional and service trades	2	2.78			2	1.17	1	0.54
Gentlemen, esquires			1	1.15			4	2.15
Miscellaneous	3	4.17	5	5.75	2	1.17	17	9.14
Total known	72		87		171		186	
Total unknown			8		2		7	
Total	72		95		173		193	

SOURCE: 1532–1542: D. Hollis, ed., *Calendar of the Bristol Apprentice Book, 1532–1565. Part 1: 1532–1542* (Bristol Record Society 14, 1949). 1626–1636: Bristol Record Office, *Apprentice Book*, 1626–1640, ff. 1ᵛ–333ᵛ.

[a] I.e., the occupations of apprentices whose fathers were in the textile industries.
[b] I.e., the occupations of fathers whose sons were apprenticed in the textile industries.

tailors, and other textile craftsmen who apprenticed sons in the city placed them in one of the textile industries; between 1626 and 1636 the figure was almost exactly 55 percent. The largest portion of those apprenticed in this economic sector were themselves sons of cloth and clothing manufacturers, and the increased percentage of Bristolians apprenticed in these industries in the 1620s and 1630s came primarily from among this same group. Once again, many of the new apprentices in these trades were indentured in exactly the same craft as their fathers. In the first period the figure is just over 23 percent, and in the second it is just under 33 percent. The shift suggests a hardening of social boundaries similar to that in the leather industries. By the seventeenth century, indeed, the textile crafts, even more than the leather trades, had become isolated from the upper reaches of the civic social order. Not only was the proportion of leading entrepreneurs' sons in these crafts relatively low, especially if we consider Bristol's population growth in the previous century, but the percentage of textile producers' children who entered the most lucrative of the city's trades was markedly reduced from the levels of a century before.

Whereas the leather trades were in decline in the later sixteenth and early seventeenth centuries and the textile industries in a period of stability or slow growth, the metalworking industries were experiencing something of a boom. Even though the recruitment of labor in the latter was subject to different economic pressures than employment in the leather and textile trades, metalworking shows the same general pattern of limited occupational mobility as the other two. From 1532 to 1542, only one hundred and twenty-one men were apprenticed in metal trades in Bristol, of whom thirty-seven, or about 30 percent, were Bristolians. From 1626 to 1636, three hundred and seventeen men were apprenticed in these same trades, of whom one hundred and forty-four, or about 45 percent, were Bristolians. During the first of these periods, only about 30 percent of those apprenticed in these crafts were themselves the sons of metal craftsmen.[65] In addition, only about 16 percent of the apprentices in the metal industries were placed in exactly the same craft as their fathers (Table 14). This suggests that the metal trades in this period were less able than other industries to provide livelihoods for the sons of their own members. But the avenues of mobility were not significantly more open than for sons of the other tradesmen. Rather than showing an even distribution of metal craftsmen's sons throughout the economy, the data reveal a marked concentration in the textile trades, especially in cloth production, which perhaps reflects the location of the metal

TABLE 14 BRISTOLIANS IN THE METALWORKING INDUSTRIES, 1532–1542 AND 1626–1636

| | 1532–1542 | | | | 1626–1636 | | | |
| | Sons[a] | | Fathers[b] | | Sons[a] | | Fathers[b] | |
	No.	%	No.	%	No.	%	No.	%
Leading entrepreneurs								
Merchants			1	2.70	3	3.70	1	0.72
Major retailers			1	2.70	1	1.23	7	5.07
Soapmakers, chandlers	1	4.17					1	0.72
Total	1	4.17	2	5.41	4	4.94	9	6.52
Textile industries[c]	9	37.50	4	10.81	7	8.64	19	13.77
Leather industries[c]	1	4.17	3	8.11	5	6.17	16	11.59
Metal industries	11	45.83	11	29.73	50	61.73	50	36.23
Building trades					4	4.94	13	9.42
Shipping and related trading and port activities	1	4.17	3	8.11	9	11.11	9	6.52
Woodworking			4	10.81	1	1.23	1	0.72
Food production	1	4.17	2	5.41	1	1.23	10	7.25
Professional and service trades								
Gentlemen, esquires								
Miscellaneous			3	8.11			11	7.97
Total known	24		32		81		138	
Total unknown			5				6	
Total	24		37		81		144	

SOURCE: 1532–1542: D. Hollis, ed., *Calendar of the Bristol Apprentice Book, 1532–1565. Part 1: 1532–1542* (Bristol Record Society 14, 1949). 1626–1636: Bristol Record Office, *Apprentice Book, 1626–1640*, ff. 1^r–333^v.
[a] I.e., the occupations of apprentices whose fathers were in the metal industries.
[b] I.e., the occupations of fathers whose sons were apprenticed in the metal industries.
[c] For purposes of this analysis, both production and secondary use have been combined.

industries in the same city neighborhoods as the clothmaking crafts in this period.[66] It is also significant that only a small percentage of new apprentices in the metal industries were the sons of the city's leading entrepreneurs. By the early seventeenth century, however, the state of this sector of Bristol's economy had vastly improved. In the period from 1626 to 1636, almost 62 percent of the sons of metal craftsmen indentured were placed in the metal trades themselves. At the same time, the proportion of those bound in exactly the same occupation as their fathers increased to 27 percent. The remaining Bristol-born apprentices in these industries came from a relatively wide range of family backgrounds. But only a very small percentage of metal craftsmen's sons ever entered the service of the city's leading entrepreneurs. Although pewterers and goldsmiths were among Bristol's wealthier inhabitants and attracted some apprentices from the families of merchants and other major dealers, the sons of metal craftsmen rarely could enter the upper echelons of Bristol's social order.

The picture appears to have been the same everywhere in Bristol. Between the second quarter of the sixteenth century and the second quarter of the seventeenth a growing percentage of Bristolians were apprenticed in the same craft as their fathers. The evidence of apprenticeships within the city of Bristol-born young men whose social backgrounds we can determine shows almost 25 percent in the first period, and over 33 percent in the second. This evidence suggests not only that Bristol's social order was composed increasingly of kin-based occupational groupings but that social barriers were becoming higher as well. Early sixteenth-century Bristol was by no means an open society in which individuals and families readily changed social station from generation to generation, but movement from trade to trade, at least within a given group of industries, was markedly easier in this period than it would be a hundred years later.[67] Taken by themselves, these changes are important enough. But they gain significance when considered in the light of Bristol's commercial expansion in the later sixteenth and early seventeenth centuries, and its 25 percent or more increase in population. Under these new conditions, maintenance of the status quo, if not an actual growth in the social diversity, might have been expected. Instead, economic and demographic growth was accompanied by the development of a somewhat more rigidly hierarchical social order.

The key to understanding these changes in social mobility lies in developments among Bristol's leading entrepreneurs—its merchants, major retailers, and soapmakers—who occupied the social heights in the

city. The composition of the category we have designated "major commercial and entrepreneurial occupations" is different from that of those
previously discussed. As used here, it denotes merchants, major retailers
such as mercers, grocers and drapers, and one group of manufacturers,
the soapmakers. Hence, it links individuals whose common characteristic is command over considerable quantities of capital, rather than
participation in the same industry or the performance of the same
economic function. This is perhaps especially noticeable for the soapmakers. Although their participation in the national market made them
as much large-scale dealers as manufacturers, their place among the
city's magnates results from their financial resources and consequent
social power. It has been impossible to identify other manufacturers
whose investment in fixed capital or role in the national market would
warrant their inclusion in this category. It has been necessary, therefore,
to exclude rather arbitrarily those brewers, whitawers, glovers, pewterers, braziers, and goldsmiths whose investment in capital equipment or
raw materials and participation in a regional or national market might
have made them the equals of the soapmakers. In the textile industry,
particularly during the sixteenth century, some tailors, tuckers, and
clothworkers acted as clothiers or drapers, putting out raw material for
manufacture or selling cloth by the yard or the piece to retail customers.
But, unlike the soapmakers, nearly all of whom were significant entrepreneurs, in these other trades and industries only detailed knowledge
of each man's business would reveal whom to include among the leading entrepreneurs. Unfortunately, the surviving evidence is insufficient
for this purpose. At the other end of the scale, the category of "leading
entrepreneur" may include some individuals whose economic importance was rather small. Many haberdashers, for example, were merely
small-scale dealers in odds and ends, rather than purveyors of high-
priced, first-quality goods such as grocers, drapers, and mercers tended
to sell. Similarly, some innholders were little more than tavernkeepers,
renting their property from some major figure and acting as his agent.
But the distortion resulting from their inclusion is more than outweighed by the number of leading entrepreneurs among the tailors, whitawers, pewterers, and the like who have been excluded solely on the basis of occupation.[68]

Although a number of leading entrepreneurs apprenticed their sons
in the ranks below them, they often searched out successful masters in
the more lucrative manufacturing industries, such as whitawers, goldsmiths, and brewers, for this purpose (Table 15). Access to the upper

TABLE 15 BRISTOLIANS IN MAJOR COMMERCIAL AND ENTREPRENEURIAL OCCUPATIONS, 1532–1542 AND 1626–1636

| | 1532–1542 | | | | 1626–1636 | | | |
| | Sons[a] | | Fathers[b] | | Sons[a] | | Fathers[b] | |
	No.	%	No.	%	No.	%	No.	%
Leading entrepreneurs								
Merchants	17	28.81	16	25.40	34	25.40	25	16.89
Major retailers	11	18.64	14	22.22	30	18.52	38	25.68
Soapmakers, chandlers	2	3.39			21	12.96	22	13.10
Total	30	50.84	30	47.62	85	52.47	85	57.43
Textile industries[c]	11	18.64	10	15.87	19	11.73	11	7.43
Leather industries[c]	7	11.86	9	14.29	18	11.11	3	2.03
Metal industries	2	3.39	1	1.59	9	5.56	4	2.70
Building trades			2	3.17	2	1.23	4	2.70
Shipping and related trading and port activities	2	3.39	6	9.52	16	9.88	18	12.16
Woodworking	1	1.69			1	0.62		
Food production	4	6.78	3	4.76	8	4.94	9	6.08
Professional and service trades	1	1.69	1	1.59	4	2.47	1	0.68
Gentlemen, esquires							10	6.76
Miscellaneous	1	1.69	1	1.59			3	2.03
Total known	59		63		162		148	
Total unknown			5				9	
Total	59		68		162		157	

SOURCE: 1532–1542: D. Hollis, ed., *Calendar of the Bristol Apprentice Book, 1532–1565. Part 1: 1532–1542* (Bristol Record Society 14, 1949). 1626–1636: Bristol Record Office, *Apprentice Book, 1626–1640*, ff. 1ʳ–333ʳ.
[a] I.e., the occupations of apprentices whose fathers were leading entrepreneurs.
[b] I.e., the occupations of fathers whose sons were apprenticed to leading entrepreneurs.
[c] For purposes of this analysis, production and secondary use have been combined.

reaches of the social hierarchy was largely closed to men in lesser trades and crafts. In terms of social mobility, the civic elite lived very much in a world unto itself. Just as with other trades, throughout our period elite fathers showed a strong tendency to apprentice their sons in their own sector of the economy and to draw their apprentices from the same circles. In each period, slightly over 50 percent of the sons of Bristol's leading entrepreneurs who were apprenticed within the city were placed with masters in this same group of trades. Between the early sixteenth century and the early seventeenth, there was a 10 percent increase, from 48 to 58 percent, in the number of Bristol-born apprentices entering these trades whose fathers were leading entrepreneurs. The distribution of other occupations represented among the Bristolians apprenticed in this category also changed. Between 1532 and 1542, only twelve of the Bristol-born apprentices who became indentured to merchants, major retailers, or soapmakers came from families in the city's large-scale industries, such as brewing and whitawing. The fathers of twenty-one others came from among the minor crafts, such as shoemaking. A similar pattern appears in the distribution of occupations filled by the sons of the city's leading entrepreneurs from 1532 to 1542. Merchants and other major entrepreneurs placed twenty-nine of their sons as apprentices in manufacturing trades, but only ten of them joined in the more important crafts such as brewing and whitawing. In other words, in the early sixteenth century Bristol's leading entrepreneurs drew their apprentices from a relatively wide range of family backgrounds and placed their own sons in a relatively wide range of occupations. Between 1626 and 1636, however, both distributions were much narrower. In this period, the sixty-three Bristolians who moved from outside the city's economic leadership to apprenticeships within it came from families of generally high social standing. Ten were sons of gentlemen, two of parish clergy, and one of a physician. At the same time, the noncommercial occupations to which the sons of major entrepreneurs were apprenticed show a similar change. Fewer of them entered the lesser trades and more went into crafts that enjoyed national markets for their wares. The evidence indicates that the upper echelons of Bristol's social hierarchy were more homogeneous in family background in Charles I's reign than had been the case in Henry VIII's and that by the 1630s the cream of the apprenticeships in Bristol was being skimmed by the sons of the city's leading entrepreneurs.[69]

Over a long period these patterns of apprenticeship were bound to create networks of kinship among the active masters in every sector of the economy, as ties between father and son and brother and brother ramified throughout each trade or craft. But even in the short term, the high number of sons apprenticed to their father's fellows in one branch or another of commerce or industry suggests the existence of very intimate social bonds within each group of masters. Where the forming of an apprenticeship tie did not reflect already well-established connections of blood and business, new ones were bound to come into being by the very placing of a son under the tutelage of a fellow Bristolian. In other words, the framework within which most Bristolians carried on their social and economic affairs had a distinctly occupational character, in the sense that trade or craft determined many other social ties. This was as true for the Merchant Venturers, whose membership we know accurately only from 1605, as for any of the other identifiable groups in the mercantile community. In these circles it was fairly common for sons to leave trade for one of the professions or to live on income from land their fathers had acquired. Judging by evidence derived from the Bristol burgess records, which enroll the names of men claiming the freedom of the city, those who followed their fathers into trade usually were apprenticed to other Merchant Venturers; often they married into Merchant Venturer families as well.[70]

The model of society employed in the foregoing analysis is the social pyramid, with an undifferentiated body of wage laborers at the base and the leading overseas merchants at the apex. In such a social order the number of places available in a given rank is fixed, with only a handful of places at the top. Within this framework the meaning of the term "social mobility" is limited. Strictly speaking, it can refer only to the relative ease with which members of different social groupings attain access to the various positions in society, since no more than a small portion of the population can ever reach the heights. Using this definition, an increase in social mobility denotes an improvement in the chances members of the lower ranks have for social betterment, not a rise in the proportion of the total population achieving the upper reaches of the pyramid, which under our definition is a logical impossibility. Under this interpretation, an increase in social mobility indicates only the achievement of a more representative distribution of social backgrounds through all levels of the social hierarchy.

But a second, broader way of considering social mobility is sometimes confused with the first. If a change upward or downward is observed in the percentage of the population able to reach the pinnacle of society, what has occurred is the development of a new framework of social organization. This kind of social mobility is different in character from the first, since an increase or decrease in the percentage of the population reaching the topmost positions can result only from a change in the proportion of positions at the top. In other words, in order for there to be social mobility in this second sense, the old social pyramid has to disappear and be replaced by a structure with a different shape. The new one could be just another pyramid with steeper or more gently rising sides. But it could also be something closer in form to a Siennese tower, with a small room atop a narrow staircase, or to the Empire State Building, with a small tower perched above a larger one. Or it could be analogous to a modern glass-and-steel office block, with clean rectilinear lines. The degree of social mobility possible in a society in the first of our two senses will depend on this second, structural sense, that is to say, on what form society takes and on the consequent proportion of places in the various ranks.

The social changes experienced in Bristol between the 1530s and the 1630s were of the second type: they were changes in structure, rather than in mobility narrowly construed. During this century Bristol became a society in which the topmost positions tended increasingly to be inherited by those born into high rank. We can see this difference in several ways. Between 1532 and 1542, two hundred and eighty-two men were apprenticed to the diverse group of leading entrepreneurs, of whom sixty-eight, or about a quarter, were Bristolians. From 1626 to 1636, five hundred and sixty-four men were apprenticed in this group of trades, of whom one hundred and fifty-seven, or almost 28 percent, were Bristolians. Taking merchants separately, one hundred and nineteen of them were apprenticed between 1532 and 1542, and one hundred and forty-two between 1626 and 1636 (Table 16).[71] In other words, between the end of Henry VIII's reign and the beginning of Charles I's there was a dramatic change in the proportion of merchants to major retailers and soapmakers. In the earlier period, merchant apprentices represented about 42 percent of all those we have classified as leading entrepreneurs, but in the later period they represented only about 25 percent. Whereas the total number of merchants apprenticed in Bristol increased by less than 20 percent—in other words, below the rate of population increase—the total number of apprentices in all crafts almost doubled and the total number of apprentices among the other leading entrepreneurs increased more than two and a half times.

These figures suggest that either the size or the number of retail establishments grew faster than did merchant firms. But the expansion in Bristol's trade in the later sixteenth and early seventeenth centuries should have had the opposite effect, since the greater scope and complexity of commerce ought to have resulted either in the taking on of additional merchant apprentices to conduct business in different markets or in the establishment of larger numbers of specialized firms working in conjunction with one another. Given that between the late fifteenth century and the late sixteenth, the number of merchants entering goods in the Bristol customs records had fallen from about two hundred and fifty per year to fewer than one hundred,[72] it is clear that no such changes had occurred among merchant firms. Instead merchants must have relied on journeymen to serve as factors and supercargoes in their enterprises. This conclusion in itself suggests that entrance into full participation in the merchant's trade was more difficult in the early seventeenth century than it had been in the early sixteenth. What explains the increased demand for apprentices among the retailers? Since nothing about the scope or techniques of the drapers', grocers', or mercers' trade had changed significantly between the two periods, at least as far as we know, it is likely that the larger numbers of apprentices entering those enterprises reflect an increase in the number of retail establishments in Bristol while the number of merchant firms declined or remained at the same level as in the 1530s.[73]

Another change also occurred. In Henry VIII's reign, about a quarter of all merchants' apprentices and about a fifth of those bound to major retailers and other large-scale dealers and entrepreneurs were native Bristolians. This proportion did not change in the early seventeenth century for the retailers. In the case of the merchants, however, the ratio of Bristolians to non-Bristolians went from about one in four to one in two and a quarter. That is, at the same time that Bristol-born merchant apprentices were becoming a socially more exclusive group, a higher percentage of positions with overseas traders were being filled by residents of the city, often the sons of fellow merchants (see Table 16). From what family backgrounds did the non-Bristolians come? In the period 1532–1542, they were a relatively diverse group. Of the eighty-eight strangers apprenticed to merchants in this period, only about 15 percent were the sons of esquires and gentlemen; another 17 percent were from the families of merchants and other leading entrepreneurs. The majority came from the less exalted ranks of English society; the

	1532–1542			1626–1636		
	Bristolians	*Non-Bristolians*	*Total*	*Bristolians*	*Non-Bristolians*	*Total*
Men						
Leading entrepreneurs						
Merchants	31	88	119	63	79	142
% of total known men	8.20	8.63	8.51	6.57	4.48	5.22
% of category	26.05	73.95		44.37	55.63	
Major retailers	31	114	145	65	268	333
% of total known men	8.20	11.18	10.37	6.78	15.20	12.23
% of category	21.38	78.62		19.52	80.48	
Soapmakers and chandlers	6	12	18	29	60	89
% of total known men	1.59	1.18	1.29	3.02	3.40	3.27
% of category	33.33	66.67		32.58	67.42	
Total	68	214	282	157	407	564
% of total known men	17.99	20.98	20.17	16.37	23.09	20.72
% of category	24.11	75.89		27.84	72.16	
Textile production	56	140	196	124	229	353
% of total known men	14.81	13.73	14.02	12.93	12.99	12.97
% of category	28.57	71.43		35.13	64.87	
Leather production	51	99	150	38	65	103
% of total known men	13.49	9.71	10.73	3.96	3.69	3.78
% of category	34.00	66.00		36.89	63.11	
Clothing production and other secondary users of cloth and leather	85	202	287	146	247	393
% of total known men	22.49	19.80	20.53	15.22	14.01	14.44
% of category	29.62	70.38		37.15	62.85	
Metal crafts	37	84	121	144	173	317
% of total known men	9.79	8.24	8.66	15.02	9.81	11.65
% of category	30.58	69.42		45.43	54.57	

Building trades	7	28	35	69	128	197
% of total known men	1.85	2.75	2.50	7.19	7.26	7.24
% of category	20.00	80.00		35.03	64.97	
Shipping and related trading and port activities	26	129	155	193	328	521
% of total known men	6.88	12.65	11.09	20.13	18.60	19.14
% of category	16.77	83.23		37.04	62.96	
Food production and related industries	20	71	91	50	121	171
% of total known men	5.29	6.96	6.51	5.21	6.86	6.28
% of category	21.98	78.02		29.24	70.76	
Woodworking	6	12	18	11	9	20
% of total known men	1.59	1.18	1.29	1.15	0.51	0.73
% of category	33.33	66.67		55.00	45.00	
Professional and service industries	15	27	42	19	49	68
% of total known men	3.97	2.65	3.00	1.98	2.78	2.50
% of category	35.71	64.29		27.94	72.06	
Miscellaneous	7	14	21	8	7	15
% of total known men	1.85	1.37	1.50	0.83	0.40	0.55
% of category	33.33	66.67		53.33	46.67	
Total known	378	1,020	1,398	959	1,763	2,722
Total unknown[a]	1	6	7	5	7	12
Total men	379	1,026	1,405	964	1,770	2,734
% of total	93.58	97.53	96.43	93.14	97.41	95.86
% of category	26.98	73.02		35.26	64.74	
Women	26	26	52	71	47	118
% of total known women	6.42	2.47	3.57	6.86	2.59	4.14
% of category	50.00	50.00		60.17	39.83	
Total Men and Women	405	1,052	1,457	1,035	1,817	2,852
% of category	27.80	72.20		36.29	63.71	

SOURCE: 1532–1542: D. Hollis, ed., *Calendar of the Bristol Apprentice Book, 1532–1565. Part 1: 1532–1542* (Bristol Record Society 14, 1949). 1626–1636: Bristol Record Office, *Apprentice Book, 1626–1640*, ff. 1ᵛ–333ᵛ.
[a] In these cases either the occupation or the geographical origin is unknown.

industrial crafts, especially textile manufacture, account for just over 25 percent, and agriculture for just over 40 percent. The same general pattern is observed in this period among the apprentices to major retailers and soapmakers. In Charles I's reign, however, the picture is significantly different. Of the seventy-nine outsiders bound to merchants, only about 13 percent now came from artisan families and another 13 percent from agriculture. The fathers of the rest consist of about 16 percent merchants, 4 percent clergymen, and over 48 percent esquires and gentlemen. The contrast with apprentices in other leading entrepreneurial occupations is striking. Although about 20 percent of non-Bristolians indentured to major retailers and soapmakers had gentry backgrounds, these trades were filled primarily by the sons of yeomen, husbandmen, and minor craftsmen, not from the rural or urban elite.

These data confirm the picture we have been seeing of Bristol society as becoming increasingly rigid and hierarchical in its organization during the sixteenth and early seventeenth centuries. However, apprenticeship reveals the process of occupational and social mobility only at second hand. In and of itself it granted nothing but seven years or more of training and labor in the household of a master. Only if the servant established his own business at the end of his term would apprenticeship have contributed significantly to his advancement. In Bristol and in most other corporate towns in early modern England, this transition was accomplished when a young man entered into the freedom of the town by swearing a formal oath to preserve its liberties and abide by its customs. Performance of this ritual and payment of the appropriate fees gave him full rights to trade under the privileges and immunities of the town. This freedom to trade could be obtained in early modern Bristol in any of four ways: by apprenticeship to a freeman, by patrimony, by marriage to either the daughter or the widow of a freeman, or by redemption, which was accomplished by the vote of the Common Council and the payment of a substantial entry fine. Each signified in its own way that the newcomer possessed social connections within the city. Only apprenticeship, however, permitted an individual truly to earn his place. Even though, as we have just seen, family background limited who became apprenticed to whom, once a young man's years of service were completed his social origins were technically irrelevant. If he had sufficient resources to start a business of his own, his service in his master's household fully warranted his entrance into the freedom. The other criteria for admission were different in character, since each stressed the newcomer's social ties, not his training or economic success. Even redemption, which was purchased, depended less on wealth than on acquiring the goodwill of the Bristol common councillors. As a practical matter this meant having the patronage, and usually also the formal surety, of at least one and commonly several well-established and fiscally sound local businessmen. What is of interest for our purposes is the relative importance of apprenticeship to the other three forms of admission. Since the number of freemen who could successfully carry on business in a particular trade or craft was limited by the size and scope of the market, those admitted by patrimony, marriage, or redemption reduced the number of places available to young men seeking their economic independence by apprenticeship (Table 17).

Unfortunately, we have no long series of admissions to the freedom for the sixteenth century on which to base a comparison, but an examination of the relationship between admissions by apprenticeship to admissions by the three other means in the first half of the seventeenth century shows how difficult it was to become a merchant during this period. Although merchants were one of only three groups in which the ratio between apprenticeships and admissions to the freedom was less than two to one, this fact by itself does not tell us whether a larger than average proportion of merchant apprentices attained the freedom of the city, or whether the percentage of admissions by patrimony, marriage, and redemption was higher for merchants than for other trades.[74] The evidence supports the second conclusion. Between 1607 and 1651, nearly 45 percent of all merchants entering the freedom of Bristol were admitted by patrimony, marriage, or redemption. In some periods the figure was almost 66 percent, and at no time did it fall below 25 percent. The most usual standard was patrimony, which accounted for over two-thirds of the one hundred and thirty-one merchants who were admitted in a way other than by apprenticeship. The figures for major retailers and soapmakers show a much stronger role for apprenticeship. Over the whole period, it accounted for three-quarters of new admissions in these trades, falling only once a fraction below two-thirds. This is the same pattern as in the minor crafts and lesser trades, where typically 70 to 75 percent of new admissions were by apprenticeship. In other words, not only were merchant apprenticeships dominated by the sons of leading entrepreneurs and country gentlemen, but entrance into the seventeenth-century merchant community was more dependent upon birth and family than is true of nearly all other crafts and trades. For members of Bristol's lower social ranks, moving to the top of the social hierarchy was even more difficult than the apprenticeship data reveal.

TABLE 17 PERCENTAGE OF FREEMEN ADMITTED TO LEADING ENTREPRENEURIAL
OCCUPATIONS BY PATRIMONY, REDEMPTION, AND MARRIAGE, 1607–1651

	1607–1611	1611–1615	1615–1619	1619–1623	1623–1627	1627–1631	1631–1635	1635–1639	1639–1643	1643–1647	1647–1651	Total
Merchants	36.67	33.33	26.09	60.00	66.67	48.89	36.84	40.48	48.48	55.56	45.71	44.71
Other large-scale dealers, major retailers	20.00	24.44	32.14	24.39	23.40	21.05	26.79	18.18	26.67	25.00	34.69	25.27
Soapmakers and chandlers	—	25.00	35.71	9.09	6.67	8.33	7.14	—	5.26	20.00	16.67	10.96
Total	22.09	25.56	31.18	29.85	30.00	30.70	25.84	27.84	29.46	30.59	36.46	28.89

SOURCE: Bristol Record Office, Burgess Book (1607–1651).

The term "merchant" has undergone an evolution in meaning through three distinct phases since the early Middle Ages. According to Charles Gross,

> At first it embraced all who, in their trade, were in any way concerned with buying and selling, including petty shopkeepers and many handicraftsmen. During the fifteenth and the greater part of the sixteenth century, it applied preeminently to all who made a business of buying and selling for resale—retailers as well as wholesalers—manual craftsmen not included. It then came to have its present meaning of an extensive dealer.[75]

The earliest stage in this development corresponds to the period of the Gild Merchant, which consisted of all tradesmen of a particular borough. Such a gild is known to have existed in Bristol in the twelfth and thirteenth centuries. The Gild Merchant was an exclusive society whose constitution preserved to its sworn membership the main economic privilege possessed by a chartered borough—the freedom to buy and sell without paying local customs and tolls. Retail trade was its primary concern, and no distinction was made between overseas traders and those who limited themselves merely to buying and selling in the marketplace or keeping shops. Strictly speaking, the gild consisted of one class of individuals, all of whom possessed the same trading rights, and every gildsman was potentially, if not actually, an overseas merchant. The later Middle Ages, however, witnessed a sharp narrowing of the definition. First to be excluded were those poorer elements who used their trading privileges to "color" strangers' goods under the aegis of their own membership in the borough. Ousted next were the craftsmen, including middlemen and entrepreneurs. Finally the line was drawn between the merchant retailer and the mere merchant.[76]

The development of commercial organization in Bristol followed this pattern closely. In the fourteenth century it had been textile manufacturers, such as Thomas Blanket and William Canynges the Elder, who were Bristol's leading men. But after the mid-fifteenth century, the history of the merchant community was marked by an accelerating process of exclusion, as a class of merchant dealers who specialized in overseas trade began to differentiate themselves from these industrial entrepreneurs. As late as 1467, however, no challenge was offered to the claims of all Bristol freemen to trade overseas on their own behalf. But in 1500, when Bristol was still a major cloth exporter, this new group of merchant adventurers, as they then began to call themselves, attempted to exclude the city's clothiers from foreign commerce by prohibiting their fellows from delivering cloth abroad for nonmembers and by permitting mariners to ship no more than three whole cloths in their own name.[77] Nevertheless, at this time no distinction was made between mere merchants and merchant retailers. By the mid-sixteenth century, however, the focus was on the growing rivalry between large-scale wholesalers and prominent shopkeepers as well as clothiers and other manufacturers. Many merchants wished to exclude the latter groups from direct participation in foreign trade.

From the start these moves involved an intricate interplay of political choice and socioeconomic development. The establishment of new trading relations among merchants and between them and the rest of Bristol society led to the foundation of the Society of Merchant Venturers to provide common regulations and political protection for mere merchants. The Society, in turn, helped to crystallize the new trading practices and social and economic arrangements into a form of social organization for the city. It is hard to escape the sense that the increased rigidity of the occupational groupings we have observed in our study of social mobility and the growing differences in social background between the merchants and the rest of Bristol society were the consequence, perhaps only partially intended, of the development of the Merchant Venturers. The establishment of this company brought the mere merchants together in new ways, gave them common interests, and made it both easier and more desirable to form family alliances among the membership. As these overseas traders grew in wealth and power after 1552, they became a focus for gentry from Bristol's hinterland who desired lucrative and influential positions for their younger sons, and for merchants from other cities who wanted to establish a foothold for themselves in this increasingly prosperous merchant community.

The evolution we have described did not occur in an economic vacuum. In large part it was the consequence of the growing complexity of trade and industry in the sixteenth century. Where once a single tradesman united in his own person the production and the distribution of goods, distinct categories of entrepreneur had emerged to perform these services. This process was accompanied by the development of what George Unwin has identified as "three different capital functions" which distinguished the dealer in foreign wares, the overseas trader, and the industrial entrepreneur, who competed with each other to "secure the economic advantage of standing between the rest and the market."[78] In place of an economy in which every operating unit was a near-replica of every other, there came about a new economic order composed of specialized and interlocking elements. In it the merchant, with his command of credit, access to shipping, and connections in distant markets, was usually able to dominate both the producer and the retailer.

However, these developments were not uncontested. They arose because of the ability of Bristol's mere merchants to control the city's government and to use their influence with the Crown as extra-economic resources which in times of genuine economic crisis could be called on for assistance. But what sprang from politics could be countered by politics. Roger Edgeworth, preaching at the time of the Society's foundation, saw it even at this early moment as a source of dissension in the city. Speaking of the need for unity in the body politic, he told Bristolians:

> You haue in this citie erect a certain confederacie, which you call the companye, I pray God it may do well, but I perceiue a certaine mundanitie in it, a worldly couetouse caste to bring the gaines that was undifferent & common to al the marchaunts of this citie into the handes of a fewe persones. Wherefore good neyghbours, loue the whole brotherhed & vniuersal companie of Christes faithful people, diuide it not, & if there be any cantel broken out, pray for them that thei may returne and come home againe to the great flocke and congregation of Christian people, and that they may hereafter loue the whole fraternitie.[79]

What Edgeworth saw at the Society's birth became the recurring motif of Bristol's history in the decades to follow. To understand why this was so we need to see how these disagreements were transformed in ideology, which is the task of the next section of this book.

PART 2

In a Worshipful State, 1450–1650

CHAPTER 4

The Navel of the World

The concept of social organization concerns the ways that human beings adjust means to ends in their collective lives. For sociologists and political scientists, this focus usually yields an analysis of self-perpetuating social institutions and bureaucratic systems in which each element supports the others as part of a larger mechanism. For historians, it commonly involves tracing in narrative the reasons why individuals and groups acted as they did. Either way, however, students of social organization generally consider the significance of an action to lie in its use rather than in its place in an already existing web of symbols and values. Our approach in the previous section, mixing the methods of the social scientist with the interests of the historian, followed this line of interpretation. It told the story of how Bristol's overseas merchants built a new social order for themselves in response to the economic conditions confronting them after 1453. But these Bristolians also lived in a world of well-established cultural codes and social meanings with which they were obliged to come to terms in remaking their society. To move beyond the limited notion of functionalism and the narrow idea of rationality upon which we have so far relied, we now need to examine this social and political language and the changes it underwent.

In 1577 John Northbrooke, "preacher of the Word of God" at Bristol, published one of England's earliest condemnations of stage plays, interludes, "jugglings and false sleyghts," and other pastimes. Our duty, he says, requires us to "apply al and euery of our doings to ye glory of God," but instead "we kepe ioly cheare one with another in banquetting, surfeiting and dronkennesse; also we vse all the night long in ranging from town to town, and from house to house, with mummeries and maskes, diceplaying, carding and dauncing." Thus, "we leaue Christ alone at the aultar, and feed our eyes with vaine and vnhonest sights." Festival and holy days contribute to this spirit of dissipation, for by them "halfe the yeare, and more," is "ouerpassed . . . in loytering and vaine pastimes . . . restrayning men from their handy labours and occupations."[1]

Northbrooke's views represent a fundamental rejection of the cultural traditions that dominated English life until the sixteenth century. Nowhere had these traditions been better exemplified than in the town in which Northbrooke served his ministry. For example, on Corpus Christi in early sixteenth-century Bristol, we are told,

> [t]he members of every guild . . . assembled with music, flags and banners to join in a splendid ecclesiastical procession through the streets, where the houses were decorated with tapestry, brilliant cloth, and garlands of flowers and the afternoon was spent in the performance in the open air of miracle plays, in which every craft claimed its special part, to the enjoyment of the whole community.[2]

And on Midsummer Eve, these same gildsmen "—who emulated each other in the display of gay dresses, banners, burning 'cressets' and torches, and in the supply of minstrels and musical instruments— marched through the streets, the proceedings terminating in morris dancing and various games, in which the populace participated."[3] These celebrations, along with others in Advent and at Christmas, played an important part in the official civic calendar. The mayor and his brethren of the Common Council, far from being God's ministers in punishing "dicers, mummers, ydellers, dronkerds, swearers, roges and dauncers," as Northbrooke would have had them be,[4] participated in and even led most of the festivities. In the later fifteenth century, Robert Ricart, Bristol's town clerk and lay brother of its Fraternity of Kalendars, exhorting his readers in nearly as hearty a manner as Northbrooke, set forth these "laudable" customs in a book of remembrance so that the city's officers "may the better, sewrer, and more diligenter, execute, obserue, and minstre their seid Offices . . . to the honoure and comon wele of this worshipfull towne, and all thenhabitaunts of the same."[5] Where Northbrooke saw the activities of "idle players and dauncers" leading only to their city's moral downfall,[6] Ricart, writing a hundred years before, saw these same practices as intimately connected with Bristol's welfare.

Curiously, many of the celebrations that Ricart praised and Northbrooke damned were already something of a dead letter in England by the 1570s. I do not mean, of course, that Christmas feasting and Shrove Tuesday cock-throwing were no more, or that church ales and Sabbath-day sports did not persist. But the great public celebrations led by the civic leaders of the towns, paid for out of the funds of the town treasuries, had largely ceased. Most had been stricken from the liturgical calendar in Henry VIII's reign,[7] and although there had been an effort under Queen Mary to revive them, they never recovered their old vitality and had long been in abeyance when Northbrooke took up arms against dicing, dancing, and vain plays. Despite some massive demonstrations of nostalgia, their end had been peaceful. There was no St. Bartholomew's Day massacre in their defense. They had passed on not in fire but in ice.[8] This chapter attempts an explanation for their seemingly peaceable demise.

By choosing to examine this subject, however, we set forth into perhaps the most troubled waters of historical interpretation. It is not that the field has suffered from bitter debates, with scholars striking each other hip and thigh after the fashion of the Hebrews and Amalikites; there has been no "Storm over the Ceremonies." Rather, the methodological and theoretical issues raised by the study of festival and ritual have produced so little consensus that many historians refuse to accept the subject as history; they see no way that it can be studied according to the canons of historical inquiry and reject it as a form of misplaced sociologizing or literary criticism gone astray. Past rituals, it is widely believed, had meanings for their participants that at this distance we cannot penetrate; hence all we can do is to reduce them in some sterile and arbitrary way to epiphenomena of the social order according to some Marxist theory of base and superstructure or some Durkheimian scheme of functionalism.[9] But the problem of understanding ritualistic action is not unique to students of lost religions. Historians of every type face it whether they are studying diplomatic negotiations, election stump oratory, or factory life. Interpreting ritual means making intelligible highly formalized actions that manifestly are intelligible to the actors themselves, and as such it is a problem of human understanding not confined only to one branch of history or, indeed, to historical study alone. It is a problem of everyday life.

A simple analogy drawn from one of Roger Edgeworth's sermons may help to convey what I mean. In speaking of correct behavior, Edgeworth says:

> [I]f a man woulde syng in the middle of the market, or in a court at the barre afore the iudge when ther be weighty matter in hand, he should offend against modestie, & against al good humanitie, so that he may be called modest or manerly that in al his behaviour vseth good maner and measure, and a mean.[10]

Why should singing in these circumstances amount to an offense? Nothing would be amiss if this same man sang a psalm in church or a tune in the alehouse: such behavior would be appropriate to the setting and thereby conform, in Edgeworth's sense, to the Aristotelian mean. The answer lies in the relationship between meaning and context. The market and the law court are places intended for the conduct of particular kinds of business, solemnly undertaken. Those engaged in them are governed by tacitly accepted rules of conduct which not only dictate their behavior but make it understandable to their fellows. When in the marketplace, it is proper to cry out one's wares and to bargain. Both situations dictate highly ritualized patterns, not amenable to hymn-singing or balladeering. In bargaining, for example, there are accepted procedures of offer and counteroffer the use of which helps the parties to come to agreement upon a price. Each side employs the common language of haggling to signal his wishes and to discover his opposite's intentions. Each side tries to read the other's situation in his offers and adjusts his actions accordingly. Should one of the bargainers break into song in the midst of such a negotiation, his tune would seem the raving of a madman, because it would defeat the common purpose of the exchange. Similarly, in a law court it is proper to make motions and to give arguments in the specialized language of the law. A lawyer who sings his pleas would be judged—quite rightly—as deranged. There would be no conventions against which to weigh his songs, and his actions would become unintelligible. In other words, it is by properly understanding the context in which we find ourselves and adjusting our behavior to it that we begin to make our meanings known and grasp the meanings of others.

We could hardly proceed in our lives if our social actions were not amenable in this way to interpretation by others. But to understand social action requires an understanding of the social setting in which the action takes place. This raises two important points, one regarding the way the action is viewed by outside observers and the other the way it is seen by the actors themselves. For the outsider, discovering the rules of intelligibility shared by those he observes demands an understanding not only of their gestures but of their frame of reference as well. This task, as has been pointed out by many theorists, is somewhat like translating from one language to another, a difficult enterprise when there are large differences between cultures. To do it effectively requires attention not only to grammar, syntax, and logical connections but to what is sometimes called the speaker's "form of life." As Hilary Putnam puts it, comprehension of the words or behavior of a stranger begins with assumptions about what he "wants or intends" and is relative to "the nature of the environment" in which he speaks or acts. In Putnam's terms it is "interest-relative," a concept he illustrates with the following example. "Willie Sutton (the famous bank robber)," he tells us, "is supposed to have been asked 'Why do you rob banks?,' to which Sutton gave the famous reply: 'That's where the money is.' Now . . . imagine," Putnam says,

> (a) a priest asked the question; (b) a robber asked the question. . . . The priest's question means: "Why do you rob banks—*as opposed to not robbing at all?*" The robber's question means: "Why do you rob banks—as opposed to, say, gas stations?" And Sutton's answer is an answer to the robber's question, but not the priest's.[11]

In interpreting language and other forms of social action, we need to know what issue is being raised in order to understand the response, and this means understanding the context—the environment—in which the actors find themselves. Is it a confessional, or a den of thieves?

When the social setting in which we live is changing rapidly, it is possible that some of us will move in a context that differs in significant ways from everyone else's, and that as a result the same social behavior will be open to systematically different interpretations—in which one party, as it were, asks the priest's question and the other answers the robber's. In extreme circumstances, moreover, a traditional form of social behavior can completely lose its intelligibility if the social setting in which it previously made sense is sufficiently transformed. By ceasing to have social relevance, it ceases to be acceptable or useful behavior and fades from view. In a den of thieves the priest's question is rarely in order.

This way of thinking about ritual and social change establishes the conditions under which the meaning of social action can be determined. It tells us that the performers and their audience belong to the same community of discourse. But this does not imply that all participants in this community will necessarily agree on every interpretation of meaning. Confusion, misunderstanding, disagreement, and conflict about troubling issues can be as much a part of community life as harmony and agreement. This approach neither reduces meaning to the way ritual symbolizes or expresses the social order nor subsumes meaning into social function. Instead, it views meaning and context in relation to one another without conflating the two. Let us see whether this formulation can aid us in understanding the strange death of civic ceremony in Reformation Bristol.

In the early Middle Ages, when Bristol's Gild Merchant was transforming the borough into an effective corporate body, the principal line of tension in the city was between its sworn brotherhood of freemen and all non-freemen, that is, between those who enjoyed the liberty to trade freely by retail within the borough and those, whether inhabitant or stranger, who did not. Until the fourteenth century the freemen had a certain unity, despite differences in wealth and power among them, because they had to define themselves against dangers that came to the borough from outside, including threats from the Crown to Bristol's political independence.[12] By the later fourteenth and early fifteenth centuries, however, the fabric of social life had begun to alter, as various stages of cloth production migrated into the countryside, as the trade in woolens looked more and more to foreign markets, as a class of merchant entrepreneurs differentiated themselves from the other members of the old mercantile community, and as local governance fell into the hands of the borough's "better and more worthy men" serving on a select council. Moreover, after Bristol had achieved a form of incorporation in 1373, relations between freemen and non-freemen became somewhat less problematic, and the principal focus of the city's political life turned from protecting the independence of the borough to regulating relations among the freemen.[13] In this era, more than before, the burgesses of Bristol lived according to the ideals of social unity but the realities of social division.[14] They bound themselves in a compact body by oaths promising complete devotion to the city's commonweal and thorough commitment of their wealth and power to its aid.[15] Yet they resided in a town whose topography segregated them into distinct neighborhoods and whose economy placed them in separate social groupings.

The celebrations of the Feast of St. Clement, patron of the mariners and merchants,[16] on 23 November, and of the Feast of St. Katherine of Alexandria, patroness of the weavers, two days later, were very much a product of this later period. Although there was a chapel dedicated to St. Katherine in Temple Church from 1299, and a gild of weavers from at least the 1340s—and probably a good deal earlier—the grant of the first indulgences to the gild for its chapel dates only from 1384, and the chapel itself became a permanent chantry only in 1392. It is in this same period, that is, the middle and late fourteenth century, that the city acquired its Common Council.[17] Thus it is unlikely that St. Katherine's Day could have received an elaborate *official* celebration—engaging both the gild and the civic leadership—before the mid-fourteenth century. About St. Clement's Day we can be somewhat more definite. The chapel and gild associated with him were founded only in 1445 or 1446.[18] Hence to grasp the significance of this pair of feast days, we must begin with the peculiarities of late medieval Bristol.

Bristol was first and foremost a river port, located at the confluence of the Avon and the Frome, which, in the words of John Leland, "dothe peninsulate the towne."[19] In consequence, the urban territory in the fourteenth and fifteenth centuries was divided into three separate segments. In the center, between the two rivers, there were eight small and three large parishes, all completely built up. To the east and south of the Avon, across the bridge that had given Bristol its name, lay three relatively large and also well-inhabited parishes. By the fifteenth century, Bristol also extended to the west and north in an arc of important suburbs beyond its old medieval walls (Figure 3).[20] Jurisdictional considerations further increased this complexity. Until 1373 the river Avon divided the city legally, politically, and administratively, as well as geographically. On its western and northern bank, it lay in the county of Gloucester; on its eastern and southern bank, it lay in Somerset.[21] Moreover, even after Bristol became a county in its own right in 1373, it still stood in two different dioceses, with the fifteen parishes west and north of the Avon subject to the bishop of Worcester and the three parishes to its east and south under the authority of the bishop of Bath and Wells.

Finally, two ecclesiastical enclaves existed within the city: the liberty of the Augustinian Abbey in the parish of St. Augustine to the west, and

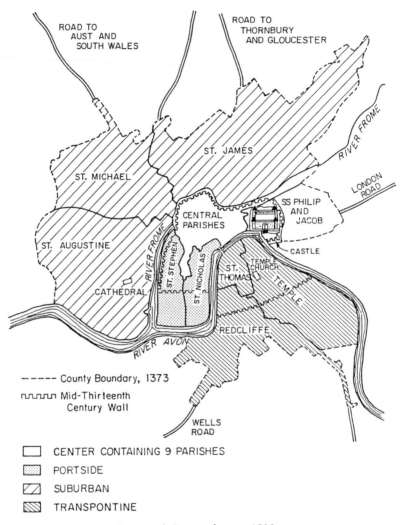

Fig. 3. Bristol's Ecclesiastical Geography, ca. 1500.

the franchise of the Order of St. John of Jerusalem, known as Temple
Fee, in the parish of Temple to the south. The holders of both claimed
for themselves wide immunity from the jurisdiction of Bristol's government in such matters as payment of local tolls and taxes and freedom
from suit in court; in addition, fugitive criminals, including murderers
and men outlawed in civil cases, could claim sanctuary within the
boundaries of each liberty.[22] These facts directly affect our story. When
Ricart wrote, St. Clement's Chapel was located at the Hospital of St.

Batholomew in the College Green, within the enclave of St. Augustine's Abbey. St. Katherine's Chapel was located in Temple Church itself, and the weavers' gildhall, also dedicated to St. Katherine, stood nearby in St. Thomas Street; both were situated in the heart of Temple Fee.[23]

Although mariners or merchants might seem from our modern viewpoint to have little in common with weavers, from the perspective of the late medieval urban polity they shared several important characteristics. In Bristol, the community of freemen was by definition a community of retailers.[24] But in the later Middle Ages, mariners and overseas merchants depended more on distant markets than on the local one, and many of them traded principally by wholesale, not retail. Their actions in the community, then, were not readily controlled by official disenfranchisement or discommoning, which merely deprived them of their right to trade legally by retail at a shop or market stall. A similar difficulty arose with the weavers, since they too depended for their economic activities primarily on markets outside the city proper. By the fourteenth century, as we know, Bristol was one of England's leading cloth exporters, and every year thousands of fabrics made their way to the continent in return for such goods as wine and woad. In a very real sense, the whole life of the city centered on this trade. It not only supplied the necessary infusions of wealth to keep the city running but set a rhythm to city life, as wool gathered in the spring shearings was turned into cloth to ship in time to purchase French wine from the autumn harvest. This process reached its climax toward the end of November, as the great cloth fleet sailed for Bordeaux,[25] and the festive days of St. Clement and St. Katherine came at just the right moment in the year to bless the major events in the city's annual economic cycle.

In popular celebration, St. Clement's Day and St. Katherine's were often treated as an interrelated pair. In many places, the former was a special day for boys and the latter for girls. In some, the two feasts were collapsed into one and celebrated on the same day.[26] For late medieval Bristol, the pairing seems focused especially on the structural tensions that characterized the community—those arising from the geographical divisions in the city, from the existence of large jurisdictional enclaves within its borders, and from the important but peculiar place of weavers and overseas traders in the social order.

Unfortunately, we know very little about how the city celebrated St. Clement's Day. From Ricart's *Kalendar* we can see that there was at least one procession, occurring on St. Clement's Eve, in which the members of the Bristol Corporation, almost certainly coming from the

Guildhall in the city center, crossed the river Frome into the heart of the
sanctuary of St. Augustine's Abbey. The following day, a mass with
communion was celebrated.[27] The celebration, with its crossing of the
boundaries and its taking of the sacrament, seems very much a ceremony of unification.

A similar pattern is to be observed in the Feast of St. Katherine,
about which Ricart tells us somewhat more. The celebration divides
into three parts, typical of rites of passage as they have been described
and analyzed by Arnold van Gennep and Victor Turner.[28] It began with
a procession to evensong at Temple Church, passed through a long transition, and ended with a second procession and a mass.[29] To understand
this sequence of events we need to study each of these stages in turn. In
doing so, we can not only examine the particular significance of St.
Katherine's Day but perhaps also see something of the significance of St.
Clement's Feast as well.

Processions were a commonplace of urban life in the Middle Ages,
and the members of the Bristol city government attended many public
functions in this fashion, each man in his scarlet robe walking in the
place appropriate to his rank and seniority.[30] In general, these processions had a double social meaning. Most obviously, they expressed in
visible form the organization of the municipal government; the persons
holding each of the principal offices were publicly advertised. Not only
were observers made aware of the hierarchy of power within the city,
they were reminded through this symbolic expression of political authority of their own proper position in the community and of the need
to show deference to its leaders.[31] But in this particular case, the procession stood for something more. The presence of the magistrates in full
regalia in the church asserted the legitimacy of their authority in a place
where ordinarily they could not exercise control. Although technically
they had power over the Bristol freemen—most of them weavers and
other clothworkers—who lived within Temple Fee, they could not enforce that power directly should they meet resistance there. The procession, then, raised the problem of Temple Fee's anomalous jurisdictional
status and introduced in a dramatic way the theme of its underlying
unity with the civic community as a whole. The same can be said for the
procession on St. Clement's Eve, two days earlier, to the College Green.

The transition stage of St. Katherine's festivities shifts our attention
from the status of Temple Fee to the relationship between the weavers'
gild and the municipal authorities, and from St. Katherine's Chapel to
St. Katherine's Hall, where there were "drynkyngs" of "sondry wynes"

and where "Spysid Cakebrede" was eaten by the assembled celebrants. At the Hall the mayor and his brethren became the guests of the weavers, which gave the latter the opportunity to display their wealth and manifest their importance.[32] Moreover, Ricart says, "the cuppes" were "merelly filled aboute the hous," which signifies the drinking of "healths" among the participants; it is with the same or similar phrases that this time-honored social ritual is often identified in the late medieval and early modern period. By its nature this is a reciprocal process; healths are not merely given but exchanged. In this way the weavers secured the "amity and affection" of the city's political leadership and, if need be, forgiveness for any wrongs. In the drinking of healths and the eating of spiced cake the sharply delineated hierarchy apparent in the processional breaks down, most probably in a degree of inebriation, a kind of licensed drunkenness. Drunkenness is the opposite of order. It wreaks havoc on both body and mind, and, as was commonly said, "nothing can be found stedfast" in it.[33]

Suitably inebriated after thus passing the cups, the membership of the city government found their way "euery man home" alone.[34] What had started as an ordered procession into Temple Fee now became a leaderless and unorganized—a disordered—movement away from it. Viewed in this fashion, the transition stage of the festival seems devoted primarily to the ceremonial stripping away of the hierarchical structure and pretensions of Bristol's leadership.[35] This effect was only reinforced as events moved further into the night. When they reached home, the mayor, sheriff, bailiffs, and other worshipful men received "at theire dores Seynt Kateryns players, making them to drynk at their does, and rewardyng theym for theire playes."[36] Unfortunately, Ricart tells us nothing about the nature of these plays or about the social makeup of the group of wandering performers. But we know enough to draw some tentative conclusions.

By tradition, St. Katherine was a special guardian of the Christian community against evil secular authority. The essential elements of her life concern her challenge and ultimate defeat of the emperor Maxentius, a cruel persecutor of Christians. In the end, her righteous authority triumphed over Maxentius's injustice, fulfilling her prophecy that if he failed to correct his ways he would "be a servant." In local festivities on her day, the figure of St. Katherine usually appeared with her assistants—sometimes children or, more commonly, lesser members of some gild—to demand tribute from the leading citizens, usually the civic authorities. The event was one of ritual submission which gave social inferiors an opportunity to exact symbolic homage from their betters. The treats they received from the leading men gave recognition that these notables were part of the same community as the players; they were a kind of toll or entry fee. By giving them, the city's governors subordinated themselves symbolically to Katherine's divinely inspired authority and, therefore, not only to the virtues she exemplified but to the community she represented.[37]

If this interpretation is correct, it leads us by a natural progression to the final stage of St. Katherine's rite in Bristol: the unification of Temple Fee and its weavers with the borough community as a whole. Once again the event centers on a procession, but now the Corporation members, purged or purified by the proceedings of the previous night, join the parishioners of Temple to make a circuit of the town, ritually integrating the population of Temple Fee into the borough community. This union is sealed with a mass and offering, which combined, as John Bossy has emphasized, the principles of order and unity within social divisions. In their solemn communion, with its focus on the Kiss of Peace, the members of the Corporation were finally joined together with their fellow citizens from the parish of Temple, each in his legitimate place as members of the larger Christian commonwealth.[38] Again a similar point can be made about the celebration of St. Clement's Day at College Green.

In this way the Feast of St. Katherine together with its companion Feast of St. Clement confirmed the principle of unity proclaimed by the late medieval borough community. According to theory, a saint was the representative in heaven of a community, ready to intercede for its members individually and collectively, so the community gained in solidarity from its veneration of his or her image or relics. In other words, a spiritual bond, mediated through sacred objects, tied together life in this world with life in the next and made the social body also a holy one, the symbol of godly order and harmony. The community represented by a saint necessarily was a microcosm of the world. It marked off within its boundaries a series of structured relationships that distinguished it from other communities and made it unique at the same time as it replicated the divine order.[39] The result in Bristol of celebrating such a saint's day was a territorial unity that defined the boundaries of the community; a jurisdictional unity that linked its members together in a set of common rights and privileges; and a social, or even spiritual, unity that was the ideal of their common enterprise. Tension, dissent, and conflict there might well be, but not without resolution, at least in theory. These two festivals recognized the fact of territorial, jurisdictional, and social cohesion within the divided city and reaffirmed its ideals of harmony, uniformity, and solidarity.

The borough community of the high Middle Ages in theory was a bounded world, a communion of interests and purposes separating the townsmen and their life of trade from the agrarian existence of the rest of England. The feasts of St. Clement and St. Katherine confirmed these ideals of community in the face of social and economic tensions that by 1400 had begun to threaten their foundations. In symbolic form they integrated the weavers and mariners into the body politic of the city. Robert Ricart, in his map of the city at its foundation, also conveyed this vision of Bristol as an emblem of the cosmos (Figure 4).[40] This map, in which Bristol sits upon a little hill between four gates, portrays a nearly perfect example of what Werner Müller has identified as the Gothic town plan. It is a city built as "the navel of the world," a cross within a circle, representing the heavenly Jerusalem, in which the four main streets divide the world into its four component parts.[41] It puts into visible form, then, the ordered community which found its highest expression on Corpus Christi, when the civic body, the crafts, and the other citizens proceeded through the town, each in his proper place, in veneration of the host.[42]

In general, all of Bristol's late medieval festive life encouraged its citizens to conceive of their city in this way, as a microcosm embedded in the larger order of God's universe. It also yielded a subtle commentary on the nature and distribution of political authority. In ritual and festival the civic community appeared as a bounded world of reciprocal relations—of harmonies and correspondences—not of absolutes. For, taken together, events like the celebration of the feasts of St. Clement and St. Katherine emphasized the social limitations on authority, not the sovereignty of those who exercised it. They focused on the membership of the mayor and his brethren in the commonalty of burgesses and freemen, and on the need for communal acceptance of their earthly rule.

The ceremonial practices we have just analyzed survived intact until the middle of the sixteenth century, but long before they disappeared there were signs that many Bristolians had come to doubt their efficacy. By the early fifteenth century, for example, most townsfolk had become indifferent to the great Corpus Christi processions, which had once been among the most popular religious celebrations and the preeminent

Fig. 4.   Robert Ricart's Plan of Bristol at Its Foundation. (Robert Ricart, *The Maire of Bristowe Is Kalendar,* Bristol Record Office, MS 04720 (1), f. 5. By permission of the City of Bristol Record Office.)

means of expressing the town's hierarchical organization and spiritual kinship.[43] Even Ricart's loving codification of the annual cycle of feast and ceremony may be a sign that some Bristolians—like Mayor William Spencer, who commissioned Ricart's book—thought their ancient customs needed to be preserved and reinforced among the civic elite. By the 1530s, moreover, the city had begun welcoming organized troupes of

players to the city to perform their entertainments indoors in the Guildhall for a small elite, competing with St. Katherine's players in both substance and form.[44]

But the old ceremonies themselves persisted into the era of Reformation. With the combined attack on popish "superstitions," religious orders, and chantries, however, the framework described by Ricart suffered permanent and irreversible change. In 1541 Henry VIII ordered
the abolition of the "many superstitious and chyldysh obseruances . . .
observed and kept . . . vpon Saint Nicholas, Saint Catherine, Saint
Clement, the Holy Innocents and such like."[45] Corpus Christi suffered
a similar fate, disappearing from the church calendar with the publication of the Edwardian prayer books.[46] Of course, deep religious divisions persisted in the city in the mid-sixteenth century, as Roger Edgeworth made clear in the sermons he delivered during this period of
upheaval.[47] At the same time, many tradition-minded laymen, including
the great Spanish merchant Robert Thorne, and such clergymen as
Edgeworth himself and Paul Bush, the Marian bishop in Bristol, still ardently upheld the old forms of piety.[48] But this cultural politics did not
extend its defense of customary practices to the excesses associated with
the old holidays and pastimes. Against the surge of Protestant reform,
the defenders of tradition in Bristol advanced their sober new vision of
devotion, which preserved the crosses and the images but condemned
the "gluttony" and "lechery" of traditional culture.[49] By Elizabeth I's
and James I's time, learned Protestant ministers such as Northbrooke,
Thomas Thompson, and Edward Chetwyn were striking even more vigorous hammer blows against idle pastimes and drunkenness. Under
these strictures, celebrations such as those that honored St. Katherine
and St. Clement stood utterly condemned for their depravity.[50]

Although many of Bristol's late medieval gilds, like St. Clement's and
St. Katherine's, survived the dissolution of the chantries into the later
sixteenth century and beyond, they did so as a result only of the reas-
signment of their properties for charitable purposes, not of the survival
of their old religious spirit.[51] At the same time, the feasts of St. Clement
and St. Katherine disappeared from the civic calendar. One reason for
the quick and relatively painless demise of the two saints' days is supplied by Henry VIII's attack on the church. With the dissolution of the
monasteries and the suppression of the religious orders in England,
the liberty of St. Augustine's Abbey, already under vigorous attack
by the city and the Crown in the 1490s,[52] ended in December 1539,
with the dissolution of the monastery. In 1541, when the Knights

Hospitallers were disbanded, the liberty of Temple Fee was also quashed.[53] These changes transformed the spiritual geography of Bristol. No longer did the civic map contain hot spots of great religious power but temporal pollution, where debtors could dodge creditors, illicit traders could keep open shops, and outlaws could flaunt their disregard of all just authority.[54] Now the command of the mayor and his brethren was efficacious in every quarter of the city, and every inhabitant, burgess and stranger, was subject to their rule. The city was freed from the potential for lawlessness and violence always inherent in the existence of the religious enclaves. In consequence, crossing the Frome into St. Augustine's or the Avon into Temple no longer had the political or social significance it once did. As these districts became legally integrated into the city's body politic, they became in a sense demystified. At the same time, the city achieved a new kind of religious unity, for in 1542 the property of St. Augustine's Abbey became the foundation of the diocese of Bristol, carved out of the old bishoprics of Worcester and Bath and Wells.[55] For the first time, Bristol was under one episcopal administration.

But along with these alterations in traditional church administration came deeper changes in the fabric of social life in Bristol, changes in the structure of authority and distribution of power that provide the wider context for the rituals we have been examining. These developments transformed the medieval community and robbed the ceremonies of their old efficacy. We have already studied the emergence of a new form of commercial community in Bristol as the city's economy shifted decisively away from France to focus on southern Europe and the Atlantic. By the mid-sixteenth century, control of overseas trade had fallen into the hands of a small and exceedingly tight-knit group of dealers. As the scale and internal organization of the merchant community changed, so too did its relations with the larger English economy. The city was no longer a restricted market in which all citizens had an equal opportunity to buy the goods of strangers. As we know, the common practice now was for outside dealers to have fixed contracts with particular Bristolians, using the old fairs and market hall not as places for free buying and selling but to meet regular customers or agents, settle accounts, and strike new bargains. From 1546, even the collection of tolls at the city gates had been abandoned, and in consequence the ancient distinction between strangers and citizens lost much of its economic and cultural force.[56]

Accompanying these changes were shifts in the social geography of the city. From wills and deeds we know a good deal about where the

leading men in Bristol resided in the fourteenth and early fifteenth centuries. For some of the richest citizens, such as the great Canynges family, the favored places were great stone mansions in Redcliffe and other
southern parishes where land was available for gardens and orchards.
Others preferred locations on the city wall, where stone towers made
imposing residences. And, of course, many lived in the city center, where
they enjoyed maximum command of the urban market.[57] Hence the
city's "better and more worthy" men were rather evenly distributed
through the neighborhoods. We can see this quite clearly by examining
the residences of the city's common councillors at this time. We know
the names of the forty-two councillors in 1381 and of fourteen others
added between that date and 1409; of these, the residences of thirty-
eight can be established. Twenty lived in the central city, and eighteen
in the three parishes east and south of the Avon.[58] On St. Katherine's
Eve in the late fourteenth century, therefore, the procession from the
Guildhall to Temple Church would have taken many Corporation
members back toward their homes and about equal numbers away from
them. And when St. Katherine's players went from door to door to perform for these men, they would have toured the whole town.

The same list of common councillors allows us to establish something of the occupational structure of the city's governing elite. Nearly
all its members, wherever they lived, engaged in overseas trade to some
degree. Most identified themselves as "merchants and drapers," and
many had properties both in the center and in the southern parishes.
They were entrepreneurs who organized the woolen industry and
traded its products in foreign markets without any differentiation of retail shopkeeping from wholesale trading or from the financing of cloth
production. At least two councillors seem to have been members of St.
Katherine's gild.[59] Given the close ties between mariners and merchants, we can assume that a number of councillors became members
of St. Clement's when it was founded in the 1440s. Hence intimate economic and social connections linked the members of Bristol's corporation and the members of the gilds of St. Clement and St. Katherine. In
this period, on the feast days of the two saints it was not a distant body
of strangers who came to the gild chapels but men with whom the gildsmen dealt week in and week out.

By the early sixteenth century much of this had changed radically.
Where the evidence for the late fourteenth century suggests an even distribution of wealth through the city, in the 1520s we find quite distinct
differences. According to statistics derived from the records of the subsidy in 1524, the center and portside parishes possessed 72 percent of

TABLE 18 GEOGRAPHICAL DISTRIBUTION OF WEALTH IN BRISTOL, 1524

Parishes / Mean Assessment	Assessments in £[a]	No. Assessed	%	Total Assessed Valuation (£-s-d)	%
Center and Portside / £12-10-00	101 +	11	1.93	2,040-00-00	28.63
	21 to 100	60	10.53	2,950-00-00	41.40
	6 to 20	122	21.40	1,369-00-00	19.21
	2 + to 5	85	14.91	325-04-00	4.56
	2	96	16.84	192-00-00	2.69
	1 to 2	196	34.39	249-05-00	3.50
Total		570		7,125-09-00	
Transpontine and Suburban / £5-13-04	101 +	3	0.62	430-00-00	15.56
	21 to 100	24	4.93	1,173-00-00	42.46
	6 to 20	48	9.86	475-13-04	17.22
	2 + to 5	52	10.68	193-13-04	7.01
	2	101	20.74	202-10-00	7.31
	1 to 2	259	53.18	288-10-00	10.44
Total		487		2,762-16-08	
City Total / £9-07-02	101 +	14	1.32	2,470-00-00	24.98
	21 to 100	84	7.95	4,123-00-00	41.70
	6 to 20	170	16.08	1,844-13-04	18.66
	2 + to 5	137	12.96	518-17-04	5.25
	2	197	18.64	392-00-00	3.98
	1 to 2	455	43.05	539-15-00	5.44
Total		1,057		9,888-05-08	

SOURCE: Public Record Office, E 179/113/192 (lay subsidy roll dated 10 January, 15 Hen. VIII). For purposes of analysis the city's parishes have been divided as follows: Center: All Saints; Christ Church; St. Ewen; St. John; St. Lawrence; St. Leonard; St. Mary-le-Port; St. Peter; St. Werburgh. Portside: St. Nicholas; St. Stephen. Transpontine: St. Mary, Redcliffe; St. Thomas; Temple. Suburban: St. Augustine; St. James; St. Michael; SS. Philip and Jacob.

[a]The subsidy statute covering this assessment, Stat. Realm 14 & 15 Hen. VIII c. 16, provided that individuals would pay on land, on goods valued 40 s. or more, or on wages of 20 s. and up. Almost everyone in Bristol paid either on goods or wages. Hence I have converted the few valuations on land to their equivalents in goods or wages, which together were taxed according to a different scale. In a number of instances the Bristol assessors recorded individuals paying on less than 40 s. on goods, which appears to have violated the statute. I have assumed that this is merely a clerical error and that all assessments under 40 s. were for wages. Those explicitly designated as having been assessed on wages break down by district as follows: center, 85; portside, 21; transpontine, 45; suburban, 63; city total, 214.

the city's taxable wealth, although during the second quarter of the sixteenth century only about 48 percent of the city's population resided there (Table 18).[60] In this district now dwelled Bristol's richest inhabitants, as well as a large number of middling types. Although a number of wage earners also lived there, they were concentrated primarily in a few streets near the city's wharfs and the butchers' shambles. Not only did the suburban districts to the north of the Frome and to the east of the Castle and in the transpontine district to the south of the Avon contain fewer wealthy residents, but those who did live there possessed smaller holdings than their counterparts in the center, and in place of the middling men we find larger numbers of individuals living on wages.

Evidence derived from the subsidy records from 1545 and other documents from this period gives us a more detailed view of the geographical distribution of occupations. The picture is of a city in which overseas merchants, rich retailers such as grocers, mercers, and drapers, and small shopkeepers such as shoemakers and tailors dominated the city's center, while large-scale manufacturers such as clothiers, brewers, and tanners lived in the outdistricts, along with small artisans such as weavers and wiredrawers and servants and wage-earning employees; the leather and brewing industries were located to the north of the Frome and the cloth industry to the south of the Avon. Overseas trade accounted for the richest citizens, although the retailing of luxuries and the manufacture of leather also produced significant numbers of wealthy men (Table 19). Since the Corporation drew its membership only from among the city's "better and more worthy men," it was now made up primarily of figures drawn from these sectors of the economy, not from the textile industries. Patterns of residence among the Corporation members also changed. Nearly all of them now lived near the Guildhall in the city center or in the two immediately adjoining portside parishes. There was almost no participation by those dwelling in the clothmaking district across the Avon or in the other outparishes.

In the midst of these developments Bristol's civic constitution also changed, in a manner that reinforced the building relationship between the community and the wider world and further broke down the old fabric of self-enclosed communal life. In 1499, Henry VII confirmed Bristol's liberties and immunities but altered the structure of its governing body, primarily by creating a bench of aldermen. The mayor and aldermen received designation as justices of the peace, which brought the city into conformity with the national system of administration then emerging in the counties. At the same time, the recorder—usually an

TABLE 19 SOCIAL GEOGRAPHY OF BRISTOL, 1545

Occupations	Center	Portside	Trans-pontine	Suburban	City Total	Mean Assessment in £
Male householders						
A. Leading entrepreneurs:						
Merchants	38	27	1	1	67	25.70
Major retailers						
draper	5	14			19	19.47
fishmonger	4				4	7.00
grocer, apothecary	21	1	2		24	19.81
haberdasher	2	1			3	16.67
innkeeper, vintner	5	1	4		10	16.60
mercer	9	2			11	27.75
Subtotal	46	19	6		71	19.64
Soapmakers	3	1	3		7	14.86
Total A	87	47	10	1	145	22.21
B. Textile production:						
Clothier	1	1			2	5.50
Dyer			5		5	9.80
Sherman			8		8	6.25
Tucker			8		8	11.17
Weaver			5		5	6.40
Total B	1	1	26		28	8.26
C. Leather production:						
Currier	1		2		3	9.33
Skinner	5				5	12.20
Tanner	2	1		10	13	25.62
Whitawer	4		1	7	12	15.08
Total C	12	1	3	17	33	18.27

D. Clothing production:					Total	
Capper	2		3	5		9.00
Glover, purser	4			4		9.25
Hosier	2			2		6.50
Pointmaker	1			1		12.00
Saddler	1			1		5.00
Shoemaker	5		3	8		6.75
Tailor	11	6	3	20		9.43
Upholsterer			1	1		17.00
Total D	26	6	10	42		8.85
E. Metal crafts:						
Bellfounder	1			1		5.00
Cardmaker	1		1	2		7.50
Pewterer		2	1	3		19.67
Smith	2		1	3		9.67
Wiredrawer	1		2	3		11.33
Total E	5	2	3	2	12	11.83
F. Food production:						
Baker	5	1	2	1	9	12.89
Brewer	1	2	1	5	9	13.59
Butcher	4			1	5	19.20
Total F	10	3	3	7	23	14.54

(continued)

TABLE 19 (continued)

Occupations	Center	Portside	Trans-pontine	Suburban	City Total	Mean Assessment in £
G. Shipping industry:						
Hooper, cofferer	2	8			10	11.63
Mariner, ship's captain		2			2	11.50
Ropemaker		4			4	13.58
Ship's carpenter		1			1	12.00
Total G	2	15			17	12.10
H. Professional, etc.:						
Attorney, lawyer	2				2	12.00
Barber			2		2	7.00
Clerk			1		1	30.00
Government official			1		1	19.33
Scrivener		1	1		2	10.50
Stationer	1				1	5.00
Surgeon		1			1	7.00
Total H	3	2	5		10	12.03
I. Miscellaneous:	3		3		6	6.17
Total known A–I	149	77	63	27	316	16.66
Total unknown A–I	22	8	13	6	49	13.09
Total male householders	171	85	76	33	365	16.18
Female householders	13	4	4		21	25.18
Servants	3		1	2	6	2.69
Grand Total	187	89	81	35	392	16.46
Mean Assessment in £	18.17	18.10	9.98	18.64	16.46	

SOURCE: Public Record Office, E 179/114/269 (lay subsidy roll dated 4 March, 37 Hen. VIII). The districts are defined as in Table 18.

up-and-coming London lawyer—became fully integrated into town government as one of the aldermen. His presence was required at gaol delivery, of which the mayor and aldermen were now to be justices. Since the mayor also served as one of the two justices of assize, the civic body was formally bound into the judicial and administrative structure of the nation. This meant that the status and power of the leading men in town government were increased, whether they were acting at any given moment as royal or as purely local officials. It also meant that the Crown, through the mayor and aldermen, now had a direct and continuous link to the city government upon which both the city and the Privy Council could rely.[61]

Occasionally the tensions inherent in these new political and social arrangements flared into open conflict. For example, in the disputes that arose in 1543 over the existence of the Candlemas fair in the parish of St. Mary, Redcliffe, the opposing parties reflect almost exactly the new geographical and sociological divisions we have been discussing. The supporters of the fair were primarily artisans resident in the city's outdistricts, most from south of the Avon and a few from north of the Frome. Its critics, who supported the city government's Star Chamber suit to quash the fair, came from the central district, and especially from the richest and most powerful groups living there, the great merchants and the major retailers.[62] As a result, the city's social divisions, which the old festivals had sought to overcome in favor of unity and harmony in communal life, now seem to have become wounds in the body politic.

The development of Bristol's economy in the later fifteenth and early sixteenth centuries had made it increasingly difficult for the old festivals to mark the community's separation from the wider world and to reinforce its internal order. Mervyn James has sought to explain a similar transition by referring to the ways that the sixteenth century "progressively upset" the "social and political balance" of the late medieval urban community. "The degree of impoverishment of gild organizations," he says,

> the pauperization of town populations, the changing character and role of town societies, increasing government support of urban oligarchies were all factors tending toward urban authoritarianism. As a result urban ritual . . . no longer served a useful purpose; and [was] indeed increasingly seen as potentially disruptive of the kind of civil order which the magistracy existed to impose.[63]

This interpretation suggests that the members of a strident, secularized urban elite in the end forced their new views of the social world on their social inferiors. But it seems clear that in Bristol the ruled as well as the rulers no longer found the ancient ceremonies acceptable or efficacious, with the former perhaps preceding the latter to this conclusion.

Late medieval Bristol was one of England's great centers of Lollardy, which anticipated many of the ideas of early Protestantism. Indeed, the presence of Lollards there in the early fifteenth century was sufficiently important that Robert Londe, schoolmaster at New Gate in Bristol, made them the subject of one of his *vulgaria*, designed to teach his young charges the finer points of Latin grammar and syntax through the use of socially and culturally relevant materials.[64] In its early years the movement in Bristol had a large clerical leadership headed by John Purvey, Wycliffe's companion during his last days. The city even supplied six chaplains to Sir Thomas Oldcastle's army on St. Giles Field in 1414. But from the outset the movement also enjoyed significant lay support in Bristol. Along with the six chaplains at St. Giles Field, for example, came forty other townsmen, the largest contingent of supporters from a single community in the Lollard army in this rebellion. Most of these men were weavers from the three southern parishes of the town. Moreover, despite the persecution of this group and of other Bristol Lollards in the fifteenth century, Lollardy had too strong a hold in the city to be eliminated. Throughout this century and into the next, ecclesiastical authorities continued to uncover groups of heretics professing Lollard beliefs. Like those who went to join Oldcastle, these men and women came primarily from the cloth industry, and from the city's southern parishes; most were weavers.[65]

The connection between the cloth industry and Lollardy in Bristol draws us again into the world of the cloth gilds. In late medieval Bristol, these bodies were not only fraternities of craftsmen, organized in a fellowship of common interests for the protection and regulation of their mystery, but brotherhoods of the faithful, united in the name of their patron saint for prayer and for honoring the dead. Moreover, their seemingly distinct functions were inextricably intertwined. Gildsmen were expected to come to the general processions of their fellowship on Corpus Christi and on feast days, to support the gild's chapel if it had one, and even to make payment of fines for violating the economic regulations of their craft in wax, for the maintenance of their saint's candle.[66]

Under these conditions, resistance to the economic policies reinforced by the gilds could hardly help taking a religious form among
many of the disaffected. Here the doctrines of Wycliffe and the Lollards
offered an especially potent weapon. Wycliffe's emphasis on the authority of the Bible, his rejection of transubstantiation, his stress on predes-
tination, and his criticism of the doctrine of penance and its liturgy all
were important elements in the beliefs of his followers.[67] But among the
laity, especially after Oldcastle's defeat, particular attention was paid to
his rejection of the Real Presence and of the veneration of saints. In Bristol this focus was especially strong. Again and again its Lollards crudely
attacked the main beliefs and practices of late medieval Catholic piety.
They complained against worship in Latin, and they argued that "the
sacrament of thalter is not the very body of our lorde but material
brede." But most of all they professed hostility to the saints, claiming
that prayer should be made directly to God, not through holy interces-
sors, offerings to whose images were damnable.[68] But if religious obser-
vance was but the obverse of economic regulation in the life of the gilds,
an attack on prayers for the dead, the veneration of saints, and the honoring of holy images such as the Bristol Lollards had mounted became
at the same time an attack on the governing institutions of the domestic
economy, the gild leadership, and the city government that supported it.
Many of these Bristolians must have found Wycliffe's harsh criticisms of
the craft gilds congenial to their views.[69]

A series of ordinances of 1419 exemplify this combination of religion
and economics. In that year, coming at the height of official reaction to
Bristol Lollardy, the four Masters of the weavers' gild petitioned the
mayor and the Common Council for new ordinances. They complained
that their own authority "had been greatly and grievously vexed" by violators of the weavers' ordinances, "because they had not the same ordinances" under the common seal of the town. They desired, therefore, to
have the old ordinances, with their mix of economic and religious precepts, confirmed under the city's seal, a request to which the city government readily agreed.[70] Clearly a strong challenge to gild rule had been
mounted. At the same time, two other ordinances, even more revealing
in their nature, were also passed. These required, first, that all the masters and servants of the craft "come to the general processions and to
the other precepts of the Mayor" and, second, that they "shall be con-
tributors to all kinds of costs and expenses which shall be incurred . . .
on their light and torches against the feasts of Corpus Christi" and the

midsummer vigils.[71] The breakdown of gild authority in this period thus affected both its secular and its spiritual aspects.

Lollard rejection of gild practices was the most extreme form of opposition to the system of gild regulation in force in late medieval Bristol. However, because gild ordinances often advanced some economic interests against others, there were also many other reasons for criticism and resistance to them. Unfortunately, we have no way of knowing for certain when we should attribute such troubles within the gilds primarily to the Lollards, although we know the names and beliefs of many of Wycliffe's adherents in the city. But there can be no doubt that resistance to gild governance based on many of the same grievances the Lollards complained about persisted among the weavers until well into the fifteenth century. In 1463, for example, the "pore artificers" of the gild complained that the four Masters annually elected by the livery put the "poure Craftymen daily to grete iniuries wronges and importable fynes the which fynes . . . is not hadd to the sokour and Comyne weele of the seide crafte but only to a synguler avayle of the seid Maisters and their owne Purs." The fines in question, of course, went not into the Masters' own pockets but to the support of the gild's activities: the hall, the chapel, the processions, the gild dinner on St. Katherine's Eve, and the like. To resist the fines was to leave these gild traditions, spiritual as well as temporal, without proper enforcement, or possibly even to reject them outright. The main remedy the commons requested from the Bristol Corporation is also revealing, for they argued that the Masters were chosen "yerely notte by the will and assent of the hoole crafte but by the xii men" of the livery "sucche as they wolle call thayme self whereof we byseeke yow that they may be choszen by the hoole body of the crafte."[72] They desired a restoration of the gild's old constitution, under which all had united in common effort. A gulf had opened between the views of the gild elite and its commoners, a gulf characterized by the view that the elite no longer ruled for the common good but only for their own benefit.

These difficulties among the weavers are evidence of disaffection in their ranks in the mid-fifteenth century, not of heresy. They were not necessarily caused by the Lollards, although Lollard activity persisted among weavers and other clothworkers during this period and after.[73] Nevertheless, signs of resistance to gild practices reveal a general cultural or moral malaise in the cloth industry, a sense that the old ways no longer had significance for current problems. This mood may have resulted, in part at least, from the shifting nature of woolen manufacture in later fourteenth- and early fifteenth-century Bristol. As country clothmaking grew, more and more of the cloth woven within the city seems to have been of much cheaper quality than had been the case a century before.[74] Probably the number of Bristol weavers also declined, though, judging from the frequent mention of weavers among the sixteenth-century burgesses, they seem to have declined more in wealth than in total numbers.[75] These changes would have made it increasingly difficult for the weavers to maintain their former gild practices, either in the vigorous supervision of ordinances or in the dutiful performance of rituals. But economic distress by itself cannot explain the weavers' apparent indifference to or rejection of their gild's traditional religious practices. One might expect that, if the gildsmen's faith in their traditions had remained strong, under these troubled economic conditions they would seek solace, protection, and guidance from their processions, their vigils, and their lights. However, many of the weavers chose a different course. Rather than drawing together under the name and effigy of their patron saint, they strayed from the community and the discipline of their gild.

Thus, about the same time that St. Katherine's festival had acquired the form that Ricart describes, or soon thereafter, a significant group of weavers, her earthly clients, not themselves a part of the gild leadership, had tired of its religious foundations. Some had even rejected them outright, though their masters and social betters still supported them. Similarly the town's leaders remained faithful in the fifteenth century to the celebration of Corpus Christi, when lesser men not only among the weavers but in other gilds such as the shoemakers had lost their enthusiasm for it. Already in the 1420s punitive ordinances existed requiring participation in the great procession which once had been so overwhelmingly popular.[76]

By the 1530s this rejection of the cult of the saints was very general in Bristol. The theme was struck almost at the very outset of the Reformation by Hugh Latimer, who won the support of large numbers of leading townsmen, both in the Common Council and out, when he preached in Lent 1533. In these extremely popular sermons he lashed out particularly against the old Lollard target, the idolatrous worship of saints, which Latimer saw all around him:

> I said this word "saints" is diversely taken of the vulgar people: images of saints are called saints and inhabitors of heaven are called saints. Now by honouring of saints is meant praying to saints. Take honouring so, and images so, saints are not to be honoured: that is to say, dead images are not to

be prayed unto, for they have neither ears to hear withal, nor tongues to
speak withal, nor heart to think withal &c. They can neither help me nor
mine ox, neither my head nor my tooth, nor work any miracles for me more
than another.[77]

Such views carry with them large social and political as well as philosophical and religious implications. Although they do not necessarily
preclude adherence to some principles of Catholic belief or lead directly
to radical Protestantism, they reject a regime as well as a liturgy. They
show that many Bristolians, like the disaffected weavers of the fifteenth
century, no longer found meaning in some of the most important rituals
around which they had organized their public and private lives.

Within a few short years, moreover, these reformist views were put
into action all over the city. "[A]t the dissolucion of Monasteries and of
Freers houses," we are told by Roger Edgeworth,

> many Images haue bene caryed abrode, and gyuen to children to play wyth
> all. And when the chyldren haue theym in theyre handes, dauncynge theim
> after their childyshe maner, commeth the father or the mother and saythe:
> What nasse, what haste thou there? the child aunsweareth (as she is taught)
> I haue here myne ydoll, the father laugheth and maketh a gaye game at it.
> So saithe the mother to an other, Iugge, or Thommye, where haddest thou
> that pretye Idoll? John our parishe clarke gaue it me, saith the childe, and
> for that the clarke muste haue thankes, and shall lacke no good chere.[78]

Although Edgeworth greatly lamented this desecration of images and
fought desperately against it, he could do little to restore the faith many
Bristolians once had in them. The most solemn devotions had taken on
the character of childish things.[79]

⁓⊱⋇⊰⁓

Among the possible explanations for this decline in the traditions of late
medieval piety, the history we have been recounting suggests an association with two quite closely related changes in social setting: first, the
rise of regional or national or international networks of trade and industry, which undermined an individual's sense of participation in a
self-enclosed economic world; and, second, the growth of social strati-
fication in urban society, which by driving a wedge between the rich
and powerful, on the one hand, and the mere craftsmen and small shopkeepers, on the other, made it difficult for many to think of themselves
as brothers and sisters in a fellowship of common purposes and interests. The great civic ceremonies of the later Middle Ages emphasized the

inherent unity of city life under its apparent diversity, but they could have meaning only within certain limits. As the horizons of economic activity opened and social distances grew, the members of the community must have found it increasingly difficult to conceive of Bristol as a world unto itself. For these citizens the town had opened to the larger world, which penetrated the community and reshaped it. Hence the ceremonies that once had marked the community's separation from its surroundings and unified its structure became archaisms. Like antiquated words or phrases, they had lost their context and therefore passed from use.

CHAPTER 5

The Sanctification
of Power

We have been arguing throughout this book that an early modern English town, unlike the great city-states of the ancient world or of Renaissance Italy, was not self-sufficient. It was, rather, a legal and political unit within the larger order of the realm, defined by privileges and immunities that granted it only a modicum of self-government under royal command and that enabled it only partially and intermittently to regulate and contain the social and economic processes upon which its way of life depended. Where Aristotle's Athens or Dante's Florence, with their independent governments, diverse social structures, and wide hinterlands, had plausible claims as autonomous communities capable of satisfying within their own boundaries most of the earthly hopes and wants of their members, Tudor and Stuart London or Bristol were but parts of an interlocking web of urban and rural places that no one believed could stand on their own. What held each of them together was its corporate existence and sense of community, which separated the freemen from their surroundings and gave them a unity and a capacity for collective action they otherwise would not have possessed. This capacity in turn depended on the ability of each city's governors to convert their authority into actions in the interest of the urban community.

We know with some accuracy who among the Bristolians could claim authority in the city from the end of the fifteenth to the middle of the seventeenth century. At the head, of course, were the forty-three members of the civic body: the mayor, recorder, aldermen, sheriffs, and common councillors, all of whom had been co-opted into this duty by their predecessors. The governing group of the city also included the paid assistants of the Corporation, such as the chamberlain, the town clerk, and the sergeants-at-mace, as well as the officers of the gilds—the master, wardens, assistants, and so on—and of the parishes—the church-wardens, vestrymen, overseers of the poor, constables, and the like. Hence, in a city of ten to twelve thousand souls, of whom perhaps as many as a sixth or even a fifth were free burgesses, the proportion of citizens who shared in rule at one time or another during their lives was relatively high. At any given moment, something like 10 percent of them might have held one or another of these positions.[1] However, as with so much else in the history of this period, we know far more of the membership of the elite, who consistently left marks in the surviving municipal records, than about the lesser figures in the urban hierarchy. Nevertheless, the impression we derive from the existing sources is very much in keeping with Sir Thomas Smith's depiction of urban political sociology in his *De Republica Anglorum,* first published in 1583. According to Smith, it was not only wealthy and independent citizens who exercised the authority of municipal office and bore its charges, but for default of sufficient numbers of them even "Taylors, Shoomakers, Carpenters, Brickmakers, Bricklayers, Masons" and other artificers might share in rule in the towns, sitting on "enquests and Juries" or being "Commonly made Churchwardens, alecunners, and manie times Constables."[2] Bristol could not have conducted its daily affairs without such assistance.

Wide participation in local governance was an important feature of social and political life in Bristol, one that gave considerable substance to the ideals of communal fellowship and common duty that traditionally had been manifested in the city's festivals and that still were conveyed in the oaths taken by every freeman. But here, as everywhere in English society, only a handful of individuals, in Bristol's case primarily the members of the Bristol Corporation, exercised genuinely large powers in shouldering the burdens of service to the commonwealth. This elite, the very top of the city's social hierarchy, not only occupied the principal municipal offices but held the leading posts in gild and parish as well. For example, the right fell to them, as members of the Common Council, to impose economic regulations on citizens and strangers, to administer those regulations, and to levy and collect taxes to pay for municipal government. With the Reformation, these same individuals took on added religious duties, among which were those of appointing the chaplain in the Mayor's Chapel and the minister in Temple Church and arranging for and selecting weekly lecturers to provide theological edification and moral guidance to the populace.[3] This role became even more important after 1627, when Bristol's government acquired the advowson of seven of its eighteen parishes.[4] To a degree perhaps not reached again until the creation of the welfare state, they oversaw the lives of the citizenry from the cradle to the grave. The governance of Bristol generally followed the pattern in the nation at large: the exercise of rule depended on the participation and tacit consent of the ruled, but the duty of government belonged to an exclusive group who alone enjoyed the legal authority to administer and judge. Fortunately, our evidence allows us to take a close look at the changing social makeup of this body under the Tudors and early Stuarts.

Throughout Bristol's premodern history, the acquisition of public office by its citizens was a direct outgrowth of their economic and social success. If a man accumulated riches, he was expected to accept the burdens of borough government, bearing from his own funds, if necessary, a portion of the financial charges. Refusals to serve were met by heavy fines. The expenses of office could sometimes be very large, as William Dale discovered when he served as sheriff in 1518, but this made it all the more essential for wealthy men to undertake responsibility for local administration. By the charter, membership in the central governing body, the Common Council, was vested in "the better and more worthy men" of the town, who in 1635 were said to consist of those freemen possessed of at least £1,500 in goods and credit.[5]

This application of an economic standard for public office meant, however, that the composition of the Common Council tended to reflect the distribution of wealth in Bristol. Although some eligible freemen would inevitably fail to be elected, the leading occupations in the city were likely to be represented roughly in proportion to their socioeconomic weight in the community at large, for otherwise the political domination of a particular group might lead to the economic ruin of its members. Hence as the patterns of social mobility altered and the social organization became transformed, the structure of civic politics also tended to change. By the early sixteenth century, as we know, the economic changes Bristol had experienced in the wake of the loss of Bordeaux were already apparent in the new social geography of the city, with the common councillors now concentrated in the city center. We can develop this picture further by looking at municipal election results for the sixteenth and early seventeenth centuries.

Bristol's new charter of 1499 authorized the mayor then in office, Nicholas Browne, and two aldermen nominated by him to name the new group of Corporation members, which assured that the new body would be amenable to the spirit of hierarchy evident throughout the charter.[6] Thereafter, the system of election was co-optative. Vacancies in the Common Council were filled by vote of the remaining members of the body, who chose between two candidates for each position, one nominated by the mayor and one nominated at large. Because only a limited number of citizens were wealthy enough to serve, however, the same candidates tended to reappear from election to election until they eventually were chosen and sworn. They did not always do so willingly; some preferred to pay heavy fines rather than accept the time-consuming burdens and indeterminate expenses of municipal office. Occasionally coercion was used to dragoon a reluctant individual into service, as when Luke Hodges, grocer, was threatened with a £200 penalty for his refusal.[7] But Common Council membership also had its rewards, since this body exercised considerable power, especially in economic regulation. As a result there was always a tension in the electoral process as the councillors tried to insure that no one who could bear office would escape, but tended to seek friends and supporters for their own points of view. The outcome was a body that was never overwhelmed by a single faction but was always controlled by a majority who held common views on the key issues of the day.

The exact membership of the Common Council is unknown for most of the sixteenth century, but it can be reconstructed almost in its entirety by using the names of the sheriffs elected each year during the period. Because these officials were responsible for, among other duties, that of collecting and paying the city's fee farm, the office was a very burdensome and costly one to hold. New members of the council usually were chosen as sheriff as a kind of entry fee or tax soon after joining the body; normally they held the post just once. A few refused to serve, and some were passed over, but in practice nearly all the common councillors held the office at one time or another during their municipal careers. By the terms of the 1499 charter, two sheriffs were elected each year, with vacancies created by death filled during the year. Between 1500 and 1600, two hundred and two Bristolians were elected to the office, which almost certainly represents more than 90 percent of the council's membership during this period. What bias there is favors the wealthiest councillors, since these men would have been the least likely to have been passed over or to have refused to serve.[8]

The occupations of one hundred and eighty-three of Bristol's sixteenth-century sheriffs are known. For the whole century, almost 80 percent were either overseas merchants or major retailers or soapmakers, and this proportion was on the increase—under 70 percent in the first fifty years, over 85 percent in the second. Among the grocers, drapers, mercers, and vintners, moreover, many would have abandoned their retail shops to deal exclusively by wholesale as "mere merchants." After 1550, the cappers, tuckers, whitawers, glovers, pointmakers, tanners, pewterers, smiths, and other artisans contributed much smaller numbers or disappeared entirely from the list. In particular, the participation of the once preeminent textile industries was minimal—just over 5 percent (Table 20). In the late Middle Ages, as we know, councillors had come from a relatively undifferentiated body of shopkeeper-merchants, who bought and sold a great variety of wares by retail as well as wholesale. It is hard to escape the conclusion that after 1499 the Corporation, though apparently more diverse in the occupations represented among its membership, in fact was far more homogeneous in social makeup than it had been, and that it was becoming only more so in the course of the sixteenth century.

For the early seventeenth century, the council membership is known directly from the town clerk's minutes of its meetings. Between 1605 and 1642, when Civil War events disrupted the election procedures, one hundred and twenty-three Bristolians were chosen for service, including one who was elected, dismissed, and reelected. The occupation or status of one hundred and twenty of these men is known. The overall pattern is very similar to what we have just seen for the later sixteenth century. Over 80 percent came from among the city's leading entrepreneurs, with a third being major retailers. There was a small increase in the percentage of merchants at the expense of retailers and soapmakers. For this period we are also able to establish the connection of the council members to the Society of Merchant Venturers, which gives us a more precise idea of their economic interests. Seventy-one councillors, or nearly 60 percent, were associated with the Society during their careers. Sixty-two served at one time or another as its master, treasurer, or warden, an indication that their connections were close. Moreover, the dominance of the Merchant Venturers in the government was strengthening during the early seventeenth century. From 1605 to 1623, 57 per-

TABLE 20   OCCUPATIONS OF BRISTOL SHERIFFS, 1500–1600

	1500–1550		1550–1600		1500–1600	
	No.	%[a]	No.	%[a]	No.	%[a]
A. Leading entrepreneurs:						
Merchants	30	33.71	39	41.49	69	37.70
Major retailers						
apothecary, grocer	12	13.48	8	8.51	20	10.93
draper	6	6.74	15	15.96	21	11.48
fishmonger			1	1.06	1	0.55
haberdasher	4	4.49			4	2.19
mercer	7	7.87	9	9.57	16	8.74
vintner			2	2.13	2	1.09
Subtotal	29	32.58	35	37.23	64	34.97
Soapmakers, chandlers	2	2.25	7	7.45	9	4.92
Total A	61	68.54	81	86.17	142	77.60
B. Textile industries:						
Capper	2	2.25			2	1.09
Tailor			2	2.13	2	1.09
Tucker, clothier	3	3.37	1	1.06	4	2.19
Upholsterer			2	2.13	2	1.09
Total B	5	5.62	5	5.32	10	5.46
C. Leather industries:						
Shoemaker			1	1.06	1	0.55
Tanner	4	4.49	2	2.13	6	3.28
Whitawer, glover, pointmaker	5	5.62	1	1.06	6	3.28
Total C	9	10.11	4	4.26	13	7.10
D. Metal industries:						
Bellfounder	1	1.12			1	0.55
Cardmaker	1	1.12	1	1.06	2	1.09
Goldsmith			1	1.06	1	0.55
Pewterer	1	1.12			1	0.55
Smith	1	1.12			1	0.55
Total D	4	4.49	2	2.13	6	3.28
E. Woodworking:						
Hooper, cooper			1	1.06	1	0.55
F. Food production:						
Baker	2	2.25			2	1.09
Brewer	6	6.74	1	1.06	7	3.83
Total F	8	8.99	1	1.06	9	4.92
G. Professional and service trades:						
Scrivener	1	1.12			1	0.55
Tidewaiter	1	1.12			1	0.55
Total G	2	2.25			2	1.09
Total known A–G	89		94		183	
Total unknown A–G	13		6		19	
Grand Total	102		100		202	

SOURCE: William Adams, *Adams's Chronicle of Bristol*, ed. F. F. Fox (Bristol: J. W. Arrowsmith, 1910); A. E. Hudd, "Two Bristol Calendars," *Bristol and Gloucestershire Archaeological Society, Transactions* 19 (1894–95): 105–41.

[a] Percentage of total known for period.

TABLE 21   OCCUPATIONS OF MEMBERS OF
THE COMMON COUNCIL, 1605–1642

	No.	%[a]
A. Leading entrepreneurs:		
Merchants	56	46.67
Major retailers		
apothecary, grocer	7	5.83
draper	11	9.17
fishmonger	2	1.67
haberdasher	1	0.83
hardwareman	3	2.50
mercer	13	10.83
vintner, innholder	3	2.50
Subtotal	40	33.33
Soapmakers, chandlers	4	3.33
Total A	100	83.33
B. Textile industries:		
Clothier	5	4.17
C. Leather industries:		
Pointmaker	1	0.83
D. Metal industries:		
Cardmaker	1	0.83
Wiredrawer	1	0.83
Total D	2	1.67
E. Food production:		
Brewer	7	5.83
F. Gentlemen, yeomen	5	4.17
Total known A–F	120	—
Total unknown A–F	3	—
Grand Total	123	—

SOURCE: A. B. Beaven, *Bristol Lists: Municipal and Miscellaneous* (Bristol: T. D. Taylor, Sons and Hawkins, 1899).
[a] Percentage of total known for period.

cent of the new councillors were members of the Society; but from 1623 to the outbreak of the Civil War, the figure was 75 percent. These changes reflect the growing importance of the "mere merchants" in Bristol. As council vacancies fell open they were increasingly filled by Merchant Venturers (Table 21).[9]

A similar pattern is apparent among the mayors and aldermen, who as Bristol's justices of the peace were the dominant forces in local affairs. For the mayors a complete list of those holding the office is available from the high Middle Ages. Over the whole period from 1500 to 1642, between 70 and 80 percent of them were merchants, major retailers, or soapmakers, with the merchants once again representing the largest single share.[10] The figures are virtually the same for the aldermen in the early seventeenth century, when we can first establish an accurate list of their names. But since almost all of them eventually served as mayor, this similarity in proportion is only to be expected. For the early seventeenth century we can once again establish the affiliation of these men with the Merchant Venturers. Just over 60 percent of the mayors and just under 60 percent of the aldermen were members during their lifetimes. Again, the connection was strengthening in the early seventeenth century. Between 1605 and 1623, for example, just over half of the mayors were Merchant Venturers. In the following nineteen years the proportion rose to more than four out of five (Tables 22 and 23).

The Bristol Corporation was never intended to be a cross-section of civic society. Unlike the governing body of London, its membership was not even selected according to gild affiliation. It was, rather, an organization of the community's social and economic leaders, chosen primarily because their personal fortunes could bear the costs of service. It should occasion no surprise, therefore, that only a small portion of the city's trades and industries were represented among the mayors, aldermen, and common councillors and that the mercantile and industrial elite held the vast majority of the offices. Nor is it especially remarkable that this exclusivity was reinforced by a pattern of close personal relations among these men. Given the nature of trade and industry in this period, it is only to be expected that the richest citizens of Bristol would also have shared family ties, business associations, and close friendships. But for all the predictability of these facts, they are nonetheless important in understanding how Bristol was ruled in this period.

It is not possible to review all the significant personal connections that linked the members of the Common Council. There were undoubtedly many important ties that the extant evidence has not brought to light. Enough survives, however, to give a glimpse of the general pattern. During the early seventeenth century, almost 80 percent of the Corporation members were linked to at least one other councillor by a family tie or by personal dependency, and nearly 40 percent of this group were connected to more than one of their fellow councillors. The most common bonds were those of kinship, but apprenticeship also played a very large role. Between 1598 and 1642 almost 37 percent of the members of the Common Council were related to one another by blood or marriage and a further 30 percent were tied to one another as master and apprentice.[11] Many of the ties cut across occupational lines.

TABLE 22   OCCUPATIONS OF BRISTOL MAYORS, 1500–1642

	1500–1550		1550–1600		1600–1642	
	No.	%[a]	No.	%[a]	No.	%[a]
A. Leading entrepreneurs:						
Merchants	21	45.65	18	36.00	20	47.62
Major retailers						
apothecary, grocer	2	4.35	5	10.00	2	4.76
draper	4	8.70	7	14.00	2	4.76
fishmonger			1	2.00		
haberdasher	4	8.70				
hardwareman					1	2.38
mercer	2	4.35	4	8.00	7	16.67
vintner			2	4.00		
Subtotal	12	26.09	19	38.00	12	28.57
Soapmakers, chandlers			2	4.00	2	4.76
Total A	33	71.74	39	78.00	34	80.95
B. Textile industries:						
Tailor			1	2.00		
Tucker, clothier	1	2.17			3	7.14
Upholsterer			1	2.00		
Total B	1	2.17	2	4.00	3	7.14
C. Leather industries:						
Tanner	4	8.70	3	6.00		
Whitawer, glover, pointmaker	3	6.52	1	2.00		
Total C	7	15.22	4	8.00		
D. Metal industries:						
Bellfounder	1	2.17				
Cardmaker					1	2.38
Pewterer			2	4.00		
Total D	1	2.17	2	4.00	1	2.38
E. Food production:						
Baker	1	2.17				
Brewer	1	2.17	3	6.00	2	4.76
Total E	2	4.35	3	6.00	2	4.76
F. Gentlemen, yeomen	2	4.35			2	4.76
Total known A–F	46		50		42	
Total unknown A–F	7		0		1	
Grand Total	53		50		43	

SOURCE: William Adams, *Adams's Chronicle of Bristol*, ed. F. F. Fox (Bristol: J. W. Arrowsmith, 1910); A. E. Hudd, "Two Bristol Calendars," *Bristol and Gloucestershire Archaeological Society, Transactions* 19 (1894–95): 105–41; A. B. Beaven, *Bristol Lists: Municipal and Miscellaneous* (Bristol: T. D. Taylor, Sons, and Hawkins, 1899).
[a] Percentage of total known for period.

George White, for example, was apprenticed to Rice Jones, grocer, was the brother-in-law of William Barnes, clothier, and was the close friend and business associate of Henry Hobson, hardwareman, and Mathew

TABLE 23   OCCUPATIONS OF BRISTOL ALDERMEN, 1605–1642

	No.	%[a]
A. Leading entrepreneurs:		
Merchants	19	45.29
Major retailers		
apothecary, grocer	2	4.76
draper	3	7.14
hardwareman	1	2.38
mercer	6	14.29
vintner	1	2.38
Subtotal	13	30.95
Soapmakers, chandlers	2	4.76
Total A	34	80.95
B. Textile industries:		
Clothier	2	4.76
C. Metal industries:		
Cardmaker	1	2.38
D. Food production:		
Brewer	2	4.76
E. Yeomen	3	7.14
Total known A–E	42	
Total unknown A–E	1	
Grand Total	43	

SOURCE: A. B. Beaven, *Bristol Lists: Municipal and Miscellaneous* (Bristol: T. D. Taylor, Sons, and Hawkins, 1899).
[a] Percentage of total known for period.

Warren, clothier.[12] But connections were most commonly related to the members' economic positions. This meant that personal relationships among the councillors tended to reinforce the differences among the various occupational groups on the council, with many of the older generation of masters relying on their sons and former apprentices to support their points of view on key issues.

Hence the possibility of deep factional division existed within the Corporation and, as we shall see in the next chapter, it was made manifest in fierce disputes that erupted at various times in the Elizabethan and early Stuart periods. But despite the strong potential for political faction in the city, the proceedings of the Common Council were usually free of political strife. Most decisions were reached by consensus, not majority vote, with the more difficult matters referred to committees for preliminary discussion and possible resolution. Election to high city office also showed few signs of bitter division. Because the offices at stake were costly to hold, a practice of rotation was followed by which nearly every member was selected as he became eligible and few served more than once in any particular post. Even more important were the demands for political harmony imposed by the Corporation's role as the ruling authority in the city. Without the collective efforts of its members to maintain order, enforce the laws, ameliorate the city's economic and social ills, and exercise moral leadership over the general population, the fabric of urban community would have been rent by the same divisions that always lurked near the surface of politics in the Common Council. In other words, the fact that the Corporation held genuine authority within the city worked against the temptation for one group or another to use it to the detriment of some rival. Yet the advancement of particular interests and the pursuit of private benefits could never be entirely suppressed in a body so heavily dominated by one of them. This meant not only that conflict was inevitable but that the Corporation's role as the upholder of the common welfare required periodic justification and regular reinforcement. Before examining the actual processes of political engagement in Bristol between the beginning of the sixteenth century and the middle of the seventeenth, we should first explore the methods used to legitimate them.

Although we are reasonably certain of who exercised authority in Bristol, we are less clear about what it meant for them to do so and how their understanding of their roles might have changed during the reigns of the Tudors and the first two Stuarts. By any standard, authority is a deeply ambiguous concept.[13] It can refer in a variety of ways to rights. Someone in authority has the right to act and to be obeyed within his jurisdiction. He is at liberty to act, but he need not do so every time the opportunity arises. In terms of rights, authority is a legalistic concept, and we often speak of those holding it as having "legal" or "constitutional" authority. But "authority" can also refer in a variety of ways to capacities or powers. Someone who is exceptionally competent in a given realm is an authority: he has the power to produce results. Through his reputation for expertise he also has the title to be believed and the capacity to influence the opinions and judgments of others. In this way he exercises power over their conduct or action, and he is said to have "moral" authority. His authority not only enables him to act within his areas of competence, but imposes upon him the duty to do so. As an authority he has an obligation to perform right actions; he is not morally free to use his skills on some occasions and to withhold them on others.

For some purposes these two ideas complement one another. He who authorizes an action has a right; he who is authorized has a duty. The former works autonomously to perform as he chooses in the realm in which he is entitled to act. The latter works for the good or the interest of those who have granted him his power, and he must perform this service if he is to meet his obligation to them. This formulation, however, assumes that the fundamental unit of analysis is the individual and that the fundamental question is how individuals come to accept authority. It neglects the way the very concept of authority presupposes the existence of community. It is not enough to claim authority for oneself; it is also necessary that it be recognized by others according to some mutually agreed-upon rules. Otherwise, one is applying force, not exercising authority.[14]

The problem of community proves just as troubling as the problem of authority, since communities are not all of the same type. We can speak with equal clarity of linguistic communities, where large numbers of people residing in different countries share the same tongue, and academic communities, where small numbers working in the same institution pursue common goals in their various disciplines. But to modern social scientists and historians the term has come to distinguish tight-knit collectivities of people living in close proximity in village or town, separated from the larger society and the state. In keeping with this kind of understanding, it is often assumed that authority in a community is what Max Weber called "traditional authority," that is, authority that rests on "an established belief in the sanctity of immemorial traditions and the legitimacy of the status of those exercising authority under them." Here is where "moral authority" holds sway. Authority in a more broadly gauged modern society is what Weber called "legal authority," that is, authority that rests on "a belief in the 'legality' of patterns of normative rules and the right of those elevated to authority under such rules to issue commands."[15] In this interpretive scheme, the early modern period is often treated as the time when the second type of authority first took hold. It is widely considered to be the era that saw the rise of the bureaucratic state and that consequently produced the inevitable collisions between society and the state. But this new rational form of authority, the interpretation goes, did not succeed all at once. Instead it made itself felt initially only in certain advanced political settings, namely, the great cities of Italy and the courts of the great northern monarchs. The provinces, and especially the provincial towns, remained centers of the older, sanctified forms of authority, subject to the predatory challenges of power-mongering state officials.[16]

But no one living in an early modern English town could have made the distinctions between community and society or traditional and legal authority upon which such an interpretation depends. As used in modern scholarship, these are terms of art. They may help us locate ourselves amid the complexities we study, but they do so by obscuring the uncertainties and ambiguities with which contemporaries lived. They make it difficult to see how those who experienced the changes understood them. If we are to grasp this reality, we must turn our attention to the ways that ideas of authority were represented at the time. In the provincial towns authority was present at every turn, but on certain festive occasions—at the annual election of the mayor, for example—it received particular notice by the townsmen. Here ideas, so difficult to come by in words, were revealed .n gestures and actions.

In the late medieval era it was not possible to think of a community without also attending to the place of leadership within it. According to the common understanding, every social organism was a body politic in which head and members worked together for the common good. A community lacking a head was, like the human body on which it was modeled, either dead or an enormity. This theme was especially important in cities, since what held them together was their corporate existence, which in turn depended on the ability of their governors to act for the whole polity. Their governing powers required constant justification and continuous reinforcement. Not surprisingly, celebrations of authority became one of the great subjects of urban culture in the period. Embedded in them was a particular view of authority according to which the right to make decisions for the community depended on public recognition of the individual's worthiness for the task. The activities of St. Katherine's players in uniting the members of the city's most important craft with the officials of the Corporation was only one among the many ceremonial means addressing this issue.

In the fifteenth century, Bristol's government, established by Edward III's charter of 1373, was a self-perpetuating, closed institution of forty-two citizens. Its members were chosen by co-optation, and its chief officers, the mayor and a single sheriff, were elected exclusively from among its own membership. As described by Ricart, election proceedings began on St. Giles Day, 1 September, when the mayor's four sergeants officially warned the membership of the Common Council of the impending election. The election itself was held on 15 September, and failure to appear subjected each absent councillor to a fine of £10, very steep for the period. Candidates were nominated as well as chosen on 15 September, and each election was conceived to be a spontaneous judgment by the councillors about who was best suited to serve the city. The voting proper began with the current mayor "first by his reason" naming and giving "his voice to some whorshipfull man of the seide hows," that is, nominating and voting in the same motion. "[A]fter hym the Shiref, and so all the house perusid in the same, euery man to gyve his voice as shall please him." In theory, it was possible for each council member to nominate a new candidate, including himself, when his time came to give his voice. The victor was "hym that hathe moste voices." In fact, contests appear to have been exceedingly rare. But participation by the entire membership in this way helped to bind them in obedience to the new regime, since the councillors were much less free to criticize or oppose the new officers at a later date if they had played a part in selecting them. The vote of every member was to be based on the principles of spontaneity and openness. An election was the free choice of the assembled civic leadership made according to the community's highest ideals. Reason and good conscience were to be used to find the best person to serve the commonwealth for the coming year.[17]

Election to the mayoralty was a great honor in the city. In recognizing the worthiness of the man for this office of trust, it enhanced his social importance both by the deference that his fellow townsmen would now show him and by the opportunity his office gave to display his wealth to the city. The office was also a burden, requiring time away from personal business and the outlay of large sums to support the ceremonial requirements of officeholding. The mayor had little independent political power, however, since his freedom of action was restrained by the legal forms he was obliged to follow and by the council, which acted as a check upon his formulation of policy. Nevertheless, because the office brought enhanced status it carried political weight: status, especially when given official recognition, rewarded the recipient with greater influence in local affairs and brought his fellow townsmen to him for wise counsel.[18]

In the public presentation of the new mayor, all these considerations played a role. The process began at once. Having been in "due form electid," the successful candidate was to "rise fro[m] the place he sat in, and come sytt *a dextris* by the olde maires side," there to participate in subsequent deliberations. Once these "communications" had been completed, attention was turned to making the new mayor known to the town. With the adjournment of the election meeting, he was

worshipfully accompanyed, with . . . certein of the seid hous, home to
his place," in effect publicly announcing the election to all who observed this mayoral party pass through the streets.[19]

The official date for the new mayor's installation into office was
Michaelmas, 29 September, fully two weeks after the election. In the interval, Ricart tells us, "the seide persone so electid maire shalle haue his
leysour to make his purveyaunce of his worshipfull householde, and the
honourable apparailling of his mansion, in as plesaunt and goodly wise
as kan be devised." When his house was readied for the festivities to
come, the new mayor was to come to the Guildhall in a full-scale procession in which he took his proper place as the head of the government,
"accompanyd with the Shiref and all his brethern of the Counseill, to
feche him at his hows and bring him to the seide hall, in as solempne
and honourable wise as he can devise to do his oune worshippe." Since
the mayor was the head not only of the government but of the community, it was proper for him to enter office "to the honour, laude, and
preysyng" of all Bristol, whose inhabitants perforce witnessed the procession as it made its way through the streets.[20]

Because of the preeminence of the mayor in the civic hierarchy, the
ceremony at his inauguration was extremely rich in meaning and detail.
His formal installation into the seat of authority was accomplished only
after he had been reminded of his responsibilities to the borough community and sworn to his duties. Before administering the oath, the outgoing mayor made a speech to his brethren and the others assembled
that stressed the commonweal of the city and the maintenance of unity
among the citizens. According to Ricart, he apologized to his fellow
townsmen for any offense he might have given and offered to make
amends for his errors from his own goods or to "ask theym forgevenes
in as herty wyse" as he could, "trusting verilly in God they shal haue
no grete causes of ferther complaynts." If he could not heal all the
wounds that his government might have caused, the mayor continued,
the "worshipfulle man" chosen to be the new mayor "of his grete wise-
dome, by goddes grace, shal refourme and amende alle such thinges as
I of my sympileness haue not duely ne formably executed or fulfilled."
Finally, the outgoing mayor thanked his fellow citizens for their "gode-
ness" according to their "due merits" in showing "trewe obedience to
kepe the king our alther liege lorde is lawes, and my commaundment in
his name, at all tymes," and he prayed that God would reward them
with "moche joy, prosperitie and peas, as evir had comens and true
Cristen people."[21]

After the speaking of these significant words came the swearing-in of the new mayor (Figure 5). The oath, as it was taken in Ricart's time and with some small changes at least to the end of the sixteenth century, was preoccupied with the formal and specific tasks undertaken by the mayor that had been laid out in the city's charters.[22] Ricart shows the incoming mayor swearing on a book, almost certainly the Bible, held by the outgoing mayor; the common councillors sit or stand around the council table. A number of citizens appear at the periphery. The town clerk reads the oath, the swordbearer holds the cap and sword of justice, and an assistant holds the seal mentioned by Ricart. On the council table we see a large pouch (probably containing monies to be received into the new mayor's care), a scroll, and an account book. The room itself is decorated with the royal arms in the center, the Cross of St. George to the left, and the arms of the town of Bristol to the right. Standing at the "high deise" of the Guildhall, before his fellow common councillors and members of the "Comyns," the inauguree swore allegiance to the monarch to "kepe and meyntene the peas of the same toune with all my power." Under this authority he then promised to "reproue and chastice the misrewlers and mysdoers in the forsaid toune," to maintain the "fraunchises and free custumes whiche beth gode," to put away "all euell custumes and wronges," to "defende, the Wydowes and Orphans," and to "kepe, and meyntene all laudable ordinaunces." Most important, he also swore "trewely, and with right," to

> trete the people of my bailly, and do every man right, as well to the poer as to the riche, in that that longeth to me to do. And nouther for ghifte nor for loue, affeccion, promesse, nor for hate, I shall do no man wronge, nor destourbe no mannes right.[23]

In these clauses the mayor is viewed largely in his capacity as a judge. The underlying theme, even where the enforcement of municipal ordinances is concerned, is one of judiciousness and evenhandedness.[24] By the formula of the oath, the mayor's role within the city rests almost entirely on his position as the king's vicegerent in the city. This same emphasis is apparent at the conclusion of the oath. After kissing the book held for him by the outgoing mayor, the new mayor received from the hands of his predecessor the essential symbols of his office: the king's sword and the cap of justice, the casket containing the seal of his office as escheator, the seal of the Statute of the Staple, and the seal of the Statute Merchant, all signifying the judicial authority the mayor derived from the Crown.

When taken together with the outgoing mayor's speech, however, the inauguration conveys a more complex picture of the mayor's role.

Fig. 5. The Swearing of the New Mayor at Michaelmas in the Late Fifteenth Century. (Robert Ricart, *The Maire of Bristowe Is Kalendar*, Bristol Record Office, MS 04270 (1), f. 152. By permission of the City of Bristol Record Office.)

Although his authority derived from a royal grant, its base was local. He was the king's lieutenant in the city, but the borough's servant. As head of the community he could act as a buffer between the Crown and the city, protecting it from corrosive outside interference and permitting it the maximum autonomy by carrying out the king's business and maintaining peace in his name. The mayor's duty was, with the aid of the Holy Trinity, to keep the city "in prosperouse peas and felicite" and to preserve its internal solidarity by maintaining the social fabric against all damage, especially that caused by misgovernment.[25]

Along with the formal oath-taking, which renewed the bonds of authority, there were also informal proceedings which were intended to promote the internal solidarity of the civic body. The first of these festive events occurred immediately after the mayor had taken his oath. Once the symbols of office had been handed over to him, he immediately changed places with his predecessor and "all the whole company" brought "home the new Maire to his place, with trompetts and clareners, in as joyful, honourable, and solempne wise as can be devised . . . there to leve the new Maire, and then to bring home the olde Maire."[26] These honorific processions were followed by communal dinners, the majority of the council dining with the new mayor at his house and a smaller number, including all the officers, dining with the outgoing mayor. After they had eaten, "all the hole Counseille" assembled at the High Crosse, in the town center,

> and from thens the new maire and the olde maire, with alle the hole company, to walke honourably to Seint Mighels churche, and there to offre. And then to retorne to the new Maires hous, there to take cakebrede and wyne. And then, evey man taking his leeve of the Maire, and to retray home to their evensong.[27]

This ceremony repeated in a symbolic way the transfer of authority from the outgoing to the incoming mayor. First the council was divided to honor, some one man, some the other, by being his guests. The two mayors then jointly led a slow and stately procession uphill to St. Michael's Church. The mood seems to have been one of reluctant farewell to the outgoing mayor. But after the offering at St. Michael's the tone would have changed. The return to the town center, downhill, undoubtedly conveyed a lively spirit of energetic and joyful new beginning. To conclude the celebration, all were united at the new mayor's house, where they sealed the transition of power by sharing his cheerful hospitality.

The mayor's role as both the king's and the community's servant received special emphasis when royalty visited the city. Between 1461 and

1509 there were five such visits to the city, of which only Henry VII's in 1486 is documented in detail.[28] These rare events stressed Bristol's dual character as a legal corporation and a moral community. Although in planning each of these celebrations the Bristolians must have paid great attention to the monarch's tastes and views, they also had a chance to express their own outlook, since the arrangements were all made and financed by the citizenry themselves. Henry VII visited Bristol in 1486 on his progress through the realm to secure the loyalty and obedience of his kingdom's major cities after his victory at Bosworth Field.[29] Hence much attention was bound to have been paid to Bristol's subordination to royal authority. But the principal theme of the performances put on during his stay was, not the power of the king, but the corporate autonomy of the city.

The most important pageant took place amid "great Melodie and singing," immediately as the king passed through the town gate. Henry was accompanied there by "the Maire, Shriffe, the Bailiffs, and ther Brethern, and great Nomber of other Burgesses al on Horseback," who had ridden out of the town to greet him. "But the Mair of Bristow bar no mase, nor the Shrif . . . no rodde, unto the tyme they came to the gate . . . wher beginneth ther Fraunches." Here the mayor and the sheriff took up the symbols of their offices as the representatives of royal justice in the borough, in the process accentuating the boundaries of the community and their own authority within it.[30]

When the king had passed the gate and entered Bristol proper, he was greeted at once by a figure representing the legendary British "King Bremmius," according to tradition the founder of the city. Bremmius welcomed his "moost dere Cosine of England and Fraunce" to the town, thanking God highly on behalf of the Bristolians "for such a Soueraigne Lorde." But his main purpose was to ask Henry for assistance. "This Towne lefte I in greate prosperitie," he said,

> Havyng Riches and Welth many Folde;
> The Merchaunt, the Artyficer, ev'ryche in his Degre,
> Had great Plentye both of Silver and Golde,
> And lifed in Joye as they desire wolde,
> At my departing; but I have been so long away,
> That Bristow is fallen into Decaye
> Irrecuparable, withoute that a due Remedy
> By you, ther herts Hope and Comfort in this Distresse,
> Proveded bee, at your Leyser convenynetly,
> To your Navy and Cloth-making, wherby I gesse
> The Wele of this Town standeth in Sikerness,

> May be mayteigned, as they have bee
> In Days hertofore in Prosperitie.
>
> Now farwell, dere Cosyn, my Leve I take
> At you, that Wele of Bountie bee
> To your saide Subjects for Maries Sake,
> That bereth you ther Fidelitie.
> In moost loving wise graunte ye
> Some Remedye herin, and he wille quite your Mede,
> That never unrewarded leveth good Dede.[31]

This may seem no more than a straightforward petition for aid from the Crown, but the speech has another, more subtle dimension.[32] According to Geoffrey of Monmouth and his followers, King Bremmius, or Brennius as he is more frequently called, was one of the noble race of Trojans who ruled Britain after Brutus had conquered and settled the land. In one version of the story, made prominent in Bristol by Ricart's *Kalendar,* this Brennius is identified as the founder of Bristol, just as Brutus founded London and King Ebrancus founded York.[33] Since Henry Tudor himself claimed descent from the British kings,[34] King Bremmius gave Bristol a form of kinship tie to the new monarch which was of use in requesting assistance from him. At the same time, reference to the mythic founder helped avoid the worst implication of the petition—the apparent dependency of the borough community upon the royal will for its maintenance. Since Bristol was in existence from the first beginnings of the "British realm," the Bristolians seem to have been saying, its status could hardly depend on a later royal patent. Any special exemptions or privileges it received were offered, not by the king's mere motion and sovereign will, but as a moral obligation to preserve the noble work of his great and famous ancestor. As Bremmius says, he founded the city and "called it Bristow" after himself, "for a Memoriall," so that the British would never forget him.[35]

Along with advancing Bristol's claim on Henry for aid, this form of petition upheld Bristol's independent honor. It was clear in law that each of the city's liberties and franchises, including that of corporate status, required royal warrant. In this sense the borough community was founded by the royal will. But the existence of the borough, with its sworn membership and its reciprocal and interlocking social relationships, transcended this dependency, since its citizenry formed a moral community as well as a legal corporation. History was called upon to resolve this dilemma. Because the city was obviously the creation of men, it could not be thought a part of the natural landscape. It required a founder. But if the community was to preserve its independence, its foundation had to be set in the distant past. By stressing Bristol's antiquity, King Bremmius pointed not only to the borough community's continuity but also to its autonomy. Autonomy went hand in hand with unity. The city presented itself to the larger world as a single, integrated whole, existing independently of its surroundings.

As expressed in ceremony, the unity of late medieval Bristol was a living unity like that of the human body. The city was understood to be a highly structured organism whose parts worked together to preserve the well-being of its members. But to maintain this unity required constant vigilance, because there were always divisive interests, such as craft rivalries, ready to undermine the general welfare. Bristol's social and political rituals were aimed at purging the disruptive forces from the community and reinforcing the moral and spiritual foundations of the community by direct confrontation with the most vulnerable points in the social body.[36] The ceremonies and festivities at the annual inauguration of the mayor addressed only the yearly transfer of authority from one individual to another, a threatening and dangerous moment in the life of any body politic. It was also necessary, however, to deal with the even greater source of potential trouble, the fact that Bristol's public officials were also private men who might be tempted to put themselves or their families and friends above the common good. They needed to be reminded of their duties as servants to the community: hence the promises of fairness in the mayor's oath, and the presence of the Commons in the Guildhall to hear it.

On St. Michael's Day, however, the Commons played only a passive role, standing in the Guildhall outside the ring of councillors merely to witness the oath-taking, and thronging the streets to watch deferentially as the procession passed by. In other festivities they were more assertive, intervening to mock the civic authorities for their folly, to chastise them for their failures, and to instruct them in their duties. As we have already seen, this was probably the work of St. Katherine's players on 25 November. Similarly, at Christmas a Lord of Misrule issued satiric proclamations and ordinances endorsing licentiousness, approving disorder, and encouraging drunkenness, idleness, and other misdemeanors, thereby standing authority on its head and criticizing its shortcomings.[37] But the most intriguing of these celebrations is the festival of the Boy-Bishop.

Much of what we know of this popular custom relates to its use in cathedral chapters, university colleges, and schools such as Eton. At Salisbury Cathedral, for example, a young chorister was elected to serve in this mock-episcopal capacity from 6 December, St. Nicholas' Day, to Childermas, 28 December. According to the account given by a seventeenth-century antiquary, he was not only "to beare the name and hold up the state of a *Bishop* . . . habited with a *Crozier* . . . in his hand and a *Mitre* upon his head," but to perform everything the "very Bishop himself" did, except the mass. And "his fellows," a group of boy choristers, "were to take upon them the style and counterfeit of Prebends yielding to their Bishop . . . no less than canonical obedience." The Sarum use also provided elaborate processionals and services for the mock bishop, including his giving the sermon and benediction on Holy Innocents' Day.[38] But in Bristol the custom made the municipal authorities as much the focus of the occasion as the church hierarchy was. Ricart describes the festival as follows:

> [O]n Seynt Nicholas Eve . . . the Maire, and Shiref, and their brethern to walke to Seynt Nicholas churche, there to hire theire even-song: and on the morrow to hire theire masse, and offre, and hire the bishop's sermon, and have his blissyng; and after dyner, the seide Maire, Shiref and theire brethern, to assemble at the maires counter, there waytyng the Bishoppes comming; pleying the meane whiles at Dyce, the towne clerke to fynde theym Dyce, and to have I d. of every Raphill; and when the Bishop is come thedir, his chapell there to synge, and the bishope to geve them his blissyng, and then he and all his chapell to be serued there with brede and wyne. And so departe the Maire, Shiref, and theire brethern to hire the bishopes evesonge at Seynt Nicholas chirch.[39]

In most respects it appears that the authority of the Bristol Boy-Bishop corresponded quite closely to the usage at Salisbury. He had a chapter, gave sermons, offered benedictions, and sang evensong.[40] But his blessing of the civic body during its game of dice appears to be unique.

The role of the Boy-Bishop in this encounter is both satiric and didactic. Although the throwing of dice was a common pastime in the later Middle Ages, this form of gambling was also understood to be a pernicious vice, one that indicated the corruption of those who played at it. In Chaucer's *Canterbury Tales*, for example, dice-playing appears again and again as the symbol of folly and evil. The Pardoner speaks of it, together with drunkenness, as the "devels sacrifice"; the Franklin indicates that it is the very opposite of virtue and frugality; the Shipman shows it to be the negation of the merchant's craft. In "The Cookes Tale" it is portrayed as a form of sin which, along with dancing, lechery, and drunkenness, leads to idleness and theft.[41] These views were commonplaces of the moral teaching not only of Chaucer's time but for the three centuries following. According to Sir Thomas Elyot, writing in 1531, dice-playing was the devil's invention:

> For what better allective coulde Lucifer deuise to allure or bringe men pleasauntly in to damnable seruitude, than to purpose to them in fourme of a playe, his principall tresory; wherin the more parte of synne is contained, and all goodnesse and vertue confounded?[42]

The governor of the game of dice, of course, is Fortune, which by nature is changeable, alternately bringing good and bad to those who are at her mercy.[43] Accordingly, to play at dice is to abandon God's will and moral purpose to go over to mere chance. At the same time, it is to deny one's capacity to reason and to act. In the words of Elyot again,

> there is nat a more playne figure of idleness . . . For besides that, that therin is no maner of exercise for the body or mynde, they which do playe herat must seme to haue no portion of witte or kunnyng, if they will be called faire plaiars.[44]

In the Bristol Common Council this understanding of dice-playing took on added significance. By the city's charters, the principal duties of the councillors were, first, to establish competent ordinances "that shall be consonant with reason and useful for the commonalty," and, second, to levy local tallages and rates for common purposes and oversee their proper expenditure.[45] To sit at the mayor's counter throwing dice represents the absolute abandonment of these responsibilities. Where reason and prudence were supposed to prevail, we find chance and profligacy; where the councillors were supposed to act as the better and more worthy men of the community, we find them idly playing with no apparent regard to their standing. As Chaucer tells us,

> Hasard is verray mooder of lesyngs
> And of deceite and cursed forswearings
> Blaspheme of Crist, manslaughtre, and wast also
> Of catle and of tyme, and furthermo
> It is repreeve and contrarie of honour
> For to ben holde a common hasardour
> And ever the hyer he is of estaat
> The moore is he yholden desolaat
> If that a prince useth hasardry

> In all governaunce and policye
> He is, by commune opinioun
> Yholde the lasse in reputacioun[46]

The significance of the Boy-Bishop's visit to the Guildhall may perhaps be better understood by looking briefly at a surviving sermon of a Boy-Bishop given at St. Paul's, London, in the early 1490s. Beginning with the exhortation "Prayse ye childerne almyghty God," this sermon likens man in childhood to animal kind:

> A childe fyrste whan he is in his infant age is not contreyned unto no lawes; he is not corrected nother beten; and there is no defaute layde unto hym, but utterly he is lefte unto the lawe of kynde. Do he what somever he will no man doth blame hym. Morally the state of man immedyately after synne was verely the state of chilhode and infans hauinge no nouryce.

Adult life, of course, was to be just the opposite: under law, and subject to blame and punishment when it failed to obey. But if it fell under the control of the passions, it became childhood again. As the Boy-Bishop says,

> whan that man was utterly without ony expressyd lawe, havynge no mayster to his owne naturall inclynacyon as to his lawe, there was no lawe of God newe put to hym.

The message is double-sided. Quoting St. Paul in Corinthians, the young preacher says,

> Be not chylderne in your wyttes; but from all synne and malyce be ye childerne in clennesse. And in this fourme all maner of people and al maner of ages in clennese of lyf ought to be pure as childrine.[47]

Viewed in light of these remarks, the presence of the Boy-Bishop at the mayor's counter offers a telling commentary upon the dice game. The city fathers are shown to act without a child's cleanness but with his wit. They abandon themselves to the "lawe of kynde" and the whims of chance, being for the moment without a "nouryce or guyder." To them comes a child bishop, exercising a supremely adult authority and signifying the high purposes for which they were elected. In this way the festivity not only criticized the mayor and his brethren for their inevitable failings but purged them of their official sins. It also emphasized that the civic authorities served the community and thus were subject to the chastisement and the approbation of those they governed.

As we know from John Northbrooke, by the late sixteenth century the combined effects of religious revolution and economic change had

already profoundly transformed the cultural forms that Ricart had so
lovingly calendared. These same changes in outlook also took their toll
on the conception of political authority in Bristol. No longer was the
city conceived as a quasi-religious brotherhood, in which authority was
celebrated and legitimized at feasts and on holy days. Rather, the ideals
of godly rule, linking the authority of the local governors to the monarchy and from thence to God himself shaped the new conception of officeholding. Thomas Thompson, lecturing his Bristol congregation on
the virtues requisite of a magistrate, best articulates this viewpoint.
Government officials, he says, are to be

> such as are most perfect in knowledge, hence in conscience, and expert in
> practice. . . . But since all the praise of vertue is in action, we cannot make
> knowledge only the Magistrates complement: and therefore with those Intel-
> lectual abilities they must adioyne those morall vertues of *Fortitude* and *Ius-
> tice* . . . both to endure the troubles, looses and dangers of gouernment . . .
> in warres, and . . . in peace.[48]

A magistrate was expected to be a Christian exemplum of civic virtue,
not only living according to God's law and with the blessing of his
grace, but also endowed with a practical understanding of worldly affairs and the courage to use that understanding wisely and well.

There was no doubt that government service was considered a duty
for such a man. As Thompson says,

> it is not . . . for him to refuse it as either too base or troublesome, vnlesse hee
> will bee accounted either an idle, or a proud man . . . since hee is a member
> of that body politique which by all meanes hee must preserue, and since he
> must not hide what God hath giuen him for the benefit of the Common-
> wealth vnlesse he will partake of the punishment inflicted vpon the idle ser-
> uant, whose talent was given vnto another. For (as *Chrysostome* saith well)
> *hee that receiveth the grace of learning for the profit of others, and doth not
> use it, doth wholly loose that grace.*[49]

Thompson also makes clear that the principal responsibilities of city officers "were to keep order," without which there is "Anarchie, wherein
every man is kinge in his owne conceite, vndertaking what him list to
doe as when there was no King in Isreal." And, in proper fulfillment of
their judicial duties, they were to "both scatter the wicked, *and Iudge
the poore in truth.*"[50] Their failure to accept these responsibilities or
their neglect of them in their rule would only bring ruin to the commonwealth:

> For I pray you shall not all the body bee troubled, when the head is shaken
> asunder? As shall not the tree be subiect to falling, when the root is bared?

Some flatter the great men telling them, that they by reason of their wealth, and high estate neede not doe any thing else, but to live at ease, eat and drinke, and take their pastime, as the retchlesse rich glutton said to his secure soule. But the wisest king that euer liued said Wo bee to thee O Land when thy King is a child and thy Princes eate in the Morning.[51]

To a degree these are commonplaces of late medieval and early modern political culture; little about them would have been foreign to Ricart. But in the Elizabethan and early Stuart periods, the mechanisms of communal control that the citizens had previously imposed upon their governors—for example, in the performances of St. Katherine's players and of the Boy-Bishop—had been replaced by a different form of ritual, according to which the common councillors reminded *themselves* of their high calling. To open each council session, they prayed:

Especially (O Lord) wee beseech thee in they great and infinite mercyes to look uppon this Citye and uppon us nowe assembled and uppon all the corporacion and commons here that wee both for our selves and for them may consulte of those thinges which concern our dutyes towards thee our gratious God and towardes the Kinge under our gratious Lorde that both wee and all the people of this Citye may glorifie they name [and] may live in brotherly love, and charitye one toward another.[52]

Prayer, of course, could bind political actions as forcibly as could social obligation. But prayer involved a very different kind of ritual exchange from that which had regulated political authority in late medieval Bristol. It linked the prayer-giver to God, not to the community which, as a microcosm of the universe, mediated between the individual and his Maker.

Not surprisingly, these early modern magistrates set themselves in the wider world of the nation by the principle of hierarchy. Indeed, much of Bristol's ceremonial life in the later sixteenth and the early seventeenth century conveyed precisely this quality. Its most characteristic form was the procession. Eleven major feast days were recognized. On them the mayor and his brethren were to wear the scarlet robes signifying their particular rank in the civic body—cloaks with fur and felt trimming for the mayor and former mayors, gowns alone for the rest. These so-called "Scarlett days" were Michaelmas, when the new mayor was installed—preceded and followed by solemn processions, as in the past—All Hallows Day, Christmas, St. Stephen's Day, Twelfth Day, Easter Sunday, Easter Monday, The Feast of the Ascension, Whitsunday, Trinity Sunday, and St. James Day, for the great summer fair. On every one of these important religious festivals, with the exception of St.

James Day, there was a full-scale procession of the city government, wherein all could observe the civic hierarchy in its proper order making its way through the town. Except for the absence of the festivals of St. Clement, St. Katherine, St. Nicholas, Corpus Christi, St. John, and St. Peter, all of this would have been familiar enough to Ricart and his contemporaries. But there is one all-important difference. In the later sixteenth and the early seventeenth century, the Corporation members dressed themselves in their scarlet garments not to hear mass, still less to participate in a drunken revel, but to attend a lecture by one of the city's preachers. Sitting together in church, the mayor and the councillors must have stood out as an honored elite among the congregation.[53]

Not only did these changes bring a new earnestness and sense of sobriety to officeholding, they also raised the magistrates above criticism from their inferiors. No longer was emphasis placed primarily upon their membership in the borough community. Instead, their role as the agents of royal authority was given special attention. Authority now meant sovereignty; it conveyed rights and yielded majesty and power. The magistrates revealed this viewpoint especially in the symbolism they chose for asserting their position. In 1606, for example, the Common Council agreed that a convenient place ought to be built in the Bristol Cathedral where they and their wives might "sytte . . . to heare the sermons on the Sabaothe and after festival dayes."[54] After some discussion, the dean and the chapter agreed to the proposal, and a gallery was built "over against the pulpit." William Adams, Bristol's early seventeenth-century chronicler, who no doubt himself saw the finished work, gives the following description:

> It was not only a fair and comely ornament to the church, but also a fit and convenient place for the council to sit and hear the word preached, leaving the room below for gentlemen and others. They placed there our King's arms gilded, and under [it] reserved a fair seat for the King or any nobleman that should come to this city: and under the same [gallery] also fair seats for the council's and clergy's wives and other fit place also for the bishop, dean and others of the clergy.[55]

There could be no clearer hierarchical symbolism, nor a more revealing insight into how the Bristol Corporation viewed their place in God's order. Seated in honor above the pulpit, with the bishop, the dean, and even the king himself perhaps among them, they were to hear the Holy Word. This self-image was a powerful one. Less than two years later, Bishop Thornborough, returning to Bristol from a long absence at York, where he was dean of the Cathedral Chapter, found its symbolism so much an affront to his own episcopal dignity that he ordered the gallery removed.[56]

These new attitudes were given added depth when royalty appeared in the city. Two such visits were made between 1558 and 1640: one by Queen Elizabeth I in 1574, and the second by Queen Anne of Denmark in 1613. Both occasioned magnificent displays of civic pomp. Since much honor accrued from these rare opportunities to entertain royalty, every effort was made to show the city at its best. But these two events reveal a very different profile than had appeared for the visit of Henry VII. In both instances the celebrations took the form of massive military displays in which the prowess of the city's Trained Bands went hand in hand with their show of loyalty and obedience to royal rule. Instead of stressing the city's antiquity and independence, the mayor and his brethren emphasized their city's place in the larger organization of the state and their own subordination to the monarchy.[57] We can see this clearly in the description of Queen Elizabeth's visit.

When Elizabeth came to Bristol in 1574, "the mayor and all the council riding upon good steeds, with footcloths, and pages by their sides" received Her Majesty within Lawford's Gate, just outside the boundaries of the city. There an interesting series of exchanges took place, in marked contrast to the symbolism adopted in 1486. At the gate "the mayor delivered [his] mace unto her Grace," thus relinquishing the sign of his authority as her lieutenant, "and she delivered it unto him again," reinforcing her authority over the city and his dependence upon her for favor. After an oration by John Popham, the recorder, and the delivery of a gift of £100 in gold to her, the queen was escorted through the city in a procession in which "the mayor himself rode nigh before the Queene, betweene 2 serjeants at arms."[58] This procession, with each rider holding his proper place in relation to the queen and the others in the order of march, set the tone for the military displays that occupied the queen's time for the rest of her three-day stay.

To give the displays added meaning, the city hired the poet Thomas Churchyard to supply an allegory, which was presented to the queen in speeches and in a little book interpreting for her the actions of the armed bands.[59] The allegory pitted peace against war and put the city on the side of peace:

> Dissenshion breeds the brawll,
> and that is Pomp and Pried:

> The Fort on law and order stands,
>   and still in peace would bied.
> The Warrs is wicked world,
>   as by his fruets is seen:
> The Fortres representith peace,
>   and takes thy part O Queen.[60]

Later we learn that the Fort stands for the "Citie." The "Citie" resists
war and shows "what follies and conflicts rise in Ciuill broyls, and what
quietnesse coms by a mutual loue and agrement."[61] "Our traed doth
stand on Siuill lief / and thear our glory lies," it says,

> Wee Marchants keep a mean vnmixt,
>   with any iarrying part:
> And bryng boeth Treble and the Baess,
>   in order still by art.[62]

However, it required human reason and will to tune the parts of a community into harmony with one another, for order in this allegory is conceived as an active principle; it must be created and not merely preserved. "Our orders maks the roister meek," says the "Citie,"

> and plucks the prowd on knees.
> The stif and stubborne kno the yoek,
>   and roets vp rotten trees
> That may infect a fruetfull feeld,
>   what can be sweet and sownd:
> But in that soyl whear for offence,
>   is due correction fownd.
> Wee make the siuill laws to shien,
>   and by example mield
> Reform the rued, rebuek the bold,
>   and tame the contrey wyeld.[63]

Nevertheless, vanity could undermine this harmony, by encouraging
people "to prowl about for pens and piuish pealf" to the neglect of their
fellows. Such selfishness was shortsighted, however; it bred dissension
and blinded one to danger. To overcome this threat it was necessary for
citizens to move beyond their petty, private interests into the service of
the queen and the nation. All were members of her "staet," and hence
must be "a true and loyal stock . . . reddy . . . with losse of lief" to battle her foes.[64] Thus the "Citie" declares that "though our ioy be most
in peace, and peace we do maintain . . . Yet haue we soldyars" that

> ... daer blade hit with the best,
> when cawse of contrey coms
> And cals out of courage to the fight,
> by sound of warlike Droms.[65]

It was only from the monarch, however, that peace and order could come to the city. She was a "Prince in deed of princely minde . . . the toutchstoen . . . the Pillar, Prop and stay [o]f eury region far or neer." She was the "noble Judge" who stood above the fray to decide great quarrels. Hence her "helpyng hand" was needed "to cord disorders" wherever they appeared:[66]

> And blest be God we haue a Prince,
> by whom our peace is kept:
> And vnder whom this Citie long,
> and land hath safly slept.
> For whomliekwyse a thousand gifts,
> of grace enioy we do:
> And feell from God in this her rayne
> ten thousand blessyngs to.
>
> . . . .
>
> And mark how mad Dissension thriues,
> that would set warres abroetch:
> Who sets to saell poer peoples liues,
> and gets but viell reproetch.
> And endles shaem for all their sleights:
> O England ioy with vs:
> And kis the steps whear she doth tread,
> that keeps her countrey thus.
> In peace and rest, and perfait stay,
> whearfore the god of peace:
> In peace by peace our peace presarue,
> and her long lief encrease.[67]

The dependence upon the queen so clearly articulated in these verses was repeated in the mock battle itself. The third and last day of the maneuvers ended with three assaults upon the fort, but the enemy, having been repulsed, agreed to a parley. The attackers offered the "good Citizens and Soldiors" of the fort a chance to surrender and "depart with bag and bagaeg," honorably but in defeat. "To which the Fort maed answer, that the Cortaynes nor Bulwarks was not their defence, but the corrage of good peple, & the force of a mighty prince (who saet and beheld all these doyngs) was the thing they trusted to." With this the enemy was defeated and peace was declared. "[A]t which pece boeth sides shot-of their Artillery, in sien of triumphe, and so crying God saue the Queen, these triumphs and warlik pastimes finished."[68]

Throughout these three days the underlying theme was the city's place in the royal chain of command. The queen came to town "with princely trayn and power," and to honor her the city called out the Trained Bands to guard and wait upon her. The citizens thus fell "with all orders and marshall manner" into line with this princely train. Churchyard's allegory, moreover, gave added stress to the queen's position as commander. He arranged, for example, to have the gentlemen waiting upon the queen join with the citizens in defense of the fort. In addition, during one of the mock engagements, John Robartes, a common councillor, came to the queen to crave her aid "in their defence that peace desiers." Later, on the third day, "nue suckors commyng from the Court to the Forts great comfort" turned the tide of battle. To cap this symbolism, the queen exercised the prerogative of commander in rewarding the Trained Bands with a gift of 200 crowns for a banquet.[69] Whereas Henry VII's stay in Bristol had stressed the city's independence from the ruling monarch, Elizabeth I's emphasized just the reverse. Instead of arising from autonomy, as was claimed in the fifteenth century, civic unity now required the authority of the monarch.[70]

The spirit of this new urban order is captured in a sermon given in 1635 by Thomas Palmer, vicar of St. Thomas and St. Mary, Redcliffe, in Bristol. "This honorable City," he says,

> may be compared unto the sea-faring Tribe of Zebulon, that was a Haven for ships. . . . And so is this. The men of that Tribe were expert in warre: they could keepe ranke, they were skilfull at all the Instruments of warre. . . . And so may the men of the City.[71]

Warfare is understood to be the scourge of God upon the wicked; it "is sent into the world for our sinnes, to correct us for them, to deterre us from them." In consequence, military service is a divine calling. "As warre is from the Lord," Palmer says,

> so let it be for the Lord. If *Caesars* honour was touched, his souldiers were so prodigall of their blood, so desperately furious, that they were invincible. They gave unto *Caesar* that which was *Caesars*: let us give unto God, that which is Gods; the expense of our dearest blood for the maintenance of his Cause.[72]

This militant Christianity was highly political, with the soldier viewed as the counterpart of the government official; each in his own realm battled in God's name against iniquity and evil. As their roles were conceived by Palmer,

> [t]he sword of the Warriour findes an honourable Parallel with the sword of the Magistrate. They are both drawn for the execution of Justice. Experience and skill are requisite to the managing of them both. Let the Magistrate countenance the souldier in time of Peace. And the souldier shall defend the Magistrate in the time of warre.[73]

The two coexisted under the Lord of Hosts,

> [t]hat as that God of Peace hath taught us those things which belong unto our peace: so that Man of warre would teach our hands to warre, and our fingers to fight; that neither the sword of the Magistrate, nor of the warriour may bee drawne wrongfully, or in vaine. That the end of our temporall warfare may be a blessed peace upon earth: and of our spirituall, an eternall peace in the heavens. Unto which Peace the God of Peace brings us all.[74]

In contrast to the social vision of the late medieval community, whose hierarchical structure was mediated by a series of ritualized exchanges and mocking reversals of role, this new model of society was a military one, with sharply defined ranks, rigid organization, and harsh discipline. There is no room here for the carnival spirit of abandon that Mikhail Bakhtin argues offered "a second world and second life outside officialdom," through which "all hierarchical rank, privileges, norms and prohibitions" are suspended, and people are permitted to enter "for a time . . . the utopian realm of community, freedom, equality, and abundance."[75]

In this light, the history of Bristol's midsummer watches on St. John's Eve and St. Peter's Eve, 24 and 29 June, is especially instructive. In the fifteenth century, these were convivial gild events involving candlelight processions through the town and gild drinkings, which were generally such bibulous and violent affairs that in 1450 the Common Council took to distributing wine to each gild in strictly limited quantities paid for out of the town coffers.[76] In 1572–73, however, Mayor John Browne ended the drunken revels and "the delightful shows" that traditionally had accompanied these festive occasions and, according to William Adams, "turned the same into a general muster in war-like sort; and all the burgesses being fully armed with all sorts of warlike weapons, every craft and science several by themselves with their drums and colours," which, Adams says, "was well used and made a comely show."[77] In

making this change Browne was anticipating the view of John Northbrooke, who in his *Treatise* against dicing, dancing, and vain plays, published only five years later, argued that military exercises "trayning vp
men in the knowledge of martiall and warrelike affaires and exercising"
and imparting "knowledge to handle weapons" were acceptable forms
of play.[78]

⁓ᴥ⁓

For Bristolians in the sixteenth and seventeenth centuries, the controlling social metaphor was the idea of the body politic. A body politic is
a commonwealth; its component parts form an integrated whole and
cannot exist separately from one another. In consequence, not only must
there be a head to rule, but everything else must be proportionately organized and in its proper place. The vision is one of a hierarchical division of labor in which some parts have greater importance or value than
others but each performs a function vital for the rest. If this body politic
should fall into disorder, the ruling authority was to restore it to health
by reestablishing the proper arrangement of organs and limbs.

This hierarchical image of society rested on two competing ideals.
On the one hand, there was the ideal of reciprocity, by which the ruler
and the ruled worked together for the common good, thereby creating
a moral community. On the other, there was the ideal of rank or function, by which each member of the community contributed to the
commonwealth according to his station, but only established rulers had
responsibility for government. Implicit in the notion of a body politic
was a connection between commonwealth and rule. The commonwealth involved the mutual relations of the members of society; rule involved the use of authority by governors to bring order and security to
them. Proper coordination of the commonwealth with the exercise of
such authority produced a harmonious polity. But at bottom these concepts offered alternative visions of order. In the former, every member
of the polity had an obligation to uphold justice, the foundation of order; in the latter, the governors alone dispensed justice.

Authority in late medieval Bristol had arisen from within the community of burgesses, which as a microcosm of the world replicated the
order of the universe and displayed in small its harmonies and correspondences. Those who ruled the borough did so by virtue of their
moral leadership in it, which was sanctioned not only by the legalities
of election but by rituals of recognition and acceptance which criticized

and purified as well as exalted those in power. In Queen Elizabeth I's time, authority arose in a much wider field. Those who held authority were no longer merely citizens of their borough. Their community could no longer be thought of as a microcosm of the world. It was instead part of a larger commonwealth; it did not stand alone. Those who governed the community were agents of royal rule, subject to the tutelage of the Crown and privileged to associate themselves with its majesty and power.

CHAPTER 6

Little Businesses

In late medieval Bristol, the prevailing ideology of urban life centered on the desire to maintain communal harmony in the face of increasing evidence of social differentiation and political division. When unity means holiness, the smallest sign of disagreement is a sign of disease, corruption, and sin. The higher the value placed on social unity, the greater the risks attendant on social conflict. For this reason the threshold of conflict was very high in the city, since once it had been crossed it would be difficult to limit its course. Strong factions, each convinced that their opponents were transgressing against the common good, each actively seeking the others' destruction, would lead the social body away from the Kiss of Peace to bitter enmity and recurring political struggle. In consequence, both ceremony and politics were largely devoted to suppressing disagreement and disorder before they irreversibly disrupted community life. At the same time, the magistrates depended on their fellow townsmen's acceptance of their moral authority in enforcing order. It was widely understood, as we have seen, that a man's prior standing in the community led to office. Office, in turn, yielded power—power to shape and enforce the lawful practices and policies of the community. Service in government was a recognition of a person's authority, not its source; and political power was understood to follow from authority rather than produce it.[1]

The new vision of order that had emerged among the Bristol magistrates in the later sixteenth and the early seventeenth century altered this relationship between authority and power in the city. Even though older ideas of office could still be drawn upon after 1499, the changed context of relations with the Crown deeply affected their meaning. Now the source of authority in the civic community could be considered to lie outside its sworn membership. Power came to its governors not only through selection by their fellows for municipal office but also through their dependent relationship to the king or queen, whose servants they were. Or, to put this another way, the monarch, the fount of all governmental authority, could no longer be thought of as a distant, if benevolent, suzerain, someone who might occasionally visit the city as did Henry VII in 1486. Instead, he or she was now understood to be present within the community immanently or spiritually, giving form to its hierarchy of authority. In a sense, the monarch, acting in the everyday world of human affairs, came to play a role parallel to the one once played by the saints in heaven, whose mediations unified the earthly community under God; with the demise of the saints only the king or queen, representing the image of godly majesty and divine authority on earth, could fix the community within God's ordering of the world. In this view, the possession of power, the capacity to enforce one's will, yielded authority, the ability to command respect and deference. The former arose from royal sanction, the latter from the community's acceptance of it.

This way of envisioning the civic world carried with it new openings for dissension and disorder, since there were now two sources of legitimacy in the city, the community of citizens and the Crown, which potentially could compete with one another. Although most of the time these two lines of authority flowed as the treble and bass of a mutually supportive harmony, after 1499 those who served as royal lieutenants might find themselves from time to time lacking the moral force necessary to command voluntary obedience from the citizenry, or at any rate from a significant portion of it. Of course, under the old dispensation as well as the new, the city's governors could be challenged by some members of the community for failing to act on behalf of the commonweal. But now a new kind of politics became available when this happened, a politics that involved a complex interplay of local and national forces. Whereas, previously, political conflict tended to remain bottled within the confines of the civic community, antagonistic groups could now appeal for favor or support beyond the city's boundaries, to the central institutions of the state. Local politics would sometimes become an exercise in calling on the royal court, the Privy Council, or Parliament to redress the balance of factions at home.

These considerations bring us to what we may call, following Conrad Russell, the "little businesses" of the localities.[2] "Little businesses" in Russell's usage are primarily administrative or economic issues concerning such matters as the provision of local justice or the regulation of local trade, which may have been troubling to the communities in which they arose but commonly were of small interest to the great men who ruled at the center of affairs, whence the interested parties turned for their remedy. But were these little businesses exclusively local in their significance? On their face they may seem to be, for the repair of bridges and the maintenance of lighthouses—to use Russell's examples—or the erection by statute of a local trading monopoly—to follow the case of Bristol—hardly appear the "great matters" of grand politics. How can we find the foundations of dynastic marriages, the sources of aristocratic factionalism, or the origins of international war in them? Nor are they of much interest to legal or constitutional history, since the resolution of local problems had been the stock-in-trade of royal government from the Conquest, if not before. There is seemingly no story to tell. But from the viewpoint of the history of the state, "little businesses" suggest the local community's inability to accomplish its goals or resolve its difficulties with its own resources. Seen in this perspective, they indicate the need of the local community to call upon the state to help to perform its necessary services and to cope with its own internal problems, including social rifts and political divisions. Here there may be somewhat more history.

In the present chapter we shall explore the interpenetration of national and local politics in order to show how changes in what we might call Bristol's political economy heightened the interrelation between the community and the state. The approach will be somewhat different than the one we have used in most of the previous chapters. Modern social scientists conducting research on contemporary political choice normally rely on sophisticated statistical techniques to study the complex interplay of ideological and social forces that shape their subjects' action. Lacking evidence of all the relevant variables, however, we must rely on a more old-fashioned method: the method of political narrative. This chapter will take us from the economic, social, and cultural analysis that has dominated the previous discussion to the telling of stories that emphasize specific events and detail the actions of particular individuals.

During the Elizabethan and early Stuart period, Bristol's Society of Merchant Venturers stood at the center of the highly energized field of forces in which the city was situated. As we have already indicated, the Society was never a simple commercial organization. With its membership drawn from the city's social elite and with many of its leaders also serving on the Common Council of the city, often as mayor and aldermen, it not only performed social functions but also regularly crossed from the realm of economic profit narrowly construed into the realm of political power and back again. For this reason, the Society should be seen metaphorically as the very heart of Bristol's body politic in this era; it kept up the pressure and gave impetus to the fluid political forces that circulated through the community. Although in their communal relations most Bristolians no doubt found disharmony and dissension illegitimate and abhorrent, the Society's receipt of royal letters patent in 1552 set in motion a recurring process of conflict, accommodation, and renewed conflict that was the defining feature of the city's history in this period.

The privileges granted to the Merchant Venturers by Edward VI did not take long to erode. By early in Elizabeth I's reign, some of the city's artificers and retail shopkeepers were openly offering resistance to the Society's newfound authority. In 1566, the Merchant Venturers responded by acquiring a royal confirmation of their letters patent and by obtaining a parliamentary statute to strengthen their corporate powers.[3] The principal issue for the Merchant Venturers was that Edward VI's grant had provided no penalties against nonmembers who engaged in overseas trade contrary to its terms. Hence, the Merchant Venturers said, many in the city, "being neither admitted into the saide Society" nor apprenticed "to the same Arte by the space of Seaven yeares," continued to "exercise recourse of merchaundise beyond the Seas" contrary to "the good intention" and "expresse words" of the letters patent, "to the great hindraunce and decay of all the . . . Cittie."[4] In response, the statute granted the Society explicit enforcement authority against violators of its charter and strictly limited the membership to those engaged exclusively in wholesale trade. The Society was to be made up of mere merchants and mere merchants alone.[5]

This parliamentary act had explosive effects in Bristol. Almost immediately, violent protests arose from various quarters about its terms. The Tuckers' gild openly complained that they were the result of a "sutell fetch" by William Carr and Thomas Chester, the city's two members of Parliament in 1566, who used petitions for the relief of poverty from the clothworkers of the city to persuade the Privy Council "that the cheffe decay of bristowe was for that the marchauntes and the

navigacion of the Cytie and porte weare in decay by meanes of so many
occupying unto the sea in the trade of marchaundise and did lade uppon
Strayngers bottomes and having non experyence ne skyll therein" and
thus "optayned to be a crafte."[6] This bitterness quickly turned into a determination to have the new statute quashed whenever the next parliament was convened.

Maneuverings began before the municipal elections on 15 September
1570, in expectation that there would soon be a new Parliament, which
had been under consideration by Sir William Cecil and the Privy Council since the previous February.[7] Three days before the annual city
elections, a new ordinance on nominations to office was passed by the
Bristol Common Council to assure that ordinary common councillors
would have nominees they could support.[8] This aim was to wrest control of the city elections from the previous mayor, the same Thomas
Chester who as a member of Parliament in 1566 had helped to procure
passage of the Merchant Venturers statute. With their own men in municipal office, the anti-monopolists hoped to control the upcoming elections for Parliament and assure a favorable representation for their
position. The gambit worked. When the writs for the election of MPs
were finally issued in February 1571, the mayor's office belonged to
William Tucker, clothier, and one of the two sheriffs' places belonged
to John Barnes, another clothier, whom Tucker had nominated. Of
the leading elective offices, only the second sheriff's post was held by a
merchant, William Hickes, closely associated with the city's leading
Spanish traders, who had been nominated by Chester in his capacity as
outgoing mayor.[9]

Despite these preparations, the parliamentary elections themselves
proved extremely divisive, "so that the Sheriffs were at great debate a
long time after."[10] The two MPs from 1566, Chester and William Carr,
both mere merchants, were opposed by John Popham, a prominent
West Country lawyer who was also Bristol's recorder, and Philip Langley, a grocer who lived by retail as well as wholesale. In the end,
Popham and Langley were the victors. In addition, John Young, a client
of the earl of Pembroke and a prominent gentleman resident in Bristol,
sat for Old Sarum and stood ready to speak for the Bristol retailers. He
and Popham could be counted on to hold their own with the Privy
Council and in Parliament against any counterattack from the mere
merchants. With the backing of the mayor speaking officially for the
commonalty of the city,[11] these three MPs therefore enjoyed a good

chance of securing the repeal of the 1566 statute. But the Merchant Venturers were not without their own resources.

The "Bill for Bristowe," as the *Commons Journal* refers to the repeal measure, was formally introduced into Parliament on 10 April, only eight days after the beginning of the session. In the estimation of John Hooker, chamberlain of Exeter and one of its members in this Parliament, "among the private bills" considered in this session "none was more important."[12] At the time of its introduction, Sir James Croft, recently appointed comptroller of the queen's household and privy councillor, attempted to compromise the differences between the Bristol merchants and their rivals by asking that "both parties might bee heard and the controversie appeased."[13] This opened the door for the merchants, who showed immediately that they had taken pains on their own behalf. Since they had no voice among the Bristol MPs, they enlisted the aid of William Fleetwood, recorder of London and one of the more experienced and flamboyant parliamentary speakers, who did not let them down. In a characteristically loquacious and wide-ranging speech, he quickly "entred into a good discourse of the prerogative." His argument, after it is stripped of its willful obfuscation and its citation of numerous precedents from the reigns of Edward I, Edward III, Henry IV, and the Irish Parliament, made the point that prerogative "might . . . bee touched, if they should enter to overthroughe her letters patentes, to whom by law there is power given to encorporat any towne," and, he warned, perhaps from his own experience in the previous Parliament, "she is sworn to preserve her prerogative."[14]

Fleetwood's principal opponent in debate was John Young, who, according to John Hooker, "very pithely" presented the case for repeal of the 1566 act,

> first shewinge the losse which hath growne to the Queene of her customes; then the private monopoly wrought and occasioned by the Marchants, the controversies which have ensued by this means amonge them; then the subtill meanes whereby the statute was procured without the consent of the Maior and commons of the city.[15]

After Young, the matter was debated in somewhat confusing fashion by a number of prominent Parliament men, during which it was alleged by Popham in answer to Fleetwood that through the Bristol company "the publick and free trading of others was restrained." Although the queen by the due exercise of her prerogative could create a body with special privileges, Popham said, by "the Greate Charter of England" she could not, according to this argument, harm any of her subjects by her grant.[16] Fleetwood, recognizing that his point had suffered a serious political setback, if not also a legal one, closed the day's debate by obtaining a delay in the appointment of a committee to take up the bill.[17] In the interval, however, he was not able to find support for quashing the measure, though his efforts did assure that when the committee was finally appointed it would hear "both parties" touching the bill and that he would be among its membership.[18]

Thereafter the bill experienced extremely tough going. In committee, which included Young and Popham and an important group of interested members as well as Fleetwood,[19] the merchants, represented by learned counsel, attacked it vigorously but could convince the MPs only to change some of its words, which were deemed "somewhat sharp," not to amend it in "substance or matter." Nevertheless, when it was read for the third time it was only "after many Arguments" that it finally passed "upon the Question."[20] Nor did this end the controversy, for the measure also met considerable resistance when it was sent up to the Lords, where it was immediately committed on its first reading without being engrossed. The presence on the committee of seven privy councillors, including Burleigh, Leicester, and the Lord High Admiral, indicates that it had caused a great stir among the queen's leading advisers. This committee kept the bill for fifteen days without amending it in substance. During the interval the queen's officers appear to have sought to calm the Bristol anti-monopolists in their passion for vengeance by binding their principal spokesman, Philip Langley, and others to obey orders of the Privy Council concerning, as we are told, "the trade of marchandize of Bristowe."[21] Once this had been done, the "Bill for Bristowe" received its final reading and was approved.[22]

The terms of the act as they finally appear in the statute book indicate that John Young's arguments in the Commons had been convincing. According to the preamble, the monopoly of the Merchant Venturers had enhanced the prices of "all maner of merchandize," consumed the wealth of the city, and caused the customs to be reduced and the navy decayed,

> for that a great many of welthye inhabitantes and citizens of the said citie which before that tyme occupied greate stockes were thereby cut of[f] from the trade of the Seas. And thereof followith that the poore craftes men are not wrought as they might be to the great ruyn and decay of all the saide Cit-

tye and theinhabitauntes of the same and to the great damage of the countrye envyroning the same.[23]

In remedy, the act ordered full restoration of "the wonted libertye of the said citizens . . . to trafficke for merchaundize beyond the Seas."[24] But it left the original charters intact, "to have their validitie according to the lawe," as Popham argued.[25]

In 1566 the issue between the Society and its opponents was cast as a rivalry between "Merchant Venturers" and "Artificers" who had not been trained in the art of merchandise. But it was not poor handicraftsmen but middlemen who were the primary target of the merchants' monopoly. The tuckers, for example, became engaged in the debate not so much as manufacturers of finished cloth but as clothiers who organized production and interposed themselves between those who made the cloth and those who bought it in the market. We have already seen that as their new role evolved they had acquired a trading function which included the importation of such raw materials as oil and dyestuffs and the export of finished cloth. Soapmakers became enmeshed in the controversy because they too had developed an interest in trade, including the import of olive oil to supply their workshops. But given the new structure of Bristol's trading economy, with its heavy emphasis on profits from imports, the main focus was on the retailing of these wares. When the Merchant Venturers fought for their monopoly their principal targets were grocers, mercers, haberdashers, vintners, and soapmakers, who dealt in imported wares. Dealers in domestic commodities, such as chandlers, victualers, and even drapers and clothiers, were not directly mentioned in the parliamentary debates.[26]

In the late sixteenth and early seventeenth centuries, the members of the Society had conceived of Bristol's mercantile community as a great chain of being, with themselves mediating between the domestic and the international market. As John Browne wrote in his *Marchants Avizo* during Queen Elizabeth I's great war with Spain,

> . . . when the marchant was free,
> His ventures for to make:
> Then every art in his degree
> Some gaines thereof did take.

> The merchant made the clothier rich
> By venting of his cloth:
> The Clothier then sets many at worke
> And helpeth every craft.

> . . . .

> The Grocer and the Vintner
> The Mercer profit reape:
> When Spices, Silks and Wines, come store
> By Marchants ventures great.[27]

At bottom, the merchant monopolists saw the art of merchandise as a craft "where in there is more skill than every man judges." If handicraftsmen and shopkeepers were to overturn this order, economic chaos would ensue. "Unskilfullness in merchandies and great numbers going over the seas," the Merchant Venturers argued, "must greatly abase our English commodities and advance the price of foreign wares; for the more there are to sell there, the worse market they will make, and the more buyers of strange commodities the dearer they must be." "The rich retailers," moreover, "must needs undo all the poorer sort who do not venture, and eat out the mere merchants, who have but those to whom they make their vent."[28] The inevitable results would be the decay of trade, the loss of shipping, the diminution of the navy, the decline of the royal customs, the unemployment of clothworkers and others, and the collapse of all charity. We can almost hear them say, "Take but degree away, untune that string, / And hark what discord follows."[29]

These views were especially attractive to those among the Merchant Venturers who focused their trade primarily on Bristol's southern markets, where the drive to maximize profits from imports was especially strong. These traders, who numbered in their ranks the city's richest and most powerful men, were the leaders of the Society. However, men who devoted the majority of their trade to the northern markets, where bulky items with low profit margins were preeminent, would not only have been rather less threatened by the trading activities of the so-called rich retailers but somewhat less inclined to see the economic world in terms of a rigid hierarchy of crafts. Trade in salt, canvas, naval stores, and other goods that came from the French coasts and the Baltic simply did not lend itself to systematic differentiation of the economic functions of merchant and retailer, since the primary market for many of these products was the merchant community itself. At the same time there were always Merchant Venturers who valued their relations in the city at large as much or more than their devotion to the Society's ideals or their connections with particular members and who therefore were reluctant to press their demand for monopoly to the point of lasting conflict with their fellow Bristolians. But among the leadership of the Merchant Venturers, the dominating view in this period and for decades to follow was the one articulated by John Browne. Restricting each art and craft to its proper bounds alone would benefit Bristol's commonweal.

Not all Englishmen, and certainly not all Bristolians, agreed with the view of the proper urban social and economic order that prevailed among the Merchant Venturers. Many of the retailers and artificers saw freedom to trade—their "wonted libertye"—as a natural concomitant of their status as burgesses, secured by their freeman's oath. At the end of Elizabeth's reign Thomas Dekker's London comedy *The Shoemaker's Holiday* presented in dramatic form just such a vision of urban life. There Dekker tells the story of Simon Eyre, the simple London shoemaker who rose to wealth and the lord mayoralty through his good fortune in the merchants' trade. It is a fantasy of social mobility and urban achievement. Pretending to be of great standing and credit, Eyre bought at a bargain a rich cargo of sugar, almonds, and other luxuries imported to London by a debt-ridden merchant who needed a quick sale. Eyre's progress to greatness depended on the special customs of London—still in force, though perhaps in modified form, at the time Dekker wrote his play—whereby every freeman of London enjoyed the right to buy and sell by wholesale any goods that came his way. Hence he could also change his occupation from craftsman to trader, even though he had not apprenticed in his new calling.[30] Late medieval Bristol had operated by somewhat similar rules, at least as regards the right to engage in overseas commerce. All freemen could do so without hindrance. As we have seen, in the fifteenth century Bristol's merchants still traded by retail as well as wholesale.

Those excluded from foreign trade saw the Merchant Venturers' monopoly as usurping the ancient rights of citizenship and those who performed this act as violating the bonds of community. "O mercifull lorde god," some of them had lamented after Thomas Chester had obtained the Society's monopoly in 1566,

> who wolde have thought that Mr Chestre beyeng a free Citizen borne and sonne unto the naturaleste Cytizen that was in Bristol in our tyme . . . wee say who wolde have thought that Mr Thomas Chestre by name wolde consent to have the cytie of bristowe made bond. . . . [W]hat hath happened to thee o bristowe, bondayge bondaige and mysery for before Bristol withall for inhabitaintes were free and theyre lybertie alwayes to sende theyr goodes unto the sees.[31]

This language represents a very early expression of the arguments mounted time and time again by Elizabethan and early Stuart lawyers and parliamentary debaters in attacking monopolies. By granting an exclusive right to trade to particular individuals, it was said, a monopoly deprived free men of their livelihoods and thereby turned them into villeins or slaves.[32] Even the merchants recognized the strength of this view and were obliged to accept its underlying premise. The existence of ancient rights was in no danger from their corporation, they alleged, because

> no man is exempted that ever occupied the seas, but such as voluntarily sequestered themselves from the same, for every retailer, leaving off his retailing, may be a merchant, so that he will content himself with the only trade of merchandise.[33]

But they would not yield the main point. For them, overseas trade was a separate craft.

In this way two rival concepts of the urban community found particular expression in 1571. The Merchant Venturers envisioned a society in which specialized economic functions were arranged in hierarchical order, with foreign commerce at the pinnacle. The retailers and manufacturing entrepreneurs saw all freemen of the city as members of the same undifferentiated legal and economic group, all possessed of an equal right to trade abroad. The struggle between these views, which had previously coexisted in the city's culture of community and authority, remained the recurring theme of local politics for the next century or more.

Although the repeal of the 1566 act removed the Merchant Venturers from the parliamentary agenda for the time being, it did not end the turmoil in Bristol. Within twelve days of the dissolution of Parliament, the bitter rivalry between the merchants and their opponents surfaced again. On 10 June, Mayor William Tucker reported to the Common Council that Thomas Chester had been behind the appeal to the Privy Council "to have reasonable articles drawen as well for the Norishinge of Aymitie betweene the marchants of this Citie and other Inhabitants of the same As for the makinge and concludinge of good orders for the Comon Welthe and profit of the same citie." It was this effort that resulted in Langley and Bristol's other anti-monopolists becoming bound to the Privy Council for their obedience to its orders. Chester's participation in that search for accommodation is significant. Despite his evident support for the Merchant Venturers' monopoly, he was the son of a pointmaker and had close ties with the city's clothworkers. He had also been associated in a business venture with John Young.[34] Hence he was well placed to calm the political seas in Bristol. Nevertheless, his efforts were a failure; the Common Council majority seems to have had deep suspicions of his motives, as well as strong partisan feelings of their own. In response to Tucker's announcement, a majority of twenty common councillors ordered the chamberlain to draw a bond "to save harmless" those who stood bound to the Privy Council.[35]

We are fortunate in knowing the names and something of the connections of these twenty men, whom we may identify as Bristol's anti-monopoly faction. Perhaps not surprisingly, Mayor Tucker headed the list with Sheriff John Barnes; as we know, both of these men were clothiers. In addition, three aldermen were in this group, all of them grocers. Of the remaining fifteen, the occupations of fourteen are known. Four were grocers, two were clothiers or drapers, two were mercers, two were coverlet makers and upholsterers; a tailor, a tanner, a skinner, and a soapmaker made up the rest. No one among this group could be identified as a "mere merchant" by the usual standards. This party of anti-monopolists was also a relatively tight-knit social group which had strong interlocking ties of business association, family, and friendship. But the anti-monopolist party in the city was not primarily a social clique isolated from the major overseas merchants by birth, marriage, and commercial connection. Although the ties of its members with the merchants were neither so numerous nor so strong, regular cross-cutting links bound Bristol's retailers and industrial middlemen to the leading Merchant Venturers.[36] But in 1571, political and economic circumstances drove these social bonds into the background and made connections with other retailers and manufacturing entrepreneurs more important. The key to the anti-monopolists is not the social relations of its members with each other, but their opposition to the Society of Merchant Venturers.

Because family connections and other social ties reinforced the economic interests of the Society's opponents, the political wounds of 1571 went very deep. Bitterness lingered for more than a year following the dissolution of Parliament, with contentious debates marring a number of council sessions as merchants and their opponents angrily attacked each other with "contumelious words." This was a period in which calling someone "knave in his ear," as George Snygg, merchant, did to John Jones, skinner, or claiming "you belie me," as Philip Langley said to Alderman Robert Saxey, one of the leading Merchant Venturers, could itself become the cause of violent hatred. Even levying fines against the wrongdoers, as the Common Council quickly did on each occasion, could not completely erase the dishonor associated with the public insult.[37] Nor was the spirit of partisan rage limited to a few individuals. In April 1572 the Common Council majority sought to avenge itself in a fiscal way on their Merchant Venturer opponents by ordering a tax of eight pence in the pound on all inhabitants, to cover Philip Langley's charges for repealing the 1566 statute. Had this extraordinary levy ever been enforced, it could have been used by the assessors to cripple those with cash reserves and well-stocked storerooms, that is to say, principally the merchants.[38] But before the council majority executed the ordinance, calmer heads seem to have prevailed and the tax measure was repealed in favor of an award to Langley of just £50 for his expenses at the last Parliament.[39]

But even this prudent backing away from further confrontation did not end the troubles. Within just five years new controversies were at work in the city. They came with the establishment of the Spanish Company in 1577. This new commercial organization was founded with powers greatly surpassing those that had belonged to its predecessor, the Andalusia Company of 1530.[40] Like the Andalusia, however, the Spanish Company's main purpose was to give England's Spanish merchants a common policy and single voice with which to face the difficult conditions they found in the Iberian peninsula. Plans for establishing the Company were well underway as early as 1573, and although it was Londoners who primarily pressed the Privy Council for new letters patent, a party of Bristolians seems to have joined them.[41] Recent experience had unfortunately made the latter all too aware of the need for a protective organization in Counter-Reformation Spain: the religious persecution and subsequent legal problems of their fellow townsman, John Frampton, a resident factor in Andalusia, had touched the goods many had left in his charge.[42]

The new Spanish Company also filled an even more important need for the Bristol Merchant Venturers, since retailers and artificers were expressly excluded from membership.[43] Bristol had its own branch of the Company, including resident assistants to enforce ordinances. Hence membership provided the mere merchants with a way to rebuild their monopolistic control of local trade, so heavily dependent in this period on Spain, without controlling the Common Council or electing supporters to Parliament.[44] However, the participation of Bristol's mere merchants in the new Spanish Company quickly reopened the battles of 1571 and 1572. The Bristol membership was headed by Alderman Robert Saxey and Thomas Chester, the latter being named among the three

Bristol assistants to the Company. Many of the other members were also among the principal protagonists in the earlier dispute. It was perhaps inevitable, therefore, that there would be trouble when in August 1577 the Privy Council ordered Chester and three other Bristol members "to require all such of that cittie as are retaylers and artificers trading Spaigne to forbeare any more traffique in that countrye."[45]

Since the queen's councillors stood ready to use their extensive powers to back the new Company's privileges and ordinances, open resistance was no longer a fruitful course for the city's merchant retailers. For this reason Langley and the others ostensibly accepted restrictions on their retailing as the condition of their continued participation in the Spanish trade. But rather than giving up their retail activities, they took them underground. By December 1578, Langley and his supporters were again subject to the attentions of the Privy Council, which at the request of the Merchant Venturers commanded the mayor and sheriffs of Bristol, with the assistance of their brethren on the Common Council, to call the merchant retailers before them and advise them "to yeilde to suche order as by that Societie hath ben taken against that kynde of retailing." If they refused, the mayor and sheriffs were to take bonds from them "to her Majesties use for . . . apparence fourthwith before their Lordships that such order may be taken . . . as shalbe thought convenient."[46] If they could not be persuaded to comply, they would be constrained.

Neither Langley nor his allies appear to have found the prospect of a visit to the Council Board very attractive. Faced with the Privy Council's threat, they yielded. When a year or so later a similar dispute regarding the Spanish Company's prohibitions against retailing opened in Chester and spread to Liverpool, the Bristolians refrained from using it as an occasion for renewed protests of their own.[47] By the early 1580s the local branch of the Spanish Company was vigorously enforcing its rules, placing violators in the Bristol Newgate, and levying heavy fines against interlopers, without encountering the leading merchant retailers again.[48] Although this fact does not necessarily mean that Langley and the others had entirely left off overseas trading or completely abandoned their retailing, it does suggest that by the 1580s retailing by merchants had been sharply curtailed and that an accommodation had been reached between the mere merchants and their rivals.

Dependent as the Bristol Merchant Venturers had become upon the privileges of the Spanish Company, however, their renewed local monopoly could not survive for long after war broke out between the

English and the Spanish in 1585. Although trade with Spain did not cease during the war years, it took place illicitly through French ports and was so closely associated with privateering as to make the two almost indistinguishable. Since war made trading in Spain and Portugal more risky and more costly, there were also increased incentives to push commerce into the Mediterranean and in general to rely on non-Spanish and non-Portuguese markets for business. At the same time, the scarcity of Iberian goods in the market increased the pressure among merchants to indulge in retail enterprise; doing so helped make up lost profits. Even if the Spanish Company had continued to operate, its ability to discipline its members would have been all but destroyed. But the authority of the Company did not simply erode under the pressure of war; it collapsed. In May 1586 the Privy Council was already complaining of the Company's failure to meet its obligations, and by February 1589 its general court had ceased to meet; thereafter no financial accounts were kept. With it went the effective existence of the Bristol branch. In whatever capacity the Merchant Venturers managed to stay together during the 1590s, and there is evidence that the Society did survive through the war years, their hard battles of the 1570s had been for naught.[49]

With the succession of James I and the end of open hostilities with Spain that followed, the Spanish Company attempted a revival. Official meetings began in March 1604, and by mid-May assistants for the principal outports were named, including John Barker and John Hopkins for Bristol.[50] But almost immediately a hitch occurred when a group of leading merchant retailers in London, perhaps joined by others from the outports, entered objections with the Privy Council against the Spanish Company's old privileges, arguing that its charter had become "voyde by Non User, during the longe tyme of Contynuance of the warr, which doth therefore dissolve the said Corporation." To quiet this rather technical complaint and to forestall difficulties from the outports to which it opened the door, new letters patent were issued in May 1605, granting provincial merchants a larger role in this Company than they had enjoyed in its predecessor. There were now to be sixty-one assistants, in place of the forty established in 1577, with thirty from the outports and thirty from London. Since the remaining place belonged to the Company's secretary, who was also a Londoner, the merchants of the metropolis remained in control. But among the new Company's five hundred and fifty-seven original members, only two hundred and thirty-seven were Londoners. The Bristolians fared especially well, with ninety-seven members, four of whòm were appointed to the first Court of Assistants.[51]

By early June 1605 the new Spanish Company was once again capable of filling the role it had played earlier for the Bristol Merchant Venturers. Not only had the new climate of relations between England and Spain resulted in the confirmation of the old English privileges in the Iberian peninsula, but the Company showed every intention of once again eliminating retailers from the Iberian trades. It instituted its own campaign to end the practice of partnership between mere merchants and retailers,[52] and it secured from the earl of Dorset, Lord Treasurer, a broadly worded order to the Customers prohibiting them from taking

> any entry of any merchaundizes to be transported into Spaine or Portugall, or make any agreement for Custome, but only with such as are or shalbe free of that Company, and thereby excluding all retaylours Artificers Inholders ffarmors Comon Marryners and handycrafts men, out of the said society.[53]

Former retailers were not permitted to join until they had been mere merchants for at least seven years, while all present members were to give over their retailing activities or leave the Company.[54] But there is perhaps more here than meets the eye, for the initial enumeration of the membership seems to have been based on a rather more generous interpretation of mere merchant status than before, at least in the case of Bristol. In 1577 there had been but seventy-five Bristolians named to the Spanish Company; in 1618 there were but seventy-two Bristolians listed as Merchant Venturers in its first official membership roll.[55] It is very likely, therefore, that the ninety-six men named in 1605 included among their number more than a few whom the Bristol mere merchants would have rejected as ineligible. Possibly the refounded Spanish Company was seeking to avoid the troubles with the larger merchant retailers that had punctuated the life of its predecessor in the later 1570s and early 1580s.

Nevertheless, from the perspective of Bristol's history in the early Jacobean age, it matters little whether the new Company was harshly exclusionary or generously welcoming, since only a minority of the city's leading merchants were enthusiastic participants in its affairs. Of the four Bristol assistants, for example, only John Whitson, who was in London in 1605 as one of the city's members of Parliament, ever attended meetings of the fellowship, perhaps because he found its new admissions policies to his liking. But even he did so just three times.[56] The Bristolians' indifference, if not caused by the liberal membership policies of the new Company, resulted from two other interrelated factors. First, the city's trading interests were less heavily based in the Iberian peninsula than they had been before the war. It was no longer possible to control the city's economy by controlling this one aspect of it. And, second, they were suspicious of the Londoners, in part because the Bristolians feared that the merchants of the capital would control the new trade between Newfoundland, the Iberian Peninsula, and the Mediterranean, in which Bristol and other western ports had a geographical advantage, and in part because it was still necessary to appeal to London many important Company matters vital to the Bristolians' interests.[57] With the Mediterranean and trans-Atlantic trades playing an ever greater role in Bristol's economy, there simply was less reason to rely for help upon a London-dominated corporation.

Two months after the sealing of the Spanish Company's new charter, the question of London's role produced an incisive protest from the merchants of the outports, led by those from Exeter, Plymouth, and Barnstable, who wanted to elect their own officers, make their own ordinances, and admit their own freemen rather than going to the Company in London.[58] In response the Company agreed that each branch could lay down its own bylaws, provided they were ratified by a general court in London before being put into execution. It also decided to send officers to the outports to enroll new apprentices and freemen and to swear in local officials rather than requiring them to come to London for the purpose.[59] This seemingly conciliatory approach apparently encouraged Whitson to attend his last two London meetings, in hopes probably of keeping the Company alive in Bristol.[60] But by now the majority of Bristol's merchants were determined to take no further part in it. When the Company's agents arrived in the city in September to swear in the local officers, the Bristolians, who had elected their own officers the previous May, refused to submit to the agents' authority or the orders of the Company, pretending, as the Londoners said, "to stande and governe of themselves."[61]

After this action the dénouement was not long in coming. On 31 December 1605, the Bristol Common Council regularized the independent existence of the local merchant company with a remarkable ordinance requiring the "merchant adventurers" of the city to exempt themselves from the London-based company and establishing in its place a company of merchant adventurers

to be ordered and governed amongest them selves by such Orders Constitutions and pollycyes as shalbe hereafter set downe and agreed on by the
Mayor aldermen and Common Counsell . . . according to the Charters of the
said Cytie and by the Master Wardens Communytee and Corporacon of
merchaunts within the Cytie of Bristoll.[62]

In place of membership in a chartered national company with large and
secure powers, the Merchant Venturers had decided to reestablish themselves on a purely local basis.

The Common Council ordinance of 1605 represents a remarkable
turn of events in the history we have been following. For over a century,
commercial organization in Bristol had oscillated between purely local
institutions and participation in one or another national company. The
first approach rooted Bristol's trade in the civic polity; the second recognized the city's connections to the wider world of commerce and
industry in the realm. As the city's trade networks expanded, the available forms of national organization, focused as they were on controlling
particular markets, had become less and less useful to its mere merchants, but so too had reliance on civic authority. Nevertheless, the
Merchant Venturers now had in essence been refounded by a Common
Council ordinance; its powers to enforce its regulations rested on the
city's right to legislate for the well-being of its burgesses. The presence
on the council of a powerful contingent of merchants made this arrangement eminently workable. But the Society's new status was not much
different now from that of an ordinary craft gild. In legal terms, Bristol's merchants had returned to their position of a century before. They
were once again dependent upon the Bristol Corporation for their
regulatory powers.

If history had thus repeated itself, it was only to a very limited degree. The urban world into which the merchant company of 1500 had
been introduced could still be represented in that period as a self-
contained community of brothers in which the general welfare of the
polity took precedence over the particular good of any of its members.
Although even at this early date the city's gates were already opening
to commerce from southern Europe and the Atlantic, the effects of this
revolution on social organization and mental outlook were only just becoming apparent. By 1605, however, Bristol was completely enmeshed
in an open-ended commercial network, ramified throughout western Europe and the north Atlantic, and its inhabitants were therefore affected
by events in places far from the control of their local government. Its
merchants in particular were as much citizens of the world as freemen

of Bristol. To reintroduce a local trading company into this new commercial context was not merely anachronistic, or even reactionary; it was also radical. In borrowing ideas from a past age to advance particular interests in the present one, the Common Council sought to grant the merchants effective control of these new trading networks and to place the new pattern of merchant domination in the social and political order of the city. Given the bitter antagonisms engendered by such monopolistic aspirations, it could not hope to succeed without a fight. Before long one was in the offing.

On the central question of requirements for admission to the refounded Society of Merchant Venturers, the ordinance of 1605 endorsed exclusionary principles similar to those laid down in 1566 and upheld in the Spanish Company of 1577. But with a difference. It ordered that every burgess not already free of the Society who desired to use the "trade of marchandyzes" was to be admitted during the next year for a modest entry fine of twenty shillings, "geving over the exercise of all other trades occupations and professions of getting his or thire Lyvinge." John Whitson and two other aldermen were appointed to enroll any who sought entrance under this ordinance, apparently in hopes of drawing the merchant retailers and the overseas trading artisans into the Society without a fuss. After this first year of relatively easy admission to the Society, however, all others who were neither the sons nor apprentices of current members were to be admitted only as redemptioners, paying much larger entry fines.[63] Whitson's involvement in the enrollment of new members was intended to encourage compliance and tranquillity. From his recent experience in the Spanish Company and in James I's first Parliament, where free trade had been such an important issue, Whitson accepted the principle that no Englishman could be deprived of entry into overseas trade so long as he would submit to its proper regulation. Indeed, Whitson was among the aldermen who approved Lawrence Hyde's selection to the Bristol recordership in 1605, and Hyde, the scourge of monopolies in 1601, was the principal architect of the free-trade agitation in 1604.[64]

Reliance on a local ordinance rather than royal letters patent, however, made these new rules exceptionally vulnerable to political challenge from the Merchant Venturers' old rivals within the city. By as early as 1612, if not before, they were in question from those quarters, and the Common Council found it necessary to give its prior consent to the drafting of a new Merchant Venturer ordinance providing that no member of the Society should "vse or exercise any other trade but onlye the trade of a merchaunte adventurer" so long as he used "the trade of a merchante" and that all who would practice the merchant's trade must be members of the Society.[65] But this only stirred further controversy when economic conditions began to tighten at the end of the decade. By the summer of 1618 there were renewed difficulties in enforcing the Society's ordinances, and the Merchant Venturers felt obliged to order that no inhabitant of Bristol should be considered a member of the Merchant Venturers unless he subscribed to its ordinances, was admitted in open court of the company and had his name entered into its register in the presence of the master, wardens, and assistants. In August the Society paid Nicholas Hyde, who had succeeded his brother as Bristol's recorder in 1615, for his opinion regarding the "validity of the marchantes Charters," further suggesting that the Society's authority was under challenge.[66] We have no record of his views, but given the repeal of the 1566 statute and the subsequent record of legal decisions and parliamentary actions against monopoly wherever they appeared, it is hard to believe that Hyde would have found legal support for the monopolistic implications of the 1605 and 1612 ordinances governing membership in the Society. In any case, the upshot in 1618 was the adoption of a new strategy on this issue among the Merchant Venturers.

The Society's new ordinances, perhaps drafted on Hyde's instructions, offered membership to three categories of candidates: the sons or apprentices of mere merchants or those who served their apprenticeships with lawfully admitted redemptioners and were "ymployed in the trade and recourse of marchandize onely" during their terms; redemptioners; and the sons of redemptioners. The first were to be admitted at their own request, paying only a modest fine; the second were to enter only by vote of the Hall, paying a substantial composition established at a special meeting; their sons "exerciseing the trade of marchandisinge onelie and haveinge served noe apprenticeshippe therevnto" were treated as a special class, paying a forty-shilling fee in addition to the regular fees paid by the sons of mere merchants. Once a family was established as having redemptioner status, moreover, all its future members were to be subjected successively to this regulation.[67] These new ordinances also made room for the admission of retailers and artificers, since they provided that such individuals might be admitted "whilest they remaine Retailers or Artificers" for a fine at "a speciall Courte holden for that purpose."[68] These new procedures avoided the legal shortcomings of the old; under them the Merchant Venturers could no longer be accused of maintaining an unauthorized monopoly. But making it necessary for retailers and artificers to win the approval of the present membership before admission meant that only those few individuals who were found acceptable to the majority of the Merchant Venturers would be allowed to enter.

Two other ordinances of 1618 were designed to tighten this control. Brothers of the Society were forbidden to join in partnership with Bristolians who were not members for the sale of any goods within the city or its environs. Similarly, ships' pursers, factors, and attorneys employed by Merchant Venturers were not to act as agents for non-members. Violators were subject to a fine of £20 for the first offense and disenfranchisement thereafter. A second measure explicitly forbade Merchant Venturers to deal in partnership with any retailer or artificer for any merchandise to be transported to or imported from "anie the partes beyond the Seas." Violators here were to lose 25 percent of the value of all illicitly traded goods.[69] These seemingly contradictory rules suggest that partnerships with retailers and artificers were the more common violation and could not be controlled effectively by the threat of disenfranchisement.

The same day these new ordinances were approved, the Merchant Venturers began, as we have just noted, a membership register, which listed seventy-two men who had been "legally admitted into the Societie." In the following two years, eleven more Merchant Venturers were added, eight of them in the first year.[70] This influx suggests that the new ordinances confining overseas trade to members of the Society had had some effect. Four of the new admissions were redemptioners, that is, men who lacked apprenticeship in the "art of merchandise." One had been trained as a brewer; two others earned their livings in part as manufacturers of methaglin, a distilled brandy made from honey usually imported from Brittany. One, Christopher Whitson, was also sometimes identified as a sugar refiner. All three had been resident in Bristol for some time. Whitson, cousin of John Whitson, had been a member of the Common Council since 1611.[71] Presumably these traders were admitted under the new rule governing retailers and artificers and were bound in obedience to the Society's authority by their solemn oaths upon election. But it was not until 1647 that another redemptioner was permitted to enter.

The Merchant Venturers' ordinances of 1618 attempted to establish a modus vivendi between Bristol's mere merchants and its retailers and shopkeepers. By permitting a small number of the latter to enter the Society as redemptioners, they had removed the taint of monopoly that had shrouded the Merchant Venturers' legal status and had thereby quieted the most serious complaints against their corporation. But they did not open the floodgate to newcomers. Participation in the most lucrative enterprises depended as much on what the structure of trade allowed as on the legal rights of the traders freely to pursue their interests. Hence, even though the concessions of 1618 could not completely end the overseas trading activities of nonmembers, by controlling relations among the Society's membership and preventing partnerships with outsiders they could nonetheless limit the scope and scale of such activities. So long as Bristol's commerce remained concentrated on the importation of exotic foreign wares from a small number of specialized markets, few merchant retailers or overseas trading artisans could successfully compete with the major wholesale merchants. Without the aid of the latter, they lacked the necessary shipping, the well-developed local connections, and the secure credit relations required to sustain large-scale commerce to those parts. In the aftermath of the loss of Bordeaux, the trade of Bristol naturally lent itself to oligopoly, whether or not the mere merchants could effectively maintain a monopoly through their exercise of political power.

Although after 1571 the Merchant Venturers' letters patent still remained in their hands, available to be cited from time to time as a sanction for their corporate activities, the events of that fateful year put them in doubt, since the statute of 1566 contained a general confirmation of Edward VI's patent. The repeal of the statute, accepted by the queen, left the original document in a curious state, vulnerable to various kinds of attack in the law courts.[72] For this reason much effort was devoted by the Society, still committed to the need for a monopoly, to reversing the events of 1571. In 1606, for example, only two months after Bristol's overseas traders had separated themselves from the Spanish Company, the Merchant Venturers were seeking an exemption for themselves from the terms of the parliamentary act for "free trade" into Spain, Portugal, and France, which had opened Iberian commerce to all who would engage in it. Had they been successful, they would have reestablished parliamentary sanction for their local monopoly. But even though the measure was read twice, it failed to receive approval.[73] In the Parliaments of 1621 and 1624 the Society again attempted to secure itself, petitioning on these occasions for a confirmation of its charters and explicitly requesting the renewal of its earlier statutory monopoly.[74]

On these occasions they bolstered their case by analogy to the Exeter merchants, who unlike the Bristolians had managed to save their monopoly in the free-trade debate of 1606 because of the alleged antiquity of their charter, their service to the Crown, and their maintenance of almsmen, teaching of children, and other charitable works. "[I]n all which respects . . . wee doe equallize if not exceed them," the Bristolians claimed in 1621, citing their overseas explorations, their provision of ships for Crown service, and their maintenance of an almshouse and a free school for mariners' children. They could no longer support these works, they said, "vnlesse wee may obteyne lawfull aucthoritie for the better ordering of their trade" to end the losses caused by untrained shipmasters, mariners, and sailors, dishonest Severn boatmen, and, above all, "the indisscrecion and excesse of vnexperienced enterlopers."[75] In support, the mayor and aldermen of Bristol provided a detailed certificate outlining the history of the merchants' monopoly and arguing against the 1571 repeal act because it had been procured "by certeyne shopp keepers and tradesmen" when the mere merchants were weakened by great losses. Since the repeal of the statute and the opening of the Spanish trade at the beginning of James I's reign, they alleged, many Bristol "shoppe keepers, and men of manuell occupacions, forsakeing their vsuall trades and exerciseing the traffique and recourse of marchandice being altogether vnexperienced therein, are fallen to decay." By these means, and because the Merchant Venturers could not effectively regulate their own membership or seafarers who depended on overseas trade, the Society and the citizens of Bristol "are much prejudiced to the great hindrance of the weale and prosperitie of the same Citty, the Decrease of Navigation and the Diminucion of his Majesties Customes." Hence, the mayor and aldermen heartily endorsed the Society's petition for the renewal of its charters.[76]

Despite this impressive local support, all efforts to reestablish the Merchant Venturers' monopoly through parliamentary statute failed. Here the analogy with Exeter is instructive, for, unlike Bristol, that city's mere merchants had been able to accommodate their differences with the other freemen within a year of acquiring their monopoly privileges, which henceforth remained in place. The monopoly survived without a defeat in the courts or in Parliament. When the Exeter merchants asked Parliament to exempt their charter from the provisions of the free-trade measure in 1606, they had history on their side, and no angry local voices to challenge their claims.[77] In the national political climate of James I's reign, during which the House of Commons placed monopolies of all types under the most intense scrutiny, an appeal by the Bristol Merchant Venturers, who lacked the advantages of their Exeter counterparts, for parliamentary restoration of their monopoly privileges was hardly likely to succeed.

So long as the Merchant Venturers' authority remained a purely local issue, however, the support of the Common Council was sufficient to sustain it under most of the difficulties it might encounter. But in the 1630s the Merchant Venturers came under direct attack from the Crown, which threatened the very existence of the Society. The point of crisis was the so-called wharfage duty on imported goods, created by the Common Council in 1606 for the maintenance of the port facilities and collected after 1611 by the Merchant Venturers, who from that time expended the proceeds for their own purposes, as their principal source of revenue.[78] From the start there was a question about the legality of this new levy, but during the 1620s the Privy Council had given its support to uphold it.[79] In the mid-1630s, however, the Crown's officers, searching for new sources of royal revenue, changed this policy in response to a complaint from the merchants of Barnstable.[80] By November 1637 the matter had become the subject of a formal inquiry conducted by a commission headed by the marquis of Hamilton, in which the rapacious and violent Lord Mohun, together with Robert Pawlett, Esq., and Charles Fox, Esq., acted as principal investigators. The terms of their commission included authority to inquire under what warrant wharfage had been imposed.[81] To the Merchant Venturers this was a frightening threat. Not only was their chief source of income under challenge, but their legal status was put in doubt as well, since inquiry into the warrant for the collection of wharfage duty called into question their authority to enforce their own ordinances. The marquis of Hamilton's commission raised the possibility that the Merchant Venturers would not merely lose the wharfage duty, from which they could recover, but would be stripped of their enforcement authority and damaged beyond repair.

To guard against this prospect the Merchant Venturers and their supporters in the city government began a process of calculated delay. The commissioners' primary interest was in the Society's account books and other records. But the Society's officers—with the aid of the town clerk, James Dyer, who was a well-connected barrister—contrived, by keeping these records from them, to provoke the commissioners, especially the notoriously ill-tempered Lord Mohun, into overstepping their authority. Dyer's advice led to the arrest of the Society's warden, while his own harsh words to the commissioners caused him to be placed under security to appear before the solicitor-general. But this "purposed opposition," as Mohun called it, spurred the commissioners on to forcing entry into the Merchants' Hall to seize the account books from their locked chest. And so the pot was stirred.[82]

These proceedings resulted in a letter of outrage from Dyer to Sir Edward Nicholas, by now a prominent privy councillor, who was an old and influential friend of the city. Next came a petition to the king complaining of the excesses of the commissioners, carried to London by a party of leading merchants among the aldermen and common councillors.[83] This in turn produced a hearing in the king's presence at which Charles ordered the Bristolians and the commissioners each to present bills in Star Chamber detailing their grievances, in effect delaying further action. It was just the respite the Bristolians wanted.[84] The litigation came before Star Chamber in April 1638. At about the same time the Society decided to petition the king for a confirmation of its charter. Nothing is known of the negotiations, but approval came quite quickly; new letters patent were sealed on 7 January 1639.

This new charter not only brought the intrusive commission on wharfage to an abrupt halt but granted the Merchant Venturers new powers of enforcement, focused on a new Court of Assistants named in the patent, that guaranteed the Society's ability to impose its ordinances even on nonmembers. The membership of this initial Court of Assistants is especially important, since to it were named those leading merchants whose trade had long focused on the Iberian Peninsula, the Mediterranean, and the Atlantic islands, where the pursuit of high-profit imports was of preeminent importance. Since this body would perpetuate itself by co-optation, the Society was now securely in the hands of men fully devoted to the ideals of monopoly that had first emerged in the sixteenth century. The Merchant Venturers' efforts, and an expenditure of £400, according to their *Hall Book,* had brought an end to the uncertainty about their legal position that had haunted them since 1571.[85]

With this authority, the Society set about drafting new bylaws, which were completed and approved on 4 April 1639. Many measures, such as the rules excluding retailers and craftsmen from membership without a special meeting of the Hall and forbidding members from acting in partnership with nonmembers, were repeated verbatim from the 1618 ordinances, though the Society's new enforcement powers gave them added bite. In addition, all Merchant Venturers were required to refrain from selling any cloth or other goods or from buying any merchandise beyond the seas for the benefit of nonmembers, and all were forbidden to allow any but a fellow Merchant Venturer to freight ships with them. Finally, new inspection procedures were introduced to assure that shipmasters, mariners, and other seamen did not use their ancient privilege of lading their own trading goods aboard vessels in order to conduct illicit trade for retailers and manufacturers.[86]

The acquisition of the charter and the passage of these new ordinances seemed to end an era in the history of the Merchant Venturers. Once again the Society enjoyed the secure legal position and effective enforcement authority it had achieved in 1566. Although technically it did not have a monopoly, by controlling its own membership it could now keep nearly all shopkeepers and artisans from conducting overseas trade. The effect was immediate. By June 1639 the Society's Court of Assistants was meeting to recover outstanding debts owed the Society for wharfage and other duties. On two days, twenty-nine individuals were summoned to the Merchants' Hall to arrange for early payment. Twelve of them were not members of the Society at the time.[87] This new power in turn had an effect on the size of the Society's membership, since it was now not only more difficult for nonmembers to engage in foreign commerce but also more beneficial to be a member. During the twenty-one years between the ordinances of 1618 and the charter of 1639, only sixty-three members had been added to the Society. But now, within three years, fifty-one overseas traders entered the fellowship, including five of the twelve men previously chastised for failing to pay their port duties.[88]

The connection of the Merchant Venturers to the membership of the city government that had sustained their Society through its long sojourn in the institutional wilderness after 1571 also made possible their great success in 1639. Merchant domination of the city government resulted in such a close alliance that in the decade preceding the issuance of the 1639 charter the Society and the city government almost formed an interlocking directorate. During these years, for example, Alderman Humphrey Hooke held the office of master for six years, and Alderman Richard Long for two more. In the same period, Hooke and Long each served as mayor for one year, with Long's term coinciding with one of his two years as master. Alderman Richard Holworthy also was simultaneously mayor and master during this period. Moreover, when Parliament was summoned, it was the same merchant leadership that was sent. In the early Stuart period, Merchant Venturers held both Bristol seats in every session, except in the 1625 Parliament and the Short Parliament, when the city's recorder served along with a Merchant Venturer. Alderman Hooke sat in both the Short and the Long Parliament, and Richard Long sat in the Long Parliament with him.[89]

Although there were certainly differences in outlook among the Merchant Venturers, with some more committed than others to the Society's monopolistic policies, control of the city government gave their corporation enormous advantages both at home and in Westminster. As we have seen, not only could the Merchant Venturers count on the Common Council to sustain their Society's activities, as it did in passing the ordinance of 1605 and again by granting the wharfage duty, but it also often acted on the Society's behalf when favors were sought from the national authorities, as in 1621 and 1624, when the Society attempted to regain its monopoly through a parliamentary statute, and again in the 1630s, when its letters patent were under challenge.[90] These efforts were supported to a considerable degree by the wider membership of the city's elite, in part because many who were not members of the Merchant Venturers enjoyed close family and business ties to merchants of the fellowship. For example, among the nine aldermen who in 1621 signed the certificate sent to Bristol's members of Parliament in support of the Merchant Venturers' claims to monopoly, one was a soapmaker, one a mercer, one a brewer, and two, identified only as yeomen, were probably innkeepers.[91] At least three of these men also had close family ties to leading Merchant Venturers. In other words, by the 1620s a measure of peace appears to have been achieved in relations between the Society and the elder statesmen among the shopkeepers and artisans. Nevertheless, resistance to the Merchant Venturers' claims to monopoly survived down to the Civil War and beyond. As we have already seen, opposition arose after the Common Council's attempt in 1612 to restrict overseas trade to mere merchants. Even the compromise of 1618 did not end the controversy. The aldermen's certificates in support of the Society in 1621 and 1624 attest that some retailers and craftsmen continued to resist the Society by participating in overseas trade without joining its membership or submitting to the 1618 ordinances. Only with the Merchant Venturers' victory of 1639 did the Society reacquire the necessary powers to end these challenges.

These controversies only rarely found their way into local electoral politics in Bristol. Because high city offices such as mayor or sheriff were costly to hold, a practice of rotation was commonly followed by which nearly every common councillor was selected as he became the most senior figure who had not yet served. Moreover, the council itself was so heavily dominated by the Merchant Venturers that their rivalry with the retailers and manufacturers rarely could surface there. Nevertheless, this rivalry did manifest itself occasionally in the period. The election of Christopher Whitson to the mayoralty in 1626 can serve as our illustration.[92]

Whitson appears to have been among the leading protesters in 1612 against the Common Council's ordinance excluding retailers and manufacturers from overseas trade; and, as we have already seen, he became one of the few redemptioners admitted to the Society after the Merchant Venturers had been forced to liberalize their admissions requirements in 1618. Not surprisingly, his place in the city government excited dissension from the mere merchants. When he was proposed for sheriff in 1613 a dozen votes were cast against him, an almost unheard-of occurrence in elections for this burdensome office. Although not all of this opposition came from Merchant Venturers, Whitson's main adversaries were a closely linked group of great Spanish and Mediterranean traders, longtime proponents of the monopolistic ideals of the Society, who were led by Alderman Robert Aldworth, perhaps the richest and best-connected Bristol merchant of his generation. Whitson may also have been behind the resistance to the Merchant Venturers' appeals for monopoly in the parliaments of 1621 and 1624 and the subsequent demand for the vote by all the freemen in the elections to the Parliament of 1625.[93] In any case, by 1626 the leading Merchant Venturers thought of Whitson as an overly "puntuall" man, as was said by one of them, rigid in outlook, whom the leading Merchant Venturers could not trust to act in their interests.[94]

Whitson's main rival for the mayoralty in 1626 was Aldworth himself, who was nominated by the outgoing mayor, John Barker, a Merchant Venturer in Aldworth's camp. Analysis of the final vote shows the leading Spanish and Mediterranean traders on the council pitted against the retailers and manufacturers. Aldworth received nineteen of the forty-two votes cast; seventeen of these came from Society members. Whitson received twenty-two votes, only eight of which were from Merchant Venturers.[95] The division among the Merchant Venturers is revealing in its own right. The eight votes from Society members for Whitson came from lesser members, men who traded primarily in the bulky and less profitable wares of the Baltic, Normandy, Brittany, and the Bay of Biscay. They were in the following of Alderman John

Whitson, Christopher's powerful cousin. John Whitson's own rivalry with Aldworth and his clique went back to the beginning of James I's reign when, as we have noted, Whitson was the only Spanish merchant in Bristol willing to accept the newly refounded Spanish Company, including its apparent welcoming of retailers and craftsmen into the Bristol branch.[96]

These rivalries between the mere merchants and their anti-monopoly opponents penetrated deeply into the structure of politics in Bristol in this period, becoming in the process a foundation for controversies seemingly very distant from the main arena of conflict. Take, for example, what happened in 1639 when the city needed to elect a new chamberlain. By letters patent of 1499, the Bristol chamberlain, with duties modeled on those of his London counterpart, was to be elected by the mayor and the Common Council and to hold office during their pleasure. Because of his central importance as comptroller of the city's revenues, agent in its dealings with the Crown, and enforcer of its economic regulations, the Corporation took great pains not only to assure that he would be a man of known character but to control his activities when he was in office.[97] Normally, the office was a source of strength in municipal affairs. In 1639, however, the death of Nicholas Meredith, who had been Bristol's chamberlain for the previous thirty-six years, provoked a crisis with the Crown. At the election of his successor in October, eight candidates presented themselves, only four of whom received votes. The winner was William Chetwyn, a well-connected merchant, the choice of twenty-four of the forty-one councillors present.[98] Among the disappointed, receiving no votes at all, was one Ralph Farmer, gentleman, a minor official of the Chancery and an associate of the earl of Berkshire in the monopoly of malt kilns. At the time of the election, however, Farmer, though the son of Thomas Farmer, brewer, late alderman of Bristol, had not yet sought admission to the freedom of the city, possession of which was required for the office according to the city's charters.[99] Nevertheless, before a month had passed the Common Council received an ominous letter directly from King Charles I, quashing the election on the grounds that Chetwyn was a man "out of this our realm" and that his election had been for private ends, "to the prejudice of common libertie." In his place the king recommended "Ralph ffarmer a man not vnknowne vnto yorselves and by many of you much desired, of whose abilities & fitness we have receaved an ample testimony and assurance."[100] Just how the king became cognizant of this matter is unclear. The common councillors placed the blame on

Ralph Farmer himself, whom they accused of casting "some aspersion" on them by some "vndue suggestions" to the king.[101] But probably Farmer's connection with the earl of Berkshire, recently sworn to the Privy Council, explains how he was able so quickly to obtain the ear of King Charles.

The Common Council's reaction to the king's letter showed prudence but determination. They immediately quashed Chetwyn's election and replaced him with Farmer, who by now had become a sworn burgess of the city. But at the same time they appointed a committee to go forthwith to the court to insure that "the City . . . stand right in his Majesty's opinion."[102] The upshot was a petition to the king describing what they had done in response to his letter, denying that the councillors had acted in any way out of faction, reminding him of the city's charters, confirmed by him, which placed the right to elect the chamberlain in the hands of the mayor and the Common Council, and asking that he "ratify" the first election or permit them to proceed to a new election between Chetwyn and Farmer. When the king ordered a new election, Farmer received eighteen votes, including those of the mayor and two sheriffs, while Chetwyn again received twenty-four votes.[103]

Curiously, the forces at work in this election show social and political cleavages similar to the ones we have seen at work between Aldworth and Whitson. In the first vote in October, no identifiable faction supported Chetwyn or any of his active opponents.[104] But at the second election fifteen of Farmer's eighteen votes came from leading Merchant Venturers, including four who had previously voted for Chetwyn. This shift made Farmer the candidate of the mere merchants, including the surviving members of the Aldworth clique, many of whom had been named to the Society's powerful Court of Assistants in its recent charter. Chetwyn's supporters came from a wider range of occupations, including, besides merchants, mercers, brewers, drapers, and grocers. Although fourteen of Chetwyn's votes also came from Merchant Venturers, most of these were northern traders, and less influential in the Society than were Farmer's supporters. Quite surprisingly, the latter had spent most of the 1630s fending off one royal commission after another in search of unpaid debts owed the Crown or its officials.[105]

How can we explain this division? Unlike in the Whitson election case, the answer cannot be found primarily in the economic activities of the two candidates. Chetwyn himself was a well-connected merchant who had been a Merchant Venturer since before 1618; he had been apprenticed to one of Aldworth's regular business partners. Farmer apparently did not engage in overseas trade at all. Rather, the deciding factor seems to have been the social horizons and aspirations of Farmer's party. They were politically wary and politically adept men, dependent upon foreign trade and therefore upon the Crown and national policy for their economic positions. With the granting of the Merchant Venturers' new charter in 1639, these individuals had received a great boon from Farmer's nominator, King Charles I. To them it must have seemed only prudent to follow his leadership in filling the chamberlain's office.

We have moved decisively from the realms of economic structure, social organization, and cultural form to the world of political choice and action. Although large-scale historical developments like the opening of the Atlantic to trade and the coming of the Reformation conditioned the course of political events in this period, they did not determine them. Rather, individuals, acting from motives that pulled them, sometimes at cross-purposes, to advance their personal or family interests and to uphold their communal obligations, were confronted by dilemmas of commitment that could be resolved in a variety of ways. Their decisions depended on how they weighed the efficacy and rectitude of the available courses of action and the importance and value of their various goals. In these circumstances, we can no more expect to find uniformity of choice within identifiable groups than between them. The patterns, instead, were probabilistic or statistical, with the members of a particular group mostly following the same line as their fellows but by no means always doing so. Nevertheless, the Merchant Venturers, particularly those specializing in trade with southern markets, had come to believe that only a form of monopoly could assure Bristol's prosperity, whereas a wide group of retailers and artisan entrepreneurs saw such a monopoly as a threat to their ancient rights as freemen of the city and of England. These little businesses reveal a complex interplay of local issues and national policies, notable citizens and Crown officials, communal factions and central institutions. They were little only in scale, not in significance.

CHAPTER 7

Looking Backward

Politics is never just the effect of impersonal economic and social processes. It drives developments in society as well as responds to them; it transforms social facts into social forces. Social facts—facts about the varying distribution of wealth, the growth or decline of population, or the alteration of social structure—operate largely below the threshold of everyday awareness. They are usually discernible only to the trained eye looking in retrospect at the accumulated evidence of slow and steady processes of change. Present-day historians armed with the weapons of modern scholarship can often learn more about social facts than could those who lived through their various twists and turns. But the facts of social change can never be kept entirely below the surface of daily events. By showing the fault lines and rifts in society, they move individuals and groups to concerted action. They enter into consciousness and are transformed into ideology. Often this process involves assimilating the new into the old, first in order to find the right language by which to understand it, and later to try to contain it. In this respect the shaping of an ideology has a great affinity with the formation of ritual, especially of the kind that the Bristolians made for themselves in the later Middle Ages. There is both an inability to grasp the scale and significance of change and a hope of holding the community together as the pressures for change build within it. But as with those late medieval rituals, a backward-looking approach can only bottle up so much before its vocabulary of containment can no longer cope with the energies it tries to control.

Something of this process can be gathered if we look briefly to the Petition of Right. This document, justly famous in English history, also has a unique place in Bristol's local history. In August 1628 the city's two members of Parliament, John Doughty, an alderman, and John Barker, who had been mayor in 1625–26, brought into the Council House "six paper books containing the several arguments made in the Parliament house of the liberties of the subject," which the council "thought fit" to be "entered into some of the register books of this citty there to remain of record forever."[1] Why were the councillors so interested in these debates?

Much of the answer lies in the nature of the events that originally provoked the Petition of Right. Since war with Spain and France depended on sea power, Bristol, England's second port, inevitably found itself in the thick of the action and thus bearing what its magistrates considered a disproportionate share of the burden. They were required to lay out money to supply the king's ships and to offer him the services of their own, all without timely payment or clear purpose. Again and again they found themselves dutifully answering requests from the Privy Council for the pressing of sailors and staying of ships, only to be faced with countermanding orders and with seemingly inexplicable administrative confusion and delay.[2] As merchant shipowners deprived by the wars of the late 1620s of their principal markets, they could do little else with the ships, their main capital resources, except engage in privateering, which brought their enterprises into conflict with other naval activities and brought them into all too frequent dealings with the corruption of the Lord Admiral's agents.[3]

Wartime frustrations had been building in Bristol from the inception of Charles I's reign to the summoning of the 1628 Parliament, as the actions of naval commanders, press masters, Admiralty officials, and the like became increasingly intrusive. The climax came in the winter of 1628, when Captain William Buxton, under orders from the Admiralty, attempted to press into royal service seven of Bristol's best ships and eight barques, totaling about eighteen hundred tons and carrying four hundred and forty-four men and one hundred and six pieces of valuable ordnance. The owners of two of the vessels refused to fit their ships, saying they would "not disburse any money in setting them forth." The "stubbornnesse" of these two men, Giles Elbridge, son-in-law and partner of Robert Aldworth, and Humphrey Hooke, already a prominent councillor and leading Merchant Venturer, encouraged others to resist. Buxton found himself unable to complete his orders without paying "theise stiffnecked people" for everything in advance. "[F]or if possible," he said, "I will not be beholding to none of this towne for the smallest courtesie."[4]

The crisis of 1628 hit the city's merchants hardest. They wanted relief from the heavy fiscal burdens of the war,[5] and by the summer of 1628 all those who were owed large sums by the Crown had begun what can only be called a lenders' strike. On 22 August, the very day the six paper books were registered in Bristol, the mayor wrote to the Privy Council that until the debts were repaid "noe man will contribute to any further charge."[6] But the Bristol merchants were prepared to undertake some necessary burdens, such as guarding the coasts against piracy, provided they were guaranteed in advance that their costs would be met by the Crown. In June, for example, they had set forth two ships on condition that the expense would be covered by the Exchequer from the proceeds of the first two subsidies recently granted in Parliament. Indeed, the city's two members of Parliament had brought this good news with them from Westminster, along with the arguments in Parliament that they wished preserved in the city's records.[7] No wonder the leading common councillors found the issue of liberty as expressed in the Petition of Right so worthy of special treatment.

The Bristol magistrates' concern for the "liberties of the subject" carries with it some important implications about their idea of the state. These men saw themselves in a coordinated relationship with the central government, with which they were jointly to preserve order and protect the subjects. They were willing to accept state power so long as it helped them perform these vital functions. Order to them meant the union of authority with property, a union expressed in their own leadership of their community, and they feared any use of state power that threatened this union. For this reason, no Bristol magistrate was anticipating an all-out breach with the monarch in defense of community against the encroachments of the king's officers upon the city's body politic. Many of the councillors, however, were concerned about the best way to distribute power between the local and the central authorities for the preservation of order and property, and in the later 1620s they feared that the unrestrained exercise of royal power might result in social chaos.

The same sense of danger to hierarchical order also troubled them in the 1630s, when a plague of royal commissions seeking concealed prizes

and unpaid customs descended upon them in the aftermath of the Spanish and French wars. The commissioners, acting "as lords and judges
over them, as if all law and justice lay in their hands," threatened the
networks of cooperation and deference in the city. They forced merchants to tell what they knew "of others their friends and partners . . .
[w]hereby some are constrained (for discharging of their consciences) to
accuse one another." Even worse, they "tempted" the merchants' factors, servants, and seamen "to accuse the Marchants and owners by
whome they liue and are maintayned."[8] Hence the Bristol magistrates
faced the question of political choice by concentrating on what would
best promote the maintenance of the national polity as they had come
to understand it. For most of them, this was a polity in which men who
had roots in the community, not strangers with few local ties and little
comprehension of local conditions, properly exercised authority for
the king. The Bristol magistrates envisioned a political world in which
community and state were related to one another as parts to the whole,
not as opponents. In this sense they measured the events of the early
years of Charles I's reign against the model of society made evident in
Elizabeth I's visit to Bristol in 1574 and confirmed in Queen Anne's visit
in 1613.[9]

The responses of the Bristol magistracy to the events of 1628, then,
could not become the city's first step along the "high road to civil war,"
since the motives behind them were linked to ideals of hierarchical authority. Though these men were harshly critical of current policies, their
grievances did not provide a firm footing for systematic opposition to
the Crown. Even their experience in the 1630s of intrusions and usurpations by Charles I and his agents could not force them into rebellion
against their king. When the Civil War finally came to Bristol in 1642
and 1643, the majority of the common councillors, and others of similar
social and economic position, sided with the king against Parliament.
Their long, if tumultuous, association with the Crown as its suitors and
servants, culminating in the Merchant Venturers' receipt of their new
letters patent, seems to have anointed their loyalty with the chrism of
self-interest. As Sir Ronald Syme tells us of another era of revolution,
"liberty and the law are high-sounding words. They will often be ren-
dered, on a cool estimate, as privilege and vested interest."[10]

But words have a political efficacy of their own, since politics depends in part on how the parties express the issues. In this instance, the
words used were corrosive of the very regime of privileges and immunities which those who uttered them sought to uphold. To secure for

themselves the "liberties of the subject," the Bristol common councillors adapted to their purpose a well-established procedure for registering the royal concessions and favorable judicial rulings affecting their corporate franchises.[11] By making the six paper books "of record" they showed their intention of using them as precedents in the law courts at Bristol and Westminster against future encroachments and usurpations by the Crown. But in doing so they transformed the nature of the issue from one of communal privileges and immunities to one of individual and collective legal rights. In a sense, they saw their particular problems as part of a larger dilemma of fundamental law affecting everyone, not as a series of separate challenges to them alone that were to be met one at a time using makeshift defenses.[12] Is it too much to say that these Bristolians—for a brief moment at least—conceived that their English liberties preceded their burghal rights? And that their civic franchises alone could not protect them against the arbitrary actions of the Crown or its officials? If most of these men saw their interests as allied with the king in 1642, that hardly diminishes the importance of this "declassification" of liberty, as J. H. Hexter has called it.[13] It represented a profound and irreversible shift in the conception of contemporary political problems that entered the general political culture, made it possible to juxtapose the claims of authority to those of rights, and—as we shall see—affected Bristol's affairs in the ensuing period.

In Bristol, relations between the town authorities and the Crown had long worked at cross-purposes. They not only linked the local community to the English state but drove a wedge between the increasingly dominant faction in that leadership and the larger community over which it ruled. As we know, the roles of mayor, alderman, and common councillor served to separate the officeholders from the body politic at large and to give them advantages in dealing with the state on matters vital to their private interests. For members of this merchant elite, the later 1620s and the 1630s had been a period of conflict with the Crown that had ended in accommodation. Other groups in the city were not so fortunate, since they lacked the political resources of the Merchant Venturers. After 1634, for example, the city's soapmakers had no one of their Company in the Bristol Corporation. Nevertheless, their difficulties with the Crown were just as great as those of the merchants. First, the royal patent granted to the Society of Soapmakers of Westminster resulted in a sharp cutback in legal soap production in Bristol; then the king's impost on soap almost destroyed the industry in the city. By the late 1630s only four of eleven soap-houses survived in Bristol, and a full dozen of the soapmakers were lodged in Fleet Street prison for non-payment of the impost. Yet no one from the Bristol Corporation came to the aid of the soapmakers. As a result, several prominent Bristol soapmakers struck private bargains with the Westminster company and the Crown, leaving their fellows to struggle to find a livelihood, a task made all the more difficult by the Merchant Venturers' new charter, which deprived them of the right to trade overseas free of Merchant Venturer control. Such were the disadvantages of exclusion from civic office.[14]

The various Bristol responses to the summoning of the Long Parliament also show the existence of a divided community in pre–Civil War Bristol. When Parliament was summoned, the freeholders of the borough, namely the members of the Corporation and a few others of similar social rank, selected two Merchant Venturers, Alderman Hooke and Alderman Long, to sit for the city. In January 1641 these men were presented with the two grievances Bristol's Common Council wished redressed in Parliament: the violation of Bristol's rights as a staple town for trade in wool, and the actions of those persons who had given false or misleading information to the king about the merchants, causing them "to be Pursuivanted up and unjustly handled and ill dealt with."[15] In other words, the grievances were the complaints of the narrow merchant group that dominated the city. But the excluded members of Bristol's community did not go unheard at this time. In October 1640, as the Long Parliament was about to be elected, "a great number of burgesses of the Citie" petitioned the Common Council for the right to vote in the parliamentary elections. This renewed a request made as recently as 1625, which the council had denied. The result was the same in 1640. The Corporation preserved its hold over parliamentary elections.[16]

In the absence of evidence naming the petitioners or information about whom they wished to elect, it would be a mistake to overinterpret this petition. Nevertheless, knowing what we do of the social and political structure of Bristol in the Elizabethan and early Stuart period, we can be reasonably certain that among the main beneficiaries of the requested change would have been precisely that excluded group of retailers and manufacturers whom the Merchant Venturers had sought to oust from foreign trade, since they vastly outnumbered the Merchant Venturers among the city's freemen.[17] The petition called upon the same principles of freeman's rights and community values that this group saw as being violated by the Society's privileges. In 1571 their predecessors had responded to the Merchant Venturers' monopoly with a similar demand for the right to vote in the forthcoming parliamentary elections.[18] The redress they wanted involved gaining access to the one institution they might use to counter the wide political influence so long enjoyed by the Merchant Venturers.

For ordinary citizens as well as magistrates, the social and political changes of the previous century or more could not be completely covered by Bristol's ancient traditions. The burghal rights of the former and the civic authority of the latter were now too deeply enmeshed in the institutions of the state and too dependent on events and developments occurring far from Bristol itself. Accommodation of differences would have to occur in a much wider field. The resulting division was deeply ideological. It touched the way various Bristolians understood their social and political world. What mattered was the distribution of authority, the capacity to rule. For one group the social order was arranged in a hierarchy headed by the monarch, with whom the local governors were associated as his lieutenants. In this view the requirements of justice provided that each rank receive its due according to its proper place in the hierarchy and that authority be concentrated at its head. On the other side, the principle of hierarchy, while hardly rejected, was subject to considerations of community and legal rights. Authority depended on recognition and acceptance by those over whom it was exercised, and justice demanded that the community's governors act for the commonweal, which could override the claims of individuals or particular groups. Any claim for privileges and immunities at the expense of the rights of fellow citizens violated this rule. In consequence, what was necessary and proper in the first view might be a sore grievance in the second.

In the early modern period, political ideology normally was never far from religious outlook. Was there a religious dimension to the factional conflicts that had developed in Bristol from the middle of the sixteenth century? Although the prehistory of the Merchant Venturers is centered on a religious gild and its chapel, nothing we have learned about the earliest stages of the disputes between the monopolists and their shopkeeper and craftsman rivals suggests that differences about doctrine, liturgy, or church government might have colored the rivalry. There were certainly many in the city who desired further reform in the church and others who wished to return to the comforts of traditional practices, if not the authority of the bishop of Rome. For example, Roger Edgeworth, writing at the height of the Reformation, saw a city in which som wil heare masse, some will heare none by theyr good wils, som wil be shriuen, som wil not, but for feare, or els for shame. some wyll pay tithes & offeringes, some wil not, in that wors then the Iewes which paid them truly, and fyrst frutes & many other duties besides. Som wil prai for the dead, som wil not, I heare of muche suche discention among you.[19]

But these differences did not play themselves out in controversies over the merchant monopoly in the second half of the sixteenth century. When Edgeworth lamented the dissension caused by the Merchant Venturers' 1552 charter, it was not because he favored one side or the other for its religious views, but because he saw social and political conflict to be undermining the communal harmony he deemed essential to a proper religious life.[20] Moreover, the Common Council during the reigns of Elizabeth I and James I seems to have been dominated by godly men of a moderate Calvinist outlook, who viewed the Anglican settlement as the exemplum of what Patrick Collinson has called "the religion of Protestants."[21] The ministers they selected for town lecturerships, such as Thomas Thompson, Edward Chetwyn, and Thomas Palmer, certainly seem to fit this mold.[22]

But there was an important intellectual link between the desire to maintain the art of merchandise as a separate craft and some forms of religious conservatism. As Roger Edgeworth viewed the matter in the mid-sixteenth century, those in the priesthood, no less than in any other occupation, needed training and skills. Just as a tailor ought not to meddle in the work of a Merchant Venturer, and a shoemaker ought not to practice the grocery trade, the priesthood should be left to those called to it. "I have knowen many in this towne," Edgeworth said, "that studienge diuinitie, hath kylled a marchaunt, and some other occupations by theyr busy labours in the scriptures, hath shut vp the shoppe windowes, faine to take Sanctuary." What was needed instead was "a true instructour, not infected with wylful and newfangled hereseyes."[23] Edgeworth's reason for believing so was that Christ had distributed his gifts "as doth please his goodnes . . . to some more of them, to some fewer and not so many." To some God had given "knowledge and cunning in spiritual causes, to some in temporall matters, to some learning in physicke, to some in surgerye, to some in handy craftes, to some in marchaundise or in such other occupying."[24] In each craft, moreover, some were more fit to lead than others.

As if there should be a matter of the trade of marchaundise to be intreated of among the marchauntes of this citie, if there came in a marchaunte of graue and longe experience, all the others woulde geue eare and lysten to his talke, and would be gladde to followe his counsell. . . . Euen so it is in matters of higher learnynge pertaining to our soule['s] health.[25]

Hence those in Bristol who believed in the priesthood of all believers were as wrong in their outlook as those who interloped on the trade of the Merchant Venturers.

For conservatives like Edgeworth there was a strong link between God-given skill and divinely ordained authority. Without authority, such figures were convinced, there would be nothing but disorder. "Experience teacheth," Edgeworth argued,

> that a great housholde wythout good officers is a troublous and vnruly busines. For where there is no quiet order of the subiectes among them selues, and of theym all in theyr degree toward theyr great mayster, soueraygne or ruler, euery man taketh his owne way, and so foloweth streife, brawling, and variaunce, and at the last destruction. The housholder must be fain to breake vp houshold if his folkes amende not. The great housholder almighty god hath a great & chargeable familie, that is the vniuersal multitude & company of al mankinde, which thoughe he could rule at his plesure accordinge to his own wil, yet it hath pleased him to put an order in this houshold, som head officers, som mean, som lower in auctoritie, som subiectes & seruantes.[26]

In such a social order everyone was "to do his office in his degree" and to cherish and help his fellows in safeguarding the whole. This view, of course, was but a commonplace of sixteenth-century social theory, as codified, for example, in the famous "Homily on Obedience."[27] Most Bristolians, like most other Englishmen, would have accepted its general premises and its broad conclusions.

But could ardent Protestants make its details consistent with the doctrine of justification by faith or election, which focused on the individual Christian's relationship to God, not on the special skills of the priesthood? If so, could they also make its claims on behalf of a strict division of labor among the crafts consistent with the principles of justice owed to all Bristol freemen according to the spirit of civic brotherhood? Unfortunately, nothing in the evidence for the reigns of Elizabeth I and James I tells us how Bristolians answered these questions or shows us that those who responded to the first of them in opposition to strong claims of clerical authority consistently answered the second in opposition to the Merchant Venturers' monopolistic claims. Given the complexity of these issues, we can hardly expect a clear-cut pattern to have appeared. However, by the 1620s and 1630s the city's sociopolitical factions may possibly have taken on some characteristics of a religious rivalry, although the evidence is extremely fragmentary and must be viewed with caution.

We can see such a rivalry surface, perhaps, in the election for mayor contested between Robert Aldworth and Christopher Whitson. Aldworth and some of this supporters seemed to have favored the Laudian or Arminian position in the church and would have found Edgeworth's view of the world congenial to themselves. Aldworth himself was a distant kinsman of Archbishop Laud.[28] In the 1630s, he and some of his allies favored church beautification and church music in their wills.[29] Unfortunately, we know nothing directly about Christopher Whitson's religious views, though the use of the word "puntuall" to describe him may hint that his enemies viewed him as a Puritan, overly precise in his morality and public observances.[30] It is also possible that his cousin, John Whitson, was favorably disposed toward Puritan views, at least at the end of his life. The moral and religious reflections he left behind at his death and his charitable bequests conform nicely in thought and action to many teachings of Puritan divines.[31]

A bit more is known about Christopher Whitson's brother-in-law, Mathew Warren, clothier, whose election to the mayoralty in 1633 also was disputed by Robert Aldworth and thirteen other Merchant Venturers.[32] In Queen Elizabeth I's reign Warren had been servant to William Tucker, clothier, who as mayor in 1571 led the fight against the Merchant Venturers' monopoly.[33] Warren's wife was probably active in Rev. William Yeamans's circle of Puritans, which met regularly in his house in St. Philip's parish to discuss sermons and difficult matters of Bible interpretation; she and many others from this group were important sectaries after 1640 and later became early Quakers. Mathew Warren was also tied to George Bishop, one of Bristol's leading sectaries of the 1640s and 1650s.[34] Most of the members of Yeamans's group were small shopkeepers and craftsmen, exactly those most likely to see injustice in the Merchant Venturers' monopolistic pretensions. But since they were not common councillors, their role in disputed municipal elections was, at most, indirect.[35] Although we have no direct evidence of Warren's own involvement in Yeamans's meetings, we can see that in his relations with his family and with the city's craftsmen in the cloth industry he lived in intimacy with some of its most faithful attenders.

This evidence suggests, but only very tentatively, the possibility that the different social visions of the rival parties in Bristol sometimes went together with membership in different religious camps. Some of the monopolists, with their strongly hierarchical views, tended toward Arminianism, while some of the anti-monopolists, with their strong sense of a brotherly fellowship of freemen, tended toward a community-minded Puritanism and even toward what Patrick Collinson has called "voluntary religion."[36] However, we are looking here at the extremes in the religious spectrum. They illustrate the ideological and cultural forces at work in the city, not the actual distribution of religious opinion among the various groups. It would be wrong to think that the majority of leading overseas traders were likely to be high churchmen while the majority of their opponents tended to be sectaries. Instead, difference in outlook turned on the relative weight given in each quarter to the demands of order and of fellowship. Divergent views on these issues could be readily expressed within the bounds of orthodox Calvinist Protestantism. We can see this point in the 1639 chamberlain's election, where the evidence of religious affiliation is ambiguous and confused.

William Chetwyn was the cousin of Edward Chetwyn, former city lecturer and late dean of the Bristol Cathedral chapter, who died only months before the October 1639 chamberlain's election. As we have already noted, Dean Chetwyn was an old-fashioned Calvinist.[37] He possessed a good library of Puritan books, including a Geneva Bible and the works of William Perkins, and he had strong views on the limited authority of bishops. He was also the brother-in-law of Sir John Harington of Kelston, whose Christian humanist learning and moderate Puritanism are well known. Edward's son, moreover, was an outspoken Presbyterian in the 1640s and 1650s.[38] Hence it is possible that some of the opposition to William Chetwyn arose from the city's Arminians in disagreement either with him directly or with his cousin and his cousin's family. He certainly seems to have received little support from the old Aldworth clique, even in the first of the two elections, despite his apprenticeship to one of its leading members.[39]

If it was Chetwyn's religious affiliation that drove opposition to him, however, support for Ralph Farmer was a poor way to have shown it. His patron, the earl of Berkshire, was hardly a friend or ally of Archbishop Laud or his party; indeed, he was rather the opposite. In April 1639, Laud had written Viscount Wentworth describing Berkshire as one of the "miserable builders" in the king's council, working "at Babel," "a very thin tree in a storm, and he will soon be wet that shelter there."[40] Farmer, for his part, seems to have been anything but a Laudian. He was an "Independent" in the 1640s and later a Presbyterian.[41] Finally, there seems nothing in William Chetwyn's service in the chamberlain's office from 1639 to his death in 1651 to show obvious religious partiality.[42] He was almost certainly no Arminian, or he probably would not have survived the parliamentary purge of Bristol's government in 1645, but he also does not appear to have been an outspoken Puritan, since he remained in office during the Royalist occupation of Bristol from 1643 to 1645, when the crown removed the leading Puritans and parliamentary supporters from their civic offices. Overt doctrinal differences seem distant from the rivalry between Chetwyn and Farmer.

Nevertheless, we cannot dismiss the importance of religion even here, at least for some common councillors. It was Chetwyn who had well-known connections to a prominent clergyman whose orthodox Calvinist views would have been very familiar to the Bristolians from the days he had lectured to them on "The Strait Gate and the Narrow Way" and other subjects, and it was Farmer who had the backing of the king. For those leading Spanish and Mediterranean merchants who were emotionally and intellectually committed to hierarchical order in society and the beauty of holiness in liturgy and who understood their authority in the city to descend from God and the king, the choice between Farmer and Chetwyn would not have been a difficult one. They could vote but one way, even if they knew of Farmer's dependence upon the earl of Berkshire and of Berkshire's rivalry with Archbishop Laud. Laud and his followers, after all, were hardly likely to back Chetwyn even to thwart the patronage of the "thin tree" they so despised.

The choice would have been more difficult for the rest of the Common Council, whether they were content with the moderate Calvinism that had prevailed in the Anglican hierarchy before Charles I's reign and that still engaged most Englishmen or whether they favored further reform in the church, since it required them to weigh their respect for the king's nomination against their own commitment for or against Chetwyn. In the highly charged atmosphere of this election, the choice was likely to be made ideologically, depending on whether or not the voter honored the role of royal authority in overseeing the city more than the civic community's liberty to decide the matter for itself. Yet no well-developed rules existed for making such a choice. The king and the community were understood to be joined in harmony in the body politic, not to be opponents or enemies. They were believed to receive mutual benefits from their union, not losses on one side to balance gains on the other. Ordinarily a choice between king and community never arose. Among the councillors who switched their votes in the second election—to Chetwyn from his previous opponents, and from Chetwyn to Farmer—the necessity of deciding between competing values, mixed with the need to make judgments regarding their own self-interest, must have posed a major dilemma. Out of such ethical ambiguity we cannot expect to find intellectual clarity.

We come away with a picture of Bristol in the 1630s as a city in which small but significant groups of high churchmen, many of whom where wealthy Spanish and Mediterranean merchants, and proto-sectaries, the vast majority of whom were shopkeepers and artisans, lived in a place populated by moderate Anglicans, for whom the potentially competing ideals of order and community remained in what at times became an uncomfortable equipoise, exemplified as much in the small disputes over local politics and commercial organization in the city as in the great controversies of church and state.

The force of events in the 1640s, during which Bristol found itself the focus of contention by opposing parties both within and without the city, gave its politics a new and harder edge. But in the face of continued uncertainty on the part of many Bristolians about the best course to follow, political necessity and the opportunity for material advantage took the place of intellectual clarity in the debates. Given the effect of the Merchant Venturers' 1639 letters patent on the trading activities of non-members, it is no surprise to find that the old rivalry between the merchant monopolists and the retailers and craftsmen resurfaced with the calling of the Long Parliament. As we know, from the very moment of its foundation the Society of Merchant Venturers had engendered bitter conflict within the city whenever it triumphed in its battle for effective monopoly powers. The attempt by some of the freemen to win the vote in the October 1640 elections is only the first hint of the troubles. Signs of the character of the political alignments appear in the fate of Aldermen Long and Hooke, Bristol's members in the Long Parliament. In 1642 both were ousted from their seats for participating, along with many other Merchant Venturers, in Alderman Abell's wine license. In 1645 the Long Parliament removed them from the municipal office as delinquents.[43] Their replacements, elected in 1642 under the same franchise as Long and Hooke, had similar histories. Both John Glanville, the city recorder since August 1630, and John Taylor, an alderman since January 1640, were adherents of the same social, economic, and political view held by the conservative leaders of the Merchant Venturers. Taylor went to Oxford when the king set up a Parliament there, and in 1645 he died in Bristol defending the city against Fairfax and Cromwell.

Glanville, who had been Speaker of the Commons in the Short Parliament, also joined the king in Oxford in 1643, was disabled from future service by the Long Parliament, and was imprisoned for a time in the Tower before compounding for his delinquency. Bristol purged him as its recorder in 1646.[44]

According to John Corbet, minister in the city of Gloucester and ardent supporter of the parliamentary cause in this period, with the outbreak of Civil War Bristol was "much distracted" between the "well-affected and malignant parties," with the "basest and lowest sort" together with "the wealthy and powerful men" supporting the "King's Cause and Party," while "the middle rank, the true and best Citizens," were on the parliamentary side. "[T]he present state of things," he says, "had taught men to distinguish between the true Commons of the realm and dreggs of the people, the one the most vehement assertors of Publike Liberty, but the other the first rise of Tyrannical Government and the foot-stoole upon which Princes tread when they ascend the height of Monarchy." The shortcomings of "the needy multitude" he attributed not only to "their natural hatred of good Order," but also to the fact that they "were at the devotion of the rich men," who, he tells us, were "des-affected to reformed Religion" and "conscious of delinquency" and therefore "did much distaste the wares of the Parliament." By implication, he saw the virtue of the true Commons resulting from their support of "good Order" in civic affairs, their independence from the patronage of the powerful, and their affection for "reformed Religion."[45]

In offering this analysis Corbet refers specifically to events in December 1642, when Bristol was garrisoned by parliamentary forces under the command of Colonel Essex. Fearful that a garrison would make Bristol the target of attack from the king's forces, the city government, already committed to the Western Association in support of Parliament, sought to man the fortifications on its own. As Corbet tells the story, Essex found himself blocked "by the multitude" at one of the gates and had to force his way into the city at a less well-manned place to which he received direction "from a Party within."[46] But Corbet may also have been thinking of the events of the following spring, when a band of Bristolians, including the two sheriffs for the year, organized a plot to reverse these events by opening the city's gates to Prince Rupert. The attempt was thwarted when a considerable number of sailors and portside laborers, along with many of the leading merchants, were arrested by Colonel Nathaniel Fiennes and his soldiers. Although there were certainly men of "the middling sort" in this conspiracy, its leaders came from that same group of Merchant Venturers who had supported Robert Aldworth in his bids for a second term as mayor in 1626 and 1633.[47]

Many of these men had also been behind the effort in the spring and fall of 1642 to send petitions to both the king and Parliament urging an "accommodation" of their differences. At first glance this petition campaign appears to support the claim that a large number of Bristolians, if not most, preferred a form of neutrality to partisan commitment in the Civil War.[48] But a closer look shows that even neutrality had its partisan edge. Unfortunately, only the city's petition to the king has survived. It is focused primarily on the grievances of its great merchants but openly follows the very similar petitions mounted in London in 1642 by a group of its prominent citizens, many of whom later became involved in Edmund Waller's plot to turn the metropolis over to the king. Comparison of London's petition to the Lords and Commons, which has survived in a copy printed by the king's supporters in Oxford in 1642, with Bristol's somewhat later petition to the king, also printed in Oxford, shows them to be very similar in their ideological outlook and political purpose, though somewhat different in their emphasis. There can be no doubt that each city's petitions had an independent history, but in genesis and ideology Bristol's shares a great deal with its London counterpart.[49]

The Londoners in their petition to Parliament stressed how "by a knowne Law" the realm had "setled and preserved our protestant Religion, our Liberties, and properties, with a right understanding betweene King and Subjects, which produced peace and plenty in our streets." Continued civil war, they said, threatened "the destruction of Christians, the unnatural effusion of bloud; Fathers against Sons, brothers by brothers, friends by friends slaine, then famine and sicknesse, the followers of civill war, making way for a generall confusion, and invasion by a forraigne Nation, while our Treasure is exhausted, our Trade lost, and the kingdome dis-peopled."[50] The emphasis was on the danger to true religion, public order, and social hierarchy engendered by the "divisions" between the king and Parliament. The Bristolians, too, were concerned about these matters. They lamented that the realm was now "as full of horror and wrath as any object which can incounter humane eye-sight, appearing meerly the Ghost of that *England* which it was so lately." They complained that they were "overwhelmed with an increasing perpetuity of cares and troubles, such as not time nor history had scarce mentioned in this Kingdome, neither in the Barons nor any other civill warres: Your Majesty being, as it were divorced from those husbands of the Common-wealth, the honourable the high Court of Parliament." And they spoke bitterly of the "strange and uncouth distractions that have lately broken forth into the Church of *England*."[51]

Somewhat more than the Londoners, however, they emphasized the disastrous toll on trade created by the outbreak of war. "[I]nstead of the continuall and gainful trade and commerce, which all maritime towns, in especial this City of *Bristoll* had into forraigne parts," they said,

> [o]ur ships lie now rotting in the Harbor without any Marriners or fraught or trade into forraigne parts, by reason of our home-bred distractions, being grown so contemptible and despised there, that our credits are of no value, wee being (through the misfortune of our nation) reputed abroad as men meerly undone at home; and what detriment this discontinuance of traffique with forrainge nations may beget and bring forth, both to your Majesties particular revenue, by decay of the emolument of customes, and to the Subject in generall by want of exportment and importment of commodities, cannot to your sacred wisdome be unknowne.[52]

As a result, "no man injoyes his wife, children, family or estate in safety this day . . . so that unspeakable is our misery, unutterable our grievances, fathers being ingaged enemies against sons; and sons against fathers; every good Towne and City, as this your City of *Bristoll,* being inforced to their great and infinite expence, to maintaine garrisons and courts of guards for their security."[53] The debt to the Londoners' language is apparent enough in these sentiments, but the differences suggest how much the Bristol petitioners saw a well-established trade as one of the principal sources of good order in their community.

The logic of the London petitions of 1642 had linked support of the Crown with the defense of liberty and the church. With the 1643 plot in Bristol to turn the city over to Prince Rupert, this same conjuncture of ideas became apparent among the conspirators, although again with something of a Bristol twist.[54] Their motives were heavily colored by the economic and financial burdens imposed upon the city by the war, the blame for which was placed by the conspirators squarely on the shoulders of the parliamentary forces resident within their walls. As an anonymous pamphleteer said in commenting on the martyrdom of Robert Yeamans and George Bowcher in the Royalist cause, "it is no wonder . . . that a city thus robbed of its wealth and libertie, groaning under the insupportable yoke of bondage and tyranny should endeavor by restoring the king to his rights, to restore themselves to their former freedome," which could not be done but by casting off the bonds in which the parliamentary garrison had ensnared them.[55] According to one source, the plotters considered themselves as standing for "the King, the Protestant Religion, and the Liberties of this City."[56] Yeamans said as much in his own defense. His commission from the king, he argued, was

> for the mayntenance of the true Protestant Religion established in the Church of *England*, the King's Prerogative and safety of his Person, Priviledges of Parliament, and the liberty and propriety of the Subject, and the defense of the City against all forces without the joynt consent of the Maior, Aldermen and Common Councell amongst whom there was some difference at that time concerning the admission of any Forces.[57]

Earlier, in their petition to the king, these same men had indicated that they were also pained by the "too much power of the Prelacie in forcing new Canons and unheard of doctrines upon us." They saw them as "the immediate and efficient causes of the many dissentions and troubles now raigning in this Realm, no oppression being so forcible or oppressive to mens consciences, as that which is intruded on them concerning their Beliefe and the worship of God."[58] They were neither Laudians nor sectaries in their religious beliefs. Their identification of local liberties of self-rule with the more general liberties of the subject, however, gives us an insight into the inherent royalism of their position. Serving as a member of the Corporation meant to Yeamans, Bowcher, and many of their colleagues on the Common Council being a royal officer, acting according to the city's charters for the mutual benefit of the urban community and the kingdom at large. Among those committed to this vision, any action that threatened the political role of the mayor, aldermen, and Common Council as the proper agents of royal authority in the city would be met with resistance, whether it came from the king's principal officers, as in the late 1620s and 1630s, or from the parliamentary army, as in 1642 and 1643. Since their own position in Bristol, and more generally in the English polity, depended in large measure on their relationship to the Crown, preserving the "liberties" of the city in the 1640s required restoring the king to his proper place at the head of the state.

Those who called for "accommodation" in 1642 and 1643 followed this same line of thinking. As we have seen, they spoke of the "strange and uncouth distractions that have lately broken forth into the Church of *England*," the "many dissentions and troubles now raigning in this Realm," and even of the king being "divorced from . . . the honourable

the high Court of Parliament."[59] This language carries with it a theory
about what has gone wrong. "Distraction," for example, refers to the
physical rending asunder what organically belongs together; it is what
happens when a traitor is beheaded, drawn, and quartered. "Divorce,"
a relatively new word in the early modern period, refers to the separation of the head of a family from his helpmate.[60] From its earliest usage
it carried a sense similar to "distract." In the Third Book of Sir Philip
Sidney's *New Arcadia,* for example, Pamela's executioner is said to have
used his sword "to divorce the fair marriage of the head and body."[61]
"Dissent"—used especially in relation to religious matters—is the opposite of "consent" and implies a failure to apprehend and submit to the
unifying truth. It depends on the existence of a natural union of parts
that together form a harmonious whole. Taken together, the use of these
terms to describe the disorder of the times gives us the image of a body
politic—with head and members—torn apart. "Accommodation" was
the proper remedy for this condition. In a strict sense it means bringing
things into measure. In other words, it signifies putting back together in
proper order that which belongs together. In the 1640s this could only
mean restoring the king to his leadership, just as healing "divorce" in
a family meant restoring the husband to its head. Bristolians who
adopted this language were neutralists only in a tactical sense; their
hierarchical vision of the social order, which made them desire peace
within their community, also allied them with the king as the one force
ultimately able in their vision of the world to bring harmony and proportion to the body politic.

For most of the Bristol magistrates this desire for unity was very
strong in the early days of the Civil War.[62] In November 1642, when
they decided to go ahead with the petitions that they had first discussed
the previous May, they declared themselves "to be in love and amity one
with another and doe desire a friendly assotiacion together in all mutuall accomodation." At the same time, they ordered the parish clergy to
meet with a committee for an "amiable accomodacon one with another
throughout the whole Citty to the end the Ministers themselves and
other of the inhabitants may be drawn" into discipline and order.[63] But
it is clear that the possibility of preserving harmony was growing very
dim. Not only had it taken them from May to July to agree on a first
draft of their petitions and from November to January to redraft and
send them,[64] but in the interval strong political forces were beginning
to stir elsewhere in the city. By the end of November, the Common
Council even found it necessary to forbid the wearing of colors and

ribbons on hats to signify affiliation with the king's party or the Parliament's.[65] The aim was to prevent street violence as the political issues of the era diffused into the lower echelons of Bristol society and factionalism threatened to undermine authority in the city.

Despite its shortcomings, then, Corbet's analysis of the politics of Bristol in the early 1640s has much to commend it. However, its efficacy depends precisely on avoiding a reductionist interpretation of his language.[66] Like the ancient writers from whom he derives his threefold system of categorization, Corbet's understanding of the concept of class is never exclusively economic. It turns instead on understanding political power and wealth to be intertwined precisely because the possession of wealth typically carried with it the obligation of service and the capacity to command. It is true, of course, that no city's politics can be made to fit neatly into a simple sociopolitical framework. It would be an oddly utopian world if all members of a given group, however defined, were found to conform their lives to a single formula. Nevertheless, Corbet was certainly right in seeing the majority of leading merchants taking sides with the king when events forced them, sometimes against their will, to decide where they stood. Their view of the world as well as their interests lay with him. And the king, for his part, knew well how to seal their allegiance to his cause. After his forces had seized Bristol in 1643, for example, he rewarded the Merchant Venturers for their "loyalty and fidelity" to him "in these late tymes of difficulty" by granting them the right to trade freely in the heretofore protected markets of the Company of the Merchant Adventurers of England and the Eastland, Russia, and Turkey Companies.[67] Although this patent had no more efficacy than Charles could give it, and his power in commercial matters was very limited in the mid-1640s, it was politically as well as legally the kind of grant that only a king could make. The leading Merchant Venturers lived according to a vision of public order that depended for its coherence on exactly this type of authority. They had spent decades in pursuit of favors of a similar sort. Hence Charles I's generosity harmonized with their understanding as well as their self-interest.

    Corbet was also right in thinking that many of the most ardent supporters of the parliamentary cause during the Civil War came from the ranks of the city's shopkeepers and craftsmen. We can perhaps see this from the list of witnesses who appeared at Colonel Nathaniel Fiennes's court-martial in December 1643 to support charges made by William

Prynne and Clement Walker against Fiennes for his surrender of Bristol
to Prince Rupert the previous July. These witnesses joined with Prynne
and Walker in vigorously attacking Fiennes, the son of Lord Saye and
Sele, for what they considered his lukewarm commitment to victory
against the king and thoroughgoing reform in church and state. Where
the leading Merchant Venturers had played the most important role as
supporters of the Yeamans-Bowcher conspiracy, here we find on the
parliamentary side precisely those middling men whom Corbet had argued were the greatest strength in Bristol. They were figures like Robert
Bagnall, Henry Hassard, James Powell, William Deane, Abell Kelly, and
John Batten, shopkeepers and artisans who later in the period would
be prominent both as interlopers in overseas trade and as leaders in radical politics. Several came from William Yeamans's circle in St. Philip's,
among them Dorothy Hassard, daughter of a prominent scrivener, sister
or sister-in-law to other small dealers, and wife of Matthew Hassard,
who had succeeded Yeamans as minister at St. Philip's.[68] Given the links
between the leading mere merchants and the Crown, it is hardly surprising that many men and women in the city's middling ranks were
filled with zeal for the good old cause. By the early 1640s, as we have
already seen, a rich legacy of antagonism between figures from these
groups and the Merchant Venturers had already been sustained for at
least ninety years.

It would be a mistake to think that those who sided with Parliament
in the Civil War did so primarily because of their grievances against the
Merchant Venturers. No doubt most of them acted, as did the members
of Yeamans's circle, from deeply held religious and ideological convictions, not narrow self-interest. But for many Bristolians those convictions had taken shape in the context of long-standing grievances against
the mere merchants' claims of monopoly. The grievances themselves depended not only on the actual damage done by the Merchant Venturers
to the social prospects or material welfare of their opponents but the ag-
grieved citizens' beliefs about the requirements of justice owed to all of
Bristol's freemen. These views in turn helped define what it meant for
them to live in a properly ordered and godly community. It is perhaps
only to be expected that as a result of this process of ideological self-
definition, men who opposed the Merchant Venturers' monopolistic
practices would be stirred into support for the parliamentary cause in
the early 1640s, when politics continuously cut the middle ground from
under the feet of those who might wish to stand upon it. The history of
the Society was so deeply embedded in Bristol's life and culture by this

time that a person's views about it could readily tip the balance one way or the other when large and difficult political decisions had to be made. The Merchant Venturers' receipt of new letters patent in 1639 seems to have provided a number of the Society's old opponents with a good reason to take the parliamentary side.

The careers of several leading supporters of the Long Parliament in Bristol can illustrate this connection between political radicalism and opposition to the Merchant Venturers' monopoly. One of these supporters was Richard Vickris, trained as a fishmonger. He served on the commission appointed by the Long Parliament in 1645 to purge Bristol's government of "delinquents" after Prince Rupert had been ousted from the city and to settle affairs in the interests of the parliamentary side. Although he had become a member of the Society of Merchant Venturers in the 1630s, he was among those resisting its authority to collect wharfage in 1638–39.[69] During the 1630s he had also regularly traded in partnership with nonmerchants, in violation of the Society's strict ordinances forbidding this practice. So had another ardent parliamentary supporter, Richard Aldworth, cousin to Robert and a member of the Merchant Venturers, although he had been trained as a mercer. Aldworth was one of the Recruiter members of the Long Parliament added in 1646. Like Vickris, and perhaps John Whitson before him, Richard Aldworth seems to have held a view of the Merchant Venturers as a useful institution for commercial regulation but not as an exclusive organization for promoting the interests of a few. The other Recruiter member for Bristol was Luke Hodges, a grocer and sometime partner of Vickris, though never himself a member of the Merchant Venturers. In 1635 he had fallen afoul of the Bristol Corporation and was threatened with a heavy fine when he resisted election to the Common Council.[70] Although neither Aldworth nor Hodges was an extreme radical, both were politically committed members of the Long Parliament who conformed themselves to the revolution as it unfolded in the late 1640s and early 1650s. Hodges eventually became an excise commissioner for the Commonwealth in 1652.[71] For these three men, the shaping experience of opposition to the Merchant Venturers' monopolistic claims and practices in the 1630s seems to help account, though by no means completely, for their alignment with Parliament in the 1640s.

Finally, we can also see something of the way the Merchant Venturers' monopoly had entered into politics in the history of relations between the Society and its opponents in the aftermath of the New Model Army's victorious siege in 1645. Parliament's purge of the Common

Council in 1645 removed ten men for their military service in the Royalist cause and for other forms of "delinquency." Eight of them were Merchant Venturers, drawn from that same group of Spanish and Mediterranean traders who in the 1630s had looked to Robert Aldworth for leadership. In the years from 1645 to 1650, eighteen men were either restored to or newly elected to the Common Council. Only eight were Merchant Venturers. One of these members of the Society was Richard Vickris, who had been ousted from his council post by the Royalists in 1643. A second was his son Robert, who was probably an early sectary in his own right and who later married the daughter of George Bishop, one of the city's leading radicals and a founding member of the Society of Friends in Bristol.[72] Two more were men who joined with the large throng of interlopers who entered the Merchant Venturers after the crackdown on illicit trade that followed the grant of new letters patent in 1639. A further two became members only after 1645, when the Society had markedly relaxed its old standards of admission.[73] In other words, not only did the proportion of Merchant Venturers added to the council drop from about 75 percent in the 1620s and 1630s to about 45 percent in this period, but even among the Merchant Venturers on the council there was no longer the same support for the old monopolistic policies and practices.

Because Bristol's history in this era was so dominated by the relations of the Merchant Venturers to their fellow freemen, whether friends and associates or competitors and opponents, it is perhaps not surprising that the city should have faced the cataclysm of the Civil War by looking backward to this history. When victory came to the antimonopolists in 1645, the remedy desired was the restoration of what they considered the rightful order of city life, an order in which the members of each trade or craft had their due place in the fabric of the community. Insofar as the reformed Common Council had a program in these years it was devoted to this end. Not only did the council seek to fill its ranks with a more even distribution of the wealthier occupational groupings in the city—mercers, grocers, soapmakers, and the like, as well as mere merchants—but it set out to put the city's crafts on a footing equal to that enjoyed by the Merchant Venturers. In 1647, for example, the mercers and linendrapers organized themselves into a gild for regulating their trade; the turners did the same in 1649, the milleners in 1651, and the woolendrapers in 1658.[74] At the same time, several of the older gilds strengthened their enforcement powers by passing ordinances permitting them to recover fines by legal action before city

courts rather than by the traditional but difficult and dangerous procedure of seizing goods directly from wrongdoers. The whitawers did so
in 1646, the weavers in 1649, and the newly revived company of barber-
surgeons in 1652.[75] In these various ways a concerted effort was made
to use the old mechanisms of social and economic control, strengthened
by new procedures, to bring balance and order to the civic community.
The same principle was at work in 1647 when the Common Council ordered the city's law courts, the Tolzey and the Mayor's Court, to "be
kept & continued as antiently."[76] In 1652 it carried its purposes further
when it made general the use of legal process to collect fines for violation of its own ordinances and regulations.[77]

This evidence also hints at another important feature of the period—
its social and economic turmoil. The very fact that the gilds and the city
government needed to revive or revise their old regulatory schemes suggests that enforcement had fallen into disarray. During a half-decade or
more of strife, Bristol's affairs had been marked by two full-scale sieges
in 1643 and 1645, a major outbreak of plague, the garrisoning of the
city by Parliament, by the king, and by Parliament again, and the corresponding turnover of power in the city from one local faction to another. It is no wonder that the traditional mechanisms of social and
economic control required renovation. Moreover, the presence of a substantial parliamentary garrison at Bristol Castle after 1645 made the
city something of an open market for strangers who might wish to come
to the city to take advantage of the new, more fluid economic and political situation this created.[78] In response to these chaotic conditions, the
reformed Common Council of Bristol was anxious to establish a social
order in which each trade and craft received its due according to the
council's understanding of the ancient traditions of the city.

In a sense, the reformers had accepted the main premise behind the
Merchant Venturers' own desire for control of its trade. They saw a city
composed of functionally interrelated economic specialties, each supporting the others through the proper management of its own affairs.
To assure this outcome the council wanted all the crafts to have the necessary powers to protect themselves against encroachments from others,
and it willingly granted them new privileges to assure that they could.
Where a particular group could not defend itself on its own, or where
economic disorder arose outside the bounds of craft organization, the
city government was ready to assist in imposing its tradition-minded vision of order, employing its own new techniques to do so. This conception of policy implied that the Merchant Venturers would take their

place—inevitably, an important one—within the prevailing division of labor. They would no longer be guaranteed superiority in rights and privileges, as they had long desired. Instead, they would become the first among equals in an economy of coordinated and mutually supportive parts.

⚘

No matter how fervently the Common Council sought to restore the old vision of order in this newly purified form, they were bound to have difficulty in doing so. Between the late 1630s and the early 1650s, the economic world in which they lived had undergone a profound and irreversible change. We can get a brief glimpse of that change in the preamble to the ordinances of yet one more new gild founded in 1652, the Company and Fellowship of Tobacco Pipemakers. According to this document, "the Art and Skill of makeing Tobacco Pipes" had now "become a Trade . . . very usefull and beneficial to the makers of them within this Citty," one capable of supporting "many Inhabitants and Free Burgesses," their wives, families, and apprentices. At its foundation there were already twenty-five active masters in the Company, who had "been bread and brought up Apprentices in the same Art."[79] Tobacco had been a highly valued trading item for decades, of course, but this new industry could never have taken hold in Bristol on this scale during the 1620s or 1630s, when only tiny quantities of Spanish and Virginia tobacco found their way to the city. We have here the first hint that a major new market in American commodities had emerged in Bristol between the granting of the Merchant Venturers' letters patent in 1639 and the founding of this Company of Tobacco Pipemakers in 1652.

In the next section we shall examine the effects of the extraordinarily rapid growth of this market on Bristol's life in the second half of the seventeenth century. Previously we explored the history of the city from William Smith's double perspective, laying it in platform, if you will, in its changing landscape of socioeconomic practices and political and ideological structures. Now we shall use a microscope to study the new form of life that emerged in the city after 1650. When we have completed this task we will be in a position to evaluate Bristol's transition from a medieval commercial center to an entrepôt of early modern capitalism.

PART 3

The Capitalism of the Spirit, 1650–1700

CHAPTER 8

A Shoemakers' Holiday

Through much of its history, Bristol had looked to the Atlantic for its fortune. Its sailors were already busy in Iceland's waters at the beginning of the fifteenth century.[1] But until the mid-seventeenth century, their inner eye was always elsewhere. When they surveyed the ocean they saw either the fish they needed in their quest for the wealth of the Iberian and Mediterranean markets or the passage that would take them directly to the riches of the East. It was only in the 1620s and 1630s that the English settlements in the Americas began to produce goods that attracted Bristol's merchants and suggested the genuine possibility that America might be as lucrative as the markets of southern Europe or even the pleasure domes of Asia. At first this new trade, profitable though it could be, was conducted on a very small scale. But by the 1650s it had grown considerably in volume. Now ships were returning to Bristol from the Chesapeake and the West Indies by the dozen, not just in twos and threes. This growth, however, represents more than a change in the character of this trade. It also reveals a change in the nature of the trading community that conducted it and in the political economy governing the city's life. Trans-Atlantic commerce became in an almost literal sense a shoemakers' holiday, an arena in which small men—artisans and shopkeepers—could, like Thomas Dekker's Simon Eyre, play the merchant.

Sometimes historical processes of this magnitude are captured in a single source. Such a document, when we are lucky enough to come upon one, can let us see a whole world in a grain of sand, as it were.

It can show us its larger structures in interaction. For late seventeenth-century Bristol we have just such a source in the city's *Register of Servants to Foreign Plantations*, calendaring the indentures of over ten thousand individuals who migrated from England to America through Bristol between 1654, when the *Register* begins, and 1686, when the last entries were recorded. It reveals a city at the center of colonial trade, supplying Virginia, Maryland, and the West Indies with the labor necessary to make their settlement successful. This source has long been known to students of seventeenth-century colonization in the New World and of geographical mobility in England itself.[2] But along with evidence of the early migration to the West Indies and the Chesapeake, it also yields insight into the economic, political, and ideological developments affecting Bristolians in the era that followed the Civil Wars. Within it, the main facts and forces of change affecting early modern Bristol have converged. To pursue the story of social and political change we have been telling, then, I propose to examine the history of this *Register* in some detail, as a way of understanding Bristol's encounter with the newfound land into which it and its people had now entered. As we shall soon see, the *Register*'s dry-as-dust pages contain within them something of the world of the shoemaker merchant.

The story of the Bristol *Register* has been colored from the outset by the social problem it professed to remedy. According to the September 1654 city ordinance that established this book of enrollments, it originated in response to the

> many complaints . . . oftentimes made to the Maior and Aldermen of the inveigling purloining carrying and Stealing away boyes Maides and other persons and transporting them beyond Seas . . . without any knowledge or notice of the parents or others that have the care and oversight of them.[3]

Not surprisingly, these dramatic words have attracted the attention of nearly every modern writer who has discussed the ordinance or the *Register*.[4] But no one has asked what prompted these charges of man-stealing or whether they present a satisfactory explanation for the *Register*'s existence. An answer to the first question will show on reflection that they do not.

In September 1654, Bristol's government had only one relevant case before it. It involved Farwell Meredith, an orphaned, runaway apprentice, who had importuned passage aboard the *Dolphin of Bristol*, bound for Barbados, and upon arrival had been sold as a servant to a planter there. According to a deposition given by several of the *Dolphin*'s crew, Meredith first came to the ship on 14 October 1653, when he was rescued from the tidal flats at Kingroad onto which he had ventured in his efforts to board the vessel. The following morning Marlin Hiscox, the ship's carpenter, asked the young man whether he would go ashore, but, according to the crewmen, Meredith responded that "he would leape overboard rather than goe on shore and yt he would goe to ye Barbadoes where he said he had a brother." With this the runaway entered himself into the "Merchants booke" by the name of John Chetwind of Gloucester, and only later at sea did he reveal his true name to be Meredith. When the *Dolphin* reached Barbados, Hiscox and John Blenman, the ship's supercargo, put young Meredith in service in a plantation "according to the Custome of the Iland," in return for which John George, the planter, promised Hiscox and Blenman a quantity of sugar. But Meredith refused to serve, saying "he would not worke for he did not come thither to worke for he was a gentlemans sonn & if he had thought he should have been sold he would never have come along with . . . Hiscox." His refusal resulted in severe beatings from the planter. Meredith arrived in Barbados just before Christmas 1653. At about the same time, efforts began in Bristol to recover the young man. By July 1654, his guardian had initiated proceedings in the Bristol Mayor's Court on actions of trespass and assault. The matter was still before the court on 11 September, when the last of a series of depositions was taken.[5]

Instead of a case of kidnapping in the strict sense of the word, what we have here is an allegation of "spiriting"—that form of treachery through which, according to contemporaries, countless men and women in the mid-seventeenth century were "enticed" or "seduced" into bonds of servitude in the plantations.[6] In this story, the runaway Farwell Meredith apparently learned only at the end of his journey of the custom of paying in service for passage to the colonies. But his case differs little in practice from the more common cases in which "spirits" gulled their victims into voluntarily sailing to Virginia or the West Indies with false tales of rich prospects upon completion of their service. In all these instances the hapless person found himself bound in a contract for labor which he had entered without his informed consent.

There can be little doubt that "spiriting," and perhaps also kidnapping, were sometimes practiced in mid-seventeenth-century Bristol. As early as 1644, for instance, an accusation arose against Michael Diggens, a Bristol mariner, for being "an old Roge" who "Cozened . . .

many men and brought them out of the Country." In the mid-1650s and
early 1660s the Bristol archives record examples of nearly half a dozen
man-stealers, kidnappers, and spirits.[7] But granting the prevalence of
this evil and the widespread desire to crush it, the question remains: in
September 1654 did the Bristol Common Council intend only to remedy
this wrong, or did it have broader aims?

The ordinance established a simple arrangement for regulating the
traffic in servants from Bristol. To prevent "mischeifes," it required

> all Boyes Maides and other persons which for the future shall be transported
> beyond the Seas as servants . . . before their going aship board to have their
> Covenants or Indentures of service and apprenticeship inrolled in the Tolzey
> booke as other Indentures of apprenticeship are and haue used to be and
> that noe Master or other officer whatsoever of any ship or vessell shall
> (before such inrolment be made) receive into his or their ship or vessell
> or therein permit to be transported beyond the Seas such Boyes Maides or
> other persons.[8]

However, this seemingly straightforward procedure conceals a rather
puzzling fact.[9] By treating servants' covenants as in the same class as
indentures of apprenticeship, it placed them in a category of contract
into which minors could freely enter without their parents' consent.[10]
Apprenticeship indentures were normally bipartite agreements, with reciprocal obligations made exclusively in the names of the master and the
servant.[11] In the mid-seventeenth century, English law on this subject
was clear and unchallengeable. Coke, in his *Commentary upon Littleton*, for example, laid it down as "common learning" that "an infant
may bind himself . . . for his good teaching or instruction, whereby he
may profit himself."[12] Even though the courts held that ordinarily a
master could not sue an underage apprentice for damages upon such a
covenant, the indenture remained binding.[13] As the judges say in the
case of *Gylbert v. Fletcher* (1630), if the servant "misbehave himself,
the master may correct him in his service, or complain to a justice of
the peace to have him punished." In this fashion local police powers
rather than private litigation insured the apprentice's adherence to his
covenants.[14]

Requiring indentures from all servants bound to the plantations
might prevent future complaints of the type made by Meredith and his
guardian, but it could neither halt the activity of "spirits" who chose to
operate within the rules nor prevent the escape of runaways who chose
to abuse them. At best, it placed only a minor obstacle in their paths.
Provided the "spirit" had induced his underage victim into signing an

indenture, no real hindrance stood in the way of transporting him beyond the seas to the complete ignorance of his family or master. Moreover, any runaway willing to conceal his past could easily avoid detec-
tion, as the *Dolphin*'s crew claimed Meredith had done. In 1654,
therefore, the Bristol Common Council acted more to set the trade in indentured servants on a secure legal footing than to attack the evil of
"spiriting" proper.[15]

The registration procedures themselves lend some credence to this
view. Although servants usually appeared at the Tolzey to acknowledge
their indentures as they were being drawn and enrolled,[16] nothing in the
Bristol legislation required them to do so, and it was possible—as with
apprenticeship—for the master to present indentures already in being
for the clerks merely to enroll.[17] During some periods servants seem already to have been aboard ship when their indentures were presented,
a fact which must have made seeking acknowledgment of the contracts
no more than perfunctory.[18] Moreover, nothing in the Bristol ordinance
demanded consent from parents or masters before indentures for underage servants could be entered, and the Bristol *Register* mentions such
consent only once in all its ten thousand entries.[19] A master could even
legitimately avoid bringing a servant before the clerks to acknowledge
his indenture, "for feare of [his] running away."[20] If the problem of
runaways was the primary concern of the Bristol magistrates, these
arrangements appear woefully inadequate to their task. The welfare of
the servants hardly seems to have been what was at issue.

We also miss the point, however, if we look at the Bristol ordinance
primarily as a means of securing the servant trade in the interests of the
traders. The ordinance's most salient feature, its lengthy enforcement
clause, suggests that the Common Council's main purpose was not to
protect either servant or master, but to require the use of indentures by
traders not otherwise disposed to employ them. The enforcement clause
imposed a £20 fine on all ships' masters who received servants for transportation before the enrollment of their indentures. Violators were to be
punished either by distress and sale of their goods or by action of debt
sued before the Mayor's Court by the city chamberlain.[21] Those who informed against violators stood to gain one-quarter of the fine. Finally,
the councillors provided that the water bailiff should from time to time

> make strict and diligent search in all ships . . . after all Boyes Maides and
> other persons that are to be transported as Servants beyond the Seas and if
> vppon examinacon he find any such Boy maide or other person which haue
> not their . . . Indentures of service and apprenticeship so inrolled in the

TABLE 24   OCCUPATIONS OF THE COMMON COUNCILLORS
PRESENT AND VOTING ON 29 SEPTEMBER 1654

	No.	Merchant Venturer Members as of 29 September 1654[a]
Merchant	21	20
Mercer-Linendraper	8	3
Woolendraper	2	1
Grocer	2	
Ironmonger	1	
Vintner	1	
Soapmaker	1	
Brewer	4	
Total	40	24

SOURCE: Bristol Record Office, *Common Council Proceedings*, vol. 5, p. 72, compared to Bristol Record Office, MS 04220 (1), and Society of Merchant Venturers, *Wharfage Book*, vol. 1. The occupations of council members are based on prosopographical research using wills, court records, apprenticeship and burgess books, and similar sources. Membership in the Society of the Merchant Venturers was established from Patrick V. McGrath, ed., *Records Relating to the Society of Merchant Venturers of the City of Bristol in the Seventeenth Century* (Bristol Record Society 17, 1952), pp. 27–32, 261. I am grateful to Dr. Jonathan Barry for his assistance in assembling the data from the *Wharfage Book*.
[a] Members of the Society of Merchant Venturers before 1646 = 20.

Tolzey booke as aforesaid then the Water bailiff shall immediately give an Accompt thereof to the Maior or some of the Aldermen who are desired . . . to take such speedy course therein as by Law they are enabled to doe.[22]

Presumably the water bailiff also stood to collect £5 for each fine that was recovered. No more thoroughgoing administrative arrangement for the enforcement of a local ordinance existed in mid-seventeenth-century Bristol.[23] The councillors clearly wanted each servant, of whatever age or description, to have an indenture, yet they expected some of the servants' masters and some of the ships' captains to resist the requirement. In order to see the significance of this simple administrative point we must turn our attention from legislative interpretation to political history.

The men who passed the servant ordinance of 1654 represented the same mercantile elite that had long dominated Bristol. They came from a narrow range of the city's most lucrative occupations (Table 24). Of the twenty-one merchants who attended the council session on 29 September, some had themselves participated in the colonial trades during the 1650s (Table 25). However, most of them engaged much more heavily in traffic with Bristol's main continental markets in France, the Iberian peninsula, and the Mediterranean. Only a handful of the coun-

TABLE 25   COLONIAL TRADERS AMONG THE COMMON
COUNCILLORS OF 29 SEPTEMBER 1654

Traders[a]	Merchant Venturers	Non–Merchant Venturers	Total
Certain	17	3	20
Possible	2	2	4
Total	19	5	24

SOURCE: Bristol Record Office, MS 04220 (1), and Society of Merchant Venturers, *Wharfage Book*, vol. 1, compared to Bristol Record Office, *Common Council Proceedings*, vol. 5, p. 72.
[a] The records for colonial traders provide evidence for those who imported between May 1654 and May 1656 and those who exported servants from Michaelmas 1654 to Michaelmas 1656. If we continue the importers to 25 March 1657, we add just one more common councilman, namely Alderman John Locke, a Merchant Venturer.

cillors appear, directly or through their agents, among the dealers in servants. The council's American traders—slightly over half the membership—primarily enjoyed the fruits of the import trade in sugar and tobacco, not the difficulties of the export trade in human labor. Of the twenty-four councillors who belonged to Bristol's Society of Merchant Venturers, twenty had become members before the marked liberalization of admissions standards in 1646.

In order for us to understand what disturbed these men about the traffickers in servants, we need to return to the case of Farwell Meredith. The men responsible for "spiriting" Meredith to Barbados represent a nearly ubiquitous but largely unregulated element in Bristol's mercantile community in the mid-seventeenth century. They were "interlopers" according to the Merchant Venturers' definition. John Blenman, the *Dolphin*'s so-called merchant, was in fact a shipwright's apprentice. His master, Richard Basse alias Philpott, probably owned all or part of the vessel and with it engaged in overseas commerce as an adjunct to his trade of shipbuilding. To the tradition-minded overseas merchant, such an individual threatened the stability of the market both at home and abroad and usurped the rightful place of the true merchant, whose skills alone assured a steady trade at reasonable prices. Marlin Hiscox, the *Dolphin*'s carpenter, symbolized an even greater challenge to the traditional commercial order. Unlike Basse, he did not enjoy the freedom of Bristol. Never having sworn the burgess oath, he possessed no ordinary trading rights within the city. The sugar that John George owed him for Meredith's labor might as well have belonged to a foreigner or stranger who legally could bring goods to port only under economic restrictions.[24]

TABLE 26   BRISTOL TRADERS WITH THE AMERICAN COLONIES, 1654–1656

	Importers[a]		Shippers of Servants[b]		Both		Total	
	No.	%	No.	%	No.	%	No.	%
Men								
Leading entrepreneurs								
Merchants	80	26.23[c]	34	15.11[d]	18	21.69	96	21.48
Other leading entrepreneurs[e]	80	26.23	20	8.89	11	13.25	89	19.91
Total	160	52.46	54	24.00	29	34.94	185	41.39
Lesser crafts and trades[f]	30	9.84	11	4.89	5	6.02	36	8.05
Gentlemen, professionals, etc.[g]	4	1.31	5	2.22			9	2.01
Shipping industry[h]	100	37.79	121	53.78	41	56.63	180	40.27
Planters	11	3.61	34	15.11	8	9.64	37	8.28
Total known	305		225		83		447	
Total unknown	88		5		1		92	
Total	393		230		84		539	
Women	30		8		2		36	
Total men and women	423		238		86		575	
Importers, 15 May 1656– 24 March 1656/7	38				6		44	
Adjusted total[i]	461		238		92		619	

SOURCE: Bristol Record Office, MS 04220 (1); Society of Merchant Venturers, *Wharfage Book*, vol. 1; the names were cross-checked with other sources, including wills, Merchant Venturer records, apprenticeship and burgess books, and the Bristol deposition books.

[a] Mid-May 1654 to mid-May 1656.

[b] 29 September 1654 to 19 September 1656.

[c] Percentage of total of known men shipping inward.

[d] Percentage of known men shipping servants.

[e] Grocer, apothecary, haberdasher, mercer-linendraper, woolendraper, soap-boiler–chandler, vintner, innkeeper, fishmonger, ironmonger, tanner, clothier.

[f] Tailor, bodicemaker, hosier, glover-whitawer, upholsterer, feltmaker, milliner, pewterer, goldsmith, cutler, wiredrawer, watchmaker, gunsmith, butcher, baker, tobacco pipe–maker.

[g] Gentleman, yeoman, clerk, minister, scrivener.

[h] Mariner, cooper, shipwright, ship's carpenter, surgeon, pumpmaker, cook, sailmaker, ropemaker.

[i] If we include all the exporters of servants from 30 September 1656 to 29 September 1657, we increase the number of those trading both ways only by an additional two.

John Blenman, Richard Basse, and Marlin Hiscox were typical of the men who engaged in Bristol's American trades in the 1650s. In contrast to the city's traffic with the European continent, still largely in the hands of the Merchant Venturers, this trans-Atlantic commerce was not conducted primarily by traditional wholesale merchants. A broad spectrum of crafts was represented among the hundreds of individuals who indentured servants to themselves between 1654 and 1660. Judged by the entries in the *Register*, as David Souden has noted, "the whole Bristol trading community appear to have been involved in the trade of sending servants to the colonies."[25] However, this is only part of the picture.

As a practical matter, a profit could only be returned from the West Indies and the Chesapeake markets in the form of commodities.[26] In general, the shippers of servants seem to have initiated transactions as speculative ventures and were paid in colonial products only when they sold their cargoes in the colonies.[27] Fortunately, we can study the import side of Bristol's trade with these markets by using the records of the wharfage duty kept by the Society of Merchant Venturers.[28] Viewed together with the *Register of Servants*, the wharfage records yield an astonishing picture of Bristol's colonial trading community. Even the importers were far from being a body of traditionally trained merchants. In the two-year period after May 1654, when the *Wharfage Books* begin, four hundred and twenty-three individuals imported colonial sugar and tobacco. Thirty were women; some of these were themselves planters, but most were the wives or widows of mariners and shopkeepers who engaged in the trans-Atlantic traffic. Of the three hundred and ninety-three men, we know the occupations of three hundred and five. The vast majority were Bristolians, but on the whole they were not merchants. Somewhat surprisingly, only about 26 percent of the list can be identified with this occupation, at least as it is narrowly defined (Table 26). For the rest, soapboilers, grocers, and mercers were especially prominent among major retailers and manufacturers, and tailors, shoemakers, and metal craftsmen among those in the lesser trades. In the shipping industry, mariners, coopers, and shipwrights account for the majority of those engaged in the traffic.[29]

The representation of Merchant Venturers among the colonial importers is also revealing. In all, only seventy-six importers of Virginian and West Indian commodities in this two-year period were associated with the Society at some point during their lifetimes, and only twenty-four had entered the organization before 1646. Twenty-nine became members only after 1656, eight of them after 1670 (Table 27).

TABLE 27   MERCHANT VENTURERS TRADING WITH
THE AMERICAN COLONIES, 1654–1656

Merchant Venturers	Importers	Shippers of Servants	Both	Total
Admitted before 1646	24	6	2	28
Admitted 1646–1656	23	5	5	23
Admitted after 1656	29	12	6	35
Total[a]	76	23	13	86

SOURCE: Comparison of Bristol Record Office, MS 04220 (1); Society of Merchant Venturers, *Wharfage Book*, vol. 1; Patrick V. McGrath, ed., *Records Relating to the Society of Merchant Venturers of the City of Bristol in the Seventeenth Century* (Bristol Record Society 17, 1952), pp. 27–32, 261.

[a] If we add in those who imported goods from 15 May 1656 to 24 March 1657, we increase the number of importers admitted by one, the number of exporters admitted between 1646 and 1656 by two. But none of these shipped both ways.

According to the *Wharfage Book*, many of the older members of the Society who engaged in trans-Atlantic commerce still bought sugar at Lisbon, while others who did not engage in colonial trade at all also frequented Lisbon for sugar.

If we analyze the exporters of servants during the first two years of the *Register*, we get a picture of trade dominated yet more heavily by those who were not Merchant Venturers. Men identified as merchants represent only about 15 percent of the servant traders, and the role of the Merchant Venturers was smaller still, amounting to only 10 percent of the total (see Tables 26 and 27). Although some of Bristol's better-established overseas merchants, like Joseph Jackson, John Knight, and William Merrick, imported substantial quantities of colonial products in these years, such men did not dominate the colonial trades in the way they did the European ones. Instead, members of the shipping industry appear to have taken the largest share of the business (see Table 26).

These characteristics of the colonial trading community become even clearer when we consider trans-Atlantic commerce as a two-way traffic, with each shipment of servants resulting in a return cargo of sugar or tobacco. Between 30 September 1654 and 29 September 1656, two hundred and thirty-eight persons appear as masters in the *Register of Servants*, but only slightly more than a third of these traders imported any colonial products through Bristol from mid-May 1654 to late March 1657. During this overlapping thirty-four-month period, a total of six hundred and nineteen individuals traded with the American colonies, vastly exceeding the numbers who regularly traded in any way with Bristol's traditional markets in Europe and the Mediterranean. But only ninety-two men and women, or about 15 percent, were two-way traders who exported servants as well as importing colonial sugar, tobacco, and other goods.

Since many of the importers must have sent manufactured goods and other items to the colonies rather than servants, the absence of their names from the *Register of Servants* should be no surprise. But how did the servant traders who, according to Table 26, appear to have done no importing manage their affairs? A number of possible explanations suggest themselves. Returns from the colonies may have gone to another English port, such as Plymouth or London, though no evidence of such a pattern has come to light. Perhaps some Bristolians sought to avoid English customs by bringing their imports directly to market in Europe, in violation of the Navigation Acts. If such illicit transshipments occurred we should find some evidence of them when the traders returned to Bristol with European goods paying wharfage duty. We find just the contrary. The vast majority of colonial traders rarely, if ever, imported continental commodities to the city.[30]

The true explanation of the imbalance between exporters of servants and importers of sugar and tobacco lies in the social organization, not in the economics of the colonial trade. Most of the "masters" who appear in the *Register* and not in the *Wharfage Book* must have been agents for principals who actually financed the trade, enjoyed its profits, and appear only in the *Wharfage Book*. Many of the figures designated in the *Register* as masters, such as Gabriel Blike, William Rodney, Henry Daniel, John Vaughan, and Robert Culme, in fact were apprentices acting as factors or supercargoes for their own masters, on whose account trading took place.[31] Blike, for example, shipped eight servants, mostly to Barbados, between 1654 and 1656 while he was apprenticed to Walter Tocknell, but imported no colonial goods during that time. Tocknell, by contrast, shipped no servants but imported large quantities of sugar and tobacco.[32] Seafaring men such as mariners, shipwrights, coopers, and surgeons, sailing aboard vessels bound for American waters, could offer the same service to those in Bristol who traded to the colonies less frequently or who could not spare an apprentice for the long journey.

This seafaring population represented a potential threat to the principles and practices of the traditional merchant. Ships' crews had a long-standing right to conduct trade on their own account in the vessels on which they sailed, and, as we have just seen, many mariners took advantage of this custom to import colonial products in their own name. But the mariners' privilege sometimes concealed illicit trade by non-freemen who merely used the good offices of sworn burgesses to escape restrictions imposed on the commerce of "foreigners." As we know, from the Middle Ages onward this "colouring" of strangers' goods had been roundly condemned as a violation of the spirit of the urban community. Every freeman took a solemn oath against the practice. Mariners, however, had strong incentives to violate this oath, if they had ever sworn it. Not only did they often lack the capital with which to conduct trade on their own, but they spent far too much time at sea to dispose properly of the goods they imported. By allowing other individuals to trade through them, they could profit from a privilege that they might otherwise never use. Sometimes the strangers for whom they colored goods were colonial planters. However, trade by resident non-freemen was a far greater challenge to the principles by which the mercantile community operated.[33] Young merchants, serving aboard ship as factors, supercargoes, or pursers, fell into a somewhat similar category. Although by custom they also could trade on their own account, even during their apprenticeship,[34] they often lacked the capital and the commercial outlets at home to take full advantage of the privilege. Hence they too might be tempted to color strangers' goods, not only against local ordinances but against the interests of their employers as well.[35]

Bristol's Merchant Venturers were acutely aware of the problems that the trading privileges of mariners and young merchant factors posed for the control of overseas trade. Their 1639 ordinances complained that mariners

> have of late very often taken, vpon theire credit and other waies, divers goods and marchandice of great value, And carried the same . . . vnto the partes beyond the Seas, and in Returne thereof have brought home . . . divers other wares and marchandice . . . the most part thereof, without the leave, privitie, or knowledg of the Ouners of the said Shippes, or Marchants whoe tooke the saide Shippes to Fraight . . . Whereby his maiesty is much deceyved and the marchants disheartened in theire trade.[36]

For this reason, the Society forbade any ship's captain or crew member from putting goods aboard his vessel without the specific approval of two of the chief laders and two of the chief owners. A fine of double freight was imposed for every violation. Moreover, the ship's purser, under pain of losing his wages, was to inform his principals of the quantity and type of goods brought aboard by crew members. For their part, the factors and apprentices of Merchant Venturers were forbidden to act for "any Stranger or Forreiner not free of [the] Societie." They were neither to lade any export goods on behalf of the ineligible traders nor to buy any goods abroad for them. The penalties imposed were heavy, amounting to over 15 percent of the value of goods for a first offense and over 30 percent for a second offense.[37] Nevertheless, judging by the number of non–Merchant Venturers in the *Wharfage Books* and *Register of Servants*, it is clear that these efforts had failed.

Roger North long ago observed the same peculiarities in Bristol's trading community that we have just examined. "It is *remarkable* there," he said,

> that all men that are dealers, even in shop trades, launch into adventures by sea, chiefly to the West India plantations and Spain. A poor shopkeeper, that sells candles, will have a bale of stockings, or a piece of stuff, for Nevis, or Virginia, &c. and, rather than fail, they trade in men.[38]

At the Restoration, the London merchant John Bland portrayed the Chesapeake traders—especially those he believed had procured the passage of the Navigation Acts—in much the same way. "They are no Merchants bred," he complained,

> not versed in foreign ports, or any Trade, but to those Plantations, and that from either Planters there or whole-sale Tobacconists and shopkeepers retailing Tobacco here in England, who know no more what belongs to the commerce of the World, or Managing new discovered Countries, such as Virginia and Mariland are, than children new put out Prentice.[39]

North and Bland present a dark vision—to them, a nightmare—of a bustling, disorderly world of small men advanced beyond their stations. Bristol's old-line Merchant Venturers would have deemed their description a prophecy of doom all but come true.

Their viewpoint, upheld largely unchanged down to 1639, not only reflected their economic interests but had conformed to the economic and social realities of overseas trade as well. So long as commercial profits were derived primarily from scarce and high-priced imports drawn from a small number of continental markets, successful trade depended on the maintenance of regular mercantile networks abroad and a complex form of organization at home. As we know, merchants habitually acted as agents, partners, creditors, and brokers for one another, switching roles as circumstances required. They chartered ships together and used each other's servants as factors in overseas trade, and much of their business abroad proceeded through fellow Bristolians resident in the principal foreign markets trading for commission on behalf of their brethren at home.[40] Even though Merchant Venturers had reason to concern themselves with the overseas trade of artificers and shopkeepers, the actual conditions of foreign commerce limited the danger, since the Society of Merchant Venturers could readily control that trade. Only the Society's membership commanded the necessary capital and organization to conduct such commerce on a consistently large scale. They owned the shipping; they had the foreign contacts; and they enjoyed the services of fellow merchants to help them drive the trade. The high prices of the luxury goods in which they dealt, moreover, would have kept all but the wealthiest of retailers from competition with them. In 1618 and 1639, the Merchant Venturers had relied on these truths when framing their ordinances. Since others who would attempt to trade could be barred from the services of the factors, servants, and mariners traveling abroad for the Merchant Venturers, craftsmen and shopkeepers would need to acquire their own shipping, establish their own credit network, and build their own organization in foreign markets to conduct their trade. The Merchant Venturers counted on them being unable to do so.

Across the Atlantic, however, a new commercial world was taking shape. The inhabitants of the colonies were Englishmen with family and business ties in their home country. The social composition of the colonial communities therefore provided commercial connections between planters and traders which elsewhere required specially established resident factors, commission agents, and brokers to achieve.[41] In a sense, the settlement of a colony already contained within itself the seeds of a mercantile organization to cultivate commerce as it was needed. Moreover, many of the colonists came from the west of England, and even from Bristol itself, which gave the city some particular advantages in the trade.[42]

Among these West Countrymen, a number of Bristol-based merchants and mariners stand out. For example, Anthony Dunn, a Bristol merchant though not a Merchant Venturer, resided in Barbados in the 1650s, leaving his wife behind in Bristol to supply him with servants. He may also have been connected with Richard Dunn and Ann Dunn of Bristol, each of whom also traded between Barbados and Bristol in these years. Another emigrant Bristol merchant was John Yeamans, brother of Robert, the Bristol martyr to Charles I's cause in 1643, and himself an ex-colonel in the Royalist army. He settled on Barbados in

1650, later to become one of the great men of the island, governor of Carolina and a baronet. Other members of his family, however, remained in Bristol to trade with him. In 1654–55, when his Barbados holdings probably were still undeveloped, one hogshead of sugar was registered in his name for wharfage duty owed at the Backhall.[43] Richard Allen, a ship's surgeon with political views nearly opposite to those of Yeamans, also became a colonial planter in these years, although in Virginia, not Barbados. And Robert Glass, mariner, reversed the process. In the 1640s he lived as a planter in Barbados, doing business with Bristol, but by 1655 he had set up as a merchant in the western port to conduct trade with his former West Indian neighbors. Finally, in 1657, he became a freeman of the city after marrying the daughter of John Dee, cooper. Dozens of such stories could be told.[44]

The early Chesapeake and West Indian colonists, moreover, traded under conditions far different from those experienced by commercial dealers in Europe. Rather than develop production in a variety of necessary goods for home consumption, they used their comparative advantage in natural resources—in this case, land—to produce one highly valued commodity, which they exported in return for the manufactured items and other resources that they needed.[45] This type of economy had a profound effect on the character of trade. At the major European ports a merchant could buy a variety of goods, each governed by its own market conditions. To maximize his profits he needed to play these markets with great care, neither committing all his capital to one commodity whose home price might later collapse nor buying everything that seemed quickly merchantable.[46] To purchase these wares, the merchant needed cargoes of quite specific items in high demand and scarce supply among his foreign customers. At Cádiz he might choose among sherry, wine, olive oil, oranges, almonds, and even sugar and tobacco. To acquire them, however, he could use only lead, calfskins, Welsh butter, salt fish, or certain varieties of English cloth. Each of these commodities, of course, also had its own market which needed careful cultivation. A trading venture, therefore, usually involved a complex series of transactions, often requiring numerous brokers and go-betweens, sales at San Lucar de Barrameda and purchases at Jerez de la Frontera, with bills of exchange drawn on Seville.[47]

How different trade looks in the Chesapeake and the West Indies during the mid-seventeenth century. At Jamestown in Virginia, a merchant found tobacco and little else; at Bridgetown in Barbados, he found sugar, with perhaps small quantities of ginger, cotton, or tobacco as well. To get these goods he could bring the most varied of cargoes; the early colonists lacked practically everything in the way of household wares, manufactured items, clothing, and even food and drink—hence the bales of hosiery and pieces of stuff mentioned by Roger North. Most of all they lacked labor. This need was answered by huge shipments of servants that arrived every year from Bristol and London. Since the colonies possessed no system of currency, the colonial merchant operated by a form of barter: so many pounds of tobacco or sugar for so much of this or that. Although by the 1660s elements of a more complex commercial organization had begun to appear,[48] many colonial traders still operated on the same speculative basis that Richard Ligon described for the 1640s, using their vessels as both warehouses and trading counters, bringing mixed cargoes of servants and manufactures to the colonies in hope of finding a market for them. This pattern in much of colonial commerce would have struck the itinerant merchant of the Middle Ages as thoroughly familiar.

The survival of speculative commerce along these lines depended on the settlers as much as the traders. So long as the colonists relied so heavily on sugar or tobacco as a cash crop, they could hardly escape the market economy for many of the goods they needed. Only a few had the capital to serve this market themselves by becoming merchant planters or industrial producers. The others, even those with skills in highly valued manufacturing crafts, looked upon the acquisition and development of land as their best hope of gain. Even the early Chesapeake factors, with their important business connections in England, rarely became shopkeepers trading exclusively at their own risk and on their own account. The more successful among them used their accumulated profits to buy land, not to expand their trading operations.[49] According to Richard Ligon, the Barbados merchants operated in just the same way, pyramiding their commercial gains until they had amassed the funds to set up a sugar plantation for themselves.[50] Under such conditions the growth of sophisticated and well-capitalized commercial institutions was bound to be slow, at first utilized only by the biggest and most ambitious planters, while the others made do with more primitive forms of organization. Until the final decades of the seventeenth century, the trade remained largely decentralized, despite evident signs of increasing concentration.

In its formative years, this emerging Atlantic economy conformed poorly to the economic theories advanced by Bristol's Merchant Venturers. From the point of view of the settlers, sugar and tobacco, still luxuries in England, were staples. They represented the lifeblood of their economic activities. If they did not have them to sell, the colonists could purchase little they needed.[51] Thus planters were unable to restrict production to uphold prices. Doing so would only idle servants, who nonetheless continued to require maintenance, and waste the labor already expended in clearing land for cultivation. For this reason, planters met falling prices for sugar or tobacco by more intensive efforts at production, not less. As Russell Menard has shown, until about 1680 the faster tobacco prices fell, "the more rapid the growth of output."[52] Sugar production reveals the same relation to declining prices.[53] Above all, the colonial economy's dependence upon land conditioned the expansion. During the mid-seventeenth century, planters simply had no alternative ways to use their capital. They could either employ it in growing sugar or tobacco, or they could save it by buying land for later use. Thus, contrary to the Merchant Venturers' expectations, the prices of sugar and tobacco did not automatically rise when large numbers of traders competed for the goods. Rather, production grew in order to uphold income as prices fell. As a result, the colonial trades in the mid-seventeenth century could not be regulated in the same way as the European. Trade proceeded through too many outlets, and production remained high and continued to grow. Although to the Merchant Venturers, with their traditional viewpoint, the American trades represented the very image of disorder, their Society could offer no ready and easy way to bring discipline to the market.[54]

Not all Bristolians, as we know, agreed with the Merchant Venturers' view of the proper urban social and economic order. Many of the retailers and artificers saw freedom to trade as a natural concomitant of their status as burgesses. For these shopkeepers and craftsmen, the American trade represented a shoemakers' holiday of its own. It offered an opportunity to trade abroad in an area outside the control of the Merchant Venturers. It gave small men the chance to use their capital and their contacts to become merchants. Of the many who did so, some indeed were shoemakers. James Wathen, for example, ran a steady business in the American colonies in the mid-seventeenth century. During the early 1650s he traded with both Virginia and Barbados, importing tobacco and sugar and shipping servants. During these same years his brother Richard acted as servant to a Barbados planter, providing James with a business connection on the island. Although Wathen never achieved Simon Eyre's eminence, like the London shoemaker his commercial activity continued unabated through his later life. After the Restoration we find him still plying the colonial trade just as he had under the Commonwealth.[55]

Wathen's career not only reveals the ways the emerging Atlantic economy disrupted traditional patterns of commercial life in Bristol but also illustrates how the troubled politics of the 1640s and 1650s had thrown the city into turmoil. For Wathen not only "interloped," as the Merchant Venturers might have said, in foreign commerce, but in his kinship ties he represented the forces of political and religious radicalism in the city. He came from a large family of middling men—tanners, wiredrawers, shoemakers, pinmakers, and mariners—who not only engaged in American trade but challenged the civic establishment as well.[56] For example, James Wathen, Senior, a pinmaker and cousin of James the shoemaker, was one of Bristol's more outspoken sectaries in the early 1650s; so was John Wathen, apothecary, another kinsman. John Wathen eventually became a partner in the Whitson Court sugar refinery founded by Thomas Ellis, merchant, in 1665, while other Wathen relations also engaged in American trade. Moreover, Ellis, a leading Bristol Baptist, had gotten his start in the sugar trade in the 1650s by shipping large cargoes of shoes to Barbados, which perhaps links him directly with James Wathen, shoemaker, as well.[57]

The men who "spirited" Farwell Meredith to Barbados share this same combination of religion and economics. Marlin Hiscox and Richard Basse also were tied to a group of active sectaries. The Hiscox clan was closely connected through apprenticeship with William Philpott, a cooper who was Richard Basse's stepfather—a fact which makes the crew of the *Dolphin* almost as cosy as an eighteenth-century cousinage. Basse himself grew up in the same household as William Bullock, a shipwright who was one of Bristol's truly large-scale dealers in colonial goods in the mid-seventeenth century. Both Philpott and Bullock, like James Wathen, pinmaker, and John Wathen, apothecary, appear among the supporters of the radical Colonel John Haggatt in the 1654 elections to the first Protectorate Parliament. Moreover, Bullock and some of the Hiscox family were early Quakers.[58]

Numerous other Bristol sectaries also engaged in colonial commerce during these years. For example, Christopher Birkhead, a mariner who sometimes voyaged to the West Indies and the Chesapeake, was one of Bristol's more militant saints. In the mid-1650s, Birkhead, by then a follower of George Fox, had already acquired an international reputation as a troublemaker for disrupting Presbyterian services at Bristol,

Huguenot services at La Rochelle, and Dutch Reformed services at Middleborough.[59] Captain George Bishop, a New Model Army man, an Agitator at Putney, onetime secret agent to the Commonwealth's Council of State, Haggatt's colleague in the 1654 parliamentary election, and early sectary, also engaged in colonial trade in this period.[60] Captain Thomas Speed, another New Model Army man and also by 1655 a leading defender and propagandist for the Bristol Friends, was if anything an even more important American merchant. In the early 1650s he engaged with several other Bristolians in a series of projects to transport Irish prisoners to the colonies.[61] By the middle of the same decade he had become almost as important as William Bullock in American commerce, importing over seventeen tons of Barbados sugar during 1654–55 and accounting for considerable quantities of Virginia tobacco during the following year.[62]

Other American traders among the sectaries led somewhat more sedate political and economic lives. The Baptists Major Samuel Clarke and Robert Bagnall, for example, were the merchants of the *Samuel Pinke of Bristol*, which Christopher Birkhead sailed for the Caribbean in August 1653.[63] Both of them traded in West India sugar and Virginia tobacco in the mid-1650s. Samuel Clarke's brother Joseph, a scrivener, and Robert Cornish, a sailor, were also Baptists dealing in American imports in these years. Among the Quaker traders we find such men as the grocers Thomas Ricroft and John Saunders, the ironmonger Henry Roe, the mariner Latimer Sampson, and the merchant Jasper Cartwright. These were middling traders, importing smaller quantities of American goods than Bullock and Speed but maintaining a steady commerce nonetheless. Unfortunately, it is impossible to make a complete tally of the Bristol Baptists and Quakers who invested in colonial enterprise during the mid-seventeenth century, since we do not know the names of all the city's sectaries in this period. But for the ten years following the establishment of the *Wharfage Book* and the *Register of Servants* we can identify more than sixty such individuals in the city who engaged in trans-Atlantic commerce, some trading only once or twice, some like Bullock and Speed among the city's largest dealers in colonial commerce, but many, like Wathen, conducting a modest but continuous traffic with America.[64]

These men possessed ideals of community and individual commitment different from the hierarchical views held by conservative Bristolians such as the leading Merchant Venturers. In their congregations they had long since rejected the structures of authority of the established church. They believed in a community of the spirit, and they governed themselves through regular meetings at which a democratic ideal of brotherhood prevailed.[65] To men and women reared with these religious convictions, Simon Eyre's world, as depicted by Dekker, would have seemed far more congenial than the Merchant Venturers', for the idea of a rigid structure of occupations ranked in a neat hierarchy bore little resemblance to their most profound experiences of community life. It is perhaps no surprise to find them often acting to break down the strict boundaries separating stranger from Bristolian and mere inhabitant from full citizen. The "coloring of strangers goods" was a commonplace of business practice among them. When the civic authorities made a concerted effort to end this ancient misdemeanor in the mid-1660s, they found Thomas Ellis and his Baptist associates heavily engaged in it.[66] Some of the sectaries even began their careers in Bristol as "interlopers" pure and simple. Major Samuel Clarke, for example, only entered the freedom of the city in 1652 after a shipment of imported fruit belonging to him had been seized as "foreign bought & sold."[67] Moreover, the merchant sectaries, especially the Quakers, could not follow Clarke's lead in becoming Bristol freemen, since their consciences prevented them from swearing the burgess oath. Many traded illicitly all their lives. Among them perhaps was John Wathen, whose name never appears in the Bristol burgess books.[68]

The year 1654 brought many of these issues of economics, politics, and religion to a head. According to James Powell, Bristol's chamberlain at the time, there were two causes for the "distempers" of that year: the dispute over the parliamentary election, and "the comeinge of the quakers." The election, he said, "bred an extreame feud" between the magistracy and the two defeated candidates, Colonel Haggatt and his cousin Captain George Bishop. These men looked upon their opponents as Cavaliers; they accused Alderman Miles Jackson, one of the newly elected members of Parliament, of royalism, made similar charges against those electors who voted for Jackson, and accused the sheriffs and their fellow common councillors of complicity in a plot to defeat "the godly party" in the town. Afterward, Powell continues, "they waited occasions to blast the cittie by all possible meanes."[69]

Although Powell does not tie the arrival of the Quakers explicitly to the election, in truth they were closely connected. The Quakers first came to Bristol in the spring of 1654; by June they already had won some important converts. Moreover, John Audland and John Camm made one of their initial visits to the city at the time of the poll itself, although for what reason we cannot tell. Many of their early converts appear as parties to the election squabble. George Bishop soon became one of Bristol's most outspoken Quakers, his tireless pen turning out pamphlet after pamphlet for the cause from 1655 on. Haggatt never went so far, but he was allied through his family with many of Bristol's first Friends, his wife among them. Their supporters too appear connected to the Quaker movement. A third of them became Friends in the waves of conversion following the visits of Audland, Camm, and other first publishers of Truth.[70] In Powell's view, the "franticke doctrines" of these Quakers had not only "made . . . an impression on the minds of the people of this cittie" but also "made such a rent in all societies and relations which, with the publique afront offered to ministers and magistrates, hath caused a devision, I may say a mere antipathy amongst the people, and consequently many broyles."[71]

As a result, these events ushered in a period of nearly unprecedented dissension within the city. Haggatt and Bishop, using their allies among the Bristol garrison, mounted a concerted attack on the loyalty of the Bristol Common Council. A broad body of their supporters petitioned the Lord Protector to quash the election results, and George Bishop filed information accusing the magistrates of complicity in Royalist plots. By the end of 1654 the effects of the Quaker conversions had become all too apparent to the civic authorities. Individual Quakers began disrupting religious services in the city's churches and resisting the authority of the aldermen to punish them for their breaches of the peace. At the same time, large public meetings were held, some drawing over one thousand participants. As the movement grew, fear of Quakerism also grew in many quarters. Riots ensued in which bands of apprentices assaulted Quakers on the streets and threatened their public meetings. Moreover, George Cowlishay confirmed the worst suspicions of many Bristolians by spreading a rumor that he had picked up from an Irishman. The Quakers, he charged, really were Franciscan and Jesuit subversives, in England to undermine Protestantism. Many Baptists, their ranks severely depleted by losses to the Quakers, accepted the story as gospel.[72]

These developments certainly did not grow only from seeds planted by the expansion of Bristol's trans-Atlantic trade, nor were they mere reflections of economic divisions within the city. The election and its aftermath hardly reveal the conflict as one simply between the mere merchants and their rivals. Differing views on the constitution and on religious settlement lay at the bottom of the troubles. Nevertheless, the

TABLE 28   OCCUPATIONAL BACKGROUND OF THE DISPUTANTS IN
THE PARLIAMENTARY ELECTION OF 1654

	Haggatt		Aldworth and Jackson	
Occupations	No.	%	No.	%
Merchants	7	5.83[a]	26	15.76[a]
Major retailers and other leading entrepreneurs	38	31.67	76	40.06
Lesser crafts and trades	49	40.83	39	23.64
Shipping	23	19.17	18	10.91
Gentlemen, professionals	3	2.50	6	3.64
Total known	120		165	
Total unknown	8		17	
Total	128		182	
Members of the Society of Merchant Venturers	5	4.17	26	15.76

SOURCE: The names of those who supported Aldworth and Jackson are known from H. E. Nott and Elizabeth Ralph, eds., *The Deposition Books of Bristol*. Vol. 2: *1650–1654* (Bristol Record Society 13, 1948), pp. 181–83. The names of those who supported Haggatt have been established by collating ibid., pp. 180–81, and Public Record Office, SP 18/75/14vi (two slightly different copies of the list drawn by Haggatt's teller at the 12 July poll) with Public Record Office, SP 18/75/14ii (the petition made to the Protector on Haggatt's behalf protesting the election). The petition contains ninety-five names, thirty-eight of which do not appear on either of the teller's tallies. Thirteen of the ninety-five later swore they never signed the petition, but eight of those appear on one or both of the tellers' lists. A further two are known to have been early Quakers and Baptists. I have counted all thirty-eight among Haggatt's supporters. It appears likely that they were not counted because they were deemed ineligible. Bishop's supporters walked out without voting, after protesting against the eligibility of many of their opponents' supporters.
[a] Percentage of the total known.

two political factions do show some interesting socioeconomic differences. Although many of Aldworth's and Jackson's supporters had interests in the American trade, just like Haggatt's supporters, the latter consisted much more heavily than the former of men in the lesser crafts and in the shipping industry. Only seven of Haggatt's votes came from men identified in any way as merchants, and only five from Merchant Venturers. Although both factions in the election found considerable support among soapmakers, grocers, and other major retailers and entrepreneurs, a higher percentage of Aldworth's and Jackson's votes came from this quarter. In addition, twenty-six of their backers identified themselves as merchants and the same number were Merchant Venturers, most of them older members of the Society (Table 28).[73] Jackson himself had been a member since at least 1618, and Aldworth, a lawyer by profession, was the son of a Merchant Venturer of the 1620s and 1630s.[74] The impression is strong, therefore, that Aldworth's and Jackson's supporters on the whole came from the richer segments of Bristol's population and were closely tied to the Merchant Venturers.

Despite the resistance of conservative-minded Bristolians to the excesses of the colonial traders, these citizens could no longer look backward to the traditions of commercial organization for relief of their grievances, since the Society of Merchant Venturers had long since ceased to protect against the competition of interlopers. Not only did the conditions of colonial trade defeat the techniques of regulation available to the Society, but the Society itself no longer possessed the political power it once had had to control the trading community. The politics of the 1640s had broken its once united leadership and reduced its significance in local affairs. After the parliamentary victory in Bristol in 1645, the new regime in the Corporation and the Society does not seem to have shared the old order's prejudices against artisan and shopkeeper merchants. Perhaps political allegiances made it difficult even for veteran Merchant Venturers to insist on their exclusion. Between December 1646 and December 1651, seventeen of the thirty-five men admitted to the Society were redemptioners of one sort or another. Some were highly irregular appointments by pre–Civil War standards.[75] Among these redemptioners, we find Thomas Speed, William Bullock, George Bishop, and at least one other sectary, who came to play important roles in the government of the Society in the early 1650s. Speed was one of the Society's wardens in 1651, and he often served on committees engaged in negotiations with the Rump Parliament or the Council of State. He and Bullock also served on the Court of Assistants, as did Captain Henry Hassard, the fourth sectary and redemptioner. Finally, Bishop used his leverage with the Commonwealth's officialdom to gain trading privileges for the membership.[76]

However, this was not an era of good feeling in the Society's history. Although on paper the membership continued to grow, the records of the Merchants' Hall in the mid-seventeenth century reveal a deep malaise. All through the 1650s and 1660s, considerably less than half of the membership appeared at the quarterly meetings, including the annual election meeting; fewer still turned out for special assemblies. Many of the members stayed away for years on end, prompting the passage in 1652 of a stiff ordinance against all who "wilfully refuse to come to the Hall upon reasonable summons" or who failed to leave proxies when they traveled from town on business.[77] The Society's finances also appear in disarray. Time and time again the *Hall Book* says that the payment of fines and of wharfage were seriously in arrears.[78]

The crisis appeared to be one of authority as much as economics. In 1650 the Hall felt obliged to cite its ancient patent from Edward VI, the parliamentary statute of 1566, and Charles I's charter of 1639 in insisting on the "power and authority not only to make laws and ordinances agreeable to reason for the good of the said Company, But to impose and assess such reasonable paynes, penaltyes and punishments by ffynes and amerciaments for breach of them." To better collect these fines, the Society adopted the procedure by action of debt, bill, or plaint in the name of the wardens and treasurer before the Mayor's Court in the Guildhall.[79] Despite this measure, the collections of fines and wharfage remained a continuing problem throughout the 1650s and 1660s.[80]

If the established Merchant Venturers could no longer rely on the Society to achieve their ends, however, they could still use the Common Council to do so. There, as we have seen, they still enjoyed a clear majority of the membership. Moreover, most of the Merchant Venturers on the council had joined before the Civil War, and even before the issuance of the new charter in 1639. Their commercial lives showed a commitment to the principles upon which the Society had stood for so long. The dominance of these men in the city government is clear from the way they handled the election of the first Protectorate Parliament. They controlled the poll both through the sheriffs and through insisting that their voices be heard before the others could vote,[81] and thus they assured victory for candidates who would act in the Society's interest. Once the members were in Westminster they became spokesmen for this dominant interest, as they had been in the 1620s, using their positions to advance the Merchant Venturers' claims in such matters as the trade in Welsh butter, and attacking the roots of radicalism in the city as well. According to instructions sent by the magistrates, the MPs were not only to help "establish and settle order in the Church" and to rid the city of the Cromwellian soldiers who had so ardently supported Bishop and Haggatt but were also to address some symptoms of the breakdown in the civic social order arising from the American trade. "The Privildges & liberties of the Citty," the magistrates complained,

> are very much incroached upon to the great discouragement of the Inhabitants, especially young men who thinke it much that they should serve apprentishippe for many yeares; whilst other men that have never served halfe their time & others that were never apprentices at all, are permitted to keepe shope in as free away as themselves.[82]

The common councillors proposed no specific remedy for this last ill, perhaps because it sprang from a number of separate, if interrelated, sources. Most of all, they could no longer urge the principle of monopoly as the solution to their troubles, since even the conservatives of the Protectorate could not be expected to endorse it. However, one of the acts of the Long Parliament, arising from political circumstances similar to those we have found in Bristol in 1654, offered a start toward a cure. In May 1645, the House of Commons received word that Edward Peade, a London merchant, had engaged in child-stealing in the course of his trade. Peade served, along with such radicals as Maurice Thompson, Cornelius Holland, and Owen Rowe, as a commissioner for Somers Islands, and he and Rowe were associated with John Goodwin's congregation at St. Stephen's, Coleman Street.[83] During 1645 this intimate connection between the leading London Independents and the Somers Islanders, also noted for their religious zeal, appeared as one theme in London's "counter-revolution" mounted by the so-called Presbyterians in the capital.[84] The information against Peade only confirmed for these conservatives that Goodwin's followers were without scruple in all they did. Enemies of London radicalism such as William Spurstow pounced upon the accusation as a means to punish their opponents.

We have no evidence that the parliamentary ordinance of May 1645 or the measures later taken to strengthen it were ever enforced, but they provided the legal authority upon which the Bristol Common Council rested its own registration scheme.[85] With it the common councillors took a first but vital step in regulating the disorder of the colonial trades—a disorder produced largely by the trading activities of their political enemies. The *Register* worked against those shoemaker merchants and shopkeeping interlopers in various ways. It authorized the water bailiff to board ships in harbor to make inquiry about the indentures of servants and thereby placed the trading activities of all those who used the port under far closer official scrutiny. In this way illicit traders—especially traders who had not paid the entry fees for admission to the freedom of Bristol and had not sworn the freeman's oath—became somewhat more vulnerable to arrest and to payment of local duties. But the requirement that indentures be used for all servants did something more: it placed the traffic of marginal traders under new economic restraints, which reduced their threat to the established merchant community.

The new registration scheme introduced in Bristol raised the transaction costs associated with conducting the servant trade, since shipping a servant across the Atlantic now required coping with a cumbersome administrative system and with the need to pay for the drawing and registration of the servants' indentures. Although the charges were small, they had to be paid in coin, as did the fee for admission to the freedom of Bristol. Even for the relatively well-to-do, coin was not always easy to come by. Since most of the servants exported to the colonies in the 1650s were poor men and women seeking subsistence and without money in their purses, it seems clear that these charges would have had to be borne by the servant traders. The trade in servants also operated under certain constraints unusual in other types of commerce. Conditions in the Chesapeake and the West Indies were devastating to newcomers in the seventeenth century. According to some estimates, about 40 percent of those who arrived in these regions died during their terms, many in the first year. The others went through a period of severe "seasoning" during which they were ill for much of the year. As a result, planters usually tried to protect their investment in valuable labor by keeping the new servants free from work during the hot months. Only in the second year, if these newcomers had survived, could the planter expect to get a full year's work from them.[86] Thus a difference of a year or more in a servant's term represented a significant difference in his value. As it turns out, servants with indentures had, on average, shorter terms by a year or more than those who came on the custom of the country, since they enjoyed far more leverage to negotiate their terms while in England than after they had crossed the Atlantic. Once the servant had received his payment in the form of passage, he could do nothing but accept the custom as it existed. He had no freedom to return.[87] The use of indentures to regulate the trade therefore had the effect of cutting into its profitability for the trader. In this way it might be thought to bring the evil of "spiriting" under some control, since the poorer traders, those most easily tempted to inveigle or purloin servants to the colonies, were more susceptible than their richer competitors to the disincentives created by the new registration scheme.

For the marginal traders such as the mariners, shopkeepers, and artisans so heavily represented among the sectaries, the forced shift in operation instituted by the registration scheme of 1654 was especially significant, since the price of tobacco and sugar was already in decline in the 1650s. For the large merchants the losses involved would have been easier to absorb, especially because these men could more readily trade in other goods not affected by the same market conditions as servants. Thus the *Register* sought to accomplish what other economic regulations could not. Since it was no longer possible to exclude marginal traders from the use of ships and the services of factors, it sought to take advantage of the wealth of established merchants to reach the same end. In doing so it conceded an important point. If the larger retailers and manufacturers, such as those we find supporting Aldworth and Jackson in the election, could no longer effectively be barred from overseas trade, at least the Quaker shoemakers might.

To cope with the disorder of the colonial trades the Bristol common councillors sought a new market-based discipline in foreign commerce, something that would overcome the apparent anarchy of the sectaries while avoiding the self-defeating rigidities of the old regime. Although in the context of Interregnum politics their action had only limited significance, seen in the light of the history of Bristol's political economy this new strategy signaled the beginnings of a revolution at least as important as the one it sought to end. It employed political authority to regulate the market so that in turn the market could regulate the distribution of political power. It was a move fraught with possibilities, to which we now turn.

CHAPTER 9

Registering
the Pilgrimage

The growing importance for Bristol of trade with the American colonies had the paradoxical effect of diminishing the power of the city's mere merchants in its economy. For decades these men had been pursuing high-profit imports—tobacco and sugar, as well as other wares—to their first markets. This process had led them from the Iberian peninsula into the Mediterranean and the Atlantic islands. With dreams of their city becoming a new Venice or a new Lisbon, they searched for the Northwest Passage to the riches of the East, only to find Newfoundland and begin their quest for wealth on American shores. But the very openness of the trans-Atlantic markets and their nearly unquenchable demand for strong backs and small wares had made most of Bristol's old techniques of commercial regulation ineffective. The damage done to conservative aspirations was only enhanced by the turmoil of the Civil Wars and Interregnum. As a result, the merchants' long-standing efforts to control the city through the maintenance of an exclusive organization of traders, exercising political as well as social and economic power, gave way to a new approach, one employing regulations geared to the disciplines of the market in an attempt to protect the interests of the civic elite. By increasing the transaction costs associated with the servant trade, the Bristol common councillors sought to give an advantage to those dealers who could bear them and thereby to concentrate the trade in the hands of a small number of large-scale entrepreneurs, traders whose economic behavior would be predictable. Since the export of servants was paid for through the import of sugar and tobacco, such a system of economic regulation, if it worked, would give order to the American trades in ways that the Society of Merchant Venturers desired but could no longer accomplish through its corporate powers.

By some measures the Merchant Venturers' new strategy may be counted a success, since the servant trade, which had reached enormous heights in the 1650s and early 1660s, settled down after 1662. The average number of servants shipped annually from Bristol in the period from 1662 to 1678, the last full year for which a separately kept *Register of Servants* has survived, was more than 50 percent below the peak annual averages reached in the previous period (Table 29).[1] But in other respects it might seem that the project had failed, since the servant trade never became concentrated in a small number of hands. Most servant traders still limited themselves to shipping one or two servants a year. For example, in 1667–68, when four hundred and forty-nine servants left Bristol for America, two hundred and forty individuals took responsibility for their indentures; in 1677–78 ninety-four men and women took responsibility for the indentures of one hundred and forty-four servants.[2] A similar pattern can be observed in other aspects of trade as well. Leaving the Irish trade and coastal enterprise aside, seaborne traffic to and from the American colonies in the early 1670s accounted for about 45 percent of the vessels and 60 percent of the tonnage frequenting the port of Bristol. But this expansion in the colonial trades was accomplished primarily by numerous small exporters, most of them Bristolians, who still sent every variety of manufactured item along with servant labor to the planters in return for their produce, primarily sugar and tobacco. The concentration of colonial enterprise in the hands of large firms was a phenomenon primarily of the eighteenth century.[3]

The above conclusions assume, in part, that the *Register of Servants* offers a consistently accurate record of the scale and structure of the servant trade over the full life of the registration scheme. But perhaps this premise is mistaken. In order for the *Register* to provide us with a trustworthy tally of the movement of servants to the colonies, the Bristol magistrates would have had to maintain efficient enforcement of the law over a long interval, something they could rarely accomplish even when the policy being enforced was not controversial. Given the political emotions behind the scheme, the policy is all the more unlikely to have been carried out with a steady hand. Can we turn this possible shortcoming for economic history to the advantage of the story we have been telling? Since the *Register* was created as a weapon of war in a period

TABLE 29   EMIGRATION AND THE ENGLISH ECONOMY, MICHAELMAS 1654 TO MICHAELMAS 1678

Harvest Year	Servants	Wheat Prices, England (s./quarter)	Wheat Prices, Exeter (s./quarter)	Index of Consumer Prices	Real Wages
A. 1654–55	228	21.04	26.41	531	565
1655–56	318	35.13	44.56	559	537
1656–57*	538	36.77	44.84	612	490
1657–58***	727	44.43	47.78	646	464
1658–59**	884	50.13	43.66	700	429
1659–60***	667	47.42	45.50	684	439
1660–61***	822	48.30	50.78	648	463
1661–62***	805	64.04	58.37	769	390
Total A	4,989				
Annual average	624				
B. 1662–63	471	41.30	42.16	675	444
1663–64	266	41.61	39.50	657	457
1664–65	212	35.93	36.76	616	487
1665–66	227	32.25	34.94	664	452
1666–67	379	25.13	30.16	577	520
1667–68	449	27.53	29.32	602	498
1668–69*	417	35.43	45.07	572	524
1669–70	362	32.83	41.16	577	520
Total B	2,783				
Annual average	348				

C. 1670–71	299	33.72	595	35.15	504
1671–72	206	31.08	557	31.17	539
1672–73	142	32.48	585	34.19	513
1673–74***	281	49.57	650	54.77	462
1674–75***	445	47.79	691	52.11	434
1675–76	263	32.02	652	30.69	460
1676–77	216	27.26	592	30.77	509
1677–78	144	38.94	633	43.20	478
Total C	1,996				
Annual average	250				
Total A–C	9,768				
Annual average	407				
Correlations					
1654–1662 (significance level)		+.87 (.01)	+.72 (.05)	+.87 (.01)	−.91 (.01)
1662–1678 (significance level)		+.13 (N.S.)	+.25 (N.S.)	+.16 (N.S.)	−.07 (N.S.)
1654–1678 (significance level)		+.68 (.001)	+.60 (.01)	+.49 (.02)	−.58 (.01)

SOURCE: The symbols for harvest years, and the wheat prices, are derived from W. G. Hoskins, "Harvest Fluctuations and English Economic History, 1620–1759," *Agricultural History Review* 16 (1968): 15–31; * = Harvest deficient or bad in West only; ** = Harvest generally bad, but average in the West; *** = Harvest generally deficient or bad. Servant data from Bristol Record Office, MSS 04220 (1–2). Price index data from E. H. Phelps-Brown and Sheila V. Hopkins, "Seven Centuries of the Prices of Consumables, Compared with Builders' Wage-Rates," in E. M. Carus-Wilson, ed., *Essays in Economic History*, 3 vols. (London: Edward Arnold, 1954–1962), vol. 2, p. 195. Wage data from E. A. Wrigley and R. S. Schofield, *The Population History of England, 1541–1871, A Reconstruction* (Cambridge, Mass.: Harvard University Press, 1981), p. 693. These figures are derived from those provided by Phelps-Brown and Hopkins, "Seven Centuries of the Prices of Consumables," p. 195.

of political turmoil, did political considerations affect—even distort—
the data we can derive from this source? The main targets of the original ordinance, as we know, were the Bristol radicals who had come to
play a large role in the increasingly important colonial trades. After the
Restoration, they were an even greater source of concern to the local authorities than they had been under the Protectorate. In this chapter we
shall use the *Register* to provide clues to the history of political conflict
and revenge in Bristol we have been following.

The Bristol *Register* presents evidence of an anomaly in the statistics of
the servant trade. The number of servants leaving the port was relatively low in 1654 and 1655, then rose steadily through the later 1650s
and early 1660s, only to drop off during the summer and fall of 1663,
never again to recover the old peak. The largest number to leave in a single year, measured from Michaelmas to Michaelmas, was over eight
hundred, but after the fall of 1662 the totals exceed four hundred only
four times and never exceed five hundred (see Table 29).[4] Calendar-year
totals show the same pattern as those for harvest years (Table 30).
When measured against the best available estimates of total migration
to the colonies, these figures seem rather puzzling. Between 1654 and
1662, for example, Bristol's share of average annual emigration from
the British Isles to America may have been as high as 9.6 percent. But
from 1662 to 1669, the city's share appears to have dropped to 8.1 percent, and by the 1670s it seems to have amounted to no more than 5.0
percent. Yet Bristol's involvement in trans-Atlantic commerce became,
if anything, even stronger in these years than it had been in the 1650s.
We would expect it to have maintained its share of the servant trade
or at least to have experienced a less precipitous decline.[5] The relation
of servant enrollments in Bristol to English population trends also
points to another puzzle. In the years from 1655 to 1662, emigration
from the city was closely correlated to net migration from England. After 1662 there is no longer any correlation between the figures for Bristol and those for the country as a whole.[6] Was there in fact an abrupt
change in the nature of the servant trade after 1662, or are we observ-
ing an artifact of the registration system itself? Why did it cease working uniformly and effectively in the period after 1662?

 In recent years we have come to know a good deal about the overall
pattern of migration from England in the seventeenth century. The peak
years of this migration were the 1650s, when perhaps as many as
seventy-two hundred individuals, many of them servants, went each

year from England and Wales to the American colonies. In the decades thereafter, the pace slackened to between 60 and 70 percent of this total.[7] A number of explanations have been presented for this course of development. Mildred Campbell has argued that decayed conditions in the clothmaking districts of the West Country and economic pressures on West Country leaseholders at renewal of their tenures account for much of the emigration of the 1650s and that religious persecution of the Quakers may also have been important in the later 1650s and early 1660s. Wesley Frank Craven has added to this list the harvest failures of 1657 to 1661, which, he argues, drove many of the hungry to migrate. His reading of the evidence suggests that improved conditions after 1662 account for the drop in servant registrations at Bristol. Other hypotheses have appeared. Some scholars, for example, point to rising real wages in England and the increased demand for labor caused by the rebuilding of London after the great fire. In addition, changes in the colonies, such as the introduction of black slavery in the sugar plantations and the falling prices of tobacco, have been suggested. To this we might add the effects of war with the Dutch.[8] How do these explanations square with what we have learned about Bristol?

Seventeenth-century emigration was of course a highly complex social phenomenon. Each year hundreds of men and women of assorted ages and backgrounds left Bristol for a variety of overseas plantations. Some undoubtedly felt conditions at home to be pushing them abroad, while others almost as certainly found the opportunities for a new life in the colonies calling them forth. Many probably responded to pressures of both kinds. We can hardly expect a single explanation to account completely for their movement. In a sense, history has presented us with too many explanations. Not all of them are testable with the surviving data. For example, we shall probably never know enough about the West Country land market to assess whether the renewal rate for West Country leases corresponds in any way to the rate at which migrants from this region headed for America. However, a quick examination of the evidence we do have calls in doubt a few proposed hypotheses, at least as they might apply to Bristol.

Take the case of the trade in slaves, which competed with the servant trade in supplying agricultural labor to the American colonies. At first glance, the grant in January 1663 of a new charter to the Company of Royal Adventurers Trading to Africa might seem to explain the precipitous decline in the enrollment of servants at Bristol during this year, especially to Barbados, where the Africa company made most of its slave

TABLE 30   EMIGRATION AND TOBACCO PRICES, 1655–1678

Calendar Year	Total No. of Servants	Servants to the Chesapeake[a]				Farm Price of Tobacco
		1	2	3	4	
A. (1654)	—	—	—	—	—	2.65
1655	267	112	112	113	113	2.30
1656	336	70	110	123	117	2.20
1657	616	58	115	165	140	2.40
1658	779	103	188	210	199	1.90
1659	903	99	266	305	286	1.65[b]
1660	603	76	181	170	176	1.50[b]
1661	723	89	349	338	344	1.50
1662	836	374	506	501	503	1.60[b]
Total A	5,063	981	1,827	1,925	1,878	
Annual average	633	123	228	241	235	
B. 1663	397	158	159	159	159	1.55[b]
1664	251	121	121	121	121	1.35
1665	309	242	244	243	244	1.10
1666	332	257	257	257	257	0.90
1667	355	222	222	222	222	1.10
1668	402	291	291	291	291	1.25
1669	344	201	201	201	201	1.15
1670	334	168	172	172	172	1.15[b]
Total B	2,724	1,660	1,667	1,666	1,667	
Annual average	341	208	208	208	208	

	Col 1	Col 2	Col 3	Col 4	Col 5	Tobacco price
C. 1671	284	152	152	152	152	1.05
1672	255	208	208	209	209	1.00
1673	93	69	69	69	69	1.00
1674	369	194	194	197	196	1.00
1675	395	294	294	295	295	1.00
1676	223	171	172	172	172	1.05
1677	202	129	129	129	129	1.15
1678	177	138	138	138	138	1.15
Total C	1,998	1,355	1,356	1,361	1,360	
Annual average	250	169	170	170	170	
Total A–C	9,785	3,996	4,850	4,952	4,905	
Annual average	408	167	202	206	204	

Correlations

	Col	Col	Col
1655–1662 / (significance level)	-.72 (.05)	-.66 (.10)	-.69 (.10)
Time lag[c] / (significance level)	-.78 (.05)	-.75 (.05)	-.77 (.05)
1663–1678 / (significance level)	+.12 (N.S.)	-.23 (N.S.)	-.23 (N.S.)
Time lag[c] / (significance level)	-.20 (N.S.)	-.20 (N.S.)	-.20 (N.S.)
1655–1678 / (significance level)	-.03 (N.S.)	-.02 (N.S.)	-.03 (N.S.)
Time lag[c] / (significance level)	-.17 (N.S.)	-.10 (N.S.)	-.14 (N.S.)
1659–1678[d] / (significance level)	+.40 (.10)	+.42 (.10)	+.41 (.10)
Time lag (1660–1678)[d] / (significance level)	+.23 (N.S.)	+.21 (N.S.)	+.22 (N.S.)

SOURCE: Servant data are from Bristol Record Office, MSS 04220 (1–20); tobacco prices, given in pence sterling per pound of tobacco, are from Russell Menard, "The Tobacco Industry in the Chesapeake Colonies," *Working Papers from the Regional Economic History Research Center* 1, no. 3 (1978): 158–59. The figures for 1654 to 1658 are Virginia prices; thereafter they are Maryland prices.

[a] Column 1 gives the raw figures as derived from the *Register*. Column 2 adjusts the figures on David Galenson's assumption that the annotation "on the same conditions" means "same destination as the last listed" (David Galenson, *White Servitude in America: An Economic Analysis* [Cambridge: Cambridge University Press, 1981], pp. 220, 224). Column 3 is calculated by assigning the "unknowns" in each month to destinations according to the proportion of the knowns. Column 4 halves the difference between Column 2 and Column 3. Since the "unknowns" do not seem to have been randomly distributed, Column 4 probably comes closest to the correct totals.

[b] Fewer than eight observations.

[c] These correlations are given on the assumption that the demand for servants fluctuated with a year's time lag to allow for news of tobacco price variations to reach England.

[d] These correlations test the relationship between emigration and Maryland prices.

shipments. But Bristol's servant trade operated independently of this competition. During the 1650s and early 1660s it exported large numbers of servants to Barbados, even though slaves were already in heavy use there. There is no reason to think that the Africa company's activities in the island changed the situation enough to explain the decline in the servant figures. Since the fall in the number of servant enrollments after 1662 also affected Bristol's traffic to Virginia, where the demand for slaves did not yet match that in the West Indies, some other factor must have been at work limiting the market.[9] As regards the role of war in disrupting Bristol's servant trade, the timing seems to be somewhat off. Although warfare with the Dutch certainly affected English enterprise in American waters, the Second Dutch War began only in March 1665, albeit after a year of earnest preparations. The decline in servant enrollments in Bristol had already set in more than a year before the talk of war with the Dutch had become serious.[10] Again we are driven to look for further explanations.

Many of the proposed economic explanations, taken individually, seem plausible enough in accounting for the general pattern of change in the servant trade during the second half of the seventeenth century. Undoubtedly, the state of food prices and real wages in England and Wales and of tobacco and sugar prices in the international market affected the numbers of servants indentured and shipped from England and Wales to the colonies during this period. Yet when we trace the history of any particular causal factor in relation to Bristol's own servant trade, we find that its effects vary widely from period to period. For example, if we lay out our data from Michaelmas to Michaelmas, the state of the harvest is significantly correlated with emigration. This result is almost entirely a consequence of famine conditions during the first eight years of the registration. During these years, the annual peak of servant registrations, which always occurred in the summer and early fall, appears especially high, just as we would expect if food shortages were driving the emigration.[11] But for the period after 1662 the pattern does not hold. The correlation of enrollment with wheat prices breaks down completely: emigration rates appear relatively high in some bad years and relatively low in others. Indeed, 1667–68, with its low grain prices, yields the highest emigration figures for the period following 1662–63 (see Table 29), a fact made all the more puzzling by the increased demand for labor in London that is said to have begun in this year.[12]

One possible explanation for this uneven effect of grain prices on emigration may lie in the character of the food market, which had changed after the Restoration, when substitutes for wheat became more widely used. It has been argued that this change diminished the threat of famine in England and thus reduced the effect of high wheat prices upon population trends.[13] Use of the Phelps-Brown/Hopkins index of consumer prices, based on a wide variety of foods and other commodities, permits a test of this hypothesis, even though the data are drawn primarily from the southeast of England. The results are almost exactly the same as those obtained using wheat prices alone. There is a strong and significant positive correlation, but it is heavily dependent on the results for the first eight years of the series; this relationship disappears after 1662 (see Table 29).[14]

Food prices alone, however, tell us little about the economic pressures on population in periods without famine, since a rise in food prices may be matched by a corresponding increase in wages. To correct for this limitation we can look at real wages. These were on the increase in the later seventeenth century, as population growth leveled and then entered a thirty-year period of stagnation or even decline.[15] This change has been used by historians not only to explain the slackening pace of emigration to the colonies but even to account for the shift from indentured servitude to slavery as the preferred labor system in some of them.[16] However, comparison of our Bristol data with real wages yields almost exactly the same results as before. Once again, a strong and significant correlation appears for the years up to Michaelmas 1662, though this time a negative one, but after 1662 the relationship no longer seems meaningful.

If economic conditions in England cannot account for the pattern of servant migration from Bristol after 1662, perhaps economic conditions in the colonies can. Although we know that in general sugar prices fell during the later seventeenth century, no reliable series of them exists against which to test our data. We are somewhat better off for the tobacco trade with the Chesapeake, for which it has been shown that the number of new servants indentured in this region each year rose and fell with the farm price of tobacco.[17] But the same direct relationship does not appear to hold for the registration of indentures at Bristol, even if we allow a year's time for the news of changing prices to reach the city (see Table 30). In fact, Bristol's trade in servants to Virginia and Maryland appears at times to contradict the price trends. In the late 1650s and early 1660s, emigration rose at a steady pace despite falling prices; the correlation is a negative one. The years after 1662 witnessed something of the same confused relationship between emigration and prices.

According to Russell Menard, the period from 1665 to 1667 was among the worst for the Chesapeake tobacco industry in the century, yet Bristol's shipments of servants to the region recovered in these years from the low figures of 1663 and 1664.[18] When tobacco prices rose between 1668 and 1671, however, Bristol's recorded shipment of servants dropped. In the following decade the arrival of new servants in the Chesapeake was disrupted by the Third Dutch War, but recovery is said to have begun in 1674, rising to a peak in 1678 or 1679.[19] Bristol's recorded shipments fall significantly only in 1673, and they rise to a peak in 1675, on stagnant tobacco prices. With more buoyant prices, the export of servants from the city appears to have fallen to about 45 percent of the level in 1675.

Of course, we are working with a rather blunt instrument, one based only on scattered prices primarily from Maryland, which did not receive the majority of Bristol's servant exports. Still, this evidence, taken together with our examination of the effects of the Africa company's new charter, the coming of the Dutch War, and domestic prices and wages on emigration, makes it hard to escape the conclusion that after 1662 some intervening factor, not already accounted for, affected the number of servants registered from year to year. Up to that year the servant trade followed a steady course in which the impetus of hard times in England overcame the effects of poor commodity prices in the colonies to produce a pattern of enrollments in the Bristol *Register* explicable in economic terms. Even though there must have been considerable underregistration in these years, what there was appears to have occurred at an even rate, with enrollments closely following the rhythms of migration itself. As a result, the figures we have derived for the period from 1654 to 1662 give us a reliable idea of the secular trend in the trade, though probably not of its true volume. After 1662, however, the administration of the *Register* seems much more haphazard, with the numbers of enrollments rising and falling in an erratic fashion.

If economics alone cannot explain the patterns revealed by the Bristol *Register*, can politics provide a further understanding? Did the registration of servants respond to the rhythms of politics as well as to the ebb and flow of economic or demographic trends? For example, does the persecution of the Quakers and their despair over religious conditions in England account in part for the large numbers of emigrants in the late 1650s and early 1660s?[20] There can be no doubt, of course, that the

Chesapeake and the West Indies had significant Quaker communities in the mid-seventeenth century and that Bristol was a way station for them and for other sectaries on their pilgrimages to the New World.[21] Bristol's Quakers, many of them heavily engaged in colonial trade, certainly did not shy away from helping their fellows on both sides of the Atlantic. George Bishop acted as such a conduit for emigrant Friends in 1656, continuing a tradition among the Bristol sectaries that went back to the earliest days of colonial migration.[22]

The role of persecution in accounting for this movement during the 1650s, however, cannot be demonstrated so readily. Between 1654 and 1656, only twenty-one Bristol Quakers were actually imprisoned for their religious activities, although there were several serious riots and warrants were issued in the city for the arrest of John Camm, John Audland, George Fox, James Nayler, and Edward Burrough as members of "the Franciscan Order in Rome." Moreover, the Bristol Quakers carefully disassociated themselves from the James Naylor affair in 1656 and as a result suffered little serious trouble with the authorities in the aftermath of this scandal.[23] Although the Quakers themselves complained loudly of persecution in Bristol in these years, the pattern seems much the same in other prominent Quaker strongholds. In London and Middlesex, for example, there were clashes between the Friends and their opponents, but no systematic persecutions.[24] For all the upheavals caused by the Quakers in the mid-1650s, it appears that they enjoyed a degree of religious toleration from the authorities, even if they were subject to periodic attacks from their religious enemies and to regulation of their nonreligious activities.

The same could not be said, however, for the early 1660s. As the decade began even James Powell, no friend to the Quakers, could see the signs of a terrible change about to wreck the delicate balance that had been reached in the 1650s. Just before the king's return in 1660 Powell wrote to acquaint John Weaver of the Council of State "in what sad state and condition we are fallen unto."

> How the old good cause is now sunke and a horrid Spirit of Prophanenes Malignity and revenge is risen vp Trampling on all those that have the face of godlinesse and have been in ye Parliament party insomuch that if the Lord doe not interpose I doubt [not] a Massacre will follow on the godly. And the very name of fanaticke shall be sufficient to ruine any sober Christian as the name of Christian amongst the Heathens Lollards amongst the Papists and Puritan of Late amongst the Prelaticks. . . . The Lord prepare us for the great storm that is approaching.[25]

Even before the Restoration, the sectaries, especially the Quakers, became targets of violent apprentice riots encouraged by many of their masters.[26] With the return of the monarchy, the persecution took on an official character and proceeded with depressing regularity through the decade. As Edward Terrill of Bristol's Broadmead Baptist Church reported when the Second Conventicle Act came into force in 1670, this "trouble was our seventh Persecution in Bristoll, since K. Charles II returned." He noted persecutions in 1660, 1661, 1662, 1663, 1664, and 1666, as well as in 1670.[27]

These persecutions sprang from a variety of motives, ranging from a wish for revenge against Commonwealthmen to a desire to suppress all heterodox religious practices. But one recurring theme was fear of the sectaries as a source of disorder or even insurrection.[28] In 1660, for example, Richard Ellsworth, one of Bristol's most ardent scourgers of dissent, urged the imprisonment of those who refused the oaths of Supremacy and Allegiance, noting

> [t]hat noe Quaker or rarely any Anabaptist, will take those Oathes, soe that the said Oathes are refused by many hundreds of those Judgments, being persons of very dangerous principalls, & euer Enimies (in this City) to his Majestie's royall person, gouernment, & restauration, & some of them, petitioners to bringe His Martired Majestie of blessed Memory to his Triall; & will vndoubtedly fly out againe, & kicke vpp the heele against his Soueraigne Authority, should it lie in theire Power.[29]

The large public meetings favored by the sectaries were one source of this fear, for throngs, often composed of strangers as well as citizens, gathered at them. As Ellsworth says,

> These ... Monsters of Men with uss, are very, yea more Numerous, then in all the West of England ... on this side [of] London; & heere they all Confer, & haue Their Meetings, att all seasons till 9 of the clock att night, & later, sometymes aboue 1000, or 1200 att a tyme, to the greate affrighting of this City, as to what wilbe the Consequent thereof, If not restrained.[30]

At Bristol, moreover, the existence of the two fairs, at St. Paul's tide in January and at St. James's tide in July, only made matters worse; for these were not only great clearinghouses for trade but gathering places for the sectaries, many of whom, of course, were traders themselves.[31] At the same time, the city was well recognized by the authorities as a center vital to the control of the West, for, as a Somerset gentleman observed in 1663, it was "one of the most Considerable Townes vnder his

Majesty's subiection, beeing a good Port, and furnished with a well stored Magazine of Wealth & all ammunitions of warre, and able to se-cure themselves and give assistance to the neighbouring Countrys."[32]

Not surprisingly, the authorities at Bristol displayed a marked skit-tishness at the first hint of danger.[33] Reacting perhaps to news of Ven-ner's Fifth Monarchy plot in London, they struck at once in January 1661, when Henry Roe, the Quaker ironmonger, and Samuel Clarke, the Baptist merchant, both former Cromwellian soldiers, were found to have large trading stocks of powder and shot in their cellars. These stocks, of course, were primarily to supply merchant vessels with the arms they needed on the high seas. Nevertheless, the ammunition was confiscated, and the magistrates in their zeal shut the city gates against impending insurrection.[34] Similar rumors of insurrection abounded in this period, forcing the civic authorities repeatedly into a posture of defense. The city gates had to be guarded again in November 1661, when wild stories of a fanatic uprising spread through the West, though these precautions were soon left off on "hearinge ye designe was quasshed."[35] At the time of the St. James Fair of 1662, new rumors of trouble surfaced but could not be confirmed; still, the Trained Bands had to be called to keep watch over the fair-goers.[36] In the fall rumors spread again, and the deputy lieutenants resolved to raise part of the mi-litia and to secure all suspected persons.[37] By December this vigilance had turned up evidence of what the deputy lieutenants called a "very dangerous" design to begin at Whitehall on 1 January and spread throughout the realm. Six or seven hundred persons were said to be en-gaged around Bristol alone, requiring "the speedy raising of the Militia for the safety" of the city.[38]

These conditions demanded vigilance from the authorities both against sectarian meetings and against the wanderings of vagrants and other masterless men, two issues closely connected in national politics from the outset of the Restoration, if not before.[39] Fear of sectarian vaga-bondage seemed to take precedence, partly to halt the work of the Quaker missionaries and partly to prevent the mass gatherings which caused such apprehension. For example, the very first day of business in the Convention Parliament saw a bill "against Vagrants, and wandering idle, dissolute persons," which, having failed of passage in 1660, was entered again on the first day of business in the Cavalier Parliament and incorporated in part in the Quaker Act of 1662.[40] Moreover, this link-age of issues prevailed in Parliament even after the passage of the Quaker Act. It is no surprise, perhaps, that many of the MPs involved in the passage of the Act of Settlement in 1662 were also interested in the attack on the sects.[41]

Among these MPs we find John Knight, Senior, one of the members for Bristol. Not only did he work as a committeeman on the Act of Settlement and on later measures to explain and expand it, but he was similarly engaged in the Commons work on the Conventicle Act, and he is even said to have wept for joy on receiving news of its passage.[42] In Bristol this combination of issues had a special local flavor, conditioned by the city's prominence both as a commercial center and as a sectarian stronghold. As we have seen, in the 1650s politics had already been penetrated by a mixture of religious and economic rivalries. Many of the old issues flared with new force at the Restoration. With Charles II's return, the Smiths, the Bakers, the Barber-Surgeons, and the Shoemakers all complained that those not free of their gilds took apprentices and practiced their crafts outside gild regulations. As a result, the mayor and aldermen ordered the city clerks in each case to refrain from registering any apprentice in these crafts without the certificate of the master of each gild, and in 1667 the Common Council passed a comprehensive ordinance on the matter.[43] In these same years the Merchant Venturers made yet another try to halt the "interloping of Artificers & others . . . tradeing into forreigne parts, not haveing beene bounde Apprentices to ye Art & mistery."[44] At the Restoration, the civic authorities turned their attention to the colonial trades, appointing as water bailiff John Towgood, son of a prebend in the Bristol Cathedral, and an enemy of the sectaries.[45] From early in 1660 evidence appears in the city of careful searches aboard ships for unindentured servants, and in Parliament in 1662 John Knight became engaged in an attempt to legislate against the stealing of children and servants.[46] When his efforts failed, Nathaniel Cale, mayor in 1662–63, petitioned the Crown, apparently without success, for letters patent to bolster his authority to enforce the procedures established in 1654.[47] The search for settlement at the Restoration revived with even greater force the heady mixture of religion, politics, and economics already present at the creation of the Bristol *Register*.

Although the scourging of the sects in England might well have encouraged some dissenters to seek relief in the colonies,[48] at the Restoration these places had become almost as incommodious for nonconformists as England itself. In Barbados, for example, official objections to the Quakers and other separatists began within weeks of Charles II's return to the throne, and by the spring the Assembly of Barbados complained that the island's many sectaries have declared an absolute Dislike to the Government of the Church of *England* as well by their Aversion and utter Neglect or Refusal of the Prayers, Sermons and Administration of the Sacraments, and other Rites and Ordinances thereof . . . as by holding Conventicles in private Houses and other places, scandalizing Ministers, and endeavouring to seduce others in their erroneous Opinions, upon Pretence of an alteration of Church-Government in *England*. All which their Misdemeanours have begotten many Distractions, a great Reproach and Disparagement to the Church and Ministry, and Disturbances of the Government of this Island.[49]

In response to an order from the Council of Foreign Plantations to settle religion, the legislature required all residents of the island to conform themselves to English law governing the practice of the Anglican church.[50] As a result, at least thirty-six of the island's Quakers were imprisoned for their meetings and their subsequent refusals to take the oath of allegiance to the king.[51] During these same years the sectaries in Maryland, Nevis, Antigua, and other American plantations also suffered persecutions.[52]

Probably the most significant attacks on religious dissent, however, occurred in Virginia. Events there demand a close look, since the Bristol *Register* shows this colony to have experienced the greatest decline in the number of enrolled servants after 1662. Action against the sectaries in Virginia began even before the Restoration itself. In March 1660, at the same time as the Quakers in Bristol were being threatened by the city's apprentices, the Virginia General Assembly enacted legislation forbidding ships' captains from bringing Quakers to the colony and ordered the suppression of Quaker publications, the punishment of those who held conventicles, and the arrest and deportation of all Quakers already there.[53] But the colony remained interested in attracting new population and seems not to have enforced this measure vigorously; in any case the legislation did not stem the tide of Quaker migration. With the Restoration a somewhat less harsh approach was tried for a time, using fines and other punishments short of outright banishment.[54]

By the winter of 1661, the Virginia General Assembly had taken its first tentative steps to settle the church.[55] A year later, more comprehensive legislation appeared arranging church finances, subjecting all nonconformists to heavy fines for failing to attend the services of the established church in the colony—now fully restored in Anglican practice—and specially punishing the Quakers "for assembling in unlawful assemblies and conventicles."[56] In December 1662 the General Assembly extended this policy of intolerance by ordering the punishment of all those who refused to have their children baptized, a direct confrontation with all the sects.[57] These measures were given teeth by vigorous

enforcement, for in 1662 it was reported that many of the Virginia
Quakers were imprisoned or even banished because they would not aid
the established church, promise to abstain from their own meetings, or
swear oaths.[58]

The climax of this process of persecution came in 1663. September
saw the passage of an act against the "Quakers and any other separatists" that signaled a renewed desire to destroy the sects. The Virginia
General Assembly, liberally plagiarizing the English Parliament's Quaker
Act of 1662 and anticipating the language of the English Conventicle
Act of 1664, called the nonconformists a threat to "public peace and
safety" and "a terror to the people." It forbade all conventicles and
again subjected all ships' captains to heavy fines for transporting Quakers to the colony.[59] This measure put the final touches on an anti-
sectarian code in Virginia almost as strict as the Clarendon Code taking
shape in England itself. Moreover, at about the same time, news came of
a "barbarous designe" of what Robert Beverley called "several munti-
nous and rebellious *Oliverian* Soldiers, that were sent thither as Servants," who, "depending upon discontented People of all sorts, form'd
a villanous Plot to destroy their Masters, and afterwards to set up for
themselves." This event caused an immediate shock in the colony. The
militia was called at once, the plot thwarted, and arrests made. Even after the execution of the leaders, fear of its nearly successful "subversion
of . . . religion lawes libertyes, rights and proprietyes" lingered in memory, and as late as 1670 the colony enforced an act to keep 13 September, the day of the plot, "holy" and "in perpetual commemoration."[60]

As a result, Virginia in 1663 and 1664 was not an especially congenial place for the sectaries. Persecutions were harsh and, according to
Beverley, made many of the nonconformists "flie to other Colonies, and
prevented abundance of others from going over to seat themselves
among 'em."[61] It is possible that the sharp decline in servant enrollments in Bristol in the summer of 1663 and after owes something to this
history. Virginia nevertheless continued to draw some dissenters to it even
in the years after 1663, since the anti-Quaker legislation of the 1660s
was used only against those Quakers who engaged in controversy; others remained free as long as they lived peaceably in the colony.[62]

In Bristol, as in Virginia, the chronology of persecutions also made
1663 and 1664 an especially dangerous period for the sectaries. Despite
the Declaration of Indulgence of 1662, throughout the winter and early
spring of 1663 there was considerable uneasiness about an impending
insurrection in England, particularly in the West.[63] By the end of May

word had come of a major plot set in Ireland for taking Dublin Castle in which, as the king reported in a speech before the Commons, "many parliament men were engaged." "You will not doubt," he said, "but that those seditious persons there had a correspondence with their friends here."[64] And although this conspiracy had been nipped in the bud, evidence of further plots in England began to appear.[65] The threat to Dublin Castle, moreover, drew Bristol into the center of these affairs. Not only was the city the major English port for travel to and from Ireland, but some of the conspirators, such as Captain John Gregory and John Casbeard, who had been uncovered earlier by the city's magistrates, appeared to be deeply involved in the Irish matter.[66]

As the year went on conditions seemed to worsen. In July, news of the Derwentdale plot broke in Yorkshire,[67] and the king issued orders to the justices of assize to "prevent and punish the scandalous and seditious Meetings of Sectaries." In addition, he asked the members about to return home at the proroguing of Parliament to use their vigilance and authority in their counties to prevent disturbances by "the restless spirits of ill and unquiet men," securing their persons if need be.[68] At the same time, a new militia act came into force, authorizing the lieutenants and their deputies to call up contingents of the Trained Bands for fourteen-day intervals, a course followed in many places in the north and west.[69] Although no direct evidence of Bristol's reaction to these events in the summer of 1663 has survived, careful precautions by the commanders of the militia, similar to those taken in the previous year, would have been in order as the time of the St. James Fair approached in July. Early in September, the king and queen journeyed to Bath and Bristol, only to be met by sectarian disturbances in the region, for which Charles Baily, the Bristol Quaker, was among those arrested.[70] Finally, in October definite word came of a plot set especially in the western counties, in which Bristol was to have been one of the principal targets.[71] On receiving word from the Privy Council, two companies of foot soldiers were immediately put on guard, and the following day the whole regiment was mustered. Sir John Knight, the new mayor, whom we have already met as one of Bristol's MPs, quickly took the opportunity to "putt in Execution his Majesties pleasure against the Sectaries in this Citty & theire seditious meetings."[72]

Knight's entrance into the mayoralty at Michaelmas 1663 began one of the most violent periods of religious persecution in Bristol's history. Even before news of the plot reached him in mid-October, he was already at work suppressing the sects, arresting Thomas Ewins and other

Baptists and threatening the Quakers.[73] By the end of November he had begun a series of attacks on sectarian meetings designed to procure, as reported by the Quakers, "the rooting of us, and the generation of us, out of this City."[74] Over a four-week period he and the deputy lieutenants repeatedly disrupted the Quaker meetings, closed the meeting house, and arrested the sect's leaders and imprisoned them.[75] On Christmas Day these attacks reached a level of genuine barbarity when three Quaker servants at work in their masters' shops were caught by members of the militia, "tied Neck and Heels with half hundred Weights and Muskets about their Necks, in extreme cold Weather, till the Eyes of two of them were thought to be drawing out, their Faces being black."[76]

The remainder of Knight's year in office proceeded in much the same vein. From Christmas on, he and his officers repeatedly interrupted Quaker meetings, made arrests, and at one point even had the meetinghouse door nailed shut. In February Knight, joined by two aldermen, one of the sheriffs, and "sundry officers," broke up a meeting of three hundred at Samuel Tovey's house in Broadmead and arrested and imprisoned eighty men and women.[77] When January brought word of another plot of the "fanaticks" to surprise Bristol, the civic authorities again struck at the Quakers, this time arresting fifteen of them for unlawful assembly.[78] Yet all of this was but a prelude to the outburst of persecutions that occurred when the Conventicle Act came into force at the beginning of July. On the first Sunday in the month, Knight and two aldermen came to the Quaker meetinghouse and opened a court for the judgment of the violators of the act. On this day alone, one hundred and seventy persons were fined for a first offense under the statute.[79] During the following weeks Knight returned again and again to the Quakers to close down their meetings and to arrest their membership. In all, he succeeded in convicting two hundred and nineteen for a first offense, a further one hundred and five for a second offense, and twenty-three more for a third offense, a dozen of whom were sentenced to banishment in the West Indies. When he left office, one hundred and forty-five Quakers remained in prison under the act. Moreover, the new legislation placed other dissenting sects in the same jeopardy as the Quakers. The Bristol Baptists also found themselves targets for arrest and conviction and "were forced to . . . meet more Privately" and "to move from house to house."[80]

After reviewing this dismal narrative, we can hardly be surprised to find intolerance contributing in some measure to emigration from England.

Between 1659 and 1662, attacks on the dissenters must have added considerably to the pressures already produced by poor conditions in the English economy. Yet no simple explanation is possible. During this same period, religious oppression also grew in the colonies, although in Virginia the persecution of the sects in 1659–1660 abated somewhat just after the Restoration, and broke forth anew only in 1663. Until that year, Virginia may have remained reasonably attractive to the sectaries as a possible place of safety; afterward it could no longer have seemed very secure. This change in the practices of persecution in the colonies, taken together with improvements at the same time in English grain prices and real wages, may help explain the decline in servant enrollments at Bristol after the peaks reached in the late 1650s and early 1660s. Nevertheless, the whole story cannot turn on these two considerations alone, if only because sectarian migrations continued to Virginia itself and to other colonies throughout the Restoration period.[81] If religious persecution played a significant role in driving Englishmen to the colonies before 1663, we must wonder why, according to the Bristol *Register*, its effects diminished so dramatically just as the attacks grew to their most intense. Nothing in the history of intolerance in the colonies could have outweighed the oppressions in England in the mid-1660s.

To see what mechanisms were at work in determining the rate of servant enrollments in Bristol we need to return to England once again. Unfortunately, we can say little about whether events outside the city played a decisive role in limiting the registration of servants there. It might be, for example, that West Country justices of the peace, apprehensive about insurrection in 1663 and 1664, used the Act of Settlement to turn back migrants before they reached the city, especially at fair time, when large numbers of indentures were usually drawn. But no evidence has come to light to confirm such actions. An examination of Bristol's own Restoration politics, however, can show us something of the way noneconomic events governed the administration of the servant *Register* during this period. Even though the policy of persecution followed by Sir John Knight and his allies had considerable support within the city, there was also much opposition to it from moderate members of the Restoration Common Council, as well as from the larger body of citizens. As the Quakers said with only slight exaggeration, Knight's zeal "set-up to counter-buff the stability of the City, and to overturn . . . the well poized Government of unity and peace into disunion and troubles."[82]

Bristol's politics in these years are difficult to unravel, for a number of rivalries were at work both inside and outside the government.[83] For example, Richard Ellsworth, the Customer for Bristol who during the last days of the Commonwealth had played a major role in organizing Royalist efforts in the city, looked upon Knight as "disaffectious to the interest Royall" and used his connections in Westminster to advocate an even more vigilant and extreme policy against the sects.[84] On the other side, a number of officials had close ties to the sectaries. Many were engaged in the colonial trades, which regularly brought them in contact with the sectarian community. Of the twenty-seven Bristolians who petitioned the Crown for a convoy to Virginia in September 1665, eleven were members of the Common Council, and one a recently retired member. Yet along with them were James Wathen and Thomas Ellis, whom we have already met, and Gabriel Deane, who voted for John Haggatt in the parliamentary election of 1654 and who was purged from the council in 1661.[85] With such shared business interests, councillors and sectaries sometimes entered into partnership. In the Commonwealth period, Robert Cann, mayor in 1662–63, had invested in ventures with Thomas Speed, with whom his relations remained good even after the Restoration, when Cann became a planter in Barbados.[86] In 1661 William Willett, another councillor, owned the ship *Resolution* with Speed, Gabriel Deane, and five others.[87]

At about the same time, Sir Humphrey Hooke, a man with important family and political ties in Bristol, Gloucestershire, and Barbados who was deputy lieutenant for the city in 1664, received from the king an extensive grant of land in Virginia which he held jointly with Robert Vickris, whose wife and children were Quakers.[88] Kinship ties also affected the relations of the civic authorities to the sectaries. Richard Streamer, sheriff in 1663–64 and sometimes a colonial trader himself, was George Bishop's brother-in-law, and Sir Robert Yeamans, sheriff in 1662–63 and a former Royalist officer, was a kinsman of Thomas Speed's wife, who was a prominent Quaker in her own right.[89] As George Bishop reminded Knight, the Bristol sectaries were

> a considerable body of people in this City, we, our families, our relations, our estates; we are of the City, and in the City, and inhabitants thereof, and enterwoven we are therein, and with the people thereof, as a mans flesh is in his body, and his spirit in his flesh.[90]

Business and kinship connections, of course, could not always counteract the power of religious conviction or political principle among the Bristolians. Sir John Knight, whose zealous hatred of sectarian and republican ideas went back to the 1640s, did not alter policy because of his own close family ties to the dissenters.[91] Nor did the rather similar family relations of Sheriff Streamer prevent his conscientious, though reluctant, performance of duty.[92] But they made full enforcement exceedingly difficult, because many Bristolians did not share Knight's bloody-mindedness. Though prepared to resist public outrages by sectarian incendiaries, they preferred to ignore those dissenters who lived peaceably in the city. For example, juries at the Sessions in January 1664 would not find the Quakers guilty of unlawful assembly as charged: one group of defendants was acquitted, and a second convicted, after considerable debate, by special verdict covering only a part of the indictment.[93] Later in the same year, when the authorities attempted to transport three Quakers for their third conviction under the Conventicle Act, the crew of the *Mary Fortune* refused to take them, saying that "their Cry, and the Cry of their Family and Friends, are entered into the Ears of the Lord, and he hath smitten us even to the very Heart, saying, *Cursed is he that parteth Man and Wife.*"[94] Many others were moved to acts of compassion as well. Sir Robert Cann, by now a baronet, and Sir Robert Yeamans visited the arrested Quakers in jail, and Robert Yate and John Knight, of the Sugar House on St. Augustine's Back, both of whom had extensive business connections with Speed and other Quakers, offered to stand surety for the jailed sectaries.[95]

These events illustrate the degree to which Bristol was torn by political division in the 1660s. Sir John Knight, Senior, was among the leaders of a significant group of Cavaliers in the city. His principal allies were men like Nathaniel Cale, soapmaker, who had been purged from the city government as a Delinquent in 1645, and John Locke, merchant, who had left in 1656 because of his Royalist views.[96] These men and a few others like them, including several prominent members of the local gentry, served as deputy lieutenants for the city. Although in law, as some of them said, they had "no Authoritie to exercise any Ciuil power as magistrates in the Citty agaynst any man for delinquency," their military office gave them considerable ability to control events, especially when the mayor was in sympathy with their cause, as in Sir John Knight's term. When necessary, a large body of citizens under their command could be relied upon for political aid.[97] For most of the period, however, only a handful of leading aldermen held the office of deputy lieutenant concurrently. In any case, the Common Council did not consist entirely of men of similar background. At the outset of Knight's mayoralty in 1663, only five aldermen and three common councillors were old Royalists, either having been ousted for their political views in the 1640s or 1650s or, like Knight himself, having refused to swear the oath of office until the Restoration.[98] By contrast, four aldermen and five common councillors had served in the civic body during the Interregnum and thus had worked closely at times with the members of the sects. Furthermore, a number of those elected to the council after the Restoration served only with great reluctance, in some instances caused by their unwillingness to enforce harsh government policy against friends and kinfolk. Among the latter may have been John Knight, the sugar refiner, who though elected in 1661 would not be sworn until September 1664, and then only under the Privy Council's threat of a stiff fine.[99]

Under these conditions, it should come as no surprise to find the city government rent by fierce battles for political primacy in this period. During Sir John Knight's term, the conflict took the form of a challenge to the precedence of the local leadership, in which Sir Robert Cann, Baronet, and Sir Robert Yeamans were in the vanguard. Cann and Yeamans claimed on behalf of those titled members of the council that they should have precedence before all others regardless of their seniority. In large measure the issue was a symbolic one that served to draw political support for Cann and Yeamans from aldermen who possessed knighthoods. But more was at stake than mere symbolism, since nominations and votes in the civic body proceeded by order of precedence. In effect, Sir Robert Cann was seeking to use his baronetcy to oust the mayor from his privileged place in directing the affairs of the city. For Yeamans, who was not yet an alderman, the issue also had special importance; had he won his point, he would have gained precedence over all but those aldermen who had received knighthoods before him. It is no wonder, therefore, that the issue created an explosion of antagonism in the city that quickly evinced itself in challenges to Knight's actions against the dissenters.[100]

To a large degree, the rate of servant enrollments in Bristol depended upon which faction controlled the civic administration at the time. After Sir John Knight's year of terror, no other mayor before the 1670s undertook an all-out attack on the dissenters.[101] John Lawford, Knight's immediate successor, aided by Knight himself, vigorously enforced the Conventicle Act; yet he did not make mass arrests or attempt to impose the penalty of banishment.[102] During 1667–68, peace and quiet were said to have reigned in Bristol, and in 1669 little was done to suppress the sects, even after the issuance of a royal proclamation against conventicles.[103] The mayors during these years were Alderman Edward

Morgan, father of John Morgan, upholsterer, one of Bristol's great exporters of servants to the colonies, and Alderman Thomas Stevens, a grocer much of whose business must have been in colonial products. Both of these men had joined the Common Council in the Interregnum, and, interestingly, both had resisted accepting high office in the 1660s until forced by threats of confiscatory fines.[104]

In addition to Lawford, Sir Thomas Langton, mayor in 1666–67, and Sir Robert Yeamans, mayor in 1669–70, receive mention as prominent persecutors in these years. But neither man was hellbent on routing the sects. Langton acted only on direct evidence of apparent seditious activity, to which he was especially alert because of the threat of a Dutch attack during his term.[105] Yeamans, for his part, had the misfortune to hold office when the Second Conventicle Act came into force. Thus he found it his duty to execute a policy his enemy Sir John Knight had helped create.[106] This act gave substantial authority to the deputy lieutenants to aid in enforcement and subjected the justices of the peace and the chief magistrates of the towns to stiff fines for each failure to respond to informations duly presented them.[107] Even so, Yeamans acted only reluctantly, prodded by the bishop of Bristol, whose informers made it impossible to disregard the dissenters' meetings. Furthermore, many of his colleagues, assistants, and fellow citizens refrained from supporting his efforts. Statutory fines were imposed; but when the cases arose, numerous aldermen absented themselves from the bench, and the goods distrained to pay the fines often found no buyers. With the aid of the Trained Bands, Yeamans managed to close the meetinghouses for a time, but the Baptists and the Quakers took to the streets to hold their services. For two months, in fact, Yeamans's persecution amounted to little more than halfhearted threats against the sectaries put forth in combination with plaintive letters of apology to the Privy Council for failing to do better. Yeamans confined himself to his duty narrowly construed; he attacked sectarian religion according to law, but had no interest in abusing the dissenters in their businesses or everyday lives. Perhaps to indicate his distaste even for this task, he ended his term by nominating as his successor the moderate-minded sugar refiner Mr. John Knight, although the king had previously ordered that only aldermen were eligible for the office.[108]

The years following Sir John Knight's mayoralty brought with them a moderation of religious persecution in Bristol. These same years also saw the beginning of an era of more favorable material conditions for English labor. As population growth ceased and agricultural production diversified, England no longer suffered periodic subsistence crises and real wages improved, with the result that everywhere in the country the rate of emigration to America fell to levels significantly below those reached in the 1650s. In a general way the decline in the number of indentured servants enrolled at Bristol after 1662 parallels the development nationally. Had the registrations for these years recovered their earlier peaks, we would have every reason to be surprised. From the beginning of 1663, however, a number of factors other than wages and prices intervened to affect the flow of servants through Bristol. War in colonial waters and the plague in London, though not the fire, appear to have played a short-term role. Religion and politics, in both England and the colonies, seem more significant, sometimes stirring religious discontent at home and at other times threatening equal danger abroad.

But Bristol itself is where the most important intervening factors can be found. As we have seen, the city was at times an exceedingly dangerous place for sectaries. In 1663–64, many of the leading colonial traders found themselves in jail for their religious beliefs and no doubt were unable to attend to their businesses. In other years, religious persecutions must have thoroughly distracted them, even though they did not result in long imprisonment. When persecutions raged in Bristol, emigrating dissenters may have avoided the city on their way abroad, using other and safer ports instead. However, the greatest effect was probably administrative, rather than economic. The system of registration could not be enforced for long without cooperation from the traders. The city's administrative resources simply were far too small to do the work day in and day out. In July 1662, when Mayor Nathaniel Cale was maintaining his vigilance against impending insurrection, the whole registration scheme had come under challenge. Periodically during the previous two years, city officials had boarded ships to assure themselves that all servants were properly registered. But resistance by the ships' captains and traders seems to have halted this practice, causing Cale to petition the Privy Council for authority to make these inquiries.[109]

No such grant was forthcoming, and the practice of boarding ships did not begin again until August 1670, at the very end of Yeamans's mayoral term.[110] Thus for most of the 1660s the city seems to have employed no effective means of checking the indentures of servants. During periods of persecution it was easy enough for servants to embark on Bristol ships far from the scrutiny of the city authorities, boarding, as Farwell Meredith had done in 1654, at Kingroad at the mouth of the Avon, rather than nearer to the sources of trouble. In other words, persecution served to increase underregistration. Only when the city was relatively free of attacks on the sects or when those attacks were accompanied by vigilant searches for unindentured servants, as was the case from 1660 to 1662 and again during Ralph Olliffe's troubled mayoralty in 1674–75, can the Bristol *Register* give us a reasonably accurate picture of the servant trade.[111]

The scheme to register indentured servants in Bristol was never exactly what it pretended to be. Instead of offering genuine protection for boys, maids, and other persons who might be spirited beyond the seas by the rogues who plied the servant trade, it sought to control the commercial activities of the numerous men and women, some of them religious and political radicals, who pursued profit in the American colonies. The entries in the *Register* responded as much to the fortunes of politics as to the economics of trade and agriculture. Since Bristol was a commercial city whose very social structure and social geography rested on its role as a major port, its community life was dominated by its connections with distant markets on the continent and in the Atlantic. Its politics and its economy had been inextricably intertwined ever since it received its first grants of privileges in the twelfth century, if not before.[112] This meant that the exercise of power never took a single form. Those who contested for command of the city's markets also vied for control of its government and of its rituals and symbols, sacred and profane. Political strife centered on the regulation of trade and manufacture, which in turn became the means to enhance economic power and advance an ideology. As Bristol's commerce with America increased in importance during the middle and late seventeenth century, not surprisingly it became the arena within which these battles for local domination were fought.

CHAPTER 10

The Spirit World

For most scholars, the history of the Bristol *Register* has been the story of servants making their way to America. But it turns out to be as much, if not more, the story of their masters making their way in England. To stretch seventeenth-century usage only slightly, it is a register of spirits as well as of servants. To those who invoked the word "spirit" in the seventeenth century, it was a term charged with significance. It fit into folklore as well as theology, and into more than one branch of the natural sciences. In general it meant the principle or force that animates or directs a physical organism. In man, it could refer to the soul. But, as with the soul, it was a force for good or evil, a force that might impel one toward either God or Satan. It is to this turbulent world of the spirits that we must now turn.

To those who sought to regulate the servant trade, the spirit was a devil. For example, Lionel Gatford believed many children and servants sent to the plantations were

> cheatingly duckoyed without the consent or knowledge of their Parents or Masters ... and ... sold to be transported; and then resold ... to be servants or slaves to those that will give most for them. A practice proper for Spirits, namely the Spirits of Devils, but to be abhorred and abominated of all men that know either what men are, or whose originally they are, or what their relatives are, either natural, civil, or Christian.[1]

Like the devil, the spirit cozened, enticed, or tempted his, or sometimes her, victims into base servitude by taking advantage of their idleness.

With false demeanor and engaging words, he appealed to their lust for fleshly pleasures and convinced them that "they shall goe into a place where food shall drop into their mouthes: and being thus deluded, they take courage, and are transported."[2] Spirits especially prized children, and, like the evil demons of folklore, stole them whenever they could.[3] Hence they could be said to copy their counterparts of the invisible world in studiously endeavoring "to deprave and corrupt Mankind, and to enlarge their own Empire by the Accession of frail man, whose weakness they abuse and triumph over."[4]

In this view, the servant trade brought depravity and disorder with it and fed the worst in human nature. In consequence, "spirit" was "so infamous a name" that riotous mobs "wounded to death" many who had been tarred with it, and convicted spirits ranked among the most vilified of criminals.[5] According to the Bristol magistrates, spirits took advantage of the moral and intellectual shortcomings of their victims. Many of the servants who came to the city to sail to America, the Bristolians said,

> prove to be husbands that upon discontents & humor haue forsaken their wiues & children & thereby exposed them to misery or Parish mercy; otherwhile wiues out of a peevish passion haue abandoned their husbands and houses; children & apprentices y^t runaway from their parents & Masters & often times vnwary & credulous persons haue been tempted & betrayed on shipboard by Men-stealers comonly called Spirits & many also which haue been persued by Hue & Cries either for robberies Burglaries or breaking Prison doe thereby escape ye persecucon of Law & Justice.[6]

Among the traders the traffic in servants encouraged covetousness and pride in the form of a supervening desire to abandon their calling for undeserved gain. Moreover, by trading abroad from their shops and workbenches these dealers in servants shared one further trait with the inhabitants of the world of darkness: like witch's familiars, they shifted their shapes "at their pleasures" by changing places in the natural order of the economy from retailer or artisan to long-distance merchant.[7]

Because it was laden with such heavy implications, the word "spirit" also provided a handy weapon with which to slander opponents. The cases of Edward Peade in London and Marlin Hiscox in Bristol were by no means the only ones in which the technique was employed. For example, in 1652 Hugh Peter was called the "chief Agent, Actor or Procurer" among "the Spirits that took Children in England, said to be set awork first by the Parliament."[8] Similarly, Secretary Thurloe was smeared in 1659 with a charge of selling Rowland Thomas, a Royalist agent, into slavery in Barbados.[9] The tactic was employed yet again in the aftermath of the Exclusion crisis when John Wilmore, merchant of London, faced charges of spiriting. Wilmore suffered less as a merchant than as a figure with strong Whig connections. He not only had served on the Middlesex grand jury that indicted the duke of York for recusancy, but also was foreman of the London jury that disregarded the charges of treason against Stephen College, the arch anti-papist follower of Shaftesbury.[10] In Bristol, too, party politics in the 1680s were brought near to the boiling point by similar charges of spiriting leveled against some common councillors. When Chief Justice Jeffries came to Bristol in 1685 to mete out his punishments to Monmouth's rebels, he opened the assizes with a biting attack on Sir William Hayman, then the mayor, and Sir Robert Cann, among others, not only for neglecting to punish dissenters but for kidnapping. The mayor was fined £1,000 "for suffering a boy committed to Bridewell to go beyond the sea," and Cann and four others were required to find £5,000 surety each to answer similar charges.[11]

From the beginning the best targets for these charges were the sectaries, whose political principles and religious practices gave them a reputation, among their enemies, for demonic possession. In Richard Baxter's view, Satan himself had "notoriously deluded" the Anabaptists, Ranters, Fifth Monarchists, and other "Enthusiasticks," as he called them, and they in turn had deluded more foolish men and women by "their pretended Angelical Revelation."[12] The Quakers often bore the brunt of such criticism. Orthodox Calvinists like William Grigg and Ralph Farmer of Bristol were convinced that the sect merely put into practice what other separatist doctrines already implied.[13] "When the Quakers first arose," it was said,

> their Societies began like witches with Quaking, and Vomiting; and Infecting others with breathing on them, and tying Ribbons on their Hands. And their Actions as well as their Doctrines shewed their Master. When some as professying, walked through the Streets of Cities naked; and some vainly undertook to raise the Dead.[14]

Moreover, by attacking the ordained ministry, permitting women to speak at Meeting, refusing to uncover before superiors or magistrates, and denying titles of honor, the Quakers seemed to stand for all that threatened the prevailing social order.[15] Their enemies therefore singled them out as men and women "big with swollen pride . . . as if neither *God* nor *Nature* nor *State* hath made any difference of persons."[16] Worse yet, in Ralph Farmer's words, they were high-minded lovers of their own "fancy"; they threatened "breaking the bonds of duty in all relations . . . Husband and Wife, Parents and Children, Masters and Servants, Magistrates and Subjects, Ministers and People."[17] As the authorities in Virginia said, the Quakers were, therefore,

> an vnreasonable and turbulent sort of people . . . teaching and publishing lies, miracles, false visions, prophecies and doctrines, which have influence vpon the comunities of men both ecclesiasticall and civil endeavouring and attempting thereby to destroy religion, lawes, communities and all bonds of civil societie, leaving arbitrarie to everie vaine and vitious person whether men shall be safe, lawes established, offenders punished, and Governours rule.[18]

In the aftermath of Bristol's troubles in 1654 and of James Naylor's infamous ride in 1656, the sober-minded magistrates and ministers of that stronghold of the sects could only concur with this trans-Atlantic view. "The damnable and blasphemous Doctrines of the Quakers," William Grigg argued, "tend in their own nature, to the utter ruine of the true Christian Religion, and Civil Government; both in Cities, Families and all Relations, as would soon appear, had they power in their hands."[19] To the city's governors, then, the religion of the Spirit represented in the extreme many of the dangers inherent in the capitalism of the servant trade, and they readily identified the two. In this they did no more than recapture the logic of an earlier persecution. In the fourth century, Julian the Apostate himself identified the *agape* of the early Christians with

> those who entice children with a cake, and by throwing it to them two or three times induce them to follow them, and then, when they are far away from their friends cast them on board a ship and sell them as slaves, and that which for the moment seemed sweet, proves to be bitter for all the rest of their lives.[20]

Among the city's sectaries a very different view prevailed. For many of them the religion of the Spirit was a religion of liberation.[21] It freed them not only from doubts about their personal salvation but also from unwanted restrictions imposed on them by worldly institutions. Nearly all of them resisted the notion that their practices in any way undermined legitimate authority. "As to Government," the Quakers told Sir John Knight in 1664, "they were not against it, but did own the Second Table as well as the First, Masters, Parents, and Magistrates &c., but all in the Lord; and . . . where they could and not sin against the Lord they were obedient; and where they could not, they did quietly suffer."

"What they did," they insisted, "was not in obstinacy and contempt . . . but in Conscience to the Lord, whose worship was in the Spirit." This test of conscience came first, and they would accept no authority of whose righteousness they were not personally convinced. What would "thou . . . have them do," they asked, "seeing their Conscience was not satisfied? Suppose . . . that we are mistaken . . . wouldst thou have us do that which our conscience is against, because of what may be done to our bodies, before we are convinced of the contrary?"[22] Not even the devil could force them from their spiritual freedom; for, as George Bishop argued, "if he could compel, what man should be free? and in what condition were man, if he could be compell'd? and how could man be charged with evil, if he could not do otherwise?"[23]

Bristol's Baptists, however, shied away from such forthright challenges to the established political order. Many of those who remained in the Broadmead congregation after the coming of the Quakers adhered to a version of election theology and would have agreed with Robert Purnell, their ruling Elder, "that nothing in the world . . . renders a man . . . more like Sathan then to argue from mercy, to sinfull liberty; [and] from Divine goodnesse, to licentiousnesse, which is the Devill's Logick."[24] Nevertheless, they maintained an open communion and shared many sympathies with their former brethren among the Quakers. Like them, they believed in a way of life guided by religious conviction, in which each person took absolute responsibility for his own actions. If man could not by himself achieve salvation, he still remained free to resist evil and was obliged to seek righteousness.[25] "Our omissions and commissions be charged upon ourselves," Robert Purnell said, for the sin "lodging in our hearts . . . doth mischief us more then Satan, for he can but tempt, but our deceitful hearts do yield."[26] Moreover, the soul was no passive thing, but reached out to fulfill God's commandments. "Hath the Lord . . . made man an empty creature and void of reason?" Purnell asked.

> [H]ath not man many members in his body and faculties in his soul? . . . for . . . is there not an understanding to understand? is there not a mind or memory to minde or remember? is there not a judgement to judge and determine of things? is there not a will to will the things that the Judgment doth judge as good? Are there not Affections to affect that, which the Judgment presents as good? Or else doth God speak to man as a stock or a stone?[27]

For these reasons, Purnell believed that God approached man by appealing to his rational judgment and his interest, as well as his conscience. "He doth not only offer mercy," he told his brethren, "but doth labour with strong reasons, and arguments, and motives to draw the soul to himself" and "to out bid all other comforts we have in sin." To counter the persuasions of the devil, the world, and our own corruption, he offers "honey, milk, rayment" and "such things as do most take with our hearts." It is "as if the Lord hath said, well, though thou hast been a great sinner . . . yet if thou wilt but turn at my reproof . . . I will pour out my Spirit upon thee, I will give grace and glory, a House, a City, a Kingdome, Life, and all things." In this way the Lord, appealing to our rational instincts, "doth . . . out bid them all, and so win our soul to himself."[28]

With many of the Baptists, the test of "experience" had much the same force as Quaker "conscience." Important truths came "experimentally," either through "immediate inspiration" in which God "darted" his teachings directly into the heart, or through painstaking study and lengthy discourse with fellow Christians.[29] For this reason, the life of the Broadmead church centered upon its weekly conference, in which the experiences of individual members were employed to interpret Scripture "that so there was liberty for any brother (and for any Sister by a brother) to propose his doubt of, or their desire of, understanding any Portion of Scripture," which the others sought to answer as the Lord moved them. In this way, Baptists came to understand the truth, not by authority, but as a thing living in their own souls.[30] They also knew they could not always confine their confessions of faith to these meetings. As one of them said in the face of Sir John Knight's persecutions, "there is a time to speak, that we may not be dumb."[31] Like the Quakers, they found it necessary to bear witness to their faith by the testimony of civil disobedience, following the rule that "every man look to his own heart" and that "no man can be forced beyond his freedom." To honor Christ's "prerogative," they offered up their liberty "upon the service and sacrifice of the faith" and "in opposition to the inventions and usurpations of men therein."[32]

Among the Quakers and the Baptists there was also a strong leveling impulse. George Bishop declared that in this earthly world "all are in the like state . . . and all have the same dependency . . . on the Lord," whether "Rich or Poor, High or Low, Governours or governed, King or people, Master or Servant, Bond or Free."[33] Robert Purnell also argued for the equality of men before God. "Justice hath no respect of persons," he stated, and God brings "down the mighty from their seat . . . exalting them of low degree."[34] Under heaven, he said, we should distinguish only saints and sinners, and accept the truth wherever it is to be found, "either in noble or ignoble, old or young, weak or strong, learned or unlearned."[35] As is well known, the Quakers and the Baptists put these principles into practice in the organization of their own meetings. The Quakers, of course, had no professional pastor to head their community, but waited in silence upon the Lord. "We know his voice from a Strangers," Bishop said, "and can try the spirits: and even those who oppose themselves have and may come to our Assemblies freely, and speak, whom we judge in the spirit of Jesus Christ."[36] The Baptists, for their part, chose their teachers and pastors from among religious men, many of whom lacked formal education in theology and Scripture.[37] Among these early sectaries, we find servants as well as masters, youths as well as elders, and women as well as men taking on the obligations of religious leadership in their communities. The first Quaker sufferers in Bristol were Elizabeth Marshall, widow, and John Warren, an adolescent servant, both jailed in 1654 for their outcries against the "priests" in the "steeplehouses."[38] Later, in 1682, when first the Quaker men and then the Quaker women were seized and imprisoned, their children, according to William Sewel, "now performed what their Parents were hindred from" and "kept up their religious Meetings as much as was in their Power."[39] Among the Baptists, Mrs. Nethway, "a woman very eminent in her godlinesse," played the leading role in selecting the Broadmead church's teacher in 1651.[40] In other words, both groups lived by the doctrine that "God is no respecter of faces; but among all nations he that feareth him and worketh righteousness is acceptable to him."[41]

These powerful ideas translated into an equally powerful vision of a new social order. Implicit in them was a conception of society which, though hardly devoid of distinctions of status and wealth or even of party, rejected the static hierarchical structure of the old regime and assumed a much more open communion of individuals. Both the Baptists and the Quakers accepted a degree of social diversity as an element of social unity and would not permit the state to override the freedom of individuals to choose their own way. Robert Purnell, for example, reminded Parliament in the early 1650s that, "next under God, all power fundamentally was in the people of God," of whom those in authority were merely "Trustees."[42] What he wanted was a new "Church-state," in which the poor and forlorn would receive succour, the godly would go free from the meddlings of excisemen and contribution-collectors, and the sects would continue to have their separate existences, but now based upon a spiritual union; for, as he says, "the body is not one member, but many."[43] Differences about discipline and about "how, and when, and in what places . . . God is to be worshipped" were to be tolerated.[44] "And when this day is dawned," he prophesied,

> and this Day-star is risen in our hearts, Ephraim shall not envy Judah, nor Judah vex Ephraim; Presbyterians shall not so bitterly cry out against Independents, nor Independents have such hard thoughts of the Presbyterians. Yea, they will be ashamed to own one another by these fleshy titles, but look upon and love one another as Christians, members of the same Body, heirs of the same promise, children of the same Father, having all the same Spirit, all cloathed with the same Robe, inclined to the same Work, ruled by the same Word and Spirit, and so their love to each other, shall arise from the Union in the Spirit.[45]

For Purnell and his brethren, the religion of the Spirit permitted or, rather, demanded the communion of men and women in outward difference with one another. But for the Quakers it went even further, since in their doctrine, liberty of conscience was the keystone of all personal freedom. "Ye know," George Bishop said, "that the Good Old Cause, was (chiefly) Liberty of Conscience . . . and the Liberties of the Nation were bound up and joyned together (with it), as two lovely Twins that cannot be divided." Moreover, liberty of conscience was the preeminent civil right, "and where this Liberty is abridged by a State, that State is not free, For a free mind, and a free speech, and a Free State, go together, and weere the two former are wanting, the later is not."[46] This meant, in effect, that the exercise of authority must rest on the acquiescence or consent of those subject to it. An individual who was not personally convinced of the righteousness of a governmental action was bound, not by it, but by his conscience. Consider, for example, the case of William Foord, a Quaker serge weaver, who first came to attention in 1655 when the Company of Milleners in Bristol accused him of keeping a stranger in his employ, contrary to their ordinances. The mayor ordered Foord "to turn the stranger a way and not to teach him." But Foord refused, saying "he was not of their trade, and therefore their Ordinary had no power over him."[47]

Foord's remark might well be read as a manifesto for a host of sectarian small traders and dealers. These men and women envisioned a world in which arbitrary economic distinctions created by actions of the law or the state had no force. They insisted on the rights of Englishmen to "freely come into, and live in any place, within the English jurisdiction, giving an accompt of their names, former habitations, business, places of birth, and last abode, and freeing the parish from charge if it be demanded."[48] In other words, they rejected the basic premise of urban life, which separated freeman from foreigner and gave the magistrates authority to remove unwanted strangers, vagrants, and rootless persons from the town.[49] They believed instead that the "Law of God" required "strangers to be entertained, and cherished, and loved as thy self, not to be vexed or oppressed," and that the "Rights, Liberties, [and] Fundamental Laws" of the English demanded that "Justice be open and free to all" and that "the Magistrates without respect of persons, judge according to the Law, not their own wills or lusts."[50] Their beliefs would not let them accept anyone's exclusive trading privileges. For example, when George Bishop acted during the Commonwealth to defend the Merchant Venturers' rights to trade in calfskins and butter, he would not limit his protection to merchants alone, but extended it to the shoemakers and shopkeepers who also traded in these goods.[51] For him and those like him, all who violated these basic principles were agents of the devil and "Merchants of Babylon."[52]

These ideas come very near to the views upheld in more systematic seventeenth-century discussions of liberty in politics and society. They envision a social order grounded in personal choice and individual commitment. If William Foord had voluntarily placed himself under the rule of the Milleners, he could have no claim to disobey; but since he had not, he assumed a right to pursue his business free from outside interference. His own choice, based on a personal judgment of his rights and interests and of God's will and its demands upon him, governed his activities. This freedom was far from unlimited, since he could not hope to succeed without God's aid and blessing. But how was God to make his will manifest? For a trading man like Foord, the test of whether to continue in his enterprise was a test of the market. If the enterprise prospered, he would maintain it. The same sentiment seems to have prevailed among the sectaries in the colonial trade. They asked no more than for the market to decide whether they should engage in it. By implication, they also placed the colonial servant under the same regime, free to sell his labor to whom he wished, according to what the market would bear.[53]

Since R. H. Tawney's time it has been something of a commonplace that the medieval conception of a social theory based ultimately on religion was discredited in the mid-seventeenth century. Where once the theory of a just price had ruled, Restoration Englishmen are said to have relied more upon the idea of an impersonal market that regulated all economic affairs.[54] The members of the dissenting sects, however, had a distinctively religious view of the market and their relation to it. Many of them believed it wrong to haggle over the price of a commodity. They thought instead that a good Christian should set one fair price and hold to it.[55] In the words of Charles Marshall, one of the leading Bristol Quakers of the Restoration period, a tradesman was to "use but a few words" in his dealings

> and be Equal, Just and Upright; and . . . be not drawn forth in many words, . . . but after you have put a price on your Commodities, which is Equal, and as you can sell them, then if the Persons you are Dealing with, multiply words, stand you silent in the Fear, Dread and Awe of God, and this will answer the Witness of God in them you are dealing with.[56]

According to George Fox, Christ himself required this practice in his Sermon on the Mount when he ordered that all our communication be "Yea, yea; Nay, nay: for whatsoever is more cometh of evil."[57] "[Y]ou tradesmen, merchantmen of all sorts whatsoever, buyers and sellers," Fox says,

> set no more upon the thing you sell in exchange, than what you will have; is it not better and more ease to have done at a word, than to ask double or more? Doth not this bring you into many vain words, and compliments, and talk, that fills the vain mind? This is deceitful before God and man. And is it not more savoury to ask no more than you will have for your commodity, to keep yea and nay in your communication, when you converse in your calling, than to ask more than you will take? and so is not there the many words where is the multitude of sins? This is the word of the Lord to you, ask no more than you will have for your commodity . . . and here will be an equal balancing of things.[58]

These ideas were developed most systematically by the Quakers, but other dissenters, such as John Bunyan, agreed with them in principle.[59] They thought that in the ordinary course of business affairs each commodity should have one price, which the buyer was free to take or leave as he wished. In other words, they believed in what John Locke, writing in the mid-1690s, called "the common rule of traffic," namely, the obligation to sell goods to one and all at the price set at the point of sale by the current state of supply and demand, i.e., by the prevailing market price. According to this view, as Locke outlined it, a merchant or shopkeeper who "makes use of another's ignorance fancy or necessity to sell ribbon or cloth etc dearer to him than to another man at the same time, cheats him." Similarly, if by "artifice" he raises his customer's "longing" for his wares or by his great "fancy" sells them "dearer to him than

he would to an other man he had cheated him too." But so long as there
is no deceit and each side is equally subject to the same trading conditions, the demands of justice are served. For this reason, Locke argues
that "what any one has he may value at what rate he will and transgress
not against justice if he sells it at any price provided he makes no distinction of Buyers but parts with it as cheap to this as he would to any
other Buyer."

In a market of this sort, the buyer guarantees no assured profit to the
seller, but buys "as cheap as he can" even if it is to the "merchant's
downright loss when he comes to a bad market." Conversely, the merchant or shopkeeper is at "liberty . . . to sell as dear as he can when he
comes to a good market." In this fashion they each expose themselves
to the risks inherent in trade. Without this sharing of the dangers, Locke
says, there would be "an end to merchandising," since the possibility of
loss would not be counterbalanced by the chance of gain. Trade would
also halt if in practice the burdens were not distributed equitably, if either the buyer or the seller was more likely than his counterpart to suffer loss. "The measure that is common to buyer and seller," Locke concludes, and that therefore moves the continuous exchange of goods
between the parties

> is just that if one should buy as cheap as he could in the market the other
> should sell as dear as he could there, everyone running his venture and
> taking his chances which by the mutual and perpetual changing wants of
> money and commodities in buyer and seller comes to a pretty equal and fair
> account.[60]

There is perhaps nothing new in the idea that the just price for a
commodity is the market price and that this price ought to be the same
to all. A number of scholastic thinkers had so argued in the Middle
Ages, among them San Bernardino of Siena.[61] Nevertheless, the understanding of mercantile morality set forth by George Fox and Charles
Marshall and given sharper theoretical form by John Locke makes a significant break from one of the most fundamental aspects of earlier economic practice, the full meaning of which becomes apparent only in the
context of mid-seventeenth-century affairs. From the Middle Ages into
the seventeenth century, most buying and selling were inseparable from
bargaining. A price was set only after agreement between the parties.
Gerard Malynes defined the process as "an estimation and price demanded and agreed upon . . . according to a certaine equalitie in the
value of things . . . [s]o that equalitie is nothing else but a mutuall voluntary estimation of things made in good order & truth."[62] On its face,

nothing would appear to uphold the idea of a modern, free market more than this. But in fact this regime of bargaining served an economic order that was anything but free.

Outside of the trade in staples, the market was highly opaque. Commodities were not standardized, communications were slow, and, consequently, the overall state of the market was unknown and unpredictable. As a result, the needs and interests of the different buyers and sellers were not immediately apparent. The market was small both in number of dealers and number and variety of commodities traded within it. Buyers could not readily abandon one supplier for another when dissatisfied with the goods they were offered, or shift their preference from one type of goods to another. Bargaining helped remedy these shortcomings. The price asked and the price offered set the limits of the market, and the haggling permitted each of the parties to judge the other's situation as it compared to his own. In the end the transaction was to give a profit or benefit to both sides. Hence Malynes's insistence on the word "equality," for this type of market was not inherently a competitive one.[63]

In such a market, transaction costs necessarily were high. It was difficult for sellers and buyers to locate each other; large risks were involved in the extension of credit; and little genuine recourse was available if the goods purchased turned out to be defective. To minimize these costs, however, a host of regulatory devices existed. Trade in "market overt" was a supervised trade, whether it occurred at a dealer's stall in the market square or at the tradesman's counter in his shop. In the towns, as we know, only sworn freemen enjoyed a right to trade in shops; and they were subject to a host of local regulations, including in many cases gild ordinances, intended not only to assure honesty and good quality but to limit competition. All others were confined to the market square, the market hall, or the fairgrounds, where local dealers had advantages and transactions were subject to close scrutiny by city officials. When disputes arose, they were subject to the decisions of a local market court, operating under the principles of law merchant and staffed by local tradesmen. Failure to obey its rulings would lead to a loss of trading privileges in the town. In other words, bargaining represented only a limited degree of freedom, designed to overcome the difficulties inherent in an opaque market. The economy itself was a restrictive one, subject to "custom and command."[64]

The economic practices advocated by the Quakers and other dissenters stood in sharp contrast to this older regime. These tradesmen were, in a sense, market democrats. In their view, the seller was not merely to be consistent in all his dealings with his fellows; he was literally to be "no respecter of faces," or, as the King James version has it, "no respecter of persons." Once he had decided, without the benefit of bargaining, on a price for his goods, he was to welcome all comers without distinction. If he had found a price that would attract customers and still leave him a modest profit on which to maintain his enterprise, he would thrive, provided no outside authority interfered in the conduct of his affairs beyond setting down the common rules of fairness to be maintained by all parties.[65] The decision on what price to charge was his, and so was the risk. Customers would be equally free to take what was offered or go elsewhere. The requirement that dealers set one price and stick to it was tantamount to insisting on the creation of a free, competitive market of a modern type along the lines suggested by Locke. What had once required haggling now was to be done by one party's judgment alone. How had this transformation of commercial practice come to be? What does it signify?

The new economic circumstances of the second half of the seventeenth century offer one element of the explanation. As Joan Thirsk has shown, England in these years experienced a veritable consumer revolution, conditioned by a secular rise in real wages, by the growing concentration of population in the towns, and by the expansion of the colonial markets. These changes not only assured a larger and more stable demand for non-staple items but were accompanied by the establishment of new trades and industries as new commodities, domestic and colonial, and new manufactures appeared in quantity for the first time. Consumers, in consequence, had much greater freedom to shift preferences from one type of goods to another, as well as from one dealer to another. This change in turn supported the development of new principles of business ethics. In these ways, then, the consumer revolution brought with it the rise of a new type of market society in England. It was a revolution that especially affected the small craftsmen and shopkeepers in the towns. Many of them very much depended for their livelihood on meeting the burgeoning demand for new wares.[66] In places like Bristol, where religious dissent was strong in these same circles of small tradesmen, it was also a revolution that especially affected the sectaries.

These new economic conditions affected everyone in the trading community, however, not just the Quakers and other dissenters. Why, then, did the sectaries become the first and strongest advocates of the new marketing practices? To find an answer to this question we need to place seventeenth-century economic practice in the context of the wider world of politics and culture. It is too easy to think of the economy as an autonomous realm of human behavior and to forget that for many purposes individuals or groups may be able to choose between economic and political solutions for a particular problem. This point has been made by Albert O. Hirschman in his *Exit, Voice, and Loyalty.* Hirschman begins his discussion by considering the case of a customer who is dissatisfied with the goods he has bought from a firm. To register his protest, the customer has two choices. He can use the market mechanism and take his business elsewhere, a strategy Hirschman calls "exit." Alternatively, he can return the goods with a complaint or appeal to the government for a remedy, a process Hirschman calls "voice." The first is an economic solution, the second a political or quasi-political one, and Hirschman's work has been concerned to understand the conditions under which individuals or groups would prefer one or the other, setting up a spectrum of possible actions between complete withdrawal from the market into a kind of autarky, and reliance upon open violence to obtain redress for one's grievance. Given this polarity, individuals and groups can sometimes find themselves caught up in a process of what Hirschman has called "shifting involvements," in which people move in a cycle from "voice" to "exit" and back to "voice," as political engagement first attracts, then repels, them, then attracts them again. The great power of this insight is its treatment of these modes of behavior as alternatives, not as mutually exclusive categories. It sees them as opposite poles on a single, graded scale, not as an absolute dichotomy.[67]

This understanding of economic behavior illuminates the history of the dissenters. Adopting the viewpoint of the merchant and tradesman, they advocated a regime of "exit," not "voice." Why? Their arguments were universal ones, intended not merely to set ethical standards for themselves but to transform the actions of all traders in the market and therefore to change the economy as a whole. But the position they advanced was very much in their own interest. In the 1640s and early 1650s, the sectaries had been among the leading practitioners of "voice" in its most overt form. Some had been in the Cromwellian army, and many had pressed for social, moral, and religious reform by the Long Parliament and the Commonwealth. They had been especially active in the Rump and in Barebone's Parliament. But their hopes had been frustrated by politics, and with the coming of the Protectorate they no longer had the leverage to exercise "voice" very effectively.[68] A number of sectaries, especially the Quakers, withdrew from politics in these years, or, to put this more precisely, from active efforts to win command of the institutions of the state. As we have seen in Bristol, many found themselves more likely to be the victims of "voice" than its beneficiaries—victims, that is, of attacks by their political and religious enemies who now had command of the instruments of the state.

The history of the Society of Merchant Venturers shows how the "voice" of the influential could win privileges for them to the detriment of their competitors. Similarly, the history of the Bristol *Register of Servants* demonstrates how the "voice" of political grievance, when exercised by those who controlled the institutions of force and coercion in society, could be turned against the economic activities of political opponents. With the Corporation and the Conventicle acts of the early 1660s, these trends became even more general. Not only did they force convinced dissenters out of political office, they placed the weapons of persecution in the hands of their long-standing social and political enemies. Under these conditions, "exit" was the only strategy available to the sectaries, and they expressed it both by disengaging from active politics and by advocating a free market economy in which to work. The strategy of "exit," understood in this way, offers those who choose it a chance to achieve purity, where "voice" with its continuous engagement with political ambiguity is, as Hirschman puts it, "treacherous": it sometimes requires compromising one's principles to gain practical advantage.[69]

We should not think that for the sectaries this withdrawal into economic activity necessarily represented an abandonment of the public life for a completely private one. Just the contrary: the Quakers and other dissenters thought of it as a witness to their righteousness, which in the end would achieve what could not be accomplished by politics alone. Setting a fair and fixed price, Charles Marshall argued,

> will answer the Witness of God in them you are dealing with; and if this should not please People at first, yet you will see it will Overcome; so that you in your Dealings therein keep out of the Spirit of the World, out of all Covetousness, Over-reaching, and Craftiness, in the harmless Life, seeking the Kingdom daily, and let other Things come as Additional: So all being diligent in the pure Fear of the Lord . . . you will see great Opportunity in your Dealings of reaching unto People, and thereby Thousands may be reached, convinced and brought to Truth.[70]

According to George Fox, such action inevitably would lead to triumph in this world, for

> a child shall trade with you as a man, because of the equity, and yea and nay, and righteousness, and true weighing of things, and true consideration of

things, and people shall not be afraid of one cheating the other, of destroying the other, where truth and equity is among them, and mercy and righteousness, and no more is set upon the thing than what they will take, who are in their yea and nay in their communication.[71]

For Marshall and Fox, therefore, economic activity was not politically passive, but a form of attack. It did not tame the old passions, but redirected them into new social realms. Far from abandoning the good fight, the Quakers and other dissenters redefined the arena of public action to include their ordinary engagements in everyday life and then sought to gain by their commercial interests and personal example what they had failed to achieve by their militant evangelism.[72]

What gave the sectaries an advantage in this form of warfare was the discipline imposed upon them by their meetings. Whereas they followed a doctrine of "exit"—of free and open market relations—in dealing with outsiders, they maintained a regime of "voice" in relations among themselves. Baptists and Quakers regularly assumed the obligation to offer moral guidance to individual members and to chastise them for their moral failings. They attacked drunkenness, gluttony, licentiousness, and evil conversation, and sought to assure that all brothers and sisters lived frugal, sober, and disciplined lives. These interventions extended to the members' business practices, especially among the Quakers, whose Men's Monthly Meeting, established in 1667, was specifically charged with this responsibility. These duties turned the Men's Meeting into something akin to a medieval merchant gild that regulated the trading relations of its members among themselves and with the larger economic world. It assured that all members would uphold the reputation of the Friends for fairness in their dealings with outsiders. It intervened with merchants and shopkeepers to keep them from spendthrift practices and to prevent them from overreaching themselves in their investments. It set standards for manufacture and for honest dealing, and it arbitrated business disputes between members when they arose. If necessary, it acted as an agency for collection of their outstanding debts, and, when all else failed, it supported those in need, often helping them to cover their business obligations and to start anew. Where Quaker, and to a lesser extent Baptist, businessmen were individualists in regard to the state and the market, they were subjects of an egalitarian spiritual fellowship in regard to one another. Their dealings together were founded on the reasonable assurance that a promise made was a promise performed.[73]

What made this necessary was the prohibition against swearing which dominated the teachings of the Quakers and many other dissenters. Until Parliament passed the Affirmation Act in 1696, the unwillingness of the Friends and other sectaries to swear oaths cut them off from ordinary recourse to law, where oath-taking was essential.[74] The prohibition marked those who upheld it as a people apart, willing to suffer for their "testimony"; in a sense it drove them back upon one another's assistance in all vital matters, economic and social as well as religious. A Quaker or Baptist tradesman who felt a scruple against swearing necessarily bore a large risk in offering credit in his trade, and outsiders bore a large risk in selling on credit to him. Yet, as we have seen, trade in the early modern period was virtually impossible without credit. This forced dissenters to deal primarily with other members of their sects whenever credit transactions were required. Here the moral discipline and economic intervention of the religious institutions gave them a measure of security that other Englishmen lacked. Not only did the sects promote among their members the development of a psychology of striving and hard work, but their meetings enforced this ethic with group efforts and real sanctions. In addition, the religious associations provided networks of business contacts both within and between communities that helped lubricate the wheels of commerce. Among the Quakers this was especially the case, for the Men's Meeting, which formally controlled apprenticeships and marriage arrangements, provided a ready means for mobilizing capital among large groups of small investors.[75] Among the Baptists and other nonconformists, similar though less formal sources of social solidarity also reinforced the bonds created by shared religious convictions. Through these mechanisms the Quakers and other dissenters could play a prominent role in industries demanding large-scale investment in fixed capital, such as shipowning, sugar-refining, soapmaking, and metalworking, and in long-distance trades with lengthy turnarounds, such as commerce with the colonies.

This same point can be put another way. The old ideal of the town market had depended on the existence of a body of sworn freemen who alone fully enjoyed the benefits of the town monopoly. However, the restrictions imposed on the trade of non-freemen had economic purposes beyond guaranteeing a crude competitive advantage to the privileged body. We can see this if we look again at the various ways freemen could be made in most towns: patrimony, apprenticeship, marriage to a freeman's daughter or widow, and redemption. Each method had its own significance, but each in its own way also assured that the new freeman had a strong tie to the community he was entering. A craftsman or shopkeeper who became a burgess after his apprenticeship, for example, would be well known to his master's customers and business associates. His training not only would have taught him skills but would have woven him into the fabric of urban society and established his reputation for honest dealing. Similarly, admission by patrimony and, to a lesser extent, admission by marriage and by redemption relied on family or social ties within the city to certify and guarantee the good character of the new freeman.

By assuring that the sworn citizenry would have such strong local connections, these methods of admission to the freedom reinforced the most fundamental values upon which urban society depended. On the one hand, the town as a political community needed a body of men able and willing to pay local rates and bear the heavy burdens of office. Citizens with a long-term personal interest in the community were more likely to do so, if only for fear of losing face before their family, friends, and neighbors.[76] On the other hand, the town as a trading community needed a body of men honor-bound to pay their debts. In an economy habitually scarce of money, all business, even the most petty, depended on credit. Ordinarily a merchant or shopkeeper could not pay his suppliers until he had sold the goods and himself received payment for them. One trader along the line breaking faith could cause a credit crisis for everyone else in the chain. So long as most such trade was between fellow townsmen, however, community pressure acted to prevent such crises, both by encouraging debtors to pay if they could and by keeping creditors from unnecessarily destroying a debtor's business by going to law too early or by refusing the efforts of local arbitrators to settle on mutually acceptable terms.[77]

Before the development of modern markets and modern methods of market discipline, there was a very close link in many towns between the desire to assure that citizens would perform public service and the need to guarantee the payment of personal debts. Under the trading conditions prevailing in the late medieval and early modern economy, a man's good name was his principal capital asset. It bound him to the community in which he was known and reduced the risk that he would break faith with its members, either by refusing to meet his public obligation to serve them or by failing to meet his private obligation to fulfill his promises and contracts. Failing in the performance of these duties would hurt, even destroy, his ability to maintain his way of life in the city. At the same time, every improvement in his status was also an improvement in his fortune. Officeholding not only gave official recognition to his reputation for good judgment and reliability but enhanced it and thereby furthered his capacity to conduct his private affairs. For these reasons, the pursuit of gain in the market, which we have been calling the strategy of "exit," was not distinguished in the medieval town from the strategy of "voice." If one wished to advance in business one could not withdraw from political involvement or the demands of service to the community.

This regime was always somewhat fragile, even in its heyday in the high Middle Ages, but it became more and more frail as industry migrated out of the towns and as internal trade became regional or national in scope. It should be no surprise to discover that from the early sixteenth century, at about the same time as Bristol's fairs and other old market institutions were taking on new functions and the city abandoned the collection of the traditional tolls at its gates, the tendency of its citizens to refuse service in civic office also grew. Such refusals persisted throughout the ensuing period.[78] The migration of George Monox, Paul Withypool, Robert Thorne, and other major cloth exporters to London in the early sixteenth century should be seen in this same light. Their public service followed their business interests.[79] By the second half of the seventeenth century these civic traditions in Bristol were in an advanced state of decay. As we have seen, the city became filled with shopkeepers and craftsmen who conducted retail trade without being sworn freemen and in many cases without even having been apprenticed in their occupations. Furthermore, Bristol found its substantial men refusing office with unheard-of frequency. Between the Restoration and 1680, for example, some fourteen Bristolians elected to be common councillors refused to serve and had to be discharged, and a further seven were sworn only after having put up considerable resistance.[80] Under these conditions, it became possible to separate "exit" from "voice," to pursue alternative strategies for obtaining one's ends.

But in examining the relation between credit and the scheme of admission to a town's freedom, a question immediately arises. What mechanisms for assuring credit discipline developed to substitute for those that used to be in force in the cities? A partial answer to this question can be supplied if we look again at the economic implications of religious politics after the Restoration. The Clarendon code, especially the Corporation Act, had removed from the *cursus honorum* of the towns all those unwilling to conform themselves, even occasionally, to the Anglican service. Insofar as officeholding marked one's rank in the social hierarchy, these men no longer stood on the same ladder of mobility as their fellows. Moreover, some nonconformists refused to swear oaths and thus found themselves unwilling—or, as they would have said, unable—even to enter into the freedom of their home communities. In Bristol and similar places, it is these religious dissenters we find most frequently arrested for illicit retail trading or fined for refusing to serve in office. Indeed, in many instances nonconformists were purposely elected to office in order that they could then be fined. The fines served both as a way of taxing their wealth, which would otherwise not be employed for civic purposes, and as a form of persecution. At least three of the fourteen unsworn common councillors elected between 1660 and 1680 fall into this category.[81]

However, the members of the dissenting sects had their own mechanisms for maintaining credit discipline when they were cut off from the older civic and gild forms. Those mechanisms were of a type that remained useful after the trader had left the jurisdiction of the town. The concept of "calling," which demanded hard work, sobriety, honesty, constant striving to do one's best, and, above all, a religious devotion to keeping one's word, played an all-important role. As a dissenter went about his business, he showed his creditworthiness by the same means he used to manifest his commitment to God's law. Among some groups, moreover, this psychological scheme of credit discipline was reinforced by a social one. Their religious meetings in many ways performed similar functions to the clubs, Masonic lodges, and pseudo-Masonic organizations that John Brewer has shown to have been essential in stabilizing the credit system of the eighteenth century.[82]

The world of the shopkeeper, the peddler, and the itinerant craftsman was the environment from which such religious dissent drew its greatest strength. It was peopled by individuals whom Christopher Hill has termed "masterless men" because they depended primarily upon their own resources, psychological as well as economic, in earning their livelihoods.[83] Far from being masterless, these men were their own masters. They viewed life as a pilgrimage on which they progressed along a straight and narrow path guided by a religious and ethical compass within them. They represented at one and the same time the two principles of independence and trustworthiness. Once they had bound themselves by a promise, whether it was to God or to creditor, they would do everything in their power to keep their word. It was this outlook, inculcated and reinforced by the work of the religious meeting, that made possible the dissenters' participation in the economic revolution of the later seventeenth century.[84]

Take, for example, the sugar refinery established in 1665 at Whitson Court in Bristol by a group of Baptists headed by Thomas Ellis and Edward Terrill.[85] Its history in the 1660s and 1670s gives a good picture of how connections within the dissenting community could be employed to build up an enterprise from relatively small beginnings. Ellis, who became a freeman of Bristol in 1641, was the son of Walter Ellis, a prominent Merchant Venturer from before 1618, a common councilor in the 1620s and 1630s, and keeper of the Backhall under the reformed city government in 1647–48. Both Thomas's father and his grandfather had been importers of sugar to the city in the years before the development of the West Indies trade. Ellis was also the cousin of John Gonning, Junior, another prominent Merchant Venturer and well-connected supporter of the parliamentary cause in the 1640s, who from 1651 to his death in 1662 was part owner of St. Peter's sugar house, the first such establishment in Bristol, founded by Alderman Robert Aldworth in 1612. In Ellis, therefore, we have a man who not only had family ties to and personal interest in the sugar trade but who no doubt also benefited from a comfortable inheritance from two generations of successful trade in the city and who enjoyed close connections to the wealthiest and most prominent elements in the city's commercial leadership.

By the later 1650s and early 1660s, however, Ellis's religious convictions had almost certainly undermined his position in the city at large. We find him in the city's commercial records only as a small-scale trader in West Indian sugar. At one point, for example, he shipped a modest cargo of shoes to Nevis for his supplies. When he started his own sugar refinery he turned primarily to his dissenting brethren, first buying the old priory property in Lewins Mead in St. James parish from William Davis, merchant, and John Teague, leatherseller, who were almost certainly co-religionists. Within two years of this purchase he was made Ruling Elder of the Broadmead Baptist Church, located not far from his new sugar house. To get started he depended on the expertise of two fellow Baptists as his sugar bakers: Anthony Wood, a colonial merchant who also became a trading partner and key supplier of sugar to Ellis's enterprise, and Godfridt von Ittern, a recent émigré from Hamburg. To build up a capital stock for equipment and supplies, Ellis also looked for credit to his fellow Baptists, receiving it from Thomas Harris, an apothecary; Edward Terrill, a scrivener; and John Wathen, apothecary, kinsman of James Wathen, shoemaker, whom we have already met. In this way, capital of approximately £800 was built up to pay for the property and equipment on the site.

Although we find both William Colston of St. Peter's sugar house and John Knight, Junior, who had a sugar house at the Great House on

St. Augustine's Back, importing sugar "ten tons at a time," Ellis and his associates rarely made entries in the Customs House on their own. Instead of sending their servants to buy directly from the planters, they relied for their supplies on the large numbers of small traders who brought sugar to Bristol. At the same time, they undertook to secure further supplies by "coloring" sugar and molasses belonging to strangers as their own. In most cases the suppliers were American planters who were probably also fellow Baptists. Using these techniques, a risky investment in one of the few early modern industries requiring significant stocks of fixed capital was turned into a success. By 1682, when Ellis sold the sugar works to Edward Terrill and a partnership of three Presbyterian grocers headed by Michael Pope, the enterprise had multiplied in value. The three grocers each had invested £1,000 to start their business. These figures suggest that the original £800 investment had grown in value to perhaps between £4,000 and £6,000 in less than twenty years.

The nature of the shipping industry also offered room for pooling resources and talents. Ships were inherently complex pieces of machinery, demanding large outlays of funds and a variety of skills to build and maintain. To work efficiently they demanded a cohesion or solidarity among all the parties—investors, merchants, and crew—that could only be enhanced if these individuals also shared extra-economic loyalties.[86] Often these ties were promoted by kinship, but it is not surprising to find interconnected groups of dissenting shipowners, builders, and sailors operating in a fashion not unlike that of Ellis and his associates. We have already seen such a connection at work among the Quakers in the makeup of the crew of the *Dolphin of Bristol,* which brought young Farwell Meredith to Barbados in 1654. A similar pattern can be observed in the history of the ship *Love's Increase,* which William Bullock employed to transport Irish prisoners to the West Indies as indentured servants in the 1650s. It was built in the 1640s by a team of sectaries headed by Bullock's father and was owned in the 1650s by Thomas Speed's sister-in-law, Ann Yeamans, herself a prominent Quaker. It was from Ann Yeamans that Bullock contracted for its use. Its name, chosen for it in the 1640s, was not a mere fancy but an expression of the fondest hopes of those associated with it.[87]

The link among the dissenters between the pursuit of gain in the wider world and the maintenance of solidarity in their own communities was an intimate one. Their external strategy of "exit" could not have succeeded so well without their internal practice of "voice."

Indeed, in the dissenters' own minds these two methods of addressing humankind were conceived as interconnected parts of the same design. Both turned on their abhorrence of false swearing, since they understood bargaining in the traditional manner as simply another form of oath-taking. Their practice of setting a single price for the sale of a particular commodity thus arose from interpretation of the same scriptural passages that had produced their prohibition against swearing of any kind. In the Sermon on the Mount, they argued, had not Christ required "Yea, yea" and "Nay, nay" as an alternative to oath-taking? Had he not said, "Swear not at all"?[88] And in the Epistle of St. James were not Christians told, "above all things . . . swear not, neither by heaven, neither by the earth, neither by any other oath: but let your yea be your yea; and your nay, nay; lest ye fall into a condemnation."[89] In conventional Protestant commentaries, such as those of William Ames, these words were not interpreted as absolutely prohibiting oaths or forbidding all bargaining—far from it.[90] The dissenters, who had experienced the defeats of the Interregnum and the religious and economic persecutions of the Restoration, used these doctrines to define their place in the world as an embattled remnant. At one and the same time they were able to face their enemies as militant proselytizers for the Truth and to draw together for moral guidance and material support.[91]

Anglican Royalists such as Sir John Knight saw religious uniformity as the only sound basis for a civilized society. So long as men and women remained united in their deepest convictions and devoted to a common heritage of worship, harmonious social relations and an orderly and productive economy were assured. In the face of dissent, only political and social upheaval and economic chaos could be expected. The dissenters, however, viewed the enforcement of an outward uniformity as no more than tyranny, out of which no public good could come. It not only destroyed the fabric of community but made the free course of economic exchange all but impossible.[92] When the dissenters put forth the idea of a free market, therefore, it was a counterattack to their Anglican Royalist opponents. But it also provided a mechanism for settlement with those Bristol common councillors who sought to use the constraints of competition to control the sectarian colonial traders. On the whole, the great servant traders among the sectaries—such men as Speed, Bullock, and even the irrepressible Christopher Birkhead—accepted the use of the indenture for servants bound for the plantations as right and proper and in their interest, and they continued to register servants most of the time throughout the Restoration.[93] Both parties seemed willing to let a man's ability to compete determine whether he would remain a colonial merchant. Possession of the necessary investment capital, rather than training in the merchant's craft or membership in the Merchant Venturers, became the primary determinant of one's ability to engage in the traffic.

Nevertheless, it was not mere accommodation that the dissenters sought in accepting the challenges of the free market. It was spiritual victory, which would come in the form of converts to their religious way. But even if they could not draw large numbers by their personal example, they expected that their commercial successes would bring customers to them and thereby produce a harmonizing of interests and meeting of minds even with opponents. As Charles Marshall put it,

> [W]hen the People of the World come to your Houses, to have Converse and Commerce with you, all being in Dread, Fear and Awe of the Lord God, in the Sweet, Savoury Chaste Life, the Witness of God will arise, and make them acknowledge, You are the People of the Lord, and that he is with you.[94]

The result would be a unified city. In the words of George Bishop, men could "begin to forget the old Engagements wherein they had been mutually exercised to the detriment of each other, and . . . apply themselves to things that concerned their Own, and the good of each other."[95] Political moderation would guarantee this social harmony. So long as each man could pursue the dictates of his conscience and tend to the prospering of his estate, free from the meddlesome interference of the authorities, the city would be "at peace and unity within its self; men of all perswasions, as to Religion, well perswaded amongst themselves, and as to the Civil peace united in the hearts, and love of each man to another, and the public benefit." With this guarantee of a unified social order, "every individual might rest assured of the peace and safety of his estate and Person, in the persuance of the publick."[96]

By removing themselves from politics, the realm of the passions, to economics, the realm of the interests, the dissenters had come a long way toward intellectual agreement with their enemies. What remained was for those in authority to move toward them. We have already seen that the social history of dissent had laid the groundwork for this modus vivendi. The dissenters in Bristol were no newcomers lacking roots in the city. They had kinship and business ties with a wide variety of their fellow Bristolians and could neither be confined to a sectarian ghetto nor be driven from the town into exile. These conditions were only reinforced by economic developments in the second half of the seventeenth century. As the dissenters became established in their chosen trades, some, like Thomas Ellis among the Baptists and Thomas Gouldney among the Quakers, grew wealthy and could not be ignored. This was due to their importance in the colonial trades, whose role in Bristol's economy grew at an extraordinary pace from 1660 to 1700. So long as the Quakers and Baptists owned ships and sugar refineries, they would have support from at least some Anglican traders and shopkeepers.

As we know, even in the 1660s these facts had helped promote a policy of religious toleration among some of the leaders of Anglican Bristol. By the end of the century, this view had won the support of statute and had become very widespread among Bristol's elite. In 1695, John Cary, merchant of Bristol and member of Parliament for the city, himself the son of an Anglican minister, argued for "liberty of conscience" as one of the essentials necessary for the improvement of England's trade. Although he believed that the Toleration Act had already helped to remedy the breach in the body politic, he still thought "it were to be wisht some way be found to make Methods of Trade more easie to the Quakers than now they are. I am apt to think," he said, "that he who appears in the Face of a Court to give Evidence on his word, if he be a Man of Conscience looks on himself equally obliged to speak the Truth as if he is sworn, and nothing will deter a dishonest Man like the fear of punishment."[97] In Bristol and many other places, the sectaries had become sufficiently important to the economy to make it necessary for their neighbors to accept them in peace and work with them in trust and harmony. In these respects Cary had accepted in principle the dissenters' most profound teachings on the ethics of work and of charity.[98]

By the late seventeenth century, the English commercial economy had become dependent on a national market in which diverse activities were integrated over ever wider fields. Whereas in the late Middle Ages each of the major towns was a replica of its rivals, urban centers were now parts of a large, interconnected network in which each element had distinct functions to perform.[99] In this new economic order the insights of Marshall and Fox had a special place. As political economists such as

Charles Davenant had come to recognize, a well-developed division of labor meant that human beings could not survive without the assistance of others to supply their wants. Commerce had the capacity to bring men together in peaceable intercourse, where, in addition to depending on judgment of their own self-interest,

> [t]hey will find, that no trading nation ever did subsist, and carry on its business by real stock; that trust and confidence in each other, are as necessary to link and hold a couple together, as obedience, love, friendship, or the intercourse of speech. And when experience has taught each man how weak he is, depending only upon himself, he will be willing to help others, and call upon the assistance of his neighbours.[100]

Economic development, at first the source of social conflict, had become a wellspring of social cohesion. Davenant, of course, refers only to the market for trade and credit and neglects the market for labor, which did not always bring men together in harmonious and mutually beneficial relations. Even though he disregards the world of the servant, he tells us a penetrating truth about the world of the spirit. Its history in the later seventeenth century is one of political and religious rivalry transformed into economic and social cooperation. It is a view that sees economic activity itself, optimistically, as an example of *"Love's Increase."*[101]

Conclusion:
The Widening Gate
of Capitalism

For most English men and women of the Tudor and Stuart period, change never brought progress, though it might produce reform, renascence, or restoration. A perfect world was a stable world, unaltered and unalterable in its essentials. To signify this certainty Queen Elizabeth had adopted as her motto *semper eadem,* "always the same," expressing her sense that the good and true were good and true for all times and all places. But the era through which she and her compatriots lived challenged the very premises of their thought, including the notion that change always represented either a falling away from perfection or a return to it. Bristol offers us a paradigmatic example of this great transformation, as much intellectual and cultural as social and economic in its character. Bristol's history between 1450 and 1700 created a center of early modern capitalism out of a medieval commercial town. So fundamental were these changes that to a Bristolian born in the first half of the fifteenth century the world of the late seventeenth-century city, had it been possible to describe it to him, would have seemed almost as foreign and exotic as the cities of China had been to Marco Polo. At the end of the two hundred and fifty years of history we have been reviewing, Bristol had become in its own way a newfound land, as different from the old city as North America was different from the world that John Cabot and his Bristol colleagues had known in Europe.

We have seen how England's loss of Bordeaux in 1453 marked the end of a long-stable pattern in the history of Bristol's trade wherein every year cloth was exchanged in Gascony for huge quantities of wine, and how the Bristolians began a series of adjustments in the trade, society, and politics of their city. By the end of the sixteenth century, Bristol's commerce, driven by its merchants' quest for the highly profitable and scarce commodities of southern Europe, had come to focus on the Iberian peninsula, and new forms of merchant organization had emerged to exploit this traffic. A half-century later the pattern had changed again as Bristolians, still driven by "Bristol's hope" for quick turnover and large gains in the luxury trades, transformed their city into an entrepôt of the trans-Atlantic economy. As recently as the 1630s, only a handful of vessels using the port annually had made the journey to and from the American plantations. But by the late seventeenth century about half of the shipping leaving British waters from Bristol was bound for Virginia, the West Indies, or Newfoundland, and a similar portion of the incoming traffic had originated there. As a result of this concentrated commercial effort, American sugar and tobacco had become by 1700 almost as much a staple of the city's trade as French wine had been in the fifteenth century.

This transformation, so fundamental to bringing Bristol into the modern world, was as much a matter of outlook as of action. It could not have been accomplished without the will and ingenuity to break from the conventions of the past shown by many Bristolians, and it could not have been sustained without the growth among them of a new economic understanding. In Bristol as elsewhere, new economic ideas had been slow to emerge, and no single moment can be named as the turning point. But, fortunately, we can observe the main outlines of this important intellectual transition in the writings of three men: Roger Edgeworth in his *Sermons,* delivered in the 1540s and 1550s; John Browne in his *Marchants Avizo,* which appeared in 1589; and John Cary in his *Essay on the State of England in Relation to its Trade, Its Poor and its Taxes,* published in Bristol in 1695, and *Essay on the Coyn and Credit of England: As they stand with Respect to its Trade,* which appeared the year following. When looked at closely, these writings reveal a profound change in worldview of which Browne, who wrote in the late 1570s or early 1580s, represents the turning point between Edgeworth's religious and ethical approach and Cary's political economy.

As a city preacher in the 1540s and 1550s, Roger Edgeworth found it useful to draw many of his analogies and examples from the experiences of trade and the handicrafts familiar to most of his listeners. His sermons allow us to glimpse their world through its commonplaces.

Edgeworth was well aware that this world, which involved the seeking of "gaynes" or "wynnynge," operated according to ethical principles peculiar to it. "[T]he occupying that well besemyth som man," he says,

> is vnfitting and euil besemyng som other man . . . A Draper, a Mercer, a Shoemaker, and a hardwareman may stand in the open Market and sel hys ware to the most aduauntage and gaine, thereby sufficientlye to sustayne hym selfe, and hys familye or housholde. A knyght, a squyre, or a well landed manne maye not so do wyth hyse honestye. It were filthye, shame, and dishonestye for hym so to dooe, and hys winning shoulde not bee but fylthye wynnynge . . . and shamefull gaines.[1]

Nevertheless, even in the commercial environment of the city, the pursuit of gain was likely to be tainted. Covetous men, Edgeworth said, were like moles, blind to godly or heavenly counsel, who would rather descend "headlong" into the depths "to their lucre and aduantages" than feed on the "wine and wastel" of divine wisdom. Their lives were filled with "the temporall woe and paine they have in keping their goodes: for they be rather possessed and holden of theyr goods, then possesseth and holdeth them. And they haue their goodes as we say a man hath a paire of fetters or shackles vpon his legges, more to his paine then to his pleasure."[2]

For Edgeworth, life in this urban world was fraught with unpredictable risks. It demanded courage as well as judgment and skill. To survive it was necessary to persist in one's enterprises without regard to uncontrollable dangers and unforeseen losses. Since this was especially true for overseas traders, they became his model for fortitude in the face of adversity. If one or two storms or one or two losses should cause the shipman or the merchant to "abhorte and giue of going to the sea," he says, "there would at the last no man aduenture to the seas, and then farewell this citye of Bristow, and all good trade of marchaundyse and occupying by sea."[3] A merchant, although he has experienced many losses by shipwreck, still seeks out "straunge lands" and adventures "on his olde busynes" with a stock "gathered of borowed money, and dothe full well, and commeth to great substaunce and riches."[4] But because survival required taking advantage of every opportunity to earn profit, this trading community was also a world of temptations to evil. Out of "couetousness to get the penye" men were driven to "sell false or noughty ware, or by false weightes or measures [to] deceiue [their] neighbours."[5] We have all known "some Marchuntes and other occupiers," Edgeworth says,

> that in their prenticeshippe, and while they were iourneymen or seruauntes haue feared God deuoutlye, and the worlde busilye. And when they haue set

vp and occupied for them selues, haue growen to muche riches in a little space, in so muche that within seuen or eight yeres they haue bene able to be shyriffes of the Citye, but when they were fatte, that their prouender pricked them, they haue begon to kycke against GOD, and to do noughtelye. . . . They haue take their pleasures moste voluptuouslie, and haue contemned all others dispitefully which is a signe that the feare of GOD was cleane gone.[6]

For this reason, fearlessness in the face of danger could never be enough. It was also necessary to "sticke stedfastlye to thy fayth, doing accordinglye to Gods holye worde."[7] According to Edgeworth, "He that feareth God will do good dedes, and will eschue the contraries, and his thrifte shall come accordinglye."[8]

Since it was from God that men "had their thrift," the only way to assure success was to live according to His will. All citizens were to do "their dutye in their tythes and offeryngs" to Him, keeping themselves "in the feare and awe" of His majesty, and "liuynge charitablye" toward their neighbors.[9] To illustrate these truths, Edgeworth told his listeners a little story. He asked them to consider two young men who had come to a town together as apprentices, "came forth to libertie together," and set up in their occupations at about the same time. "[T]he one was more expert in his occupation then the other, the more quycke more liuelye, and more pregnant of witte, and he laboured . . . bothe earlye and late, as the other did, and yet he could not come forwarde, but euer almoste in beggars estate." After a time the man "that was so farre behind" met his old acquaintance "and marueylynge of the chaunce of them boothe considerynge (sayth he) that when we were yong I was more likely to come forward then thou. And that I labour and studie . . . as many waies to haue the world, and to come to welthines, and more then euer diddest thou, & yet it wil not be, and the more I labour yet neuer the nere." He suspected the reason must be that his fellow had "founde some bagges or treasure trouvy, some hid riches that bringeth thee alofte." The second man agreed that his success was because he had indeed "founde some hydde ryches" and offered to bring his friend to where he "mayest finde like riches."[10]

On the appointed day, the rich man brought his old acquaintance to church, where the first man "fell on hys knees and saide his prayers deuoutly as he was wont to do," while "the other man called busily on him to shewe him his treasure. Tarye a while," said the rich man,

we shall anone haue a Masse or some diuine seruyce compiled or gathered of the word of God, or some sermon of exhortation that may do vs good.

Anone a prieste was ready & wente to masse: After masse this poore mannes minde was on the money, and called vppon his frende whiche at the laste aunswered after this maner. Frende, thou haste hearde and sene parte of the treasure that I haue founde. Here in this place I haue learned to loue GOD, heare I haue learned to feare God, Heare I haue learned to serue GOD. And when I haue done my duetye to God, home I go to my woorke about suche businesse as I haue, and all thinges goeth forward and so I am comne to this honeste Almes that GOD hathe lende me, wyth whiche I am well contented, and do thanke God for it, it commeth of God, and not of my deseruynge.[11]

His recommendation to his friend was to emulate this example if he wanted riches. "I see thy fashion," he said, "thou little regardest God or his seruice, and lesse regardest his ministers. Thou haddest leuer goe to the market then to Masse, and on the holye daye, to idle pastimes, then to heare a Sermon." Hence, "if thou thriue it is meruayle. And surely if thou prosper and go forwarde for a season, thou shalte haue one mischaunce or another that shall set thee further backwarde in a daye, then two or three good yeares hath set thee forward."[12]

Skill, diligence, and the capacity for hard work were as nothing in Edgeworth's economic world. By themselves they could not keep one from beggary. Even a successful enterprise was worthless, since it could not be counted upon as a firm foundation on which to build future successes. The world was simply too unpredictable, too likely to turn one's days from good to bad in the twinkling of an eye. Only if one foreswore the market for the mass, respected the ministry, and performed the proper godly devotions would one receive a lasting reward. Hence the moral of Edgeworth's tale was that "[t]hey that feare God haue no pouertie, for eyther they be ryche, or at leaste wyse be verye well pleased wyth that little that they haue, which passeth all gold and precious stoones. . . . Pietie or mercie with a hart content wyth that a manne hathe, is a greate gaynes and winnynge."[13] Religious devotion also gave more than contentment with one's lot; the spiritual merit built up through good works became the treasure upon which one could draw to go steadily forward in one's everyday affairs. In this sense, the spiritual and material orders were united. God blessed those who gained His favor through their piety. In another way, however, they were radically disjoined, since there was little that one's earthly endeavor could do to promote one's earthly reward. Such success as one might have in one's affairs came, as it were, from grace and not from works.

John Browne shared many of Edgeworth's assumptions about the nature of the economy and its inherent dangers. The son of a Bristol draper, he was among the early Merchant Venturers in the city. Born about 1525, he was apprenticed in 1538 to a leading merchant, was married to the daughter of another in 1545, became mayor in 1572, and died in 1595. Hence he lived through the sixteenth-century climax of Bristol's transition from being a specialist in cloth and wine to its new role as the entrepôt of the Iberian trades. His *Marchants Avizo* was intended as a handbook—or, as Browne himself says, "a patterne"—of merchant practice, designed especially for merchant apprentices in this era of economic change.[14]

Browne does not describe a modern economy. For him, the economy simply lacked the stable and predictable markets in which prices could be set without extensive haggling. As a result, a merchant could only use his "best indeuoure to sell as the time serueth." If he could not "sel to some reckoning" in one place he took his goods to another "there to sell . . . as well as you may please."[15] For this reason, the practice of merchants remained an art, subject to the wisdom of experience where nothing was hard and fast, and the best advice was "to haue good insight your selfe, and to do according as is your hast and necessities for your sales."[16] No self-sustaining market mechanism could adjust the interests of buyers and sellers and control the dealings of merchants with each other. Browne believed, with Edgeworth, in a providential universe in which God's visible hand could "destroy both thy bodie and soule."[17] Trade, in this world, depended on personal relations among the traders, and the preservation of one's good standing with them was more important than maximizing profit on a particular transaction. In Karl Polanyi's phrase, the economy remained "submerged . . . in social relationships,"[18] subject to the unpredictable interplay of individual actions and chance events.

As if to mark this fact, Browne ends his book with "certain Godly sentences" which combine worldly wisdom and sage counsel on human frailty with admonitions to "first seeke the kingdome of God" and "remember often thy Creator." Some of these sentences stress right actions, as in the admonition that "when thou promisest any thing: be not slacke to performe it, for he that giueth quickly, giueth double." Others warn of dangers to be avoided from fellow merchants. "Be not hasty in giuing credit to euery man; but take heed to a man that is ful of words, that hath red eyes, that goeth much to law, and that is suspected to liue vnchaste." For, through proper management of his relations with his fellows, a merchant "may liue with honestie and credit in time to come" and thereby have "prosperitie in all his wayes." These moral precepts ring with an old-fashioned condemnation of covetousness and all that

goes with it. "The godly and diligent man," we read, "shall have prosperitie . . . but he that followeth pleasure and voluptuousnesse shall
haue much sorrow." Nevertheless, this condemnation was not in itself
a critique of business enterprise. It focused instead on the morality of
whoever might acquire wealth, no matter what his social rank or occupation. Did he gain it honestly, or by deceit? Did he act with reason and
restraint, or rapaciously? Did he use his profits to maintain his family,
to employ others, and to provide charity, or did he turn them to gluttony, wasteful luxury, and dissipation? If he was honest, selfless, and responsible, he was not covetous, even though he might be exceedingly
wealthy. Browne's overall aim was to encourage the merchant to live
frugally and without greed, so as to avoid the threats of disaster around
him. "Be circumspect and nigh in all your expenses," he says, "that
what you now spare and save . . . may grow the more to your owne
benefit in time to come." Here Browne differs from Edgeworth, since
Browne believes that prudent conduct can limit risks and improve
chances for prosperity.[19]

In the course of providing this tutelage Browne gives us a picture of
the economy as he understood it. Since he saw its foundation in the exchange of goods, he dwelled primarily on relations among merchants.
Nowhere in his book did he instruct the merchant apprentice in how to
acquire domestic wares for export or how to dispose of imports once
they had reached England. Instead, he focused on the manner in which
a group of English traders, mostly from Bristol, worked together to dispose of their wares on the continent and to purchase the most profitable
goods they could from foreign dealers. However, Browne had a clear
comprehension of the mechanisms that made his economic world work.
He knew the importance of foreign exchange and the role of credit, and
he understood the necessity of organization and regulation in maintaining the vital networks. But the community of merchants was always
at the heart of this world. Its success in mediating between domestic
and foreign markets affected every craft—spinsters and sailors, weavers
and dyers, landlords and tenants, husbandmen and victualers, grocers,
clothiers, vintners, and mercers. If the merchant prospered through
God's blessing and his own prudence, those who depended on him
would do so as well.

In other words, Browne had a sense of the economy as an integrated
system, though not yet one separate from the larger social world. Its
trades and crafts formed a social body in which each part worked
to support the welfare of the whole. But his hierarchical ordering of

occupations was concerned primarily with social distinction—"degree," as he says—not functional economic integration. The merchant stood at the apex of a social pyramid, where he was the outlet for surplus domestic goods and the source of scarce foreign ones. His work, although it was of social benefit to each rank beneath him, did not promote the creation of trades and industries; it only redistributed their wares. Its very nature prevented this hierarchy from being a self-regulating mechanism of interconnected parts, since what was valued within it was set by absolute standards of virtue and not by the workings of the system itself. Nevertheless, this emphasis on the virtue of the trader placed some of the responsibility for the general welfare on his experience, choices, and effective actions.

Browne's moral precepts, though familiar enough to men of Edgeworth's outlook and their medieval predecessors, were conjoined to a growing sense that the merchant was a public figure, like the gentleman, the lawyer, and the cleric. The merchant's activities affected the harmony of the commonwealth, because if he neglected his duties or failed in his enterprises those dependent on him would suffer. Hence his work required close regulation and demanded protection. This was a theme of the Commonwealthmen of the mid-sixteenth century, who usually are read more for their criticisms of trade and industry than for their vision of a new social hierarchy.[20] The same ideas became a theme for the merchants themselves as they petitioned for privileges and as they joined the royal court to advise the Crown.[21] Although Browne, writing at the age of sixty or so, appears to have held no hope for political advancement or personal benefit, he shared this new understanding. He looked on his book as the product of his public duty to aid his "profession." When his profession prospers, he argued, "then common weales in wealth increase," and everyone gains thereby:

> Let no man then grudg Marchants state,
> Nor wishe him any ill:
> But pray to God our Queene to saue,
> And Marchants state help still.[22]

Nevertheless, *The Marchants Avizo* is not a work of policy. Its chief purpose was "to worke a generall ease to all Marchants: whereby they may the lesse trouble themselues either with writing, invention, or thought of these matters," and also to "be some stay to young and weake wits: yeelding them therby the more freedome of mind towards their other businesses."[23] To accomplish these goals, it provided models of accounting procedures and of letters to and from servants sent abroad, drafts of various types of commercial instrument, and guides to weights, measures, exchange rates, and the qualities of certain imported wares.

John Cary wrote, however, with a deep concern for high matters of political economy. The son of Shershaw Cary, a Merchant Venturer, he was also a Merchant Venturer in his own right. Born about 1650, he was admitted to the Society in 1677 and became its warden for the year in 1683. He was briefly a member of the Bristol Common Council in 1687–88, helped to found Bristol's famous Corporation of the Poor in 1696, and died about 1720.[24] He too witnessed a major transition in Bristol's history, as the city moved from its focus on Spain and southern Europe to become an entrepôt of trans-Atlantic commerce. Writing in a genre that first became prominent during the economic crisis of the early 1620s, Cary attempted a systematic analysis of the present economic order with the goal of promoting national trade, increasing wealth, and improving government revenues. Of course, he had his own viewpoint, one that, if implemented, would have specially benefited the kind of commerce practiced by his fellow Bristolians. Far from advocating a single interest, however, he adopted the dispassionate and disinterested tone of the public commentator explaining the "Foundations of the Wealth of this Kingdom."[25] "The general *Trade* of the Nation (which is the support of all)," he says,

> requires as much Policy as Matters of State, and can never be kept in regular Motion by Accident; when the frame of our *Trade* is out of Order, we know not where to begin to mend it, for want of a Sett of Experienced Builders, ready to receive Applications, and able to judge where the defect lies.[26]

The ends advocated by Cary resulted from his belief that "true Profits" result, not from trade, but from "that which is produced from Earth, Sea and Labour . . . our Growth and Manufacture."[27] Therefore, trade that neither exported English products or manufactures nor supplied things necessary to promote manufactures at home, to carry on trade abroad, or encourage navigation

> cannot be supposed to be advantageous to this Kingdom, for there must be a difference made between a Nations growing rich and particular Mens doing so by it, and I humbly propose that it may be possible for private Men to be vastly improved in their Estates, and yet at the Years end the Wealth of the Nation cannot be a whit greater than at the beginning. . . . [W]hilst the thrifty Shopkeeper buys at one Price, and sells at another to the prodigal *Beaux,* and the industrious Artificer rents his Labour to the idle Drone, and the politick Contriver outwits the unthinking Bully, one raises his Fortunes on the other's decay, the same for our *Outland Trade,* if we Export the true

Riches of the Nation for that which we consume in our Luxury, tho' private-
Men may get rich by each other, yet the Wealth of the Nation is not any way
encreased.[28]

On this basis he rejected the trade with the East Indies, since it ex-
tracted England's wealth for high-priced goods without promoting
domestic employments. But he had high praise for trade with the American plantations, which, in his view, had spared England a crisis of over-
population. "People are or may be the Wealth of a Nation," he argued,

> yet it must be where you find Imployment for them, else they are a Burthen
> to it, as the Idle Drone is maintained by the Industry of the laborious Bee,
> so are all those who live by their Dependence on others, as Players, Ale-
> Houses Keepers, Common Fidlers, and such like, but more particularly Beg-
> gars, who never set themselves to work.[29]

The plantations not only employed the poor but encouraged navigation,
were a market for England's own goods, supplied commodities that
could be wrought up at home or exported again, and made unnecessary
the purchase of similar goods from the territories of other princes.

> [F]or I take England and all its Plantations to be one great Body, those being
> so many Limbs or Counties belonging to it, therefore when we consume their
> Growth we do as it were spend the Fruits of our own Land, and what thereof
> we sell to our Neighbours for Bullion, or such Commodities as must pay for
> therein, brings a second Profit to the Nation. . . . This was the first design of
> settling Plantations abroad, that the People of England might better main-
> tain a Commerce and Trade among themselves, the chief Profit whereof was
> to redound to the Center.[30]

All in all, Cary's work depicted an economy transformed. Browne,
a century earlier, had portrayed a commercial economy concentrated on
Spain, Portugal, and France, and on only a handful of commodities—
spices, sugar, wine, dyestuffs, oils, soap, iron, and salt—from which the
greatest portion of a merchant's profits ordinarily could be expected.
Nothing was said directly about exports, although of course they are
mentioned in various of the letters Browne used to give examples of
form. But Cary's economy encompassed the whole world—Asia, Africa, and especially America, as well as Europe, and the domestic as
well as the international market—and valued the widest range of raw
materials and finished goods, from the small and high-priced to the
bulky and cheap. Its foundation lay in the relations between merchants
and producers and in the creation through labor of new wealth.

Cary was no less religious than Edgeworth and Browne. Indeed, he
is probably best known for his public acts of charity on behalf of the

poor in Bristol. He was also no out-and-out free trader in the manner
of the Bristol Quakers. He believed in state intervention to protect commerce and industry. Though he thought an outright "Monopoly by Law
a thing very contrary to the Genius of the People of *England*"—something that "seems to barr the Freedom and Liberty of the Subject"—he
nevertheless agreed with the old Merchant Venturer theme about the
need to prohibit "the Merchant from being a Shopkeeper, or Retailer,
and the shopkeeper from being a Merchant or Adventurer at the same
time." If "neither would interfere in the others business," he said, each
"would be better managed."[31] But in so saying he was offering advice
to tradesmen based on his analysis of the workings of the economy, not
on a program of regulations and laws. Unlike Edgeworth and even
Browne, Cary understood the economy to operate according to its own
demonstrable rules. For him the market was a mechanical system,
reaching a balance according to a scheme of weights and counter-
weights and working on a principle of the division of labor in which all
the parts were linked by the circulation of wealth. "As the wealth and
Greatness of the Kingdom of *England* is supported by its Trade," he
said, "so its Trade is carry'd by its Credit, this being as necessary to a
Trading Nation, as Spirits are to the Circulating of Blood in the Body
natural; when those Springs . . . Decay, the Body languishes, the Blood
stagnates and the Symptoms of Death soon appear."[32] If the economy
depended on cogs to direct the wheels, it required only minimum adjustments "to keep them true."[33]

One influence on Cary's thinking was his acquaintance with major
developments in the natural sciences. His papers even contain descrip-
tions of three comets and a sketch of one of them.[34] He felt comfortable, as we have just seen, with analogies drawn from William Harvey's
path-breaking work on human circulation and had grasped the mecha-
nistic paradigm emerging in astronomy and other branches of science in
his day. He probably was familiar as well with the writings of John
Locke and his circle; his work obviously owes a debt to Locke's thinking on the role of labor in creating wealth. But the development of the
economy in the second half of the seventeenth century also played a
large role in accounting for Cary's vision. He could easily see in his own
city the integration of trade and industry about which he theorized. The
plantations alone supplied it with

> great Quantities of *Sugar, Tobacco, Cotten, Ginger* and *Indigo* . . . which be-
> ing bulky for their transporting hither, and the greater Number of ships, im-
> ploys the greater number of Handicraft Trades at home, spends more of our

Product and Manufactures, and makes more Saylors, who are maintained by a separate Imploy.[35]

The same was true for every trade. "For," he argued,

if One Raised the Provision he eat, or made the Manufactures he wore, Trade would close, Traffique being a variety of Imployments Men set themselves on adapted to their particular Genius's, whereby one is serviceable to another without invading each others Province; thus the Husbandman raises Corn, the Millard grinds it, the Baker makes it into Bread, and the Citizen eats it; Thus the Grazier fats Cattle, and the Butcher Kills them for the Market; Thus the Shepard shears his wool, the Spinster makes it into Yarn, the Weaver into Cloth, and the Merchant exports it; and every one lives by each other: Thus the Country supplies the City with Provisions, and that the Country with Manufactures.[36]

As Cary envisioned this interlocking of trade, it extended far beyond the boundaries of England. For example, according to him, the use of Indian calicos drove Silesian and German linens from the market and encouraged those who made them to convert their looms to the production of woolens. This in turn deprived England of a market for woolen cloths and even touched the manufacture of hats, which depended on central European wools for felt.[37] The same principle applied everywhere. In place of Browne's hierarchical view, in which everyone depended on the merchant to succeed, Cary's functional view stressed the reciprocity of all economic relations. "I comprehend all transferring of Properties under the general Notion of Trade; the *Landlord*, the *Tenant*, the *Manufacturer*, the *Shopkeeper*, the *Merchant*, the *Lawyer* all are Traders so far as they live by getting from each other, and their Profits arise from the Waxing and waning of our Trade."[38] The guiding principle was indeed that "every one lives by each other."[39] The merchant had a vital role to play, because he stimulated production, but he was only one among many, each of whom depended absolutely on his fellows in the division of labor.

Because Cary's economy was subject to the laws of cause and effect, it was capable of development. "The first Original of Trade," he tells us,

was Barter; when one private person having an Overplus of what his Neighbour wanted furnished him for his Value in such Commodities the other had, and stood in need of ... And as People increased so did Commerce; this caused many to go off from *Husbandry* or *Manufacture* and other ways of living; for Convenience whereof they began Communities; this was the Original of Towns, which being found necessary for *Trade*, their Inhabitants were increased by expectation of Profit; this introduced *Forreign Trade*, or *Traffick* with Neighbouring Nations.[40]

This economic evolution created increasingly complex relationships among people. As they came more and more to depend on trade, the "buyer not only sold his commodities at home, but also dispersed them among those who were seated in the Country at a distance . . . and thence came in a skill and cunning to foresee their Rise and Fall according to their consumption and prospect of supply."[41] Differences arising among buyers and sellers led next to the need for laws and lawyers, courts and judges, while the advance of "Trade brought Riches, and Riches Luxury, Luxury Sickness, Sickness wanted Physick and Physick required some to separate themselves" to become doctors. "[M]any also of ripe parts were fitted for Service of the Church, others of the State; great numbers were Imployed in providing Necessaries of Meat, Drink and Apparell both for themselves and other People . . . others fit things for their Pleasures and Delights."[42] In this way economic growth produced civilization, with its benefits and discontents. As "Mens knowledge increases by Observation," Cary concluded, "one Age exceeds another . . . because they improve the Notions of Men."[43]

Roger Edgeworth could not conceive of improvement in our lives as in any way the consequence of human will. Only an ever-present God, working according to His own judgment of our true wants, could produce worldly satisfaction of them. Although John Browne had a more positive view of men's ability to cope with the ways of the world, he too looked to God as the primary source of human welfare. "First seek the kingdome of God and the righteousness thereof," he advised, "and then all things shall be giuen thee that thou hast neede of."[44] He was also unable to contemplate a world ordered in any other than a static, hierarchical fashion. For John Cary, however, the social world was in a continuous process of change. It had begun in simplicity, but, driven by man's need to balance existing supplies against his wants, it had grown day by day in complexity. Only the underlying laws of economic action, themselves open to human understanding and application, remained constant.

The history we have been recounting in this book tells of the transition from Edgeworth's form of economy to Cary's. But it was also a history that took Bristolians from one form of social and political order to another. Although it was possible at the end of the period to think of political economy, if not economics itself, as an autonomous subject, this was only part of a process of change that was as much social, political, and cultural as it was economic. To citizens of the fifteenth-century city,

Bristol had appeared as a replica of the cosmos, an ordered and harmonious arrangement of parts that made a unified whole. Its trade
may have extended their reach far beyond the city's boundaries, but
in theory the city remained a compact community of sworn brothers
who acted with common interests and for the common good. By the
fourteenth century a group of wealthy men, mostly engaged in the overseas trade in cloth, had emerged as a distinct body of civic leaders in
Bristol. Although their prosperous circumstances had distinguished
them from their fellow townsmen, as citizens they were but members
of the commonalty, enjoying equal liberties and franchises with all
other sworn burgesses. The loss of Bordeaux, however, and the course
of change it helped set in motion had undermined the foundations of
this community.

The first signs of a significant shift in social outlook had come
quickly. In 1467, when the level of Bristol's trade stood near its nadir
for the fifteenth century, the city government created the first organization exclusively for overseas merchants. Although this special fellowship of merchants, comprised of officers, hall, and regulatory functions,
appears to have been short-lived, ending when economic conditions
improved, it marked a change and set a precedent. From this moment
on, merchants would become increasingly separate from those in other
occupations who engaged in buying and selling. In 1500, the idea of
a separate fellowship of merchants became even more definite when
the newly reformed Bristol Corporation issued an ordinance establishing a company "separate and distincte from every other companyes
of handecraftymen."[45] During the second half of the sixteenth century
this concept crystallized further, first with the acquisition of a royal
charter of incorporation for the Society of Merchant Venturers of Bristol, and then with the concerted efforts of its members to exclude all but
wholesale merchants from overseas trade. The attempt at monopoly became the recurring theme in Bristol's history until well into the seventeenth century.

At the same time a parallel development occurred in the realm of politics. The medieval borough had long been governed by a mayor, annually elected at a general meeting of the burgesses. It was not until the
mid-fourteenth century that a select body of councillors joined him in
rule. Until then, government seems to have had a communal form; all
major decisions were made at the same sort of general meeting as that
which elected the mayor. In Edward II's reign, when a group of fourteen
local magnates set themselves up as a governing body, their rule was met
with violent resistance from the townsmen. Finally, in 1344, the city es-

tablished a Common Council of Forty-Eight, whose members were chosen from among the wealthier men engaged in cloth manufacture and
trade. When Bristol was incorporated as a county in its own right in
1373, this body was reformed into a council consisting of the mayor, the
sheriff, and forty of the "better and more worthy men" of the borough.
At the same time, the mayor became the king's lieutenant in the city and
one of the justices of assize, and the mayor and the sheriff jointly became keepers of the peace and justices of gaol delivery, which linked the
city to national administrative and legal institutions. Nevertheless, their
elevation to these national offices did not break the mayor's and the
sheriff's ties to the community. The Bristolians still considered them
and their brethren on the Common Council as the representatives of the
whole body politic of the town, not its overlords. They served by communal acceptance of their rule, ritually given and received by the shouts
of acclaim at the annual mayoral elections and in the festivals of the
civic year that followed.

The new Bristol constitution of 1499 altered this delicate balance between the role of royal official and communal representative for these
civic leaders. By creating a bench of aldermen, who along with the
mayor served as justices of the peace, and by adding as recorder a
learned lawyer who was also an alderman, it integrated the city government into the same national regime of administration then emerging in
the counties. In consequence, the members of the Corporation more
and more were identified by their new status as a separate body of officials within the city, partaking of the authority of royal rule. What
made this development especially potent was the way it connected with
the changing character of the overseas trading community. Since the
leading men in the council were also the leading men in commerce, the
power and influence they enjoyed in government could be used to advance their interests in the economy. Time and again the city government intervened to support the leading merchants in their petitions for
royal favor and in their quest for monopoly. Bristol had evolved a
strongly hierarchical social order in which the great wholesale merchants dominated the economy, interposing themselves between other
domestic dealers and foreign markets, and in which the magistrates—
who in most instances were the same men—dominated the polity, interposing themselves between the ordinary citizenry and the central institutions of the state.

However, the rivals of the mere merchants among the city's retailers and craftsmen of the city perceived issues very differently. To
them the attempts at merchant monopoly usurped the ancient rights of

citizenship, and those who performed this act violated the very bonds of community. This communitarian undercurrent surfaced only occasionally to produce political strife among the citizenry, but it seems to have been present in latent form throughout our period. Whenever the mere merchants' efforts to secure a monopoly resurfaced, the retailers and craftsmen mounted stiff resistance to the Merchant Venturers' claims as best they could. Among some of these rivals of the Merchant Venturers, an undercurrent of communitarian social feeling converged with religious ideals of community to create a revolutionary party in the city, anxious for fundamental reform in church and state. Indeed, many of the most radical Bristolians in the 1640s and after came from just those sections of the city's economy most affected by the monopolistic claims of the merchants. To match the religious passions of some of the enemies of monopoly, among the monopolists themselves a small but powerful group emerged who favored a Laudian view of religion and society and who supported the king with fervor in the battles of the 1640s.

In these ways the central place of a state-supported, regulated merchant company in Bristol's history contributed to the growing radicalization of the city's politics. Clashes between rival economic interests, fueled by changing patterns of social mobility and political recruitment, took on increasingly more significance as the ideological edge already apparent in the battles of the 1560s and 1570s transformed the issue of monopoly into one of high morality and linked it to affairs of state. The Merchant Venturers' new charter of 1639 only added kindling to the flames, since the antagonisms aroused by it became one element in the partisan rivalries of the Civil War period in Bristol. The coming of the Civil War also meant that the Merchant Venturers' great victory of 1639 was short-lived. Once Parliament's forces had defeated the Royalists, control of Bristol fell into the hands of citizens with no sympathy for monopoly, while in Westminster little support with which to challenge the new local regime remained for the Merchant Venturers. As the instrument of national economic policy and the product of political conflicts played out in Westminster as well as Bristol, the Merchant Venturers could not help being caught up in the upheavals of the 1640s; they were nearly destroyed by them. Just as the Society's formation was the local expression of national politics, so was its fate.

It is sometimes said that all politics is local politics, since ultimately it must be played out by people in the context of their daily lives. However, local politics can either draw in upon itself and make the connections and rivalries of local inhabitants the foundation of local affairs, or it can reach beyond its boundaries to participate in the larger world of governmental institutions and political movements. Late medieval Bristol attempted with increasing difficulty to maintain the first kind of politics. Sixteenth- and seventeenth-century Bristol was an example of the second type. In ordinary times, the focus of political action was the exploitation of the state for local advantage, but when a national crisis developed, it engaged Bristolians immediately because they were a politically integrated part of the realm.

Moreover, the seventeenth century witnessed a significant transformation in the ways the local effects of politics were experienced in the city. Before 1640, the main political issues concerned the role of the city in the state. The magistrates saw themselves in a coordinated relationship with the central government to preserve order and protect the subjects. They were willing to accept state power so long as it helped to perform these vital functions. When they found it necessary to defend their role as local governors, they were not acting because they considered themselves as buffers against the king but because they saw themselves as essential parts of royal government. Order to them meant the union of authority with property, as expressed in their own leadership of their community, and they feared any use of state power that threatened this union. For this reason they made their political choices by concentrating on what would best promote the maintenance of the national polity as they understood it. In the Tudor and early Stuart years, most of Bristol's magistrates conceived of this polity as one in which authority was exercised for the king by men rooted in the community, not by strangers with few local ties and no comprehension of local conditions. In other words, during this period they envisioned a political world in which community and state were related to one another as parts to the whole, not as opponents.

This "country" attitude, which the Bristolians shared with many of the gentry, persisted into the Restoration and beyond. But after the Civil Wars the underlying structure of politics was vastly complicated by ideological and religious differences, which on the one hand drew many more Bristolians into the vortex of political conflict and on the other connected the city's affairs in new ways with national political developments. Religious divisions founded on rival conceptions of universal truth touched men and women in the city who rarely, if ever, had engaged in public controversy. Local politics were no longer confined to the city's better and more worthy men and their immediate opponents,

but now involved many servants and apprentices, craftsmen, and shopkeepers in the lesser trades and their wives and daughters. Moreover,
the efforts of the 1650s to regulate the trading activities of the sectaries
and the attempts of the 1660s to purge the civic community of their
presence were linked directly to shifts in the configuration of national
politics and thus tied to extralocal institutions—Parliament, the national executive, and the leaders of sects, among others. When the
Army in Bristol came to the support of the radical candidates for Parliament in 1654, when Cromwell ordered the demolition of the Castle and
the disbanding of its garrison in 1656, when Sir Humphrey Hooke
stood down from his parliamentary seat in favor of the earl of Ossory
in 1661, and when the Conventicle Act became the weapon of Sir John
Knight's persecution in 1663, the gates of local politics widened. These
events not only confirmed Bristol's connection with the ever-present
powers of the state but also revealed its participation in political conflicts that had their center far outside the city's boundaries.

Another, deeper dynamic was also at work in this period to challenge
Bristol's standing as a closed arena. So long as commerce was confined
to a few markets in Europe or the nearby Atlantic possessions of the European powers, where only a limited range of export goods could be
sold and where only those with established reputations and trading connections could flourish, the members of Bristol's merchant elite could
use the Society of Merchant Venturers to protect themselves from all but
the most determined interlopers. But the emerging American trade
could not be managed through a regulated trading company, since the
colonies had such high demand for small wares and for labor. Moreover, many Englishmen with the necessary supplies and the desire to
profit from them had kinfolk and friends among the colonists with
whom they could deal confidently on credit. Under these conditions, attempts to regulate trade according to the models of the sixteenth century were doomed to failure.

Once this new reality had been recognized in Bristol, the terms of
conflict between the Merchant Venturers and their rivals shifted. Since
overseas commerce with the colonies could not be controlled by limiting
access to the market, a concerted effort was made to raise the marginal
costs of enterprise, at least for those engaged in the lucrative trade in
servants. The requirement that every servant leaving Bristol for the
American plantations have an indenture allowed the larger traders to

compete more effectively against the small, with the goal of driving the part-time merchant completely out of the traffic. Although this effort proved unsuccessful, in large measure because illicit dealing was far too easy, it marked a major shift in understanding. Now, to be a merchant was no longer an issue of training and status but one of wealth. The market was to control who entered and who survived the competition for power and riches.

It was not the Merchant Venturers alone who had come to this conception of the economy. Among the sectaries, whose numbers swelled with small shopkeepers and craftsmen, it became a matter of religious conviction and political wisdom to trade in a free market. The urban market they knew was a regulated market, subject to the political control of those who governed the city. In the 1640s, these sectaries had fought to gain control over this system of regulation in order to make it more equitable. But by 1654 their efforts had failed, and they became the victims of the city government, especially after the Restoration. It now made better sense for them to seek a free market, where their economic successes could be achieved without political hindrance. This strategy was not only a defensive one. Those who argued for it saw in it a way to win support for their point of view as their economic success drew more and more of their old enemies into peaceful intercourse with them, converted many to the virtues of their views, and convinced the authorities to desist from their persecutions. In this competition the sectaries had some advantages. Among themselves they represented a closed community of known and trusted members whose word was their bond. They could mobilize capital and deal together on credit with confidence that their fellows would uphold their promises, thus providing the necessary competitive edge to overcome their rivals. As a result, many of them found it convenient to comply most of the time with the new regulations imposed on their trade. In the end, their views converged with those of their enemies, and the basis for settlement became apparent.

Between 1450 and 1700, therefore, Bristol had become, not only a port specializing in trans-Atlantic commerce, but a society organized after the same fashion as the newly emerging economic order. The city, which in the fifteenth century had been thought the microcosm of a world of harmonies and correspondences, was now for many a network of functional relations, subject to the laws of cause and effect. Just as dealers were to compete for buyers in a free market, ideas were to compete for acceptance and men for power in an open forum. As the gates of Bristol widened, the logic of life moved from a theologian's dialectic to a political arithmetician's calculus.

What made this development so significant was the way it reinforced the changes in Bristol's life wrought by the widening of its economic gates. Bristol had always been a comparatively complex community. From the time it became a great center of cloth manufacture and trade in the high Middle Ages, it had depended on an intricate division of labor. Clothmaking, even in those early days, involved numerous stages of production, many of which were performed by specialists. Overseas commerce also depended on the work of numerous specialists. When combined, these two aspects of Bristol's medieval economy produced a relatively complex occupational structure. With the collapse of the cloth trade and Bristol's development as a regional center for imports, this pattern became even more complex. Between the 1530s and 1540s sixty-eight different trades are mentioned in Bristol's apprentice book; by the late 1620s and early 1630s there are one hundred and four different trades.[46] Although it is impossible to be as precise for the years after 1650, when the apprentice records become much less reliable, it is clear that growth was continuous into the second half of the seventeenth century. New trades such as sugar-refining and tobacco-pipe–making appeared, while older crafts, particularly in metalworking and clothmaking, showed a greater division of labor. We even find such specialized arts as "Gingerbread maker."[47] In consequence, by 1675 there might have been as many as one hundred and seventy-five or even two hundred recognized crafts within the city.[48] Even the merchants, who never quite became the specialists in wholesale enterprise that some thought desirable, exhibited such a division. Only a small number engaged in trade with all of Bristol's markets. Most, especially those interested in colonial commerce, concentrated their efforts in only one or two places.

These changes signaled not only a greater complexity of social life within Bristol but a greater degree of integration between the city and the larger economy. Throughout our period Bristol was preeminently a center of distribution. Its role in England was largely to provide a transfer point for goods produced elsewhere, although of course many of its inhabitants devoted themselves to altering those goods in one way or another to make them more marketable. But the seventeenth century brought Bristol an increasingly intricate and specialized pattern of commercial relations, as well as more diverse commodities to buy and sell.

In the fourteenth and early fifteenth centuries the city had played a somewhat specialized role in trade with England's possessions in France. If we visualize a map of commerce on which are recorded Bristol's markets, with smaller or larger circles depending upon where its enterprise was most concentrated, there would be but few such circles, and only the one marking Bordeaux would be large in size. In this period Bristol's trade rarely left the well-known ports of nearby France and northern Spain. In the sixteenth and early seventeenth centuries, however, the web of commerce was cast somewhat more widely, to cover the whole of the Iberian peninsula and the western Mediterranean, as well as the Atlantic islands off the African coast. Our map would show not only more circles but more large ones as well, as Bristol came to specialize in the commerce of southern Europe. Cádiz, San Lucar, Málaga, Marseilles, Toulon, Leghorn, Madeira, and the Canaries would now have to join San Sebastian and Bilbao and the ports of western France as Bristol's main points of contact. By the end of the seventeenth century, this picture had changed again. Now the West Indies and the Chesapeake provided Bristol's principal markets, although the city's traders never lost interest in their older markets. Hence Bristol's trade increased in density and complexity with its increasing concentration upon American colonial commerce.

As the development of Bristol's commerce resulted in a wider and more intricate network of markets, with both an increased concentration of enterprise and a greater number of significant points of contact, the city's place in the domestic economy underwent specialization of another sort. We can see the changing pattern by looking at the locations from which the city recruited its apprentices. Apprentices usually followed trade routes in seeking service; they made their contacts in those places with which their families had connections. In the early sixteenth century Bristol drew its apprentices from nearly everywhere in England. The main concentrations were in the nearby counties, but many came from the Midlands and there were even a number from the north of England and from East Anglia and the home counties. By the early seventeenth century, the percentages of apprentices coming from distant places had shrunk drastically. Nearly all now came from Gloucestershire, Wiltshire, Somerset, the Severn Valley, and South Wales, and this pattern persisted into the later seventeenth century.[49] In other words, as trade became denser and more diverse, Bristol's hinterland became more clearly circumscribed, and the city moved from its indefinite place as England's second port, a ranking that could only pale in the face of London's vastly greater trade, to being what W. E. Minchinton has called "the metropolis of the West," a center serving as the focus for the region's economy.[50]

These changes in Bristol's foreign and domestic commerce defined a particular function for it in an increasingly elaborate and interdependent economic order. They meant that Bristol's prosperity was grounded more firmly in the health of the national economy and in the nation's ability to protect its trading interests abroad. Moreover, this link between political and economic developments grew stronger in the period. In the sixteenth or the early seventeenth century it was far from unusual for Bristolians to recognize that their welfare depended on national policy and to seek to influence that policy accordingly. The Society of Merchant Venturers existed in part for just such a purpose. By the early 1620s, men like John Guy were well aware that their own prosperity could be deeply affected by economic actions taken in places with which they had no direct trading contact.[51] But John Guy's memorandum on the crisis of the 1620s was only the forerunner of Charles Marshall's and John Cary's more systematic contributions to economic understanding. Guy implicitly recognized that economics and politics were inextricably connected. Later Marshall argued much more directly that economics could be used to direct the power of the state, and Cary wrote in the belief that proper public policy could improve the economy. Increasing interdependence meant that it was not sufficient to look to one's own narrow interests in devising cures for problems. They now required systematic remedies. Since general solutions could only be political ones, political complexity grew as the economy developed.

It is a commonplace of historical study to conceive of social change according to one of two models: that of entropy, or that of evolution. For those who shared Roger Edgeworth's and John Browne's conservative sensibility, change meant declension, a move from order to chaos. For those of John Cary's outlook, change held the hope of redemption. It brought a possible perfection of order as society moved from amorphous homogeneity to greater organization. Students of the early modern period have usually favored one of these views, either despairing at the loss of community or delighting in the improvement of the age. The story we have told about Bristol, however, has been ecological in character, concerned with the relationship between the city understood as a social organism and its environment. It presents a narrative of change from one kind of complexity to another—from a complexity based on the city's political integration with the state to a complexity based also on its integration into the emerging Atlantic economy.

In Henry VIII's reign the population of Bristol had stood at about ninety-five hundred or ten thousand persons, not far different from what it had probably been in the aftermath of the Black Death in the fourteenth century.[52] Late in Elizabeth I's reign it began to grow, and by the beginning of James I's reign it had reached twelve thousand or perhaps even a bit higher. In the early 1670s it seems to have been about sixteen thousand, and at the end of the seventeenth century it had exceeded twenty thousand. In other words, the period we have studied shows about a 25 percent increase in population in Elizabeth's reign, a further 33 percent during the first three-quarters of the seventeenth century, and yet another 25 percent in its last quarter. The next century witnessed a doubling in size, as Bristol's built-up area burst beyond the boundaries of the medieval city and spread into the surrounding countryside.[53] This history sets the seventeenth century apart as the beginning of a new period in Bristol's long-term development. No longer was its population essentially stable in size, with every increase in the number of inhabitants almost immediately cut back by epidemic disease, as had happened periodically from the late fourteenth to the late sixteenth century. Even the great plague that killed between twenty-five hundred and three thousand Bristolians in 1603 and 1604 was unable to stop the steady growth of the city. Within five years the population had already made up between 50 and 75 percent of the loss. A second great plague in 1645, which killed three thousand inhabitants in the course of the New Model Army's siege of the city in that year, also resulted in a rapid recovery. By 1600 Bristol had become a city of ever-expanding numbers, growing in size slowly at first but with increasing momentum. In 1700 it was twice as large as it had been in 1550.[54]

The face of Bristol was transformed as a consequence of this rapid population growth. We have already seen William Smith's map of Bristol (Figure 1), which he sketched on his visit there in July 1568. It gives an aerial view of the city as it would be seen moving from southwest to northeast. About a century later, James Millerd, a mercer by occupation, executed a detailed plan of Bristol, drawn to scale, giving a similar bird's-eye view of the city in the early 1670s (Figure 6).[55] Smith's map shows us a city still largely contained within its medieval walls. To the north, there are large open spaces near the Cathedral and on St.

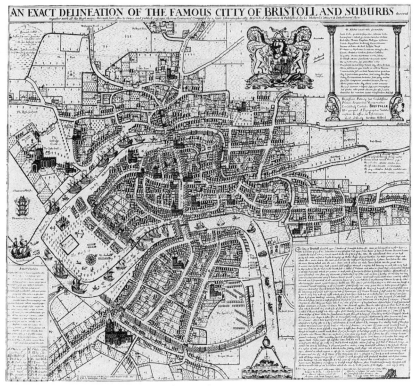

Fig. 6.   James Millerd's View of Bristol, 1673.

Michael's Hill; to the east, the Castle still stands as a fortress and the
streets running near its walls are only sparsely settled. The Avon Marsh
to the west is also relatively undeveloped, as are the lands just beyond
Redcliffe and Temple gates. A large amount of open space also remains
inside the walls. Throughout the city, in the central parishes as well as
the southern ones, were scattered numerous gardens and orchards as
well as large expanses of vacant ground, especially along the marshy areas on the river banks. The walls built in Henry III's reign to allow for
growth still left room for substantial development.

   In contrast to this small and seemingly underpopulated city of 1568,
Millerd's Bristol is a large and thriving center. Although only about a
third of the city's territory is substantially built up, and large expanses
of vacant land are still to be seen in the Avon Marsh and in the southern
parishes, the city center is now fully developed, the Castle has been replaced by a thriving city district, and the extramural districts all show

a large number of dwellings. Both Redcliffe and Temple to the south have greatly expanded beyond the old walls. Still more densely occupied are St. Michael's Hill and the neighborhood around the Cathedral, which seem to have been transformed from thinly populated, almost rural parishes to burgeoning urban districts. The Avon Marsh has also begun a new life; not only has it been carefully landscaped, but King Street has changed from a mere pathway below the city wall into a thoroughfare with handsome houses on both sides. But the most dramatic changes occurred in the parishes to the east of the Castle. Numerous gardens and orchards are still interspersed among the dwellings, but the Old Market, Broadmead, and Horsefair have all become significant new neighborhoods. Most of this expansion beyond the city walls can be dated to the second half of the seventeenth century, following Oliver Cromwell's demolition of the Castle in the mid-1650s.[56] This picture is confirmed by the hearth tax records of 1671.[57] Again we see evidence of considerable growth in the transpontine and suburban districts. In the early sixteenth century only about 45 percent of Bristol's population lived in these neighborhoods; at the later date almost 60 percent did so. There were also great gains in the north and east of the city. In 1524 only about 23 percent of Bristolians had resided there. In 1671 almost 35 percent did so, with the largest increase coming in the neighborhoods to the east of the city center.

Hearth tax records also allow us to see something of the distribution of wealth in the city. As in the early sixteenth century, the central and portside parishes were still the richest, but they no longer dominated the city as they once had. In 1524 they accounted for about 54 percent of its taxable wealth; in 1671 the figure was only 44 percent. In addition, the rank ordering of the neighborhoods had shifted. In 1524 the suburban districts were the poorest in the city, judged by mean assessments. In 1671 the transpontine parishes held this position. The portside wards came next. Taxpayers from the rapidly developing suburban neighborhoods now ranked second, behind those in the city center, in the average number of hearths on which they were obliged to pay taxes. The distribution of poverty through the city also shows a striking pattern, although here we cannot make a comparison to the figures for 1524, since the sixteenth-century subsidy rolls for that year did not note the number of paupers in each district. The hearth tax listings for 1671 show that about 20 percent of the city's population were paupers by the standards of the assessors of the tax. The city center harbored the smallest share of these poor; less than 13 percent of its inhabitants were classified as paupers in this year. The next smallest proportion, amounting to just 16 percent, is to be found, somewhat surprisingly, in the transpontine neighborhoods. Both the portside and the suburban districts had relatively high levels of poverty, with the poor making up just over 19 percent of the population of the former and about 22 percent of the latter.

By 1671, then, Bristol had a social composition rather different from what we observed for the early sixteenth century. In the center we still find high concentrations of the rich and relatively small numbers of the poor. In the transpontine parishes we find a far narrower range of social types living in close proximity. Judging by the numbers of hearths possessed by each group in this district, those able to pay taxes inhabited dwellings not very much larger than those who could not. In these two parts of the city, little seems to have changed in the distribution of wealth from what we saw in 1524, although the evidence suggests that there was perhaps a decline in the number of independent craftsmen and shopkeepers in the transpontine district from the levels of a hundred and fifty years before. In the portside and suburban districts, however, the pattern had broken with the past. There we see significant concentrations both of the well-to-do and of the poor. However, subtle differences also appeared between these two sections of the city. In the portside parishes, where many merchants still resided, the houses of taxpayers were on the whole somewhat larger than in the suburban neighborhoods. In the newly formed Castle district and the other neighborhoods to the east of the city center especially, a picture emerges of a district with a heavy concentration of middling men and women—shopkeepers and artisans—living comfortably but not quite as well as the merchants and ship owners who resided near the port facilities and in the Avon Marsh.

The Restoration period also gave Bristol's religious geography a new face. To a surprising degree, its dissenting communities concentrated themselves in the districts experiencing new growth. By the 1670s the Baptists had meetinghouses in Broadmead, in the vicinity of the Old Market to the east of the city center, and at the Pithay, near the south bank of the Froome to the northwest of the center. The Quakers, who once had occupied the Broadmead, now had two meetings: one near the Old Market in the Friary in St. James's, and the other across the Avon in Temple Street. The Congregationalists had a chapel in Castle Street in the heart of the newly formed Castle ward and also met at a house on Philip Street nearby; Presbyterian congregations gathered at John

Lloyd's house on St. James Back, also near the Castle and the Old Market, and at Jeremy Holwey's house in Corn Street in the city center.[58] Along with the separatists who attended services exclusively at these places, there were almost certainly also occasional conformists to Anglicanism and numerous other laymen who sought spiritual comfort and religious guidance from conformist and nonconformist ministers alike and who would have swelled the attendance at these dissenting meetings from time to time.

According to the surviving figures from the so-called Compton census of 1676, which attempted to tally the number of dissenters over sixteen years of age in each parish, about 11 percent of the city's population were nonconformists. This figure probably understates the true total, since the Bristol returns are fragmentary and inconsistent in their presentation of the results. Nevertheless, judged by the results for the census as a whole, this was a high figure, since in the province of Canterbury the census showed dissenters to have amounted to only slightly over 4 percent of the entire population. For the diocese of Bristol, excluding the city of Bristol proper, the figure was between 2.5 and 3 percent. Not surprisingly, the heaviest concentrations of the city's nonconformists came from the neighborhoods in which we find the churches, chapels, and meetinghouses of the dissenting sects.[59] According to the census, about 13.5 percent of the population of the transpontine and suburban districts were dissenters, with the areas around the Castle holding the largest numbers; only about 8.5 percent of the inhabitants of the center and portside neighborhoods were so designated, with the two portside parishes having the smallest share—each with less than 5 percent. Although the city's old parish structure remained intact, the uniformity it had represented was shattered beyond repair. Bristol was now as complex a place in spirit as it was in economics, politics, and social organization.[60]

We can now return to the image with which we opened our story, the image of the castle and the gate. The early modern English city was always something of both: a stronghold with a distinctive way of life, and a point of communication and exchange. From one perspective, its Guildhall and law courts were its center and its high walls its symbol. They gave tangible form to its existence as a community, a body politic. However, from another point of view, its life focused on the boundaries where this community connected with the larger world. This was as it must be, for every boundary is potentially also a threshold; it is marked not only by barriers but by passing places. Indeed, there could be no meaningful frontier to separate friend from enemy or kindred from stranger without there also being figures who would traverse it. Only in the presence of outsiders do boundaries become necessary; and just as a world of infinite abundance would need no economics, a homogeneous world would be a boundless one.

The ancient Greeks viewed the god Hermes as both the protector of boundaries and the patron of the professional boundary-crossers. He guarded the home ground, making it safe against danger from outsiders, and aided merchants and others who went abroad to trade.[61] In his dual nature he captured the paradoxical character of trade before modern times. Since all commerce depended on the fragility of credit, its practitioners necessarily concerned themselves with the reduction of risk. The common method was to rely on highly restricted credit networks, entrance into which was limited to those of known reputation. Good fame and good name, established through long association with other traders, alone sufficed to guarantee trustworthiness. In this respect a trading community was a closed fellowship that distinguished between brothers, who enjoyed the privileges of full membership, and strangers, who either were required to pay a premium to participate or were excluded entirely. In the high Middle Ages whole towns had operated on this principle. Later, specialized groups of tradesmen, eventually including long-distance merchants, adopted the same idea to protect themselves even from fellow townsmen. But to trade meant to reach beyond one's own borders, not only to move goods but to participate, at least briefly, in communities where the trader was himself a stranger. For this reason many in early modern England viewed the trader's activity with skepticism, since his mobility raised doubts about his stake in his home community. By its very nature, a merchant's life could never be a purely local one.[62]

These conditions left merchants in a state of constant tension, since they could not easily find safe methods for securing their wealth. Even in the sixteenth century, large-scale industry with its demands for fixed capital investment hardly existed, and trade itself was still little more than an adjunct to agriculture. In the absence of banking institutions and of a well-established market in stocks and government debt, traders could do little more than buy property, an opportunity open to only a few. Hence a trader's commercial investments usually represented the vast majority of his wealth, and it was necessary to turn them over continuously if he was to survive. By the end of the sixteenth century, these severely restrained conditions began to ease somewhat for the Bristolians, as they moved into a wider world of commerce and as domestic trade and industry grew larger and more sophisticated. More opportunities became available for successful enterprise.

Yet the story is far from an epic of victorious expansion. Not only were there periodic crises that affected everyone and highly unstable markets that required constant vigilance, but the lives of individual artisans and merchants were subject to unpredictable disasters, for trade was an inherently uncertain undertaking. No matter how cautious or wealthy the entrepreneur, a great variety of events, often of the most prosaic kind, stood ready to disrupt his affairs and threaten his business establishment. The vicissitudes of wind and weather could destroy his fortune overnight, or the bankruptcy of a customer could create havoc with his own credit.

This dialogue between the need for security and the desire for expansion provided the prime stimulus for development in early modern commercial society. There was no ready and easy way to resolve the tension. Enterprise entailed risk, and no system of security could entirely remove that risk. Moreover, as commercial contacts grew and the market increased accordingly in scope and scale, it became more difficult to control trading activity through coercive organization. Neither the trading fellowship nor the state was sufficient to provide the discipline, especially the credit discipline, necessary for stability. What was needed was a new set of moral imperatives that impelled traders not merely to pursue gain but to pay debts. It has been the argument of this book that the rise of capitalism results as much from changes of this kind in the trader's spirit as from new developments in the external circumstances in which he worked.

Max Weber's *The Protestant Ethic and the Spirit of Capitalism* rightly holds the preeminent place in the study of religion's relationship to the rise of modern capitalism; he framed the questions and set the agenda for an ongoing and fruitful field of scholarship.[63] For eighty years now, the Protestant work ethic has been revisited time and again by historians of nearly every intellectual bent and ideological persuasion. In the main, this outpouring of research has examined the psychological effects of Protestant, and especially Calvinist, teachings on economic behavior, either to show how it impelled some groups to a single-minded pursuit of investment and production or to deny that it played any such role. Albert O. Hirschman, however, has offered another perspective. "Weber," he says,

> claims that capitalistic behavior and activities were the indirect (and originally unintended) result of a desperate *search for individual salvation*. My claim is that the diffusion of capitalist forms owed much to an equally desperate search for *avoiding society's ruin*, permanently threatening at the time because of precarious arrangements for internal and external order. Clearly both claims could be valid at the same time: one relates to the motivations of the aspiring new elites, the other to those of various gatekeepers.[64]

But the theorists to whom Hirschman and other scholars have referred are not the only figures in the period to make "political arguments for capitalism before its triumph."[65] As we have seen, the English dissenters made a similar argument, but for a very different purpose. In response to a political challenge that would have crushed them if it could, they advocated a free market, not so much because it would yield universal peace, but because it would bring them universal victory. Only as they found relief from their persecution and made their way in the world did their ideas begin to coincide with those of the "intellectual, managerial, and administrative elite" whom Hirschman properly calls the gatekeepers.[66] The success of the dissenters, moreover, depended as much on their social connections and religious institutions as on their ideology. Their family and business ties, their inability to deal on a large scale with creditors from outside their sects, and their reliance upon their meetings for moral guidance and economic assistance all gave material support to the doctrines of hard work and frugality in which they believed. Ideas and institutions went hand in hand to transform individual psychology into a social force.

Weber and his followers missed this political, social, and institutional framework for religion's contribution to capitalism. They emphasized only the relation of religious belief to the spirit that underpinned the economy. According to them, Protestant thought, especially English Puritanism and nonconformity, promoted a moral commitment to hard work and achievement and thus led a Protestant to improve his property and to invest his profits, which made for business success in an expanding economy. Most of Weber's critics have concentrated on this argument, pointing out that, far from encouraging moneymaking, Puritans, like their medieval predecessors, condemned as covetousness the pursuit of private profit. According to this view, only with the Restoration did Englishmen, including the Puritans, come to see the striving entrepreneur as anything but an upstart and a danger. As Paul Seaver has pointed out, however, there is also a third position, namely, that many religious-minded merchants and tradesmen

> may have heard the Puritan message in its fullness, have accepted its strictures regarding the temptations and dangers of economic enterprise, and have perceived no contradiction between the values preached and their business practices, because what was in fact preached was supportive of, rather than at variance with, their way of life.[67]

This religion of Protestants, especially in the form of Puritanism and nonconformity, well served the kind of economic world in which the men and women of the early modern period found themselves. For those like the merchant John Whitson in the 1620s or the apothecary Charles Marshall in the 1670s, true Christianity stressed the importance of things higher than worldly wealth. They envisioned life on earth as a struggle to overcome obstacles and resist temptation; final triumph would come in the next world, not this. Disaster, if it occurred, was a test to be met and defeated. In the meantime every possible precaution was to be taken to prevent it. The sense of perspective and duty, reinforced by religious institutions and social networks, gave the pre–Civil War Puritans and the Restoration Baptists and Quakers advantages in the seventeenth century that others lacked. They lived in an economy fraught with danger and risk, but their religious confidence, their personal sobriety and frugality, and their reliance on their brethren's guidance and assistance gave them the strength to bear whatever came to them.

✦

"Be not conformed to this world," St. Paul beseeched Christians, "but be transformed by the renewing of your mind."[68] In order to make one's way in early modern England, it was necessary to achieve just such a transformation. Complexities abounded everywhere, and only a self-disciplined soul could provide a true center of stability. In a sense, each individual had to carry his own ordered world within him as he journeyed through the uncertainties. Community could begin only with the understanding that each of us possesses our own identity, our own world, and that to achieve social solidarity required an exchange among independent human beings. But this meant that every person must act according to his own will and judgment and bear his own risks. Insofar as capitalism is the rational pursuit of gain, this kind of ethical individualism is its necessary cultural and intellectual prerequisite. It depends on each person's recognition that his inner life affects his world; it does not divide him from it. By his actions he can transform it, but he also remains forever open to its shaping influences.

The capitalism born in coping with the new demands of the Atlantic economy and the new conditions of politics in the Restoration was not only a set of beliefs but a system of organization for carrying them out, a way of doing as well as seeing—a distinct form of life. Forms of life have origins just as species do. They connect with past forms. Even though they live in environments different from those of their forebears, they use many of the characteristic features of their ancestors, if for quite unexpected ends. Moreover, just as with the origin of species, the rise of forms of life is unpredictable, contingent both on the nature of their surroundings and on the kind of adaptations they have been able to make. This means that they are not universal. The truths that apply to one form of life will be meaningless or false in others. It also means that they are not eternal. After they come into existence, they can experience catastrophic change or suffer extinction. The form of life whose emergence we have described here, based as it was on an uncertain system of credit, undependable trading conditions, and an unstable structure of politics, did not—could not—long remain as it was. As Britain underwent its financial and industrial revolutions in the eighteenth century and moved toward representative democracy in the nineteenth, the features of this form of capitalism were altered or passed out of use; and Bristol—England's gate to the Atlantic—lost its central place in the still-widening economy to Birmingham, Liverpool, Manchester, and other industrial cities of the Midlands and the North. Nevertheless, Bristol's contribution was a lasting one, for as it helped to open England to the world, it also helped to teach the world what it meant to live by the disciplines of the market, "ship shape and Bristol fashion."

Abbreviations

Adams's Chronicle	William Adams, *Adams's Chronicle of Bristol*, ed. F. F. Fox (Bristol: J. W. Arrowsmith, 1910)
AHR	*American Historical Review*
APC	*Acts of the Privy Council*
Beaven, *Lists*	A. B. Beaven, *Bristol Lists: Municipal and Miscellaneous* (Bristol: T. D. Taylor, Sons, & Hawkins, 1899)
BGAS	*Bristol and Gloucestershire Archaeological Society, Transactions*
BL	British Library, London
BRO	Bristol Record Office, The Council House, Bristol
BRS	Bristol Record Society
CJ	*Journals of the House of Commons*
CSP	*Calendar of State Papers . . . Preserved in the . . . Public Record Office*
DNB	*Dictionary of National Biography*
EcHR	*Economic History Review*
Edgeworth, *Sermons*	Roger Edgeworth, *Sermons Very Fruitful, Godly and Learned* (London, 1557)
Hayden, ed., *Records*	Roger Hayden, ed., *The Record of the Church of Christ in Bristol, 1640–1687* (BRS 27, 1974)
HMC	Historical Manuscripts Commission
JBS	*Journal of British Studies*

JEcH	*Journal of Economic History*
L. and P.	*Letters and Papers, Foreign and Domestic, of the Reign of Henry VIII, 1509–47*, ed. J. S. Brewer, James Gairdiner, and R. H. Brodie, 21 vols. in 33 parts; 2d ed., vol. 1 in 3 parts, ed. R. H. Brodie; addenda, vol. 1 in 2 parts (London: Longman, 1862–1932)
LJ	*Journals of the House of Lords*
Latimer, *Annals*	John Latimer, *The Annals of Bristol in the Seventeenth Century* (Bristol: William George's Sons, 1900)
Latimer, *Merchant Venturers*	John Latimer, *The History of the Society of Merchant Venturers of the City of Bristol, with Some Account of the Anterior Merchant Guilds* (Bristol: J. W. Arrowsmith, 1903)
LRB	*The Little Red Book of Bristol*, 2 vols., ed. F. B. Bickley (Bristol: W. C. Hemmons, 1900)
McGrath, ed., *Merchants and Merchandise*	Patrick V. McGrath, ed., *Merchants and Merchandise in Seventeenth-Century Bristol* (BRS 19, 1955)
McGrath, ed., *Records*	Patrick V. McGrath, ed., *Records Relating to the Society of Merchant Venturers of the City of Bristol in the Seventeenth Century* (BRS 17, 1952)
Marchants Avizo	I[ohn] B[rowne], *The Marchants Avizo very necessary for their sonnes and seruants, when they first send them beyond the seas, as to Spaine and Portingale or other countreyes* [London, 1589], ed. Patrick V. McGrath (Boston: Baker Library, Harvard Graduate School of Business Administration, 1957)
Mortimer, ed., *Minute Book*	Russell Mortimer, ed., *Minute Book of the Men's Meeting of the Society of Friends in Bristol, 1667–1686* (BRS 26, 1970)
PRO	Public Record Office, London
Seyer, *Memoirs*	Samuel Seyer, *Memoirs Historical and Topographical of Bristol and its Neighbourhood*, 2 vols. (Bristol: John Mathew Gutch, 1821–1823)
SMV	Society of Merchant Venturers
Stat. Realm	*Statutes of the Realm*
TRHS	*Transactions, Royal Historical Society*
VCH	*Victoria County History*
WMQ	*William and Mary Quarterly*

Notes

PREFACE

1. See, e.g., Elizabeth Fox-Genovese and Eugene D. Genovese, *Fruits of Merchant Capital: Slavery and Bourgeois Property in the Rise and Expansion of Capitalism* (Oxford: Oxford University Press, 1983), chap. 1.

2. Stephen Greenblatt, *Shakespearean Negotiations: The Circulation of Social Energy in Renaissance England* (Berkeley and Los Angeles: University of California Press, 1988), p. 5.

3. F. J. Fisher, "The Sixteenth and Seventeenth Centuries: The Dark Ages of English Economic History," *Economica* n.s. 24 (1957): 2–3.

4. See, e.g., Robert W. Fogel, "The Reunification of Economic History with Economic Theory," *American Economic Review* 55 (1965): 92–98; Robert W. Fogel, "The Limits of Quantitative Methods in History," *AHR* 80 (1975): 329–50.

5. See David Landes, "On Avoiding Babel," *Journal of Economic History* 38 (1978): 3–12, esp. p. 7.

6. Marc Bloch, *The Historian's Craft*, trans. Peter Putnam (New York: Alfred A. Knopf, 1953), pp. 27–29.

7. Greenblatt, *Shakespearean Negotiations*, p. 7.

8. Steven Ozment, ed., *Three Behaim Boys Growing Up in Early Modern Germany: A Chronicle of Their Lives* (New Haven: Yale University Press, 1990), p. xii.

9. I have discussed these ideas more fully in David Harris Sacks, "The Hedgehog and the Fox Revisited," *Journal of Interdisciplinary History* 16 (1985): 267–80.

10. David Harris Sacks, "Trade, Society and Politics in Bristol, Circa 1500–Circa 1640," 3 vols., Ph.D. dissertation, Harvard University, 1977; revised as *Trade, Society and Politics in Bristol, 1500–1640*, 2 vols. (New York: Garland Publishing, 1985).

INTRODUCTION

1. Oscar Handlin, "The Modern City as a Field of Historical Study," in Oscar Handlin and John Burchard, eds., *The Historian and the City* (Cambridge, Mass.: MIT Press, 1963), p. 2.

2. BL, Sloane MS 2596, f. 77: William Smith, *The Particular Description of England. With the Portraitures of Certaine of the Cheiffest Citties & Townes, 1588,* f. 77; a facsimile appears in William Smith, *The Particular Description of England, 1588; with views of some of the chief towns and armorial bearings of nobles and bishops,* ed. Henry B. Wheatley and Edmund W. Ashbee (London: privately printed, 1879), plate 25; see also William George, "The Date of the First Authentic Plan of Bristol," *BGAS* 4 (1879–80): 296–300.

3. H. A. Cronne, ed., *Bristol Charters, 1378–1499* (BRS 11, 1945), pp. 33, 37, 38.

4. Smith, *The Particular Description of England, 1588,* pp. vi ff.; *DNB,* "William Smith."

5. On the history of Bristol's common seal, see James Dallaway, "Observations on the First Common Seal Used by the Burgesses of Bristol," *Archaeologia* 21 (1827): 79–87; J. R. Planché, "On the Municipal Seals and Armorial Ensigns of the City of Bristol," *Journal of the British Archaeological Association* 31 (1875): 180–89.

6. Thomas Churchyard, *The Firste Parte of Churchyardes Chippes, contayning twelue severall Labours* (London, 1575), f. 118^r.

7. Alan Everitt, " The County Community," in E. W. Ives, ed., *The English Revolution, 1600–1660* (London: Edward Arnold, 1968), p. 49.

8. Mrs. J. R. Green, *Town Life in the Fifteenth Century,* 2 vols. (New York: Macmillan, 1894), vol. 1, pp. 1–2.

9. Thomas Hobbes, *Leviathan, or the Matter, Forme, & Power of a Common-wealth, Ecclesiaticall and Civill,* ed. C. B. MacPherson (Harmondsworth: Penguin, 1968), pp. 368, 375.

10. Everitt, "County Community," p. 48.

11. The classic account of *Gemeinschaft* is to be found in Ferdinand Tönnies's seminal work of 1887, *Community and Society,* ed. and trans. Charles P. Loomis (New York: Harper and Row, 1963). See also Max Weber, *The Theory of Social and Economic Organization,* trans. A. M. Henderson and Talcott Parsons, ed. Talcott Parsons (New York: Oxford University Press, 1947), pp. 136–39; and Emile Durkheim, *The Division of Labor in Society,* trans. George Simpson (New York: Macmillan, 1933). By the Second World War the idea of community as a special kind of social form had reached general currency in English usage: Raymond Williams, *Keywords: A Vocabulary of Culture and Society* (New York: Oxford University Press, 1976), pp. 65–66. Cf. H. P. R. Finberg, *The Local Historian and His Theme* (Leicester University, Dept. of English Local Hist., Occasional Papers 1, 1952), pp. 5–8; Alan Everitt, "The Local Community and the Great Rebellion," reprinted in K. H. D. Haley, ed., *The Historical Association Book of the Stuarts* (London: Sidgwick and Jackson, 1973), p. 76; Alan Everitt, *New Avenues in English Local History* (Leicester: Leicester University Press, 1970), p. 6; Alan Everitt, *Ways and Means in Local*

History (London: National Council of Social Service for the Standing Conference for Local History, 1971), p. 6.

12. Finberg, *The Local Historian and His Theme*, pp. 5, 6, 7, 9, 15.

13. Ibid., pp. 7–8.

14. Thomas Wilson, *The State of England, 1600*, ed. F. J. Fisher, in *Camden Miscellany* 16 (Camden Society, 3d ser., 52, 1936), pp. 20–21.

15. Ibid., p. 21.

16. John Stowe, *A Survey of London, Reprinted from the Text of 1603*, ed. C. L. Kingsford, 2 vols. (Oxford: Clarendon Press, 1908), vol. 2, pp. 206–7.

17. Ibid., p. 198.

18. Frederick Pollock and F. W. Maitland, *The History of English Law before the Time of Edward I*, 2 vols., 2d ed., rev. by S. F. C. Milsom (Cambridge: Cambridge University Press, 1968), vol. 1, pp. 635–36. For Maitland's more general statement of this view, see pp. 687–88. For later statements along these same lines, see Wallace T. MacCaffrey, *Exeter, 1540–1640*, 2d ed. (Cambridge, Mass.: Harvard University Press, 1976), ch. 9; Clive Holmes, "The County Community in Stuart Historiography," *JBS* 19 (1980): 54–73; see also David Harris Sacks, "The Corporate Town and the English State: Bristol's 'Little Businesses,' 1625–1641," *Past and Present* 110 (February 1986): 69–75.

19. Everitt, *Ways and Means in Local History*, p. 6.

20. See, e.g., Everitt, *New Avenues in English Local History*, p. 6.

21. For a classic statement of this social theory by a British social anthropologist, see A. R. Radcliffe-Brown, *Structure and Function in Primitive Society: Essays and Addresses*, foreword by E. E. Evans-Pritchard and Fred Eggan (London: Cohen and West, 1952).

22. See, e.g., Alan Everitt, *Change in the Provinces: The Seventeenth Century* (Leicester University, Department of English Local History, Occasional Papers, 2d ser., 1, 1969), pp. 35ff.; Charles Phythian-Adams, *Desolation of a City: Coventry and the Urban Crisis of the Late Middle Ages* (Cambridge: Cambridge University Press, 1979), pp. 249ff.

23. Karl Marx, "The Eighteenth Brumaire of Louis Bonaparte," in David McLellan, ed., *Karl Marx: Selected Writings* (Oxford: Clarendon Press, 1977), p. 300.

24. Eric Wolf, *Europe and the People Without History* (Berkeley and Los Angeles: University of California Press, 1982), pp. 3, 385.

25. Finberg, *The Local Historian and His Theme*, p. 11.

26. Thomas Kuhn, *The Structure of Scientific Revolutions*, 2d ed. (Chicago: University of Chicago Press, 1970), pp. 174–210.

27. "A Catalogue of Some Books and Treatises Relating to the Antiquities of England," in William Camden, *Camden's Britannia, Newly Translated into English, with Large Additions and Improvements*, ed. Edmund Gibson (London, 1695), unpaginated.

28. See, e.g., [John Graunt], *Natural and Political Observations mentioned in a following Index, and made upon the Bills of Mortality by John Graunt* (London, 1662; 5th ed. 1676), ed. W. F. Willcox (Baltimore: Johns Hopkins University Press, 1939); Gregory King, *Natural and Political Observations and Conclusions upon the State and Condition of England*, reprinted in G. E.

Barnett, ed., *Two Tracts by Gregory King* (Baltimore: Johns Hopkins University Press, 1936); William Petty, *The Economic Writings of William Petty*, 2 vols., ed. C. H. Hull (Cambridge: Cambridge University Press, 1899); Karl Pearson, *The History of Statistics in the Seventeenth and Eighteenth Centuries against the Changing Background of Intellectual, Scientific and Religious Thought: Lectures by Karl Pearson Given at University College London during the Academic Sessions 1921–1933*, ed. E. S. Pearson (London: C. Griffin, 1978), pp. 1–140; William Letwin, *The Origins of Scientific Economics: English Economic Thought, 1660–1776* (London: Methuen, 1963), pp. 79–146; Ian Hacking, *The Emergence of Probability: A Philosophical Study of Early Ideas about Probability, Induction and Statistical Inference* (Cambridge: Cambridge University Press, 1975), pp. 92–121; Barbara Shapiro, *Probability and Certainty in Seventeenth-Century England: A Study of the Relationships between Natural Science, Religion, History, Law and Literature* (Princeton, N.J.: Princeton University Press, 1983), pp. 129–30; Lorraine Daston, *Classical Probability in the Enlightenment* (Princeton, N.J.: Princeton University Press, 1988), pp. 127–29; Lorraine Daston, "The Domestication of Risk: Mathematical Probability and Insurance, 1650–1830," in Lorenz Krüger, Lorraine Daston, and Michael Heidelberger, eds., *The Probabilistic Revolution*, 2 vols. (Cambridge, Mass.: MIT Press, 1987), vol. 1, pp. 237–60.

29. See Herbert Butterfield, *The Whig Interpretation of History* (London: G. Bell and Sons, 1951).

30. For a view of evolutionary biology as historical narrative which has much in common with the approach followed here, see Stephen Jay Gould, *Wonderful Life: The Burgess Shale and the Nature of History* (New York: W.W. Norton, 1989).

31. See, e.g., Immanuel Wallerstein, *The Modern World-System: Capitalist Agriculture and the Origins of the European World-Economy in the Sixteenth Century* (New York: Academic Press, 1974); Immanuel Wallerstein, *The Modern World-System II: Mercantilism and the Consolidation of the European World-Economy, 1600–1750* (New York: Academic Press, 1980); see also Fernand Braudel, *Civilization and Capitalism, 15th-18th Century*, 3 vols., trans. Siân Reynolds (New York: Harper and Row, 1979–1982), vol. 3, esp. chap. 1; Fernand Braudel, *Afterthoughts on Material Civilization and Capitalism*, trans. Patricia M. Ranum (Baltimore: Johns Hopkins University Press, 1977), esp. chap. 3; Wolf, *Europe and the People Without History*, esp. chap. 1.

32. Hilary Putnam, *Meaning and the Moral Sciences* (London: Routledge and Kegan Paul, 1978), p. 42; for a fuller discussion of this point see below, chap. 4.

CHAPTER 1

1. Charles M. MacInnes, *A Gateway of Empire* (Bristol: J. W. Arrowsmith, 1939), p. 9.

2. Latimer, *Merchant Venturers*, p. 27.

3. For a brief overview, see E. M. Carus-Wilson, *The Merchant Adventurers of Bristol in the Fifteenth Century* (Historical Association, Bristol Branch, Pamphlet 4, 1962).

4. See H. R. Fox Bourne, *English Merchants: Memoirs in Illustration of the Progress of British Commerce*, 2 vols. (London: R. Bentley, 1866), vol. 1, p. 106; Nikolaus Pevsner, *The Buildings of England: North Somerset and Bristol* (Harmondsworth: Penguin, 1958), p. 403.

5. E. M. Carus-Wilson, *Medieval Merchant Venturers*, 2d ed. (London: Methuen, 1967), pp. 72, 75, 79, 89–90; see also William Worcestre, *Itineraries*, ed. John Harvey (Oxford: Clarendon Press, 1969), pp. 130–33.

6. Carus-Wilson, *Medieval Merchant Venturers*, pp. 67–73.

7. Carus-Wilson, *Medieval Merchant Venturers*, pp. 248, 257; Y. Renouard, "Les Relations de Bordeaux et de Bristol au Moyen Age," *Revue Historique de Bordeaux* n.s. 6 (1957), pp. 105–6; M. K. James, *Studies in the Medieval Wine Trade*, ed. E. M. Veale with introduction by E. M. Carus-Wilson (Oxford: Clarendon Press, 1971), pp. 93–108.

8. Carus-Wilson, *Medieval Merchant Venturers*, pp. 269–71; James, *Medieval Wine Trade*, pp. 1–37; Renouard, "Les Relations de Bordeaux et de Bristol," pp. 106–8; J. W. Sherborne, *The Port of Bristol in the Later Middle Ages* (Historical Association, Bristol Branch, Pamphlet 13, 1965), pp. 9–13; Théophile Malvezin, *Histoire du Commerce de Bordeaux depuis les Origines jusqu'à nos Jours*, 2 vols. (Bordeaux: A. Bellier, 1892), vol. 2, p. 199.

9. James, *Medieval Wine Trade*, pp. 38–42; Carus-Wilson, *Medieval Merchant Venturers*, pp. 40–43; Sherborne, *Port of Bristol*, pp. 21–22; Renouard, "Les Relations de Bordeaux et de Bristol," pp. 109–10, 111; see below, Tables 1 and 2.

10. Carus-Wilson, *Medieval Merchant Venturers*, pp. 50, 58–59, 257; V. M. Shillington and A. B. Wallis Chapman, *The Commercial Relations of England and Portugal* (New York: E. P. Dutton, 1907), pp. 13, 14, 18, 49, 56, 68; Sherborne, *Port of Bristol*, p. 11.

11. Carus-Wilson, *Medieval Merchant Venturers*, pp. 28–40, 246–48, 269–71; Y. Renouard, "Les Conséquences de la Conquête de la Guienne par le Roi de France pour le Commerce de Vins de Gascoigne," *Annales du Midi* 61 (1948–49): 16–18; Renouard, "Les Relations de Bordeaux et de Bristol, " pp. 104–5; M. G. A. Vale, *English Gascony, 1399–1453: A Study of War, Government and Politics during the Later Stages of the Hundred Years War* (London: Oxford University Press, 1970), pp. 11–26; Robert Boutruche, *La Crise d'un Société: Seigneurs et Paysans du Bordelais pendant la Guerre de Cents Ans* (Paris: Belles Lettres, 1947), pp. 141–65.

12. Malvezin, *Histoire du Commerce de Bordeaux*, vol. 2, p. 199.

13. The history of Bristol's trade just before and just after the English loss of Bordeaux shows how precipitous was the decline in both cloth exports and wine imports. Between 1440 and 1460 an average of 4,231 whole cloths were exported annually from Bristol; in the same period an average of 1,738 tons of wine were imported annually. But during the first five years of this period, from 1440 to 1445, the annual averages were 5,427 whole cloths and 2,411 tons of wine. In the last five years, the annual averages were 2,943 whole cloths and 814 tons of wine. In three years in this half-decade, wine shipments were under 800 tons for the year. For detailed figures see E. M. Carus-Wilson and Olive Coleman, eds., *England's Export Trade, 1275–1547* (Oxford: Clarendon Press,

1963), pp. 95–100. See also Carus-Wilson, *Medieval Merchant Venturers*,
pp. 41–45, 265–78; James, *Medieval Wine Trade*, pp. 40–45, 111–12; Renouard, "Conquête de la Guienne," pp. 18–24; Boutruche, *La Crise d'un Société*, pp. 170–71, 219–31, 399–411.

    14. Bristol produced about £1,450 of customs revenue per year in the 1490s.
In the same period London produced about £8,520 per year, Southampton
about £6,365 per year, and Exeter about £1,000 per year; see Georg von
Schanz, *Englische Handelspolitike gegen Ende des Mittelalters mit besonderer
Berücksichtigung des Zeitalters der beiden ersten Tudors, Heinrich VII. und
Heinrich VIII.*, 2 vols. (Leipzig: Duncker und Humblot, 1881), vol. 2, pp. 37–
46; Sacks, *Trade, Society and Politics*, vol. 1, p. 284. Note, however, that the
ratio between customs rates and market prices varied somewhat from item to
item, so port totals never reflect the volume of trade in exactly the same way
for each port. These totals also vary according to the proportion of denizen,
alien, and Hanseatic merchants in each port's trade, since these groups paid customs on different scales, with foreigners paying higher rates. In the case of Bristol and its near neighbor and rival Exeter, 90 to 95 percent of trade was consistently in the hands of denizens. For London, however, the figure was
approximately 50 percent, and for Southampton, 25–30 percent. Finally, those
totals apply properly to customs jurisdictions, not just to one port. In the fifteenth century, Bristol did include some adjacent ports in Wales and in the
Severn River valley, but with Bridgewater under a separate jurisdiction, Bristol's
totals are for a relatively well-defined area. Indeed, most of the traffic from the
minor ports associated with it passed through Bristol both to and from overseas. London was perhaps even better defined, extending only to Gravesend and
Tilbury. With Southampton and Exeter, however, the areas covered by the
above customs totals are larger and more diffuse. Southampton included Ports-
mouth, and Exeter included Dartmouth. Hence the figures represent the significance of each port in the system of customs collection better than their actual
place in the hierarchy of port cities. Nevertheless, they undoubtedly give us the
right order of precedence and suggest in terms of order of magnitude something
of the differences among these ports.

    15. I. S. Leadam, ed., *Select Cases before the King's Council in the Star
Chamber commonly called the Court of Star Chamber, II: 1509–1544* (Selden
Society 25, 1911), p. 266.

    16. Ibid., p. 268.

    17. See Sacks, *Trade, Society and Politics*, vol. 1, p. 284; E. M. Carus-
Wilson, *The Expansion of Exeter at the Close of the Middle Ages: The Harte
Memorial Lecture in Local History, University of Exeter, 12 May 1961* (Exeter:
University of Exeter, 1963).

    18. See G. D. Ramsay, *English Overseas Trade during the Centuries of
Emergence: Studies in Some Modern Origins of the English Speaking World*
(London: Macmillan, 1957), pp. 134–38; D. Burwash, *English Merchant Shipping, 1460–1540* (Toronto: University of Toronto Press, 1947), pp. 161–63,
234.

    19. A. K. Longfield, *Anglo-Irish Trade in the Sixteenth Century* (London: G.
Routledge and Sons, 1929), p. 216.

20. On Anglo-French commercial relations in the early sixteenth century, see P. Boissonade, "Le Mouvement Commercial entre la France et les Iles Brittaniques au XVIᵉ Siècle," *Revue Historique* 134 (1920): 192–228, and 135 (1921): 1–27; Robert Boutruche, ed., *Bordeaux de 1453 à 1715* (Bordeaux: Fédération Historique du Sudouest, 1966), p. 93; M. Mollat, *Le Commerce Maritime Normand à la Fin du Moyen Age: Etude d'Histoire Economique et Sociale* (Paris: Plon, 1952), pp. 139–45; Gordon Connell-Smith, *Forerunners of Drake: A Study of English Trade with Spain in the Early Tudor Period* (London: Longmans, Green, 1954), pp. 41, 60–61; Burwash, *English Merchant Shipping*, pp. 163, 235–36; Jacques Bernard, *Navires et Gens de Mer à Bordeaux (vers 1400–1550)*, 3 vols. (Paris: SEVPEN, 1968), vol. 2, p. 508; vol. 3, Appendices.

21. Shillington and Chapman, *Commercial Relations of England and Portugal*, pp. 133–34.

22. Connell-Smith, *Forerunners of Drake*, pp. 34, 41, 54, 60–62, 105–6, 124, 207–12; T. S. Willan, *Studies in Elizabethan Foreign Trade* (Manchester: Manchester University Press, 1959), pp. 84–85; D. M. Woodward, *The Trade of Elizabethan Chester* (Hull: University of Hull Publications, 1970), p. 40n.

23. For discussion of the idea of an urban crisis in the later Middle Ages see Charles Phythian-Adams, "Urban Decay in the Later Middle Ages," in Philip Abrams and E. A. Wrigley, eds., *Towns and Societies: Essays in Economic History and Historical Sociology* (Cambridge: Cambridge University Press, 1978), pp. 159–85. For a general overview of the concepts of urban function, urban network, urban system, and urban hierarchy, see Jan de Vries, *European Urbanization, 1500–1800* (Cambridge, Mass.: Harvard University Press, 1984), esp. pp. 118, 167–68, 171; E. A. Wrigley, "Urban Growth and Agricultural Change: England and the Continent in the Early Modern Period," in E. A. Wrigley, *People, Cities and Wealth: The Transformation of Traditional Society* (Oxford: Basil Blackwell, 1987), pp. 157–93. For additional discussions, see Alan Dyer, "Growth and Decay in English Towns, 1500–1700," in *Urban History Yearbook, 1979* (Leicester: Leicester University Press, 1979), pp. 60–72; Charles Phythian-Adams, "Dr Dyer's Urban Undulations," ibid., pp. 73–76; S. Rigby, "Urban Decline in the Later Middle Ages," ibid., pp. 46–59; A. R. Bridbury, "English Provincial Towns in the Later Middle Ages," *EcHR*, 2d ser., 34 (1981): 1–24; R. B. Dobson, "Urban Decline in Late Medieval England," *Transactions of the Royal Historical Society*, 5th ser., 27 (1977): 1–22; N. R. Goose, "In Search of the Urban Variable: Towns, 1500–1650," *EcHR*, 2d ser., 39 (1986): 165–86; D. M. Palliser, "A Crisis in English Towns? The Case of York, 1480–1640," *Northern History* 14 (1978): 108–25; Charles Phythian-Adams and Paul Slack, "Urban Decay or Urban Change?" in Charles Phythian-Adams et al., *The Traditional Community under Stress* (Milton Keynes, England: Open University Press, 1977), pp. 5–29.

24. See Tables 3 and 4, above; C. G. A. Clay, *Economic Expansion and Social Change: England, 1500–1700*, 2 vols. (Cambridge: Cambridge University Press, 1984), vol. 2, pp. 108ff.; Steve Rappaport, *Worlds within Worlds: Structures of Life in Sixteenth-Century London* (Cambridge: Cambridge University Press, 1989), pp. 87–96; D. M. Palliser, *The Age of Elizabeth: England under the Later Tudors, 1547–1603* (London: Longman, 1983), pp. 278–91; D. C.

Coleman, *The Economy of England, 1450–1750* (London: Oxford University Press, 1977), p. 51; W. G. Hoskins, *The Age of Plunder: King Henry's England, 1500–1547* (London: Longman, 1976), pp. 178–80; Ramsay, *English Overseas Trade*, pp. 1–33; F. J. Fisher, "Commercial Trends and Policy in Sixteenth Century England," in E. M. Carus-Wilson, ed., *Essays in Economic History*, 3 vols. (London: Edward Arnold, 1954–1962), vol. 1, pp. 153–55; Lawrence Stone, "State Control in Sixteenth-Century England," *EcHR* 17 (1947): 104 ff.; J. D. Gould, *The Great Debasement: Currency and the Economy in Mid-Tudor England* (Oxford: Clarendon Press, 1970), pp. 115ff.; Carus-Wilson, *The Expansion of Exeter*.

25. Leadam, ed., *Select Cases before the Star Chamber*, II, p. 146.

26. *L. and P.* 13, part 2, p. 322; *Stat. Realm* 32 Hen. VIII, c. 18, lists Bristol in 1540 among the thirty-six English towns which "nowe are fallen downe decayed and at this day remaine unreedified and doo lye as desolate and vacante groundes"; see also Jean Vanes, ed., *Documents Illustrating the Overseas Trade of Bristol in the Sixteenth Century* (BRS 31, 1979), pp. 28–31.

27. Leadam, ed., *Select Cases before the Star Chamber*, II, p. 250; SMV, *Book of Trade*, p. 36; BL, Lands. MS 86/13; Ramsay, *English Overseas Trade*, p. 137.

28. G. C. Moore Smith and P. H. Reaney, *The Family of Withypoll, with Special Reference to the Manor of Christchurch, Ipswich, and Some Notes on the Allied Families of Thorne, Harper, Lucar and Devereaux* (Walthamstow Antiquarian Society Official Publication 34, 1936); George F. Bosworth, *George Monoux: The Story of a Waltamstow Worthy—His Foundations and Benefactions* (Walthamstow Antiquarian Society Official Publication 3, 1916); George F. Bosworth, *George Monoux: The Man and His Work* (Walthamstow Antiquarian Society Official Publication 17, 1927); George S. Fry, *Abstract of Wills Relating to Walthamstow, co. Essex (1335–1559)* (Walthamstow Antiquarian Society Official Publication 9, 1921), pp. 20–46; A. H. Johnson, *The History of the Worshipful Company of Drapers of London: Preceded by an Introduction on London and Her Gilds up to the Close of the XVth Century*, 3 vols. (Oxford: Clarendon Press, 1914–1922), vol. 2, pp. 14–15, 21, 79, 136; Connell-Smith, *Forerunners of Drake*, pp. 8–10, 19–20, 60–65; Ramsay, *English Overseas Trade*, pp. 135–36.

29. Connell-Smith, *Forerunners of Drake*, pp. xii–xiv, 9–19; Gordon Connell-Smith, "English Merchants Trading to the New World in the Early Sixteenth Century," *Bulletin of the Institute of Historical Research* 23 (1950): 53–67.

30. Johnson, *Drapers of London*, vol. 2, p. 79; Smith and Reaney, *Family of Withypoll*, pp. 14–23. Withypoll was a Merchant Adventurer and even governor of the Company.

31. PRO, PROB 5/18 Thrower; a copy appears in E. W. W. Veale, ed., *The Great Red Book of Bristol*, 5 vols. (BRS 2, 4, 8, 16, 18, 1931–1953), vol. 16, pp. 124–29.

32. Gordon Connell-Smith, "The Ledger of Thomas Howell," *EcHR*, 2nd ser., 3 (1950–51): 365–66, 368–69; Connell-Smith, *Forerunners of Drake*,

pp. 10, 19–21, 24, 67, 69, 75–76; Connell-Smith, "English Merchants Trading to the New World," p. 61; Johnson, *Drapers of London*, vol. 2, pp. 251, 252–54; PRO, PROB 5/24 Alen.

33. Johnson, *Drapers of London*, vol. 2, pp. 252, 253; Connell-Smith, "Ledger of Thomas Howell," p. 365; Connell-Smith, *Forerunners of Drake*, pp. 61–65, 69.

34. Johnson, *Drapers of London*, vol. 2, pp. 252–54.

35. SMV, *Book of Trade*, p. 36. On Bristolians becoming non-resident members of the London Drapers' Company, see Johnson, *Drapers of London*, vol. 2, pp. 258–59, 261; Connell-Smith, *Forerunners of Drake*, pp. 35, 61.

36. See Rappaport, *Worlds within Worlds*, pp. 96ff.

37. E. M. Carus-Wilson, ed., *The Overseas Trade of Bristol in the Later Middle Ages*, 2d ed. (New York: Barnes and Noble, 1967), pp. 37–39, 70–71, 83–85, 101–2, 104–5; Veale, ed., *Great Red Book of Bristol*, vol. 8, p. 1; Carus-Wilson, *Medieval Merchant Venturers*, pp. 9–10, 64–65; A. A. Ruddock, *Italian Merchants and Shipping in Southampton, 1270–1600* (Southampton, England: University College, 1951), pp. 18, 41, 44–45, 115, 188, 265; Olive Coleman, "Trade and Prosperity in the Fifteenth Century: Some Aspects of the Trade of Southampton," *EcHR*, 2d ser., 16 (1963–64): 11–12.

38. Carus-Wilson, ed., *Overseas Trade of Bristol*, pp. 84–85, 113–15, 117–18; Carus-Wilson, *Medieval Merchant Venturers*, pp. 67–68, 70, 71–73; James Dallaway, *Antiquities of Bristow in the Middle Centuries Including the Topography by William Wyrcestre and the Life of William Cannynges* (Bristol: Mirror Office, 1834), pp. 78, 109; Robert Fabyan, *The New Chronicles of England and France in Two Parts*, ed. Henry Ellis (London: F. C. and J. Rivington, 1811), p. 633; Robert Ricart, *The Maire of Bristowe Is Kalendar*, ed. Lucy Toulmin Smith (Camden Society n.s. 5, 1872), p. 41; *Calendar of the Patent Rolls* (1452–1461), p. 517; see also Jacques Heers, "Les Genois en Angleterre: La Crise de 1458–1466," in *Studi in Onore de Armando Sapori*, 2 vols. (Milan: Instituto Editoriale Cisalpino, 1957), vol. 2, p. 810.

39. Fernand Braudel, *The Mediterranean and the Mediterranean World in the Age of Philip II*, 2 vols., 2d ed. trans. Siân Reynolds (London: Collins, 1972–73), vol. 1, p. 612.

40. Carus-Wilson, ed., *Overseas Trade of Bristol*, pp. 234–35, 260–64; Carus-Wilson, *Medieval Merchant Venturers*, pp. 60, 92. A similar relation probably also existed with the Canary Islands, with trade proceeding through Cádiz, Puerta Santa Maria, San Lucar de Barremeda, and Seville: J. A. Williamson, *The Cabot Voyages and Bristol Discovery under Henry VII* (Hakluyt Society, 2d ser., 120, 1962), pp. 14–15; J. A. Williamson, *Hawkins of Plymouth: A New History of Sir John Hawkins and the Other Members of His Family Prominent in New England* (London: Argonaut Press, 1949), pp. 16–17; Carus-Wilson, ed., *Overseas Trade of Bristol*, p. 267.

41. J. A. Williamson, *The Voyages of the Cabots and the English Discovery of North America under Henry VII and Henry VIII* (London: A. and C. Black, 1929), pp. 18, 128; Williamson, *Cabot Voyages and Bristol Discovery*, pp. 14–15; D. B. Quinn, *England and the Discovery of America, 1481–1620, From*

the Bristol Voyages of the Fifteenth Century to the Pilgrim Settlement at Plymouth: The Exploration, Exploitation and Trial-and-Error Colonization of North America by the English (New York: Alfred A. Knopf, 1974) p. 57.

42. See T. E. Reddaway and A. A. Ruddock, *The Accounts of John Balsall, Purser of the Trinity of Bristol, 1480–1*, Camden Miscellany 23 (Camden Society, 4th ser., 7, 1969).

43. There were two Brasil traditions of the Middle Ages. One was the product of Celtic legend, which spoke of a Land of the Blest (Hy-Brasil, in Gaelic). Maps of the fourteenth and fifteenth centuries usually depicted it as a round or semicircular island located near the west coast of Ireland. The second tradition was Italian and Portuguese in origin. It postulated an Isle of Brasil in the mid-Atlantic, southwest of the Iberian peninsula. Usually maps depict it, together with several larger land masses which were identified as the Island of the Seven Cities and Antilla, somewhere in the mid-Atlantic along the tropic of Cancer. It was almost certainly this Brasil that the Bristolians were seeking in the 1480s; see Samuel Eliot Morison, *The European Discovery of America: The Northern Voyages, A.D. 500–1600* (New York: Oxford University Press, 1971), pp. 102–4; Quinn, *England and the Discovery of America*, pp. 59–60; Williamson, *Voyages of the Cabots*, pp. 125–26, 132–33; Williamson, *Cabot Voyages and Bristol Discovery*, p. 21; see also Kenneth R. Andrews, *Trade, Plunder and Settlement: Maritime Enterprise and the Genesis of the British Empire, 1480–1630* (Cambridge: Cambridge University Press, 1984), pp. 41–43.

44. Carus-Wilson, ed., *Overseas Trade of Bristol*, pp. 157, 161–65; Williamson, *Cabot Voyages and Bristol Discovery*, pp. 20, 188–89; Quinn, *England and the Discovery of America*, pp. 8–10, 72–73; Worcestre, *Itineraries*, pp. 308–9; W. E. C. Harrison, "An Early Voyage of Discovery," *Mariner's Mirror* 16 (1930): 198–99; D. B. Quinn, "Edward IV and Exploration," *Mariner's Mirror* 21 (1935): 283–84. For evidence of other voyages in the 1480s and 1490s see *CSP (Spanish)* (1485–1509), p. 177; H. P. Biggar, *The Precursors of Jacques Cartier, 1497–1534* (Ottawa: Government Printing Office, 1911), pp. 27–30; L. A. Vigneras, "New Light on the 1497 Cabot Voyage to America," *Hispanic American Historical Review* 36 (1956): 506–9; L. A. Vigneras, "The Cape Breton Landfall, 1494 or 1497?" *Canadian Historical Review* 38 (1957): 219–28; Quinn, *England and the Discovery of America*, part 1; Williamson, *Voyages of the Cabots*, pp. 23–24, 149–52; Williamson, *Cabot Voyages and Bristol Discovery*, pp. 19–32, 210–12, 310–14; A. A. Ruddock, "John Day of Bristol and the English Voyages Across the Atlantic before 1497," *Geographical Journal* 132 (1962): 225–33; Morison, *European Discovery of America*, pp. 166, 205–9, 220; Andrews, *Trade, Plunder and Settlement*, pp. 43–44, 46–47. Quinn provides a strong circumstantial case for a Bristol discovery of America predating 1497; Morison has firmly questioned several of the assumptions upon which Quinn's case is built. Andrews cuts to the heart of the matter by arguing that the Bristolians' quest for Brasil "led to the discovery of North America" whether the actual landfall occurred in 1497 or before.

45. Morison, *European Discovery of America*, p. 166; Quinn, *England and the Discovery of America*, pp. 30, 47–54; Carus-Wilson, *Medieval Merchant*

Venturers, pp. 129–30; Williamson, *Voyages of the Cabots*, pp. 8–10, 128–30; Williamson, *Cabot Voyages and Bristol Discovery*, pp. 13–14, 23, 175–77; Harold A. Innes, *The Cod Fisheries: The History of an International Economy* (New Haven: Yale University Press, 1940), p. 11n.; C. B. Judah, *The North American Fisheries and British Policy to 1713*, Illinois Studies in the Social Sciences 18, nos. 3–4 (Urbana: University of Illinois, 1933), p. 13.

46. Biggar, *Precursors of Jacques Cartier*, pp. 7–10.

47. Williamson, *Voyages of the Cabots*, pp. 24–32, 144, 148, 149–58; J. A. Williamson, *Maritime Enterprise, 1485–1558* (Oxford: Clarendon Press, 1913), ch. 3; Williamson, *Cabot Voyages and Bristol Discovery*, pp. 33–53, 201–14; Morison, *European Discovery of America*, pp. 159, 165–66; Quinn, *England and the Discovery of America*, pp. 14–17; Andrews, *Trade, Plunder and Settlement*, pp. 50ff.

48. Vigneras, "New Light on the 1497 Cabot Voyage," pp. 507–8; Vigneras, "Cape Breton Landfall," pp. 226–28; Morison, *European Discovery of America*, pp. 170–72, 178–79, 209; Andrews, *Trade, Plunder and Settlement*, pp. 44–46, 47.

49. *CSP (Milan)*, vol. 1, no. 552, see also no. 535.

50. Biggar, *Precursors of Jacques Cartier*, pp. 13–15.

51. *The Great Chronicle of London*, ed. A. H. Thomas and I. D. Thornley (London: George W. Jones at the Sign of the Dolphin, 1939), pp. 287–88; introduction to Williamson, *Cabot Voyages and Bristol Discovery*, pp. 93, 101–15; Morison, *European Discovery of America*, pp. 189–91; Polydore Vergil, *The Anglica Historia of Polydore Vergil*, ed. and trans. Denys Hay (Camden Society, 3d ser., 74, 1950), pp. 116–17; Biggar, *Precursors of Jacques Cartier*, pp. 27–29.

52. Based on analysis of PRO, E 190/1129/11 and 1129/12. For a full discussion of the reasons for using this method and some remarks on trade conditions in 1575–6 and the limitations of the Port Books as a source, see Sacks, *Trade, Society and Politics*, vol. 1, pp. 309–14; vol. 2, Appendix 1 (pp. 723–44), and p. 846n.1.

53. See Table 6 below. The figure of seven hundred and forty-nine cloths refers only to exports to the Continent. A bit less than twenty-eight cloths plus a small quantity of new draperies were shipped to Ireland in this year. Sacks, *Trade, Society and Politics*, vol. 1, p. 351.

54. Sacks, *Trade, Society and Politics*, vol. 1, pp. 322–46.

55. Ibid., pp. 314–22.

56. Braudel, *Mediterranean*, vol. 1, p. 298; Sacks, *Trade, Society and Politics*, vol. 1, pp. 321–22.

57. Sacks, *Trade, Society and Politics*, vol. 1, pp. 322–28.

58. Sacks, *Trade, Society and Politics*, vol. 1, pp. 329–45.

59. Sacks, *Trade, Society and Politics*, vol. 1, pp. 356–57; vol. 2, pp. 745, 749. About 80 percent of the inward and 95 percent of the outward trade was in the hands of the Irish.

60. Woodward, *Trade of Elizabethan Chester*, p. 5; Longfield, *Anglo-Irish Trade*, chap. 2.

61. Sacks, *Trade, Society and Politics*, vol. 1, pp. 351–54.

62. J. E. Thorold Rogers, *A History of Agriculture and Prices in England from the Year after the Oxford Parliament (1259) to the Commencement of the Continental War (1793)*, 7 vols. (Oxford: Clarendon Press, 1882–1887), vol. 4, pp. 409, 689; William Beveridge, *Prices and Wages in England from the Twelfth to the Nineteenth Century* (London: Frank Cass, 1939), pp. 36, 75.

63. Braudel, *Mediterranean*, vol. 1, pp. 442–43; see also Braudel, *Civilization and Capitalism*, vol. 2, chap. 4.

64. The discussion in this and the following section is based on analysis of PRO, E 190/1129/11, 1129/12, 1130/5, 1131/5, 1131/10, 1132/8, 1132/12, 1133/ 1, 1133/8, 1133/11, 1134/3, 1134/7, 1134/10, 1135/6, 1136/3, 1136/1, 1136/8, 1139/10. The results are tabulated and explained in Sacks, *Trade, Society and Politics*, vol. 1, chaps. 8 and 9, and in Appendix 2 (vol. 2, pp. 745–51).

65. The following account is based on analysis of PRO, E 190/1135/6. This year is the best available in this period, in part because we have a complete set of Port Books on which to base our analysis. For discussion of trade conditions in this year, see Sacks, *Trade, Society and Politics*, vol. 1, pp. 372–73.

66. Sacks, *Trade, Society and Politics*, vol. 1, pp. 373, 377, 380.

67. But definite conclusions as to the scale of the increase cannot be reached, because the rates upon which the Port Books relied were twice revised upward early in James I's reign: see T. S. Willan, ed., *A Tudor Book of Rates* (Manchester: Manchester University Press, 1962), p. xlii. Still, the increase in wine shipments suggests considerable growth in the size of Bristol's trade, even if the improvement in ad valorem duties is only illusory.

68. See Sacks, *Trade, Society and Politics*, vol. 1, pp. 429–54.

69. PRO, E 190/1134/7.

70. See, e.g., *Adams's Chronicle*, pp. 185–86; Latimer, *Annals*, p. 34.

71. PRO, E 190/1134/3, 1134/10, 1135/6. For evidence of Bristol's trade elsewhere in this region, see PRO, E 190/1134/3, 1136/8, 1136/10; Sacks, *Trade, Society and Politics*, vol. 1, pp. 384–85.

72. Reddaway and Ruddock, eds., *Accounts of John Balsall*, pp. 1–29; Antonio de Capmany Surís y de Montpalau, *Memorias Históricas sobre la marina commercio y artes de la antigua ciudad de Barcelona*, 2 vols. (Madrid: A. de Sancha, 1779–1792), vol. 1, part 2, p. 137; Jean Vanes, ed., *The Ledger of John Smythe, 1538–1550* (BRS 28, 1974), pp. 97, 106–7, 154, 158, 188, 217, 233, 235, 253, 262.

73. The Bristol merchant John Browne makes no mention in his *Marchants Avizo* of ports beyond Gibraltar. On Gibraltar as a barrier to shipping see Braudel, *Mediterranean*, vol. 1, pp. 117–20, 609–10, 622–23.

74. See, e.g., PRO, E 190/1134/3, 1134/7.

75. Braudel, *Mediterranean*, vol. 1, pp. 587ff.

76. Braudel, *Mediterranean*, vol. 1, p. 523; Earl J. Hamilton, *American Treasure and the Price Revolution in Spain, 1501–1650* (Cambridge, Mass.: Harvard University Press, 1934), pp. 262–82; E. H. Phelps Brown and Sheila V. Hopkins, "Seven Centuries of Building Wages," in Carus-Wilson, ed., *Essays in Economic History*, vol. 2, pp. 168–78; E. H. Phelps Brown and Sheila V. Hopkins, "Seven Centuries of the Prices of Consumables, Compared with

Builders' Wage-Rates," in Carus-Wilson, ed., *Essays in Economic History*, vol. 2, pp. 179–96.

77. See, e.g., Vanes, ed., *Ledger of John Smythe*, pp. 4, 13, 20, 89, 169, 287, 295.

78. *Marchants Avizo*, pp. 16–17; Ruth Pike, *Enterprise and Adventure: The Genoese in Seville and the Opening of the New World* (Ithaca: Cornell University Press, 1966), chap. 4; Henri Lapeyre, *Une Famille des Marchands: Les Ruiz* (Paris: A. Colin, 1955), pp. 113, 120, 122–23, 146.

79. Braudel, *Mediterranean*, vol. 1, p. 536; Hamilton, *American Treasure*, pp. 33ff., 278–81; Pierre Chaunu, *Séville et l'Atlantique (1504–1650)*, 8 vols. in 11 (Paris: SEVPEN, 1959), vol. 8, part 2, section 2, pp. 1263–64.

80. Chaunu, *Séville et l'Atlantique*, vol. 8, part 2, section 2, pp. 1158–87, 1458–1569.

81. Sacks, *Trade, Society and Politics*, vol. 1, pp. 394–95.

82. Reddaway and Ruddock, *Accounts of John Balsall*, pp. 1–29; Roger Barlow, *A Brief Summe of Geography*, ed. E. G. R. Taylor (Hakluyt Society, 2d ser., 69, 1931), p. 100.

83. Richard Hakluyt, *The Principal Navigations, Voyages, Traffiques & Discoveries of the English Nation, Made by Sea or Over-land to the Remote and Farthest Distant Quarters of the Earth at any Time within the Compasse of These 1600 Yeeres* (Hakluyt Society, extra ser., 12 vols., 1903–1905), vol. 6, pp. 136, 138–39; Willan, *Elizabethan Foreign Trade*, pp. 92ff.

84. See, e.g., PRO, E 190/1133/1, 1133/8; Willan, *Elizabethan Foreign Trade*, pp. 163–87, 279ff.

85. See, e.g., PRO, E 190/1134/3, 1134/10; "Special Direction for Divers Trades," in R. H. Tawney and E. Power, eds., *Tudor Economic Documents, Being Select Documents Illustrating the Economic and Social History of Tudor England*, 3 vols. (London: Longmans, 1924), vol. 3, p. 202; Willan, *Elizabethan Foreign Trade*, pp. 104, 107–14, 240–68.

86. PRO, E 190/1129/11; Braudel, *Mediterranean*, vol. 1, pp. 555, 606–42, and vol. 2, 1139–42; Fernand Braudel and R. Romano, *Navires et Marchandises à l'Entrée du Port de Livorne (1547–1611)* (Paris: A. Colin, 1951), pp. 50–51; Sacks, *Trade, Society and Politics*, vol. 1, pp. 311, 342–43.

87. Lewes Robertes, *The Marchants Mappe of Commerce wherein the Universal Manner and Matter of Trade is compendiously Handled* (London, 1638), pp. 40, 42.

88. See, e.g., PRO, E 190/1135/6; Sacks, *Trade, Society and Politics*, vol. 1, pp. 389–92.

89. Innis, *Cod Fisheries*, pp. 12–13; Biggar, *Precursors of Jacques Cartier*, pp. 134ff.; Williamson, *Voyages of the Cabots*, ch. 8; Judah, *North American Fisheries*, pp. 11–17; Gillian T. Cell, *English Enterprise in Newfoundland, 1577–1660* (Toronto: University of Toronto Press, 1969), p. 3.

90. E. G. R. Taylor, ed., *The Writings and Correspondence of the Two Richard Hakluyts*, 2 vols. (Hakluyt Society, 2d ser., 76, 1935), vol. 1, p. 123; see also Cell, *English Enterprise*, pp. 22–23; Innis, *Cod Fisheries*, pp. 30–33; R. G. Loundsbury, *The British Fishery at Newfoundland, 1634–1763* (New

Haven: Yale University Press, 1934), pp. 22–23; D. W. Prowse, *A History of Newfoundland from the English, Colonial and Foreign Records* (London: Macmillan, 1895), pp. 31–50; Judah, *North American Fisheries*, pp. 17–23.

91. Taylor, ed., *Writings and Correspondence of the Two Richard Hakluyts*, vol. 1, pp. 123, 128; Cell, *English Enterprise*, pp. 23–25, 78, 132, 135; Innis, *Cod Fisheries*, pp. 33ff.; Judah, *North American Fisheries*, pp. 24ff.; Sacks, *Trade, Society and Politics*, vol. 1, p. 403.

92. Hakluyt, *Principal Navigations*, vol. 8, p. 155; Pauline Croft, "Free Trade and the House of Commons, 1605–6," *EcHR*, 2d ser., 28 (1975): 21.

93. See PRO, E 190/1131/3; Cell, *English Enterprise*, pp. 24, 31–33, 47–52, 134; Innis, *Cod Fisheries*, pp. 39, 50, 52; Judah, *North American Fisheries*, pp. 31–39; Prowse, *History of Newfoundland*, pp. 79–84; Sacks, *Trade, Society and Politics*, vol. 1, pp. 404–6.

94. Taylor, ed., *Writings and Correspondence of the Two Richard Hakluyts*, vol. 1, pp. 123–34.

95. Samuel Purchas, *Hakluytus Posthumus or Purchas His Pilgrims Contayning a History of the World in Sea Voyages and Lande Travells by Englishmen and Others*, 20 vols. (Glasgow: J. MacLehose and Sons, 1905–1907), vol. 19, pp. 405–24; C. T. Carr, ed., *Select Charters of Trading Companies, A.D. 1530–1707* (Selden Society 28, 1913), pp. 51–62; J. W. Damer Powell, "The Explorations of John Guy in Newfoundland," *Geographical Journal* 86 (1930): 512–18; Cell, *English Enterprise*, pp. 53–61; Gillian T. Cell, "The Newfoundland Company: A Study of Subscribers to a Colonizing Venture," *WMQ*, 3d ser., 23 (1966): 611–25; Innis, *Cod Fisheries*, pp. 53–56.

96. SMV, *Book of Charters*, vol. 1, p. 57; McGrath, ed., *Records*, p. 200; Cell, *English Enterprise*, pp. 87–88.

97. SMV, *Book of Trade*, pp. 104–11, 123, 141–45; Miller Christy, "Attempts toward Colonization: The Council for New England and the Merchant Venturers of Bristol, 1621–23," *AHR* 4 (1898–99): 678–702; Henry S. Burrage, *The Beginnings of Colonial Maine, 1602–1658* (Portland, Maine: Printed for the State, 1914), pp. 142–43, 144–59; R. A. Preston, "Fishing and Plantation: New England in the Parliament of 1621," *AHR* 46 (1939–40): 29–43; Sacks, *Trade, Society and Politics*, vol. 1, p. 408.

98. Burrage, *Beginnings of Colonial Maine*, pp. 26, 142–43, 143n., 180n., 217–19.

99. Hakluyt, *Principal Navigations*, vol. 9, pp. 338ff., and vol. 10, p. 6; Connell-Smith, "English Merchants Trading to the New World," pp. 57–60.

100. Hakluyt, *Principal Navigations*, vol. 10, pp. 82–88, 193; I. A. Wright, ed., *Documents Concerning English Voyages to the Spanish Main, 1569–1580* (Hakluyt Society, 2d ser., 71, 1932), pp. 102–8, 187–88, 192–93, 196–99, 204, 208–10; PRO, E 190/1134/3; Sacks, *Trade, Society, and Politics*, vol. 1, pp. 412–13.

101. Quinn, *England and the Discovery of America*, pp. 139, 143–47; G. P. Winship, *Cabot Bibliography, with an Introductory Essay on the Careers of the Cabots* (New York: Dodd, Mead, 1900), pp. xvii–xviii; Biggar, *Precursors of Jacques Cartier*, pp. 134–42; PRO, SP 12/115/35, 122/62; George Best, *The Three Voyages of Martin Frobisher in Search of a Passage to Cathay and India*

by the North-west, A.D. 1576–8, 2 vols., ed. Vilhjalmur Stefansson and Eloise E. McCaskill (London: Argonaut Press, 1938), vol. 2, pp. 109–10, 123–26; David B. Quinn, ed., *The Voyages and Colonizing Enterprises of Sir Humphrey Gilbert,* 2 vols. (Hakluyt Society, 2d ser., 83–84, 1940), vol. 2, pp. 347, 350–51; Miller Christy, ed., *The Voyages of Captain Luke Foxe of Hull and Captain Thomas James of Bristol in 1631–32,* 2 vols. (Hakluyt Society, 88–89, 1894), vol. 1, pp. cxxxiv–clxviii, 455, 456, 594.

102. T. S. Willan, *The Moscovy Merchants of 1555* (Manchester: Manchester University Press, 1953), p. 118; T. S. Willan, *The Early History of the Russia Company, 1553–1603* (Manchester: Manchester University Press, 1956); Sacks, *Trade, Society and Politics,* vol. 2, pp. 735–37; MacInnes, *Gateway of Empire,* pp. 74–86; McGrath, ed., *Merchants and Merchandise,* p. 51n.; Alfred Lewis Pinneo Dennis, "Captain Martin Pring: Last of the Elizabethan Seamen," in *Tercentennary of Martin Pring's First Voyage to the Coast of Maine, 1603–1903* (Portland, Maine: Maine Historical Society, 1905), pp. 24ff.

103. See W. E. Minchinton, "Bristol—Metropolis of the West in the Eighteenth Century," *TRHS,* 5th ser., 4 (1954): 69–85.

CHAPTER 2

1. For general discussion see B. E. Supple, *Commercial Crisis and Change, 1600–1642: A Study in the Instability of a Commercial Economy* (Cambridge: Cambridge University Press, 1959), chap. 7; Clay, *Economic Expansion,* vol. 2, pp. 108–41.

2. See, e.g., Reddaway and Ruddock, *Accounts of John Balsall,* pp. 1–29; for an early sixteenth-century example of this form of trading see Vanes, ed., *Overseas Trade of Bristol,* pp. 58–59.

3. Malvezin, *Histoire du Commerce de Bordeaux,* vol. 2, p. 199.

4. Carus-Wilson, ed., *Overseas Trade of Bristol,* pp. 218–89; see also Sherborne, *Port of Bristol,* p. 27; David Harris Sacks, "The Demise of the Martyrs: The Feasts of St. Clement and St. Katherine in Bristol, 1400–1600," *Social History* 11 (1986): 157.

5. *LRB,* vol. 2, pp. 1–22, 29–30, 38–41, 51–55, 59–61; Ephraim Lipson, *The History of the Woollen and Worsted Industries* (London: A. and C. Black, 1921), p. 79; Sacks, *Trade, Society and Politics,* vol. 1, pp. 121–23.

6. *LRB,* vol. 2, pp. 5, 7–9, 15–16, 29–30, 39, 53.

7. *LRB,* vol. 2, pp. 7–16; cf. pp. 51–53.

8. Ibid., pp. 7–8, and compare the names there to T. P. Wadley, ed., *Notes or Abstracts of the Wills Contained in the Volume Entitled The Great Orphan Book and Book of Wills in the Council House at Bristol* (Bristol: Bristol and Gloucestershire Archaeological Society, 1886), pp. 12, 18, 26, 28, 32, 35, 52, 55, 75, 78, 103–4, 110; compare *LRB,* vol. 2, pp. 10–12 to pp. 51–53; see also Carus-Wilson, ed., *Overseas Trade of Bristol,* pp. 180–89; *Calendar of the Patent Rolls* (1330–1334), p. 29; *Calendar of the Patent Rolls* (1334–1338), p. 268; for fifteenth-century developments in the organization of the textile industry, see Veale, ed., *Great Red Book,* vol. 4, pp. 27, 29, 30, 126, 157–62; vol. 8, pp. 53, 66–69; vol. 16, pp. 121–24.

9. Lipson, *History of the Woollen and Worsted Industries*, p. 221.

10. *LRB*, vol. 1, pp. 114–15; compare to Wadley, ed., *Great Orphan Book*, passim, and the surviving commercial records printed in Carus-Wilson, ed., *Overseas Trade of Bristol*; see also Sacks, "Demise of the Martyrs," pp. 159–60.

11. Carus-Wilson, *Medieval Merchant Venturers*, pp. 73–97; Worcestre, *Itineraries*, pp. 130–33.

12. Sacks, *Trade, Society and Politics*, vol. 2, p. 759.

13. BRO, *Old Ordinance Book*, ff. 1^r, 33^r; F. F. Fox and John Taylor, eds., *Some Account of the Guild of Weavers in Bristol, Chiefly from MSS.* (Bristol: William George's Sons, 1889), pp. 69, 70–71, 97–99; Sacks, *Trade, Society and Politics*, vol. 1, pp. 134–36, 433–45, and vol. 2, pp. 478–79, 506.

14. Sacks, *Trade, Society and Politics*, vol. 2, pp. 469–78, 496, 507–9; for discussion of differing occupational structures, see W. G. Hoskins, "English Provincial Towns in the Early Sixteenth Century," *TRHS*, 5th ser., 6 (1956): 13–14; Hoskins, *The Age of Plunder*, chap. 4; John Patten, *English Towns, 1500–1700* (Hamden, Conn.: Archon Books, 1978), chap. 4; Palliser, *The Age of Elizabeth*, pp. 205, 238, 242–46, 251, 392–93; J. F. Pound, "The Social and Trade Structure of Norwich, 1525–1575," *Past and Present*, no. 34 (July 1966): 49–69; A. D. Dyer, *The City of Worcester in the Sixteenth Century* (Leicester: Leicester University Press, 1973), esp. pp. 81–92; L. A. Clarkson, *The Pre-Industrial Economy in England, 1500–1750* (London: B. T. Batsford, 1971), pp. 80–81, 88–92; D. M. Palliser, *Tudor York* (Oxford: Oxford University Press, 1979), chap. 6.

15. *L. and P.*, Addendum, part 1, p. 238.

16. For the course of Bristol's population history in the medieval and early modern periods see Sacks, *Trade, Society and Politics*, vol. 1, p. 205 and chap. 5 passim.

17. Vanes, ed., *Ledger of John Smythe*, pp. 315–17.

18. PRO, E 190/1129/11, 1129/12, 1135/6.

19. *Marchants Avizo*, p. 55; for a similar view see Gerard Malynes, *Consvetvdo, vel, Lex Mercatoria, or The Antient Law-Merchant, Diuided into three parts; According to the Essentiall parts of Traffike. Necessarie for All Statesmen, Iudges, Magistrates, Temporall and Ciuile, Lawyers, Mintmen, Merchants, Mariners and all others negotiating in all places of the World* (London, 1636), p. 156.

20. On the etymology of merchant "venturer" and merchant "adventurer," see Carus-Wilson, *Medieval Merchant Venturers*, pp. xv–xvi.

21. John Whitson, *The Aged Christians Final Farewell to the World and Its Vanities*, ed. George Symmes Calcott (Bristol, 1729), pp. 31–32. Internal evidence suggests that this work was written in the summer or fall of 1626; see Patrick V. McGrath, *John Whitson and the Merchant Community of Bristol* (Historical Association, Bristol Branch, Pamphlet 25, 1970), pp. 4, 16–17.

22. McGrath, ed., *Merchants and Merchandise*, pp. 80–89; W. K. Jordan, *The Forming of the Charitable Institutions of the West of England, 1480–1660* (Transactions of the American Philosophical Society, n.s. 1, part 8, 1960), p. 24n.43.

23. See, e.g., PRO, SP 14/97/96; PRO, STAC 8/49/15, 174/15.

24. See above, p. 60; Vanes, ed., *Ledger of John Smythe*, pp. 315–17. There are one hundred twenty-six entries on the list, but one is "the Wilsones," making the total at least one hundred twenty-seven.

25. More is said about the political background and significance of this list below, pp. 97–99.

26. Vanes, ed., *Ledger of John Smythe*, pp. 14–15, 20, 89, 127–28, 169, 177, 235, 254, 280, 295.

27. Ibid., pp. 58, 96–97, 108, 128–29, 256, 270.

28. Ibid., pp. 9, 191.

29. Ibid., pp. 67–68, 95, 96, 105–6, 127, 128–29, 139, 196, 217, 225.

30. Ibid., pp. 46, 52–53, 58, 60–61, 95–96, 127–28, 137–38, 147–48, 227–29, 263–64, 301.

31. Ibid., pp. 34–35, 125, 141, 151, 181–82, 251, 252.

32. Ibid., pp. 19–20, 67–69, 127–29, 228–29, 253.

33. For reason to believe that the documents printed by Browne derive from an actual trading venture see the introductory remarks by Patrick McGrath in *Marchants Avizo*, pp. xiv–xvi.

34. See C. R. Cheney, ed., *Handbook of Dates for Students of English History* (London: Offices of the Royal Historical Society, 1961), pp. 10–11.

35. *Marchants Avizo*, pp. xiv–xvi, xxv, 13, 14–16, 34, 53–54.

36. Ibid., pp. 18–19, 28–43.

37. Ibid., pp. 16–19, 47.

38. Ibid., pp. 16–18, 49–53. For an account of the working of bills of exchange see Raymond de Roover, *L'Evolution de la Lettre de Change, XIVe–XVIIIe Siècles* (Paris: A. Colin, 1953); Raymond de Roover, *Gresham on Foreign Exchange: an essay on early English mercantilism with the text of Sir Thomas Gresham's memorandum for the understanding of the exchange* (Cambridge, Mass.: Harvard University Press, 1949), pp. 94–172.

39. Willan, *Elizabethan Foreign Trade*, pp. 3–4; Vanes, ed., *Overseas Trade of Bristol*, pp. 98–99, 128–29; L. C. Wroth, "An Elizabethan Merchant and Man of Letters: John Frampton," *Huntington Library Quarterly* 17 (1953–54): 302–3; McGrath, ed., *Merchants and Merchandise*, pp. xvi–xvii, 175–76; *High Court of Admiralty Examinations (MS Volume 53), 1637–1638*, ed. Dorothy O. Shilton and Richard Holworthy, with an introduction by Eric G. M. Fletcher, Anglo-American Records Foundation Publications, vol. 2 (Washington, D.C.: Frome, 1932), pp. 15, 186, 276.

40. Vanes, ed., *Overseas Trade of Bristol*, pp. 117–22.

41. See PRO, E 190/1136/8, 1136/10; McGrath, ed., *Merchants and Merchandise*, p. 175.

42. McGrath, ed., *Merchants and Merchandise*, p. xix; Malynes, *Lex Mercatoria*, p. 145.

43. Malynes, *Lex Mercatoria*, p. 151.

44. PRO, C 1/406/5, 3/210/87; McGrath, ed., *Merchants and Merchandise*, pp. 5, 6; PRO, E 190/1136/8, 1136/10; PRO, REQ 2/167/27, REQ 2/286/52, among others.

45. PRO, SP 16/39/50 ii, 137/4; Patrick V. McGrath, "Merchant Venturers and Bristol Shipping in the Early Seventeenth Century," *Mariner's Mirror* 36 (1950): 69–80; Patrick V. McGrath, "Merchant Shipping in the Seventeenth

Century: The Evidence of the Bristol Deposition Books," *Mariner's Mirror* 40 (1954): 282–93; 41 (1955): 23–27; McGrath, ed., *Merchants and Merchandise*, pp. xix, 207–14.

46. For discussion of this method of accounting, see Jean Vanes, "Sixteenth-Century Accounting," *The Accountant* 155 (1967): 357–67; Vanes, ed., *Ledger of John Smythe*, pp. 16–22; F. C. Lane, *Andrea Barbarigo, Merchant of Venice, 1419–1449* (Johns Hopkins Studies in Historical and Political Science, ser. 62, 1, 1944), pp. 153–81; F. C. Lane, "Venture Accounting in Medieval Business Management," *Bulletin of the Business History Society* 19 (1945): 168, 173; A. H. Woolf, *A Short History of Accountants and Accountancy* (London: Gee, 1912), pp. 117–18; B. S. Yamey, "Scientific Bookkeeping and the Rise of Capitalism," *EcHR*, 2d ser., 1 (1949): 111–12.

47. PRO, E 134/12 Jac. I/Mich. 42; Sacks, *Trade, Society and Politics*, vol. 2, pp. 735–37.

48. The Parliamentary Diary of John Holles, 1624, BL, Harl. MS 6383, f. 91ᵛ; I have used the Yale University Center for Parliamentary History transcript, pp. 38–39. See also the Parliamentary Diary of John Pym, 1624, Northampton Record Office, Finch-Hatton MS 50, f. 22, Yale University Center for Parliamentary History transcript, p. 79.

49. McGrath, ed., *Merchants and Merchandise*, pp. 90–92.

50. The Parliamentary Diary of John Holles, 1624, BL Harl. MS 6383, f.92ʳ, Yale University Center for Parliamentary History transcript, p. 39.

51. *Marchants Avizo*, pp. 22–25.

52. Ibid., p. 10.

53. Ibid., pp. xi–xiii, 18–19, 48; Vanes, ed., *Ledger of John Smythe*, pp. 4, 13, 20, 89–90, 168–69, 279–80, 287, 295–96; SMV, *Book of Trade*, pp. 53–54, 207.

54. Vanes, ed., *Ledger of John Smythe*, pp. 90–92, 105–6, 131–32, 144–46, 211–12; on the sources for lead exports see Ian Blanchard, "English Lead and the International Bullion Crisis of the 1550's," in D. C. Coleman and A. H. John, eds., *Trade, Government and Economy in Pre-Industrial England: Essays Presented to F. J. Fisher* (London: Weidenfeld and Nicolson, 1976), p. 22.

55. Veale, ed., *Great Red Book*, vol. 8, pp. 50–52, 58–60; vol. 16, pp. 80–82; BRO, *Old Ordinance Book*, ff. 5ʳ⁻ᵛ, 6ʳ⁻ᵛ, 8ʳ, 25ʳ⁻ᵛ, 39ʳ, 57ᵛ, 63ᵛ, and loose paper dated 19 Eliz. I; Elizabeth Ralph, ed., *Great White Book of Bristol* (BRS, vol. 32, 1979), pp. 112–16; Sacks, *Trade, Society and Politics*, vol. 1, pp. 112ff., and vol. 2, pp. 520–26.

56. Veale, ed., *Great Red Book*, vol. 16, pp. 60–61; Robert Latham, ed., *Bristol Charters, 1509–1899* (BRS, vol. 12, 1947), pp. 58, 83–84, 116–18; *L. and P.*, Addendum 1, pp. 238–39; Leadam, ed., *Select Cases before the Star Chamber*, vol. 2, pp. 248ff.; Vanes, ed., *Overseas Trade of Bristol*, pp. 31–32. On the economic and financial functions of the fairs and their persistence, see Vanes, ed., *Ledger of John Smythe*, pp. 4–5; Johnson, *Drapers of London*, vol. 2, pp. 251ff.; Connell-Smith, "Ledger of Thomas Howell," pp. 363–70; G. D. Ramsay, ed., *John Isham, Mercer and Merchant Adventurer: Two Account Books of a London Merchant in the Reign of Elizabeth I* (Northamptonshire Record Society 21, 1962), p. xxiv; PRO, SP 16/343/25, 343/25i; Corporation

of London, *Analytical Index to the Series of Records Known as the Remembrancia Preserved among the Archives of the City of London* (London: E. J. Francis, 1878), pp. 345–46; Minchinton, "Bristol," p. 80; Sacks, *Trade, Society and Politics*, vol. 2, pp. 513–20.

57. Henry Bush, ed., *Bristol Town Duties: A Collection of Original and Interesting Documents, Intended to Explain and Elucidate the Above Important Subject* (Bristol: J. M. Gutch, 1828), pp. 57–60; Vanes, ed., *Ledger of John Smythe*, pp. 33–34, 81–82, 293, 308; Fox and Taylor, eds., *Guild of Weavers*, p. 93.

58. Fox and Taylor, eds., *Guild of Weavers*, p. 93; Vanes, ed., *Ledger of John Smythe*, pp. 80–81.

59. PRO, SP 15/20/19.

60. PRO, STAC 8/49/15.

61. Wadley, ed., *Great Orphan Book*, pp. 243, 263; BRO, *Great Orphan Book*, vol. 2, ff. 2^v–3^v 143^r–144^v, and vol. 3, 188^r–89^v; BRO, MS 09467 (13a); Gloucester Record Office, Dyrham Park MSS, D. 1799 T. 36.

62. Malynes, *Lex Mercatoria*, p. 226; T. S. Willan, *The Inland Trade: Studies in English Internal Trade in the Sixteenth and Seventeenth Centuries* (Manchester: Manchester University Press, 1976), pp. 68–91, 93.

63. See Vanes, ed., *Ledger of John Smythe*, pp. 34, 59, 103, 123, 151, 162, 198, 214, 234, 296; Willan, *Inland Trade*, pp. 67, 93–94, 124–26.

64. PRO, SP 12/131/87.

65. SMV, *Hall Book*, vol. 1, p. 2.

66. Malynes, *Lex Mercatoria*, p. 152.

67. *Marchants Avizo*, pp. 28, 36, 63nn. 51 and 54.

68. PRO, SP 15/20/19.

69. See J. W. Burgon, *The Life and Times of Sir Thomas Gresham*, 2 vols. (London: R. Jennings, 1839), vol. 1, p. 493.

CHAPTER 3

1. Raymond Firth, *Elements of Social Organization: Josiah Mason Lectures Delivered at the University of Birmingham*, 3d ed. (Boston: Beacon Press, 1961), pp. 30, 33.

2. Peter M. Blau and W. Richard Scott, *Formal Organizations: A Comparative Approach* (London: Routledge and Kegan Paul, 1963), p. 2.

3. Firth, *Elements of Social Organization*, pp. 36–40.

4. Blau and Scott, *Formal Organizations*, p. 5. The classic definition of "formal organization" is to be found in Chester Barnard, *The Function of the Executive* (Cambridge, Mass.: Harvard University Press, 1938), pp. 65–95.

5. See Charles Gross, *The Gild Merchant: A Contribution to British Municipal History*, 2 vols. (Oxford: Clarendon Press, 1890), vol. 1, p. 49.

6. Veale, ed., *Great Red Book*, vol. 16, pp. 82–84; Latimer, *Merchant Venturers*, pp. 16–18; McGrath, ed., *Records*, p. x; Patrick V. McGrath, *The Merchant Venturers of Bristol: A History of the Society of Merchant Venturers of the City of Bristol from Its Origins to the Present Day* (Bristol: Society of Merchant Venturers of Bristol, 1975), pp. 6, 8; Gross, *Gild Merchant*, vol. 1, pp.

45–46. The histories of previous organizations are associated primarily with the old Gild Merchant. A fraternity of merchants was founded in 1370 by one hundred and forty of the richest and most worthy townsmen, together with "plus ours aultres merchauntz et drapers," for the purpose of regulating the sale of cloth in Bristol and of controlling dealings with strangers who frequented the town. But this was merely a reform of the Gild Merchant and, after 1372, when the gild's right to admit freemen was successfully defended, there was no further reference to it. In the late Middle Ages, merchants were also organized through the Staple and its court in Bristol: *LRB*, vol. 2, pp. 51–55; Stella Kramer, *The English Craft Gilds: Studies in Their Progress and Decline* (New York: Columbia University Press, 1927), p. 29; Gross, *Gild Merchant*, vol. 2, pp. 353–55; Cronne, ed., *Bristol Charters, 1378–1499*, pp. 64–65; McGrath, ed., *Records*, p. ix n. 2.

7. Veale, ed., *Great Red Book*, vol. 16, pp. 120–30; McGrath, *Merchant Venturers of Bristol*, p. 7. Nevertheless, the city's leading merchants may have maintained some institutional association throughout the later fifteenth century. In 1493, thirteen of the most prominent of them joined together with thirteen mariners to build a new chapel in honor of St. Clement on what was later to be the site of the Merchants' Hall and Almshouse. But it is by no means certain that the thirteen merchants were performing their charitable work on behalf of an existing gild or society. The years between 1467 and 1499 yield no solid evidence of the activities of any such company nor any record of the election of a master or other officers: *LRB*, vol. 2, pp. 186–92; Latimer, *Merchant Venturers*, pp. 19–21; McGrath, ed., *Records*, pp. x, xi, 66; McGrath, *Merchant Venturers of Bristol*, p. 6 and 6n. 20.

8. Latimer, *Merchant Venturers*, pp. 26–35. For a discussion of the implications of the new city charter of 1499, see Sacks, *Trade, Society and Politics*, vol. 1, pp. 45–101; Sacks, "The Corporate Town and the English State," pp. 86–87; Latham, ed., *Bristol Charters, 1509–1899*, pp. 1–19.

9. Latimer, *Merchant Venturers*, p. 26; Veale, ed., *Great Red Book*, vol. 8, pp. 57–60.

10. Latimer, *Merchant Venturers*, p. 30. Many other clauses point in this same direction. For example, it was ordered that no merchant or other burgess of the city send any wine, wax, woad, iron, or other merchandise out of the city without being able to demonstrate that it had first been sold in open market or had been explicitly requested by a letter from an out-of-town customer; ibid., pp. 27–28. Rules were also laid down governing the treatment to be accorded all vessels arriving in Bristol laden with wine, wax, iron, woad, cochineal, oil, or any other merchandise shipped by strangers. Bristolians were forbidden to receive these goods and store them for their owners without the consent of the assembled fellowship: Gross, *Gild Merchant*, vol. 1, pp. 48–50.

11. Latimer, *Merchant Venturers*, pp. 32–33.

12. Ibid., pp. 32–33.

13. Ibid., p. 27.

14. Ibid., p. 35. The intent was to avoid time-consuming and socially disruptive suits.

15. Ibid., pp. 21–22; BRO, *Old Ordinance Book*, esp. ff. 2^r–3^v.

16. Carr, ed., *Select Charters of the Trading Companies,* pp. 1–3; Connell-Smith, *Forerunners of Drake,* pp. 67, 70, 76, 81–82, 90–97; Pauline Croft, ed., *The Spanish Company* (London Record Society 9, 1973), p. viii.

17. Connell-Smith, *Forerunners of Drake,* pp. 82, 89.

18. Connell-Smith, *Forerunners of Drake,* pp. 94–97; Croft, ed., *Spanish Company,* p. viii.

19. Chaunu, *Séville et l'Atlantique,* vol. 8, part 2, section 1, pp. 244–47, 273, 298.

20. Ibid., vol. 8, part 2, section 1, pp. 248–49, 299; Connell-Smith, "English Merchants Trading to the New World," pp. 53–67; Connell-Smith, *Forerunners of Drake,* pp. 70–75.

21. Chaunu, *Séville et l'Atlantique,* vol. 8, part 2, section 1, p. 307; Hamilton, *American Treasure,* pp. 189, 198.

22. Hamilton, *American Treasure,* pp. 321, 340–41.

23. Ibid., p. 261.

24. See Gould, *Great Debasement,* pp. 81–86, 94, 96, 133ff.; C. E. Challis, *The Tudor Coinage* (Manchester: Manchester University Press, 1978), pp. 81–134, 223–31; C. E. Challis, "The Circulating Medium and the Movement of Prices in Mid-Tudor England," in Peter Ramsey, ed., *The Price Revolution in Sixteenth Century England* (London: Methuen, 1971), pp. 117–33, 134–35, 139, 146; C. E. Challis, "Currency and the Economy in Mid-Tudor England," *EcHR,* 2d ser., 25 (1972): 313–22; Albert Feaveryear, *The Pound Sterling: A History of English Money,* 2d ed., rev. E. Victor Morgan (Oxford: Clarendon Press, 1963), pp. 64–69; Y. Brenner, "The Inflation of Prices in Early Sixteenth-Century England," in Ramsey, ed., *Price Revolution,* p. 78; de Roover, *Gresham on Foreign Exchange,* pp. 49–60; Fisher, "Commercial Trends and Policy in Sixteenth Century England," pp. 155–57; Stone, "State Control," p. 106; Sacks, *Trade, Society and Politics,* vol. 2, pp. 583–85.

25. De Roover, *Gresham on Foreign Exchange,* pp. 57–58; Gould, *Great Debasement,* pp. 85, 90, 91–93; Stone, "State Control," p. 106.

26. Stone, "State Control," p. 106.

27. Unfortunately, the absence of local trade statistics for 1551 and 1552 makes it impossible to know the exact course of events there. By 1553–54, however, Bristol's cloth exports were 18.1 percent below the average figure for 1549–1551, a decline that continued at a precipitous rate until the end of the decade: Sacks, *Trade, Society and Politics,* vol. 2, pp. 583, 902n. 39.

28. When the Bristol Corporation struck its deal with Sadler, it apparently was concerned to maintain the charitable functions associated with the chapel, particularly the care of poor seamen. But this act canceled the authority of the thirteen merchants and the thirteen mariner feoffees who had previously held the property. Among the first recorded acts of the newly founded Society of Merchant Venturers was its effort to recover the property directly from Sadler. In October 1553 the property passed by deed to Edward Pryn, one of the founders of the Society and at the time its first master. Pryn appears to have been acting in a private capacity and not as the Society's agent. He later resold it to the Society. But by 1561 the Merchants' Almshouse, called St. Clement's Almshouse, was already on the site, which suggests that the Society's association with Pryn's

purchase of the property was close and that it had been in possession, if not ownership, for some time; *LRB*, vol. 2, pp. 186–92; Latimer, *Merchant Venturers*, pp. 18–21; McGrath, ed., *Records*, pp. 66, 96; SMV, *Merchants Records*, Box 5, Bundle A2; William Barrett, *The History and Antiquities of the City of Bristol; Compiled from Original Records and Authentic Manuscripts in the Public Record Office or Private Hands Illustrated with Copper-Plate Prints* (Bristol: W. Pine, 1789), p. 180; Sacks, *Trade, Society and Politics*, vol. 2, pp. 903–4nn. 51–52.

29. Edgeworth, *Sermons*, f. 43ᵛ. At the time this collection was printed, Edgeworth was canon of the cathedral churches of Salisbury, Wells, and Bristol, and resident at Wells, where he was also chancellor. The sermon from which this quote comes was part of a series on the "Seven Gifts of the Holy Ghost" preached at St. Mary, Redcliffe, sometime during the years 1544–47.

30. See also below, pp. 125–26.

31. Latimer, *Merchant Venturers*, p. 42.

32. Ibid., pp. 42–43.

33. Ibid., p. 43.

34. Ibid., p. 44.

35. Ibid., pp. 44–45.

36. Ibid., p. 45.

37. See above, p. 61. The Bristol merchants were not alone in this period in seeking to exclude retailers and artisans from overseas trade; see, e.g., W. E. Lingelbach, *The Merchant Adventurers of England: Their Laws and Ordinances, with Other Documents* (Translations and Reprints from the Original Sources of European History, Department of History, University of Pennsylvania, 2d ser., vol. 2, 1902), pp. 111–16; Burgon, *Life and Times of Sir Thomas Gresham*, vol. 1, p. 464; Woodward, *Trade of Elizabethan Chester*, p. 74; W. Cotton, *An Elizabethan Guild of the City of Exeter* (Exeter: W. Pollard, 1873), pp. 6, 15–16; MacCaffrey, *Exeter, 1540–1640*, p. 137.

38. See above, pp. 62–66.

39. *APC* (1550–52), p. 485.

40. See D. Hollis, ed., *Calendar of the Bristol Apprentice Book, 1532–1565.* Part 1: *1532–1542* (BRS 14, 1949); Elizabeth Ralph and Nora M. Hardwick, eds., *Calendar of the Bristol Apprentice Book, 1532–1565.* Part 2: *1542–1552* (BRS 33, 1980); BRO, *Apprenticeship Book, 1552–1565.*

41. F. F. Fox, *Some Account of the Ancient Fraternity of Merchant Taylors of Bristol, with Transcripts of Ordinances and Other Documents* (Bristol: J. Wright, 1880), pp. 40–54, 68; Veale, ed., *Great Red Book*, vol. 16, pp. 64–69; Sacks, *Trade, Society and Politics*, vol. 1, pp. 132–33.

42. Fox and Taylor, eds., *Guild of Weavers*, pp. 91–92.

43. Latimer, *Merchant Venturers*, pp. 68, 71–75, 79–80; Sacks, *Trade, Society and Politics*, vol. 2, pp. 631–33.

44. Patrick V. McGrath, "The Society of Merchant Venturers and the Port of Bristol," *BGAS* 72 (1953): 105–28; McGrath, ed., *Records*, pp. xli, 135–75; McGrath, *Merchant Venturers of Bristol*, pp. 70–77.

45. McGrath, ed., *Records*, pp. 176–98.

46. Ibid., pp. 96–116.

47. McGrath, ed., *Records*, p. xxxvii.

48. SMV, *Book of Trade*, p. 119.

49. From 1552 to 1639 the Society acquired three such patents from the Crown: Latimer, *Merchant Venturers*, pp. 39–47, 88–97.

50. See Sacks, *Trade, Society and Politics*, vol. 2, pp. 634ff.

51. SMV, *Book of Trade*, pp. 67–68, 95–96. In a pattern typical of state concessions, the patent belonged to Richard Williams and David Lewis, who assigned a portion of it to William Harbett and Thomas Morgan. Harbett then made independent arrangements for shipping the butter with Henley and Henley with the Bristolians.

52. Ibid., pp. 170–75, 237–38.

53. SMV, *Book of Trade*, pp. 104ff.

54. McGrath, ed., *Records*, pp. 110, 111–12.

55. Ibid., p. 112.

56. BRO, *Common Council Proceedings*, vol. 2, f. 96^r; see also Sacks, *Trade, Society and Politics*, vol. 2, p. 918n. 67.

57. SMV, *Book of Trade*, p. 123; see also Preston, "Fishing and Plantation," pp. 29–43.

58. SMV, *Book of Trade*, p. 111; McGrath, ed., *Records*, pp. 207ff.

59. PRO, SP 15/22/19; *Marchants Avizo*, pp. 10, 11; Latimer, *Merchant Venturers*, p. 77; Malynes, *Lex Mercatoria*, pp. 81–86; Willan, *Elizabethan Foreign Trade*, pp. 3–4; Sacks, *Trade, Society and Politics*, vol. 2, pp. 546–50.

60. Cf. *A Relation, Or Rather a True Account, of the Island of England; with Sundry Particulars of the Customs of these People and of the Royal Revenues under King Henry the Seventh, about the Year 1500*, ed. and trans. C. A. Sneyd (Camden Society 37, 1847), pp. 24–25; Lawrence Stone, *The Family, Sex and Marriage in England, 1500–1800* (New York: Harper and Row, 1977), pp. 106–8.

61. The sources for this study are Hollis, ed., *Bristol Apprentice Book*, part 1, and BRO, *Apprenticeship Book*, 1626–1636, ff. 1–333. Although ordinarily each apprenticeship enrollment identifies the trade of the apprentice's father and that of his master, such occupational classifications did not exclude an individual from engaging in other kinds of work from time to time. Where there was no gild to enforce the boundaries between trades, or where large investments in tools or capital equipment were not necessary, it was possible to move from trade to trade. Some small shopkeepers, for example, maintained fairly diversified stocks that would qualify them for inclusion in more than one category. For example, William Adams, Bristol's seventeenth-century chronicler, was identified during his lifetime as a haberdasher, an ironmonger, and a mercer. Occasionally individuals are listed as having multiple occupations, such as Thomas Howell "hooper ac bruer" or Richard Browne "haberdasher atque wierdrawer": BRO, *Mayor's Audit* (1600–1601), p. 138; BRO, MS 09467 (13a); Hollis, ed., *Bristol Apprentice Book*, part 1, pp. 115, 125, 195; Willan, *Inland Trade*, pp. 61ff. But since in general an occupational identification in the indentures gives the central focus of an individual's economic activities, we can safely use it for our present purpose.

62. See above, pp. 57–59 and Table 8; Sacks, *Trade, Society and Politics*, vol. 1, pp. 205, and vol. 2, p. 760.

63. Sacks, *Trade, Society and Politics*, vol. 2, pp. 480–81, 663.

64. Ibid., pp. 478–79, 496, 505, 506, 759–60. Note that the cappers of 1532–1542 had disappeared as an occupational category by 1626; their craft had broken up into haberdashers, on the retail side, and feltmakers, on the production side. Feltmaking appears to have been a growth industry in Bristol in the early seventeenth century.

65. Sacks, *Trade, Society, and Politics*, vol. 2, pp. 479–80, 506–7, 760–61.

66. See below, pp. 147–53; Sacks, *Trade, Society and Politics*, vol. 2, pp. 487–88.

67. The actual figures for Bristolians apprenticed in the same occupation as their fathers are: 1532–1542, 23.94 percent; 1626–1636, 34.79 percent. The figures for those apprenticed in the same industry but not the same occupation are: 1532–1542, 18.94 percent; 1626–1636, 14.12 percent. Together, these two sets of figures total: 1532–1542, 42.23 percent and 1626–1636, 48.91 percent. See Sacks, *Trade, Society and Politics*, vol. 2, pp. 670–72.

68. The consequences of these methodological difficulties for the overall picture of social mobility are small. Even if we move everyone in a "borderline" craft, such as whitawing, into the category of "leading entrepreneur," the opportunities for social advancement would still appear greater in the early sixteenth than in the early seventeenth century. The more restricted definition we have employed in determining the composition of this category is better suited to our present purposes, however, since it results in something of an overestimation, rather than an underestimation, of mobility in Bristol. If those manufacturers who relied on heavy capital investment or produced for the national market were all included with the merchants, major retailers, and soapmakers, the apprenticeship of their sons to leading entrepreneurs would be counted in favor of heightened exclusivity, not increased openness.

69. For further discussion of this evidence see Sacks, *Trade, Society and Politics*, vol. 2, pp. 672–79.

70. BRO, *Burgess Book*, 1607–1651, passim; see also Sacks, *Trade, Society and Politics*, vol. 2, pp. 706–8.

71. See Sacks, *Trade, Society and Politics*, vol. 2, p. 759.

72. See above, p. 60.

73. For the general history of consumer industries and retailing see Willan, *Inland Trade*, pp. 50–106; Joan Thirsk, *Economic Policy and Projects: The Development of a Consumer Society in Early Modern England* (Oxford: Clarendon Press, 1978).

74. See Sacks, *Trade, Society and Politics*, vol. 2, p. 495. The other groups were food producers and woodworkers.

75. Gross, *Gild Merchant*, vol. 1, p. 157.

76. Ibid., p. 10, and vol. 2, pp. 24–27, 353–55; Latimer, *Merchant Venturers*, pp. 1–7.

77. Latimer, *Merchant Venturers*, pp. 30, 33.

78. George Unwin, *Industrial Organization in the Sixteenth and Seventeenth Centuries*, 2d ed. with intro. by T. H. Ashton (London: Frank Cass, 1963), pp. 73, 96.

79. Edgeworth, *Sermons*, ff. 210^v, 211^{r-v}.

CHAPTER 4

1. John Northbrooke, *Spiritus est Vicarius Christi in terra: A Treatise wherein Dicing, Dauncing, Vaine playes, or Enterluds, with other idle pastimes, &c., commonly vsed on the Sabboth day, are reproued by the Authoritie of the word of God and auntient writers* (London, [1577]). The Shakespeare Society edition, ed. J. P. Collier (Shakespeare Society 16, 1843), has been used here; see pp. 15, 44, 52, 90. Northbrooke served as minister of St. Mary, Redcliffe, Bristol from 1568 and was an important figure in the city's religious life in the 1570s: Thomas Tanner, *Bibliotheca Brittanico-Hiberica* (London: G. Bowyer, 1748), p. 550. The Company of Stationers of London records the license for printing on 2 December 1577: E. Arber, ed., *A Transcript of the Register of the Company of Stationers of London, 1554–1640*, 5 vols. (New York: P. Smith, 1949–1950), vol. 2, p. 321. I am grateful to Katherine Pantzer of the Houghton Library, Harvard University, for advice on the history of this text.

2. John Latimer, *Sixteenth-Century Bristol* (Bristol: J. W. Arrowsmith, 1908), pp. 5–6.

3. Ibid.

4. Northbrooke, *Treatise*, p. 12.

5. Robert Ricart, *The Maire of Bristowe Is Kalendar*, BRO, MS 04720 (1). The Camden Society edition has been used here; see p. 69. For Ricart's background, see ibid., p. i.

6. Northbrooke, *Treatise*, pp. 11–13.

7. Paul Hughes and James Larkin, eds., *Tudor Royal Proclamations*, 3 vols. (New Haven: Yale University Press, 1964–1969), vol. 1, pp. 301–2; see also David Wilkins, ed., *Concilia Magnae Britanniae et Hiberniae, a Synodo Verolamiensi A.D. CCCCXLVI. ad Londinensem A.D. MDCCXVII. Accedunt constitutiones et alia ad historiam Ecclesiae Anglicanae spectantia*, 4 vols. (London: Sumptibus R. Gosling, 1737), vol. 3, pp. 823–24, 857, 859–60.

8. John Strype, *Ecclesiastical Memorials Relating Chiefly to Religion and the Reformation of It, Shewing the Various Emergencies of the Church of England under King Henry VIII, King Edward VI and Queen Mary I*, 3 vols. in 6 (Oxford: Clarendon Press, 1822), vol. 3, part 2, p. 506, and see also pp. 8–9, 14–15, 17, 18, 21, 22; J. G. Nichols, ed., *The Diary of Henry Machyn, Citizen and Merchant-Taylor of London, from A.D. 1550 to A.D. 1563* (Camden Society, 1st ser., 42, 1848), p. 119. For the efforts of Catholic apologists in Bristol to revive the traditional forms of religious observation, see Paul Bush, *A brefe exhortation set fourthe by the vnprofitable seruant of Jesu christ Paule Bushe, late bishop of Brystowe, to one Margarite Burges, wyfe of John Burges, clotheare of kyngeswode in the Countie of Wiltshire* (London, 1556); Edgeworth, *Sermons* (London, 1557); see also K. G. Powell, *The Marian Martyrs and the Reformation in Bristol* (Historical Association, Bristol Branch, pamphlet 31, 1972). For the Elizabethan reaction to this effort at revival, see Wilkins, ed., *Concilia Magnae Britanniae*, vol. 4, pp. 182–91, 196–97, 211–14; F. E. Brightman, *The English Rite being a Synopsis of the Sources and Revisions of the Book of Common Prayer*, 2d rev. ed., 2 vols. (London: Rivingtons, 1921), vol. 1, pp. 98–101. J. J. Scarisbrick has argued that popular support for the

traditional forms of lay piety persisted long into the sixteenth century: J. J. Scarisbrick, *The Reformation and the English People* (Oxford: Blackwell, 1984); see also Christopher Haigh, "Revisionism, the Reformation and the History of English Catholicism," *Journal of Ecclesiastical History* 36 (1985): 394–406; Christopher Haigh, ed., *The English Reformation Revised* (Cambridge: Cambridge University Press, 1987). A. G. Dickens has responded to these criticisms of his views in "The Early Expansion of Protestantism in England, 1520–1558", *Archiv für Reformationsgeschichte* 73 (1987): 187–222. For a systematic consideration of this debate and a telling response to some of the claims of Scarisbrick and Haigh, see Patrick Collinson, *The Birthpangs of Protestant England: Religious and Cultural Change in the Sixteenth and Seventeenth Centuries* (New York: St. Martin's Press, 1988), esp. chaps. 2, 4; see also Robert Whiting, *The Blind Devotion of the People: Popular Religion and the English Reformation* (Cambridge: Cambridge University Press, 1989), esp. chap. 13.

9. For criticisms along these lines see, e.g., Ozment, ed., *Three Behaim Boys,* pp. xi–xiii.

10. Edgeworth, *Sermons,* f. 214^r.

11. Putnam, *Meaning and the Moral Sciences,* pp. 42, 43–44. I have given further attention to some of these issues in "The Hedgehog and the Fox Revisited," pp. 267–80.

12. See Cronne, ed., *Bristol Charters, 1378–1499,* pp. 64–69, 73–80; Gross, *Gild Merchant,* vol. 1, chaps. 2–4, and vol. 2, pp. 24–25, 353–55; Susan Reynolds, *An Introduction to the History of English Medieval Towns* (Oxford: Clarendon Press, 1977), chaps. 4–5; Sacks, *Trade, Society and Politics,* vol. 1, chap. 1.

13. See N. Dermott Harding, ed., *Bristol Charters, 1155–1373* (BRS 1, 1930), pp. 120ff.; Cronne, ed., *Bristol Charters, 1378–1499,* pp. 40–56; Martin Weinbaum, *The Incorporation of Boroughs* (Manchester: Manchester University Press, 1937), pp. 54–56; Sacks, *Trade, Society and Politics,* vol. 1, pp. 22ff.

14. Carus-Wilson, *Medieval Merchant Venturers,* pp. 1–97; M. D. Lobel and E. M. Carus-Wilson, "Bristol," in M. D. Lobel, ed., *Historic Towns* (London: Lovell Johns—Cook, Hammond and Kell Organization, 1975), pp. 1–16; Sherborne, *Port of Bristol;* C. D. Ross, "Bristol in the Middle Ages," in C. M. MacInnes and W. E. Whitterd, eds., *Bristol and the Adjoining Counties* (Bristol: Bristol Association for the Advancement of Science, 1955), pp. 179–92; see also Sacks, *Trade, Society and Politics,* vol. 1, chaps. 1–6.

15. *LRB,* vol. 1, p. 51; for a later version of the oath preserving most of its original terms, see McGrath, ed., *Merchants and Merchandise,* pp. 26–27.

16. Mariners were itinerant merchants, and their gild was closely associated from the earliest days with Bristol's sedentary merchants; see above, p. 90; Latimer, *Merchant Venturers,* pp. 19–21.

17. *LRB,* vol. 2, pp. 2–6; Fox and Taylor, eds., pp. 10–14. On the history of Bristol's governing council, see Cronne, *Bristol Charters, 1378–1499,* pp. 50, 73–83. It was only in 1344 that Bristol acquired a council of forty-eight, broadly representative of the leading men in the textile trades: *LRB,* vol. 1, pp. 25ff. And only in 1373 did its council become a body consisting of mayor, sher-

iff, and forty of "the better and more worthy men" of the borough: Harding, ed., *Bristol Charters, 1155–1373,* pp. 136–37. An earlier attempt to set up a select council of fourteen in Bristol had led to a rebellion in the city: see E. A. Fuller, "The Tallage of Edward II and the Bristol Rebellion," *BGAS* 19 (1894–1895): 171–278, esp. pp. 191ff.; Seyer, *Memoirs,* vol. 2, pp. 89ff.; John Latimer, ed., *Calendar of the Charters &c. of the City and County of Bristol* (Bristol: W. C. Hemmons, 1909), pp. 42ff.

18. Latimer, *Merchant Venturers,* p. 19n.

19. John Leland, *The Itinerary of John Leland in or about the Years 1535–1543,* ed. Lucy Toulmin Smith, 5 vols. (Carbondale, Ill.: Southern Illinois University Press, 1964), vol. 3, p. 101.

20. See Lobel and Carus-Wilson, "Bristol"; for further discussion see Sacks, *Trade, Society and Politics,* vol. 2, pp. 482ff.

21. Cronne, ed., *Bristol Charters, 1378–1499,* pp. 35–39.

22. Ralph, ed., *Great White Book,* pp. 17–67; Latham, ed., *Bristol Charters, 1509–1899,* pp. 21–22, 27–29, 93–94; *VCH Gloucestershire,* vol. 2, p. 78; John Britton, *The History and Antiquities of the Abbey and Cathedral Church of Bristol* (London: Longman, Rees, Orme, Brown and Green, 1830), pp. 21–22; PRO, STAC 2/6/93–94; Latimer, *Sixteenth-Century Bristol,* pp. 16–18.

23. Ricart, *Kalendar,* p. 80; Fox and Taylor, *Guild of Weavers,* pp. 10–14.

24. Gross, *Gild Merchant,* vol. 1, pp. 43–45; *LRB,* vol. 1, pp. 36–38.

25. See above, pp. 20–21; Carus-Wilson, *Medieval Merchant Venturers,* pp. 28–49; Sacks, *Trade, Society and Politics,* vol. 1, chap. 6.

26. John Brand, *Observations on Popular Antiquities: Chiefly Illustrating the Origin of Our Vulgar Customs, Ceremonies and Superstitions,* ed. Henry Ellis, 5 vols. (London: C. Knight, 1841–1842), vol. 1, pp. 408–14, 461–66; A. R. Wright, *British Calendar Customs: England,* ed. T. E. Lones, 3 vols. (London: W. Glaisher, 1936–1940), vol. 3, pp. 167ff.

27. Ricart, *Kalendar,* p. 80.

28. Arnold van Gennep, *The Rites of Passage,* trans. Monika B. Vizedom and Gabrielle L. Caffee (Chicago: University of Chicago Press, 1960); Victor Turner, *The Ritual Process: Structure and Anti-Structure* (Ithaca: Cornell University Press, 1969), esp. chaps. 3–5; Victor Turner, *Dramas, Fields and Metaphors: Symbolic Action in Human Society* (Ithaca: Cornell University Press, 1974), chaps. 1, 5–7; Victor Turner, *The Forest of Symbols* (Ithaca: Cornell University Press, 1967), chap. 4; Victor Turner, *The Drums of Affliction: A Study of Religious Processes among the Ndembu of Zambia* (Oxford: Clarendon Press, 1968), chap. 9. See also Edmund Leach, "Time and False Noses," in Edmund Leach, *Rethinking Anthropology* (London: Athlone Press, 1961), pp. 132–38.

29. Ricart, *Kalendar,* p. 80.

30. Ibid., pp. 68ff.

31. See Charles Phythian-Adams, "Ceremony and the Citizen: The Ceremonial Year at Coventry, 1450–1550," in Peter Clark and Paul Slack, eds., *Crisis and Order in English Towns, 1500–1700: Essays in Urban History* (London: Routledge and Kegan Paul, 1972), pp. 59, 62–63; Mervyn James, "Ritual, Drama and Social Body in the Late Medieval English Town," *Past and Present* no. 98 (February 1983): 1–29.

32. See Phythian-Adams, "Ceremony and the Citizen," pp. 63–65; James, "Ritual, Drama and Social Body," pp. 16–21.

33. Ricart, *Kalendar*, p. 80; Richard Braithwait, *The History of Moderation* (London, 1669), pp. 10, 12, 15. See also John Wycliffe, *On the Seven Deadly Sins*, in John Wycliffe, *Select English Works of John Wyclif*, ed. Thomas Arnold, 3 vols. (Oxford: Clarendon Press, 1871), vol. 3, pp. 160–61; Edgeworth, *Sermons*, ff. 231^v–232^r; William Prynne, *Healthes: Sicknesse or, a Compendious and Briefe Discourse, Prouing the Drinking and Pledging of Healthes to be Sinfull, and Vtterly Unloawfull unto Christians* (London, 1628), p. 25; Samuel Ward, *Woe to the Drunkard*, in Samuel Ward, *A Collection of Such Sermons as have beene written by S. Warde* (London, 1636), p. 553; Brand, *Popular Antiquities*, vol. 2, pp. 338–39.

34. Ricart, *Kalendar*, p. 80.

35. Turner, *Ritual Process*, pp. 94–95 and chaps. 3–5.

36. Ricart, *Kalendar*, p. 80.

37. Jacobus Voraigne, *The Golden Legend; or Lives of the Saints as Englished by William Caxton*, ed. F. S. Ellis, 7 vols. (London: J. M. Dent, 1900), vol. 7, pp. 1–31; S. Baring-Gould, *Lives of the Saints: November*, 2d ed. (London: J. Hodges, 1877), part 2, pp. 540–43; E. K. Chambers, *The Medieval Stage*, 2 vols. (Oxford: Clarendon Press, 1903), vol. 2, pp. 205–27, 393, 396–402; Joseph Strutt, *Sports and Pastimes of the People of England from the Earliest Period*, ed. J. Charles Cox (London: Methuen, 1903), pp. 201–3, 269; Brand, *Popular Antiquities*, vol. 1, pp. 411–14, 461–66; William Hone, *The Every-Day Booke and Table Book*, 3 vols. (London: T. Tegg, 1830), vol. 1, pp. 1501–8. See also Wright, *British Calendar Customs*, vol. 3, pp. 177, 179, 180–85; John Nurse Chadwick, "Rope makers' procession at Catham," *Notes and Queries*, 2d ser., 5, no. 107 (16 January 1858): 47; Charles Lamotte, *Essay on Poetry and Painting* (London: F. Fayram and J. Leare, 1730), p. 126; James Orchard Halliwell-Phillipps, *Popular Rhymes and Nursery Tales* (London: J. R. Smith, 1849), p. 238; John Noake, *Notes and Queries for Worcestershire* (Birmingham, Eng.: n.p., 1861), pp. 215–16; R. A[llies], "Worcestershire Folk-lore: Cathering and Clemening," *The Athenaeum* 1001 (2 January 1847): 18.

38. John Bossy, "The Mass as a Social Institution, 1200–1700," *Past and Present*, no. 100 (August 1983): 29–61; John Bossy, *Christianity in the West, 1400–1700* (New York: Oxford University Press, 1985), pp. 64–72; see also Susan Brigden, *London and the Reformation* (Oxford: Clarendon Press, 1989), esp. chaps. 9, 14; Susan Brigden, "Religion and Social Obligation in Early Sixteenth-Century London," *Past and Present*, no. 103 (May 1984): 67–112.

39. See Peter Brown, *The Cult of the Saints: Its Rise and Function in Latin Christianity* (Chicago: University of Chicago Press, 1981); Bossy, *Christianity in the West*, pp. 11–13, 72–73; Keith Thomas, *Religion and the Decline of Magic: Studies in Popular Beliefs in Sixteenth- and Seventeenth-Century England* (London: Weidenfeld and Nicolson, 1971), pp. 26–29, and cf. pp. 40–44; Scarisbrick, *Reformation and the English People*, pp. 12, 20, 39, 41, 54–55, 59, 170–71, 180; Collinson, *Birthpangs of Protestant England*, pp. 28–29, and cf. pp. 37–38, 50, 52–53; J. A. F. Thomson, "Piety and Charity in Late-Medieval London," *Journal of Ecclesiastical History* 16 (1965): 178–95; A. N. Galpern, *The*

Religions of the People in Sixteenth-Century Champagne (Cambridge, Mass.: Harvard University Press, 1976), chap. 1; Alan Kreider, *English Chantries: The Road to Dissolution* (Cambridge, Mass.: Harvard University Press, 1979), chaps. 1–3. For the role of intercessory prayer in late medieval Bristol, see also Clive Burgess, " 'For the Increase of Divine Service': Chantries in the Parishes of Late Medieval Bristol," *Journal of Ecclesiastical History* 36 (1985): 46–85; Clive Burgess, "A Service for the Dead: The Form and Function of the Anniversary in Late Medieval Bristol," *BGAS* 105 (1987): 183–211; but compare Robert Whiting, "For the Health of My Soul: Prayers for the Dead in the Tudor South-West," *Southern History* 5 (1983): 68–94; Whiting, *Blind Devotion of the People*, chaps. 3–4; Peter Heath, "Urban Piety in the Later Middle Ages: The Evidence of Hull Wills," in Barrie Dobson, ed., *The Church, Politics and Patronage in the Fifteenth Century* (New York: St. Martin's Press, 1984), pp. 209–34.

40. Lucy Toulmin Smith identifies this map as Bristol in 1479, but from the context it is clear that it is a view of Bristol as founded by the mythical Trojan "Brynne" or Brennus: see Ricart, *Kalendar*, pp. 10–11.

41. Werner Müller, *Die heilige Stadt: Roma quadrata, himmlische Jerusalem und die Mythe vom Weltnabel* (Stuttgart: W. Kohlhammer, 1961).

42. Latimer, *Sixteenth-Century Bristol*, pp. 5–6; Robert Withington, *English Pageantry: An Historical Outline*, 2 vols. (Cambridge, Mass.: Harvard University Press, 1918–1920), vol. 1, pp. 21–22 and 22n.; E. O. James, *Seasonal Feasts and Festivals* (New York: Barnes and Noble, 1961), pp. 223–25; *LRB*, vol. 2, pp. 145–52; Veale, ed., *Great Red Book*, vol. 4, pp. 125–26; "A shorte and briefe memory by license and correcion of the first progress of our soueraigne lorde King Henry the VIIth," printed in John Leland, *De rebus Brittanicus, Collecteanea*, ed. Thomas Hearne, 3 vols. in 4 (London: Gvl. and J. Richardson, 1770), vol. 4, p. 202. See also Phythian-Adams, "Ceremony and the Citizen," pp. 58ff.; James, "Ritual, Drama and Social Body," pp. 5ff.; Bossy, "The Mass as a Social Institution," pp. 50, 59.

43. See, e.g., *LRB*, vol. 2, pp. 117–22, 147–50.

44. John Tucker Murray, *English Dramatic Companies, 1558–1642*, 2 vols. (London: Constable, 1910), vol. 2, pp. 207–19. The first evidence of these companies of players appears in the earliest extant audit book of the city's accounts, which dates from 1532. In all probability the practice of welcoming these traveling companies began somewhat earlier. The last entries in the audit books for payments to players before the closing of the theaters in 1642 is for the year 1634–1635, but the number of entries is much less frequent after 1603 than it was in the later sixteenth century. In part this may be due to the existence on Wine Street in Bristol of a regular playhouse for performances. It appears to have been opened sometime before 1605 and to have continued in operation into the later 1620s. See Kathleen M. D. Barker, "An Early Seventeenth Century Provincial Playhouse," *Theatre Notebook* 29 (1975): 81–84; Mark C. Pilkington, "The Playhouse in Wine Street, Bristol," *Theatre Notebook* 37 (1983): 14–21; Mark C. Pilkington, "New Information on the Playhouse in Wine Street, Bristol," *Theatre Notebook* 42 (1988): 73–74; Kathleen M. D. Barker, *Bristol at Play: Five Centuries of Live Entertainment* (Bradford-on-Avon, Eng.:

Moonraker Press, 1976), pp. 3–4. I thank Irven Matus for these references and for directing me to this subject.

45. Hughes and Larkin, *Tudor Royal Proclamations*, vol. 1, pp. 301–2.

46. Brightman, *English Rite*, vol. 1, pp. 98–101.

47. Edgeworth, *Sermons*, esp. ff. 209^v, 218^v.

48. Thorne's will is printed in Veale, ed., *Great Red Book*, vol. 16, pp. 124–29. See Scarisbrick, *Reformation and the English People*, chaps. 1–2, 7; and n. 8 above. For Bush see J. H. Bettey, "Paul Bush, the First Bishop of Bristol," *BGAS* 106 (1988): 169–72.

49. Edgeworth, *Sermons*, ff. 40^r, 84^v–85^r, 131^v–132^r, 157^v–158^r, 179^v–180^r, 214^v, 235^{r-v}, 273^r–274^r.

50. See, along with Northbrooke's *Treatise* against dicing, dancing, and vain plays, Thomas Thompson, *A diet for a Drunkard, Deliuered in two Sermons at St Nicholas Church in Bristoll Anno Domini 1608* (London, 1612); Edward Chetwyn, *The Strait Gate and the Narrow Way of Life opened and pointed out in certain sermons upon Luke 12, 23, 24* (London, 1612), esp. p. 4; Edward Chetwyn, *Votitiae Lachrymae; A Vow of Teares for the losse of Prince Henry in a Sermon in the Citie of Bristol, December 7, 1612 being the Day of his funerall* (London, 1612). For the effects of the Reformation and other sixteenth-century developments on popular festivities and practices, see Imogen Luxton, "The Reformation and Popular Culture," in Felicity Heal and Rosemary O'Day, eds., *Church and Society in England: Henry VIII to James I* (London: Macmillan, 1977), pp. 57–77; W. J. Sheils, "Religion in Provincial Towns: Innovation and Tradition," in Heal and O'Day, *Church and Society*, pp. 156–76; Phythian-Adams, "Ceremony and the Citizen," pp. 70–80; Peter Burke, *Popular Culture in Early Modern Europe* (London: Temple Smith, 1978), chap. 8; James, "Ritual, Drama and Social Body," pp. 3–29; Collinson, *Birthpangs of Protestant England*, chaps. 2, 4; Brigden, *London and the Reformation*, chap. 14 and pp. 633–39; Whiting, *Blind Devotion of the People*. Mervyn James, relying on the work of Charles Phythian-Adams, attributes many of the changes to the so-called urban crisis in the late fifteenth and early sixteenth centuries; see Phythian-Adams, "Urban Decay," Phythian-Adams, *Desolation of a City*. I have expressed some reservations about Burke's and James's arguments in "Demise of the Martyrs," pp. 143–44, 165–69, and about Phythian-Adams's view of the relation of urban crisis to cultural change in my review of his book in *Journal of Modern History* 54 (1982): 105–7; see also A. R. Bridbury, "English Provincial Towns in the Later Middle Ages," *EcHR*, 2d ser., 34 (1981): 1–24; Jennifer I. Kermode, "Urban Decline? The Flight from Office in Late Medieval York," *EcHR*, 2d ser., 35 (1982): 179–98.

51. Fox and Taylor, *Guild of Weavers*, pp. 18ff.; Latimer, *Merchant Venturers*, pp. 18–23; McGrath, *Merchant Venturers of Bristol*, pp. 17–18, and cf. pp. 18–20, 81–83, 203–4, 398–401, 521–25.

52. See Ralph, ed., *Great White Book*, pp. 17–67.

53. Latham, ed., *Bristol Charters, 1509–1899*, pp. 19ff., 94–111.

54. See Natalie Zemon Davis, "The Sacred and the Social Body in Sixteenth-Century Lyon," *Past and Present*, no. 90 (February 1981): 40–70.

55. Latham, ed., *Bristol Charters, 1509–1899*, pp. 21–22, 93–94.

56. See above, pp. 78–79.

57. See Carus-Wilson, *Medieval Merchant Venturers*, pp. 75–78; Wadley, ed., *Great Orphan Book*.

58. *LRB*, vol. 1, pp. 114–15 compared to Wadley, ed., *Great Orphan Book*.

59. The procedure followed here was to compare the list of common councillors to the wills in the *Great Orphan Book* and to the surviving commercial records printed in Carus-Wilson, ed., *Overseas Trade of Bristol*.

60. The figure of 48 percent is derived from PRO, E 301/22, Certificate of the Chantries in the County of Gloucester and the Cities of Bristol and Gloucester, 1548, printed in John MacLean, "Chantry Certificates, Gloucestershire (Roll 22)," *BGAS* 8 (1883): 232–51; see also Josiah Cox Russell, *British Medieval Population* (Albuquerque: University of New Mexico Press, 1948), p. 295; Sacks, *Trade, Society and Politics*, vol. 1, pp. 208–13. Analysis of these chantry certificates yields an overall population for Bristol in 1548 of approximately 9,500, about the same figure as W. G. Hoskins established for Bristol ca. 1525, using data from PRO, E 179/113/192. There is no reason to think that the distribution of the city's population by district would have changed between 1525 and 1548. See Hoskins, "English Provincial Towns," p. 5.

61. Cronne, ed., *Bristol Charters, 1378–1499*, pp. 163–204; Latham, ed., *Bristol Charters, 1509–1899*, pp. 1–19; Sacks, *Trade, Society and Politics*, vol. 1, chap. 2; Sacks, "The Corporate Town and the English State," pp. 91–92, 93ff.

62. Leadam, ed., *Select Cases before the Star Chamber*, pp. cii–cxxiv, 237–76; Vanes, ed., *Overseas Trade of Bristol*, pp. 31–32.

63. James, "Drama, Ritual and Social Body," p. 26.

64. Oxford University, Lincoln College, MS lat. 129, cited in Nicholas Orme, *Education in the West of England, 1066–1548: Cornwall, Devon, Dorset, Gloucestershire, Somerset, Wiltshire* (Exeter: University of Exeter, 1976), p. 40.

65. K. B. McFarlane, *The Origins of Religious Dissent in England* (New York: Collier, 1966), pp. 187–89; J. A. F. Thomson, *The Later Lollards, 1414–1520* (London: Oxford University Press, 1965), pp. 20–28, 33. Some of the names of these Bristol militants are available in PRO, K.B. 9/205/1, mm. 82–83.

66. For regulations requiring gildsmen to support their fraternities' religious functions, see, e.g., *LRB*, vol. 2, pp. 121–22 (weavers); for instances of fines paid in wax, see ibid., p. 59 (weavers) and Veale, ed., *Great Red Book*, vol. 18, pp. 82–84 (merchants).

67. The ideas of Wycliffe and his early followers can be gleaned from Anne Hudson, ed., *Selections from English Wycliffite Writings* (Cambridge: Cambridge University Press, 1978); Anne Hudson, *The Premature Reformation: Wycliffite Texts and Lollard History* (Oxford: Clarendon Press, 1988), esp. chaps. 6–8; see also McFarlane, *Origins of Religious Dissent*, chap. 4; Herbert B. Workman, *John Wycliffe: A Study of the English Medieval Church*, 2 vols. (Oxford: Clarendon Press, 1926), vol. 2, pp. 3–45, 149–55.

68. For Bristol Lollardy, see Thomson, *Later Lollards*, pp. 20–28, 33–35, 37, 39–40, 44, 46–47, 54, 65–66, 68, 99, 109, 114, 155, 209, 221, 240, 246; Hudson, *Premature Reformation*, pp. 78, 81, 89–90, 122–23, 125, 131, 133, 140–42, 144, 154, 172, 183, 188, 233, 234n., 456–57, 459. For Lollard views on saints and images, see Hudson, *Premature Reformation*, pp. 301–9; Margaret Aston, *England's Iconoclasts*, Volume 1: *Laws against Images* (Oxford: Clarendon Press, 1988), chap. 4; Margaret Aston, "Lollards and Images," in Margaret

Aston, *Lollards and Reformers: Images and Literacy in Late Medieval Religion* (London: Hambledon Press, 1984), pp. 135–92. On the character of later Lollard belief see also A. G. Dickens, *Lollards and Protestants in the Diocese of York, 1509–1558* (London: Oxford University Press, 1959), chaps. 1–2; A. G. Dickens, *The English Reformation* (London: B. T. Batsford, 1964), chap. 2; Thomson, *Later Lollards*, pp. 239–50; Margaret Aston, "Lollardy and Reformation: Survival or Revival?" in Aston, *Lollards and Reformers*, pp. 219–42; Hudson, *Premature Reformation*, pp. 456ff.; J. F. Davis, "Lollardy and the Reformation in England," *Archiv für Reformationsgeschichte* 73 (1982): 217–37. For the relation of Lollardy to political dissent, see Margaret Aston, "Lollardy and Sedition, 1381–1431," in Aston, *Lollards and Reformers*, pp. 1–47; Hudson, *Premature Reformation*, chap. 8.

69. See John Wycliffe, *The Grete Sentence of the Curs Expounded*, in Wycliffe, *Select English Works*, ed. Arnold, vol. 3, pp. 333–34.

70. *LRB*, vol. 2, pp. 117–21.

71. Ibid., pp. 121–22.

72. Veale, ed., *Great Red Book*, text, vol. 8, pp. 67–69.

73. Thomson, *Later Lollards*, pp. 34, 39–40, 44, 46–47, 109, 114, 155.

74. *LRB*, vol. 2, pp. 40–41, 125; Sacks, *Trade, Society and Politics*, vol. 2, pp. 442–43.

75. Sacks, *Trade, Society and Politics*, vol. 2, pp. 478–79, 509, 752–63.

76. *LRB*, vol. 2, pp. 117–22 (weavers), 147–50 (shoemakers). In the same period there is also a curious ordinance against those who "vilipend" the men of the Common Council: ibid., vol. 1, pp. 149–53.

77. Hugh Latimer, "Articles untruly, unjustly, falsely, uncharitably imparted to me by Dr Powell of Salisbury," in Hugh Latimer, *Sermons and Remains of Hugh Latimer, Sometime Bishop of Worcester, Martyr 1555*, ed. George Elwes Corrie (Parker Society 28, 1845), p. 233; see also "Letter of Hugh Latimer to Ralph Morrice, Mayor, June, 1533," in ibid., pp. 357ff. Much additional material bearing upon Latimer's preachings in Bristol and the controversies that followed is printed in John Foxe, *Acts and Monuments of the Christian Martyrs*, 8 vols. (New York: AMS Press, 1965), vol. 7, appendix 9. For a discussion of these events and a review of the religious issues raised, see Harold J. Darby, *Hugh Latimer* (London: Epworth Press, 1953), chap. 5; for analysis of official reaction to these disturbances, see G. R. Elton, *Policy and Police: The Enforcement of the Reformation* (Cambridge: Cambridge University Press, 1972), pp. 110ff. Further discussion must await the publication of Martha Skeeters's book on the history of the church in sixteenth-century Bristol.

78. Edgeworth, *Sermons*, f. 40^r.

79. This was also the fate of the feasts of St. Clement and St. Katherine in the west of England; see R. A[llies], "Worcester-shire Folk-lore," p. 18.

CHAPTER 5

1. This estimate is based on BRO, *Burgess Book* (1607–51). During the years covered by this book of enrollments an average of 97.30 freemen were ad-

mitted each year, rising from a mean of 72.00 in the years 1607–1611 and reaching a height of 126.25 in 1627–1631; see Sacks, *Trade, Society and Politics,* vol. 2, pp. 752–58. In the absence of accurate knowledge of age-specific death rates, detailed figures for life expectancy, or a reliable age pyramid for the city, it is not possible to work out precisely how many freemen would have been alive in any one year. But, given our estimates of Bristol's population, it seems plausible to think that the number might have been somewhere near two thousand in the early seventeenth century. On the number of Bristol burgesses, see ibid., vol. 2, pp. 468–69, 875n. 5. On the degree of participation in rule in urban settings, see Rappaport, *Worlds within Worlds,* chaps. 2, 6–8.

2. Sir Thomas Smith, *De Republica Anglorum: A Discourse of the Commonwealth of England,* ed. L. Alston (Cambridge: Cambridge University Press, 1906), pp. 41–42, 46.

3. Latham, ed., *Bristol Charters, 1509–1899,* pp. 26–30, 84–92, 94–111; W. R. Barker, *St. Mark's, or the Mayor's Chapel Bristol, Formerly Called the Church of the Gaunts* (Bristol: W. C. Hemmons, 1892); BRO, *Old Ordinance Book,* f. 54^{r-v}; BRO, *Common Council Proceedings,* vol. 1, pp. 52, 82, 108, 125, 128, 140, 147; vol. 2, ff. 5^r, 6^v, 7^{r-v}, 33^r, 48^{r-v}, 88^r; *Adams's Chronicle,* pp. 184–85; APC (1592–95), p. 120; Latimer, *Sixteenth-Century Bristol,* pp. 16–17, 98–99, 103–4; Latimer, *Annals,* pp. 29–31; Paul Seaver, *The Puritan Lectureships: The Politics of Religious Dissent, 1560–1662* (Stanford: Stanford University Press, 1970), pp. 99–100.

4. BRO, Deed 01075 (1); Latimer, *Annals,* pp. 97–98.

5. Cronne, ed., *Bristol Charters, 1378–1499;* BRO, *Common Council Proceedings,* vol. 3, f. 122^r; Latham, ed., *Bristol Charters, 1509–1899,* pp. 6–7; J. H. Thomas, *Town Government in the Sixteenth Century, Based Chiefly on the Records of the Following Provincial Towns: Cambridge, Chester, Coventry, Ipswich, Leicester, Lincoln, Manchester, Northampton, Norwich, Nottingham, Oxford, Shrewsbury* (London: G. Allen and Unwin, 1933), p. 34; see also Sacks, *Trade, Society and Politics,* vol. 1, chap. 2; Sacks, "The Corporate Town and the English State," pp. 87–88.

6. Cronne, ed., *Bristol Charters, 1378–1499,* pp. 167, 183; Latham, ed., *Bristol Charters, 1509–1899,* p. 4. I. S. Leadam has argued that the force of this clause, and of the charter in general, was to purge the old corporation of its Yorkist sympathizers. But this view would appear to go beyond the surviving evidence; see Leadam, ed., *Select Cases before the Star Chamber,* p. cv.

7. BRO, *Common Council Proceedings,* vol. 3, f. 122^r; see also Sacks, *Trade, Society and Politics,* vol. 2, pp. 693–94.

8. See Sacks, *Trade, Society and Politics,* vol. 2, p. 694.

9. Sacks, *Trade, Society and Politics,* vol. 2, pp. 694–706.

10. Curiously, the percentage of "merchants" among those who served as mayor fell from the first half of the sixteenth century to the second, and rose again in the early seventeenth century. Perhaps the relatively low figure for 1550–1600 conceals a number of grocers, drapers, and mercers who were in fact "mere merchants" and members of the Society of Merchant Venturers.

11. Sacks, *Trade, Society and Politics,* vol. 2, pp. 706–8.

12. PRO, PROB 6/88 Seager.

13. This paragraph and the following depend on the discussion in "Authority," a debate between R. S. Peters and Peter Winch in *Proceedings of the Aristotelian Society* 32 (1958): supplement, pp. 207–40, reprinted in Anthony Quinton, ed., *Political Philosophy* (Oxford: Oxford University Press, 1967), pp. 83–111. See also Richard Tuck, "Why Authority Is Such a Problem," in Peter Laslett, W. G. Runciman, and Quentin Skinner, eds., *Philosophy, Politics and Society*, 4th ser. (Oxford: Blackwell, 1972), pp. 194–207; Richard Flathman, *The Practice of Authority: Authority and the Authoritative* (Chicago: University of Chicago Press, 1980); Joseph Raz, *The Morality of Freedom* (Oxford: Clarendon Press, 1986), chaps. 2–4.

14. Winch, "Authority," p. 99; Tuck, "Why Authority Is Such a Problem," pp. 200–207.

15. Weber, *Theory of Economic and Social Organization*, p. 328; Peters, "Authority," pp. 86–87.

16. The classic expression in English of this view can be found in A. F. Pollard's chapter "The New Monarchy," in his *Factors in Modern History* (New York: G. Putnam's Sons, 1907), chap. 3. Among contemporary historians, G. R. Elton has done the most to explore the bureaucratic character of the emergent English state in the sixteenth century: see especially his *Tudor Revolution in Government: Administrative Change in the Reign of Henry VIII* (Cambridge: Cambridge University Press, 1953) and *England under the Tudors*, 2d ed. (London: Methuen, 1974), chap. 7. More generally, see H. R. Trevor-Roper, "The General Crisis of the Seventeenth Century," in Trevor Aston, ed., *Crisis in Europe: 1560–1660* (Garden City, N.Y.: Anchor Books, 1967), pp. 63–102. The implications of this view of the state for the treatment of provincial or local history are summarized in Finberg, *The Local Historian and His Theme*, pp. 5–8; Alan Everitt, "The County Community," in E. W. Ives, ed., *The English Revolution, 1600–1660* (New York: Harper and Row, 1971), pp. 48–63; Everitt, "The Local Community and the Great Rebellion," pp. 76–99; and Conrad Russell, *Parliaments and English Politics, 1621–1629* (Oxford: Clarendon Press, 1979), pp. 5–26.

17. Ricart, *Kalendar*, p. 70. See also *LRB*, vol. 2, pp. 46–47.

18. See Phythian-Adams, "Ceremony and the Citizen," pp. 57–85. On this point see also Edgeworth, *Sermons*, f. 282ᵛ, where priests are compared to aldermen, who have authority not because they are the eldest but "partely for their substaunce, and more for their honestye and sadnesse and wisdome."

19. Ricart, *Kalendar*, p. 70.

20. Ricart, *Kalendar*, pp. 70–71; Phythian-Adams, "Ceremony and the Citizen," p. 62.

21. Ricart, *Kalendar*, p. 71.

22. Ibid., p. 72n. For the much simpler oath used before 1373, see *LRB*, vol. 1, p. 46.

23. Ricart, *Kalendar*, pp. 72–74.

24. Ibid., p. 71.

25. Ibid., p. 72.

26. Ibid., p. 74.

27. Ibid., pp. 74–75.

28. See *Adams's Chronicle*, pp. 69–80; Ricart, *Kalendar*, pp. 42–49; "A shorte and briefe memory of the first progress," pp. 185–203. A somewhat sketchy account of King Edward IV's visit to Bristol in 1461 also survives; see F. J. Furnival, ed., *Political, Religious and Love Poems from the Archbishop of Canterbury's Lambeth Ms. No 306 and Other Sources* (Early English Text Society, orig. ser., 15, 1866), pp. 5–6.

29. John C. Meagher, "The First Progress of Henry VII," *Renaissance Drama*, n.s. 1 (1968): 45–73; Sydney Anglo, *Spectacle, Pageantry and Drama and Early Tudor Policy* (Oxford: Clarendon Press, 1969), pp. 21–45.

30. Leland, *De rebvs Britannicus*, vol. 4, p. 199.

31. Ibid., pp. 199–200.

32. It should perhaps be noted that Bristol's petition was not without effect. Two days after King Bremmius's speech, the king summoned the mayor, the sheriff, and other burgesses to inquire about the city's poverty and to offer various forms of aid. According to the herald who recorded these proceedings, "the Meyre of the Towne towlde me they hadde not this hundred yeres of noo King so good a Comfort. Wherfor they thanked Almighty God, that hath them soo good and gracious a Souveraige Lord": ibid., p. 202. See also Anglo, *Spectacle*, p. 34; Meagher, "First Progress of Henry VII," p. 72.

33. Geoffrey of Monmouth, *History of the Kings of Britain*, trans. Sebastian Evan, rev. ed. Charles W. Dunn, intro. Gwyn Jones, 2 vols. (London: Folio Society, 1958), vol. 1, pp. 46ff.; Acton Griscom, *The Historiam Regum Britanniae of Geoffrey of Monmouth with Contributions to the Study of Its Place in Early British History, Together with a Literal Translation of the Welsh Manuscript No. LXI of Jesus College, Oxford by Robert Ellis Jones* (London: Longmans, Green, 1929), pp. 276ff.; Helaine H. Newstead, *Bran the Blessed in Arthurian Romance* (New York: Columbia University Press, 1939), pp. 155–67; Frederich W. D. Brie, ed., *The Brut, or, The Chronicles of England* (Early English Text Society, orig. ser., 131, 1906), pp. 26–27; F. S. Haydon, ed., *Eulogium (historiarum sive temporis): Chronicon ad orbe condito usque ad annum Domini MCCCLXVI., a monacho quodam Malmesbriensi exaratum. Accendunt continuationes duae, quarum una ad annum MCCCXIII., altera ad annum MCCCXC perducta est*, 3 vols. (London: Longman, Brown, Green, Longman and Roberts, 1858–63), vol. 2, p. 242; Anglo, *Spectacle*, p. 33. Bremmius or Brennius is identified with the historical Brennus, who sacked Rome in 390 B.C. According to Ricart, after returning from his great victories abroad "Brynne first founded and billed this worshipfull Town of Bristut that nowe is Bristowe and set it vpon a litell hill, that is to say, bitweene Seint Nicholas yate, Seint Johnes yate, Seint Leonardes yate, and the Newe yate" (Ricart, *Kalendar*, p. 10). According to tradition, this Brennius first named the city he founded "Brenstou." On the founding of London and York, see Geoffrey of Monmouth, *Kings of Britain*, vol. 1, p. 7; vol. 2, p.7; Brie, ed., *Brut*, pp. 11, 15.

34. See Sydney Anglo, "The British History in Early Tudor Propaganda," *Bulletin John Rylands Library* 44 (1961–62): 17–48. Henry VII's "British" origins also played an important part in the pageants arranged for him at York and Worcester in 1486: ibid., pp. 27–28.

35. Leland, *De rebvs Britannicus*, vol. 4, p. 199.

36. See Sacks, "Demise of the Martyrs," pp. 146–55; James, "Ritual, Drama and Social Body," pp. 1–29.

37. Ricart, *Kalendar,* pp. 80, 85–86.

38. [John Gregory], *Episcopus Puerum in die Innocentium, Or, A Discovery of an Ancient Custom in the Church of Sarum Making an Anniversary Bishop among the Choristers* (London, 1649), in John Gurgany, ed., *Posthuma of John Gregory* (London, 1671), pp. 113–16; Christopher Wordsworth, ed., *Ceremonies and Processions of the Church of Salisbury* (Cambridge: Cambridge University Press, 1901), pp. 52–59; Daniel Rock, *The Church of Our Fathers as Seen in St. Osmund's Rite for the Cathedral of Salisbury,* ed. G. W. Hart and Witt Frere, 4 vols. (London: J. Hodges, 1903–1904), vol. 4, pp. 250–55; Christopher Wordsworth and Douglas MacLean, *Statutes and Customs of the Cathedral Church of the Blessed Virgin Mary of Salisbury* (London: W. Clowes and Sons, 1915), pp. 264–65, esp. "Roger de Mortivale's Code" (1319), p. 264. Gregory prints on the title page of his work and again on p. 117 a sketch of the Boy-Bishop statue found at Salisbury. It shows a youth in a bishop's robes, with mitre and crozier, offering a benediction while standing atop a dragon. The Boy-Bishop ceremony was practiced not only in the church but also at schools and colleges. For a useful survey of St. Nicholas's career as a saint from the days of the early Christians to the present, see Charles W. Jones, *Saint Nicholas of Myra, Bari and Manhattan: Biography of a Legend* (Chicago: University of Chicago Press, 1978). In general on the Boy-Bishop in England, see Brand, *Popular Antiquities,* vol. 1, pp. 421ff.; Strutt, *Sports and Pastimes,* pp. 272–73; G. L. Gomme, ed., *The Gentleman's Magazine Library: Manners and Customs* (London: Stock, 1883), p. 89; Wright, *British Calendar Customs,* vol. 3, pp. 194–97; J. G. Nichols, ed., *Two Sermons Preached by the Boy Bishop in St. Paul's, Temp. Henry VIII* [sic] *and at Gloucester, Temp. Mary,* intro. Edward F. Rimbault, *Camden Miscellany* 7 (Camden Society, new ser. 14, 1876), pp. v–xxxii; Chambers, *Medieval Stage,* vol. 1, chap. 15; R. T. Hampson, *Medii aevi Kalendarium, or Dates, Charters and Customs of the Middle Ages,* 2 vols. (London: H. K. Causton and Son, 1841), vol. 1, p. 80. See also Natalie Zemon Davis, *Society and Culture in Early Modern France: Eight Essays* (Stanford: Stanford University Press, 1975), pp. 97–123; Keith Thomas, *Rule and Misrule in the Schools of Early Modern England: The Stenton Lecture, 1975* (Reading: University of Reading, 1976).

39. Ricart, *Kalendar,* p. 46. It is not clear from which church or ecclesiastical house in Bristol this Boy-Bishop was selected. He might have been a chorister at St. Nicholas Church or have been attached to one of the monastic houses in the city. Bristol did not become a bishopric in its own right until 1542.

40. Unfortunately, no Boy-Bishop sermon has survived for Bristol, but at least two, and possibly three, such sermons do exist. The two that are certain date from the 1490s and 1555, respectively, and are printed in Nichols, ed., *Two Sermons,* pp. 1–29; the third is Desiderius Erasmus, *Concio de puero Iesu,* written at John Colet's request for St. Paul's School, circa 1510, which survives in an English edition of 1536, Desiderius Erasmus, *A Most Excellent Sermon and Full of Frute and Edificyon of the Childe Jesus* (London, 1536?); Desiderius Erasmus, *Erasmi Concio De Pvero Iesv: A Sermon on the Child Jesus by Desiderius Erasmus, in an Old English Version of Unknown Authorship,* ed. J. H.

Lupton (London: George Bell and Sons, 1901); see also Desiderius Erasmus, "Homily on the Child Jesus: Concio de piero Iesu," ed. and trans. Emily Kearns, in *Collected Works of Erasmus*, ed. Alexander Dalzell et al., vol. 29 (Literary and Educational Writings), ed. Elaine Fantham and Erika Rummel (Toronto: University of Toronto Press, 1989), pp. 51–70. In this little work Erasmus appears to be using the convention of the Boy-Bishop sermon to meet the needs of Colet's humanist program for St. Paul's School. But there are sufficient differences in emphasis to leave open whether this homily was really intended for use in anything like its traditional Boy-Bishop setting.

41. Geoffrey Chaucer, *The Works of Geoffrey Chaucer*, ed. F. N. Robinson, 2d ed. (Boston: Houghton Mifflin, 1957), *Canterbury Tales*, "The Pardoner's Tale," lines 463–76, 621–28; "The Franklin's Tale," lines 682–91; "The Shipman's Tale," lines 1492–96; "The Cookes Tale," lines 4365–422.

42. Thomas Elyot, *The Boke named The Gouernour*, ed. H. H. S. Croft, 2 vols. (London: K. Paul, Trench, 1883), vol. 1, p. 275. See also Northbrooke, *Treatise*, pp. 130ff.; Philip Stubbes, *The Anatomy of Abuses* (London, 1583), pp. 172–77.

43. Chaucer, *Works. Troilus and Criseyde*, Book 2, lines 1347–51; Book 4, lines 1093–99; *Canterbury Tales*, "The Knight's Tale," lines 1238–50.

44. Elyot, *The Boke named The Gouernour*, vol. 1, pp. 272–73.

45. Harding, ed., *Bristol Charters, 1155–1373*, pp. 136–37.

46. Chaucer, *Works. Canterbury Tales:* "The Pardoner's Tale," lines 591–602.

47. Nichols, ed. *Two Sermons*, pp. 5–6.

48. Thompson, *Diet for a Drunkard*, pp. 74–75.

49. Ibid., pp. 76–77.

50. Ibid., pp. 59–60, 75.

51. Ibid., p. 25.

52. BRO, *Seventeenth-Century Ordinance Book*, unpaginated frontispiece. This prayer dates from early in James I's reign, not later than 1612; it mentions prayers for Prince Henry.

53. BRO, *Old Ordinance Book*, f. 20ᵛ (1563). After 1564, at regular meetings of the council, held on the first Tuesday of each month, proper dress was gowns "of the gravest sort" and caps: ibid., ff. 61ᵛ, 67ʳ⁻ᵛ. Scarlet was reserved for formal occasions and was worn primarily to attend church services: BRO, *Common Council Proceedings*, vol. 1, p. 139; *Adams's Chronicle*, p. 185.

54. BRO, *Common Council Proceedings*, vol. 1, p. 167; Latimer, *Annals*, p. 30.

55. *Adams's Chronicle*, p. 182.

56. Ibid., pp. 183–84; Latimer, *Annals*, pp. 30–31.

57. *Adams's Chronicle*, pp. 113–14, 188–200; Churchyard, *Chippes*, ff. 100ᵛ–110ᵛ. Queen Anne of Denmark's visit is recounted in a long poem written by Robert Naile and copied into his *Chronicle* by Adams, who describes its author as an apprentice in the city.

58. *Adams's Chronicle*, pp. 113–14; we are told that "the rest of the council rode next before the nobility and trumpeters."

59. Churchyard, *Chippes*, ff. 100ᵛ, 106ᵛ. Bristol paid Churchyard £6 13s. 4d. for his efforts, and in all the city laid out almost a thousand pounds on this

three days of festivity: BRO, *Mayor's Audit* (1570–1574), p. 290; David M. Bergeron, *English Civic Pageantry, 1558–1642* (Columbia: University of South Carolina Press, 1971), pp. 26–27. Churchyard reports that some of the speeches at the end of the celebration "could not be spoken, by means of a Scholemaister, who enuied that any stranger should set forth these shoes": Churchyard, *Chippes*, f. 110^v. But in most instances the speeches were given, and in any case all were contained in the book presented to the queen.

60. Churchyard, *Chippes*, f. 102^r.

61. Ibid., ff. 103^r, 107^r.

62. Ibid., ff. 108^r [misnumbered in the text as f. 118]–109^r.

63. Ibid., f. 108^v; the punctuation of this passage has been altered to clarify the meaning.

64. Ibid., ff. 104^{r-v}, 101^v, 102^v.

65. Ibid., ff. 108^v–109^r.

66. Ibid., ff. 101^v, 102^r, 102^v, 103^v.

67. Ibid., f. 109^{r-v}.

68. Ibid., f. 109^v.

69. Ibid., ff. 101^r, 103^r, 105^r, 106^{r-v}, 109^v–110^r.

70. On this theme, see Bergeron, *English Civic Pageantry*, chap. 1; Roy Strong, *Art and Power: Renaissance Festivals, 1450–1650* (Berkeley and Los Angeles: University of California Press, 1984); Stephen Orgel, *The Illusion of Power: Political Theory in the English Renaissance* (Berkeley and Los Angeles: University of California Press, 1975); Francis Yates, *Astraea: The Imperial Theme in the Sixteenth Century* (London: Routledge and Kegan Paul, 1975), part 2; R. Malcolm Smuts, *Court Culture and the Origins of a Royalist Tradition in Early Stuart England* (Philadelphia: University of Pennsylvania Press, 1987), pp. 1–50, 73–116, 191–213, 245–92.

71. Thomas Palmer, *Bristol's Military Garden: A sermon Preached unto the worthy Company of Practitioners in the Military garden of the well Governed Citie of Bristoll* (London, 1635), p. 31.

72. Ibid., pp. 7–8.

73. Ibid., pp. 31–32.

74. Ibid., p. 32.

75. Mikhail Bakhtin, *Rabelais and His World*, trans. Hélène Iswolsky (Cambridge, Mass.: MIT Press, 1968), pp. 6, 9, 10. See also Turner, *Ritual Process*, esp. chap. 3 and pp. 168–70, 177–78, 200–203; Davis, *Society and Culture*, pp. 122–23.

76. Veale, ed., *Great Red Book*, vol. 4, pp. 125–26.

77. *Adams's Chronicle*, pp. 112–13.

78. Northbrooke, *Treatise*, p. 107.

CHAPTER 6

1. For a discussion of the persistence of these ideas into the post-Reformation era, see Mark A. Kishlansky, *Parliamentary Selection: Social and Political Choice in Early Modern England* (Cambridge: Cambridge University Press, 1986), chap. 1. For doubts about this interpretation, see David Harris

Sacks, "Searching for 'Culture' in the English Renaissance," *Shakespeare Quarterly* 39 (1988): 486–88; David Harris Sacks, "Parliament, Liberty, and the Commonweal," in J. H. Hexter, ed., *Parliament and Liberty from the Reign of Elizabeth to the English Civil War* (Stanford: Stanford University Press, 1992), pp. 85–121.

2. Russell, *Parliaments and English Politics*, p. 37.

3. Elizabeth I's confirmation is dated 8 July 1566; a translation from the Latin original appears in SMV, *Book of Charters*, vol. 1, p. 27; and both the original and translation are printed in Latimer, *Merchant Venturers*, pp. 46–47. The statute is 8 Eliz. I, c. 19, and is printed in ibid., pp. 47–50.

4. Latimer, *Merchant Venturers*, p. 49.

5. Ibid., pp. 49–50. The sanctions against illicit trading were severe: all goods conveyed "to or from beyond the seas" contrary to the original letters patent were to be forfeited, with half going to the Crown and the other half to be divided equally between the Society and the city Chamber.

6. Fox and Taylor, eds., *Guild of Weavers*, pp. 91–92.

7. John Neale, *Elizabeth I and Her Parliaments, 1559–1581* (London: Jonathan Cape, 1953), p. 177. Neale points out elsewhere that jockeying for a position in the Commons in the Elizabethan period ordinarily began at the first rumors of a new Parliament: John Neale, *The Elizabethan House of Commons* (New Haven: Yale University Press, 1950), p. 52.

8. BRO, *Old Ordinance Book*, f. 26^{r-v}. At the same time it was ordered that, in the future, nominations were to take place on St. Giles' Day (1 September), two weeks before the actual election, presumably to permit canvassing. But the provision for nominations on St. Giles' Day was repealed in the following year; ibid., f. 29^r. Otherwise the procedure laid down in this ordinance was the one followed thereafter. Nominations to office had previously been made by seniority, with each member of the Common Council, beginning with the mayor, nominating in turn. In most cases this meant that only the most senior members of the council ever made a nomination. The new arrangement provided for each rank in the council to have its own nominee: the outgoing mayor was to nominate one person for each post; the aldermen together with the sheriffs and those councillors who had previously been mayor were to name another slate; and the remainder of the council a third.

9. See Sacks, *Trade, Society and Politics*, vol. 2, p. 907n. 76.

10. Seyer, *Memoirs*, vol. 2, p. 243; John Evans, *A Chronological Outline of the History of Bristol* (Bristol: John Evans, 1824), p. 149. See also *Adams's Chronicle*, p. 112.

11. See PRO, SP 12/77/35; Bath MSS, *Dudley Papers*, vol. 1, ff. 224^r–225^r.

12. J. B. Davidson, "Hoker's Journal of the House of Commons in 1571," *Report and Transactions of the Devonshire Association for the Advancement of Science, Literature and Art* 11 (1879): 478. The version of Hooker's journal printed by T. E. Hartley omits this and several other passages relating to the Bristol bill printed by Davidson, presumably because the original document in the Devonshire Record Office had become even less legible than it was in the 1870s: see T. E. Hartley, ed., *Proceedings in the Parliaments of Elizabeth I*. Volume 1: *1558–1581* (Leicester: Leicester University Press, 1981), p. 243n. 1. G. R. Elton

offers a somewhat confused and unreliable discussion of this debate in his *The Parliament of England, 1559–1581* (Cambridge: Cambridge University Press, 1986), pp. 131–32. However, a subsequent remark on this same episode corrects the main error and provides the necessary citation: p. 257 and n. 201.

13. Hartley, ed., *Parliaments of Elizabeth I*, p. 209; see also *CJ*, vol. 1, p. 84; Simonds D'Ewes, *The Journals of all the Parliaments during the Reign of Queen Elizabeth, both of the House of Lords and the House of Commons* (London, 1682), p. 160.

14. Hartley, ed., *Parliaments of Elizabeth I*, p. 210; D'Ewes, *Journals of all the Parliaments*, p. 160. Francis Alford, a civil lawyer who was usually cautious and conservative, answered Fleetwood's point by saying that although "hee might not speak of the prerogative aptly for that hee was not learned in the lawe, but made some remembrance of what hee had there seene concerning the act of Parliament for Southampton [in 1562–63], whereby it appeared that without an act of Parliament her Majestie's letters patentes were not sufficient."

15. Hartley, ed., *Parliaments of Elizabeth I*, p. 210; D'Ewes, *Journals of all the Parliaments*, p. 160; Davidson, "Hoker's Journal," pp. 470–71.

16. D'Ewes, *Journals of all the Parliaments*, pp. 160–61; Hartley, ed., *Parliaments of Elizabeth I*, pp. 210–11. The MPs who spoke included Francis Alford, Edward Cleer, Sir Francis Knollys, Sir Nicholas Arnold, Sir Henry Norris, Mr. Christopher Yelverton of Gray's Inn, and John Popham: Hartley, ed., *Parliaments of Elizabeth I*, p. 211. For a discussion of the implications of Popham's argument see Sacks, "Parliament, Liberty and the Commonweal," pp. 93–100; David Harris Sacks, "Monopoly and Liberty in Elizabethan England," in Dale Hoak, ed., *Tudor Political Culture* (Cambridge: Cambridge University Press, forthcoming).

17. D'Ewes, *Journals of all the Parliaments*, p. 161.

18. *CJ*, vol. 1, p. 84; D'Ewes, *Journals of all the Parliaments*, p. 162; Hartley, ed., *Parliaments of Elizabeth I*, p. 247.

19. *CJ*, vol. 1, p. 84. The other members were Sir James Croft, Sir Nicholas Pointz, Sir John Thynne, Sir Nicholas Arnold, Sir John White of London, Mr. John Newton, Mr. Francis Alford, Mr. Thomas Norton, Mr. Hall of York, and Mr. John Hooker of Exeter.

20. Hartley, ed., *Parliaments of Elizabeth I*, p. 247; Davidson, "Hoker's Journal," p. 478; *CJ*, vol. 1, pp. 85, 86.

21. *LJ*, vol. 1, pp. 679, 689; BRO, *Old Ordinance Book*, f. 29^r. Our source tells us only of the bond imposed on Langley, but perhaps a similar bond was imposed on the Merchant Venturers. Unfortunately, we have no evidence as to what the order actually was.

22. *LJ*, vol. 1, p. 690.

23. Stat. 13 Eliz. I, c. 14, printed in Latimer, *Merchant Venturers*, p. 57.

24. Ibid.

25. Hartley, ed., *Parliaments of Elizabeth I*, p. 211.

26. PRO, SP 15/20/19.

27. *Marchants Avizo*, p. 5.

28. PRO, SP 15/20/19; a version is printed in Latimer, *Merchant Venturers*, p. 54.

29. William Shakespeare, *Troilus and Cressida*, ed. Kenneth Palmer, Arden Edition of William Shakespeare (London: Methuen, 1982), p. 129, Act 1, scene 3, lines 109–10.

30. Thomas Dekker, *The Shoemaker's Holiday*, ed. J. P. Steane (Cambridge: Cambridge University Press, 1965), esp. act 2, scene 3. See also Thomas Delony, *The Gentle Craft*, in *The Works of Thomas Delony*, ed. Francis Oscar Mann (Oxford: Clarendon Press, 1912), pp. 109–33. On the rules governing the occupations and trades of London freemen, see William Bohun, *Privilegia Londini: or, The rights, liberties, privileges, laws, and customs of the city of London*, 3d ed. (London: James Crokatt, 1723), pp. 178–82; Sylvia L. Thrupp, *The Merchant Class of Medieval London (1300–1500)* (Ann Arbor: University of Michigan Press, 1962), pp. 5–6; Sylvia L. Thrupp, "The Grocers of London: A Study of Distributive Trade," in Eileen Power and M. M. Postan, eds., *Studies in English Trade in the Fifteenth Century* (New York: Macmillan, 1933), pp. 261–72. The cases Bohun cites make clear that from the late sixteenth century, after the Statute of Artificers, the officials of London sought to narrow the freedom to trade so that only those apprenticed in an occupation that "useth buying and selling as Mercer, Grocer, may exercise another Trade of buying and selling." Hence a shoemaker, trained in a "manual craft," could not enter into trade. But in earlier days the custom seems to have been otherwise, and it is clear that craftsmen and others continued to claim the right to trade by wholesale throughout the seventeenth century. For a sketch of Simon Eyre's actual career, see Thrupp, *Merchant Class of London*, p. 339. Thrupp gives Eyre's original occupation as "upholder," which might mean "upholsterer" or simply "shopkeeper."

31. Fox and Taylor, eds., *Guild of Weavers*, pp. 92–93.

32. See Hartley, ed., *Parliaments of Elizabeth I*, p. 211. Popham's argument in 1571 approaches the view later articulated by such lawyers as Lawrence Hyde, Nicholas Fuller, Edward Coke, and Francis Moore; see n. 16 above.

33. PRO, SP 15/20/19.

34. *APC* (1558–1570), pp. 193–94; Sacks, *Trade, Society and Politics*, vol. 2, p. 908n. 96.

35. BRO, *Old Ordinance Book*, f. 29^{r-v}. We do not know how many councillors were present at this meet ing. The full membership of the council at this time was forty-three including the recorder (who appeared only occasionally, at the time of gaol delivery), but it was not unusual for there to be vacancies and absences at any given meeting. For example, on 12 September 1570 only thirty-seven members were present; there were even two absences among the aldermen. It is unlikely, however, that more than five members would be missing from the council at any one time. In other words, the twenty members who supported Langley on this occasion were just barely sufficient to carry the question.

36. For details, see Sacks, *Trade, Society and Politics*, pp. 606–7.

37. Latimer, *Sixteenth-Century Bristol*, p. 57.

38. BRO, *Old Ordinance Book*, f. 30^{r}; Latimer, *Sixteenth-Century Bristol*, p. 57.

39. BRO, *Old Ordinance Book*, f. 30^{v}.

40. *APC* (1577–78), p. 354; Croft, ed., *Spanish Company*, p. xiii.

41. PRO, SP 12/105/3.

42. Wroth, "Elizabethan Merchant," pp. 302–4; Croft, ed., *Spanish Company*, p. xi n. 4.

43. PRO, C 66/1158/2256, mm. 1–12, esp. mm. 4–5. The new company's jurisdiction also covered the entire Iberian peninsula, including Portugal, and it was granted wide powers to make binding ordinances for its membership and to punish interlopers. The charter is fully calendared in *Cal. Pat. Rolls, Eliz. I* (1575–1578), vol. 7, pp. 317–23, and extensive portions of the charter are printed in Shillington and Chapman, *Commercial Relations of England and Portugal*, pp. 313–26; see also Croft, ed., *Spanish Company*, pp. xii–xiii.

44. The original membership of the Spanish Company numbered 396, of whom 223 were Londoners and only 75 Bristolians: PRO, C 66/1158/2256, m. 2; *Cal. Pat. Rolls, Eliz. I*, vol. 7, p. 318; Croft, ed., *Spanish Company*, xiii, xvii. For discussion of the relationship of the Spanish Company branch with the Merchant Venturers, see Sacks, *Trade, Society and Politics*, vol. 2, pp. 913–14n. 6.

45. *APC* (1575–1577), p. 16.

46. *APC* (1577–1578), pp. 408–9.

47. On the dispute within Chester and between the Chester merchants and those of Liverpool, see Woodward, *Trade of Elizabethan Chester*, pp. 78–87; Croft, ed., *Spanish Company*, pp. xviii–xxi.

48. McGrath, ed., *Records*, pp. 81–84.

49. SMV, *Book of Trade*, p. 37; Croft, ed., *Spanish Company*, pp. xxviii–xxix.

50. Croft, ed., *Spanish Company*, pp. 1, 2, 4.

51. PRO, SP 14/21/41; McGrath, ed., *Records*, pp. 2–3; Croft, ed., *Spanish Company*, pp. xxviii–xxix, 14, 15–16, 18, 95–113; Shillington and Chapman, *Commercial Relations of England and Portugal*, pp. 161–62.

52. Croft, ed., *Spanish Company*, pp. 22–23.

53. Ibid., pp. 23–24.

54. Ibid., pp. 31, 47, 91–92.

55. See n. 30 above; McGrath, ed., *Records*, p. 26.

56. McGrath, ed., *Records*, pp. 18, 43, 46; Croft, "Free Trade and the House of Commons," p. 24.

57. Croft, "Free Trade and the House of Commons," pp. 21–22; Croft, ed., *Spanish Company*, p. 78.

58. Croft, ed., *Spanish Company*, pp. 42, 44–45.

59. Ibid., pp. 45–47.

60. Ibid., pp. 43, 46.

61. Ibid., pp. 55–56.

62. BRO, *Common Council Proceedings*, vol. 1, pp. 112–13; McGrath, ed., *Records*, pp. 3–5.

63. Ibid.

64. For the story of Hyde's appointment to the recordership and the outcries it aroused among the Common Council and Bristol's Merchant Venturers, see Sacks, *Trade, Society and Politics*, vol. 1, pp. 87–101; on the free-trade issue see T. K. Rabb, "Sir Edward Sandys and the Parliament of 1604," *AHR* 69 (1963–64), pp. 661–69; Robert Ashton, "The Parliamentary Agitation for Free Trade in the Opening Years of James I," *Past and Present*, no. 38 (December 1967);

T. K. Rabb, "Free Trade and the Gentry in the Parliament of 1604," *Past and Present*, no. 40 (July 1968), pp. 165–73; Robert Ashton, "Jacobean Free Trade Again," *Past and Present*, no. 43 (May 1969), pp. 151–57; Croft, "Free Trade and the House of Commons," pp. 17–27; Robert Ashton, *The City and the Court, 1603–1643* (Cambridge: Cambridge University Press, 1979), pp. 84–98.

65. BRO, *Common Council Proceedings*, vol. 2, f. 24^{r-v}; see also ibid., f. 25^r; Latimer, *Merchant Venturers*, p. 6n. 3; McGrath, ed., *Records*, p. 8.

66. McGrath, ed., *Records*, p. 8; Latimer, *Merchant Venturers*, p. 67; Kramer, *English Craft Gilds*, p. 31n. 30.

67. Latimer, *Merchant Venturers*, pp. 75–76. For an account of the procedures followed to assure the effectiveness of these rules, see Sacks, *Trade, Society and Politics*, vol. 2, p. 629.

68. Latimer, *Merchant Venturers*, p. 75.

69. Ibid., pp. 78–79.

70. McGrath, ed., *Records*, pp. 26–27.

71. Christopher Whitson was admitted to the freedom of the city of Bristol as a redemptioner in 1610, and a year later was selected to serve on the Common Council. His occupation at the time of his admission is not known, because when he was sworn to the burgess-ship he was listed only as a "yeoman," a signification that in urban contexts often meant simply "not a servant" or "not a dependent": BRO, *Burgess Book* (1607–1651), f. 79^v; Anthony Salerno, "The Social Background of Seventeenth-Century Emigration to America," *Journal of British Studies* 19 (1979): 37–38.

72. In 1612 the Merchant Venturers claimed to draft their new membership rules "by vertue of their Charter." They did so again in 1618, even after receiving Nicholas Hyde's opinion: BRO, *Common Council Proceedings*, vol. 2, f. 24^{r-v}; McGrath, ed., *Records*, p. 8; Latimer, *Merchant Venturers*, p. 68. Apparently they believed that the repeal of the 1566 statute affected only their exclusionary membership rules and the expanded enforcement powers granted to support them. Although their interpretation of the law may have been correct, since they were not forced to yield up the 1552 letters patent when they lost their case in Parliament in 1571, a prudent man would not lightly have risked testing this position, especially if it was challenged by the Crown: see Sacks, "The Corporate Town and the English State," pp. 78–80.

73. *CJ*, vol. 1, p. 275; See also Croft, "Free Trade and the House of Commons," p. 26; McGrath, ed., *Records*, p. 6n. 2.

74. SMV, *Book of Trade*, pp. 82–84, 85; McGrath, ed., *Records*, pp. 9–11, 14.

75. McGrath, ed., *Records*, pp. 9–12; on the Exeter merchants' success in 1606, see Cotton, *Elizabethan Guild*, p. 177; Croft, "Free Trade and the House of Commons," p. 26.

76. McGrath, ed., *Records*, pp. 12–14; for a similar certificate in 1624, see SMV, *Book of Trade*, p. 146.

77. See MacCaffrey, *Exeter, 1540–1640*, pp. 136–59; HMC, *Records of the City of Exeter*, pp. 40–41; City of Exeter Record Office, MS Book 185, *Merchant Venturers Dispute, 1558–59*; Cotton, *Elizabethan Guild*.

78. Latimer, *Merchant Venturers*, pp. 64–65; BRO, *Common Council Proceedings*, vol. 1, pp. 116, 132; McGrath, ed., *Records*, pp. 84–88; see also

McGrath, *Merchant Venturers of Bristol,* p. 71. The Society also collected duties called anchorage, crannage, and plankage by virtue of an eighty-year lease granted to twenty-four merchant feoffees in 1601: BRO, Deed 00352 (5).

79. McGrath, ed., *Records,* p. 136; SMV, *Book of Charters,* vol. 1, pp. 95, 101; APC (1623–1625), p. 485. See also BRO, *Common Council Proceedings,* vol. 1, p. 135; Latimer, *Merchant Venturers,* p. 65; McGrath, *Merchant Venturers of Bristol,* p. 71.

80. BRO, *Common Council Proceedings,* vol. 3, f. 60^v.

81. PRO, SP 16/373/84.

82. PRO, SP 16/373/84, 16/378/4, 16/379/1i, 2, 3, 34.

83. PRO, SP 16/373/84, 16/379/1i, 34; BRO, *Common Council Proceedings,* vol. 3, f. 81^{r-v}.

84. PRO, SP 16/373/1ii, 34; BRO, *Common Council Proceedings,* f. 83^{r-v}; *Adams's Chronicle,* p. 258.

85. Latimer, *Merchant Venturers,* pp. 88–97; SMV, *Hall Book,* vol. 1, p. 24. For discussion of the terms of this charter, see Sacks, *Trade, Society and Politics,* vol. 2, pp. 647–48.

86. Latimer, *Merchant Venturers,* pp. 100–101, 102, 104–5.

87. SMV, *Hall Book,* vol. 1, p. 2.

88. McGrath, ed., *Records,* pp. 29, 261.

89. Compiled from Beaven, *Lists,* and *Return of the Name of Every Member of the Lower House of the Parliament of England, 1213–1874* (Parliamentary Papers, 1878), vol. 62, part 1.

90. See, e.g., SMV, *Book of Trade,* pp. 104–13; BRO, *Common Council Proceedings,* vol. 2, f. 96^{r-v}; Miller Christy, "Attempts towards Colonization: The Council of New England and the Merchant Venturers of Bristol," *AHR* 4 (1899): pp. 678–702; Latimer, *Annals,* p. 70; MacInnes, *Gateway of Empire,* pp. 96–106; Sacks, *Trade, Society and Politics,* vol. 2, pp. 635–38; McGrath, ed., *Records,* pp. 9–14.

91. The other four were Merchant Venturers, including the mayor. The remaining aldermen were Whitson and Guy, who were in Parliament, and the recorder, who was rarely present at aldermanic meetings.

92. The conclusion on the frequency of electoral contests is based on analysis of the mayoral elections recorded in BRO, *Common Council Proceedings,* vols. 1–3. Nominations and voting were by voice until 1642, when, significantly, a secret ballot was introduced. The town clerk or an assistant recorded each man's vote after his name in the minute book with the initials of the candidate for whom he voted. Between 1599 and 1642, twenty-five mayoral elections were uncontested, and a further ten show five votes or fewer in opposition to the successful candidate: Sacks, *Trade, Society and Politics,* vol. 2, pp. 708–9. The only other hotly contested mayoral election in our period occurred in 1633. This election pitted Alderman Robert Aldworth, one of the main protagonists in 1626, against Mathew Warren, clothier, Christopher Whitson's brother-in-law. In 1633, Warren was the most senior common councillor who had not yet served as mayor: BRO, *Common Council Proceedings,* vol. 3, ff. 44^r–45^v.

93. BRO, *Common Council Proceedings,* vol. 3, f. 134^r.

94. BRO, *Common Council Proceedings*, vol. 2, ff. 40ʳ–41ᵛ; PRO, SP 16/41/8C. For the Aldworth group's leadership in opposing the membership of retailers and manufacturers in the Merchant Venturers, see McGrath, ed., *Records*, p. 7.

95. BRO, *Common Council Proceedings*, vol. 2, ff. 142ʳ–143ᵛ, compared to the register of Merchant Venturer members in McGrath, ed., *Records*, pp. 26–29.

96. The overseas trading activities of Whitson's supporters were established by comparing evidence derived from PRO, E 190/1134/10 and E 190/1135/6, to the votes registered in BRO, *Common Council Proceedings*, vol. 2, 142ʳ–143ᵛ. Evidence of Whitson's rivalry with Aldworth can be found in Croft, ed., *Spanish Company*, pp. xliii, 18, 43, 46, 101; Sacks, *Trade, Society and Politics*, vol. 2, pp. 619–25; BRO, *Common Council Proceedings*, vol. 2, f. 55ʳ⁻ᵛ. For the relationship between Christopher Whitson and John Whitson, see BRO, *Great Orphan Book*, vol. 3, f. 250ᵛ.

97. Cronne, ed., *Bristol Charters, 1378–1499*, pp. 165–66, 175–77; BRO, *Old Ordinance Book*, f. 52ʳ⁻ᵛ; BRO, MS 04273 (1), ff. 44ʳ⁻ᵛ, 48ʳ; BRO, *Common Council Proceedings*, vol. 3, ff. 38ʳ–39ᵛ; Latham, ed., *Bristol Charters, 1509–1899*, pp. 11–13; D. M. Livock, ed., *City Chamberlain's Accounts in the Sixteenth and Seventeenth Centuries* (BRS 24, 1966), pp. xii–xiv; Sacks, *Trade, Society and Politics*, vol. 1, pp. 71–84.

98. BRO, *Common Council Proceedings*, vol. 3, f. 95ʳ⁻ᵛ. The candidates were designated by initials only. The voting was as follows: "E" = 8, "ll" = 7, "T" = 2; "C" = 24. "E" may have been Giles Elbridge, a merchant and common councillor; "ll" may have been Thomas Lloyd, a brewer and common councillor; "T" was John Thruston, a soapmaker but not a common councillor; and of course "C" was William Chetwyn, a merchant but also not a common councillor. William Chetwyn was the son of Thomas Chetwyn of Rudgely, Staffordshire, gentleman, and had been apprenticed to John Barker of Bristol, merchant. He became a freeman of the city on 4 July 1617 by virtue of his apprenticeship: BRO, *Apprentice Book* (1593–1609), f. 277ᵛ; BRO, *Burgess Book* (1607–1651), f. 93ᵛ.

99. Farmer became a burgess by patrimony on 19 October 1639, three days after this election: BRO, *Burgess Book* (1607–1651), f. 283ᵛ. For Farmer's connection with the earl of Berkshire and subsequent career, see George Bishop, *The Throne of Blood* (London, 1656), p. 109.

100. BRO, *Common Council Proceedings*, vol. 3, f. 96ʳ. The letter is dated Whitehall, 1 November 1639.

101. Ibid., f. 96ᵛ.

102. Ibid., ff. 96ᵛ–97ᵛ.

103. Ibid., ff. 98ʳ, 99ʳ. The king's letter is dated 20 November 1639.

104. Ibid., f. 95ʳ⁻ᵛ. Alderman Humphrey Hooke, for example, voted for "ll" whereas Thomas Hooke, his son, voted for "T." In the second election both of these men voted for Farmer. It is clear that in the first election there was no consensus candidate, but there appears to have been no *systematic* effort to stop Chetwyn from obtaining the office.

105. BRO, *Common Council Proceedings*, vol. 3, f. 98ʳ⁻ᵛ; Latimer, *Merchant Venturers*, p. 91; see also PRO, E 134/12 Car I/East. 21, E 134/12 Car I/

Mich. 39, E 134/13 Car I/East. 132; McGrath, ed., *Records,* pp. 238–39. See
also Sacks, "The Corporate Town and the English State," pp. 77–78.

CHAPTER 7

1. BRO, *Common Council Proceedings,* vol. 3, f. 6^v, printed with an incor-
rect citation in McGrath, ed., *Merchants and Merchandise,* p. 144. The six paper books do not appear to have survived. Possibly they were a version of the
so-called "Proceedings and Debates," many copies of which were made and circulated after this Parliament: see Robert C. Johnson, Mary Frear Keeler, Maija
Jansson Cole, and William B. Bidwell, eds., *Proceedings in Parliament, 1628,* 6
vols. (New Haven: Yale University Press, 1977–1983), vol. 1, pp. 4–33; see also
Wallace Notestein and Frances Helen Relf, eds., *Commons Debates for 1629*
(Minneapolis: University of Minnesota, 1921), introduction; R. Malcolm
Smuts, "Parliament, the Petition of Right and Politics," *Journal of Modern His-
tory* 50 (1978): pp. 714–15.

2. See, e.g., PRO, SP 16/21/111, 16/23/105, 16/40/25, 16/42/84, 16/43/52,
16/47/37, 16/49/62, 16/51/31, 63, 66, 16/75/9, 16/77/10, 16/78/30, 34, 36, 16/
79/6, 16/80/36, 42, 69, 16/82/24, 16/94/58, 58i, 63, 63i, 16/95/43, 46, 16/96/14,
16/100/42, 16/101/39, 16/109/28, 16/113/46, 16/119/50; *APC* (March 1625–
May 1626), pp. 38, 272; *APC* (June–December 1626), pp. 47–49, 109–10,
129–30, 209, 415–16; *APC* (January–August 1627), pp. 33–34, 159–61, 398,
506, 508; *APC* (September 1627–June 1628), pp. 4, 55, 58, 75, 82–83, 105–6,
132–33; *APC* (July 1628–April 1629), pp. 57, 100.

3. See, e.g., PRO, SP 16/1/12, 16/21/111, 16/22/22, 16/26/45, 16/29/17, 35,
16/32/33, 16/36/96, 16/37/54, 65, 86, 16/38/77, 90, 16/41/80, 16/42/8, 14, 70,
84, 16/47/20, 37, 16/48/2, 6, 7, 28, 16/49/62, 16/51/51, 66, 16/70/48, 52, 16/72/
43, 16/73/11, 11i, 16/74/20, 16/82/52, 16/83/19, 23, 27, 16/87/25, 66, 16/91/75,
16/115/p. 19, 16/144/22, 16/177/12; *APC* (January–August 1627), pp. 353–54;
APC (September 1627–June 1628), pp. 86–87, 186–87, 277, 287–88, 323–24,
342. See also J. W. Damer Powell, *Bristol Privateers and Ships of War* (Bristol:
J. W. Arrowsmith, 1930), pp. 69–85. For a general account of Admiralty regulation of privateering, see Kenneth R. Andrews, *Elizabethan Privateering: English Privateering during the Spanish War, 1585–1603* (Cambridge: Cambridge
University Press, 1964), esp. pp. 22–31; Andrews, *Trade, Plunder and Settlement,* chap. 11.

4. PRO, SP 16/94/58, 58i, 63, 63i, 16/95/43, 16/96/14, 16/100/42. By the
spring of 1628 the resistance of the Bristolians to the Crown's demands had become focused on the duke of Buckingham. One reason Buxton had such difficulty in the city was that his commission came from the Lord Admiral, not the
Privy Council. As Buxton wrote to Edward Nicholas, many Bristolians "do
think nay in a manner say that my Lords warrant will not be sufficient": PRO,
SP 16/95/46.

5. See Livock, ed., *City Chamberlain's Accounts,* p. xxv.

6. PRO, SP 16/113/46.

7. PRO, SP 16/108/11, 16/109/6, 28, 16/112/47, 48.

8. *Adams's Chronicle,* pp. 256, 258; PRO, SP 16/273/1. See also PRO, SP
16/373/84.

9. Put another way, the Bristol magistrates appear to have been tending toward a form of "country ideology": see J. G. A. Pocock, "Machiavelli, Harrington and English Political Ideologies in the Eighteenth Century," in his *Politics, Language and Time: Essays on Political Thought and History* (New York: Atheneum, 1973), pp. 104–47, esp. pp. 123–24; Lawrence Stone, *The Causes of the English Revolution, 1529–1642* (London: Routledge and Kegan Paul, 1972), pp. 105–8; Lawrence Stone, "Results of the English Revolutions of the Seventeenth Century," in J. G. A. Pocock, ed., *Three British Revolutions: 1641, 1688, 1776* (Princeton: Princeton University Press, 1980), pp. 32–37.

10. Ronald Syme, *The Roman Revolution* (Oxford: Clarendon Press, 1960), p. 59.

11. For the materials collected in the city's register books, see *LRB;* Veale, ed., *Great Red Book;* Ralph, ed., *Great White Book.*

12. See J. H. Hexter, "Power, Parliament and Liberty in Early Stuart England," in his *Reappraisals in History: New Views on History and Society in Early Modern Europe,* 2d ed. (Chicago: University of Chicago Press, 1979), pp. 163–218.

13. J. H. Hexter, "The Birth of Modern Freedom," *Times Literary Supplement,* 21 January 1983, pp. 51–54.

14. H. E. Mathews, ed., *Proceedings of the Company of Soapmakers, 1562–1642* (BRS 10, 1939), pp. 6–8, 194ff.; PRO, SP 16/288/49, 16/289/94, 16/308/14, 16/328/33, 33i, 16/356/101, 16/377/46; *Adams's Chronicle,* pp. 256–57; Latimer, *Annals,* pp. 121–22.

15. BRO, *Common Council Proceedings,* vol. 3, f. 110^r.

16. BRO, *Common Council Proceedings,* vol. 2, f. 134^r; vol. 3, f. 198^r. Derek Hirst argues that the freemen won a victory in 1640: Derek Hirst, *The Representative of the People? Voters and Voting and the Early Stuarts* (Cambridge: Cambridge University Press, 1975), p. 195. But he misinterprets the evidence. The "allies" mentioned in the return for this election were the other freeholders, not the freemen.

17. Based on analysis of BRO, *Burgess Book* (1607–51); see Sacks, *Trade, Society and Politics,* vol. 2, pp. 752–58.

18. BRO, MS 04026 (9), f. 105^r; Jean Vanes, "The Overseas Trade of Bristol in the Sixteenth Century," Ph.D. thesis, University of London, 1975, p. 167.

19. Edgeworth, *Sermons,* f. 209^v.

20. Ibid., f. 211^{r-v}.

21. Patrick Collinson, *The Religion of Protestants* (Oxford: Clarendon Press, 1982).

22. See above, pp. 145, 183–85, and 190–91.

23. Edgeworth, *Sermons,* ff. 43^v–44^r.

24. Ibid., f. 266^r.

25. Ibid., f. 279^v.

26. Ibid., f. 265^v.

27. *Certain Sermons or Homilies Appointed to Be Read in the Churches in the Time of Queen Elizabeth I (1547–1571): A Facsimile Reproduction of the Edition of 1623,* introduction by Mary Ellen Rickey and Thomas B. Stroup, 2 vols. in 1 (Gainesville, Fla.: Scholars' Facsimiles and Reprints, 1968), part 1,

pp. 69–77. See also ibid., part 2, pp. 271–310; Richard B. Bond, ed., *Certain Sermons or Homilies (1547) and A Homily against Disobedience and Wilful Rebellion (1570): A Critical Edition* (Toronto: University of Toronto Press, 1987), pp. 161–73, 209–59.

28. See William Laud, *The Works of the Most Reverent Father in God, William Laud, D.D. Sometime Lord Archbishop of Canterbury*, ed. W. Scott and J. Bliss, 7 vols. in 9 (Oxford: John Henry Parker, 1847–1860), vol. 7, p. 31; Edward Elbridge Salisbury, *Family Memorials: A Series of Genealogical and Biographical Monographs on the Families of Salisbury, Aldworth-Elbridge, Sewall, Pyldren-Dummer, Walley, Quincy, Wendell, Breese, Chevalier-Anderson and Phillips*, 1 vol. in 2 (New Haven: Tuttle, Morehouse and Taylor, 1885), vol. 1, part 1, pp. 103–21, and "Pedigree of Aldworth-Elbridge," facing p. 142.

29. See, e.g., "Will of Alderman Robert Aldworth," BRO, *Great Orphan Book*, vol. 2, ff. 16^r–17^r, and "Will of Alderman Henry Yate," ff. 21^r–24^r. Aldworth's own funeral monument is itself an example of the high baroque style favored by many of the followers of Laud in this period; for a photograph see Damer Powell, *Bristol Privateers and Ships of War*, facing p. 72.

30. PRO, SP 16/41/80; Christopher Hill, *Society and Puritanism in Pre-Revolutionary England* (London: Secker and Warburg, 1964), pp. 13–29.

31. See Whitson, *Aged Christians Final Farewell*; "Will of John Whitson," BRO, *Great Orphan Book*, vol. 2, ff. 244^v–250^v; Jordan, *Forming of the Charitable Institutions*, pp. 23–24, 30, 33, 38, 39. But see also John Aubrey, *Brief Lives*, ed. Oliver Lawson Dick (Harmondsworth: Penguin, 1974), pp. 366–67; McGrath, *John Whitson*, pp. 1–22.

32. See above, pp. 220–21 and p. 408 n.92.

33. BRO, *Common Council Proceedings*, vol. 3, ff. 44–45; "Will of William Tucker," in Wadley, ed., *Great Orphan Book*, pp. 245–46; "Will of Christopher Whitson," BRO, *Great Orphan Book*, vol. 2, ff. 100^v–103^v.

34. "Will of William Yeamans, gent.," PRO, PROB 6/17 Essex; "Will of Mathew Warren," BRO, *Great Orphan Book*, vol. 2, ff. 36^v–39^v; George Bishop, *A Relation of the Inhumane and Barbarous Sufferings of the People Called Quakers in the City of Bristol during the Mayoralty of John Knight commonly called Sir John Knight* (London, 1665), p. 75; see also Mortimer, ed., *Minute Book*, p. 220.

35. For the early history of the group see Hayden, ed., *Records*, pp. 13, 17, 19, 84, 88.

36. See Collinson, *Religion of Protestants*, chap. 6.

37. See above, pp. 145, 232.

38. "Will of Edward Chetwyn," PRO, PROB 6/115 Harvey; PRO, SP 16/35/92; Anthony à Wood, *Athenae Oxonienses: An Exact History of all the Writers who have had their Education in the University of Oxford*, 3d ed., with additions by Philip Bliss, 4 vols. (London: F. C. and J. Rivington, 1813–1820), vol. 2, p. 641, and vol. 4, p. 375; DNB, "Edward Chetwynd," "John Chetwynd"; Thomas G. Barnes, *Somerset, 1625–1640: A County Government during the "Personal Rule"* (Cambridge, Mass.: Harvard University Press, 1961), pp. 32, 34–35, 71; David Underdown, *Somerset in the Civil War and Interregnum* (Newton Abbot: David and Charles, 1973), pp. 22, 27, 143, 171.

39. Many of them voted for "E" in the first election. If this indeed is the symbol for Giles Elbridge, it is perhaps understandable that the Aldworth faction should do so.

40. Laud, *Works*, vol. 7, p. 568. For further evidence of poor relations between Berkshire and Laud, particularly involving their respective connections with the city of Oxford and the university, see ibid., vol. 4, pp. 174–75, and vol. 5, pp. 123–24, 244, 245, 274–80, 283–84. See also Edward Hyde, *The History of the Rebellion and Civil Wars of England*, new ed., 2 vols. (Oxford: Clarendon Press, 1843), vol. 1, p. 371.

41. Bishop, *Throne of Blood*, p. 109.

42. For the outlines of Chetwyn's career in civic office see Beaven, *Lists*, p. 235.

43. Mary F. Keeler, *The Long Parliament, 1640–1641: A Biographical Study of Its Members* (Philadelphia: American Philosophical Society, 1954), pp. 220–221, 255–56; *CJ*, vol. 2, pp. 415, 567; C. H. Firth and R. S. Rait, eds., *Acts and Ordinances of the Interregnum, 1642–1660*, 3 vols. (London: His Majesty's Stationery Office, 1911) vol. 1, pp. 797–98.

44. Latimer, *Annals*, pp. 157, 158, 181, 189, 205, 210, 214; *DNB*, "Sir John Glanville, the younger."

45. John Corbet, *An Historical Relation of the Military Government of Gloucester from the beginning of the Civill Warre betweene the King and Parliament to the removall of Colonell Massie from that Government to the Command of the Westerne Forces* (London, 1645), p. 14.

46. Corbet, *Military Government of Gloucester*. See also Latimer, *Annals*, pp. 164–65; Roger Howell, Jr., "The Structure of Urban Politics in the English Civil War," *Albion* 11 (1979): 118.

47. The participation of "the middling sort" has been emphasized by Howell, "Structure of Urban Politics," p. 115. For notes on the interrogation of the leaders and others, see Bodleian Library, Portland MSS, *Nalson Papers*, N. XIII, 151, 155–71, 190; see also Historical Manuscripts Commission, *The Manuscripts of His Grace the Duke of Portland Preserved at Welbeck Abbey*, 10 vols. (London: Her Majesty's Stationery Office, 1891), vol. 1, p. 107. I am grateful to His Grace the Duke of Portland for permission to consult and photocopy this material.

48. See Howell, "Structure of Urban Politics," p. 118.

49. In their petition to the king the Bristolians refer directly to the Londoners' earlier petition, which the Bristolians say had invoked the king's "Royall assistance and suffrage for the establishing an unanimous tranquillity throughout this Realme": *The Humble Petition of the Citie of Bristoll, for An Accommodation of Peace between His Majestie, and the Honourable the High Court of Parliament As it was presented to the Kings Most Excellent Majestie, at the Court at Oxford, by foure of the Aldermen of the said Citie; on Saturday the seventh of Januarie, with His Majesties gracious Answer therunto* (Oxford, 1643), p. 3. See also *The Petition of the Most Svbstantiall Inhabitants of the Citie of London, And the Liberties thereof, to the Lords and Commons for Peace Together with the Answer to the same And the Reply of the Petitioners* (Oxford, 1642). For discussion of the campaign for "accommodation" in 1642, see Anthony

Fletcher, *The Outbreak of the English Civil War* (London: Edward Arnold, 1981), pp. 264–82. For the link between accommodation and royalism, see John Pym, *A Discoverie of the Great Plot for the Utter Ruine of the City of London and the Parliament. As it was at large made known . . . the eighth of June, 1643* (London, 1643); Edward Montague and John Pym, *Two Speeches spoken by the Earl of Manchester and Jo: Pym; as a reply to his Maiesties answer to . . . Londons Petition* (London, 1643); T. B. Howell, ed., *Cobbett's Complete Collection of State Trials*, 33 vols. (London: R. Bagshaw, 1809–1826), vol. 4, pp. 626–53; Samuel R. Gardiner, *History of the Great Civil War, 1642–1649*, 4 vols. (London: Longmans, Green, 1901–4), vol. 1, pp. 7–9, 74–75, 146–49; see also Warren L. Chernaik, *The Poetry of Limitation: A Study of Edmund Waller* (New Haven: Yale University Press, 1968), pp. 19–34; Jack G. Gilbert, *Edmund Waller* (Boston: Twayne, 1979), pp. 24–25; J. H. Hexter, *The Reign of King Pym* (Cambridge, Mass.: Harvard University Press, 1941), pp. 9–10, 31–32, 104n. 2; Valerie Pearl, *London and the Outbreak of the Puritan Revolution: City Government and National Politics, 1625–43* (Oxford: Clarendon Press, 1961), pp. 253–56, 265–66.

50. *The Petition of the Most Svbstantiall Inhabitants . . . of London*, sig. A1b.

51. *The Humble Petition*, pp. 4–5.

52. Ibid.

53. Ibid.

54. For a somewhat different interpretation of this material see Howell, "Structure of Urban Politics," p. 119.

55. *Two State Martyrs*, in Seyer, *Memoirs*, vol. 2, p. 373.

56. J. Toombes, *Jehovah Jirah, or Gods Providence in Delivering the Godly* (London, 1643), sig. A4b.

57. Clement Walker, *The Severall Examinations and Confessions of the Treacherous Conspirators against the Citie of Bristol* (London, 1643), p. 12. See also Bodleian Library, Portland MSS, *Nalson Papers*, N. XIII, 151, 155–71, 190, 210; HMC, *The Manuscripts of His Grace the Duke of Portland Preserved at Welbeck Abbey*, 10 vols. (London, 1891), vol. 1, p. 107.

58. *The Humble Petition*, p. 5.

59. Ibid.

60. The usage here seems to owe a debt to James I's speech at the opening of Parliament in 1624, when he specifically referred to the king and Parliament as husband and wife: *LJ*, vol. 3, p. 209.

61. Sir Philip Sidney, *The Countess of Pembroke's Arcadia (The New Arcadia)*, ed. Victor Skretkowicz (Oxford: Clarendon Press, 1987), p. 426. The *Oxford English Dictionary* gives this instance as the first known usage of "divorce."

62. See Howell, "Structure of Urban Politics," p. 118.

63. BRO, *Common Council Proceedings*, vol. 4, pp. 5, 6.

64. In July the Common Council decided to withhold the petitions thus agreed upon "in regards they have bin so long retarded": BRO, *Common Council Proceedings*, vol. 3, f. 122^{r-v}. The first reference to the petitions is to be found on f. 119^v.

65. BRO, *Common Council Proceedings*, vol. 4, p. 13.

66. Brian Manning falls into this trap in his *The English People and the English Revolution* (London: Heinemann, 1976), which is criticized by Howell, "Structure of Urban Politics," pp. 114–15.

67. It is evidence of the short-term political character of this grant that the original letters patent of 1643 do not survive in the records of the Merchant Venturers. The Society retained only a copy of the original, made under the Great Seal in 1669: Latimer, *Merchant Venturers*, pp. 106–7.

68. William Prynne and Clement Walker, *A True and Full Relation of the Prosecution, Arraignment, Tryall, and Condemnation of Nathaniel Fiennes, late Colonel and Governor of the City of Bristol, Before a Councell of War held at Saint Albans during Nine dayes space in December, 1643* (London, 1643), pp. 16, 17, 42, 44, and the appended *Catalogue of Witnesses*, pp. 21, 27, 28, 32, 33; Hayden, ed., *Records*, pp. 17–19.

69. SMV, *Hall Book*, vol. 1, p. 2.

70. BRO, *Common Council Proceedings*, vol. 3, f. 122^r.

71. On the politics of these men in the 1640s see David Underdown, *Pride's Purge: Politics in the Puritan Revolution* (Oxford: Clarendon Press, 1972), pp. 366, 376, 393; John R. MacCormack, *Revolutionary Politics in the Long Parliament* (Cambridge, Mass.: Harvard University Press, 1973), pp. 328, 335.

72. See Hayden, ed., *Records*, p. 103; Mortimer, ed., *Minute Book*, pp. 58, 133, 218.

73. These conclusions are based on analysis of McGrath, ed., *Records*, pp. 27–30, 261; Beaven, *Lists*, pp. 119 and 185–315.

74. BRO, *Common Council Proceedings*, vol. 3, pp. 149, 165, and vol. 4, pp. 5, 18, 19, 178, 179; BRO, MS 04369 (1), pp. 69–70; BRO, MS 08157, pp. 37–46, 51–59; BRO, MS 01244; John Latimer, "The Mercers' and Linen Drapers' Company of Bristol," *BGAS* 26 (1903): 288. The mercers' and linen-drapers' act book beginning in 1647 has survived: Bristol Central Library, MS B 4939.

75. BRO, *Common Council Proceedings*, vol. 3, pp. 160, 200; BRO, MS 04369 (1), pp. 61–67. This procedure was first adopted by the soapmakers in 1618 and later employed by the bakers in 1621, the wiredrawers in 1629, and the mechant taylors in 1640: BRO, *Common Council Proceedings*, vol. 2, f. 78^{r-v}; BRO, MS 04369 (1), pp. 125, 130; F. F. Fox, ed., *Ancient Fraternity of Merchant Taylors*, p. 90. For a discussion of the significance of this change in enforcement procedures see Sacks, *Trade, Society and Politics*, vol. 1, pp. 138–40.

76. BRO, *Common Council Proceedings*, vol. 3, p. 163.

77. BRO, MS 04273 (1), f. 72^r.

78. See, e.g., the Merchant Taylors' ordinance of 4 December 1649 complaining of the intrusions of numerous strangers in their craft and ordering that for the future only men apprenticed in Bristol could receive protection from the Merchant Taylors' Company: Bristol Central Library, MS B 4788, Ordinance.

79. BRO, MS 04369 (1), p. 127; see also John E. Pritchard, "Tobacco Pipes of Bristol of the XVIIth Century and Their Makers," *BGAS* 45 (1923): 165–91.

CHAPTER 8

1. Carus-Wilson, ed., *Overseas Trade of Bristol*, pp. 65–68, 71–73, 79–81, 87–93, 94–97, 120–22, 125–26, 127–30, 135–37, 139–40, 144, 155–56, 208, 252, 253; Carus-Wilson, *Medieval Merchant Venturers*, pp. 1, 5, 8, 11, 13, 14, 66, 73, 81, 89, 96, 98–142.

2. BRO, MS 04220 (1–2), which covers 1654 to 1679; further material covering parts of the years 1679–1681 and 1683–1686 can be found in rough form in the records of the Bristol Mayor's Court: BRO, MSS 04355 (6) and 04356 (1). The entries have now been painstakingly edited by Peter Wilson Coldham, *The Bristol Registers of Servants Sent to Foreign Plantations, 1654–1686* (Baltimore: Genealogical Publishing, 1988). See also William Dogson Bowman, ed., *Bristol and America: A Record of the First Settlers in the Colonies of North America, 1654–1685*, preface by N. Dermott Harding (London: R. S. Glover, 1931). For discussions of this source, see Mildred Campbell, "Social Origins of Some Early Americans," in James Morton Smith, ed., *Seventeenth-Century America: Essays in Colonial History* (Chapel Hill: University of North Carolina Press, 1959), pp. 63–89; Richard S. Dunn, *Sugar and Slaves: The Rise of the Planter Class in the English West Indies, 1624–1713* (Chapel Hill: University of North Carolina Press, 1972), pp. 70–71; James Horn, "Servant Emigration to the Chesapeake in the Seventeenth Century," in Thad W. Tate and David L. Ammerman, eds., *The Chesapeake in the Seventeenth Century* (Chapel Hill: University of North Carolina Press, 1979), pp. 51–95; Salerno, "Social Background of Seventeenth-Century Emigration," pp. 31–52; David Souden, "Rogues, Whores and Vagabonds? Indentured Servant Migration to North America and the Case of Mid-Seventeenth-Century Bristol," *Social History* 3 (1978): 23–39; David W. Galenson, " 'Middling People' or 'Common Sort'? The Social Origins of Some Early Americans Reexamined," with a rebuttal by Mildred Campbell, *WMQ*, 3d ser., 35 (1978): 499–540; David W. Galenson, "The Social Origins of Early Americans: Rejoinder . . . with a Reply by Mildred Campbell," *WMQ*, 3d ser., 36 (1979): 264–86; David W. Galenson, *White Servitude in Colonial America: An Economic Analysis* (Cambridge: Cambridge University Press, 1981), esp. pp. 34–39, 183–84.

3. BRO, *Common Council Proceedings*, vol. 5, p. 72. David Galenson prints the document in Galenson, *White Servitude in Colonial America*, pp. 189–90.

4. Latimer, *Annals*, pp. 254–55; Abbott Emerson Smith, *Colonists in Bondage: White Servitude and Convict Labor in America, 1607–1776* (Chapel Hill: University of North Carolina Press, 1947), p. 71; MacInnes, *Gateway of Empire*, p. 161; Dunn, *Sugar and Slaves*, p. 70; Horn, "Servant Emigration to the Chesapeake," p. 55n. 17; Souden, "Rogues, Whores and Vagabonds?" pp. 25–26; Galenson, " 'Middling People' or 'Common Sort'?" pp. 504–5, repeated verbatim in *White Servitude in Colonial America*, pp. 37–38, and see p. 183.

5. The relevant documents are in H. E. Nott and Elizabeth Ralph, eds., *The Deposition Books of Bristol. Volume 2: 1650–1654* (BRS 13, 1947), pp. 166–67, 174–75, 192. Meredith had been apprenticed on 7 March 1653, for nine years, to Anthony Barnes, baker, and his wife Anne. Meredith is identified in the apprenticeship indenture as the son of a deceased gentleman of Landovery, Car-

marthenshire: BRO, MS 04352 (6), f. 279ᵛ. The nine-year term suggests that Meredith may have been as young as twelve when his apprenticeship indenture was drawn. The sailors aboard the *Dolphin*, however, identify him as "a Young man as they conceive aboute the age of 18 yeares": Nott and Ralph, eds., *Deposition Books*, vol. 2, p. 174. But they had good reason to shade the truth in their favor. Nevertheless, their story clearly has a modicum of truth to it. Meredith looks like the runaway young son of a Welsh gentleman apprenticed in Bristol after his father's death. For doubts about the veracity of the sailors' deposition, see McGrath, "Merchant Shipping in the Seventeenth Century," 41 (1955): 29–30.

6. See, e.g., William Bullock, *Virginia Impartially Examined* (London, 1649), p. 14; Smith, *Colonists in Bondage*, pp. 67–69. The Middlesex County Records abound with references: see John Cordy Jeaffreson, ed., *Middlesex County Records*, old ser. (1886–1892), vols. 3–4, esp. vol. 4, pp. xli–xlvii.

7. See, e.g., BRO, MS 04417 (1), f. 47ᵛ; Latimer, *Annals*, pp. 254–55.

8. BRO, *Common Council Proceedings*, vol. 5, p. 72.

9. For some comments to the contrary, see Galenson, " 'Middling People' or 'Common Sort'?" p. 505; Galenson, *White Servitude in Colonial America*, p. 38.

10. See *Gylbert v. Fletcher* (4 Car. I Trin.), Cro. Car. 179, in *English Reports* 69, p. 757 and the cases cited there. There is no doubt that indentured servants were treated administratively exactly like apprentices. Servants' covenants and apprentices' indentures were recorded in the same rough entry books of the Mayor's Court: see BRO, MSS 04354, 04355 (1–6), 04356 (1); Bowman, ed., *Bristol and America*, pp. viii–ix; Elizabeth Ralph, *Guide to the Bristol Archives Office* (Bristol: Bristol Corporation, 1971), p. 52; Galenson, " 'Middling People' or 'Common Sort'?" p. 515; Galenson, *White Servitude in Colonial America*, p. 183. Indeed, the second volume of the *Register* is officially entitled "The Inrollment of Apprentices and Servants as are shipped at the port of Bristoll to serue in any of the forraigne plantations": BRO, MS 04220 (2), f. 1ʳ. The earliest known indenture for service in the plantations, dated 4 December 1626, is to be found in an ordinary apprentice book: BRO, MS 04352 (5)a, f. 23ʳ; see MacInnes, *Gateway of Empire*, pp. 151, 158.

11. See 1 Sid. 446, in *English Reports*, vol. 82, pp. 1208–9; Joseph Chitty, *A Practical Treatise on the Law Relative to Apprentices and Journeymen and to Exercising Trades* (London: W. Clarke and Sons, 1812), pp. 29–31; Henry Evans Austin, *The Law Relating to Apprentices, Including those Bound according to the Custom of London* (London: Reeves and Turner, 1890), pp. 18–19. By the 1620s all indentures involving men, even those for parish apprentices placed by the churchwardens, are made only in the names of the apprentice and the master. For early sixteenth-century practice see Hollis, ed., *Bristol Apprentice Book*, part 1, p. 14; for the standard in the seventeenth century, see BRO, MS 04352 (5)a.

12. Edward Coke, *The First Part of the Institutes of the Laws of England, or a Commentary upon Littleton* (London, 1620), p. 172a.

13. Bristol, which from very early on kept a summary of the constitutions of London as part of its precedent books, may have followed the rules of London, where the contracts of apprentices over fourteen years of age were deemed

those of an adult and those under fourteen were subject to the common law as stated by Coke: see Bohun, *Privilegia Londini*, pp. 175–78, 338; Ricart, *Kalendar*, pp. 102–3.

14. Cro. Car. 179 in *English Reports*, vol. 69, p. 757; see the astute remarks of Fry L. J. in *Walter v. Everard*, 2 Q.B. (1881), 376. See also *Staunton's Case* (K.B. 25 Eliz. I), Moore, 135–36 in *English Reports*, vol. 72, pp. 489–90; *Walker v. Nicholason* (K.B. 41 Eliz. I, Hil. 12), Cro. Eliz. 653 in *English Reports*, vol. 68, p. 892.

15. For the Privy Council's attempt to do just this in 1682, see PRO, PC 2/69/595–96, printed in Galenson, *White Servitude in Colonial America*, pp. 190–92.

16. BRO, MS 04220 (1), f. 351^r.

17. See, e.g., ibid., f. 43^r and the entry for 20 July 1659 on an unnumbered page at the end of the volume; the Statute of Artificers, Stat. 5 Eliz. I c. 4, required only that indentures be enrolled within a year of being drawn.

18. BRO, MSS 04220 (1), ff. 351^r–352^r, 355^v–367^v, 482^r–497^v, 04220 (2), ff. 187^r–231^v, 271^v, 278^r–end of volume.

19. BRO, MS 04220 (2), f. 196^r. In this case the child was apprenticed to eleven years in Montserrat, which suggests that he was below the age of fourteen—probably about ten—at the time of the indenture.

20. BRO, MS 04220 (1), entry for 20 July 1659 at the end of the volume.

21. See above, pp. 247–48; Sacks, *Trade, Society and Politics*, vol. 1, pp. 139–40. A suit could proceed even though the party was out of town or had concealed his goods.

22. BRO, *Common Council Proceedings*, vol. 5, p. 73.

23. See Sacks, *Trade, Society and Politics*, vol. 1, chap. 3.

24. Sacks, *Trade, Society and Politics*, vol. 1, pp. 104–21. According to the *Wharfage Book*, Hiscox brought five hogsheads and five butts of Barbados sugar aboard the *Dolphin* on 5 May 1654. Clearly he had exported more than just Farwell Meredith. Mary Hiscox, perhaps his wife, had an additional four hogsheads in her name aboard the *Thomas and George* on 11 August of the same year.

25. Souden, "Rogues, Whores and Vagabonds?" pp. 34–35; Horn, "Servant Emigration to the Chesapeake," pp. 87–89. Horn's figures exaggerate the number of "merchants," for many of those who identified themselves as members of this occupation appear to have apprenticed as coopers, mariners, mercers, soapboilers, and the like. By cross-checking the names in the *Register* with other Bristol sources, I calculate that only about 15 percent of the traders in servants for whom occupations are known were "merchants" by apprenticeship or patrimony, and even this figure may somewhat exaggerate the total.

26. For planters like John George, Farwell Meredith's colonial master, the produce of their own estates—sugar, tobacco, indigo—served in place of money. See, e.g., Nott and Ralph, eds., *Deposition Books*, vol. 2, p. 115; BRO, MSS 04439 (3), f. 188^r, 04439 (4), f. 89^r; McGrath, ed., *Merchants and Merchandise*, pp. 242–43, 246, 255. Virginia, in fact, lacked hard currency of any sort, but instead its economy operated with an elaborate system of tobacco equivalencies: Edmund S. Morgan, *American Slavery, American Freedom: The*

Ordeal of Colonial Virginia (New York: W. W. Norton, 1975), p. 177; Gloria L. Main, *Tobacco Colony: Life in Early Maryland, 1650–1720* (Princeton: Princeton University Press, 1982), p. 50.

27. Bullock, *Virginia Impartially Examined*, pp. 12–14, 46–47.

28. The Bristol wharfage duty fell on a variety of luxury imports, among which were sugar, tobacco, indigo, ginger, cotton, and other colonial products. The Society of Merchant Venturers' earliest surviving *Wharfage Book*, modeled on the Exchequer's own Port Books, begins in mid-May 1654. Much like the *Register of Servants*, greater care in keeping the records seems to have been taken in the mid-1650s than later. By 1662 the recording clerks no longer always took pains to distinguish entries vessel by vessel, which makes the books extremely difficult to use.

29. Of the unknowns, many undoubtedly were planters shipping goods in their own names to the English market, but a few might have been Bristolians like Marlin Hiscox who never became freemen. For further evidence of shopkeepers and craftsmen engaged in colonial commerce see BRO, MSS 04439 (3), ff. 10^{r-v}, $40^{v}–41^{r}$, 57^{r}, 66^{v}, 102^{v}, 126^{r-v}, 131^{v}, $193^{v}–94^{r}$, 04439 (4), ff. 15^{v}, 55^{r}.

30. To avoid confusion caused by ships that stopped several places in the colonies before returning to England, in Table 26 any import of colonial goods by an individual is counted as a return for the export of any servant, no matter what the servant's original destination.

31. Souden, "Rogues, Whores and Vagabonds?" p. 35.

32. On Blike's efforts on behalf of Tocknell, see BRO, MS 04439 (3), ff. $86^{r}–89^{r}$.

33. McGrath, ed., *Merchants and Merchandise*, p. 258; McGrath, "Merchant Shipping in Seventeenth-Century Bristol," 41 (1955): 29. For evidence of the magistrates' concern about this issue in the 1650s, see BRO, *Common Council Proceedings*, vol. 5, pp. 152–53. The earliest surviving example of the freeman's oath dates from 1683 and is printed in McGrath, ed., *Merchants and Merchandise*, p. 26.

34. BRO, MS 04339 (4), f. 49^{r}.

35. Latimer, *Merchant Venturers*, p. 78.

36. Ibid., p. 104.

37. Ibid., pp. 100–101, 102, 104. These ordinances repeat in somewhat different form the ordinances of 1618; see ibid., pp. 78–79.

38. Roger North, *The Lives of the Norths*, new ed. in 3 vols. (London: H. Colburn, 1826), vol. 1, p. 250; emphasis added. Although Spain remained one of Bristol's principal markets in the later seventeenth century, trade with it was largely in the hands of the great wholesale dealers—the Merchant Venturers—rather than being shared with the city's shopkeepers. North seems to mean that Bristolians in general traded with the West Indies and Spain, but the poor shopkeepers dealt primarily with the American plantations; see also Robert Brenner, "The Social Basis of English Commercial Expansion, 1550–1650," *JEcH* 32 (1972): 361–84; and Robert Brenner, "The Civil War Politics of the London Merchant Community," *Past and Present*, no. 58 (November 1973): 53–107. There are close parallels in Bristol to the developments Brenner discusses for

London, though many of the "new men" he discusses were richer and better connected than the Bristol shopkeepers who traded in the colonies.

39. "To the Kings Most Excellent Majesty: The humble Remonstrance of John Bland of London, Merchant on behalf of the Inhabitants and Planters of Virginia and Mariland," printed in *Virginia Magazine of Biography and History* 1 (1893–94): 144. Bland was asking the king for a special exemption for the Chesapeake colonies from the Second Act of Navigation. For discussion of the economic and political forces behind the First Act of Navigation, see J. E. Farnell, "The Navigation Act of 1651, the first Dutch War and the London Merchant Community," *EcHR*, 2d ser., 6 (1964): 439–54, and the critical comments of J. P. Cooper, "Social and Economic Policies under the Commonwealth," in G. E. Aylmer, ed., *The Interregnum: The Quest for Settlement, 1646–1660* (London: Macmillan, 1972), pp. 121–42.

40. See above, chap. 2.

41. Richard Ligon, *A True and Exact History of the Island of Barbados*, orig. pub. 1657 (London, 1676), p. 109.

42. See, e.g., Nott and Ralph, eds., *Deposition Books*, vol. 2, p. 160; BRO, MS 04220 (1), f. 16^v.

43. On the career of Sir John Yeamans, see "Sir John Yeamans," *Dictionary of American Biography*. Other men associated with Robert Yeamans's 1643 plot also seem to have ended up in Barbados in this period. For example, Henry Russell, a Barbados planter in 1654, was a Bristol mariner arrested with Yeamans in 1643: see *The Copy of a Letter Sent from Bristol* (London, 1643), p. 6; BRO, *Burgess Book* (1607–1651), f. 283^r.

44. For Bristolians who emigrated to the colonies, see Souden, "Rogues, Whores and Vagabonds?" p. 36. Bristol's court records abound with cases of its citizens having settled in the colonies: see particularly Nott and Ralph, eds., *Deposition Books*, vol. 2; BRO, MSS 04439 (3) and 04439 (4).

45. The literature on this theme is enormous and growing. The works I found especially illuminating in framing the following discussion are: Morgan, *American Slavery, American Freedom*, esp. chaps. 6–9, 15; Bernard Bailyn, *The Peopling of British North America: An Introduction* (New York: Alfred A. Knopf, 1986); Jack P. Greene, *Pursuits of Happiness: The Social Development of Early Modern British Colonies and the Formation of American Culture* (Chapel Hill: University of North Carolina Press, 1988), chaps. 1, 2, 4, 7; Dunn, *Sugar and Slaves*, esp. chaps. 2–3, 6–10; Richard S. Dunn, "Servants and Slaves: The Recruitment and Employment of Labor," in Jack P. Greene and J. R. Pole, eds., *Colonial British America: Essays in the New History of the Early American Era* (Baltimore: Johns Hopkins University Press, 1984), pp. 157–94; Wesley Frank Craven, *White, Red and Black: The Seventeenth-Century Virginian* (Charlottesville: University of Virginia Press, 1971); John J. McCusker and Russell Menard, *The Economy of British America, 1607–1789: Needs and Opportunities for Study* (Chapel Hill: University of North Carolina Press, 1985), chaps. 2–4, 6–7, 11, 13–14; David W. Galenson, *Traders, Planters, and Slaves: Market Behavior in Early English America* (Cambridge: Cambridge University Press, 1986); David W. Galenson, "White Servitude and the Growth of Black Slavery in Colonial America," *JEcH* 41 (1981): 39–47; Dar-

rett B. Rutman and Anita H. Rutman, *A Place in Time: Middlesex County, Virginia, 1650–1750*, 2 vols. (New York: W. W. Norton, 1984); Paul G. T. Clemens, *The Atlantic Economy and Colonial Maryland's Eastern Shore: From Tobacco to Grain* (Ithaca: Cornell University Press, 1980), chaps. 1–3; Allan Kulikoff, *Tobacco and Slaves: The Development of Southern Cultures in the Chesapeake, 1680–1800* (Chapel Hill: University of North Carolina Press, 1986), part 1, esp. chaps. 1–2; Allan Kulikoff, "The Colonial Chesapeake: Seedbed of Antebellum Southern Culture," *Journal of Southern History* 45 (1979): 513–40; Main, *Tobacco Colony*, esp. chaps. 3–7; Gloria L. Main, "Maryland and the Chesapeake Economy, 1670–1720," in Aubrey C. Land, Lois Green Carr, and Edward C. Papenfuse, eds., *Law, Society and Politics in Early Maryland* (Baltimore: Johns Hopkins University Press, 1977), pp. 134–52; Gary A. Puckrein, *Little England: Plantation Society and Anglo-Barbadian Politics, 1627–1700* (New York: New York University Press, 1984), esp. chaps. 1–5; Terry L. Anderson and Robert Paul Thomas, "Economic Growth in the Seventeenth-Century Chesapeake," *Explorations in Economic History* 15 (1978): 368–87; Brenner, "The Civil War Politics of London's Merchant Community," pp. 65–72; Stuart Bruchey, *The Roots of American Economic Growth, An Essay in Social Causation* (New York: Harper & Row, 1968), chaps. 1–2; Jacob M. Price, "The Transatlantic Economy," in Greene and Pole, eds., *Colonial British America*, pp. 18–42; Richard B. Sheridan, "The Domestic Economy," in ibid., pp. 43–85; R. C. Batie, "Why Sugar? Economic Cycles and the Changing of Staples in the English and French Antilles, 1625–1654," *Journal of Caribbean History* 8 (1976): 1–41; Carville V. Earle, "A Staple Interpretation of Slavery and Free Labor," *Geographical Review* 68 (1978): 51–65; David Galenson and Russell Menard, "Approaches to the Analysis of Economic Growth in Early America," *Historical Methods* 3 (1980): 3–18; Richard E. Caves, " 'Vent for Surplus' Models of Trade and Growth," in Robert Baldwin et al., *Trade, Growth and the Balance of Payments* (Chicago: University of Chicago Press, 1965), pp. 94–104; L. C. Gray, *History of Agriculture in the Southern United States to 1860*, 2 vols. (Washington, D.C.: Carnegie Institution, 1933), vol. 1, chap. 2; Stanley Gray and V. J. Wyckoff, "The International Tobacco Trade in the Seventeenth Century," *Southern Economic Journal* 7 (1940): 1–26; D. Klingaman, "The Significance of Grain in the Development of Tobacco Colonies," *JEcH* 29 (1969): 268–78; Russell Menard, "From Servants to Slaves: The Transformation of the Chesapeake Labor System," *Southern Studies* 16 (1977): 355–90; Russell Menard, "Secular Trends in the Chesapeake Tobacco Industry," in *Working Papers from the Regional Economic History Research Center* 1, no. 3 (1978), pp. 1–34; Russell Menard, "The Tobacco Industry in the Chesapeake Colonies, 1617–1730: An Interpretation," in *Research in Economic History: A Research Annual* 5 (1980): 109–77; Russell Menard, "Population, Economy and Society in Seventeenth-Century Maryland," *Maryland Historical Magazine* 79 (1984): 71–74; Terry L. Anderson and Robert Paul Thomas, "The Growth of Population and Labor Force in the 17th-Century Chesapeake," *Explorations in Economic History* 15 (1978): 290–312; Hilary M. Beckles, "The Economic Origins of Black Slavery in the British West Indies, 1640–1680: A Tentative Analysis of the Barbados Model," *Journal* of *Caribbean History* 16 (1982): 36–56; Hilary M. Beckles and Andrew Downes, "The Economic Transition to the Black Labor System in Barbados, 1630–1680," *Journal of Interdisciplinary History* 18 (1987): 225–47; Carole Shammas, "Consumer Behavior in Colonial America," *Social Science History* 6 (1982): 67–86; Carole Shammas, "How Self-Sufficient Was Early America?" *Journal of Interdisciplinary History* 13 (1982): 246–72; Lois Green Carr and Lorena S. Walsh, "The Standard of Living in the Colonial Chesapeake," *WMQ*, 3d ser., 45 (1988): 135–59; Edward Papenfuse, "Planter Behavior and Economic Opportunity in a Staple Economy," *Agricultural History* 46 (1972): 297–311; James F. Shepherd and Gary N. Walton, *Shipping, Maritime Trade and the Economic Development of Colonial North America* (Cambridge: Cambridge University Press, 1972), pp. 1–48; Richard B. Sheridan, *Sugar and Slavery: An Economic History of the British West Indies, 1623–1775* (Baltimore: Johns Hopkins University Press, 1974), esp. chaps. 16–17.

46. *Marchants Avizo*, p. 10.

47. "A speciall direction for divers trades" (ca. 1575–1585), in R. H. Tawney and Eileen Power, eds., *Tudor Economic Documents*, 3 vols. (London: Longmans, Green, 1924), vol. 3, pp. 199–210; Roberts, *The Merchantes Mappe of Commerce*.

48. See Ligon, *History of the Island of Barbados*, pp. 109–12; BRO, MS 04439 (3), ff. 12ʳ–13ᵛ; K. G. Davies, "The Origins of the Commission System in the West Indies Trade," *TRHS*, 5th ser., 2 (1952): 94–95; Morgan, *American Slavery, American Freedom*, p. 177; Souden, "Rogues, Whores and Vagabonds?" p. 34.

49. Clemens, *Atlantic Economy*, pp. 93–95.

50. Ligon, *History of the Island of Barbados*, pp. 109–12; see Puckrein, *Little England*, pp. 56–72.

51. See J. H. Bennett, "The English Caribbees in the Period of the Civil War, 1642–1646," *WMQ*, 3d ser., 24 (1967): 360.

52. Menard, "Secular Trends," p. 7. See also Menard, "The Tobacco Industry in the Chesapeake Colonies," esp. p. 115.

53. Sheridan, *Sugar and Slavery*, pp. 399–401; Dunn, *Sugar and Slaves*, p. 205.

54. The Merchant Venturers, moreover, could expect no help from the colonists in their efforts to control the foreign trade of Bristol, for the planters had no interest in restricting their export market: see "The humble Remonstrance of John Bland," pp. 142–55. The problem of regulation was compounded by the development of the shipping industry at Bristol. Between 1650 and 1654, the city's *Deposition Book* contains references to one hundred fifty-six vessels frequenting the port. Forty-nine name Bristol as home port. For another forty the home port is not identified, but most of these ships probably were Bristol-based as well. The remaining sixty-seven vessels came from thirty-two different places: Nott and Ralph, eds., *Deposition Books*, vol. 2. Moreover, the Bristol ships did not all belong to Merchant Venturers. In the city, shipwrights and ship's masters as well as some shopkeepers and manufacturers often had shares in vessels and sometimes even owned them outright: H. E. Nott, ed., *The Deposition Books of Bristol*. Volume 1: *1643–1647* (BRS 6, 1935), pp. 85, 104–5, 117, 214–15; Nott and Ralph, eds., *Deposition Books*, vol. 2, p. 109; BRO, MS

04439 (4), f. 55^r; McGrath, "Merchant Shipping in the Seventeenth Century," 40 (1954): 283–84. On shipowning in general, see Ralph Davis, *The Rise of the English Shipping Industry in the Seventeenth and Eighteenth Centuries* (London: Macmillan, 1962), chaps. 3, 5. Obviously, only some of these ships frequented American waters, but the important thing is that a large supply of shipping was available at Bristol for hire by non–Merchant Venturers.

55. Nott and Ralph, eds., *Deposition Books*, vol. 2, pp. 131, 140, 169; SMV, *Wharfage Book*, vol. 1; BRO, MS 04220 (2). For examples of other shoemakers in the colonial trade see BRO, MS 04439 (3), ff. 40^v–41^r, 66^v. Shoes, of course, were an important trading item in the colonies: see BRO, MS 04439 (4), ff. 44^v, 103^r.

56. On the political proclivities of shoemakers in the preindustrial period, see Eric Hobsbawm and Joan W. Scott, "Political Shoemakers," *Past and Present*, no. 89 (November 1980): 86–114.

57. Nott and Ralph, eds., *Deposition Books*, vol. 2, p. 180; I. V. Hall, "Whitson Court Sugar House, Bristol, 1665–1824," *BGAS* 65 (1944): 14, 22, 26–27. Andrew Wathen and James Wathen, sons of William Wathen, pinmaker, and nephews of James Wathen, pinmaker, were both active as mariners, Andrew with Christopher Birkhead (BRO, MS 04352 [6], f. 45^r) and James as servant to Henry Gough (SMV, *Hall Book*, vol. 2, pp. 188–89). James Wathen, Junior, was his father's apprentice while he served Gough, a mariner turned merchant in the colonial trade: see BRO, MS 04352 (6), f. 93^v.

58. BRO, MS 04359 (2)a, ff. 121^r, 148^r, 319^r, 359^r; BRO, MS 04359 (3)a, f. 1^r; Nott, ed., *Deposition Books*, vol. 1, 173; Mortimer, ed., *Minute Book*, p. 204.

59. Nott and Ralph, eds., *Deposition Books*, vol. 2, p. 120; BRO, 04220 (1–2); SMV, *Wharfage Book*, vol. 1; George Bishop, Thomas Gouldney, Henry Roe, Edward Pyott, and Dennis Hollister, *The Cry of Blood . . . being a Declaration of the Lord arising in those People of the City of Bristol who are Scornfully called Quakers* (London, 1656), pp. 90–94, 108–11, 126–27, 134–35; Joseph Besse, *A Collection of the Sufferings of the People called Quakers*, 2 vols. (London: L. Hinde, 1753), vol. 1, p. 42, and vol. 2, pp. 395–96. This is the same Birkhead to whom Andrew Wathen was apprenticed.

60. PRO, SP 18/40/40; George Bishop, *Mene Tekel, or, the Council of Officers of the Army against the Declarations, &c. of the Army* (London, 1659), p. 48; George Bishop, *A Manifesto Declaring What George Bishope hath been to the City of Bristol* (London, 1665); Henry Fell to Margaret Fell, 14 August 1656, Friends' House Library, London, Swarthmore MSS 1/65. The *Wharfage Book* indicates that Bishop imported tobacco and sugar during 1656–57. For Bishop's political career see Richard L. Greaves and Robert Zaller, eds., *Biographical Dictionary of British Radicals in the Seventeenth Century*, 3 vols. (Brighton: Harvester Press, 1982–1984), vol. 1, p. 67; G. E. Aylmer, *The State's Servants: The Civil Service of the English Republic, 1649–1660* (London: Routledge and Kegan Paul, 1973), pp. 272–74.

61. PRO, SP 25/30/11, 25/34/2. William Bullock also engaged in this sort of trade, using the *Love's Increase* belonging to Speed's sister-in-law, Ann Yeamans.

62. SMV, *Wharfage Book*, vol. 1, 1654–55.

63. Nott and Ralph, eds., *Deposition Books*, vol. 2, p. 120.

64. This conclusion is based on a comparison of the *Wharfage Book, Register of Servants*, and *Deposition Books* entries with Mortimer, ed., *Minute Book*, pp. 193–222; Besse, *Sufferings of the People called Quakers*, vol. 2, pp. 637–38; and Hayden, ed., *Records*, pp. 281–310.

65. Hayden, ed., *Records*, esp. pp. 47–56, 100, 101–2; Mortimer, ed., *Minute Book*, pp. vii, xi–xii, xviii–xxi; William C. Braithwaite, *The Beginnings of Quakerism*, 2d ed. rev. by Henry J. Cadbury (Cambridge: Cambridge University Press, 1955), pp. 130–53; Richard T. Vann, *The Social Development of English Quakerism, 1655–1755* (Cambridge, Mass.: Harvard University Press, 1969), chaps. 4–5; Barry Reay, *The Quakers and the English Revolution*, foreword by Christopher Hill (London: Temple Smith, 1985), chap. 1, esp. pp. 20–31.

66. BRO, *Common Council Proceedings*, vol. 6, pp. 6, 70, 154, 174; Hall, "Whitson Court Sugar House," pp. 24–25, 36–37; Latimer, *Annals*, pp. 341, 346.

67. BRO, *Common Council Proceedings*, vol. 5, pp. 31–32.

68. On oaths see Bishop et al., *Cry of Blood*, p. 121; George Bishop, *A Vindication of the Principles and practices of the people called Quakers* ([London], 1665), pp. 48–51. In the 1650s and again in the 1670s Quaker shops were closed because the shopkeepers refused to swear the freeman's oath, even though they were eligible to do so: BRO, *Common Council Proceedings*, vol. 5, p. 150; Mortimer, ed., *Minute Book*, pp. 93 and 93n. The Quakers in the mid-1650s thought that every citizen, whether stranger or burgess, had the right to go peaceably about his business anywhere in the realm, and they objected strenuously to the forcing of Quaker missionaries from Bristol: Bishop et al., *Cry of Blood*, pp. 9–10. The Bristol common councillors thought differently and periodically tried to root out all strangers and inmates in the town, partly to rid themselves of vagrants and partly to purge Bristol of the Quaker menace: BRO, MS 04417 (1), ff. 46^r, 62^v; Orders of the Justices of the Peace, January 1655, printed in Bishop et al., *Cry of Blood*, pp. 62–64.

69. John Thurloe, *A Collection of the State Papers of John Thurloe, Esq.*, ed. Thomas Birch, 7 vols. (London: Executor of F. Gyles, 1742), vol. 3, p. 170.

70. Henry Fell to Margaret Fell, 11 August 1656, Friends' House Library, London, Swarthmore MSS 1/81. On the Quaker missions to Bristol, see John Camm and John Audland, *The Memory of the Righteous Revived*, ed. Thomas Camm and Charles Marshall (London, 1689), esp. Charles Marshall's *Testimony*, published as an appendix; "A Book of Letters which were Sent to G. F. from John Audland and John Camm," Friends' House Library, London, MSS, pp. 7–12, 26–27; Bishop et al., *Cry of Blood*, pp. 2–14; [Robert Purnell], *The Church of Christ in Bristol Recovering her Vail* (London, 1657), pp. 1–2. Of the one hundred twenty-eight men who supported Haggatt and Bishop with their votes or in petitions, forty-one were Quakers by 1665 or, if deceased, had close kin who were Quakers by this time.

71. Thurloe, *State Papers of John Thurloe*, vol. 3, p. 170.

72. PRO, SP 18/75/14i; Thurloe, *State Papers of John Thurloe*, vol. 3, pp. 117, 153–54, 161, 165–69, 172, 176–78, 181, 183–84, 191–92, 223–25, 242, 248–49, 259–60, 268; Bishop et al., *Cry of Blood*; Hayden, ed., *Records*, pp.

105–14; BRO, MS 04417 (1), ff. 18^v, 27^v, 28$^{r–v}$, 29^r. In this period Bishop was identified with Wildman's plot: see Thurloe, *State Papers of John Thurloe*, vol. 3, pp. 147–48. On popular fear of the Quakers in this period, see Reay, *The Quakers and the English Revolution*, chap. 4.

73. I have been able to identify thirty-four (28.33 percent) of Haggatt's supporters and fifty-one (30.91 percent) of the Aldworth/Jackson supporters as engaged in the American trade; these figures undoubtedly underestimate the totals for both sides.

74. Aldworth and Haggatt were admitted to the Society at a banquet for Lord Whitelocke on 12 August 1654, in what seems to have been a peace gesture engineered by Whitelocke: SMV, *Hall Book*, vol. 1, p. 249. Bishop had been a member of the Society since January 1651, when he was admitted gratis in thanks for his efforts at the Council of State on behalf of the Merchant Venturers' interest in trading butter and calfskins: ibid., p. 187. Although occasionally he attended meetings, he does not appear to have engaged in overseas trade before 1655. Thus although after 12 August all the parties in the disputed election were members of the Merchant Venturers, only Jackson was a real merchant regularly engaging in trade. Bishop, moreover, made it clear in the early 1650s that he did not think the Society could exclude nonmembers from trade: see Bishop, *A Manifesto*, p. 22.

75. The admission of William Yeamans, for example, notes that "he hath bin bread in, and excercised the trade of a Marchant Adventurer in this Citty the greatest parte of his tyme": SMV, *Hall Book*, vol. 1, p. 91.

76. Ibid., pp. 105, 187, 221, 244, 250, 256–57, 262.

77. Ibid., p. 228.

78. See, e.g., ibid., pp. 107, 133, 153, 199, 201, 203, 234, 249.

79. Ibid., pp. 162–63.

80. For a somewhat different view see McGrath, *Merchant Venturers of Bristol* (Bristol: Society of Merchant Venturers of Bristol, 1975), pp. 33, 97, 103 and 103n. 8. McGrath is right to say that the Society applied no religious test for membership in the seventeenth century, but in fact the openness of the Society varied a good deal from period to period. For a time in the 1640s, new men of all sorts found their way into it, but between January 1651 and January 1656 only Bulstrode Whitelocke, Robert Aldworth, and John Haggatt entered as redemptioners, all gratis. The thirteen others who were admitted in this period had all been apprenticed to members, most of them of long standing in 1645. It is also true that the Quakers and other sectaries once again sought membership in the later 1660s, but by then the Society had failed to reestablish its right to exclude retailers and shopkeepers from overseas trade, and the character of the mercantile community had changed. With sectaries owning sugar refineries, the Merchant Venturers could not cut themselves off from the nonconformists without undermining their own well-being. Hence they applied no religious test for membership.

81. PRO, SP 18/75/14iii.

82. BRO, MS 04373, pp. 58–59, dated 22 October 1654.

83. *CSP (Colonial)*, vol. 1, p. 404; Edwin Freshfield, *Some Remarks upon the Book of Records and History of the Parish of St. Stephen, Coleman Street*

in the City of London (Westminster: Nichols and Sons, 1887), pp. 8–10 and facsimiles. There is little doubt that the Mr. Peate mentioned in the facsimiles is Edward Peade and that he and Owen Rowe were of Goodwin's party to the disputes in that troubled parish.

84. See, e.g., William Prynne, *A Fresh Discovery of Some Prodigious New Wandering-Blazing Stars and Firebrands* (London, 1645), which vigorously attacks Goodwin and his gathered church and to which is appended a file of letters from the Somers Islands smearing the Independents there as well. For an account of Goodwin's affairs in London, see Thomas Jackson, *The Life of John Goodwin* (London: Longmans, Green, Reader and Dyer, 1872), chap. 3. On London politics in general in this period, see Valerie Pearl, "London's Counter-Revolution," in Aylmer, ed., *The Interregnum*, pp. 29–56. On the history of the Somers Islands, see C. M. Andrews, *The Colonial Period of American History*, 4 vols. (New Haven: Yale University Press, 1934), vol. 1, chaps. 11–12; J. H. Lefroy, *Memorials of the Discovery and Early Settlement of the Bermudas or Somers Islands, 1515–1685*, 2 vols. (London: Longmans, Green, 1877–1879), vol. 1, chap. 9; Henry C. Wilkinson, *The Adventurers of Bermuda: A History of the Island from Its Discovery until the Dissolution of the Somers Island Company*, 2d ed. (London: Oxford University Press, 1958), chap. 14; and, more generally, Henry C. Wilkinson, *Bermuda in the Old Empire* (London: Oxford University Press, 1950).

85. The language of the Bristol ordinance with its distinctive phrases referring to the "Inveigling, purloining . . . and Stealing" of children was adopted from the May 1645 parliamentary ordinance, the printed version of which was bound into the front of the first volume of the Bristol *Register* to give added force to the Common Council's legislation: BRO, MS 04220 (1); a photocopy is printed in Bowman, ed., *Bristol and America*, frontispiece.

86. Lorena S. Walsh and Russell Menard, "Death in the Chesapeake: Two Life Tables for Men in Early Colonial Maryland," *Maryland Historical Magazine*, 69 (1974): 211–17; Russell Menard, "Immigrants and Their Increase: The Process of Population Growth in Early Colonial Maryland," in Land, Carr, and Papenfuse, eds., *Law, Society and Politics*, pp. 88–110; Russell Menard, "From Servant to Freeholder: Status Mobility and Property Accumulation in Seventeenth-Century Maryland," *WMQ*, 3d ser., 30 (1973): 39–40; Darrett B. Rutman and Anita H. Rutman, "Of Agues and Fevers: Malaria in the Early Chesapeake," *WMQ*, 3d ser., 33 (1976): 31–60; Lois G. Carr and Russell Menard, "Immigration and Opportunity: The Freedman in Early Colonial Maryland," in Tate and Ammerman, eds., *The Chesapeake*, pp. 207–10; Carville V. Earle, "Environment, Disease and Mortality in Early Virginia," in ibid., pp. 96–125; Dunn, *Sugar and Slaves*, chap. 9; Daniel Blake Smith, "Mortality and Family in the Colonial Chesapeake," *Journal of Interdisciplinary History* 8 (1978): 403–28; Lorena S. Walsh, "Staying Put or Getting Out: Findings for Charles County Maryland, 1650–1720," *WMQ*, 3d ser., 44 (1987): 89–103, esp. 91–93. The most illuminating remarks on this whole dismal subject can be found in Morgan, *American Slavery, American Freedom*, pp. 158–79, 395–432.

87. Smith, *Colonists in Bondage*, chap. 11; Russell R. Menard, "British Migration to the Chesapeake Colonies in the Seventeenth Century," in Lois

Green Carr, Philip D. Morgan, and Jean B. Russo, eds., *Colonial Chesapeake Society* (Chapel Hill: University of North Carolina Press, 1988), pp. 126–27; Menard, "The Tobacco Industry in the Chesapeake Colonies," pp. 144–45; Menard, "From Servant to Freeholder," esp. p. 49; Souden, "Rogues, Whores and Vagabonds?" p. 26; Galenson, *White Servitude in Colonial America,* pp. 10–15, 102–13; David W. Galenson, "The Market Valuation of Human Capital: The Case of Indentured Servants," *Journal of Political Economy* 89 (1981): 446–67; David W. Galenson, "British Servants and the Colonial Indenture System in the Eighteenth Century," *Journal of Southern History* 44 (1978): 59–66.

CHAPTER 9

1. From 1679 to 1686, rough notes of the servant indentures entered in the Bristol Tolzey appear intermittently in the records of the Mayor's Court. Between 1 September 1679 and 29 September 1680, notations of one hundred fifty-seven servant indentures were made in the Mayor's Court Action Book: BRO, MS 04355 (6). A further thirty-one such entries appear in the same source between 30 September 1680 and 12 January 1681, a very low total for this season. There are no more entries until 26 April 1684, whence they run to 12 June 1686: BRO, MS 04356 (1). Even these records appear to be incomplete.

2. BRO, MS 04220 (2), entries for 1667–68 and 1677–78; see also Coldham, *Registers of Servants,* pp. 233–46, 339–45.

3. Based on PRO, E 190/1138/1. In 1671–72, one hundred fifty-nine vessels totaling 13,387 tons were recorded by customs officials as entering Bristol from European or Atlantic ports. Seventy-two (45.28 percent) had come from American waters. They amounted to 7,830 tons, or 58.49 percent of the total. In the same year one hundred vessels, totaling 9,159 tons, left Bristol bound for European or American destinations. Forty-seven (47.00 percent), totaling 5,630 tons (61.47 percent), were headed for the American colonies. On later developments in the organization of colonial trade, see Jacob M. Price and Paul G. E. Clemens, "A Revolution of Scale in Overseas Trade: British Firms in the Chesapeake Trade, 1675–1775," *JEcH* 47 (1987): 1–44.

4. For purposes of this analysis only the data recorded in the two volumes of the Bristol Register, BRO, MSS 04220 (1–2), have been used. These volumes were redacted by clerks from original entry books kept by the Bristol Mayor's Court. The entries end in August 1679, which means that the last complete year is 1677–78. Since the purpose of this analysis is to test the reliability of the record, the data from the original entry books for the years 1680–1686 have not been included in the analysis.

5. Henry Gemery, "Emigration from the British Isles to the New World, 1630–1700: Inferences from Colonial Populations," *Research in Economic History: A Research Annual* 5 (1980): 215–16. At best this analysis can only suggest the rough dimension of the change, since Gemery gives his totals by the decade.

6. For 1655–1662 we find a correlation of −.698 (significant at .05) with population as measured by E. A. Wrigley and R. S. Schofield, *The Population History of England, 1541–1871: A Reconstruction* (Cambridge, Mass.: Harvard

University Press, 1981), p. 532. That is, migration from Bristol in these years fluctuated inversely with increases or decreases in England's population as a whole. But after 1662 the correlation is only −.249 (n.s.). For the whole period from 1655 to 1678 we get a correlation of +.464, which is significant only at .25 and should be discounted. But we should not make too much of these calculations, since Wrigley and Schofield give estimates of population for England only, whereas a considerable number of the migrants from Bristol were Welsh. In addition, given the limited number of years in our series, our results, even for 1655–1662, should be taken only as suggestive, not definitive.

7. Gemery, "Emigration from the British Isles," pp. 215–16; Wrigley and Schofield, *Population History of England,* pp. 186–87, 219–28; Menard, "British Migration," pp. 99–105.

8. Campbell, "Social Origins of Some Early Americans," pp. 82–89; Mildred Campbell, "Mildred Campbell's Response," *WMQ,* 3d ser., 35 (1978): pp. 527–28; Craven, *White, Red and Black,* pp. 19, 20–21; Menard, "British Migration," pp. 108–9, 115–17; Menard, "The Tobacco Industry in the Chesapeake Colonies," pp. 121–22, 132–37, 148; Menard, "From Servants to Slaves," pp. 379–80; Richard N. Bean and Robert P. Thomas, "The Adoption of Slave Labor in British America," in Henry Gemery and Jan S. Hagendorn, eds., *The Uncommon Market: Essays in the Economic History of the Atlantic Slave Trade* (New York: Academic Press, 1979), pp. 391–98; Dunn, *Sugar and Slaves,* pp. 71–74; Galenson, *Traders, Planters and Slaves,* esp. chap. 1; David W. Galenson, "The Rise and Fall of Indentured Servitude in the Americas: An Economic Analysis," *JEcH* 44 (1984): 1–26; Galenson, " 'Middling People' or 'Common Sort'?" p. 504n. 9; Galenson, "Social Origins: Rejoinder," p. 272n. 18; David Souden, "English Indentured Servants and the Transatlantic Colonial Economy," in Shula Marks and Peter Richardson, eds., *International Labour Migration: Historical Perspectives* (Houndslow: M. Temple Smith, 1984), pp. 19–33; Clemens, *Atlantic Economy,* pp. 47–57.

9. G. F. Zook, *The Company of Royal Adventurers Trading to Africa* (Lancaster, Penn.: Press of the New Era Printing Company, 1919), pp. 17, 82; K. G. Davies, *The Royal Africa Company* (New York: Atheneum, 1970), pp. 41–43; V. T. Harlow, *A History of Barbados, 1625–1685* (Oxford: Clarendon Press, 1926), pp. 310n., 338; Sheridan, *Sugar and Slavery,* p. 133; Dunn, *Sugar and Slaves,* pp. 74–75, 87; R. C. Batie, "Why Sugar?" pp. 1–41; Menard, "From Servants to Slaves," pp. 360–71; Bean and Thomas, "Adoption of Slave Labor," pp. 380–86; Beckles, "Economic Origins of Black Slavery," pp. 36–56; Puckrein, *Little England,* pp. 30–32; Galenson, *Traders, Planters and Slaves,* chap. 1.

10. Charles Wilson, *Profit and Power: A Study of England and the Dutch Wars* (London: Longmans, Green, 1957), chaps. 8–9. It is always difficult to judge the effect of war on commerce. In the Second Dutch War the Bristolians complained loudly of their losses at sea during 1664–65: PRO, SP 29/133/66. But in November 1665 at least thirty and possibly forty-five ships sailed from the port to the West Indies (PRO, SP 29/136/98), and in the following July a well-laden convoy of twenty-three vessels, mostly Bristol-owned, arrived in the port (PRO, SP 29/163/128; see also PRO, SP 29/175/3, and PRO, SP 29/

177/39). Although the Third Dutch War seems to have made a much more noticeable impression on servant migration than did the second, it did so only during one year, that of 1673. In the previous and following years the war seems not to have damaged the trade to a significant degree: see Table 29.

11. Andrew Appleby, *Famine in Tudor and Stuart England* (Stanford: Stanford University Press, 1978), chaps. 7–8.

12. T. F. Reddaway, *The Rebuilding of London after the Great Fire* (London: Jonathan Cape, 1940), pp. 112ff. It might be noted, however, that if the fire had only a minor effect, the plague may well have had a greater, for Bristol established a quarantine for all strangers entering the town and cancelled its fairs during this outbreak: see Latimer, *Annals*, pp. 334–35; Robert Steele, ed., *A Bibliography of Royal Proclamations of the Tudor and Stuart Sovereigns*, 2 vols. [Bibliotheca Lindesiana, vols. 5–6] (Oxford: Clarendon Press, 1910), vol. 1, nos. 3424 and 3446.

13. Andrew Appleby, "Grain Prices and Subsistence Crises in England and France, 1590–1740," *JcHR* 39 (1979): 865–87; see also Joan Thirsk, ed., *The Agrarian History of England and Wales*. Volume 5: *1640–1750*. Part II: *Agrarian Change* (Cambridge: Cambridge University Press, 1985), pp. 95–101, 325–71, 506–30, 542–71.

14. Phelps-Brown and Hopkins, "Seven Centuries of the Prices of Consumables," pp. 179–96. I am grateful to Philip Hoffman for his advice in analyzing these data and interpreting the results.

15. Wrigley and Schofield, *Population History of England*, pp. 174–91, 210–12, 412.

16. For a strong argument on the significance of real wages in determining emigration rates, see Menard, "British Migration," pp. 108–9, 108n. 18, and Bean and Thomas, "Adoption of Slave Labor," pp. 390–98. The analysis offered by Bean and Thomas is fraught with difficulties: see Galenson, *White Servitude in Colonial America*, p. 265n. 16. Menard's analysis is also somewhat problematic. The real-wage figures he employs are based on harvest years: see Wrigley and Schofield, *Population History of England*, p. 312. But the migration figures Menard takes from Galenson and from Abbott Emerson Smith are for calendar years: see Galenson, *White Servitude in Colonial America*, pp. 220–21, 224–25; Smith, *Colonists in Bondage*, p. 309. For a more general critique of the use of the Phelps-Brown/Hopkins indexes to explain trends in the preindustrial economy, see Wrigley and Schofield, *Population History of England*, pp. 312–13, 431–35, 480–81, 638–41; Peter H. Lindert, "English Population, Wages, and Prices: 1541–1913," *Journal of Interdisciplinary History* 15 (1985): 618; David Loschky, "Seven Centuries of Real Income per Wage Earner Reconsidered," *Economica* 57 (1980): 459–65; Donald Woodward, "Wage Rates and Living Standards in Pre-Industrial England," *Past and Present*, no. 91 (May 1981): 28–45; David M. Palliser, "Tawney's Century: Brave New World or Malthusian Trap?" *EcHR*, 2d ser., 35 (1982): 349–51; Menard, "British Migration," p. 108n. 18.

17. Menard, "British Migration," pp. 116–17; Menard, "The Tobacco Industry in the Chesapeake Colonies," esp. pp. 118–20; Menard, "Immigration to the Chesapeake Colonies," *Maryland Historical Magazine* 68 (1973): 327;

Menard, "Farm Prices of Maryland Tobacco, 1659–1710," *Maryland Histori-cal Magazine* 68 (1973): 80–85.

18. Menard, "The Tobacco Industry in the Chesapeake Colonies," p. 135. In July 1666, to give an example, nineteen ships, all Bristol-owned and totaling 2,770 tons, arrived in Bristol carrying tobacco. Most of these vessels must have carried some servants on the outward voyage the previous autumn: see PRO, SP 29/163/128 (20 July 1666); see also PRO, SP 29/133/66, 29/163/127, 29/164/23.

19. Menard, "The Tobacco Industry in the Chesapeake Colonies," p. 136.

20. Campbell, "Social Origins of Some Early Americans," p. 87; Campbell, "Mildred Campbell's Response," pp. 527–28. David Galenson has challenged this view by arguing, correctly, that Campbell has not "demonstrated" the pres-ence of any Quakers among the servants on the Bristol lists. But the matter should not end with this negative criticism. As we shall see, there is good evi-dence to suggest that Campbell has a point.

21. See, e.g., Besse, *Sufferings of the People called Quakers,* vol. 2, pp. 278–391; James Bowden, *The History of the Society of Friends in America,* 2 vols. (London: C. Gilpin, 1850–1854), vol. 1, chaps. 19–20; Rufus M. Jones, as-sisted by Isaac Sharpless and Amelia M. Gummere, *The Quakers in the Ameri-can Colonies* (London: Macmillan, 1911), pp. 265–356.

22. Letter of Henry Fell to Margaret Fell, 14 August 1656, Friends' House Library, London, Swarthmore MSS 1/65. In the 1630s Dorothy Kelly, one of the founders of Bristol sectarianism, whose family were among the early Quakers there, had used her house on the High Street for this same purpose: Joseph Fletcher, *The History of the Revival and Progress of Independency in England since the Period of the Reformation,* 4 vols. (London: John Snow, 1847–1848), vol. 3, pp. 197–98; David Masson, *The Life of John Milton: Narrated in Con-nection with the Political, Ecclesiastical and Literary History of His Time,* new and rev. ed., 6 vols. (London: Macmillan, 1894), vol. 2, p. 581.

23. Letter of George Bishop to Margaret Fell, 27 October 1656, Friends' House Library, London, Swarthmore MSS 1/188; George Bishop, *The Throne of Truth Exalted over the Powers of Darkness* (London, 1656); George Braith-waite, *The Beginnings of Quakerism,* 2d rev. ed., ed. H. J. Cadbury (Cam-bridge: Cambridge University Press, 1955), pp. 253, 566. Besse names only two Bristol sufferers in the years 1657–1659, both of whom were punished for fail-ing to swear the burgess oath and for refusing to remove their hats before the magistrates: Besse, *Sufferings of the People called Quakers,* vol. 1, p. 42. For an overview of the early history of dissent in Bristol, see J. G. Fuller, *The Rise and Progress of Dissent in Bristol: Chiefly in Relation to the Broadmead Church* (London: Hamilton, Adams, 1840); Russell Mortimer, *Early Bristol Quaker-ism: The Society of Friends in the City, 1654–1700* (Historical Association, Bristol Branch, pamphlet no. 17, 1967); Hayden, ed., *Records,* pp. 16ff.; see also Jonathan Barry, "The Parish in Civic Life: Bristol and Its Churches, 1640–1750," in Susan Wright, ed., *Parish, Church and People: Local Studies of Lay Religion, 1350–1750* (London: Hutchinson, 1988), pp. 158ff.

24. For Quaker complaints of persecution in this period, see, e.g., John Crook et al., *A Declaration of the People of God in scorn called Quakers to all*

Magistrates and People (London, 1659), signed by Dennis Hollister of Bristol, among others; Bishop, *Mene Tekel*. But in contrast see Besse's account of the actual persecutions in London and Middlesex, for example, Besse, *Sufferings of the People called Quakers,* vol. 1, pp. 361–65.

25. PRO, SP 18/220/80.

26. BRO, MS 04376, f. 132ᵛ; BRO, *Common Council Proceedings*, vol. 6, p. 12; HMC, *Report on the MSS of F. W. Leybourne-Popham*, p. 160; PRO, SP 29/9/41, 42, 29/30/67; letter of William Dewsbury to Margaret Fell (February 1660?), Friends' House Library, London, Swarthmore MSS 4/134; [Richard Ellsworth], *A Letter of the Apprentices of the City of Bristol* (London, 1660); William Sewel, *The History of the Rise, Increase, and Progress of the Christian People Called Quakers*, 2d ed. (London: J. Sowle, 1725), pp. 232–33; Seyer, *Memoirs*, vol. 2, pp. 507–9; Latimer, *Annals*, pp. 290–92; Braithwaite, *Beginnings of Quakerism*, pp. 364–66; Barry Reay, "Popular Hostility towards Quakers in Mid-Seventeenth Century England," *Social History* 5 (1980): 403–4; Reay, *The Quakers and the English Revolution*, pp. 73–75. The outcries against the Quakers in this year were closely tied to discontent over the depressed state of trade, as is revealed in the *Letter of the Apprentices of the City of Bristol*, and to a sense of impending release from the social restraints imposed during the Interregnum. Just before Shrove Tuesday in 1660, for example, the mayor and aldermen issued orders to the apprentices and other young men of the town banning cockthrowing, to avoid tumults (BRO, MS 04376, f. 134ʳ⁻ᵛ) and just before the king's restoration in May they issued orders to prevent their playing "farthing pitt & lead pitt" while taking the name of the Lord in vain, and their setting up maypoles (BRO, MS 04273, f. 135ʳ⁻ᵛ). On the role of the Quakers in the events leading to the Restoration, see W. A. Cole, "The Quakers in Politics, 1652–1660," Ph.D. thesis, University of Cambridge, 1955, chaps. 3–8; W. A. Cole, "The Quakers and the English Revolution," in Trevor Aston, ed., *Crisis in Europe, 1560–1660* (Garden City, N.Y.: Anchor, 1957), pp. 358–76; J. F. Maclear, "Quakerism and the End of the Interregnum," *Church History* 19 (1950): 240–70; Barry Reay, "The Quakers, 1659, and the Restoration of the Monarchy," *History* 63 (1978): 193–215; Reay, *The Quakers and the English Revolution*, pp. 81–100.

27. Hayden, ed., *Records*, p. 127. For persecutions in London in this period and their effects on dissenters there, see Tim Harris, *London Crowds in the Reign of Charles II: Propaganda and Politics from the Restoration until the Exclusion Crisis* (Cambridge: Cambridge University Press, 1987), chap. 4.

28. On this theme, see Jonathan Barry, "The Politics of Religion in Restoration Bristol," in Tim Harris, Paul Seaward, and Mark Goldie, eds., *The Politics of Religion in Restoration England* (Oxford: Basil Blackwell, 1990), esp. pp. 168–69.

29. PRO, SP 29/21/107; see also PRO, SP 29/21/87.

30. PRO, SP 29/21/107; see also PRO, SP 29/28/87, 29/81/16.

31. PRO, SP 29/28/87, 29/56/83, 29/57/87, 122, 29/58/16, 29/68/4, 44/10, pp. 38–39, 29/100/89. On the social background to the Quakers, see W. A. Cole, "The Social Origins of the Early Friends," *Journal of Friends' Historical Society* 48 (1957): 99–118; Cole, "The Quakers in Politics, 1652–60," pp.

295ff.; R. T. Vann, "Quakerism and the Social Structure of the Interregnum," *Past and Present*, no. 48 (August, 1970): 71–91; Vann, *Social Development of English Quakerism*, pp. 47–93; A. Anderson, "The Social Origins of the Early Quakers," *Quaker History* 68 (1979): 33–40; Barry Reay, "The Social Origins of Early Quakerism," *Journal of Interdisciplinary History* 11 (1980): 55–72; Reay, *The Quakers and the English Revolution*, pp. 20–31; Mortimer, ed., *Minute Book*, pp. xxvi–xxix; Russell Mortimer, "Quakerism in Seventeenth-Century Bristol," M.A. thesis, University of Bristol, 1946, pp. 525–27.

32. PRO, SP 29/81/16.

33. For this and the following paragraphs, see, in general, Ronald Hutton, *The Restoration: A Political and Religious History of England and Wales, 1658–1667* (Oxford: Clarendon Press, 1985), esp. part 3; Richard L. Greaves, *Deliver Us from Evil: The Radical Underground in Britain, 1660–1663* (New York: Oxford University Press, 1986); W. C. Abbott, "English Conspiracy and Dissent, 1660–1674: I," *AHR* 11 (1908–1909): 503–28; Mortimer, "Quakerism in Seventeenth-Century Bristol," pp. 22–40.

34. PRO, SP 29/28/87, 29/34/68, 29/43/26; see also *Stat. Realm*, 13 Car. II st. i c. 6. A portion of Roe's stock was later returned to him, however, for, as Secretary Nicholas said to the Bristol magistrates, the king did not mean to disturb him in the innocent pursuit of his calling. Nevertheless, at Nicholas's urging Roe was forced to give a weekly accounting of his purchases and sales: [Nicholas] to the mayor of Bristol, 5 October 1661, PRO, SP 29/43/25. For discussion of the Venner plot, see C. Burrage, "The Fifth Monarchy Insurrections," *English Historical Review* 25 (1910): 739–45; Sir W. Foster, "Venner's Rebellion," *London Topographical Record* 18 (1942): 30–33; P. G. Rogers, *The Fifth Monarchy Men* (London: Oxford University Press, 1966), pp. 110–22; Bernard Capp, *The Fifth Monarchy Men: A Study in Seventeenth-Century English Millenarianism* (London: Faber and Faber, 1972), pp. 199–200; Greaves, *Deliver Us from Evil*, pp. 50–57.

35. PRO, SP 29/44/39, 39i–iv, 40, 83; see also PRO, SP 44/1, pp. 19, 71–72, 29/77/74, 75.

36. PRO, SP 29/57/42, 42i, 57, 57i, 85, 87, 87i, 29/58/16, 16i–ii, 44/4, p. 62.

37. PRO, SP 29/57/1, 29/61/98, 29/64/4, 64; see also *Stat. Realm*, 14 Car. II c. 3. On the organization and operation of the militia during the Restoration period, see J. R. Western, *The English Militia in the Eighteenth Century: The Story of a Political Issue* (London: Routledge and Kegan Paul, 1965), chaps. 1–2; Lois Schwoerer, *"No Standing Armies!" The Antiarmy Ideology in Seventeenth-Century England* (Baltimore: Johns Hopkins University Press, 1974), chap. 5.

38. PRO, SP 29/65/6, 33, 33i–iii, 34, 63, 63i, 29/69/48, 49, 63, 29/86/20, 201i–v.

39. Christopher Hill, *The World Turned Upside Down: Radical Ideas during the English Revolution* (New York: Viking Press, 1972), pp. 32–40, esp. 40; Reay, "Popular Hostility towards Quakers," pp. 388, 393–94; Smith, *Colonists in Bondage*, p. 175.

40. *CJ*, vol. 8, pp. 2, 246; *Stat. Realm*, 14 Car. II c. 1. The bill against the Quakers and the bill against vagrants were so closely tied in the minds of the

MPs that the two measures were sent to the same committee after the second readings: *CJ*, vol. 8, pp. 252, 285.

41. Cf. the committees' names in *CJ*, vol. 8, pp. 285, 346, 451, 491, 509.

42. *CJ*, vol. 8, pp. 346, 451, 491, 509; Hutton, *The Restoration*, p. 210; *A Relation of the Inhumane and Barbarous sufferings of the people called Quakers in the City of Bristol* (London, 1665), pp. 76–77. The principal author of this work is probably George Bishop. As a member of the Cavalier Parliament, Sir John Knight sat on seven committees concerned with ecclesiastical legislation. Only ten other MPs sat on as many or more such committees: see Paul Seaward, *The Cavalier Parliament and the Reconstruction of the Old Regime, 1661–1667* (Cambridge: Cambridge University Press, 1989), p. 328. Later in Charles II's reign, Knight's Anglican and anti-popery views made him an active exclusionist: see Barry, "Politics of Religion," pp. 172–73. On Knight's political career, see Basil Duke Henning, ed., *The House of Commons, 1660–1690*, 3 vols. (London: History of Parliament Trust, 1983), vol. 2, pp. 692–96.

43. BRO, MS 04417 (2), ff. 136^v, 158^v, 159^v, 166^v; BRO, *Common Council Proceedings*, vol. 6, pp. 144–45.

44. BRO, *Common Council Proceedings*, vol. 6, p. 36. This complaint found its way into one of the petitions drafted by the Common Council in April 1661 requesting a confirmation of the city's charters. There was some question, however, whether it was politically wise to include this complaint in the petition, and a second petition was drawn without it; it was left to the mayor, Henry Creswick, a Merchant Venturer, to decide, after he had scouted the territory in London, which of the two to use.

45. *A Relation*, pp. 51–52.

46. On the searches, see BRO, MS 04220 (1), ff. 351^r–352^r, 355^v–367^v, 482^r–497^v. For Knight's attempt at legislation, see *CJ*, vol. 8, p. 401. The bill originated in the Commons just before the recess of the summer of 1661. It may have been a response to complaints in London about the stealing of children for transportation to Virginia, which surfaced the year before: *Acts of the Privy Council (Colonial)*, vol. 1, pp. 296–97; see also Jeaffreson, ed., *Middlesex County Records*, vol. 3, pp. 302, 303, 306, 315. The bill was left to Alderman Fowkes of London to draft. It received its first reading in January 1662 and its second reading and commitment in April: *CJ*, vol. 8, pp. 316, 349, 401. But although the committee received further instructions from the House, it did not produce the bill for a final vote. For a connection between this bill and revenge against Civil War enemies, see *CJ*, vol. 8, pp. 403, 412. Knight remained interested in the matter of child-stealing throughout most of his long parliamentary career, serving on committees when legislation was introduced in 1670 and 1673: *CJ*, vol. 9, pp. 138, 251, 286. On each occasion the bill failed, sometimes because it could not pass the House of Lords.

47. PRO, SP 29/57/71. The Long Parliament's ordinance of May 1645 no longer, of course, had any force after the Restoration. This request of the mayor, however, did not, as far as I can determine, result in the grant of any new authority to the Bristol Corporation.

48. See, e.g., *CSP (Colonial)* (1661–1668), no. 367.

49. *Acts of Assembly passed in the Island of Barbadoes from 1648, to 1718* (London: J. Baskett, 1721), p. 12. On the "Royalism" of the elites in the colonial

Chesapeake region, especially Virginia, see David Hackett Fischer, *Albion's Seed: Four British Folkways in America* (New York: Oxford University Press, 1989), pp. 207–25; on the political effects of the Restoration on the colonies in general, see Stephen Saunders Webb, *The Governors-General: The English Army and the Definition of Empire* (Chapel Hill: University of North Carolina Press, 1979); Alison Gilbert Olson, *Anglo-American Politics, 1660–1775: The Relationship between Parties in England and Colonial America* (Oxford: Clarendon Press, 1973), chap. 2; Philip S. Haffenden, "The Anglican Church in Restoration Politics," in Smith, ed., *Seventeenth-Century America*, pp. 166–91.

50. *CSP (Colonial)* (1661–1668), no. 24; *Acts passed in the Island of Barbadoes*, p. 12. The impetus for this order and legislation appears to have been the royal proclamation of 10 January 1661, suppressing conventicles in England and requiring persons found at them to take the oath of allegiance: Steele, ed., *Bibliography of Royal Proclamations*, vol. 1, no. 3278. During this same year, the island's legislature passed an act requiring that morning and evening prayers be said by the head of every household and that all those who lived within two miles of a parish church attend morning and evening services there: *Acts passed in the Island of Barbadoes*, pp. 12–13.

51. Besse, *Sufferings of the People called Quakers*, vol. 2, p. 279. In the following year difficulties for dissenters only increased when the island established a tithe on all landowners for support of the parish clergy, for everywhere it appeared the tithe was anathema to the Quakers and to many other nonconformist groups: *Acts passed in the Island of Barbadoes*, pp. 20–22; Besse, *Sufferings of the People called Quakers*, vol. 2, pp. 280–87. On the dissenters and the tithe, see Margaret James, "The Political Importance of the Tithe Controversy in the English Revolution," *History* 26 (1941): 1–18; Blair Worden, *The Rump Parliament, 1648–1653* (Cambridge: Cambridge University Press, 1974), pp. 13, 293–95, 298, 307–8, 316; Hill, *The World Turned Upside Down*, pp. 78–79, 82–83, 152, 156–57, 189, 196, 244; Barry Reay, "Quaker Opposition to Tithes, 1652–1660," *Past and Present*, no. 86 (February 1980): 98–120. For a Bristol Quaker's view of the tithe, see Thomas Speed, *Christs Innocency Pleaded against the Cry of the Chief Priests* (London, 1656), pp. 10–11.

52. Besse, *Sufferings of the People called Quakers*, pp. 352, 366, 370, 380–82; on Maryland, see Bowden, *Society of Friends in America*, vol. 1, pp. 369–71.

53. William Waller Hening, ed., *The Statutes at Large: being A Collection of all the Laws of Virginia from the First Session of the Legislature in the year 1619*, 13 vols. (Richmond: Samuel Pleasants, Junior, 1809–1823), vol. 1, pp. 532–33.

54. See Henry R. McIlwaine, *The Struggles of Protestant Dissenters for Religious Toleration in Virginia* (Johns Hopkins University Studies in History and Political Science, 12th ser., 1894, part 4), pp. 20–21; Sewel, *Rise of the Christian People Called Quakers*, pp. 264–65; Bowden, *Society of Friends in America*, vol. 1, pp. 347–49. McIlwaine says that no Quakers appear to have suffered under the act and suggests that this may have been due to the effect of the Declaration of Breda. But for evidence of such persecution, see *The Lower Norfolk County Virginia Antiquary* 3 (1901): 103–6, 138–46; Jones et al., *Quakers in*

the American Colonies, pp. 273–74. The Bristol *Register* shows that the leading Quaker ·traders in the city, such as Speed and Bullock, continued to ship servants to Virginia in the early 1660s, but of course these emigrants may not themselves have been Quakers.

55. Hening, ed., *Statutes at Large*, vol. 2, p. 37. In 1661 Virginia received the same instructions on church settlement as had Barbados, but these may not have arrived in the colony before the end of the legislative session of March, 1661: see *CSP (Colonial)* (1661–1668), no. 24; Edward D. Neill, *Virginia Carolorum: The Colony under the Rule of Charles the First and Second*, A.D. 1625–A.D. 1685 (Albany, N.Y.: J. Munsell's Sons, 1886), pp. 282–83; see also George M. Brydon, *Virginia's Mother Church and the Conditions under Which It Grew*, 2 vols. (Richmond: Virginia Historical Society, 1947–1952), vol. 1, chap. 15; Fischer, *Albion's Seed*, pp. 232–36.

56. Hening, ed., *Statutes at Large*, vol. 2, pp. 51–52, and esp. p. 48.

57. Ibid., pp. 165–66.

58. PRO, SP 29/56/134; Neill, *Virginia Carolorum*, pp. 285–86; Bowden, *Society of Friends in America*, vol. 1, pp. 344ff.; William Meade, *Old Churches, Ministers and Families of Virginia*, 2 vols., first ed. 1857 (Baltimore: Genealogical Publishing, 1966), vol. 1, pp. 255, 427; in general see Brydon, *Virginia's Mother Church*, vol. 1, pp. 191–98. In September 1662 the Council of Foreign Plantations ordered the continuance of the policies of church government already instituted in the colony, but at the same time instructed Berkeley not to molest men solely for religion, provided they "be content with a quiet and peaceably enjoying of it, not giving therein offense or scandall to the Government": *Virginia Magazine of History and Biography* 3 (1895–96): 15; Neill, *Virginia Carolorum*, pp. 292–93. The council's remarks suggest a desire to encourage some nonconformists to continue to people the colony, but since the Quakers were not thought to be peaceable or to act without offense to the government, probably they were not included. Nevertheless, see McIlwaine, *Struggles of Protestant Dissenters*, pp. 22–23.

59. Hening, ed., *Statutes at Large*, vol. 2, pp. 180–83. For a discussion of this measure see McIlwaine, *Struggles of Protestant Dissenters*, pp. 23–24.

60. Robert Beverley, *The History and Present State of Virginia*, 1705 ed., ed. Louis Wright (Chapel Hill: University of North Carolina Press, 1947), p. 69; Hening, ed., *Statutes at Large*, vol. 2, pp. 191, 510; *Virginia Magazine of History and Biography* 15 (1907–8): 38–43; A. P. Scott, *Criminal Law in Colonial Virginia* (Chicago: University of Chicago Press, 1930), pp. 155, 156; Richard B. Morris, *Government and Labor in Early America* (New York: Columbia University Press, 1946), pp. 173–74; Webb, *Governors-General*, pp. 84–85.

61. Beverley, *Present State of Virginia*, p. 68; see also Hening, ed., *Statutes at Large*, vol. 2, p. 198; Jones et al., *The Quakers in the American Colonies*, pp. 274–75. These conditions account for the specific exclusion of Virginia as a place to send those convicted of violating the Conventicle Act of 1664: *Stat. Realm*, 16 Car. II, c. 4; see also Hening, ed., *Statutes at Large*, vol. 2, p. 510.

62. Brydon, *Virginia's Mother Church*, vol. 1, pp. 197–98; see also Neill, *Virginia Carolorum*, p. 296; Jones et al., *The Quakers in the American Colonies*, p. 280 and book 3.

63. PRO, SP 29/72/11, 11i, 29/73/12, 12i–iv; William Cobbett and John Wright, eds., *Parliamentary History of England from the Norman Conquest, in 1066 . . . to 1803*, 36 vols. (London: T. C. Hansard, 1806–1820), vol. 4, pp. 257–58.

64. Cobbett and Wright, eds., *Parliamentary History*, vol. 4, p. 268.

65. PRO, SP 29/74/48, 48i–iii, 66, 66i–ii, 29/75/11, 54, 54i, 99, 105, 115.

66. On Captain Gregory, see PRO, SP 29/67/63, 63i, 44/9, pp. 206, 269, 296, 29/67/25, 29/68/4, 44/10, pp. 38–39, 29/69/48, 49, 63, 64, 29/86/20, 20i–v, 29/95/99, 29/97/81, 84. The Gregory affair implicated Henry Roe in the plots. On Casbeard, see PRO, SP 29/76/41, 71, 72, 29/77/48, 74, 74i, 75. See also Greaves, *Deliver Us from Evil*, pp. 140–50, 160–61; Abbott, "English Conspiracy and Dissent," p. 518.

67. PRO, SP 29/77/31, 50. See also Henry Gee, "The Derwentdale Plot, 1663," *TRHS*, 3d ser., 9 (1917): esp. 135; Greaves, *Deliver Us from Evil*, pp. 165ff.; Abbott, "English Conspiracy and Dissent," pp. 521–23; Hutton, *The Restoration*, pp. 204ff.; Steven C. A. Pincus, "Protestantism and Patriotism: Ideology and the Making of English Foreign Policy, 1650–1665," Ph.D. dissertation, Harvard University, 1990, pp. 332–449. I am grateful to Dr. Pincus for allowing me to consult his dissertation.

68. Cobbett and Wright, eds., *Parliamentary History*, vol. 4, pp. 288–89.

69. PRO, SP 29/78/46, 47, 29/79/64, 126, 29/80/1, 29/80/8. Cf. the king's speech of 16 March 1664: Cobbett and Wright, eds., *Parliamentary History*, vol. 4, pp. 289–90. On the operation of the militia in this period, see Western, *English Militia*, pp. 35–36.

70. PRO, SP 29/80/10, 19, 20, 29/81/16, 73, 73i–iv. Note, however, that the Bristol Quakers were willing to contribute to a gift for the king: Latimer, *Annals*, p. 319.

71. PRO, SP 29/81/29.

72. PRO, SP 29/81/73, 92, 96. Knight, responding to a specific request from the Privy Council, searched the house of Richard Moone, a Baptist stationer, for seditious pamphlets: PRO, SP 29/81/73, 73i–ii.

73. Hayden, ed., *Records*, pp. 117–18; *A Relation*, p. 11.

74. *A Relation*, p. 17.

75. Ibid., pp. 12–36; Besse, *Sufferings of the People called Quakers*, vol. 1, p. 47. Knight claimed to initiate the campaign after receiving the Privy Council's order to do so, but according to the Quakers this order in fact was solicited by Knight in a letter reporting the city in danger from them: *A Relation*, pp. 16, 24–25, 32.

76. *A Relation*, pp. 66–67; Besse, *Sufferings of the People called Quakers*, vol. 1, p. 50.

77. *A Relation*, p. 74; BRO, MS 04417 (2), f. 129^{r-v}; see also Besse, *Sufferings of the People called Quakers*, vol. 1, p. 50.

78. *A Relation*, p. 81; Besse, *Sufferings of the People called Quakers*, vol. 1, p. 50; PRO, SP 29/110/77.

79. BRO, MS 04417 (2), ff. 122^v–124^r; Besse, *Sufferings of the People called Quakers*, vol. 1, p. 51. According to the Quakers, Knight had publicly stated that with the passage of the act "he now hoped to send four Hundred Quakers

out of the Land before the Expiration of his Mayoralty": Besse, *Sufferings of the People called Quakers*, vol. 1, p. 51.

80. BRO, MS 04417 (2), ff. 107^r–121^v; Besse, *Sufferings of the People called Quakers*, vol. 1, p. 51, and vol. 2, pp. 637–38; *A Relation*, pp. 83–125; Bishop, *A Manifesto*, esp. pp. 20–27; Hayden, ed., *Records*, pp. 118–20; Sewel, *Rise of the Christian People Called Quakers*, p. 424. Sewel suggests that some of those guilty of a third offense were redeemed by kinsmen who were not Quakers but who paid the £100 fine mentioned in the statute: ibid., p. 430.

81. See, e.g., J. C. Jeaffreson, ed., *A Young Squire of the Seventeenth Century, from the Papers* (A.D. 1676–1686) *of Christopher Jeaffreson of Dullingham House, Cambridgeshire*, 2 vols. (London: Hurst and Blackett, 1878), vol. 2, p. 61; Jones et al., *The Quakers in the American Colonies*, pp. 283–300.

82. *A Relation*, pp. 3–4; on this subject, see Barry, "Politics of Religion," pp. 169–70.

83. See Latimer, *Annals*, pp. 290ff.; Latham, ed., *Bristol Charters, 1509–1899*, pp. 35–57; Henning, ed., *House of Commons*, vol. 1, pp. 327–40; Barry, "Politics of Religion," pp. 163–89.

84. PRO, SP 29/94/20. See also PRO, SP 29/92/110; McGrath, ed., *Merchants and Merchandise*, p. 155n. Ellsworth's animosity to the sectaries possibly was enhanced by the business disputes he had with William Bullock in the 1650s: see ibid., pp. 21–22.

85. PRO, SP 29/133/66.

86. PRO, SP 25/30/11, 44/25/111. On Robert Cann's family ties, politics, and career, see Henning, ed., *House of Commons*, vol. 2, pp. 5–6; Barry, "Politics of Religion," pp. 172–73 and 185n. 35 with the works cited there.

87. BRO, MS 04439 (4), ff. 156^r–157^v.

88. *CSP (Colonial)* (1661–1668), nos. 391, 520. Sir Humphrey Hooke was the grandson of Alderman Humphrey Hooke, whom we have met. Sir Humphrey was high sheriff of Gloucestershire in 1661. He was elected for Bristol to the Cavalier Parliament, but withdrew in favor of Lord Ossory. When Ossory was raised to the peerage in 1666, Hooke reclaimed the seat: Latimer, *Annals*, p. 305. For Hooke's connections in Barbados, see *CSP (Colonial)* (1661–1668), nos. 141, 1121, 1437. Robert Vickris was an officer in the militia during the Interregnum and a common councillor from 1650 to November 1662, when he withdrew or was ousted: PRO, SP 18/220/70i, 25/76A/33; BRO, *Common Council Proceedings*, vol. 6, pp. 7–8. See also BL, Stowe MS 185, ff. 157^v–158^r; Beaven, *Lists*, pp. 201, 311; Mortimer, ed., *Minute Book*, pp. 218–19.

89. *A Relation*, p. 13; Mortimer, ed., *Minute Book*, pp. 216, 222; BRO, MS 04439 (4), f. 78^v. Yeamans was the son of John Yeamans, brewer, and a nephew of William Yeamans, scrivener. The latter's family provided one of the first contingents of the separatists in Bristol when the Broadmead church was formed in 1640 and later split from the Baptists to form the first Quaker group in the city: see Hayden, ed., *Records*, pp. 13, 84–90. Ann Yeamans, the daughter of William the scrivener, first married Robert Yeamans, merchant, who in 1643, as we know, became a martyr for King Charles I for attempting to turn Bristol over to Prince Rupert. She later married Thomas Speed, who adopted her children and brought them up in his household. John Yeamans, Robert's

brother, was also involved in the 1643 plot but was not executed. After a period of time in prison, he emigrated to Barbados and soon became one of the most important people on the island. Later he served as governor of Carolina: see "Sir John Yeamans" in *Dictionary of American Biography*. For an account of the 1643 plot, see above, pp. 238–41, and Seyer, *Memoirs*, vol. 2, pp. 341ff. The Robert Yeamans who was active in Restoration politics was a Royalist supporter in the Interregnum: see David Underdown, *Royalist Conspiracy in England, 1649–60* (New Haven: Yale University Press, 1960), p. 264. He was a significant colonial trader as well: *CSP (Colonial)* (1574–1660), pp. 350, 406. He has been identified as the son of Robert the martyr (see Latham, ed., *Bristol Charters, 1509–1899*, p. 42n. 3), but this is an error; he was a close cousin.

90. *A Relation*, p. 35. See also *Some Reasons Briefly Suggested which have Prevailed with the Dissenters in Bristol to Continue Their Open Meetings, however Persecuted or Disturbed* (London, 1675); Barry, "Politics of Religion," p. 169.

91. PRO, SP 25/94/87. Knight twice refused Common Council membership in the Interregnum: Beaven, *Lists*, p. 299. Knight's sister-in-law was Joyce Warren, wife of Mathew Warren, who had been sheriff in 1639–40, and daughter-in-law of the Mathew Warren whom we have met as mayor in 1633–34. As we know, she was a leading figure among the Quakers in the 1660s: *A Relation*, p. 74.

92. *A Relation*, p. 36. For Streamer's defense of his position, see PRO, SP 29/90/10i, 76.

93. *A Relation*, pp. 53–54, 65; Besse, *Sufferings of the People called Quakers*, vol. 1, pp. 48–49. It appears that Bristol grand juries in this period were more willing to indict sectaries than petty juries were to convict them: see BRO, MS 04451–52 (1); Barry, "Politics of Religion," pp. 167, 182n. 12. There were significant numbers of indictments for religious matters in 1662 and from 1664 on. Indictments for 1661, 1663, and 1667–1675 are missing, but for 1675 see *A Sober Answer to the Address of the Grand Jurors* (London, 1675).

94. PRO, SP 29/110/42. Ironically, the crew members argued that the transportation of these individuals violated the ordinances against spiriting, because there were no indentures and because Barbados had a strict law against those who brought unindentured servants into the colony against their wills: see *Acts passed in the Island of Barbadoes*, pp. 22–23.

95. PRO, SP 29/90/10, 10i, 62, 76, 29/92/76, 83, 83i–v, 104, 105, 110; BRO, *Common Council Proceedings*, vol. 6, p. 98; *A Relation*, pp. 33–35. On the business connection of Yate and John Knight, Junior, see PRO, SP 25/30/11; BRO, MSS 04439 (3), ff. 12ʳ–13ʳ, 04439 (4), ff. 156ʳ–157ᵛ. John Knight, known as John Knight, Junior, was the cousin of Sir John Knight: *Notes and Queries* 3 (29 April 1899): 321–23; I. V. Hall, "John Knight, Junior, Sugar Refiner at the Great House on St. Augustine's Back (1654–78)," *BGAS* 68 (1949): 110–64; I. V. Hall, "The Connections between John Knight, Junior, and the Jennings, Latch and Gorges Families," *BGAS* 74 (1955): 188–99.

96. Beaven, *Lists*, p. 185; Latimer, *Annals*, p. 265.

97. PRO, SP 29/90/10; *A Relation*, pp. 14–18, 47–48; see also PRO, SP 29/11/185, 186, 44/1, pp. 71–72, 29/61/98, 29/64/4, 29/65/16, 63, 29/81/92, 96,

29/92/53, 76. On the significance of the deputy lieutenants as an inner circle of loyalists, see Western, *English Militia*, pp. 16–17. After 1679, this same function was provided by Bristol's Artillery Company, formed under the inspiration of the marquis of Worcester, whom Barry calls the city's "ultra-royalist" lord lieutenant: Barry, "Politics of Religion," p. 170; M. de L. Landon, "The Bristol Artillery Company and the Tory Triumph in Bristol, 1679–84," *Proceedings of the American Philosophical Society* 114 (1970): 155–61.

98. Beaven, *Lists*, pp. 186, 200–202; BRO, *Common Council Proceedings*, vol. 6, pp. 23, 45–47; BRO, MS 04417 (2), ff. 155^v–156^r; PRO, SP 29/14/77. See also Latham, ed., *Bristol Charters*, pp. 35–40; Latimer, *Annals*, pp. 296–98, 309–11.

99. PRO, PC 2/51/217; BRO, *Common Council Proceedings*, vol. 6, pp. 108–9. John Knight was joined by eleven others under the order, but despite it only Knight and five more took the oath and sat: see BRO, *Common Council Proceedings*, vol. 6, pp. 65ff.; PRO, SP 44/13, p. 135, 29/57/41; Latham, ed., *Bristol Charters*, pp. 40–42, 175–78.

100. BRO, *Common Council Proceedings*, vol. 6, pp. 55, 60, 68, 86, 95, 99, 104, 112, 125; PRO, SP 29/57/55, 29/92/48, 77, 78, 83, 91, 111, 118, 29/93/47, 47i, 69, 29/94/118, 29/96/39. The outcome of the dispute was an order applying the custom of London to Bristol. In London those common councillors with titles enjoyed precedence only when not exercising their public functions or appearing as members of the civic body. In the council and aldermanic meetings they proceeded by seniority of membership.

101. See Besse, *Sufferings of the People called Quakers*, vol. 1, p. 52.

102. BRO, MS 04417 (2), ff. 104^v–105^v; Hayden, ed., *Records*, p. 121; Besse, *Sufferings of the People called Quakers*, vol. 1, p. 51.

103. PRO, SP 29/217/75, 114, 29/220/44, 29/225/38, 29/265/15.

104. BRO, *Common Council Proceedings*, vol. 6, pp. 28–30, 111; Beaven, *Lists*, pp. 200, 302, 309.

105. PRO, SP 29/177/39, 29/178/135, 29/180/5, 89, 29/181/129, 29/206/1, 1i–ii, 29/209/75, 75i–ii; Hayden, ed., *Records*, p. 125; W. C. Abbott, "English Conspiracy and Dissent, 1660–1674: II," *AHR* 14 (1908–9): 709.

106. For Knight's involvement in promoting the passage of the Second Conventicle Act, see *CJ*, vol. 9, pp. 104, 130.

107. *Stat. Realm*, 22 Car. II c. 1. For evidence of Yeamans's responses to the actions of informers, see G. Lyon Turner, ed., *Original Records of Early Nonconformity under Persecution and Indulgence*, 3 vols. (London: T. F. Unwin, 1911–1914), vol. 3, pp. 51n., 52n.

108. Hayden, ed., *Records*, p. 128; Besse, *Sufferings of the People called Quakers*, vol. 1, pp. 52–53; Mortimer, ed., *Minute Book*, pp. 33, 40, 102; PRO, SP 29/275/132, 162, 163, 29/276/14, 75, 29/278/149. The king's order requiring the mayor to be chosen from among the aldermen dates from 7 September 1665: PRO, SP 44/17, p. 134. Yeamans himself appears to have been elected in violation of the order, since he was not an alderman in 1669. The king's order was to have been read before each election meeting and apparently was read in 1669, but Yeamans omitted to read it in 1670. The election of 1670 was hotly contested, with Mr. Knight winning by two votes over two conservative alder-

men, and Sir John Knight moved immediately to quash the election. Having failed to get a Privy Council order soon enough, Sir John had his cousin hauled before the House of Commons. For the aftermath of the election, see PRO, SP 29/278/181, 210, 44/31/61, 29/279/45, 29/288/44; BRO, MS 04447 (1), p. 11; Latimer, *Annals*, pp. 355–57; Latham, ed., *Bristol Charters, 1509–1899*, p. 42.

109. PRO, SP 29/57/71. Visitation of ships in Cale's term appears to have begun on 21 April 1662 and to have ended abruptly on 7 July 1662: BRO, MS 04220 (1), ff. 482^r–497^v.

110. BRO, MS 04220 (2), f. 187^r. These entries run through 5 October 1672, i.e., they end soon after the installation of Christopher Griffeth as mayor: ibid., f. 231^v.

111. Olliffe's year in the mayoralty saw almost as violent persecution as had Sir John Knight's: see Hayden, ed., *Records*, pp. 144–70; Mortimer, ed., *Minute Book*, pp. 99–100. For evidence of the visitation of ships during his term, see BRO, MS 04220 (2), ff. 271^v; these entries continue intermittently to the end of the volume in August 1679. Olliffe, an innkeeper and vintner, served as sheriff during Lawford's term as mayor in 1664–65 and so had good experience of previous persecutions: Beaven, *Lists*, p. 303. The last days of the *Register* come at the height of the Exclusion crisis and its bitter aftermath of persecution and factional strife in Bristol: see Latimer, *Annals*, pp. 388ff.; HMC, *The Manuscripts of the Duke of Beaufort, K.G., the Earl of Donoughmore, and Others*, p. 101; Barry, "Politics of Religion," pp. 172–81. These disruptive events may account in part for the apparent breakdown in the enforcement of the servant registration scheme in its last years: see above, Chapter 8, n. 1. In fall 1681 the new mayor of Bristol, Thomas Earle, whom Charles II knighted on 4 December of that year, instituted another vigorous campaign against the conventicles, for which the marquis of Worcester wrote to thank him on the king's behalf: marquis of Worcester to the marchioness, 17 December 1681, HMC, *Manuscripts of the Duke of Beaufort*, p. 87.

112. Sacks, *Trade, Society and Politics*, vol. 1, chap. 1.

CHAPTER 10

1. Lionel Gatford, *Public Good without Private Interest* (London, 1657), quoted in Neill, *Virginia Carolorum*, p. 278.

2. Bullock, *Virginia Impartially Examined*, p. 14. Compare Richard Burton, *The Anatomy of Melancholy*, ed. Holbrook Jackson (New York: Vintage, 1977), pp. 187, 196–97; Richard Baxter, *The Certainty of the World of Spirits* (London, 1691), p. 11.

3. See Burton, *Anatomy of Melancholy*, p. 204; K. M. Briggs, *The Fairies in English Tradition and Literature* (London: Routledge and Kegan Paul, 1967), p. 115.

4. Henry Hallywell, *Melampronoea, Or a Discourse of the Polity and Kingdom of Darkness* (London, 1681), epistle sig. A4.

5. Jeaffreson, ed., *Middlesex County Records*, vol. 3, p. 278. In Bristol, the mayor and aldermen nearly always took special pains to provide these culprits with protection at the pillory against mob action: Latimer, *Annals*, p. 255; see

also Jeaffreson, ed., *Middlesex County Records*, vol. 3, pp. 182, 255, 259; *CSP (Colonial)* (1661–1668), nos. 769, 770.

6. PRO, SP 29/57/71.

7. See Burton, *Anatomy of Melancholy*, p. 182; Thomas, *Religion and the Decline of Magic*, p. 472.

8. John Josselyn, *Chronological Observations of America* (London, 1674), reprinted in *Collections of the Massachusetts Historical Society*, 3d ser., 3 (1883), p. 387. I thank Karen Ordahl Kupperman for this reference.

9. John T. Rutt, ed., *Diary of Thomas Burton, Esq., Member of the Parliaments of Oliver and Richard Cromwell, from 1656 to 1659*, 4 vols. (London: H. Colburn, 1828), vol. 4, pp. 253–73; *Calendar of the Clarendon State Papers Preserved in the Bodleian Library*, 5 vols. (Oxford: Clarendon Press, 1872–1970), vol. 3, pp. 426, 428, 441, 446, 448, 453, 457, 463, and vol. 4, 159, 162, 164, 168, 170–72, 176–77; *CJ*, vol. 7, pp. 620, 622; Thurloe, *State Papers of John Thurloe*, vol. 7, p. 639; *DNB*, "John Thurloe"; Olson, *Anglo-American Politics*, p. 38. This case also implicated Mr. Thomas Noell. It was closely connected with similar charges against other prominent figures of the Interregnum put forth by Marcellus Rivers and Oxenbridge Foyle, also Royalists transported to Barbados: Rutt, ed., *Diary of Thomas Burton*, vol. 4, pp. 253–73; Marcellus Rivers and Oxenbridge Foyle, *England's Slavery, or Barbados Merchandize* (London, 1659).

10. See John Wilmore, *The Case of John Wilmore Truly and Impartially Related* (London, 1682); John Wilmore, *The Legacy of John Wilmer, Citizen and Late Merchant of London* (London, 1692); Roger North, *Examen: or An inquiry into the credit and veracity of a pretended complete history* (London: F. Gyles, 1740), p. 591; North, *Lives of the Norths*, vol. 2, p. 25n.; John Hawles, *Remarks upon the Tryall of Edward Fitzharris, Stephen College etc.* (London, 1689), esp. pp. 5, 16–17, 52; Smith, *Colonists in Bondage*, pp. 75–76. Stephen College, a London joiner and arch anti-papist, was arrested on a charge of treason for riding fully armed to Oxford in March 1681. He was first tried at the Old Bailey, where Wilmore and his colleagues returned a verdict of *ignoramus*, after which the case was removed to Oxford, where College was convicted. For his actions in the matter Wilmore was imprisoned for fifteen weeks in the Tower on a charge of treason and only released on £9,000 bail. Almost immediately afterward came a charge of spiriting involving a runaway like Farwell Meredith who had begged passage abroad. For Wilmore's own connection to Shaftesbury, see HMC, *Fourteenth Report*, app. 4, p. 128.

11. North, *Lives of the Norths*, vol. 2, pp. 24–27; Seyer, *Memoirs*, vol. 2, pp. 531–32; Latimer, *Annals*, pp. 433–36. The Bristol aldermen were accused of permitting vagrants and even felons to accept transportation to the colonies, a practice which undoubtedly went on, as North makes clear. For an instance in the 1650s, see BRO, MS 04273 (1), f. 45^r.

12. Richard Baxter, *Certainty of the World of Spirits*, p. 175.

13. William Grigg, *The Quaker's Jesus* (London, 1658), pp. 37, 38–52; Ralph Farmer, *The Great Mysteries of Godlinesse and Ungodlinesse* (London, 1655), p. 24; Ralph Farmer, *Sathan Inthron'd* (London, 1657), p. 28. See also Richard Baxter, *The Quaker's Catechisme* (London, 1651[?]), epistle; Richard

Baxter, *One Sheet for the Ministry against the Malignants of all sorts* (London, 1657), p. 5. Grigg was a Presbyterian glover in Bristol and a member of the city's Common Council during the Interregnum; Farmer we have already met, above, pp. 222–23, 235–37. At this time he was the Presbyterian minister of St. Nicholas Church in the city, as well as city lecturer.

14. Baxter, *Certainty of the World of Spirits*, p. 176. The idea that the Quakers were possessed people was widespread; see Richard Blome, *The fanatick history* (London, 1660), pp. 71–121; *The Devil turned Quaker* (London, 1656), sig. A4a–i; Grigg, *The Quaker's Jesus*, epistle, sig. A3a–b; Farmer, *Great Mysteries of Godlinesse and Ungodlinesse*, epistle, sig. A2a, pp. 21–23, 30, 81–87; Farmer, *Sathan Inthron'd*, p. 2; Ralph Farmer, *The Impostor Dethron'd* (London, 1658), epistle, sig. Bb, pp. 5–9; Mortimer, *Early Bristol Quakerism*, pp. 4–5. In general, see Reay, "Popular Hostility towards Quakers," esp. pp. 398–99; Reay, *The Quakers and the English Revolution*, chap. 4; see also Barry Reay, "Quakerism and Society," in J. F. McGregor and Barry Reay, eds., *Radical Religion in the English Revolution* (Oxford: Oxford University Press, 1984), pp. 141–64.

15. See Barry, "Parish in Civic Life," pp. 158–59.

16. *The Devil turned Quaker*, sig. A2a.

17. Farmer, *Great Mysteries of Godlinesse and Ungodlinesse*, p. 87. See Blome, *The fanatick history*, pp. 68–70, 87–99; Reay, "Popular Hostility towards Quakers," pp. 388–89, 396; Hill, *The World Turned Upside Down*, pp. 152, 186–207; Hugh Barbour, *The Quakers in Puritan England* (New Haven: Yale University Press, 1964), pp. 111, 113, 115, 116, 161, 163, 164, 166, 168; Keith Thomas, "Women and the Civil War Sects," in Aston, ed., *Crisis in Europe*, pp. 332–57.

18. Hening, ed., *Statutes at Large*, vol. 1, p. 532.

19. Grigg, *The Quaker's Jesus*, pp. 35–36.

20. Julianus, "Fragment of a Letter to a Priest," in *The Works of the Emperor Julian*, 3 vols., ed. and trans. Wilmer Cave Wright, Loeb ed. (London: W. Heinemann, 1913–1923), vol. 2, pp. 337, 339. Cf. Julian's remarks in the same letter on demon-possessed atheists, in Julianus, *Works*, vol. 2, p. 297.

21. On this theme see, in general, Hill, *The World Turned Upside Down*; Richard Ashcraft, *Revolutionary Politics and Locke's Two Treatises of Government* (Princeton: Princeton University Press, 1986), chap. 2. This is not to deny that many of them also saw it as a religion of submission to God's will. I owe this point to discussion with J. C. Davis.

22. Bishop, *A Relation*, pp. 15–16.

23. George Bishop, *An Illumination to Open the eyes of the Papists (so called) and of all other sects* (London, 1661), p. 11.

24. Robert Purnell, *The Way to Heaven Discovered* (London, 1653), epistle, sig. B4d. See also Hayden, ed., *Records*, p. 47. Purnell was a carpet-weaver by occupation. For examples of his support of the Commonwealth, see Robert Purnell, *Good Tydings for Sinners, Great Joy for Saints* (London, 1649), pp. 73–75; Robert Purnell, *No Power but of God* (London, 1651), pp. 166–67; Purnell, *Way to Heaven Discovered*, pp. 197–204; Robert Purnell, *England's Remonstrance* (London, 1653). For his attacks on the Quakers, see Robert Purnell, *A Little Cabinet Richly Stored with all sorts of Heavenly Varieties* (London,

1657), epistle; [Robert Purnell], *The Church of Christ in Bristol Recovering her Vail* (London, 1657). For a general discussion of Baptist views, see J. F. McGregor, "The Baptists: Fount of all Heresy," in McGregor and Reay, eds., *Radical Religion*, pp. 23–64.

25. Purnell, *No Power but of God*, pp. 89–90; Robert Purnell, *The Way Step by Step to a Sound and Saving Conversion* (London, 1659), p. 103.

26. Purnell, *No Power but of God*, epistle, sig. A4b.

27. Ibid., p. 80.

28. Purnell, *Good Tydings for Sinners, Great Joy for Saints*, pp. 7–8.

29. Purnell, *Way to Heaven Discovered*, epistle, sig. B3b; Robert Purnell, *The Way to Convert a Sinner* (London, 1652), pp. 20, 33; Purnell, *A Little Cabinet* (London, 1657), epistle, pp. 167–68; Purnell, *Way Step by Step*, pp. 62–65.

30. Hayden, ed., *Records*, p. 100; see Purnell, *Way to Heaven Discovered*, epistle, sig. B3b.

31. Robert Simpson to Edward Terrill, 27 June 1664, signed from Newgate, printed in Edward B. Underhill, ed., *The Records of a Church of Christ, meeting in Broadmead, Bristol, 1640–1687* (London: J. Haddon, 1847), p. 79.

32. Thomas Ewins to "the small remnant that meet this afternoon," (1664?), in Underhill, ed., *Records*, pp. 80–81; Thomas Ewins to Edward Terrill, 23 July 1664, in ibid., p. 83.

33. Bishop, *An Illumination*, p. 12.

34. Purnell, *Good Tydings for Sinners, Great Joy for Saints*, pp. 26–27; cf. Bishop, *An Illumination*, p. 19.

35. Purnell, *No Power but of God*, epistle, sig. A4ab; see also Purnell, *Way to Heaven Discovered*, p. 188.

36. George Bishop, *Jesus Christ, the Same Today as Yesterday* (London, 1655), p. 5.

37. For example, Thomas Ewins, called as teacher in 1651 and then installed as pastor in 1662, was a London tailor by trade: Hayden, ed., *Records*, p. 27.

38. Bishop et al., *Cry of Blood*, p. 102.

39. Sewel, *Rise of the Christian People Called Quakers*, pp. 556–57.

40. Hayden, ed., *Records*, p. 102.

41. Acts 10: 34–35. This was a frequently cited passage among the sectaries: see, e.g., Purnell, *Good Tydings for Sinners, Great Joy for Saints*, pp. 25, 26–27; Bishop, *An Illumination*, p. 31; Hayden, ed., *Records*, p. 102.

42. Purnell, *The Way to Heaven Discovered*, pp. 193–94; see also Purnell, *England's Remonstrance*.

43. Purnell, *Good Tydings for Sinners, Great Joy for Saints*, pp. 62–63, 73–75; Purnell, *Way to Heaven Discovered*, pp. 191–204; Purnell, *England's Remonstrance*.

44. Purnell, *Way Step by Step*, pp. 101–2.

45. Purnell, *Good Tydings for Sinners, Great Joy for Saints*, epistle, sig. A2b. On this subject, see Barry, "Parish in Civic Life," p. 161.

46. Bishop, *Mene Tekel*, pp. 4, 30–31.

47. Bishop et al., *Cry of Blood*, pp. 106–7. Foord's case shows how quickly a purely economic matter could become a religious cause célèbre. When called before the magistrates by the milleners, Foord showed them "his unmannerly

carriage . . . in ye Tolzey by keeping on his hatt on his head though commended to take it of." For this he was ordered to find sureties for his good behavior. At Quarter Sessions he reappeared to clear those who stood bond for him, and the whole matter reopened again when the town clerk, Robert Aldworth, asked him if he was sorry for keeping strangers. He said "he had committed no evill, therefore he hd no cause for sorrow, nor had he broken any Law." For all this he was recommitted to Newgate: BRO, MS 04417 (1), f. 20ᵛ; Bishop et al., *Cry of Blood*, pp. 132–34.

48. Bishop et al., *Cry of Blood*, pp. 9–10.

49. The common practice in Bristol in dealing with newcomers to the city, as a condition of allowing them to stay, was to take certificates from them that saved the parish harmless from supporting them on the poor rates. The Quakers seem to be referring to this practice in their defense of the migration of strangers into the town: see Sacks, *Trade, Society and Politics*, vol. 1, pp. 231–32; Latimer, *Annals*, pp. 13–14. In general, see Philip Styles, "The Evolution of the Law of Settlement," *University of Birmingham Historical Journal* 9 (1963): 35–42; A. L. Beier, "Vagrants and the Social Order in Elizabethan England," *Past and Present*, no. 64 (August 1974): 3–29.

50. Bishop et al., *Cry of Blood*, p. 10.

51. Bishop, *A Manifesto*, pp. 21–22.

52. Bishop et al., *Cry of Blood*, p. 2.

53. For evidence that this is just what servants were doing, see Galenson, *White Servitude in Colonial America*, pp. 102–13; Menard, "British Migration," pp. 106–9.

54. R. H. Tawney, *Religion and the Rise of Capitalism: A Historical Study*, 2d ed. (New York: New American Library, 1960), esp. pp. 11–20; see also Christopher Hill, "Protestantism and the Rise of Capitalism," in Christopher Hill, *Change and Continuity in Seventeenth-Century England* (London: Weidenfeld and Nicolson, 1974), pp. 81–102.

55. On the significance of this position for the later development of capitalism, see Max Weber, "The Protestant Sects and the Spirit of Capitalism," in H. H. Gerth and C. Wright Mills, eds., *From Max Weber: Essays in Sociology* (New York: Oxford University Press, 1946), p. 312. For discussion of the roots of this position in Quaker thought, see Isabel Grubb, *Quakerism and Industry Before 1800* (London: Williams and Norgate, 1930), pp. 9–46; Richard Bauman, *Let Your Words Be Few: Symbolism of Speaking and Silence among Seventeenth-Century Quakers* (Cambridge: Cambridge University Press, 1983), chap. 7.

56. Charles Marshall, *Sion's Travellers Comforted, and the Disobedient Warned: In a Collection of the Books and Epistles of the Faithful Minister of Christ Jesus, Charles Marshall* (London, 1704), pp. 14–15.

57. Matthew 5:38.

58. George Fox, "A Cry for Repentence unto the Inhabitants of London," in George Fox, *The Works of G. F.*, 8 vols. (Philadelphia: M. T. C. Gould, 1831), vol. 4, p. 100.

59. John Bunyan, *Life and Death of Mr. Badman and The Holy War*, ed. John Brown (Cambridge: Cambridge University Press, 1905), pp. 23, 31, 34,

37, and 118–25, esp. pp. 124–25; for discussion of this work, see Christopher Hill, *A Tinker and a Poor Man: John Bunyan and His Church, 1628–1688* (New York: Alfred A. Knopf, 1989), pp. 231–39. Richard Baxter, while permitting some bargaining and variation in pricing according to circumstances, also agreed on the whole with the principle of the fixed price: see Richard Baxter, *A Christian Directory: Or, A Summ of Practical Theologie and Cases of Conscience . . . in Four Parts* (London, 1678), part 4, pp. 97, 103–6 [misnumbered as 206]; see also part 1, pp. 353–62 [misnumbered as 382]. On these themes, see Tawney, *Religion and the Rise of Capitalism*, pp. 183–87; Grubb, *Quakerism and Industry*, pp. 28–29.

60. John Locke, "Venditio. 95," dating from 1695, in his *Commonplace Book of 1661*, as printed with modernized spelling in John Dunn, "Justice and the Interpretation of Locke's Political Theory," *Political Studies* 16 (1968): 84–87; see also Dunn's discussion of this document in the body of his article, pp. 68–84.

61. Raymond de Roover, "The Concept of the Just Price: Theory and Economic Policy," *Journal of Economic History* 18 (1958): 418–34; Raymond de Roover, *San Bernardino of Siena and Sant'Antonio of Florence: Two Great Economic Thinkers of the Middle Ages* (Boston: Baker Library, Harvard Graduate School of Business Administration, 1967), esp. pp. 16–23; Raymond de Roover, "Monopoly Theory Prior to Adam Smith: A Revision," in Raymond de Roover, *Business, Banking and Economic Thought in Late Medieval and Early Modern Europe*, ed. Julius Kirshner (Chicago: University of Chicago Press, 1974), pp. 273–305; Raymond de Roover, "Scholastic Economics: Survival and Lasting Influence from the Sixteenth Century to Adam Smith," in ibid., pp. 306–35; Raymond de Roover, "The Scholastic Attitude Toward Trade and Entrepreneurship," in ibid., pp. 336–45; see also John T. Noonan, Jr., *The Scholastic Analysis of Usury* (Cambridge, Mass.: Harvard University Press, 1957). It is possible that Locke was familiar with some of the scholastic literature on economic morality to which de Roover refers in his important articles. For example, Locke's account of the moral obligations of a merchant bringing food to a famine-stricken market is virtually the same as the argument put forward by San Bernardino: see de Roover, *San Bernardino of Siena and Sant'Antonio of Florence*, pp. 20–21.

62. Malynes, *Lex Mercatoria*, p. 67; for Malynes's debt to scholastic economics, see Raymond de Roover, "Gerard de Malynes as an Economic Writer: From Scholasticism to Mercantilism," in de Roover, *Business, Banking and Economic Thought*, pp. 346–66.

63. For a good account of how such a market operates in practice, see Clifford Geertz, *Peddlers and Princes: Social Change and Economic Modernization in Two Indonesian Towns* (Chicago: University of Chicago Press, 1963), pp. 28–47.

64. The system of regulation in Bristol is discussed in detail in Sacks, *Trade, Society and Politics*, vol. 1, chaps. 3–4; for an overview of economies run by "custom and command," see John R. Hicks, *A Theory of Economic History* (Oxford: Clarendon Press, 1969), pp. 9–24.

65. Marshall, *Sion's Travellers Comforted*, p. 14.

66. Thirsk, *Economic Policy and Projects*, esp. chaps. 1, 5–7; see also Lorna Weatherill, *Consumer Behaviour and Material Culture in Britain, 1660–1760* (London: Routledge, 1988), esp. chaps. 1–4.

67. Albert O. Hirschman, *Exit, Voice and Loyalty: Responses to Decline in Firms, Organizations and States* (Cambridge, Mass.: Harvard University Press, 1970), esp. pp. 3–5, 21–43; Albert O. Hirschman, *Essays in Trespassing: Economics to Politics and Beyond* (Cambridge: Cambridge University Press, 1981), pp. 211–65; Albert O. Hirschman, *Shifting Involvements: Private Interests and Public Action* (Princeton: Princeton University Press, 1982), esp. pp. 92–120; Albert O. Hirschman, "Exit and Voice: An Expanding Sphere of Influence," in Albert O. Hirschman, *Rival Views of Market Society and Other Recent Essays* (New York: Viking, 1986), pp. 77–101.

68. Underdown, *Pride's Purge*, chap. 9; Blair Worden, *The Rump Parliament, 1648–1653*, esp. chap. 7; Austyn Woolrych, *From Commonwealth to Protectorate* (Oxford: Clarendon Press, 1982), esp. pp. 223ff.

69. Hirschman, *Essays in Trespassing*, p. 244.

70. Marshall, *Sion's Travellers Comforted*, p. 15.

71. Fox, "A Cry for Repentence," pp. 100–101.

72. For surveys of the transformation of the Quakers after the Restoration, see William C. Braithwaite, *The Second Period of Quakerism* (London: Macmillan, 1919); Reay, *The Quakers and the English Revolution*, pp. 103–22; Christopher Hill, *The Experience of Defeat: Milton and Some Contemporaries* (New York: Viking, 1984), pp. 129–69. For comments on the Baptists in the same period, see Hill, *A Tinker and a Poor Man*, pp. 101–53. On the history of the dissenters during the Restoration in general, see, along with Hill's *Experience of Defeat*, Hill, *The World Turned Upside Down*, pp. 278–91; Greaves, *Deliver Us from Evil*; Hutton, *The Restoration*; see also Barry, "Parish in Civic Life," p. 161.

73. See Mortimer, ed., *Minute Book*, pp. xviii–xxv, 76–77, 87, 88–89, 93, 94, 95, 98, 99, 108, 117–18, 124–25, 153–54; see also Grubb, *Quakerism and Industry*, chap. 5. For an account of the operations of this system in Philadelphia, see Frederick B. Tolles, *Meeting House and Counting House: The Quaker Merchants of Colonial Philadelphia, 1682–1763* (Chapel Hill: University of North Carolina Press, 1948), pp. 73–80. The Baptists were somewhat less active in this regard, but see Hayden, ed., *Records*, pp. 55–56, 121, 128–29, 187–88, 191, 202; see also Barry, "Parish in Civic Life," p. 161.

74. See Bauman, *Let Your Words Be Few*, pp. 95–119, esp. p. 98; Craig W. Horle, *The Quakers and the English Legal System, 1660–1688* (Philadelphia: University of Pennsylvania Press, 1988), pp. 49–52, 238–42; Gerald R. Cragg, *Puritanism in the Period of the Great Persecution, 1660–1688* (Cambridge: Cambridge University Press, 1957), p. 51; in general, see Hill, *Society and Puritanism*, pp. 382–419.

75. Mortimer tells us that issues relating to marriage occupied about a quarter of the business of the Men's Meeting in Bristol; apprenticeship, while not taking as much time, was also important: Mortimer, ed., *Minute Book*, p. xxiii; for evidence on apprenticeship, see ibid., pp. 1, 2, 3, 6, 41, 59, 60, 69, 70, 74, 76, 80, 84, 85, 107, 143, 178, 183, 215, 221. References to marriage matters can be found on nearly every page.

76. On officeholding as recognition of one's worthiness and honor, see Phythian-Adams, "Ceremony and the Citizen," esp. pp. 62–64.

77. On the legal system in force in the city, see Sacks, *Trade, Society and Politics*, vol. 1, chap. 4.

78. See Leadam, ed., *Select Cases before the Star Chamber*, vol. 2, p. 150; Latimer, *Sixteenth-Century Bristol*, 12–13; BRO, *Old Ordinance Book*, f. 21^v; Latham, ed., *Bristol Charters, 1509–1899*, p. 6; Latimer, *Annals*, pp. 33, 35, 133.

79. See above, pp. 30–32.

80. See Beavan, *Lists*, pp. 201–3.

81. Beaven, *Lists*, compared to Hayden, ed., *Records*, and Mortimer, ed., *Minute Book*. If we knew more about the membership of the dissenting churches, we would probably find this number to be higher.

82. John Brewer, "Commercialization and Politics," in Neil McKendrick, John Brewer, and J. H. Plumb, *The Birth of a Consumer Society in Eighteenth-Century England* (Bloomington: Indiana University Press, 1982), pp. 203–30.

83. Hill, *The World Turned Upside Down*, pp. 32–45.

84. On these themes, see Paul Seaver, *Wallington's World: A Puritan Artisan in Seventeenth-Century London* (Stanford: Stanford University Press, 1985), esp. pp. 112–42; Paul Seaver, "The Puritan Work Ethic Revisited," *Journal of British Studies* 19, no. 2 (Spring 1980): 35–53; Hill, *A Tinker and a Poor Man*, esp. pp. 155–280.

85. The following account is based on the evidence provided in I. V. Hall, "Whitson Court Sugar House, Bristol, 1665–1824," *BGAS* 65 (1944): 1–97.

86. On the organization and sociology of the shipping industry, see Davis, *Rise of the English Shipping Industry*, chaps. 3, 5–8; see also Marcus B. Rediker, *Between the Devil and the Deep Blue Sea: Merchant Seamen, Pirates and the Anglo-American Maritime World, 1700–1750* (Cambridge: Cambridge University Press, 1987), esp. chaps. 1–2.

87. Nott, ed., *Deposition Books*, vol. 1, pp. 177–78; McGrath, ed., *Merchants and Merchandise*, p. 118.

88. Matthew 5: 34.

89. James 5: 12.

90. See, e.g., William Ames, *The Marrow of Theology*, ed. and trans. John D. Eusden (Boston: Pilgrim Press, 1968), pp. 267–70.

91. See Bauman, *Let Your Words Be Few*, pp. 103–19.

92. See Barry, "Politics of Religion," pp. 168–69; Barry, "Parish in Civic Life," pp. 157, 159; Pincus, "Protestantism and Patriotism," chap. 3. See also Steven C. A. Pincus, "Popery, Trade and Universal Monarchy: The Ideological Origins of the Second Anglo-Dutch War," *English Historical Review* (forthcoming). I owe the term "Anglican royalist" to Dr. Pincus. I have also benefited from discussions with him about the points made in this paragraph.

93. See BRO, MS 04220 (2).

94. Marshall, *Sion's Travellers Comforted*, pp. 12–13.

95. Bishop, *A Manifesto*, p. 2.

96. *A Relation*, p. 3.

97. John Cary, *An Essay on the State of England in Relation to its Trade, Its Poor, and its Taxes, For carrying on the present War against France* (Bristol, 1695), p. 43.

98. In other respects, too, Cary's ideas approached those of the dissenters. Since he believed that labor created all wealth, he argued that those economic activities were best that most encouraged productive employment. He favored the colonial trades because they supplied raw materials for manufacturers; he condemned the luxury trades because they drained away England's coin without promoting its industry. As a result he was one of England's greatest advocates for putting the poor on work, and as a member of Parliament and citizen of Bristol he led the movement for the creation of district workhouses under consolidated corporations of the poor. For further discussion of Cary's ideas, see below, pp. 339–43 and the works cited at p. 449, n. 24.

99. See, e.g., de Vries, *European Urbanization, 1500–1800*, chaps. 3–4; Wrigley, "Urban Growth and Agricultural Change," pp. 157–93.

100. Charles Davenant, "Discourses on the Public Revenues," in Charles Davenant, *The Political and Commercial Works of Dr. Charles D'Avenant*, ed. Charles Whitworth, 6 vols. (London: R. Horsfield, 1771), vol. 1, p. 152. On Davenant, see J. G. A. Pocock, *The Machiavellian Moment: Florentine Political Thought and the Atlantic Republican Tradition* (Princeton: Princeton University Press, 1975), pp. 437–46; Istvan Hont, "Free Trade and the Economic Limits to National Politics: Neo-Machiavellian Political Economy Reconsidered," in John Dunn, ed., *The Economic Limits to Modern Politics* (Cambridge: Cambridge University Press, 1989), pp. 57–95.

101. See Albert O. Hirschman, *The Passions and the Interests: Political Arguments for Capitalism Before Its Triumph* (Princeton: Princeton University Press, 1977), pp. 56–63, 69ff.; Albert O. Hirschman, *Rival Views of Market Society*, pp. 105–41; see also Pocock, *Machiavellian Moment*, chaps. 13–14. For a recent and penetrating discussion of the problems brought to political discourse by these developments in economics, see J. G. A. Pocock, "The Political Limits to Pre-Modern Economics," in Dunn, ed., *Economic Limits to Modern Politics*, pp. 121–41.

CONCLUSION

1. Edgeworth, *Sermons*, f. 288^v.
2. Ibid., ff. 6^r–7^r.
3. Ibid., ff. 13^v–14^r.
4. Ibid., f. 14^r.
5. Ibid., f. 61^r.
6. Ibid., f. 61$^{r–v}$.
7. Ibid., f. 125$^{r–v}$.
8. Ibid., f. 61^v.
9. Ibid., f. 61$^{r–v}$.
10. Ibid., f. 62$^{r–v}$.
11. Ibid., ff. 62^v–63^r.
12. Ibid., f. 63^r.
13. Ibid., f. 63^r.
14. *Marchants Avizo*, pp. v–xi, 3.

15. Ibid., p. 48.

16. Ibid., p. 11.

17. Ibid., p. 56.

18. Karl Polanyi, *The Great Transformation: The Political and Economic Origins of Our Time* (Boston: Beacon Press, 1957), p. 46.

19. *Marchants Avizo*, pp. 55–57.

20. See, e.g., *A Discourse of the Commonweal of This Realm of England, Attributed to Sir Thomas Smith*, ed. Mary Dewar (Charlottesville: University of Virginia Press, 1969).

21. The character of their rhetoric can be gauged from the documents collected in Tawney and Power, eds., *Tudor Economic Documents*, vols. 2–3.

22. *Marchants Avizo*, p. 6.

23. Ibid., p. 3.

24. Latimer, *Annals*, p. 474; DNB, "John Cary." The DNB account calls him the son of Thomas Cary, vicar of SS. Philip and Jacob, but this is in error: see McGrath, ed., *Records*, p. 48. Jonathan Barry identifies Cary's politics as "radical whig": Barry, "Politics of Religion," p. 179.

25. Cary, *Essay on the State of England*, sig. A4a.

26. John Cary, *An Essay on the Coyn and Credit of England: As they stand with Respect to its Trade* (Bristol, 1696), p. 30.

27. Cary, *Essay on the State of England*, p. 48.

28. Ibid., pp. 49–52.

29. Ibid., pp. 66–67.

30. Ibid., pp. 67–68.

31. Ibid., pp. 41, 61.

32. Cary, *Essay on the Coyn and Credit of England*, p. 1.

33. Ibid., p. 30.

34. BL, Harl. MS 5540, f. 112.

35. Cary, *Essay on the State of England*, p. 75.

36. Ibid., pp. 75–76.

37. Ibid., pp. 52–53.

38. Cary, *Essay on the Coyn and Credit of England*, p. 3.

39. Cary, *Essay on the State of England*, p. 76.

40. Ibid., pp. 2–3.

41. Ibid., p. 4.

42. Ibid., pp. 5–7.

43. Ibid., p. 17.

44. *Marchants Avizo*, p. 55.

45. Latimer, *Merchant Venturers*, p. 26.

46. See Sacks, *Trade, Society and Politics*, vol. 2, pp. 752–63.

47. McGrath, ed., *Merchants and Merchandise*, p. 15.

48. Based on BRO, MSS 04352 (6), 04357 (1).

49. Sacks, *Trade, Society and Politics*, vol. 2, pp. 502–5; J. R. Holman, "Apprenticeship as a Factor in Migration: Bristol, 1675–1726," *BGAS* 97 (1979): 85–92, esp. pp. 86–97.

50. Minchinton, "Bristol," 69–85.

51. McGrath, ed., *Merchants and Merchandise*, pp. 140–43.

52. For this paragraph and the next see Sacks, *Trade, Society and Politics*, vol. 1, chap. 5.

53. [J. Rickman], *Abstract of the Answers and Returns made Pursuant to an Act Passed in the Forty-First Year of His Majesty King George III Intitled 'An Act for Taking an Account of the Population of Great Britain, and the Increase or Diminution thereof.' Enumeration*, 2 parts (London: Parliamentary Papers, 1801–2), part 1, pp. 125–26.

54. Sacks, *Trade, Society and Politics*, vol. 1, pp. 214–34, 250–54. Bristol's demographic history in the seventeenth century, especially in midcentury, contrasts with that for England as a whole. While Bristol's population growth probably slowed after 1600 from the rate achieved in the late sixteenth century, elsewhere in England, with the exception of London and a few other major urban centers, the first three-quarters of the seventeenth century was generally a period of stagnation, not growth: Wrigley and Schofield, *Population History of England*, pp. 207–13.

55. For the history of this map, see J. E. Pritchard, "A Hitherto Unknown Original Print of the Great Plan of Bristol by Jacobus Millerd, 1673" *BGAS* 44 (1922): 203–20; J. E. Pritchard, "Old Plans and Views of Bristol," *BGAS* 44 (1922): 334–36.

56. Sacks, *Trade, Society and Politics*, vol. 1, pp. 245–50.

57. The following remarks are based on analysis of PRO, E 179/116/541.

58. Hayden, ed., *Records*, pp. 14–18, 105, 133; Mortimer, ed., *Minute Book*, pp. xxi–xxii; Turner, ed., *Original Records of Early Nonconformity*, vol. 1, pp. 230, 239, 244, 328, 439, 483, 560, 562; vol. 2, pp. 818–19, 824–25; vol. 3, p. 327; Moses Caston, *Independency in Bristol, with brief memorials of its churches and pastors* (London: Ward, 1860), pp. 39–52, 82–88.

59. Anne Whiteman, ed., *The Compton Census of 1676* (British Academy: Records of Social and Economic History, n.s. 10, 1986), pp. 547–51. In her introduction Whiteman makes a cogent case for the general accuracy of the census against the criticisms made by Thomas Richards, "The Religious Census of 1676: An Inquiry into Its Historical Value Mainly with Reference to Wales," *Transactions of the Honourable Society of Cymmordorion*, 1925–26, Supplement (London: Society of Cymmordorion, 1927). But the figures for Bristol pose special difficulties, in part because no returns have survived from half of the central parishes in the city and in part because the results in two important centers of dissent, St. James and St. Mary, Redcliffe, are either misstated or confused. Given the location of Quaker, Baptist, and Presbyterian meetings in its midst, St. James probably had more than one hundred dissenters among its twelve hundred men and women over sixteen years of age. As for St. Mary, Redcliffe, its population of men and women over sixteen was almost certainly considerably larger than the hundred and fifty persons indicated in the return; in 1696 its total population equaled that for nearby St. Thomas, for which the Compton census gives three hundred and fifty persons over sixteen years of age: see Sacks, *Trade, Society and Politics*, vol. 1, pp. 239–40.

60. On this point see Barry, "Parish in Civic Life," pp. 152–78; see also Jonathan Barry, "Popular Culture in Seventeenth-Century Bristol," in Barry

Reay, ed., *Popular Culture in Seventeenth-Century England* (New York: St. Martin's Press, 1985), pp. 59–90; Barry, "Politics of Religion," p. 165.

61. See Norman O. Brown, *Hermes the Thief* (Madison: University of Wisconsin Press, 1947), esp. pp. 6–45, 78, 85, 108; see also Jean-Christophe Agnew, *Worlds Apart: The Market and the Theater in Anglo-American Thought, 1550–1750* (Cambridge: Cambridge University Press, 1986), pp. 17–56.

62. On this theme see, e.g., Pocock, *Machiavellian Moment,* chaps. 13–14; J. G. A. Pocock, "The Mobility of Property and the Rise of Eighteenth-Century Sociology," in J. G. A. Pocock, *Virtue, Commerce and History: Essays on Political Thought and History, Chiefly in the Eighteenth Century* (Cambridge: Cambridge University Press, 1985), pp. 103–23.

63. Max Weber, *The Protestant Ethic and the Spirit of Capitalism,* trans. Talcott Parsons (New York: Charles Scribner's Sons, 1958).

64. Hirschman, *The Passions and the Interests,* pp. 129–30.

65. The phrase is Hirschman's, from the subtitle of *The Passions and the Interests.*

66. Ibid., pp. 129–30.

67. Seaver, "Puritan Work-Ethic Revisited," p. 38; see also Seaver, *Wallington's World,* chap. 5.

68. Romans 12: 2.

Index

Adams, William, 186, 191
Ad valorem duties, 25, 41, 376n.67
Affirmation Act of 1696, 320
Aldermen: and integration of city and national government, 345; merchants organized by, 88; occupations of, 167; and official precedence, 300, 301, 439–40n.108
Aldworth, Richard, 245
Aldworth, Robert: business dealings of, 66–67, 68; fishing ventures of, 50; funeral monument of, 412n.29; and import market, 73, 76; Laudian position of, 234; Christopher Whitson opposed by, 221–22
Aldworth, Thomas, 52, 66, 73, 76
Alicante, 45, 46
Allen, Richard, 265
Almería, 45
American colonies: Bristol landfall in, 374n.44; development of land in, 266; lack of labor in, 266; migration to, 289–90; religious persecution in, 292–93. See also American trades
American trades: with Barbados, 253, 265; beginnings of, 251; Bristol's role in, xvii, 251–57, 258–70; John Cary on, 340; in Chesapeake, 259–60, 265, 289–90; and control of exports, 422n.54; interdependency of Spanish economy with, 92; market-based approach to, 278; in Newfoundland, 35, 48–49, 50; by non-traditional merchants, 259, 260; occupations of importers in, 259–

60; and Protectorate Parliament, 274–75; registration scheme affects, 275–77; regulation of, 267, 273, 275, 348, 422n.54; sectaries in, 269, 328; as shoemakers' holiday, 267; as single export commerce, 265; by small exporters, 279, 427n.3; in sugar, 40, 265, 266–67, 332; in tobacco, 265, 266–67, 287, 288, 332, 430n.18; as two-way traffic, 260–61; in Virginia, 51, 259, 265–66, 293–94, 297, 307; in West Indies, 51, 259–60, 265–66, 289–90, 296
Ames, William, 326
Andalusia Company, 90–91
Anglican church, 293, 434n.50
Anne, Queen (of Denmark), 187
Anti-monopolists: artificers as, 201, 224; and "Bill for Bristowe," 198–200; and Common Council, 198, 206; control of elections by, 198; ideology of, 235, 244; levy on, 206; against Merchant Venturers, 198, 203–4, 237; occupational equality for, 246; and Rev. William Yeamans, 234. See also Monopolists
Antwerp mart, 29
Apprenticeships: agents serve, to masters, 261; children serve, 105–6; in Common Council, 167–68, 169; decline of clothmaking revealed by, 57–58; Roger Edgeworth's tale of, 334–35; exclusivity of, 119; and freedom to trade, 122, 123; home of origin of, 351; to join Merchant Venturers,

453

Compositor: BookMasters, Inc.
Text: 10 / 13 Sabon
Display Sabon
Printer: Maple-Vail Book Mfg. Group
Binder: Maple-Vail Book Mfg. Group